CITIZENSHIP IN AFRICA: THE LAW OF BELONGING

Citizenship in Africa provides a comprehensive exploration of nationality laws in Africa, placing them in their theoretical and historical context. It offers the first serious attempt to analyse the impact of nationality law on politics and society in different African states from a trans-continental comparative perspective. Taking a four-part approach, Parts I and II set the book within the framework of existing scholarship on citizenship, from both sociological and legal perspectives, and examine the history of nationality laws in Africa from the colonial period to the present day. Part III considers case studies which illustrate the application and misapplication of the law in practice, and the relationship of legal and political developments in each country. Finally, Part IV explores the impact of the law on politics, and its relevance for questions of identity and 'belonging' today, concluding with a set of issues for further research. Ambitious in scope and compelling in analysis, this is an important new work on citizenship in Africa.

Citizenship in Africa: The Law of Belonging

Bronwen Manby

•HART•
OXFORD • LONDON • NEW YORK • NEW DELHI • SYDNEY

HART PUBLISHING

Bloomsbury Publishing Plc

Kemp House, Chawley Park, Cumnor Hill, Oxford, OX2 9PH, UK

HART PUBLISHING, the Hart/Stag logo, BLOOMSBURY and the Diana logo are trademarks of Bloomsbury Publishing Plc

First published in Great Britain 2018

A catalogue record for this book is available from the British Library.

Library of Congress Cataloging-in-Publication data

Names: Manby, Bronwen, author.

Title: Citizenship in Africa : the law of belonging / Bronwen Manby.

Description: Portland, Oregon : Hart Publishing, 2018.

Identifiers: LCCN 2018023018 (print) | LCCN 2018026006 (ebook) | ISBN 9781509920792 (Epub) | ISBN 9781509920778 (hardback : alk. paper)

Subjects: LCSH: Citizenship—Africa.

Classification: LCC KQC146 (ebook) | LCC KQC146 .M365 2018 (print) | DDC 342.608/3—dc23

LC record available at https://lccn.loc.gov/2018023018

ISBN: HB: 978-1-50992-077-8
ePDF: 978-1-50992-078-5
ePub: 978-1-50992-079-2

Typeset by Compuscript Ltd, Shannon
Printed and bound in Great Britain by TJ International Ltd, Padstow, Cornwall

To find out more about our authors and books visit www.hartpublishing.co.uk. Here you will find extracts, author information, details of forthcoming events and the option to sign up for our newsletters.

ACKNOWLEDGEMENTS

First I must thank Professor René de Groot of Maastricht University for suggesting the doctorate that forms the basis of this book, and for taking on the role of my supervisor. Thanks are also due to my PhD examination committee, especially Maarten Vink of Maastricht University and Rainer Bauböck of the European University Institute, who provided additional and very helpful comments on the concluding chapters; as did Mike McGovern of the University of Michigan (with even less obligation to do so). The anonymous reviewers who provided feedback on the book proposal also gave invaluable advice.

The thesis itself drew on the publications and reports I had previously written on the right to a nationality in Africa, many of them listed in the bibliography. Much of this research was conducted on behalf of the Open Society Foundations and UNHCR. I should like to emphasise also my debts to Chidi Odinkalu and Ibrahima Kane, who have informed my thinking on these issues over many years and have been inspirational leaders and colleagues in advocacy efforts on the continent. Pascal Kambale was an early sounding-board on the political complexities of the Democratic Republic of Congo; while Mirna Adjami gave generously of her time to comment on the intricacies of the law in Côte d'Ivoire. I have benefited greatly from visiting fellowships at the Centre for the Study of Human Rights at the London School of Economics, from working with UNHCR's Statelessness section in Geneva and staff in the field, and above all from ongoing discussions with as the community of scholars and activists working on statelessness in different countries around the world with whom I have had the privilege of interacting.

Finally, thanks to Robert Cohen, whose support throughout the years I have been researching and writing on these issues has been the foundation of everything.

CONTENTS

ABBREVIATIONS

ACHPR	African Commission on Human and Peoples' Rights
ACERWC	African Committee of Experts on the Rights and Welfare of the Child
ACRWC	African Charter on the Rights and Welfare of the Child
AEF	*Afrique équatoriale française* (French Equatorial Africa)
AOF	*Afrique occidentale française* (French West Africa)
AU	African Union
CEDAW	Convention on the Elimination of All Forms of Discrimination Against Women
CERD	Convention on the Elimination of All Forms of Racial Discrimination
CPA	Comprehensive Peace Agreement (Sudan)
CRC	Convention on the Rights of the Child
DRC	Democratic Republic of Congo
EAC	East African Community
ECOWAS	Economic Community of West African States
EU	European Union
ICCPR	International Covenant on Civil and Political Rights
ICJ	International Court of Justice
IOM	International Organisation for Migration
IRIN	Integrated Regional Information Networks (formerly of the UN)
OAU	Organisation of African Unity
PALOP	*Países Africanos de Língua Oficial Portuguesa* (African countries with Portuguese as the Official Language
PCA	Permanent Court of Arbitration
PCIJ	Permanent Court of International Justice
SADC	Southern African Development Community

SPLA/M	Sudan People's Liberation Army/Movement
UK	United Kingdom (of Great Britain and Northern Ireland)
UN	United Nations
UNHCR	UN High Commissioner for Refugees
UNICEF	UN Children's Fund

PART I

Introduction

1

International Law and the Right to a Nationality

A child born in Kailahun district of north east Sierra Leone as a member of the Kissi people is likely to have extended family across three countries. The district forms a promontory of territory between Liberia and Guinea; an anomaly created by the classic ruthless division of existing socio-political units by colonial borders.

Each of the three countries has entirely different formal legal traditions, and entirely different rules on who qualifies for its nationality. Let us say that our Sierra Leonean child, we'll call him Samson, does well in school, and wishes to go and study in Freetown on a government scholarship. To qualify for the scholarship, he will need confirmation that he is Sierra Leonean. The rules applied in Sierra Leone under the 1973 Citizenship Act are that a person is a citizen if born in Sierra Leone of one parent also born there, provided the parent is of 'negro African descent'. Samson has a cousin in Guinea, we'll call him Georges. Georges wants to study in Conakry, and to get the equivalent scholarship he has to fulfil the requirements on nationality set out in the 1983 civil code, and show either that he has a Guinean parent, or that he was born in Guinea and has remained resident there until he turned 18. The third cousin, Lisa, was born in Sierra Leone, but moved to Liberia when very small with her mother, who was herself born there, and she has grown up in Liberia. Liberian law contradicts itself: the constitution says that the child of a Liberian mother or father obtains Liberian citizenship at birth; but the Citizenship and Aliens Act of 1973 says that citizenship is acquired automatically based on birth in Liberia, while women cannot transmit citizenship to their children born outside Liberia. Only 'negroes' are eligible for Liberian citizenship.

One ethnic group, three countries, three entirely different citizenship regimes; or three and a half, if Liberia's contradictions are taken into account. Add to these complications the fact that birth registration, the primary route established in law to prove a child's origins, is only around 5 per cent in Liberia, and well under 50 per cent in Guinea, though almost 80 per cent in Sierra Leone. Guinea has had a requirement to carry a national identity card since independence, but in practice less than half the adult population is estimated to hold one. Sierra Leone and Liberia only began the process of introducing national identity cards from around 2015. In Guinea, a magistrate has the power to confirm whether or not Georges is Guinean by birth; in Liberia and Sierra Leone, however, the executive branch is in complete control of the process of determining if a person is a citizen.

In practice, of course, these rules may be of little relevance. What Samson, Georges and Lisa really need for confirmation of their citizenship is the attestation of a traditional leader or other local dignitary recognised by the authorities of each State that they belong to his or her community. With such a letter or oral confirmation, they are likely to be issued the documents they need.

But hold on. Take away the family relationships and solid connections to a community. What if Lisa was the child of a war, the product of a rape by a soldier (Kailahun was the first place in Sierra Leone attacked by the Revolutionary United Front in 1991)? What if Georges was found abandoned as a baby, brought up (but, of course, never formally adopted) by the family who found him? What if Samson's parents were members of the Mandingo ethnic group, born in Guinea, who moved to Sierra Leone for better economic opportunities and because the schools were better? Take away the 'obvious' nature of belonging and suddenly the rules and procedures, coverage of birth registration, and national identification systems become much more important. Not to mention access to legal assistance and funds to support the fees, official and unofficial, that will surround the application for recognition as a national.

There is a rich field of scholarship on questions of identity and belonging in Africa, on the conundrum of nation-building in the post-independence States. This literature is concerned with the complex questions of defining the membership of the 'nation' itself, the entity usually taken for granted in similar debates in the home territories of the European colonial powers. It considers the relative contribution of ethnic identity and diversity as a cause of conflict and political dysfunction, in relation to other factors such as regional underdevelopment, or the accessibility of rich and portable natural resources. More recently, attention has been drawn to the increased intensity of '*autochtone-allochtone*' or 'indigene-settler' conflicts following the re-introduction of multi-party democracy during the 1990s. By contrast to debates over identity and belonging in other continents, however, discussion of the basis of nationality law, the rights of those born in the country, the rules on descent, and the procedures for integration of immigrants through naturalisation have not received major comparative analysis.

The lack of attention to nationality laws in Africa is understandable: on the one hand, most Africans have historically held no document that officially recognised their nationality; on the other, administration of nationality law is often highly corrupt or clearly instrumentalised (or both), meaning that the law, as it is applied in practice, may be quite distant from the law as it is on paper. In a context where censuses are highly unreliable; where many, perhaps most, children are not registered at birth; where the economy is largely informal; and where a large percentage of adults get by with no formal documentation, the definition and content of the legal tie between a person and the State where he or she lives seems less urgent to determine. The situation of those whose right to a nationality is under threat may not differ very much from their neighbours whose nationality is uncontested; while the same problems also arise in communities whose right to belong at the *national* level is uncontroversial and the issue at hand is the right to access resources in a particular local government area, not an international passport.

This book, however, advances a set of interlinked arguments for the relevance of nationality law to the broader crises of citizenship in the continent, and therefore for the role that reforms to the normative frameworks of the law may play at both national and international levels.

Firstly, an examination of the history of nationality law in Africa, from the colonial period, through the transitional provisions on the creation of the new States, and the initial frameworks of nationality applied to those born after independence, sheds light on the (often unanticipated) consequences of these different frameworks for national cohesion today. Secondly, it is worth paying attention to the detail of the ways in which nationality law has been amended and applied – or manipulated – since independence, in comparative perspective, for insights into the political process and the 'imagining' of the national (or local) community. Nationality law is relevant to broader questions of citizenship and participation in African States, as it is in other countries, despite – or because of – the history by which those States came to be created and the institutional weaknesses that resulted. Thirdly, the impact of defects in nationality law and administration on the most marginalised is real and likely to increase, as African States follow the rest of the world in strengthening requirements for identification to access services and as travel within and between countries without documents is ever more difficult. Finally, the relevance of the law means both that efforts to reform the law at national level are meaningful, but also that the weak international normative framework on nationality needs strengthening.

I argue that variations in citizenship laws and regulations may have had important impacts in their own right on the ways in which questions of autochthony or indigeneity have played out in African States since independence. These variations themselves deserve greater study, both to enrich understanding of political crises based on questions of belonging, and to inform future efforts at reform. The substantive and procedural content of nationality laws can in itself either undermine the project of nation-building that has so bedevilled the continent or, alternatively, become a tool to use in that effort.

To date, advocacy for reform of nationality laws in Africa has focused on two main issues: gender equality in transmission of nationality, led by the women's rights movement; and dual nationality, influenced by the trend to gender equality, but largely driven by African diaspora groups. They have had great success: Africa has shared the strong global trends towards equal rights of men and women in nationality, and towards acceptance of dual nationality. There has been much less advocacy around an individual's right to a nationality in the State where he or she has the strongest connections; where he or she was born and brought up, has earned a living, born children, and centred his or her life. In part, this lack of advocacy reflects – and is reflected by – the weakness of international law in this area.

While the Universal Declaration of Human Rights of 1948 proclaims that 'everyone has the right to a nationality', the precise country obliged to recognise a person's nationality has, despite some restrictions, remained quite unclear. Though the point on gender equality is now (mostly) conceded, States in Africa as elsewhere still hold strongly onto the idea of nationality being a matter of sovereign discretion and not of human rights. This book joins the chorus of those arguing that the national and international law frameworks need reform, to establish the right to nationality based on criteria recognising strong connections to a territory through birth and residence as well as descent, and records efforts at the national and African levels to do so.

1.1. What's in a Word: Citizenship or Nationality?

Some discussion of terminology is a necessary preliminary before embarking on a debate over the impact of formal legal rules on broader questions belonging and participation, starting from the words 'citizenship' and 'nationality' themselves.

Nationality and citizenship are now used as synonyms in international law, to describe the legal relationship between the State and the individual that recognises the individual as having certain rights and obligations in that State.[1] In this book, the terms will accordingly be used interchangeably, but with usage varying by context (usually the language of the country under consideration and the terminology of that country's laws).

However, it is hard to understand debates around citizenship without understanding how these terms are used in different contexts. The two dominant legal traditions considered in this book, the common law and civil law, have different approaches. 'Nationality' and 'national' are in both traditions the usual term used in international legal texts for the idea of legal membership of a country; though even there the usage is not consistent.[2] At domestic level, laws in the anglophone common law tradition (including the US, for these purposes) most commonly use 'citizenship' as the term to describe the legal bond between individual and State. The UK itself creates enormous confusion with the different terms that have been used over time (see Chapter 3.1), and the colonial distinctions have traces

[1] Paul Weis, *Nationality and Statelessness in International Law* (2nd edn, Brill 1979) ch 1; Laurie Fransman, Adrian Berry and Alison Harvey, *Fransman's British Nationality Law* (3rd edn, Bloomsbury Professional 2011) ch 1.2.

[2] eg, the Universal Declaration of Human Rights states that 'Everyone has the right to a nationality' (Art 15). Yet some treaties use 'citizenship' and 'citizen' in the same context: the International Convention on the Elimination of All Forms of Racial Discrimination refers to discrimination between citizens and non-citizens (Art 25), rather than nationals and non-nationals. French then contributes a third term, that of *ressortissant*, often used where 'national' appears in the English version of a text. A *ressortissant* is a person falling under the jurisdiction of a State, but has a wider meaning than that of *national*, covering persons under the protection of a State; though the extent to which it covers non-nationals is not entirely clear. Weis (n 1) 8–10.

till today in the several different categories of 'British national', among whom only 'British citizens' (a status created in 1981) have the full range of rights.[3] In the French and Belgian civil law tradition, meanwhile, *nationalité* is the term used at both international and national levels to describe the legal bond between a person and a political entity, and the rules for membership of the community. Where a Commonwealth State would have a national citizenship act, a member of the Francophonie has a *code de la nationalité. Citoyenneté* is not used in this context.

Moving beyond the world of law and legal definition, moreover, the two words come from different historical and academic traditions, and in practice different authors use them to mean different things, even when discussing legal issues. These etymological overtones make it hard to use the terms equally with neutral effect. In general, we can make some broad distinctions. Citizenship and its cognates in other languages – derived from city – have connotations related to civil rights and participation. Nationality and its cognates – derived from nation – have connotations related to ethnicity, family, and culture.[4]

For sociologists and political scientists, the scholarly debate over 'citizenship' is mainly about the content of citizenship: what are (or should be) the rights of members of the national community?[5] These debates have a genealogy reaching far back into European history, from the challenge to allegiance based on feudal overlordship and the divine right of kings, ascribed at birth and due to the sovereign from all in his territory. As the great dynastic monarchies began to decline, enlightenment thinkers such as Locke and Rousseau theorised the social contract that binds citizens together (meaning that citizenship should be consented to, even notionally by choice of residence, as an adult man).[6] Others favouring the city States of Switzerland rather drew on descent as a proxy for consent (since a child could be assumed to wish to share his father's citizenship, with the option to reject

[3] British legislation since 1914 has used the term 'nationality' to cover a range of statuses governed in law. The term 'citizen' was first used in 1948 (to create the category of 'citizen of the UK and colonies' for those who were formerly 'British subjects'), and the status of 'British citizen' was introduced by the British Nationality Act of 1981. The act maintains distinctions between eight different grades of nationals (some of them almost obsolete), with only 'British citizens' having full rights, including the 'right of abode' in the UK. As a result of these complications the UK has unilaterally made declarations in relation to the definition of its nationals for the purposes of the EU, while the UK has not ratified the Protocol 4 to the European Convention on Human Rights (on the right of a person to enter the country of which he or she is a national) or the European Convention on Nationality 1997. See Fransman, Berry and Harvey (n 1) 65 & 87–89.

[4] For the wealth of possible confusions, see the discussion of the meanings of 'citizenship' and 'nationality' and their equivalents in many different European languages at the website of the Global Citizenship Observatory http://globalcit.eu/terminology/.

[5] A useful overview of these debates is provided in the essays extracted in Gershon Shafir (ed), *The Citizenship Debates: A Reader* (University of Minnesota Press 1998).

[6] For an exposition of the distinction between citizenship based on ascription or consent, with particular reference to the American context, see Peter H Schuck and Rogers M Smith, *Citizenship Without Consent: Illegal Aliens in the American Policy* (Yale Univ Press 1985); also Myres S McDougal, Harold D Lasswell and Lung-chu Chen, 'Nationality and Human Rights: The Protection of the Individual in External Arenas' (1974) 83 Yale Law Journal 900 at 918–928.

it at majority),[7] and thereby also created an assumption of shared identity rather than common political allegiance.

Discussions since then have continued to swirl around the different conceptions of citizenship: whether it should be ascribed at birth or acquired through voluntary agreement; whether it is a legal status based on a notional contract between citizen and State and carrying with it rights and obligations, or rather a 'republican' (in the French sense) or 'performative' idea, in which people become and are recognised as citizens through their participation in the political and public space.[8] Some in the 'citizenship studies' tradition argue for a complete move away from the 'sovereign temporal and spatial framework' in theorising citizenship (in the broader sense).[9]

'Nationality' also has its own traditions separate from international law. The proximity of 'nationality' to the idea of 'nation', means that in some contexts the term nationality is used with the connotation that someone of a particular (legal) nationality should belong to the racial, religious or ethnic group believed to make up that nation.[10] In this sense, the difference between citizenship and nationality is seen not as the distinction between the rights of members of the polity and the rules that define who is a member, but between a definition based on active participation, and a status-based definition, in this case deriving from descent and identity.

Patrick Chabal, for example, uses 'nationality' to mean 'the cluster of historical and cultural characteristics which are (implicitly or explicitly) recognised by the national subjects as defining a particular country, if only in relation to other countries'.[11] Patricia Nanz, discussing the EU citizenship regime, uses nationality to mean belonging, and citizenship to mean legal status.[12] The frequent use

[7] The founding exponent of this view was the Swiss writer Emmerich de Vattel, highly influential in the early discussions of citizenship in the US; his book *Le droit des gens, Ou Principes de la loi naturelle, appliqués à la conduite & aux affaires des nations & des souverains*, first published 1758, was rapidly translated into English with the first definitive edition in 1797 titled *The Law of Nations, Or, Principles of the Law of Nature, Applied to the Conduct and Affairs of Nations and Sovereigns*. On citizenship, see especially Book I, ch 19, Of Our Native Country, and Several Things That Relate to It.

[8] On the connotations of *nationalité* and *citoyenneté* in French, see Patrick Weil, *Qu'est-ce qu'un Français? Histoire de la nationalité française de la Révolution à nos jours* (Grasset 2002); Gérard Noiriel, 'Socio-histoire d'un concept: Les usages du mot « nationalité » au XIXe siècle' (1995) 20 Genèses 4; Olivier Gohin, 'La citoyenneté dans l'outre-mer français' (2002) 101 Revue française d'administration publique 69.

[9] Aolileann Ní Mhurchú, 'Citizenship beyond State and Sovereignty' in Engin F Isin and Peter Nyers (eds), *Routledge Handbook of Global Citizenship Studies* (Routledge 2014).

[10] Chaim Gans, 'Citizenship and Nationhood' in Ayelet Shachar and others (eds), *The Oxford Handbook of Citizenship* (Oxford University Press 2017).

[11] Patrick Chabal, *Power in Africa: An Essay in Interpretation* (Palgrave Macmillan 1993) 121.

[12] Patricia Nanz, 'Mobility, Migrants and Solidarity: Towards an Emerging European Citizenship' in Seyla Benhabib and Judith Resnik (eds), *Migrations and Mobilities: Citizenship, Borders and Gender* (NYU Press 2009) 412. See also Stephen Castles and Alastair Davidson, *Citizenship and Migration: Globalization and the Politics of Belonging* (Palgrave Macmillan 2000) 12, on the 'contradiction between citizenship and nationality, or between the nation of a citizen as an individual abstracted from cultural characteristics, and that of a national as a member of a community with common cultural values'.

of 'nation-state' in both journalism and academic literature to mean, in different contexts, both a State based on a pre-existing culturally and ethnically unified nation, and a State that is in the process of building an idea of national identity, does not help with this confusion.[13] The very name of the United *Nations*, a collective of *States* responsible for defining the rules on these issues at international level, reinforces the problem.

In law, however, neither 'citizenship' nor 'nationality' is used (in English or French) to indicate the ethnic origin of the individual concerned: the terms refer only to the legal bond between a person and a State, and the rights and obligations that accompany that bond. Yet even in legal usage, the terms to describe the main ways in which the legal status of nationality is acquired can lead to misunderstandings. In particular, the distinction between *jus sanguinis* and *jus soli* systems for acquiring nationality encourages the sense that *jus sanguinis* – the law of *blood*, even if disguised in Latin – means membership of an ethnically defined nation; a meaning emphasised by the formerly almost universal rule that it was only a father that could pass nationality to his child, allegedly to avoid the possibility of dual nationality but in practice preserving male-line genealogies. A *jus sanguinis* principle need not have any ethnic or racial basis – the requirement is only that the parent be a citizen (including by naturalisation). Nonetheless, the principle has in some countries an explicit ethnic or racial component, so that access to legal citizenship is facilitated or restricted based on membership of the dominant ethnic, racial or religious group in a country.[14]

Similar nuances exist in other languages. In a discussion of the management of nationality in the context of State succession in Sudan, Munzoul Assal argues that:

> In Sudan… both law and common discourse focus on nationality (jinsiyya in Arabic) rather than on citizenship (muwatana in Arabic). [T]he concept of nationality valorises ethnicity… emphasising nationality instead of citizenship results in disenfranchising the less privileged segments of the population. There is a need to shift the emphasis from nationality to citizenship, which becomes particularly urgent as the constitutional foundation is being laid for two new States.[15]

[13] eg, see Richard Dowden 'The State of the African State: The Past, Present and Future of the Nation State in Africa' *IPPR Progressive Review* (Institute for Public Policy Research 2004). Jeffrey Herbst talks of finding 'alternatives to the nation-state in Africa', Jeffrey Herbst, *States and Power in Africa: Comparative Lessons in Authority and Control* (Princeton University Press 2001) 259. See also, Peter Geschiere, *The Perils of Belonging: Autochthony, Citizenship, and Exclusion in Africa and Europe* (University of Chicago Press 2009), on the idea of defining the nation in the 'republican' way; Will Kymlicka, *Multicultural Citizenship* (Oxford University Press 1996); Castles and Davidson (n 12); Arjun Appadurai, *Modernity at Large: Cultural Dimensions of Globalization* (University of Minnesota Press 1996).

[14] Even in international treaties, the use of 'national or social origin' in, eg, the list of prohibited grounds for discrimination contained in the International Covenant on Civil and Political Rights (Art 2), creates a sense of overlap between the idea of nationality and the idea of ethnic identity.

[15] Munzoul AM Assal, 'Nationality and Citizenship Questions in Sudan after the Southern Sudan Referendum Vote' (Christian Michelsen Institute 2011). For more on the distinctions between *jinsiyya* and *muwatana* see Gianluca P Parolin, *Citizenship in the Arab World: Kin, Religion and Nation-State* (Amsterdam University Press 2009).

No doubt there are further overlaps and nuances in the words used to translate these concepts into national languages across the African continent.[16]

Even in contexts divorced from ideas of ethnic affiliation, distinctions between nationality as the legal bond with a particular State applicable at the international level, and citizenship as the full right to participate in the public affairs of that State, are by no means irrelevant in the twenty first century. Most obviously, gender discrimination was the norm until very recently in most countries and, though diminishing, is still quite pervasive. In the realm of nationality law, some of the older international treaties in fact assumed that gender discrimination would be applied, while trying to minimise the Statelessness that could result (see Chapter 1.2). In relation to citizenship as political participation, adult women were of course late to be given the universal right to vote (and still cannot in some countries), and often had or have lesser rights in relation to property, family decision-making and other matters.

The distinction between the concept of citizenship as full membership and nationality as the basic legal link also allowed for – and was reinforced by – the systems of legalised racial, ethnic and religious discrimination that were implemented in the European colonial States, most of all in Africa; systems which of course also emphasised primordial membership rather than procedural systems of managing the right to belong. In African countries under colonial or white minority rule, only those of European descent had both nationality and full citizenship rights, and only a tiny minority of Africans were ever given the right to cross that line, whatever other criteria they might fulfil. Even once the 1946 constitution of the French Fourth Republic explicitly stated that there was a common citizenship across the *Union française*, the rules still allowed for different rights to political participation and civil liberties for those with French civil status and those *indigènes* or natives subject to local personal law. Britain retained similar distinctions to the date of independence.[17] Only with the departure of the colonial empires was a unified citizenship status legislated in the newly independent African countries (see Chapter 4).

These etymological variations over time are reflected in contemporary debates around the nature of 'citizenship', and whether it is something that is claimed or granted. The focus of this book is the influence that the underlying legal regime has on the ability of a particular person to claim the rights of participation implied by the broader meaning of the term.

[16] For Swahili, see Carol MM Scotton, 'Some Swahili Political Words' (1965) 3 Journal of Modern African Studies 527; Emma Hunter, 'Dutiful Subjects, Patriotic Citizens, and the Concept of 'Good Citizenship' in Twentieth Century Tanzania' (2013) 56 The Historical Journal 257.

[17] Even in Britain itself, those seeking assistance under the Poor Laws were disenfranchised until as late as 1918, when the link between economic substance and political rights was finally broken, and political rights became linked instead simply to personal status as citizen; plural voting for those graduated from university was only finally abolished by Representation of the People Act 1948 – the same year as the first major nationality law reform.

1.2. The Regulation of Nationality in International Law

The ambiguities in the concepts of citizenship and nationality are reflected in and partly derive from the history of nationality law itself. Most of all, from the fact that nationality as a legal concept was originally designed to manage relations between States, not between States and their citizens.

The two principal rules accepted as giving a State the right to attribute nationality to a person at birth were the familiar basic concepts of *jus soli*, where an individual obtains nationality simply because he or she was born in a particular country, and *jus sanguinis*, where nationality is based on descent from a parent or parents who themselves are nationals.

In its historical origins, *jus soli* citizenship was based on concepts of feudal loyalty: a person born in a particular territory owed allegiance to the sovereign of that territory, with exceptions only for the child of a diplomatic representative of a foreign power. This concept of citizenship – or subjecthood – was dominant in Britain throughout its history, and carried over into its foreign territories, including the US. The foundations of British nationality law are the early litigation around the nature of the identity and rights of those who were subjects of the English monarch, notably the 1608 judgment in *Calvin's case* relating to the rights of those born before or after the union of the English and Scottish crowns, which emphasised the importance of place (and date) of birth. This absolute *jus soli* basis for English and later British nationality law (following the formal Acts of Union between England and Scotland in 1707) remained in place until it was diluted in 1981.[18]

France started from the same framework, but the post-revolutionary government introduced *jus sanguinis* rules from the early nineteenth century, aiming to create independent citizens who were no longer the permanent subjects of a single sovereign.[19] Rules on the acquisition of French citizenship were first codified in the constitutions adopted in the wake of the French revolution, which were based on the same *jus soli* principles that had been understood as in operation under the *ancien régime*, attributing the *qualité de français* to those born in France and domiciled there, and, for the first years after the revolution, even automatically to those resident in the country for a period of time. In 1804, however, the Code Napoléon separated French nationality as a constitutional matter from the exercise of civil rights; within this new civil code, *jus sanguinis* applied, so that a person was French if born to a French father.[20] After successive debates on the issue, often dominated

[18] Fransman, Berry and Harvey (n 1) ch 5.

[19] Weil, *Qu'est-ce qu'un Français?* (n 8); Patrick Weil, 'From Conditional to Secured and Sovereign: The New Strategic Link between the Citizen and the Nation-State in a Globalized World' (2011) 9 International Journal of Constitutional Law 615.

[20] For a summary of the historical development of both English and French concepts see introductory chapter to Gerard-René de Groot and Olivier W Vonk, *International Standards on Nationality Law: Texts, Cases and Materials* (Wolf Legal Publishers 2015).

by the needs of the French State for conscripted soldiers to serve in the army, in 1851 a general reform reinstated a variant on *jus soli* principles, introducing for the first time the double *jus soli* rule for those born in France of a foreign parent also born in France; such children could also repudiate French nationality at majority.

These different trajectories of Britain and France continue to have influence in Africa today, as the remainder of this book will demonstrate.

There is also a common distinction in law between nationality enjoyed from the moment of birth (termed 'nationality of origin' in the civil law countries) and nationality that is acquired at a later date by a person who was previously a foreigner. These distinctions can have important consequences for the rights of the person concerned. In many countries, the rights of those who are nationals from birth or by acquisition are the same; but others apply distinctions, especially in relation to the holding of public office or the conditions for withdrawal of nationality. Nationality from birth/of origin may be based either on descent or on birth in the country, but implies that a child is automatically attributed a nationality from the moment of birth without any further procedures required for recognition by the State (though in practice the facts entitling a person to that citizenship will of course have to be proved).[21] Nationality by acquisition relates to those who have become citizens at a later date, usually as adults. Historically, the most common reason for acquiring a new nationality was by a woman on marriage to a foreign man; but with the expansion of the European empires, and in particular the mass emigration from Europe to the US, rules about naturalisation and change of nationality became more contentious.[22]

International norms on nationality law thus developed during the nineteenth century, as migration became much more common and individuals sought to change their allegiance from one State to another. The rules on nationality emerged from international litigation over the rights of States to intervene on behalf of their nationals when travelling abroad, or of companies registered in their territory in commercial disputes. That is, the framework for international law on nationality was developed in parallel with the rules on diplomatic protection and on conflict of laws. At the same time, States retained a very wide discretion to decide which individuals were their nationals, when to offer them diplomatic protection overseas, and what rights to grant to them at home. The grant of nationality was

[21] In some circumstances in some countries, the law provides that an individual can obtain retroactive recognition of citizenship from birth/of origin *after* birth. There is also a confusion caused by the fact that in many Commonwealth countries, the term used in law for citizenship from birth is often citizenship 'by birth', based on the laws drafted at independence which borrowed the term used in British for citizenship granted at birth on the basis of birth in a territory (by *jus soli*). This usage has continued even where *jus soli* citizenship no longer applies.

[22] The terminology for acquisition of nationality in another country is not consistent, although the Global Citizenship Observatory has developed a glossary seeking to create such consistency around the processes by which citizenship may be acquired: declaration (the lodging of a form is sufficient), registration (non-discretionary but the authorities must note the acquisition), and naturalisation (discretionary grant, usually on the basis of long-term residence), available at http://globalcit.eu/glossary_citizenship_nationality/.

regarded as being within the 'reserved domain' of States, a position affirmed by the Permanent Court of International Justice (PCIJ) in 1923.[23]

Historically, theorists and legal scholars of nationality were mainly exercised about questions of wrongful attribution of nationality. The imposition of nationality on individuals which the State could not reasonably claim as its own would infringe on the sovereignty of other States: this indeed was the issue contested between Britain and France before the PCIJ in 1923 (see Chapter 3.2).[24] Avoidance of dual nationality was also a major concern. From the State's point of view it was intolerable to contemplate that a person could have two sets of loyalties; while for the individual two nationalities implied two sets of obligations, especially the obligation of military service.[25] Similarly, many States imposed a requirement to be released from nationality if a person wished to change nationality; the requirement, based on an idea of perpetual allegiance, was largely relinquished by European States during the nineteenth and twentieth centuries (under pressure from the US, wishing the possibility of gaining naturalised citizens in the context where dual nationality was not considered a possibility), but preserved in countries with an Islamic law tradition.[26]

In 1930, the Hague Convention on Certain Questions Relating to the Conflict of Nationality Laws established the first multilateral treaty recognition that State discretion in applying these principles was not absolute. Its preamble noted the interest of the international community to ensure that all countries recognise that 'every person should have a nationality'.[27] While affirming that each State may determine its own nationality laws, Article 1 of the Convention requires other States to recognise these laws only insofar as they are consistent with international

[23] *Advisory Opinion No. 4, Nationality Decrees Issued in Tunis and Morocco*, Permanent Court of International Justice, (1923) PCIJ, Ser. B, No. 4. See also ch 3.2.

[24] Weis (n 1); Ian Brownlie, 'The Relations of Nationality in Public International Law' (1963) 39 British Yearbook of International Law 284; Ruth Donner, *The Regulation of Nationality in International Law* (Transnational Publishers Inc 1994); Serena Forlati, 'Nationality as a Human Right' in Alessandra Annoni and Serena Forlati (eds), *The changing role of nationality in international law* (Routledge 2013); Enrico Milano, 'The Conferral of Citizenship En Masse by Kin-States: Creeping Annexation or Responsibility to Protect?' in Francesco Palermo and Natalie Sabanadze (eds), *National Minorities in Inter-State Relations* (Martinus Nijhoff Publishers 2011); High Commissioner on National Minorities, 'The Bolzano/Bozen Recommendations on National Minorities in Inter-State Relations & Explanatory Note'.

[25] Alfred Michael Boll, *Multiple Nationality and International Law* (Martinus Nijhoff Publishers 2007); Michel Verwilghen, *Conflits de nationalités, Plurinationalité et apatridie*, vol 277 (Hague Academy of International Law 1999).

[26] Peter Spiro, 'A New International Law of Citizenship' (2011) 105 The American Journal of International Law 694 at pp 707–709; Parolin (n 15) 108.

[27] Among the few ratifications of the treaty (which remains in force though largely superseded) were a number of African countries. Out of 23 States total (with a much larger number of signatories who did not ratify), five are African: Lesotho, Liberia, Mauritius, Swaziland and Zimbabwe; Egypt and South Africa signed but have not ratified. Britain ratified on behalf of itself 'and all parts of the British Empire which are not separate members of the League of Nations', but only a handful of former British protectorates have formally notified their succession to these obligations. Belgium's ratification was 'Subject to accession later for the Colony of the Congo'. Status of Treaties at UN Treaty Collection Depositary, https://treaties.un.org.

conventions, custom, and 'principles of law generally recognised with regard to nationality'.[28] The Hague Convention is also the earliest international statement of the rule that, where parents and location of birth are unknown, a child found in the territory shall be presumed to have been born there of parents holding the nationality of that State. Nonetheless, the convention was essentially designed to remove any doubt about which State was entitled to exercise its authority over and on behalf of any person. It aimed to harmonise rules among States in order to reduce Statelessness while also reducing the incidence of dual nationality.[29] The Hague Convention also contained the rule that a State could not exercise diplomatic protection on behalf of its national against another State of which the person was also a national.[30] This approach was, however, rejected by the US in particular, which wished to retain the possibility of exercising diplomatic protection in favour of its citizens when visiting (but not resettling in) the countries of their birth nationality. The concept of dominant or effective nationality emerged to accommodate such cases.[31]

Since the Hague Convention, the surrounding framework of international law on the meaning of nationality has changed beyond recognition. The adoption of the Universal Declaration of Human Rights in 1948 marked the most significant step forward; in this as in other commitments shaped by the brutal history of the just-concluded war. Article 15 provides that '[e]veryone has a right to a nationality' and that '[n]o one shall be arbitrarily deprived of his nationality nor denied the right to change his nationality'. The critical omission from the declaration, however, was an indication as to which State had the obligation to fulfil the right.

The most famous judicial elaboration of the concept of nationality, the 1955 *Nottebohm* case before the International Court of Justice (ICJ), does not much elucidate. Though post-dating the Universal Declaration, its reasoning and the facts of the case were founded in the pre-Universal Declaration framework of diplomatic protection and conflict of laws. In the much-quoted judgment, the court stated that:

> According to the practice of States, to arbitral and judicial decisions and to the opinion of writers, nationality is a legal bond having as its basis a social fact of attachment, a genuine connection of existence, interest and sentiments, together with the existence of

[28] 'It is for each State to determine under its own laws who are its nationals. This law shall be recognized by other States in so far as it is consistent with international conventions, international custom, and the principles of law generally recognized with regard to nationality.' League of Nations, Convention on Certain Questions Relating to the Conflict of Nationality Law, 13 April 1930 (entered into force 1937), art 1.

[29] Weis (n 1); Boll (n 25); Verwilghen (n 25). A Special Protocol Concerning Statelessness adopted by the same Hague conference, which never entered into force, only dealt with readmission of nationals who had been deprived of their nationality after entering a foreign country.

[30] Art 4 'A State may not afford diplomatic protection to one of its nationals against a State whose nationality such person also possesses.'

[31] On dominant nationality in potential dual nationality cases, see Donner (n 24), ch II (The principle of the 'effective link' in nationality law), s 4.

> reciprocal rights and duties. It may be said to constitute the juridical expression of the fact that the individual upon whom it is conferred either directly by the law or as a result of an act of the authorities, is in fact more closely connected with the population of the State conferring nationality than with that of any other State.[32]

The key to the case was that the ICJ determined that the lack of a 'genuine connection' (often reformulated as 'genuine link')[33] between Nottebohm and Liechtenstein meant that, although Nottebohm was a naturalised citizen, Liechtenstein had no right to exercise diplomatic protection on his behalf in relation to Guatemala (a country where, as a matter of fact, he had much stronger ties).[34] The case did not concern Nottebohm's own rights to either nationality – and has been criticised on the grounds that, if applied more widely today, the 'genuine connection' requirement could leave many at risk of Statelessness.[35]

The treaty framework that built up in support of the Universal Declaration gradually buttressed the idea of the right to a nationality as belonging to the individual and not the State. First to be adopted was the 1954 Convention relating to the Status of Stateless Persons, which envisages the protection of those persons who are 'not considered as a national by any State under the operation of its law' (Article 1(1)). The 1954 Convention was conceived as a pair with the 1951 Convention relating to the Status of Refugees, and follows an almost identical format.[36] The 1961 Convention on the Reduction of Statelessness was the first treaty to make it a duty of States to prevent Statelessness in nationality laws and practices. Nonetheless, many of its articles are bound about with caveats reflecting 'the unfortunate hallmarks of an international compromise'.[37]

The two treaties do not focus on the positive right to a nationality, but rather on showing a negative (lack of nationality) and then providing protection. This is true most obviously of the 1954 Convention; but also, perhaps more importantly, of the key provision in the 1961 Convention (also included in the 1969 Inter-American Convention on Human Rights)[38] that a child who is 'otherwise Stateless' should be

[32] *Nottebohm Case (Liechtenstein v Guatemala) (second phase)*, Judgment of 6 April 1955, ICJ Reports 1955, p 23. Liechtenstein sought a ruling that Guatemala should recognise Friedrich Nottebohm as a Liechtenstein national.

[33] eg, in international treaties, Art 5(1) of the Convention on the High Seas, 1958, on the nationality of ships states that 'There must exist a genuine link between the State and the ship'.

[34] The interpretation could be justified by the fact that he had blatantly sought to abuse the rules applying to nationality for his own benefit: Nottebohm had changed nationality from Germany to Liechtenstein purely to avoid being an 'enemy alien' in Guatemala.

[35] Robert D Sloane, 'Breaking the Genuine Link: The Contemporary International Legal Regulation of Nationality' (2009) 50 Harvard International Law Journal 1.

[36] Guy S Goodwin-Gill, 'Convention Relating to the Status of Stateless Persons', United Nations 2010 http://legal.un.org/avl/pdf/ha/cssp/cssp_e.pdf.

[37] Laura van Waas, 'The UN Statelessness Conventions' in Alice Edwards and Laura van Waas (eds), *Nationality and Statelessness under International Law* (Cambridge University Press 2014) 75; Mark Manly, 'UNHCR's Mandate and Activities to Address Statelessness' in Alice Edwards and Laura van Waas (eds), *Nationality and Statelessness under International Law* (Cambridge University Press 2014).

[38] American Convention on Human Rights, Art 20 – Right to Nationality. '(1) Every person has the right to a nationality. (2) Every person has the right to the nationality of the State in whose territory

granted the nationality of the State where he or she is born.[39] For the child to claim that nationality, the parents must show that he or she is not a national of another State, a requirement that may be almost impossible to fulfil. The Convention gives no recognition to the accumulation of ties to a territory of birth and residence, even over several generations, that could give a person a right to claim status there – unless he or she can prove the lack of such a right elsewhere.

It was only as the broader framework of human rights treaties built up that the idea of nationality as a human right in itself came to be more established, especially in relation to children.[40] The International Covenant on Civil and Political Rights (ICCPR), adopted in 1966 (entry into force 1976), does not discuss the nationality of adults, but recognises the right of '[e]very child … to acquire a nationality'.[41] This provision is mirrored in the Convention on the Rights of the Child (CRC), which guarantees the right of every child to acquire a nationality, placing a duty on States' parties to respect this right.[42] The much later Migrant Workers Convention (adopted in 1990) simply provides that the children of migrant workers have the right to a nationality – though the Migrant Workers Convention has one of the lowest ratification rates of any international treaty.[43]

The international human rights treaties on discrimination have provided stronger limits on State discretion, in particular the most pervasive form of discrimination in the field of nationality: that based on sex. It was presumed by the drafters of the Hague Convention of 1930 that the nationality of a woman and her children would follow that of her husband; a protocol adopted at the same time added only that a mother should be able to confer nationality on her children at least where the father was unknown or Stateless.[44] The 1957 Convention on the Nationality of Married Women reinforced this understanding and focused on

he was born if he does not have the right to any other nationality. (3) No one shall be arbitrarily deprived of his nationality or of the right to change it.' An important advisory opinion affirmed the right to nationality as recognised in international law: *Re Amendments to the Naturalisation Provisions of the Constitution of Costa Rica*, Inter-American Court of Human Rights, Advisory Opinion of 19 January 1984, OC-4/84.

[39] Johannes MM Chan, 'The Right to a Nationality as a Human Right: The Current Trend Towards Recognition' (1991) 12 Human Rights Law Journal 1.

[40] See René de Groot, 'Preventing Statelessness among Children: Interpreting Articles 1-4 of the 1961 Convention on the Reduction of Statelessness and Relevant International Human Rights Norms', *2011* (UNHCR).

[41] International Covenant on Civil and Political Rights, Art 24(3).

[42] Convention on the Rights of the Child, Art 7(1): 'The child shall be registered immediately after birth and shall have the right from birth to a name, the right to acquire a nationality and, as far as possible, the right to know and be cared for by his or her parents.' Article 8 provides an obligation for States to respect the child's right to preserve her/his identity, which includes the preservation of nationality. For discussion of the meaning of these obligations, see J. E. Doek, 'The CRC and the Right to Acquire and to Preserve a Nationality', *Refugee Survey Quarterly* 25, no. 3 (2006): 26–32; Human Rights Committee, *General Comment No. 17: Rights of the child (Art 24).*

[43] International Convention on the Protection of the Rights of All Migrant Workers and Members of Their Families, Art 29: 'Each child of a migrant worker shall have the right to a name, to registration of birth and to a nationality.'

[44] Protocol Relating to a Certain Case of Statelessness, 12 April 1930.

avoiding Statelessness deriving from conflict of laws, while also attempting to give women more choice in the matter and withdrawing somewhat from the vision of the dependency of the whole family on the husband and father.[45] Only with the 1979 adoption by the UN General Assembly of the Convention for the Elimination of All Forms of Discrimination Against Women (CEDAW) was nationality law brought within the remit of requirements for non-discrimination on the basis of sex.[46] At least in part as a consequence, though without treaty approval, there was a major shift towards acceptance of dual nationality.[47]

Other human rights treaties mention nationality in relation to their own subject matter. For example, the Convention on the Rights of Persons with Disabilities requires States to recognise the rights of persons with disabilities to a nationality, on an equal basis with others.[48]

Discrimination on racial or similar grounds is more complex. The International Convention on the Elimination of Racial Discrimination (CERD) requires that enjoyment of the right to nationality be guaranteed to everyone 'without distinction as to race, colour, or national or ethnic origin'.[49] The 1961 Convention on the Reduction of Statelessness specifically prohibits denationalisation 'on racial, ethnic, religious or political grounds', even if Statelessness would not result.[50] However, recognising that some forms of discrimination are in fact the basis of nationality law, CERD also provides that 'This Convention shall not apply to

[45] For a comprehensive discussion of the history of international law on gender discrimination and nationality, see Karen Knop and Christine Chinkin, 'Remembering Chrystal MacMillan: Women's Equality and Nationality in International Law' (2001) 22 Michigan Journal of International Law 523.

[46] Article 9 requires that 'Parties shall grant women equal rights with men to acquire, change or retain their nationality' and 'with respect to the nationality of their children'; CEDAW also specifies that men and women should have '[t]he same rights and responsibilities as parents, irrespective of their marital status, in matters relating to their children' (Art 16(1)(d)).

[47] Thomas Faist and Peter Kivisto (eds), *Dual Citizenship in Global Perspective: From Unitary to Multiple Citizenship* (Palgrave Macmillan 2007); Yossi Harpaz and Pablo Mateos, 'Strategic Citizenship: Negotiating Membership in the Age of Dual Nationality' (2018) 44 Journal of Ethnic and Migration Studies 1.

[48] Convention on the Rights of Persons with Disabilities, Article 18: '(1) States Parties shall recognize the rights of persons with disabilities to liberty of movement, to freedom to choose their residence and to a nationality, on an equal basis with others, including by ensuring that persons with disabilities: (a) Have the right to acquire and change a nationality and are not deprived of their nationality arbitrarily or on the basis of disability; (b) Are not deprived, on the basis of disability, of their ability to obtain, possess and utilize documentation of their nationality or other documentation of identification, or to utilize relevant processes such as immigration proceedings, that may be needed to facilitate exercise of the right to liberty of movement; (c) Are free to leave any country, including their own; (d) Are not deprived, arbitrarily or on the basis of disability, of the right to enter their own country. (2) Children with disabilities shall be registered immediately after birth and shall have the right from birth to a name, the right to acquire a nationality and, as far as possible, the right to know and be cared for by their parents.'

[49] CERD, Art 5 provides that 'States Parties undertake to prohibit and to eliminate racial discrimination in all its forms and to guarantee the right of everyone without distinction as to race, colour, or national or ethnic origin, to equality before the law, notably in the enjoyment of the following rights:[…] (d) Other civil rights, in particular: […] (iii) The right to nationality.'

[50] Convention on the Reduction of Statelessness, Art 9.

distinctions, exclusions, restrictions or preferences made by a State Party to this Convention between citizens and non-citizens', and excludes from its application 'legal provisions of States parties concerning nationality, citizenship or naturalization, *provided that such provisions do not discriminate against any particular nationality*' (emphasis added).[51]

There is increasing disquiet among human rights bodies at such discriminatory provisions in nationality laws, even where expressed as preferential access to naturalisation for some groups, rather than exclusions for others in relation to access to nationality from birth.[52] In 2005, the UN Committee on the Elimination of Racial Discrimination adopted a General Recommendation which outlined States' obligations in relation to providing access to citizenship, and in particular urged States to: 'Ensure that particular groups of non-citizens are not discriminated against with regard to access to citizenship or naturalization, and to pay due attention to possible barriers to naturalization that may exist for long-term or permanent residents'.[53]

A third burst of normative endeavour on nationality arose from the disintegration of the Soviet Union and the regained independence of the countries of the Warsaw Pact, followed by the civil war in Yugoslavia and the partition of Czechoslovakia into two States. As in the context of decolonisation in Africa, the transfers of legal authority created multiple opportunities for people caught between different rules and discriminations to find themselves Stateless.[54] In 1993, the UN General Assembly endorsed the recommendation of the International Law Commission that, in light of the 'alarming' tendency in recent State successions to emphasise ethnicity rather than domicile in granting a new State's nationality, it develop minimum standards for automatic attribution of nationality in these cases.[55] A special rapporteur was appointed who produced a series of three reports on State practice and the underlying principles of international law.[56]

[51] CERD, Art 1.

[52] For a survey, see Spiro (n 26)., at pp 727–730. The leading case of the Inter-American Court on Human Rights is *Proposed Amendments to the Naturalization Provisions of the Constitution of Costa Rica*, Advisory Opinion OC-4/84, 19 January 1984, Inter-Am. Ct. H.R. (Ser. A) No. 4 (1984).

[53] Committee on the Elimination of Racial Discrimination, *General Recommendation No.30: Discrimination against Non-citizens*, 2005, paras 13–17.

[54] Donner (n 24) ch V (Nationality and State succession); Weis (n 1) ch 11 (Effect of territorial transfers on nationality); Laura van Waas, *Nationality Matters: Statelessness under International Law* (Intersentia 2008) ch VI (Addressing statelessness in the context of State succession); Francesco Costamagna, 'Statelessness in the Context of State Succession: An Appraisal under International Law' in Alessandra Annoni and Serena Forlati (eds), *The Changing Role of Nationality in International Law* (Routledge 2013); Ineta Ziemele, 'State Succession and Issues of Nationality and Statelessness' in Alice Edwards and Laura van Waas (eds), *Nationality and Statelessness under International Law* (Cambridge University Press 2014); Jeffrey L Blackman, 'State Successions and Statelessness: The Emerging Right to an Effective Nationality under International Law' (1997) 19 Michigan Journal of International Law 1141.

[55] Report of the International Law Commission on the work of its forty-fifth session (3 May-23 July 1993), Document A/48/10, reproduced in Yearbook of the International Law Commission 1993, vol. II (2), para 431 et seq. The history is recounted at the UN Audiovisual Library of International law http://legal.un.org/avl/ha/annprss/annprss.html.

[56] International Law Commission, First, Second, and Third Reports on State succession and its impact on the nationality of natural and legal persons submitted by the Special Rapporteur, Mr. Mikulka,

Then, in 1999, the International Law Commission (ILC) adopted the comprehensive draft Articles on Nationality of Natural Persons in Relation to the Succession of States, which emphasise the importance of avoiding Statelessness, reinforce the (contested) presumption in international customary law that people who are habitually resident in a territory should acquire the nationality of that State after State succession, and, perhaps most significantly, challenge the discretion of States to decide which nationals of the former State they wish to acknowledge as their own. The commentary to the Articles explores the concept of the nature of the 'appropriate connection' that would give a person the right to opt for the nationality of a particular State, including habitual residence as well as a legal connection with one of the constituent units of the predecessor State.[57]

The Articles have not been formally adopted by the UN General Assembly, and are therefore not formally binding on Member States.[58] Nonetheless, they remain the most powerful and detailed statement of the principles that should apply, and, in particular, are the strongest global level statement on the obligation of a State to grant its nationality to a person with the strongest links to that State or on the basis of option. The deliberations of the International Law Commission were also influential in the Council of Europe's adoption of the European Convention on Nationality in 1997 (entry into force 2000), which establishes as a basic principle that everyone has the right to a nationality and creates obligations in case of stateless children and adults;[59] and the specific Convention on the Avoidance of Statelessness in Relation to State Succession in 2006.[60]

Documents A/CN.4/467 17 April 1995; A/CN.4/474 and Corr.1-2, 17 April 1996; and A/CN.4/480 and Add.1, 27 February 1997.

[57] International Law Commission, *Articles on Nationality of Natural Persons in relation to the Succession of States, with commentaries*, 1999 (Annex to UNGA Res. 55/153, 12 Dec. 2000), especially Art 11, commentary para 10: 'The core meaning of the term 'appropriate connection' in a particular case is spelled out in Part II, where the criteria, such as habitual residence, appropriate legal connection with one of the constituent units of the predecessor State, or the birth in the territory which is a part of a State concerned, are used in order to define categories of persons entitled to the nationality of a State concerned. However, in the absence of the above-mentioned type of link between a person concerned and a State concerned further criteria, such as being a descendant of a person who is a national of a State concerned or having once resided in the territory which is a part of a State concerned, should be taken into consideration.'

[58] UN General Assembly Resolution 66/92, 'Nationality of natural persons in relation to the succession of States', of 9 December 2011, 'Emphasized the value of the articles in providing guidance to the States dealing with issues of nationality of natural persons in relation to the succession of States, in particular concerning the avoidance of statelessness', but 'Decided that, upon the request of any State, it will revert to the question of nationality of natural persons in relation to the succession of States at an appropriate time, in the light of the development of State practice in those matters'.

[59] European Convention on Nationality, Art 4 – Principles. 'The rules on nationality of each State Party shall be based on the following principles: (a) everyone has the right to a nationality; (b) statelessness shall be avoided; (c) no one shall be arbitrarily deprived of his or her nationality; (d) neither marriage nor the dissolution of a marriage between a national of a State Party and an alien, nor the change of nationality by one of the spouses during marriage, shall automatically affect the nationality of the other spouse.'

[60] Council of Europe Convention on the Avoidance of Statelessness in relation to State Succession, 2006, Art 2 – Right to a Nationality. 'Everyone who, at the time of the State succession, had the

Prompted by the same crisis of statelessness resulting from the break-up of the Soviet Union and its satellite States that led to the ILC's Articles, UNHCR began to expand the interpretation of its mandate under the two statelessness conventions to address the wider concerns relating to State concession in the grant of nationality and not just the protection of stateless persons seeking protection in another country.[61] In 2006, the UNHCR Executive Committee adopted a resolution deciding to make stronger efforts to identify both stateless populations *and* populations with undetermined nationality.[62] In 2012, UNHCR adopted a series of Guidelines on Statelessness elaborating on the interpretation of the 1954 and 1961 Conventions. Amongst other contributions, the Guidelines emphasised the common-sense position that the key factor in determining if a person is stateless is factual State recognition of a person as a national: thus, establishing whether an individual is stateless is 'a mixed question of fact and law'.[63]

The mirrored issues of nationality and statelessness have also come to prominence within the institutions of the African Union; partly as a result of advocacy by the UN agencies and human rights groups, but also as individuals and communities impacted by discrimination and manipulation of the law have mobilised the continental human rights bodies, and as governments themselves have realised the need to provide a stronger legal framework.

The African Charter on Human and Peoples' Rights, adopted in 1981 (entry into force 1986), does not contain a provision on nationality. Nonetheless, many of the complaints brought before the Commission have concerned issues related to arbitrary denial or withdrawal of citizenship, especially in relation to politicians,

nationality of the predecessor State and who has or would become stateless as a result of the State succession has the right to the nationality of a State concerned in accordance with the [provisions of the treaty].' See also the Declaration on the Consequences of State Succession for the Nationality of Natural Persons (the Venice Declaration), adopted in 1980.

[61] This process was first enabled by UN General Assembly Resolution A/RES/49/169 of 24 February 1995; followed by UNHCR Executive Committee Conclusion No. 78 (XLVI) on the Prevention and Reduction of Statelessness and the Protection of Stateless Persons, of 20 October 1995. See Manly, 'UNHCR's mandate and activities to address statelessness'.

[62] UNHCR ExCom Conclusion on Identification, Prevention and Reduction of Statelessness and Protection of Stateless Persons No. 106 (LVII), 6 October 2006.

[63] UNHCR, *Guidelines on Statelessness No. 1: The definition of 'Stateless Person' in Article 1(1) of the 1954 Convention relating to the Status of Stateless Persons*, HCR/GS/12/01, 20 February 2012, para 16; subsequently compiled into the *Handbook on Protection of Stateless Persons under the 1954 Convention Relating to the Status of Stateless Persons*, UNHCR, 2014. See also UNHCR, *Guidelines on Statelessness No. 4: Ensuring Every Child's Right to Acquire a Nationality through Articles 1-4 of the 1961 Convention on the Reduction of Statelessness*, HCR/GS/12/04, 21 December 2012, para 19. In adopting this position, UNHCR moved away from use of the concept of '*de facto* Statelessness', which appears nowhere in any international treaty, but was mentioned in the Final Act of the conference leading to the adoption of the 1961 Convention on the Reduction of Statelessness (Resolution I stated that 'persons who are Stateless *de facto* should as far as possible be treated as Stateless *de jure* to enable them to acquire an effective nationality'). See discussions in Hugh Massey, *UNHCR and De Facto Statelessness*, UNHCR, Division of International Protection, LPPR/2010/01, April 2010; UNHCR, *The Concept of Stateless Persons under International Law (The 'Prato Conclusions')*, UNHCR, 2010; UNHCR, *Statelessness Determination Procedures and the Status of Stateless Persons (The 'Geneva Conclusions')*, December 2010. See also Alison Harvey, 'The "de Facto" Statelessness Debate' (2010) 24 Immigration, Asylum and Nationality Law 257.

but also in the context of mass expulsions (see Chapter 5.5). The Commission has deployed other articles of the African Charter to condemn these violations, including lack of due process (Article 7), right to family life (Article 18), and recognition of legal status (Article 5).[64]

The Protocol to the Charter on the Rights of Women in Africa adopted in 2003 (entry into force 2005) permitted discrimination in relation to women's right to transmit nationality to children and spouses, responding to concerns expressed during the drafting process by the North African States.[65] No case on gender equality in citizenship laws had yet been brought to the African Commission on Human and Peoples' Rights to test the provisions of the Protocol on the Rights of Women against the African Charter itself.

The African Charter on the Rights and Welfare of the Child adopted in 1990 (entry into force 1999) provides a much stronger normative framework on nationality. It echoes the UN Convention on the Rights of the Child, providing in its Article 6 for the right of every child to a name, to registration immediately after birth, and to acquire a nationality. In addition, it integrates a requirement based on Article 1 of the Convention on the Reduction of Statelessness that 'a child shall acquire the nationality of the State in the territory of which he has been born if, at the time of the child's birth, he is not granted nationality by any other State in accordance with its laws' (Article 6(4)).

The very first decision on the merits of a communication to the African Committee of Experts on the Rights and Welfare of the Child, issued in 2011, concerned the nationality of children of Nubian descent born in Kenya, in which the Committee of Experts found Kenya in violation of its obligations.[66] In 2014, the Committee of Experts adopted a General Comment on Article 6, which recalled this decision and 'reminds African States that States do not enjoy unfettered discretion in establishing rules for the conferral of their nationality, but must do so in a manner consistent with their international legal obligations.' After noting that 'the lack of recognition as a full participant in the political and social life of the country where a person has been born and lived all his or her life, has been at the heart of many of Africa's most intractable political crises and civil conflicts', the Committee condemns discrimination in rules relating to nationality, whether on the basis of sex (thus rejecting the proposition of the Protocol on the Rights of Women) or on

[64] For a presentation of the jurisprudence of the African human rights institutions, see Bronwen Manby, *Citizenship Law in Africa: A Comparative Study* (3rd edn, Open Society Foundations 2016).

[65] See discussion of the drafting process in Fareda Banda, 'Protocol to the African Charter on the Rights of Women in Africa' in Malcolm D Evans and Rachel Murray (eds), *The African Charter on Human and Peoples' Rights: the system in practice, 1986–2000* (2nd ed, Cambridge University Press 2008). Article 6 provides that: 'g) a woman shall have the right to retain her nationality or to acquire the nationality of her husband; h) a woman and a man shall have equal rights with respect to the nationality of their children except where this is contrary to a provision in national legislation or is contrary to national security interests.'

[66] Communication 002/2009, *Institute for Human Rights and Development in Africa and Open Society Justice Initiative on behalf of Children of Nubian Descent in Kenya*, African Committee of Experts on the Rights and Welfare of the Child, 22 March 2011 (the 'Kenyan Nubian Children's case'), para 53.

the grounds of race, religion and ethnicity, and makes various recommendations in line with these principles, including that States' parties should adopt legal provisions that grant nationality to children born on their territory not only where the child is otherwise stateless, but also in other cases where the child has the strongest connection to that State.[67]

The African Commission on Human and Peoples' Rights has also returned to the right to a nationality. Resolutions adopted by the Commission in 2013 and 2014 commissioned a study on nationality and decided to move towards the adoption of a draft protocol to the Charter to elaborate this right.[68] In 2015, the Commission adopted the text of a draft Protocol on the Specific Aspects of the Right to a Nationality and the Eradication of Statelessness in Africa, a text that would then move forward to be considered for adoption by the political institutions of the African Union. The proposal for a protocol was accepted by the Executive Council of the African Union in July 2016.[69]

At sub-regional level these issues have also received attention, most notably among the Economic Community of West African States (ECOWAS), where ministers and then heads of State adopted in 2015 the Abidjan Declaration on the Eradication of Statelessness, committing 'to prevent and reduce statelessness by reforming constitutional, legislative and institutional regimes related to nationality.'[70] In 2017, the ECOWAS States adopted a plan of action for the implementation of the declaration.[71] A regional response to nationality and statelessness has been one of the issues addressed by the International Conference on the Great Lakes Region (ICGLR), created in response to the political-military crises engulfing the Democratic Republic of Congo (DRC) from the mid-1990s.[72] The Conference's 2004 Dar es Salaam Declaration committed States to 'Adopt a common regional

[67] African Committee of Experts on the Rights and Welfare of the Child, 'General Comment on Article 6 of the African Charter on the Rights and Welfare of the Child' (2014).

[68] African Commission on Human and Peoples' Rights, *Resolution 234 on the Right to Nationality*, 53rd Ordinary Session, 9–23 April 2013, Banjul, The Gambia; African Commission on Human and Peoples' Rights, *Resolution 277 on the drafting of a Protocol to the African Charter on Human and Peoples' Rights on the Right to Nationality in Africa*, 55th Ordinary Session, 28 April to 12 May 2014, Luanda, Angola; African Commission on Human and Peoples' Rights, 'The Right to Nationality in Africa' (2014).

[69] Decision on the Report of the Activities of the African Commission on Human and Peoples' Rights (ACHPR) Doc. EX.CL/968(XXIX), 15 July 2016, para 5. The draft text was debated by state experts in two meetings in 2018 with revisions to reduce the legal effect of the version adopted by the African Commission. It was due to be discussed by ministers in late 2018.

[70] Abidjan Declaration of Ministers of ECOWAS Member States on the Eradication of Statelessness, 15 February 2015; endorsed by the Communique of the 47th Ordinary Session of the ECOWAS Heads of State, 19 May 2015.

[71] Banjul Plan of Action of the Economic Community of West African States (ECOWAS) on the Eradication of Statelessness 2017–2024, 9 May 2017. See documents prepared for a meeting of representatives of ECOWAS Member States, 17–20 October, 2017, Saly, Senegal, available at http://citizenshiprightsafrica.org/ecowas-coordination-meeting-on-the-implementation-of-the-banjul-plan-of-action/.

[72] The ICGLR held its first meeting in 2004 and was formalised in 2006 with the signing of a Pact on Security, Stability and Development in the Great Lakes Region. The Member States are: Angola, Burundi, Central African Republic, Republic of Congo, Democratic Republic of Congo, Kenya, Uganda, Rwanda, Republic of South Sudan (joined 2012), Sudan, Tanzania, and Zambia. See http://www.icglr.org/.

approach for the ratification and implementation of the UN Conventions on Statelessness, harmonize related national laws and standards, and provide refugees and displaced persons with identification documents enabling them to have access to basic services and exercise their rights'.[73] In 2017, the ICGLR also adopted a declaration committing to the eradication of statelessness in the region and the harmonisation of nationality laws with the international instruments.[74]

Yet, despite these moves to limit State discretion over the grant and withdrawal of citizenship and arguments for the importance of a right to nationality to enable the fulfilment of other rights, it remains the case that there currently is no international treaty nor jurisprudence establishing that a State is obliged to recognise the nationality of a person who *has* a genuine connection to that State in more than a very limited number of circumstances.[75] The adoption of the protocol to the African Charter in the form considered by the African Commission would mark a notable step in this direction.

1.3. The Content of Citizenship Rights

The international human rights regime has also rejected the distinctions that used to exist between different categories of people holding the same nationality: between the idea of nationality as a legal bond providing the State with the right to provide diplomatic protection and treat the person how it pleased at home; and the idea of nationality as the foundation for citizenship in the sense of the full right to participate in society.

Today, the theory is that nationality is a right that must have content beyond a legal status that gives rights to the State rather than the individual. The international framework of human rights law establishes what has come to be classified as a 'peremptory norm' of non-discrimination. The norm, explicitly restated in most of the international human rights treaties, requires that all those who are nationals of a State enjoy the same rights, without discrimination (though restrictions may apply, for example, to children, the mentally incapacitated, and – more controversially – some of those in prison). Thus, in relation to the right to participate in public affairs:

> No distinctions are permitted between citizens in the enjoyment of these rights on the grounds of race, colour, sex, language, religion, political or other opinion, national or social origin, property, birth or other status.[76]

[73] Dar-es-Salaam Declaration on Peace, Security, Democracy and Development in the Great Lakes Region, 2004. See also Internal Displacement Monitoring Centre and International Refugee Rights Initiative, 'The Great Lakes Pact and the Rights of Displaced People: A Guide for Civil Society' (2008).

[74] Declaration of the International Conference on the Great Lakes Region (ICGLR) on the Eradication of Statelessness, October 2017.

[75] Alison Kesby, *The Right to Have Rights: Citizenship, Humanity, and International Law* (Oxford University Press 2012) ch 2.

[76] Human Rights Committee, *General Comment No. 25: The right to participate in public affairs, voting rights and the right of equal access to public service*, 1996.

Even though this rule is of course often not respected in practice, it has effectively removed the permissibility in international law of a distinction between citizenship (as participation) and nationality (as a legal bond not necessarily encompassing full civil rights): any person who has the nationality of the State must be an equal with all other nationals, and have the same rights to participate. That is, all nationals must also be full citizens; thus establishing nationality and citizenship as international law synonyms, even if the subliminal messages buried in their etymologies and histories still influence the way that they are heard by different audiences – and even if the application of the law may bely this conclusion.

At the same time, most human rights apply to 'everyone' whatever their citizenship. The only exceptions to non-discrimination permitted in relation to internationally recognised human rights are those between citizens and non-citizens related to entry and residence in the country and to political choice and participation. States are permitted to restrict to nationals the right to enter or to permanent residence within the State; the right to freedom of movement within the State; the right to vote, run for office, or hold a public position; and the right to diplomatic or consular protection.

Even these distinctions are becoming increasingly blurred. Perhaps most significantly for a discussion of nationality in international law, the rules on the right of States and individuals alike to assert or to claim diplomatic and consular protection are becoming less stable.[77] Meantime, even citizenship rights of participation are often extended to non-national permanent residents, including the right to vote.[78] These developments have led scholars such as Yasemin Soysal to argue that citizenship is an out-of-date concept. The source of legitimacy for a person's rights is no longer his or her citizenship of a State but international human rights law; the content of those rights is set at international and not State

[77] eg, the British government sought to exercise rights of diplomatic protection in the case of non-nationals ordinarily resident in the UK detained by the US government in Guantanamo Bay – even though this was less a product of legal pressure than of the desire to distance the UK from increasingly unpopular policies adopted by the US. See, Colin RG Murray, 'In the Shadow of Lord Haw Haw: Guantánamo Bay, Diplomatic Protection and Allegiance' (2011) 1 Public Law 115; Olivier De Frouville, 'Affaire Ahmadou Sadio Diallo (République de Guinée c. République démocratique du Congo). Exceptions préliminaires : le roman inachevé de la protection diplomatique' (2007) 53 Annuaire français de droit international 291; Annemarieke Vermeer-Kunzli, 'Nationality and Diplomatic Protection' in Alessandra Annoni and Serena Forlati (eds), *The changing role of nationality in international law* (Routledge 2013).

[78] Again in the case of Britain, citizens of Commonwealth countries who are resident in the UK are entitled to vote in national elections; while the EU requires some reciprocal voting rights across its 27 States. See, eg, Rainer Bauböck and John F Rundell, *Blurred Boundaries: Migration, Ethnicity, Citizenship* (Ashgate 1998); Seyla Benhabib and Judith Resnik (eds), *Migrations and Mobilities: Citizenship, Borders, and Gender* (NYU Press 2009); Seyla Benhabib, *The Rights of Others* (Cambridge University Press 2004); Riva Kastoryano, 'Citizenship, Nationhood, and Non-Territoriality: Transnational Participation in Europe' (2005) 38 PS: Political Science & Politics 693; Rainer Bauböck, 'Expansive Citizenship – Voting beyond Territory and Membership' (2005) 38 PS: Political Science & Politics; David Earnest, 'Noncitizen Voting Rights: A Survey of an Emerging Democratic Norm' (2003).

level: status and rights are now 'post-national' rather than national.[79] Above all, this analysis is rooted within the EU, where supra-national protection of rights has been most institutionalised.

That is, if you follow the human rights regime, all nationals should have the full rights of citizens in their country of nationality (with limited exceptions applying to children, as well as some prisoners, or persons with mental disabilities); while most human rights apply to 'everyone' whatever their citizenship (with limited exceptions relating to political rights and the right to enter a country).

Even as a theory, however, there are challenges with this conceptual framework, especially around the gap between the rights of citizens of the State where they live and the idea of human rights for all. Despite the encroachments in the area of diplomatic protection or supranational citizenships, in all States there are many rights that only citizens may exercise that go well beyond the basic human rights guaranteed in international law; and in some States the differences in treatment are very large indeed, and the class of persons excluded from citizenship very extensive.

Enforcement of human rights also remains very much concentrated at the national level: although a weak international enforcement regime exists, it is individual States that sign up for the treaties on which these rights are based, and individual States that are responsible to 'respect, protect, and fulfil' the rights guaranteed to their citizens.[80] Diplomatic protection remains an important means of protection of human rights and States retain their sovereignty in international law on nationality. Discrimination on the basis of nationality is still permitted where other forms of discrimination are not. There are many rights and services available only to citizens (varying by country) that go beyond basic international law requirements but are in practice essential for any person who wishes to interact with any public institution or formalised private body, and thus to play a full part in the political and economic life of the country: the right to hold a formal-sector job, to own land, to access scholarships for education, to have non-emergency healthcare at public expense, to claim welfare benefits, to move freely and reside anywhere within national borders. Those who hold no (proof of) nationality at all are excluded from a much wider set of rights.[81]

[79] See especially Yasemin Nuhoğlu Soysal, *Limits of Citizenship: Migrants and Postnational Membership in Europe* (University of Chicago 1994); also Kesby (n 75) 47.

[80] James A Goldston, 'Holes in the Rights Framework: Racial Discrimination, Citizenship, and the Rights of Noncitizens' (2006) 20 Ethics & International Affairs 321; David Weissbrodt and Stephen Meili, 'Human Rights and Protection of Non-Citizens: Whither Universality and Indivisibility of Rights?' (2009) 28 Refugee Survey Quarterly 34.

[81] Maureen Lynch, 'Lives on Hold: The Human Cost of Statelessness' (Refugees International 2005); Brad Blitz and Maureen Lynch, 'Statelessness and the Benefits of Citizenship: A Comparative Study' (Geneva Academy of International Humanitarian Law and Human Rights 2009); Katherine Southwick and Maureen Lynch, 'Nationality Rights for All: Global Survey on Statelessness' (Refugees International 2009); Brad Blitz, 'Statelessness, Protection and Equality' (Refugee Studies Centre 2009) 3; Brad K Blitz and others, *The Cost of Statelessness: A Livelihoods Analysis of Four Countries* (Edward Elgar Publishing Limited 2011).

Control on movement is recognised by the international human rights regime as being within State discretion, with the exception of free movement within a State for those who are legally present there. Any State has the right in international law to deny non-nationals the right to entry, effectively on any arbitrary ground.[82] Much as human rights activists seek to import human rights principles into immigration jurisprudence at national level, only the most egregious abuses associated with detention and deportation – and not even all of those – are condemned by courts as human rights abuses. Some also argue strongly that protection of the full range of citizens' rights may in practice require limits on migration and on access to nationality, as a quid pro quo for the possibility of expanding or defending human rights and measures of economic redistribution and social justice for those who are in fact nationals: in order to be 'soft on the inside' a State may need to be 'hard on the outside'.[83] As Rogers Smith observes, 'it is hard to see how a whole range of human needs can be met without some sort of bordered communities'.[84] The cost is that inequalities at the global level may be emphasised in the interests of greater solidarity at the national level; some citizenships are worth more than others.[85]

It thus remains the case, in Hannah Arendt's formulation, that in many contexts legal citizenship is the basis for 'the right to have rights'.[86] Michael Walzer notes that 'the rule of citizens over non-citizens, of members over strangers, is probably the most common form of tyranny in human history'; thus, 'the denial of membership is always the first in a long train of abuses'.[87] The case studies in this book amply bear out the continuing meaning of nationality and statelessness for those whose membership is contested. Although human rights obligations set a minimum standard that is supposed to apply to all, the very idea of the right to a nationality is, after all, founded on the understanding that the State owes more to its own citizens than to other people in the world; otherwise it becomes meaningless. Most humans are not altruistic enough to stretch their solidarity around the world at an even depth of feeling across geographies and cultures.

If the international system thus accepts distinctions between citizens and aliens in State practice as inevitable – even if some argue they are not legitimate – the

[82] For more on these issues see Amal De Chickera, *Unravelling Anomaly: Detention, Discrimination and the Protection Needs of Stateless Persons* (Equal Rights Trust 2010).

[83] Linda S Bosniak, *The Citizen and the Alien: Dilemmas of Contemporary Membership* (Princeton University Press 2006).

[84] Editor's introduction to Rogers M Smith (ed), *Citizenship, Borders, and Human Needs* (University of Pennsylvania Press 2011). See also chapters by Stephen Macedo and Rainer Bauböck.

[85] Rhoda E. Howard-Hassmann, Introduction, in Rhoda E Howard-Hassmann and Margaret Walton-Roberts (eds), *The Human Right to Citizenship: A Slippery Concept* (University of Pennsylvania Press 2015).

[86] Hannah Arendt, *The Origins of Totalitarianism* (Meridian 1958).

[87] Michael Walzer, *Spheres of Justice: A Defense of Pluralism and Equality* (Basic Books 1983) 62. Walzer's discussion of membership of a political community is of particular interest to the status of 'strangers' in African societies. See ch 2, especially pp 52–61 on alienage and naturalisation.

key question becomes the existence of pathways to citizenship for those who, whether in compliance or defiance of immigration rules, are as a matter of fact settled within the State. Above all, the recognition of citizenship for those who have no viable connections to any other State. What are the rules and processes by which long-term residents, and especially their children, become full members of the polity where their lives are lived? How can we best integrate those people who are *already* effective contributors to our States, to ensure that they have access to citizenship and to the rights of citizens? There is a delicate balancing act between the recognition of a national community in which greater levels of solidarity apply, and the idea of universal rights applying to all humans wherever they live.

1.4. The Relevance of the Right to a Nationality in Africa

Is all this effort to design an international – and continental – legal and theoretical regime around the right to a nationality in fact of any relevance on the ground, to the ordinary lives and rights of individuals suffering and smiling on the African continent?

The idea of the right to a nationality is peculiar in its dependence on the State system. The entire framework of international human rights law, as a branch of international law, of course depends on the existence of States: it is States that ratify the treaties and that accept the obligations to respect, protect and fulfil the rights they recognise. But other human rights are recognised as goods in themselves – free speech, fair trial, access to education and health care – while the right to a nationality only makes sense as a good (or at all) if there are States.

As it is a cliché to say, there are particular challenges related to the creation of a national identity and a sense of citizenship in States that were arbitrarily divided at the stroke of a pen in Berlin in 1885, whose architects treated the people they found in these territories as children (at best) while they were in charge. Among these challenges is the reality that the nature of membership of African States is not so easy to fit into the etymologies and historical frames of either nationality or citizenship: neither the idea of a 'nation' as a group of people linked by a common cultural, ethnic, linguistic, religious or other identity; nor the model of a 'republic' made up of citizens voluntarily assenting to submit to and participate in their government. African States are only too obviously neither unified cultural families nor voluntary comings-together. Since their borders were established by conquerors who have now left, even a foundation of loyalty in a Hobbesian argument for deference to a sovereign with a monopoly of force is not obvious.

Africa's States, presumptively democracies from their establishment, have thus faced an acute version of the conundrum summarised by Rainer Bauböck that, 'the democratic legitimacy of decisions affecting the boundaries of a "demos" (i.e. those citizens who are eligible to participate in democratic self-government) presupposes that the demos by whom or on whose behalf a decision is taken is already composed in a way that makes its boundaries legitimate'.[88]

As a corollary, the theorising of the means by which citizenship is acquired is also hard to fit to an African context: not the concepts of rights based on descent and marriage or on place of birth, which are universally understood, but the back-history of these legal rules as they have been framed within a European history of transition from empire and monarchy to democratic 'nation-state' and a tentatively 'post-national' European Union; or alternatively within the efforts to imagine the nature of the nation and its citizenship in the immigrant States of the Americas or Australasia. The existing non-African scholarship on the meaning of citizenship – whether as a normative or descriptive term – usually assumes that it is, as a matter of law and in practice, reasonably clear who is or is not a citizen, even if the political and legal content and rights of citizenship, the status of aliens, and the means by which an alien can become a citizen remain under debate.[89] The level of concern, but not the framing, has changed as migration flows have increased (in absolute if not in relative numbers).[90]

In Africa, the European colonial powers applied an extreme version of ascriptive membership, in two senses: both that the residents of annexed territories were ascribed the nationality of their annexing State; and that 'natives' in Africa were subsequently ascribed the identity of particular 'tribes', which further determined the legal rules to which they might be subject. In neither case was there any ability to expatriate themselves and choose another allegiance (and, notoriously, tribes were often invented as much as described).[91] Colonisation both greatly increased the number of 'strangers' in any society and also took questions of membership out of the control of the traditional systems of host communities. Ethnic identity had no relevance at all to the nationality of a 'native' at the international level (that is, in relations between European States, whose jurisdictions crashed straight through existing ethno-political boundaries); but it had absolute and exclusive relevance for the person's rights and obligations within the territory of a particular European power. While a handful of black Africans and those of mixed-race crossed the barriers to acceptance as full citizens of their colonial States, most were permanently confined to a subordinate status within the framework of

[88] Rainer Bauböck, 'Political Membership and Democratic Boundaries' in Ayelet Shachar and others (eds), *The Oxford Handbook of Citizenship* (Oxford University Press 2017) 61.

[89] Bronwen Manby, 'The Human Right to Citizenship: A Slippery Concept by Rhoda E. Howard-Hassmann and Margaret Walton-Roberts (Review)' (2016) 38 Human Rights Quarterly 526.

[90] See, eg, the series of three edited collections for the Carnegie Endowment for International Peace, culminating in Thomas Alexander Aleinikoff and Douglas B Klusmeyer (eds), *Citizenship Policies for an Age of Migration* (Carnegie Endowment for International Peace: Migration Policy Institute 2002); Rainer Bauböck (ed), *Migration and Citizenship: Legal Status, Rights and Political Participation* (Amsterdam University Press / IMISCOE 2006); Christian Joppke, *Citizenship and Immigration* (Polity 2010); Smith, *Citizenship, Borders, and Human Needs* (n 84).

[91] Terence Ranger, 'The Invention of Tradition in Colonial Africa' in EJ Hobsbawm and TO Ranger (eds), *The Invention of tradition* (Cambridge University Press 1983); Martin Chanock, *Law, Custom, and Social Order: The Colonial Experience in Malawi and Zambia* (Heinemann 1998).

customary law assigned to govern their affairs as interpreted by European judges (see Chapter 3).

Then, suddenly, at independence a new model of belonging was supposed to apply, based on the rules those colonial powers had developed at home but never applied abroad. At the same time, these new rules had to accommodate both pre-colonial traditions of membership as impacted by the interpretations of the colonial powers, and popular resentments of the economic disturbances brought by colonialism (above all, the expropriation of land and the migration of labour). The decision of the newly formed Organisation of African Unity (OAU) to respect the borders established by the colonial powers,[92] committed the continent to the task of moulding these units into political communities.

A great deal of literature deals with the challenges posed by questions of identity and belonging in the post-colonial African State, and the 'crisis of nationality and sovereignty' that result.[93] There is a fairly broad consensus within these works that:

> although the genealogy and dimensions of conflicts and civil wars in Africa are quite complex and varied, underlying most of these conflicts … is the issue of citizenship and rights.[94]

There is also a great deal of agreement that the long shadow of the colonial creation of 'two publics', of citizens and of subjects, with (presumed) loyalties to the nation-state and the ethnic group, is somewhere at the heart of these problems.[95] Stephen Ndegwa analyses these divisions in Kenya, contrasting the 'dual citizenship' felt by many between a 'civic-republican' and communitarian citizenship at the level of the ethnic group and the 'liberal' and individualistic citizenship of the State.[96]

Many commentators focus on the resurgence of primordial identities under the political stresses following independence, so that (re-invented) traditional identities have become woven into 'neo-patrimonial' politics. Among these, there are those who explicitly deny the relevance of formal rules to ideas of belonging and membership, and record the implosion of the State's ability to implement any policy at all under the weight of criminality and economic crisis.[97] A person may

[92] OAU Assembly, Res. 16(I), 1st Ordinary Session, Cairo, July 1964.

[93] Chabal (n 11) ch 7.

[94] Said Adejumobi, 'Citizenship, Rights and the Problem of Conflicts and Civil Wars in Africa' (2001) 23 Human Rights Quarterly 148 at p 148.

[95] Peter P Ekeh, 'Colonialism and the Two Publics in Africa: A Theoretical Statement' (1975) 17 Comparative Studies in Society and History 91; Mahmood Mamdani, *Citizen and Subject: Contemporary Africa and the Legacy of Late Colonialism* (Princeton University Press 1996); Mahmood Mamdani, 'Beyond Settler and Native as Political Identities: Overcoming the Political Legacy of Colonialism' (2001) 43 Comparative Studies in Society and History 651; Emma Hunter (ed), *Citizenship, Belonging, and Political Community in Africa: Dialogues between Past and Present* (Ohio University Press 2016); Edmund J Keller *Identity, Citizenship, and Political Conflict in Africa* (Indiana University Press 2014).

[96] Stephen N Ndegwa, 'Citizenship and Ethnicity: An Examination of Two Transition Moments in Kenyan Politics' (1997) 91 American Political Science Review 599.

[97] See, eg, Appadurai (n 13); Jean-François Bayart, Stephen Ellis and Béatrice Hibou, *The Criminalization of the State in Africa* (International African Inst in assoc with James Currey 1999);

be perceived as a foreigner, on the basis of last name or dress, even if entitled to and in possession of papers that attest his or her citizenship.[98] Other authors have used the concept of statelessness in Africa simply to mean the lack of effective States, rather than anything to do with the right to a nationality in national or international law.[99]

Scholars such as Peter Geschiere, who explores a rich field of investigation into the meaning of autochthony or indigeneity, highlight the 'return of the local', as democratisation and decentralisation have revitalised an obsession with belonging. He argues that the idea of national citizenship, previously 'a very icon of modernity' is being called into question in debates over special rights for minorities and the cultural meaning of citizenship.[100] In weak States where resources have come to be allocated on the basis of personal patronage, democratisation and decentralisation have often made a claim to autochthony the most accessible way to make a priority claim on those resources. While the claims of autochthony are not replacing the State, they are grafting themselves onto the State structures.

The rejection of 'strangers' has, however, from the outset often been State-led.[101] Moreover, as argued by Jean-Pierre Chauveau and Paul Richards, since 'community failure' is as much a factor as 'state failure' in Africa's civil wars, 'conflict management seeking to strengthen (a mythically cohesive) "community"' at the expense of (an allegedly over-weaning) "state" may foster the very kinds of conflicts it hopes to abate'.[102] Thus, it is argued that citizenship theory should move

Patrick Chabal and Jean-Pascal Daloz, *Africa Works: Disorder as Political Instrument* (International African Institute in association with James Currey, Oxford; Indiana University Press 1999); Patrick Chabal, *Africa: The Politics of Suffering and Smiling* (Zed; University of KwaZulu-Natal Press 2009).

[98] Bruce Whitehouse, *Migrants and Strangers in an African City: Exile, Dignity, Belonging* (Indiana University Press 2012), especially ch 6.

[99] Jennifer A Widner, 'States and Statelessness in Late Twentieth-Century Africa' (1995) 124 Daedalus 129. Compare the arguments in James C Scott, *The Art of Not Being Governed: An Anarchist History of Upland Southeast Asia* (Yale University Press 2009).

[100] Geschiere (n 13) 24; see also Jean-François Bayart and Peter Geschiere, '« J'étais là avant »: Problématiques politiques de l'autochtonie' (2001) 10 Critique internationale 126; Jean-François Bayart, Peter Geschiere and Francis Nyamnjoh, 'Autochtonie, démocratie et citoyenneté en Afrique' (2001) 10 Critique internationale 177; Bambi Ceuppens and Peter Geschiere, 'Autochthony: Local or Global? New Modes in the Struggle over Citizenship and Belonging in Africa and Europe' (2005) 34 Annual Review of Anthropology 385; Armando Cutolo and Peter Geschiere, 'Populations, citoyennetés et territoires: Autochtonie et gouvernementalité en Afrique' (2008) 112 Politique africaine 5; Peter Geschiere and Stephen Jackson, 'Autochthony and the Crisis of Citizenship: Democratization, Decentralization, and the Politics of Belonging' (2006) 49 African Studies Review 1; Peter Geschiere, 'Autochthony and Citizenship: New Modes in the Struggle over Belonging and Exclusion in Africa' (2005) 32 Forum for Development Studies 371. On the idea of autochthony in the intellectual relationship of Africa to the rest of the world, see Achille Mbembe, 'À propos des écritures africaines de soi' (2000) 77 Politique africaine 16.

[101] William A Shack and Elliott P Skinner (eds), *Strangers in African Societies* (University of California Press 1979).

[102] Jean-Pierre Chauveau and Paul Richards, 'West African Insurgencies in Agrarian Perspective: Côte d'Ivoire and Sierra Leone Compared' (2008) 8 Journal of Agrarian Change 515.

beyond the dichotomy between African traditions and Western modernities, to 'accommodate a new set of societal tensions' induced by sub-national identifications, migration, economic reforms and democratic transitions.[103]

Part of this discussion has focused on the arguments put forward (including by many armed irredentist groups on the continent) that Africa's borders should be adapted to follow more 'natural' lines of ethnicity, or pre-colonial political borders. Jeffrey Herbst, for example, argues that 'at some point, the reality of disintegrating dysfunctional African States stands in such contrast to the legal fiction of sovereign States that experimentation with regard to new States is in order.'[104] Makau wa Mutua argues for the need to 'liberate the post-colonial state by creating new consensual political entities' based on the pre-colonial order.[105]

Other scholars have noted that the colonial boundaries now also have real meaning and have, in fact, created national communities, however fragile: even in rural areas quite far from centralised administration, where members of the same ethnic group are found both sides of a border, ethnic identity does not necessarily trump citizenship and a sense of belonging to a modern State.[106] Sara Dorman, Daniel Hammett and Paul Nugent join those who highlight the surprising stability of Africa's international borders, emphasising that both States and other actors are 'insistent about having the right to define who is alien and who belongs'.[107] Morten Bøås and Kevin Dunn assert the need to 'reinsert the State into examinations of autochthony'.[108] Even in extreme circumstances, there is a paradox that 'States may entirely collapse without disappearing as nations in the social imaginary.'[109]

Regardless of perspective, however, scholars have rarely seen the detailed provisions of the laws relating to differentiation between 'native' and 'stranger' as highly relevant; except in specific cases, such as Côte d'Ivoire and Zimbabwe, where it is hard to ignore the instrumentalisation of citizenship law (see Chapter 7).

[103] CRD Halisi, Paul J Kaiser and Stephen N Ndegwa, 'Guest Editors' Introduction: The Multiple Meanings of Citizenship: Rights, Identity, and Social Justice in Africa' (1998) 45 Africa Today 337.

[104] Herbst (n 13) 266; see also Gilbert M Khadiagala, 'Boundaries in Eastern Africa' (2010) 4 Journal of Eastern African Studies 266; and, for a summary of such discussions, Elliott Green, 'On the Size and Shape of African States' (2012) 56 International Studies Quarterly 229.

[105] Makau wa Mutua, 'Why Redraw the Map of Africa: A Moral and Legal Inquiry' (1995) 16 Michigan Journal of International Law 1113 at 1166.

[106] William FS Miles and David A Rochefort, 'Nationalism Versus Ethnic Identity in Sub-Saharan Africa.' (1991) 85 American Political Science Review 393 (a survey of Hausa villagers on either side of the Niger-Nigeria border); Lauren M MacLean, *Informal Institutions and Citizenship in Rural Africa: Risk and Reciprocity in Ghana and Côte d'Ivoire* (Cambridge University Press 2010).

[107] Sara Dorman, Daniel Hammett and Paul Nugent (eds), *Making Nations, Creating Strangers: States and Citizenship in Africa* (Brill 2007) 22.

[108] Morten Bøås and Kevin Dunn, *Politics of Origin in Africa: Autochthony, Citizenship and Conflict* (Zed Books 2013) 33.

[109] Crawford Young, 'Nation, Ethnicity, and Citzenship: Dilemmas of Democracy and Civil Order in Africa' in Sara Dorman, Daniel Hammett and Paul Nugent (eds), *Making nations, creating strangers: States and citizenship in Africa* (Brill 2007) 241.

There are exceptions to this rule of course, notably Jeffrey Herbst, who considers the framework of citizenship laws as part of the challenge of institutional design to respond to high levels of ethnic diversity. Herbst notes that:

> Contrary to conventional wisdom, African boundaries have fundamentally changed the nature of population movements across the continent. As a result, citizenship has acquired a salience that is greater than the ties between ethnic groups separated by a border. However, African countries have not explored the surprising firmness of their boundaries to develop innovative citizenship regulations that might establish a strong national bond between State and citizen. As a result a critical opportunity for State consolidation has been lost.[110]

Pierre Englebert takes up the same question and argues for residence, rather than 'a hypothetical nationality', to be the condition of membership in the political community.[111] Georges Nzongola-Ntalaja reviews some of the cases of denial of citizenship rights to individuals and minorities, and emphasises that 'there is no reason why people who have resided in an area for decades, and sometimes for a century or more, should be denied economic and political rights on the basis of politically opportunistic definitions of citizenship.'[112] These authors did not, however, compare the detail of the provisions of nationality laws as adopted across the continent, or in particular countries, and modified over time.

It is undeniable that formal State institutions have collapsed in some African countries and have significant weaknesses in all. In this context, alternative forms of organisation, including the 'primordial', have gained greater currency. It is important to understand and analyse these processes. Yet attempts to redesign States along 'primordial' lines have not been notably successful. The post-secession experience of South Sudan, following recognition of the Muslim-Christian divide through its secession from Sudan, does not encourage the view that new States necessarily provide solutions. Somalia and Rwanda, both exceptionally ethnically homogeneous States, have hardly been models of peace and democracy. The safer way forward may lie in the ongoing and vital – if theoretically unexciting – work of seeking to improve and strengthen the State structures that exist, and have surprising legitimacy, to manage questions of belonging. This involves, among other things, law and policy reform and better institutional design.

African politicians themselves have clearly thought that citizenship laws are relevant. Although some States have left the laws adopted at independence virtually intact, the majority have amended them multiple times, as governments have grappled – in good or bad faith – with the conundrum of the definition of

[110] Herbst (n 13) ch 8; The Politics of Migration and Citizenship; see also Jeffrey Herbst, 'The Role of Citizenship Laws in Multiethnic Societies: Evidence from Africa' in Richard A Joseph (ed), *State, conflict, and democracy in Africa* (L Rienner 1999). Herbst's work is also discussed in Keller (n 95).

[111] Pierre Englebert, *State Legitimacy and Development in Africa* (Lynne Rienner Publishers 2000) 188.

[112] Georges Nzongola-Ntalaja, 'Citizenship, Political Violence, and Democratization in Africa' (2004) 10 Global Governance: A Review of Multilateralism and International Organizations 403.

citizenship and the nature of membership in their States. Constitution-drafting exercises and agreements to end conflict have almost invariably included discussions around entitlement to citizenship.

The rest of this book addresses these questions. Part II sets out the history of nationality law in Africa during the colonial period and at the transition to independence; Part III extends this history to examine the trends and patterns in nationality law across the continent since independence. Part IV consists of case studies of the application of nationality law in States where it has been particularly problematic: as applied to pre-independence migrants, in the context of the creation of new States since independence, and to refugees and former refugees. Part V essays a set of conclusions from this material, addressing the issues established in this introductory chapter, and some recommendations for further research, and for action. I argue that law can be an instrument of exclusion or inclusion even in States where institutions are weak and many people are undocumented.

PART II

Empire to Independence: The Invention of Nationality in Africa

2

Membership in the Pre-Colonial Era

The past is never dead. It's not even past.
– William Faulkner

Many of the problems related to citizenship law and its application today can be traced back to the history of nationality in Africa, and the ways in which the current States were created and their membership defined by the European colonial powers. Though pre-colonial traditions of belonging continue to be highly influential at sub-State level, they have had little impact on the rules for accessing nationality expressed in statute law.

Belonging and citizenship at the level of the colonial State were determined by the European power with control of the territory. However, it was a two-(or more) level nationality that was created, in which most Africans did not have full civil or political rights. Though differentiated citizenship statuses began to break down as independence approached, it was only in 1994, with the final liberation of South Africa, that the framework of equal rights for all citizens was in principle accepted across the continent.

At the same time, the practical effect of colonisation was to create new territorial units that were mostly not rooted in any pre-existing State structures, and indeed often cut through previous territorial boundaries, splitting populations speaking the same language and sharing the same political institutions. The colonisers also brought vastly increased migration, either through forced recruitment or as a side effect of the pattern of economic development produced by membership of an empire, both within Africa (as of mineworkers to South Africa or plantation labour to Congo) and from other continents to Africa (including not only white Europeans but also, for example, the south Asians brought to eastern and southern regions of Africa by the British).

At independence, the colonial powers took different approaches to the management of nationality in their former colonies – although all took care in defining those who retained entitlement to a European nationality. The British created detailed and in principle quite watertight rules, included in the negotiated independence constitutions themselves. The French left determination of their new nationalities to the independent States, though most followed the model of the French nationality code in establishing their new rules. The Belgians simply abandoned their colonies with no framework in place; as did the Portuguese.

In the long run, the transitional provisions at independence have remained most relevant in countries with a descent-based legal regime. Everywhere, however, both the substantive provisions of the law and the institutional and procedural frameworks for nationality administration have kept their roots in colonial models, even as the legal and administrative tree has been pruned and shaped by subsequent reforms.

Africa's pre-colonial political and territorial entities had highly variable systems for determining who was or was not a member of each polity. As in other parts of the world, these questions were less urgent in an era of lower population densities and lower levels of migration; but, again as in other parts of the world, there were systems for welcoming and managing travellers passing through a territory, for integrating those who wished to stay, or for determining the rights of those born within a particular community. In the densely forested areas of central or west Africa, communities tended to be small enough, and land sufficiently available, that membership was effectively determined by family linkages rather than political or religious rules. In larger communities, even in quite similar geographical zones, political structures varied widely: as for example in the case of the Yoruba kingdoms, compared to the decentralised system in the Igbo territories, both in the southern part of today's Nigeria; or the empires – Ghana, Mali, Songhai, Kanem-Burnu – that succeeded each other across the Sahel; or the non-State structures governing membership of the nomadic communities in the same region.

Membership of a political unit might be decided on the basis of kinship networks organised through male or (less commonly) female-line descent, with entry-points for strangers through initiation into membership of secret societies or age-grade structures, or acceptance into a family lineage; as well as payment of tribute as an indication of allegiance to a particular monarch, admission by a chief, or approval by an assembly of existing members. As in other continents, different levels of citizenship status were pervasive, with distinctions by noble status or caste, between slave or free, and of course between men and women.[1]

Very often, belonging and membership was related to the grant of usage rights over land for farming or grazing: so, for example, in eastern Congo, agreements for 'strangers' to use land facilitated their integration into the community. Similar procedures existed in West Africa, in the system known as the *tutorat* in Côte d'Ivoire, or through *chefs de terre* or 'earth priests' in Burkina Faso or elsewhere. In time, and depending on political circumstances, late-comers would be integrated

[1] See, eg, William A Shack and Elliott P Skinner (eds), *Strangers in African Societies* (University of California Press 1979); George BN Ayittey, *Indigenous African Institutions* (Transnational Publishers 1991); Said Adejumobi, 'Identity, Citizenship and Conflict: The African Experience' in W Alade Fawole and Charles Ukeje (eds), *The Crisis of the State and Regionalism in West Africa: Identity, Citizenship and Conflict* (CODESRIA 2005); Ralph A Austen, *Trans-Saharan Africa in World History* (Oxford University Press 2010) 49–77; John Lonsdale, 'Unhelpful Pasts and a Provisional Present' in Emma Hunter (ed), *Citizenship, belonging, and political community in Africa: dialogues between past and present* (Ohio University Press 2016).

into the community and themselves become 'autochthonous' or 'indigenous'; though an autonomous status could also be maintained indefinitely.[2] Alternatively, where large groups of people fled war or oppressive rulers they simply established new political units in a zone not actively used by others.

In North Africa, the concepts of nationality and citizenship as they developed in Islam and under the Ottoman empire remain relevant today. The notion of the Muslim community, or *umma*, developed over centuries and provided a sense of common identity across political boundaries, so that borders of even the most formalised States were blurred. The idea of a 'nation-state' and nationality started to emerge in the Arab world in the nineteenth century, and the word *jinsiyya* (ultimately derived from Greek *genos*: nation, kin-group) was used for the concept of nationality, with the same connotations of ethnic or descent-based membership of a community that exist in other languages. From the early twentieth century the new term *muwatana* (derived from the word *watan* for place of residence or homeland), was used for citizenship: the status of a person who is not a foreigner, who is a native of the place, though without the connotations of rights and political participation as exist in English or (especially) French.[3] The idea of the united *umma* was undermined by increasing resistance to the control of the Ottoman empire over Arab territories, and by Ottoman sultans themselves as they sought a secular alternative in their relations with non-Muslims to the religious sovereignty conferred by the Muslim caliphate.

The obvious dysfunctions and abuse of the *millet* system, by which non-Muslim communities within Ottoman territories had jurisdiction over their own affairs on matters of personal status, led to the adoption in 1869 of the first Ottoman Nationality Law, intended – in the face of European States' insistence on the complete extraterritoriality of their merchants' communities in Ottoman territory – to determine the reach of the sultan's authority over non-Muslims. The nationality law conferred nationality through paternal descent, as well as to a child of an alien father if both were born on the territory (following the double *jus soli* principle first introduced in France in 1851, though at that time with the option to repudiate the attribution on majority). An individual born on Ottoman soil could apply for nationality within three years of majority; in addition, naturalisation was possible on the basis of five years' residence; and a final provision stated that all those resident in Ottoman territories would be considered Ottoman nationals until their foreign nationality was established. Foundlings were presumed to

[2] Jean-Claude Willame, *Banyarwanda et Banyamulenge: Violences Ethniques et Gestion de l'identitaire Au Kivu* (Institut africain-CEDAF; L'Harmattan 1997); Jean-Pierre Chauveau, 'Question Foncière et Construction Nationale En Côte d'Ivoire' (2000) 78 Politique africaine 94, and other works by the same author; Richard Kuba and Carola Lentz (eds), *Land and the Politics of Belonging in West Africa* (Brill 2006); V Adefemi Isumonah, 'Migration, Land Tenure, Citizenship and Communal Conflicts in Africa' (2003) 9 Nationalism and Ethnic Politics 1.

[3] Gianluca P Parolin, *Citizenship in the Arab World: Kin, Religion and Nation-State* (Amsterdam University Press 2009) 24–25; Jacqueline Bendeddouche, *Notion de nationalité et nationalité algérienne* (Société Nationale d'Édition et de Diffusion 1974).

be Ottoman. Conversion to Islam was not listed as a means for acquisition of nationality, breaking with the Muslim tradition, though naturalisation continued to be granted to converts as a matter of practice. The distinction between Ottoman Muslims and Ottoman non-Muslims was theoretically done away with for political purposes.[4] The 1881 regulation on population registration, however, still provided for religion to be noted at the registration of every birth.[5]

In Ethiopia, the one country in Africa not to be colonised, the first nationality law was adopted in 1930, by the Emperor Haile Selassie, during the first year of his reign. Prior to that date, the power to admit foreigners as subjects was the prerogative of the emperor, sparingly used.[6] The 1930 law (1922, in the Ethiopian calendar), was one of the oldest to be adopted in the Ethiopian legal system; even before the first modern constitution of 1931.[7] Looking to European models (especially Switzerland and France) within a general effort to modernise the Ethiopian State, it adopted a descent-based system through the male line only, unless the child was born out of wedlock (though the concept of illegitimacy was mostly foreign to Ethiopia).[8] Women married to Ethiopian men automatically acquired Ethiopian nationality; naturalisation for others was permitted on the basis of quite stringent conditions, including fluent knowledge of written and spoken Amharic; though in 1933 the law was amended to allow the emperor to waive the conditions at his discretion.[9]

The law did not permit loss of Ethiopian nationality in any other circumstances than acquisition of another nationality; and reacquisition of Ethiopian nationality required only a return to Ethiopia, renunciation of the other nationality, and application for readmission, with no discretion. The 1931 constitution itself stated only that 'All the natives of Ethiopia, subjects of the empire, form together the Ethiopian Empire'; the details were left to the law.[10] The revised constitution of 1955, which replaced its 1931 predecessor and strengthened the powers of Parliament, left the citizenship provisions in the law unchanged; however, it restricted the right to vote and stand for office to nationals from birth only; while ministers were required not only to be subjects from birth themselves, but their parents too.[11]

[4] Parolin (n 3) 71–79.

[5] Nazan Maksudyan, 'The Fight over Nobody's Children: Religion, Nationality and Citizenship of Foundlings in the Late Ottoman Empire' (2009) 41 New Perspectives on Turkey 151.

[6] Fasil Nahum, 'Ethiopian Nationality Law and Practice' (1972) 8 Journal of Ethiopian Law 168; Robert Allen Sedler, 'Nationality, Domicile and the Personal Law in Ethiopia' (1965) 2 Journal of Ethiopian Law 161.

[7] Proclamation Promulgating the Ethiopian Nationality Law, 15 Hamle 1922 (Ethiopian calendar). See also Aberra Jembere, *An Introduction to the Legal History of Ethiopia: 1434–1974* (Lit Verlag 2000).

[8] Although the law was gender-neutral at first sight, the provisions setting out the arrangements through which children born of mixed marriages could establish their Ethiopian nationality stated that: 'Every child born in a lawful mixed marriage follows the nationality of its father.' Ethiopia Nationality Law, July 1930, ss 1 and 6.

[9] Proclamation amending the Nationality Law of 15 Hamle 1922, 25 Meskerem 1926 (Ethiopian calendar).

[10] Constitution of Ethiopia, 1931, Arts 1 and 18.

[11] Nahum (n 6). Constitution of Ethiopia, 1955, Arts 1, 67 and 95.

The nature of membership of the pre-colonial political entities was thus in some ways similar to, but in others very different from, the nationality laws attached to the State system brought to Africa by European colonisation. But even in the European territories, the concept of nationality in international law was only developed during the later nineteenth century, in parallel to the age of European empires in Africa and in part as a response to this early form of globalisation, as it became more complicated to decide who owed allegiance to whom.

The major treaties and jurisprudence came in the twentieth century, in the context of the two world wars and attempts to manage their aftermath and avoid their recurrence. Many of the rules of international law concerning State recognition and State rights and responsibilities, including rights to determine who are their nationals and the rights they have over them, were thus only elaborated during the period when Africa was already colonised, and indeed, were influenced by the expansion of European empires and the dispersal of European nationals around the globe. In the litigation before nascent international bodies that developed these rules, the nationality of a person (physical or legal) was important because it related to the rights of a State to demand the loyalty of that person and protect them against the demands of another State; not as a matter of individual rights. The European conceptualisation of the State and of nationality were imposed on Africa as part of the same package.

3

The European Colonial Period

As the European empires in Africa expanded, residents of territory annexed by a European power were considered to become nationals of that State, unless treaties provided otherwise. The rules on the duties of States in this regard developed relatively early, since, by contrast with the attribution of nationality for a person within one State, transfers of territory involved at least two States, and ceased to be a matter of only domestic concern. Nevertheless, the first rules were established in domestic legislation and courts. Thus, in the case of the British annexation of territories in Africa, the rule was that all persons who were nationals of the annexed territory become British nationals unless another provision was made in the instrument of annexation; and residents of British territory annexed by another State become aliens. It was also established by English court decisions that this rule did not apply to those who left the territory prior to the transfer of sovereignty, unless they subsequently returned or voluntarily claimed the status of British subjects: this rule applied in the case of the annexation of the Boer Republics in South Africa, for example.[1] In France, the 1945 nationality code provided that all those who remained domiciled in French-annexed territories acquired French nationality, and, conversely, that those resident in ceded territories lost French nationality.[2]

Ethiopia also followed this rule in its 1952 incorporation of Eritrea as an autonomous territory under imperial jurisdiction: a proclamation stated that 'all inhabitants of the territory of Eritrea except persons possessing other nationality are hereby declared to be subjects of Our Empire and Ethiopian nationals'; as well as 'all inhabitants born in the territory of Eritrea and having at least one indigenous parent or grandparent'. If they had another nationality they were permitted to renounce Ethiopian nationality within six months and retain the foreign nationality.[3]

[1] Paul Weis, *Nationality and Statelessness in International Law* (2nd edn, Brill 1979), ch 11. The issue is discussed in the context of the colony of Lagos by Arthur VJ Nylander, *The Nationality and Citizenship Laws of Nigeria* (University of Lagos 1973) 7–8.

[2] Ordonnance No.45/2447 du 19 octobre 1945 portant code de la nationalité française. « Article 12 : Dans le cas où le traité ne contient pas de telles dispositions les personnes qui demeurent domiciliées dans les territoires rattachés à la France acquièrent la nationalité française. Article 13: Dans la même hypothèse, les personnes domiciliées dans les territoires cédés perdent la nationalité française, à moins qu'elles n'établissent effectivement leur domicile hors de ces territoires. »

[3] Imperial Order No.C of 1952, cited in Fasil Nahum, 'Ethiopian Nationality Law and Practice' (1972) 8 Journal of Ethiopian Law 168.

Nonetheless, there were cases of annexation or incorporation in which nationality was not conferred on all inhabitants of the transferred territory. Change of sovereignty did not affect third-country nationals; that is, nationals of other States recognised by the international State system.[4]

There was, however, at that time a clear distinction between the claim of an individual to the protection of his or her country of nationality against other States, and the rights of that individual within the territory of which he or she had nationality. Not only were the conditions for grant of nationality within the sovereign discretion of the State concerned; but a nationality recognised at the international level in itself did not necessarily give the individual concerned full rights within the State of nationality. Those without property, and women, were in most countries of the world excluded from full citizenship rights until at least the early twentieth century. The context of empire only strengthened these distinctions, as those not of European descent were subordinated to the white-skinned masters. To be a 'native' (*indigène*) in Africa was to be an inferior being whose culture was denigrated, who had no right to influence the decision-making processes that governed daily life, whose property was regularly forfeited, who could be forced to work or move home, and who had only limited civil liberties protections and freedom of movement. Only a tiny minority of Africans ever achieved the right to be treated on the same legal basis as whites, even where there was an ideology of assimilation as in the French and Portuguese colonies; while those of mixed race created legal and intellectual confusions that the colonial powers struggled to resolve within their worldview.[5]

Thus, colonial rule transformed existing ideas of belonging and relations between first-comers and late-comers within African polities, first by the imposition of an additional level of political authority that radically altered the boundaries and power relationships of existing communities; and, secondly, by a vastly increased volume of migration (forced and voluntary). Although there were differences among the colonial powers, the underlying realities were quite similar.

3.1. British Territories

The territories of the British empire in Africa belonged to one of three categories. First established were the 'colonies': initially the coastal trading enclaves, including Gambia, Lagos, the Gold Coast and Freetown as well as the Cape Colony and Natal

[4] Weis (n 1) 140–149.

[5] Alexander Keese, *Living with Ambiguity: Integrating an African Elite in French and Portuguese Africa, 1930–61* (Franz Steiner 2007); Martin Deming Lewis, 'One Hundred Million Frenchmen: The 'Assimilation' Theory in French Colonial Policy' (1962) 4 Comparative Studies in Society and History 129; Kristin Mann and Richard L Roberts (eds), *Law in Colonial Africa* (James Currey 1991). On those of mixed race, see Emmanuelle Saada, *Les enfants de la colonie: les métis de l'empire français entre sujétion et citoyenneté* (Découverte 2007).

in South Africa; later joined by Southern Rhodesia, and most of Kenya excluding the coastal strip. The defeated Boer republics of Transvaal and Orange Free State became colonies also, and in 1910 joined with the Cape Colony and Natal to form the Union of South Africa, also as a colony, but with a substantial measure of self-government. In 1931, South Africa became a 'dominion', the only African territory to obtain this semi-independent status, created by the Statute of Westminster 1931 and granted to the more significant colonies, including Canada, Australia and New Zealand, as well as India, Pakistan and Ceylon (Sri Lanka). The remaining territories, including all those added in the late nineteenth century 'Scramble for Africa', were designated 'protectorates'. Colonies and dominions were 'within the crown's dominions'; while 'protectorates', including most other British-controlled territories in Africa, were nominally foreign territory managed by local government structures established under British protection.[6] Finally, there were formerly German territories mandated to British administration by the League of Nations (later trust territories, under UN mandate), including half of modern Togo (which was administered as part of the Gold Coast), part of Cameroon (administered from Nigeria), and Tanganyika. Sudan was in a category all of its own, ruled as a condominium with Egypt (see Chapter 8.2)

Until 1948, the single status of 'British subject' was applied to all those born within the Crown's dominions (including the UK); during the nineteenth century, the term 'British protected person' emerged to cover the people indigenous to a protectorate. The British Nationality and Status of Aliens Act 1914 was the first statute intended to apply throughout the empire, and retained the principal nationality category of 'British subject' previously developed through common law and a patchwork of other statutes.[7] A person born in Lagos or any other colony had the same status as one born in Britain. However, 'the simple nomenclature "British subject" affords, within the Empire, no clue as to his rights'.[8] The 1914 Act expressly allowed the self-governing territories to treat 'different classes of British subjects' differently.[9] Although a British subject had the same rights of British protection in relation to foreign countries, the status was differentiated throughout the empire, with each colony deciding its own laws, including laws that discriminated on racial

[6] Another category of territory within the empire included protected States (where Britain only controlled defence and external relations): there were no protected States in Africa, though Zanzibar was treated as a protected State for some nationality purposes, since it had its own internal nationality law from 1911. Laurie Fransman, Adrian Berry and Alison Harvey, *Fransman's British Nationality Law* (3rd edn, Bloomsbury Professional 2011) catalogue entry on Tanzania.

[7] Rieko Karatani, *Defining British Citizenship: Empire, Commonwealth, and Modern Britain* (Frank Cass 2003); Fransman, Berry and Harvey (n 6) ch 3.

[8] EFW Gey van Pittius, *Nationality within the British Commonwealth of Nations* (PS King & Son 1930) 163.

[9] British Nationality and Status of Aliens Act 1914, s 26: 'Nothing in this Act shall take away or abridge any power vested in, or exercisable by, the Legislature or Government of any British Possession, or affect the operation of any law at present in force which has been passed in exercise of such a power, or prevent any such Legislature or Government from treating differently different classes of British subjects.'

grounds; a matter fiercely disputed between representatives of India, South Africa, and others at imperial conferences.[10] Separate legislation was adopted to provide for naturalisation in each colony as a distinct process from naturalisation in the UK, which did not give rights in the UK nor in other colonies; the colonies adopted their own laws to provide local rules.[11] Of particular significance for the later development of nationality law and the rights of nationals and non-nationals were the very different rights applied to the 'different classes of British subjects' in the colonial territories in relation to land ownership. Africans in the British colonies deemed suitable for European settlement – South Africa, Southern Rhodesia and Kenya in particular – were confined to 'native reserves' where they could hold land under customary law; whereas only Europeans could have freehold title in the fertile lands expropriated for their settlement. Africans were brought in as labourers or sometimes sharecroppers in those zones, but denied the right to own land themselves.

Birth in a protectorate did not confer British subject status, unless the father was a British subject; and British protected persons were treated on the same footing as aliens for the purpose of naturalisation as a British subject. The fiction was maintained, through the concept of 'indirect rule', that the protectorates were really semi-autonomous, internally governed by indigenous 'tribal authorities', with control over their own 'tribal' subjects.[12] In practice, the British colonial administrators interfered quite freely in matters supposedly within the purview of those authorities. Whereas many pre-colonial political entities had been multi-ethnic, the colonisers had an anthropological desire to sort their subjects into different ethnic groups, and to define some as 'native' to a particular area and others as 'strangers'. The 'natives' were allocated the right to be represented by a chief, the 'strangers' were subordinate; but the boundary between native and stranger could be very difficult to define. The allocation of a person to a tribe was entirely based on primordial identity: in Nigeria, for example, a 'native of Nigeria' was 'any person whose parents were members of any tribe or tribes indigenous to Nigeria and the descendants of such persons, and includes persons one of whose parents was a member of such tribe'; there was no provision for 'naturalisation' as the

[10] Daniel Gorman, 'Wider and Wider Still?: Racial Politics, Intra-Imperial Immigration and the Absence of an Imperial Citizenship in the British Empire' (2002) 3 Journal of Colonialism and Colonial History 1. See also, Daniel Gorman, *Imperial Citizenship: Empire and the Question of Belonging* (Manchester Univ Press 2006); Clive Parry, *Nationality and Citizenship Laws of The Commonwealth and of The Republic of Ireland* (Stevens & Sons 1957).

[11] Act for the Naturalisation of Aliens, 10 & 11 Vict, cap 83, 1847; replaced by the Naturalisation Act 1870, which preserved the separate processes for the colonies; replaced in turn by the British Nationality and Status of Aliens Act 1914, which gave colonies the power to grant certificates of imperial naturalisation valid across the empire, with the same effect as those granted by the Secretary of State, while still providing powers to grant only local naturalisation as a separate status. This was endorsed, after ongoing argument, by the imperial conference of 1930. Karatani (n 7) chs 2 and 3.

[12] The policy of 'indirect rule' was most famously articulated by Lord Lugard in his book, *The Dual Mandate in British Tropical Africa*, published in 1922, which stated that Britain should allow Africans to 'develop along their own lines', rather than attempt to govern Africa according to European standards.

member of one tribe or another.[13] Migrants from neighbouring territories were 'native foreigners' (see also Chapter 7.6). The distinction between first-comers or late-comers in a particular location for the purposes of access to land and other rights was flattened by this focus on ethnicity.[14] British protected persons, as well as 'natives' within the colonies, were in general governed by the customary law of the 'tribe' concerned, as modified by statute and British interpretation; 'Native Courts' were established to adjudicate disputes between natives and sanction minor offences, applying 'native law and custom, so far as it is not repugnant to natural justice, equity and good conscience'.[15]

The British Nationality Act 1948, the first attempt to create a single comprehensive system of nationality law by statute, established the new status of 'citizen of the United Kingdom and colonies' (a status abolished in 1981).[16] British subject became an umbrella status (with limited rights in itself) derived from newly created citizenships of the Commonwealth, including both the new status of 'citizen of the UK and colonies' as well as the citizenships of those territories now recognised as 'independent Commonwealth countries' under the act (mainly the former 'dominions', including South Africa, but also Southern Rhodesia).[17] Citizenship of the UK and colonies continued to be granted on a *jus soli* basis to all those born in the UK or in one of the colonies, and an alien could naturalise as a citizen of the UK and colonies in any colony as well as in the UK. A citizen of the UK and colonies of such had the right to free movement throughout the empire; however, Africans, Europeans and others retained their separate legal systems in the remaining colonies in Africa (including Kenya), meaning that freedom of movement for those of Asian or African descent was in practice restricted a great deal more than that of those of British or other European descent. 'Pass laws' were applied across the British territories to 'non-Europeans', whether in a colony or protectorate.

This regime of linked citizenships did not extend to the protectorates, which retained their subordinate status. The status of 'British protected person' was codified by the new law, and continued to apply to persons born in a protectorate who

[13] Interpretation Ordinance 27 of 1939.

[14] For a discussion, see Carola Lentz, 'Introduction' in Richard Kuba and Carola Lentz (eds), *Land and the Politics of Belonging in West Africa* (Brill 2006).

[15] The standard language, taken here from the Sierra Leone Native Courts Ordinance, 1933. On the definition of 'native' see Christopher Joon-Hai Lee, 'The 'Native' Undefined: Colonial Categories, Ango-African Status and the Politics of Kinship in British Central Africa, 1929–38' (2005) 46 Journal of African History 455.

[16] Since 1981 the primary category of British nationality has been that of British citizen, with full rights in the UK, but several other categories remain with more limited rights, including those of British protected person.

[17] The dominions that became 'independent Commonwealth countries' were Canada, Australia, New Zealand, South Africa, Newfoundland, India, Pakistan and Ceylon. Southern Rhodesia was never a dominion but was treated as such in some respects and also became an 'independent Commonwealth country'. Robert R Wilson and Robert E Clute, 'Commonwealth Citizenship and Common Status' (1963) 57 American Journal of International Law 566; R Hansen, 'The Politics of Citizenship in 1940s Britain: The British Nationality Act' (1999) 10 Twentieth Century British History 67.

were not citizens of the UK and colonies (that is, whose parents were not citizens of the UK and colonies, previously British subjects). British protected person status provided some rights both in the protectorate concerned and in the UK, including treatment as a British national for the purposes of protection when outside his or her own protectorate; but a British protected person remained an alien in many contexts, and was a lesser status than citizenship of the UK and colonies, including being barred from seeking redress against State acts in the courts. The term British protected person was also used to refer to subjects of the local rulers in the protected States, as well as residents of the mandated territories (which became Trust Territories under the new United Nations regime) and Sudan, but this was as a matter of 'royal prerogative' rather than statute.[18]

This legal structure remained essentially unchanged until the former protectorates achieved independence in the 1960s. In southern Africa, however, the structure of nationality law in British territories took a different route, due in particular to the much larger settler populations of British and other European descent. As demands grew from Africans for self-government, so also did resistance to this process from the white 'settler' population.

Efforts to shore up defences against growing African demands for political power saw the British territories of Northern and Southern Rhodesia and Nyasaland (today's Zambia, Zimbabwe and Malawi) linked together for ten years as the Central African Federation from 1953 to 1963. The creation of the federation was supported by the white minority government of Southern Rhodesia, which had for many years sought greater access to the mineral riches of Northern Rhodesia in particular; but strongly opposed by the African leadership in the protectorates of Northern Rhodesia and Nyasaland. Promised protections for African interests in the new federal political arrangements were very weak, and the vast majority of Africans were excluded from voting in federal elections on the basis of educational and property qualifications.

At the time the Federation was established, Northern Rhodesia and Nyasaland were separate protectorates. Southern Rhodesia was an 'independent Commonwealth country', which had had its own citizenship law since 1949, following the general scheme envisaged by the 1948 British Nationality Act (see Chapter 7.1). On federation, each of the three territories retained its separate status for nationality purposes, until the Federation enacted a new law in 1957, the Citizenship of Rhodesia and Nyasaland and British Nationality Act. The Act provided for *jus soli* citizenship of the federation for those born before or after the date of creation of the Federation, and for other transitional provisions.[19]

[18] The usage of 'British protected person' is very complicated, and varied over time and in different contexts, according to definitions established by the British Protected Persons Order No.499 of 1934 and subsequent Orders in Council. It was possible in some circumstances under the 1948 legislation to be both a British protected person *and* a citizen of the UK and colonies *or* a foreign national. See Fransman, Berry and Harvey (n 6) ch 3.3.3 et seq; Weis (n 1) 20–22; Nylander (n 1) 18–19.

[19] Citizenship of Rhodesia and Nyasaland and British Nationality Act 1957 (No. 12 of 1957). Excluded from *jus soli* were children born out of wedlock in Northern Rhodesia or Nyasaland whose fathers were

However, this applied only to British subjects, and most British protected persons from Northern Rhodesia and Nyasaland did not acquire the merged citizenship automatically (though they remained British protected persons under British nationality law), creating room for later confusion.[20]

At the tip of the continent, South Africa had its own particular history, as the creation of different classes of British citizenship reached its apogee with the elaboration of extraordinarily complex race- and ethnicity-based citizenship distinctions. Like Southern Rhodesia, South Africa had its own citizenship law from 1949, providing for a right to citizenship premised on birth in the territory, though with exclusions for the children of 'prohibited immigrants'.[21] The victory of the National Party in elections in the same year of 1948, however, meant that the distinctions between natives and Europeans became even more exaggerated. Ultimately, a majority of black South Africans had their nominal nationality taken away, told that instead they belonged to one of ten supposedly independent and ethnically designated 'homelands'.[22] These same distinctions were applied in South West Africa (Namibia), administered by South Africa under an initial League of Nations mandate granted in 1920; an administration which continued illegally after the Second World War, in the face of UN resolutions condemning South Africa's failure to submit to the authority of UN trusteeship council and prepare the territory for independence.

3.2. French Territories

French territories in sub-Saharan Africa were, from the early twentieth century, divided between French West Africa (*Afrique occidentale française*, AOF), French Central Africa (*Afrique équatoriale française*, AEF), and Madagascar. Algeria, in North Africa, had a special status, forming part of metropolitan France; Morocco and Tunisia were protectorates, with nominally autonomous governments under French protection; parts of German Togo and Kamerun became French mandate territories. As in the British colonies, there was a clear division between categories

not British subjects. Those who were British subjects, Southern Rhodesian citizens or registered in one of the territories as a citizen of the UK and colonies acquired Federation citizenship automatically under the transitional provisions.

[20] Fransman, Berry and Harvey (n 6), catalogue entry on Malawi; Elspeth Guild, 'British Nationality and East African Independence' (1990) 4 Immigration and Nationality Law and Practice 99.

[21] South African Citizenship Act No.44 of 1949, s 3; the *jus soli* right was subject to the usual exceptions relating to father's status as a diplomat or enemy alien, in addition to the restriction if he were a prohibited immigrant.

[22] In fact, only four of the ten 'homelands' (Transkei, Bophuthatswana, Venda and Ciskei) were ever recognised as independent by the South African government; the remaining six (Gazankulu, KaNgane, KwaNdebele, KwaZulu, Lebowa and QwaQwa) were only self-governing. See Bently J Anderson, 'The Restoration of The South African Citizenship Act: An Exercise in Statutory Obfuscation' (1993) 9 Connecticut Journal of International Law 295, for an outline of the undoing of this process. Also Fransman, Berry and Harvey (n 6), catalogue entries on Namibia and South Africa.

of national: between French nationality – the legal link between the individual and the State, and French citizenship – the status of a person with full civil and political rights. But the legal regime to achieve this distinction was quite different.

France's first colony in Africa, Algeria, had a unique legal status throughout its occupation. From 1834, just four years after Algiers was captured, the territory was annexed to France, and in theory simply formed a continuation of French territory across the Mediterranean Sea. However, native Muslims and Jews did not obtain full rights as French citizens. Two legal systems were established, with separate laws, magistrates and tribunals for those with personal status (*statut personnel*) established by the French civil code, and those with local (religious) law personal status. Even though, in 1865, it was declared that '*tout individu musulman est français*' and that natives (*indigènes*) could acquire full rights to French citizenship, this was only if they renounced their status as Muslim (or Jewish) and showed assimilation to French culture in other ways.[23] This was the foundation of the distinction based on personal status between French citizens (*citoyens français*), who were of European stock and enjoyed full civil and political rights; and French subjects (*sujets français*), whose rights were restricted, including black Africans, Muslim Algerians, and other *indigènes* of Madagascar, the Antilles, Melanesia, and other non-European territories (although the term *indigène* was freely used, including in law, it was never defined, and the legally meaningful term was that of *sujet*). In 1870, the (much smaller) Jewish population of Algeria was collectively awarded French civil status, but the same did not happen for Muslim Algerians.[24]

In 1881, France adopted a law that further formalised the division of the residents of its overseas territories into two categories.[25] It extended the application of the *Code de l'indigénat*, a collection of legal provisions added to the Penal Code that had been developed in Algeria, across the French empire. The Code provided

[23] *Senatus-consulte sur l'état des personnes et la naturalisation en Algérie*, 1865. On the development of Algerian nationality law, see generally: Patrick Weil, 'Le statut des musulmans en Algérie coloniale: Une nationalité française dénaturée' (European University Institute 2003) HEC No. 2003/3; Jacqueline Bendeddouche, *Notion de nationalité et nationalité algérienne* (Société Nationale d'Édition et de Diffusion 1974). French legislation applicable to Algeria is available with commentary in the « Digithèque de matériaux juridiques et politiques » of the University of Perpignan, http://mjp.univ-perp.fr/mjp.htm.

[24] « Les israelites indigènes des départements de l'Algérie sont déclarés citoyens français; en conséquence, leur statut réel et leur statut personnel seront, à compter de la promulgation du présent décret, réglés par la loi française. Toutes dispositions législatives, décret, règlement ou ordonnance contraires sont abolis. » Décret du 24 octobre 1870, relatif à la naturalisation des israélites de l'Algérie, known as the *Décret Crémieux*, after its author, the minister of justice in the French Government of National Defence formed during the Franco-German war of 1870–71. The confusion between the questions of French civil status, French citizenship and French nationality were such that the process of renouncing another personal status to acquire French civil status was often termed naturalisation (as in the case of the *Décret Crémieux* and *Sénatus consulte* of 1865), even though in principle those doing so were in fact already French nationals. The rights granted by the *Décret Crémieux* were revoked by the anti-semitic laws of the Second World War Vichy regime in France, applied to Algeria in 1940, and reinstated by the *Comité français de libération nationale* in 1943.

[25] Loi No.10.680 du 28 Juin 1881, confère aux Administrateurs des communes mixtes en territoire civil la répression, par voie disciplinaire, des infractions spéciales à l'Indigénat.

for a range of offences specific to *indigènes*, applied and interpreted by colonial administrators or executive-dominated colonial tribunals; French citizens in the overseas territories were governed by the French civil code in the civil courts. These provisions remained legally in force until 1946 (though the practical effect lasted longer). Although the French imperial system did not employ the British concept of indirect rule under customary law, and the *indigénat* regime did not rely on the fiction of custom, there was a very similar distinction between French subjects governed by local personal law and the *indigénat*, and French citizens of French civil status, the vast majority of European descent.[26]

A major new nationality law was adopted in France in 1889, which confirmed a return to *jus soli* principles, integrating the provisions into the civil code. The law provided for a child born in France to acquire French nationality automatically if still domiciled there for the majority of time or if born of a parent also born on French territory. These rules also applied in Algeria, and thus allowed people of European origin born in Algeria to become French. There was never any doubt that indigenous inhabitants of the French territories in Africa had acquired French nationality on annexation of the territory. However, the decrees applying metropolitan laws to these territories only applied to French citizens, not subjects. The decree implementing the 1889 law, not adopted till 1897, excluded from its application the status both of the *indigènes* of the French colonies and of foreigners considered *indigènes* born on colonial soil.[27] Even a new nationality code adopted in 1945 with the establishment of the fourth Republic following the Second World War, initially did not extend to the natives of French overseas territories.[28] Moreover, it remained the case that Muslim Algerians and other *sujets français* could not become French citizens (rather than subjects) unless they took steps to acquire French civil status as well as French nationality. A body of texts describing the criteria to show sufficient assimilation to French civilisation to be accorded this status was steadily elaborated.[29]

Following the First World War, in which Algerians were conscripted to fight for the French army, the law of 4 February 1919 theoretically made it easier for Muslim Algerians to acquire French citizenship. The decision on whether the criteria were fulfilled became a judicial rather than administrative one, reducing the level of discretion. The reality was different, since the conditions applied were so strict as to make it difficult for Muslims to fulfil them. By 1936, only 7,817 people had been 'naturalised' under this law, with a rejection rate of more than 50 per cent.[30]

[26] Christian Bruschi, 'La nationalité dans le droit colonial' (1988) 18 Procès : Cahiers d'analyse politique et juridique 29; Gregory Mann, 'What Was the Indigénat? The 'Empire of Law' in French West Africa' (2009) 50 Journal of African History 331; Pierre Lampué, 'L'étendue d'application du statut personnel des autochtones dans les territoires français d'outre-mer' (1957) 7 Civilisations 1.

[27] Roger Decottignies and Marc de Biéville, *Les nationalités africaines* (A Pedone 1963) 15–16.

[28] Ordonnance No.45/2447 du 19 octobre 1945 portant Code de la nationalité française.

[29] Saada (n 5) 116–131.

[30] Claude Liauzu, *Histoire des migrations en Méditerranée occidentale* (Éditions Complexe 1996).

The same year, the *Front populaire* government proposed a new law[31] that would grant French citizenship and the right to vote to around 20,000 to 25,000 Algerian Muslims, even if they kept their Muslim personal status. Opposition from French *colons* afraid of becoming an electoral minority ensured that the law was never passed.

A 1944 ordinance adopted by the *Comité français de libération nationale*, representing the united forces fighting with the Allies during the Second World War also repealed the separate criminal laws applied to Muslims in Algeria under the *code de l'indigénat*, and relaxed the rules by which they could become *citoyens français*.[32] Algeria was included in the general relaxation of access to French citizenship following the Second World War, but by independence in 1962, only around 10,000 Algerian Muslims had renounced their Muslim personal status to become full French citizens.[33]

Tunisia and Morocco were both French protectorates, established in 1881 and 1912 respectively, as France was awarded control of the territories when the decaying Ottoman empire began to be divided up by the European powers. Although from a strictly legal point of view the respective treaties did not deprive the countries of their status as sovereign States, leaving the Bey and the Sultan in nominal office, France effectively took over control of the two territories, whose residents became French protected persons (*protégés français*). Following World War I, part of Togo and most of Cameroon were similarly placed under French control by League of Nations mandate, and their populations became French administered persons (*administrés français*); after 1945, this was converted to United Nations trusteeship.

French regulation of Tunisian and Moroccan nationality gave rise to the first issue of substance submitted to the Permanent Court of International Justice (PCIJ) established by the League of Nations after the First World War.[34] Decrees adopted in 1921 by France and by the French administrations in Tunis and Morocco gave French nationality to persons born in Tunis and Morocco of at least one parent also born in the same territory (with exceptions). The UK protested against the decrees, which would impose French nationality on some British subjects, and the Council of the League of Nations referred the case to the PCIJ for an advisory opinion on whether the application of the decrees was by international law solely

[31] Known as the Blum-Viollette draft, after Léon Blum, at that time president of the Council of Ministers, and Maurice Viollette, former governor-general of Algeria (1925–1927), and at that time minister of State for North Africa.

[32] Ordonnance du 7 mars 1944 relative au statut des Français musulmans d'Algérie.

[33] Weil (n 23) 14; Saada (n 5) 128; Charles-André Julien, *L'Afrique du Nord en marche: Algérie, Tunesie, Maroc, 1830–1952* (Omnibus 2002) 257–259.

[34] Tunisia had laws regulating its nationality from the late 19th century. Both Tunis and Morocco were governed by decrees on nationality adopted by France on 8 November 1921, the subject of the *Advisory Opinion No.4 (Nationality decrees issued in Tunis and Morocco)*, adopted by the Permanent Court of International Justice on 7 February 1923. The decrees are reproduced in documents submitted to the court by the French government: see publications of the PCIJ, Series B and C, available at the ICJ website http://www.icj-cij.org/en/pcij.

a matter of domestic jurisdiction. The Court found that, though in principle questions of nationality were within the 'reserved domain' of States, the dispute was not solely a matter of domestic jurisdiction because of the obligations undertaken by France towards other States in the treaties establishing the protectorates. Following the Court's ruling, the question was settled by direct negotiation, and the French government undertook to ensure that a child born in Tunis of a British subject who was himself also born in Tunis should have the right to decline French nationality (though this right would not extend to the next generation): the parties thus agreed on a right of option rather than the unilateral imposition of nationality.[35]

In AOF and AEF, almost all persons of African origin were *sujets français*. Though French subjects had the theoretical right to become full citizens with French civil status, only 94 had accessed this status by 1922; there were fewer than 2,000 by 1937; and in West Africa no more than 16 were granted this status each year between 1935 and 1949: the famed French commitment to assimilation applied only in the cultural domain until the very last years before independence.[36] The exception to this rule was the French citizenship recognised in 1916 for the inhabitants (black African as well as white) of four *communes* in Senegal – Dakar, Saint Louis, Gorée and Rufisque – who had enjoyed special privileges since the 1830s, including the option to access the courts under the civil code while remaining subject to Muslim personal law, and from 1848 the right to elect a deputy to the French Parliament.[37] There were around 25,000 French citizens from the four communes by 1921, and close to 80,000 by 1936.[38] The law was, however, primarily directed at the possibility of military conscription in those territories; it was not envisaged that the citizens of the four communes would be able to move to France and live there *as Muslims*.[39]

During the last years of colonial rule, the legal status of the French colonies went through major changes that had no parallel in the British African territories and had important impacts on the development of nationality law – and on the 'idea' of francophone Africa, especially West Africa – that still have resonance today. For a decade after the Second World War the ambition of French colonial policy became the creation of a system – either federal or more assimilationist – of fully or semi-autonomous States within an overall French polity, under the continuing leadership of the French metropolitan territory. The ambitions of African leaders were in turn shaped by this framework, leading them to organise collectively and aim in the first instance at full participation in French institutions, rather than seeking independent control of each individual territory (as in the British

[35] Weis (n 1) 71–76.

[36] Catherine Coquery-Vidrovitch, 'Nationalité et citoyenneté en Afrique occidentale français: Originaires et citoyens dans le Sénégal colonial' (2001) 42 Journal of African History 285; John D Hargreaves, *West Africa: The Former French States* (Prentice-Hall 1967) 136.

[37] Bruschi (n 26).

[38] Hargreaves (n 36) 136.

[39] Saada (n 5) 120–121.

protectorates); at least until it became apparent that true equality within the French system would not be possible.[40]

The first steps of this policy were laid during the 1944 'Brazzaville conference' between General de Gaulle and the 'Free French', and indigenous leaders from the French African territories, at which promises of greater African autonomy were made, in recognition of the support of the colonial territories in the struggle against the Vichy regime and German forces. Following the end of the Second World War and the liberation of France, these promises led to a rapid evolution in the legal arrangements for the empire.[41] In 1946, the new constitution of the fourth Republic, drafted by a constituent assembly in which the African colonies were represented for the first time in such a discussion, created the *Union française*, which granted a degree of autonomy to the sub-Saharan territories.[42] The colonies became overseas territories with decentralised local government status, and were also represented in the Assembly of the Union. In 1956 a *loi cadre* (framework law) further increased the autonomy of the individual French colonies in west and central Africa, and greatly broadened the electorate, while at the same time repatriating to France some of the powers previously wielded by the AOF and AEF administrations. The Senegalese politician Léopold Sédar Senghor and others accused the French State of the 'balkanisation' of AOF by this process.[43] Their protests were successful in reducing the scope of a proposed Saharan State carving out the territories traditionally occupied by the Tuareg from their AOF administrations.[44] The French protectorates of Morocco and Tunisia gained independence the same year.

In 1958, the increasingly violent resistance to continued French rule in Algeria led to the collapse of the fourth Republic and the renegotiation of the structure of the French Union. The new constitution for the fifth Republic provided for the free association of autonomous republics within a *Communauté française*, in which France was the senior partner. The French Community was a less

[40] For a comprehensive discussion, see Frederick Cooper, *Citizenship between Empire and Nation: Remaking France and French Africa, 1945–1960* (Princeton University Press 2014); also Frederick Cooper, 'The Politics of Citizenship in Colonial and Postcolonial Africa' (2005) 16 Studia Africana 14.

[41] Cooper, *Citizenship between Empire and Nation* (n 40); François Borella, *L'évolution politique et juridique de l'Union française depuis 1946* (Librairie générale de droit et de jurisprudence 1958); KE Robinson, 'The Public Law of Overseas France since the War' (1950) 32 Journal of Comparative Legislation and International Law 37.

[42] See Cooper, *Citizenship between Empire and Nation* (n 39), ch 2, for a detailed discussion of the two constituent assemblies (the first proposed constitution being defeated, and the second approved, in a referendum in which most Africans did not have a vote).

[43] Joseph-Roger de Benoist, *La balkanisation de l'Afrique occidentale française* (Nouvelles Éditions Africaines 1979); Benyamin Neuberger, 'The African Concept of Balkanisation' (1976) 14 Journal of Modern African Studies 523.

[44] Bruce S Hall, *A History of Race in Muslim West Africa, 1600–1960* (Cambridge University Press 2011), ch 8; Joseph-Roger de Benoist, *Afrique occidentale française de 1944 à 1960* (Nouvelles éditions africaines 1982) 335–337. A French law established the *Organisation Commune des Régions Sahariennes* in 1956, but this took the form of a development agency rather than the political entity originally envisaged, and was dissolved in 1962.

assimilationist and more federal system, and individual French colonies were given the right to approve their membership by referendum. The Community's jurisdiction as a whole was limited to foreign policy, defence, the currency, a common economic and financial policy, and policy on strategic matters; as well as, except for special agreements, justice, higher education, external and public transport and telecommunications. Although all France's sub-Saharan African colonies joined the Community as federated States sharing a common nationality – except for Sékou Touré's Guinea, which rejected the constitution and thus opted for immediate independence[45] – the momentum towards full independence as individual territories was irresistible. The Community as originally envisaged functioned only during 1959, and in 1960, the constitution was amended to allow members of the Community to claim independence more easily – and, led by Mali (initially in a union with Senegal), the territories of AOF and AEF almost all did so. Even those that formally remained members of the Community in effect became fully independent.[46] In 1962 Algeria also gained independence, ending its bloody civil war.

During this evolution of the legal framework for the relationship between France and its colonies, the nationality regime also went through important changes; which seemed dramatic from the point of view of metropolitan France, though always inadequate to respond to the aspirations of French nationals in Algeria and overseas.

The first step in this process was the adoption in 1946 of the *Loi Lamine Guèye*, by the constituent assembly that drafted the new constitution. Named after a Senegalese delegate to the assembly, its single article provided that:

> A partir du 1er juin 1946, tous les ressortissants des territoires d'Outre-Mer ont la qualité de citoyen, au même titre que les nationaux français de la métropole et des territoires d'Outre-Mer. Des lois particulières établiront les conditions dans lesquelles ils exerceront leurs droits de citoyens.[47]

The political significance of this change was enormous, even though the legal meaning remained ambiguous in practice; especially the second sentence and the degree to which individual laws in each territory could in fact detract from

[45] Georges Fischer, 'L'indépendance de la Guinée et les accords franco-guinéens' (1958) 4 Annuaire français de droit international 711.

[46] Cooper, *Citizenship between Empire and Nation* (n 40), chs 6 and 7. The Community formally remained in existence until the relevant articles of the Constitution were repealed in 1995. Some few (non-African) colonies chose instead to remain part of France, under the status of overseas *départements* (equivalent to the *départements* making up the French metropolitan territory itself).

[47] Loi 46-940 du 7 mai 1946 tendant à proclamer citoyens tous les ressortissants des territoires d'outre-mer. 'From 1 June 1946 all nationals of the Overseas territories have the status of citizen, on the same basis as French nationals in the metropolitan territory or in the Overseas territories. Individual laws will establish the conditions under which they will exercise their rights as citizens'. The law was adopted by the first constituent assembly, its adoption being a tactical manoeuvre by Lamine Guèye to ensure that the principle would be endorsed by the final constitution. See ibid 88–91.

the concept of a common citizenship.[48] In parallel, the colonial ministry adopted decrees dismantling the *code de l'indigénat* (though the lack of judicial officers to staff ordinary civil courts meant that administrative tribunals continued in practice to judge lesser crimes) and another law abolished forced labour.[49] The 1946 constitution repeated the language of the Lamine Gueye Law in its Article 80 (giving the '*qualité de citoyen*' to inhabitants of the overseas territories), created a new umbrella status of *citoyen de l'Union française* in Article 81,[50] and provided in Article 82 that those citizens who had not acquired French civil status would retain their existing personal status unless they renounced it, elevating the concept of 'personal status' to a constitutional principle.[51] No text was ever adopted specifying how the renunciation described in Article 82 of the constitution might be effected; although the earlier decrees on procedures to be admitted to the status of French citizen theoretically remained in effect.[52] In 1953, the application of the 1945 nationality code was extended to indigenous inhabitants of France's overseas territories, with some first attempts to adapt rules on establishing descent and other matters to the terms of customary law.[53]

In electoral law, however, the subordination of the French colonies remained, and thus the subordinate citizenship of French nationals 'native' to the colonies. In this distinction, the issue of *statut personnel*, regulating which rules applied to a person's relations with other individuals and the disposition of his or her property, remained critical. A person whose *statut personnel* was governed by the French civil code was a full French citizen in political rights; whereas those governed by customary or Muslim law did not have full rights, despite the statement of a single common citizenship. The laws governing eligibility to vote were gradually made more expansive, but separate electoral colleges were retained for persons with French civil status and others until 1956 (and in Algeria even

[48] Borella (n 41); James E Genova, 'Constructing Identity in Post-War France: Citizenship, Nationality, and the Lamine Guèye Law, 1946–1953' (2004) 26 The International History Review 56.

[49] Cooper, *Citizenship between Empire and Nation* (n 40) 67–68.

[50] Article 81 provided for those who were not within the overseas territories but rather inhabitants of protectorates (Tunisia and Morocco) and trust territories (Togo and Cameroon), who did not have French nationality, to have citizenship of the Union and (at least) some of the rights guaranteed in the constitution (though not to *be* French citizens): « Tous les nationaux français et les ressortissants de l'Union française ont la qualité de citoyen de l'Union française qui leur assure la jouissance des droits et libertés garantis par le préambule de la présente Constitution. » Constitution of the 4th Republic, 27 October 1946.

[51] « Les citoyens qui n'ont pas le statut civil français conservent leur statut personnel tant qu'ils n'y ont pas renoncé. Ce statut ne peut en aucun cas constituer un motif pour refuser ou limiter les droits et libertés attachés à la qualité de citoyen français. » Art 82, 1946 Constitution.

[52] On the importance of civil registration and the mechanics of changing status, see Lampué (n 26); and Cooper, *Citizenship between Empire and Nation* (n 40) 152–163.

[53] Décret No.53-161 du 24 février 1953 déterminant les modalités d'application du Code de la nationalité française aux territoires d'outre-mer. See also Decottignies and de Biéville (n 27) 16–17; Stanislas Melone, 'La nationalité des personnes physiques', *Encyclopédie juridique de l'Afrique : Vol VI, Droits des personnes et de la famille* (Nouvelles éditions africaines 1982) 84.

after that date).[54] Moreover, the colonies were granted only a limited number of seats in the legislature: by 1955 the overseas departments and territories had 83 deputies in the Assembly (of which 30 were Algerian), to metropolitan France's 544, though the comparative populations were roughly equal. Similar inequalities were apparent in the lower-ranking assemblies established in each overseas territory.[55]

The new constitution of 1958 and the establishment of the *Communauté française* gave the Member States of the Community a large degree of autonomy; but, since international relations were left to France, the inhabitants of those States retained their French nationality and a French common citizenship until bilateral accords superseded the effort to maintain the Community.[56] The exception was Guinea, which rejected membership of the Community and thus was recognised as according its own nationality, though it did not in fact adopt a nationality law until 1960.[57] In French (formerly German) Togo and Cameroon, the League of Nations mandate had prohibited the grant of French nationality, and various decrees adopted during the 1930s, 40s and 50s had respected this distinction by creating a particular status for the inhabitants of these territories that entitled them to French protection at the international level (a conundrum avoided for the British by the ambiguous status of 'British protected person'); their individual nationalities were formally recognised by 1958 ordinances giving the two territories a status in the *Communauté française*.[58]

3.3. Others

Portugal drew similar distinctions between 'European' and 'native' in its five colonies in Africa. Although Angola, Cape Verde, Guinea Bissau, Mozambique, and São Tomé and Príncipe were subject to repeated changes in political status, the basic policies on the ground remained more or less stable.[59] During the eighteenth

[54] In November 1946 under 800,000 people in French West Africa were voters; rising to one million by June 1951, 6 million in January 1956 and ten million by March 1957, the first election under universal suffrage. Cooper, *Citizenship between Empire and Nation* (n 40) 139.

[55] Borella (n 41).

[56] Décision présidentielle du 9 février 1959: 'Au sein de la Communauté, il n'existe qu'une nationalité qui est la nationalité de la République française et de la Communauté'. Cited in Decottignies and de Biéville (n 27) 17. On disagreements on this point see Cooper, *Citizenship between Empire and Nation* (n 40) 349–365; PF Gonidec, 'Note sur la nationalité et citoyennetés dans la Communauté' (1959) 5 Annuaire français de droit international 748; PF Gonidec, 'La nationalité dans les Etats de la Communauté et dans les Etats 'marginaux'' (1961) 7 Annuaire français de droit international 814.

[57] Ordonnance No.011 du 1er mars 1960 portant Code de la nationalité guinéenne. The law nonetheless followed the French model closely. See Decottignies and de Biéville (n 27) 145–147.

[58] ibid 19–20; Melone (n 53) 84–85.

[59] See Malyn Newitt, *A History of Mozambique* (Hurst 1995) 378–577. In practice, Cape Verde and São Tomé and Príncipe were subjected, at least formally, to slightly different policies from Portuguese Guinea (today's Guinea-Bissau), Angola and Mozambique. See also, Paul Nugent, *Africa since Independence* (Palgrave Macmillan 2004) 17–19 & 261–271.

century, Portuguese overseas territories were named *colónias* (colonies); they were rebranded as *províncias* (overseas provinces) in the 1820 Portuguese constitution, a status they kept in the 1911 constitution. They were once again renamed *colónias* in the 1933 constitution of the *Estado Novo* dictatorship, until 1951, when they were again called *províncias*. Two categories of citizenship were introduced in 1899, for the purposes of labour regulations: the *indígena* (native) and the *não-indígena* (non-native). The *não-indígenas,* European-born Portuguese and white-skinned foreigners were full Portuguese citizens (*cidadãos*) subject to metropolitan laws, or benefited from the diplomatic protection of their State of nationality; whereas the *indígenas* were administered under the customary laws of each territory, as modified or interpreted by Portuguese authorities, and subject to a range of coercive measures.[60] Gradually, a third category emerged, that of *assimilado*, that is, a person (initially usually Asian or Afro-Portuguese but including some Africans) who claimed the status of *não-indígena* on the basis of his or her education, knowledge of Portuguese language and culture, profession, and income. From 1917 clear procedures were adopted to establish status,[61] and a 1954 decree-law on the *Estatuto do Indigenato* established a more complete and less arbitrary framework on the status of *indígena* in the mainland territories, as well as the rules and procedures by which an *indígena* could become a *cidadão*.[62] Formal legal equality in the colonies was established by the Portuguese only in 1961, in the midst of liberation wars in Africa, when any African could formally choose to become a Portuguese citizen and the worst kinds of forced labour were abolished.[63]

Similar rules applied in the Belgian, Spanish, German, and Italian colonies while they were operational, though with less elaborated ideologies and legal structures of empire.[64] Though the systems differed, in all colonial territories those with subject status (natives, *indigènes, indígenas*) were not only subject to different

[60] Peter Karibe Mendy, 'Portugal's Civilizing Mission in Colonial Guinea-Bissau: Rhetoric and Reality' (2003) 36 International Journal of African Historical Studies 35.

[61] Newitt (n 59) 382–385 & 441–444. These formal prerequisites could be waived and the *assimilado* status granted 'to any African who had proved he had exercised a public charge, that he was employed in the colonial administration corps, that he had a secondary school education, that he was a licensed merchant, a partner in a business firm, or the proprietor of an industrial establishment.' Bruno da Ponte, 'The Last to Leave, Portuguese Colonialism in Africa' (International Defence and Aid Fund 1974) 40.

[62] Decreto-lei No.39666 of 26 May 1954; see André Durieux, 'Essai sur le statut des indigènes portugais de la Guinée, de l'Angola et du Mozambique' (Académie Royale des Sciences Coloniales 1955).

[63] B O'Laughlin, 'Class and the Customary: The Ambiguous Legacy of the Indigenato in Mozambique' (2000) 99 African Affairs 5; M Mamdani, 'Indirect Rule and the Struggle for Democracy: A Response to Bridget O'Laughlin' (2000) 99 African Affairs 43. See also Shubi Ishemo, 'Forced Labour and Migration in Portugal's African Colonies' in Robin Cohen (ed), *The Cambridge Survey of World Migration* (Cambridge Univ Press 1995).

[64] Nugent (n 59). On Italy, see Fabrizio de Donno, '*La Razza Ario-Mediterranea*: Ideas of Race and Citizenship in Colonial and Fascist Italy, 1885–1941' (2006) 8 Interventions 394. Laws for the Italian colonies are extracted in Felice de Dominicis, *Commento alla legge sulla Cittadinanza Italiana del 13 giugno 1912* (Unione Tipografico-Editrice Torinese 1916). On Belgium, see ch 7.4 discussion on the rules applied in Congo.

legal regimes but were also usually obliged to work, to pay specific taxes (in kind, but also in labour), and to obtain a pass to travel within or to leave the country; while European citizens could leave the country freely, were exempt from labour legislation, and paid taxes at different rates.

Liberia had its own very particular history with regard to citizenship, starting from its foundation in 1822 by the American Colonization Society as 'an asylum from the most grinding oppression' for former American slaves.[65] The fundamental assumption of the new State was that the body of citizens was made up of the emigrants from America and their descendants. The 'Constitution of the Commonwealth of Liberia' adopted by the board of directors of the American Colonization Society in 1839 gave the governor and council powers

> To prescribe uniform rules of naturalization for all persons of color, and all persons now citizens of any part of the Commonwealth of Liberia shall continue to be so, and all colored persons emigrating from the United States of America or any district or territory thereof, with the approbation, or under the sanction of the American Colonization Society [...].[66]

The constitution clearly established the colonists as legally separate from the 'several African tribes', from whom the purchase of land had been arranged. The first constitution of an independent Liberia, freed from the control of the American Colonization Society in 1847, described 'the people of the Republic of Liberia' as 'originally the inhabitants of the United States of North America', distinguishing themselves from 'the natives of the country'.[67] With a view to that history, it was also provided that: 'The great object of forming these Colonies, being to provide a home for the dispersed and oppressed children of Africa, and to regenerate and enlighten this benighted continent, none but persons of color shall be eligible to citizenship in this Republic'; and only citizens could own property.[68]

Gradually authority was extended over the 'native tribes', and in 1869 the Interior Department was established to govern all aspects of the hinterland, 'with due regard to native customary law and native institutions'. Thus, in a similar way to that of the European colonies, 'natives' were subject to executive power and ruled by customary law and Americo-Liberians to statutory law and the civil courts, with different forms of government in the hinterland and coastal provinces. Those natives who assimilated to Americo-Liberian culture, especially by converting to Christianity and achieving literacy, could, however, come to be recognised as citizens. Only in 1904 did President Barclay declare that all the residents of the interior were citizens (largely to establish the claims of the Liberian State to the

[65] Constitution of Liberia 1847, preamble.

[66] Constitution of the Commonwealth of Liberia, 1838, Art 9.

[67] Constitution of Liberia 1847, preamble.

[68] Constitution of Liberia 1847, Art V(15). In a 1955 revision to the constitution the phrase 'persons of color' was replaced by 'Negroes or persons of Negro descent'. A similar provision exists in Haiti, for similar reasons: see Olivier W Vonk, *Nationality Law in the Western Hemisphere: A Study on Grounds for Acquisition and Loss of Citizenship in the Americas and the Caribbean* (Brill 2015) 247–249.

territory against encroachment by France and Britain); and only in 1944 did the newly elected Tubman administration extend greater rights to political representation to members of indigenous ethnic groups as part of his 'unification' drive. Yet the 'Hinterland Regulations' adopted in 1948 effectively continued to exclude the indigenous population from meaningful participation in political power – until 1964 when four new interior counties were created with full representation in the House of Representatives.[69] The first comprehensive nationality law was only adopted in 1955, the previous announcements operating more at the political than legal level. The new law moved away from the distinctions between citizens and 'aborigines' of the territory to establish a right to citizenship for anyone born in Liberia, while retaining the racial limitation.[70]

[69] Amos Sawyer, *The Emergence of Autocracy in Liberia: Tragedy and Challenge* (Institute for Contemporary Studies 1992); Thomas P Wrubel, 'Liberia: The Dynamics of Continuity' (1971) 9 Journal of Modern African Studies 189.

[70] Aliens and Nationality Law, Title 3 of the Liberian Code of Laws of 1956; codifying and updating a patchwork of various laws on immigration and naturalisation and on nationality adopted over previous decades, including a 1938 naturalisation law and 1945–46 consular service regulations.

4

Transition to Independence

The circumstances of State creation through colonisation, followed by State recognition following decolonisation, meant that indigenous African traditions of determining membership had little influence on the post-colonial legal regime. Though these systems survived throughout the colonial period and continued to have immense influence on peoples' daily lives, for the colonisers their legal effect was for the most part at sub-national scale only. Thus, indigenous traditions of belonging had only marginal impact on the ways in which nationality laws came to be drafted at independence, or on the transitional provisions adopted to govern the succession of States. This was particularly true in the Commonwealth countries, where new constitutions agreed as part of the transitional package with Britain included quite detailed provisions on citizenship; but also in the French territories, where the new States largely adopted laws based on French templates, and to lesser extent elsewhere.

Not all States adopted formal transitional rules on the status of those resident in the territory at independence. The British-negotiated constitutions all did so, distinguishing between those with stronger and weaker connections to the new State; most nationality codes of the former French territories included a chapter with transitional provisions, but some did not; Rwanda provided such rules, Burundi did not, and the Congo situation was extremely confused; the lusophone States also varied in the extent to which they explicitly provided for those born before independence. In States where the law applicable to those born after independence gave and continued to give strong rights based on birth in the territory, these rules and omissions had less relevance; where the post-independence law was or became based on descent, the transitional rules remain important today.

4.1. The Ottoman Empire

The first external power with African territories to be broken up into independent States was the Ottoman empire, at the end of the First World War, though by that date Egypt was the only North African territory still nominally under its sovereignty. In 1918, the Armistice of Moudros ended the hostilities, as well as Islamic political unity under Ottoman rule; the treaties of Sèvres and Lausanne completed the process and included transitional provisions relating to the nationality of former Ottoman subjects. The 1920 Treaty of Sèvres provided for those who had held Ottoman nationality to acquire the nationality of one of the new States if they were 'habitually resident' in that territory (the language used in the English text; the French has *établis*, a somewhat more demanding requirement). Former Ottoman subjects resident in a territory detached from Turkey and who differed in 'race' from the majority population of that territory, also had the right, to be exercised within one year, to opt for Turkish nationality or the nationality of the State where the majority of the population was of the same race as the person concerned. Special provisions were established for Egypt and Sudan (and Cyprus). These provisions were largely incorporated into the 1923 Treaty of Lausanne, with the exception of the provisions on Egypt, which had become independent in 1922. The period for the right of option was extended to two years, but subjected to the consent of the State whose nationality was chosen.

Egypt had a particular status within the Ottoman empire, with a set of rules on 'indigenous nationality' applying only to Egypt from the late nineteenth century; though for international purposes Egyptians were treated as Ottoman nationals. Independent Egypt's nationality was first regulated in 1926, by a law aimed at sorting out the status of former Ottoman subjects in the country. The law established the 5 November 1914 as the starting point for Egyptian nationality, the date the Allies entered into war with the Ottoman empire, decided to be the day that Ottoman rule over Egypt had ended. Ottoman subjects habitually resident in Egypt on that date and up to the date of entry into force of the law became Egyptian; however, the legislation greatly restricted the right to opt for Egyptian nationality generally provided in the Sèvres and Lausanne treaties, by requiring birth in the territory as well as membership of the same 'race', and reducing the period for option to six months. In 1929, a new law removed some of the restrictions on option; in relation to those born after the entry into force of the law, it maintained a paternal *jus sanguinis* basis for nationality established by the 1926 law, and also created rights based on Arab and Muslim identity that are still present in Egyptian nationality law. A child born in Egypt of a father also born there would have Egyptian nationality if the father ethnically belonged to a country where the majority of the population spoke Arabic or practised Islam. Naturalisation was also restricted to those of a common cultural, linguistic and religious background.[1]

4.2. British Territories

Most Commonwealth countries had constitutions drafted according to the standard 'Lancaster House'[2] template that structured the negotiations with the

[1] Decree-Law of 26 May 1926 and Decree-Law of 27 February 1929. See Gianluca P Parolin, *Citizenship in the Arab World: Kin, Religion and Nation-State* (Amsterdam University Press 2009) 79–82.

[2] Lancaster House was the building in London where many of the constitutions were negotiated and finalised.

independence leaders of each African State. This template established more or less uniform rules that created three ways of becoming a citizen of the new State: some became citizens automatically; some became entitled to citizenship and could register as of right; while others who were potential citizens could apply to naturalise through a discretionary process. Those who became citizens automatically were: firstly, persons born in the country before independence who were citizens of the UK and colonies or British protected persons at the date of independence, with a parent (in the countries of east and southern Africa) or grandparent (in west Africa) also born there; and secondly, persons born outside the country whose fathers became citizens in accordance with the first provision. Southern Africa had variations on the same rules.

Those persons born in the country whose parents were both (or whose grandparents were all) born outside the country were entitled to citizenship by way of registration, as were other citizens of the UK and colonies or British protected persons who were ordinarily resident in the country. Others could naturalise if they fulfilled the normal conditions set; provision was sometimes also made for easier access to citizenship for nationals of other Commonwealth countries, both in the transitional measures and on an ongoing basis; citizens of other Commonwealth countries were not 'aliens' for the purposes of domestic law, but occupied an intermediate status. The laws were not gender neutral, and special provisions relating to married women were included, usually making them dependent on their husband's status.[3]

For those born after independence, the initial constitutions established the uniform rule of *jus soli* attribution of citizenship to those born in the territory, with exceptions only for the children of a father who was a diplomat of another country (unless the mother was a citizen). Those born outside the territory would acquire citizenship only through the father.

Mirroring rules were adopted in British law, providing for the classes of persons who would lose citizenship of the UK and colonies or British protected person status when they acquired the citizenship of the new State; and for those who would retain their British connection. These provisions were drafted with a view to retaining the citizenship of those of British descent, but initially also provided equal rights to those of Asian or African origin. This situation soon changed. In Kenya in particular, where most of the territory had been a British colony, 'within the crown's dominions' but not self-governing, the status of Kenyan Asians who

[3] Laurie Fransman, Adrian Berry and Alison Harvey, *Fransman's British Nationality Law* (3rd edn, Bloomsbury Professional 2011). Ch 3 and catalogue entries on Commonwealth countries; see also International Law Commission, 'Second Report on State Succession and Its Impact on the Nationality of Natural and Legal Persons, by Mr. Vaclav Mikulka, Special Rapporteur, A/CN.4/474 and Corr.1 and 2' (1996) II Yearbook of the International Law Commission. Some people with a residual connection with the UK (through birth, descent or marriage – if a woman) retained their previous status. So too did people who, though closely connected with the new State, failed after independence to qualify for citizenship of the newly independent country. They remained citizens of the UK and Colonies or British Protected Persons.

were citizens of the UK and colonies at the date of independence created alarm at the prospect of immigration into Britain; especially as it became clear that the new Kenyan government would not be sympathetic to the Asian population. Those who had not become citizens of the new State (which required renunciation of other citizenships) remained citizens of the UK and colonies. The Commonwealth Immigration Acts of 1962 and 1968 were designed to restrict and then remove the right of abode in the UK from the Kenyan Asians, distinguishing between passports issued in the UK or in a colony, and exempting from immigration control only those citizens of the UK and colonies who had one parent or grand-parent born, adopted, registered or naturalised in the UK.[4]

Tanganyika followed the same model as Kenya and Uganda, despite its different status within the British empire as a mandate and then trust territory rather than a protectorate. The transfer of authority and citizenship for Zanzibar was somewhat different, thanks to pre-existing nationality laws adopted in 1911 (perhaps Africa's oldest) and 1952 and the decision not to restore sovereignty over any part of the coastal strip. A series of letters governed the transfer of jurisdiction over the northern part of the coastal strip and its residents to the newly independent Kenya on 12 December 1963.[5] The 1952 Nationality Decree remained in force in the islands of Zanzibar on their independence two days before Kenya, until the merger of Zanzibar with Tanganyika to create the United Republic of Tanzania in 1964.

In southern Africa, the creation of the Central African Federation could not halt the move to independence. Elaborate schemes to provide Africans with some greater but limited political power did not hold back public protest in the two protectorates at the prospect of domination by while Southern Rhodesians, and frantic negotiations did not prevent the ultimate agreement for Nyasaland and Northern Rhodesia to secede and become independent on their own terms.[6] The Federation was dissolved on 1 January 1964; in November 1965 Southern Rhodesia declared it was leaving the Commonwealth to become independent, enabling it to preserve white minority rule (see Chapter 7.1)

Northern Rhodesia and Nyasaland adopted slightly different provisions as they became the independent States of Zambia and Malawi. In Malawi, the standard terms applicable to other British protectorates applied: those born in the territory of one parent also born there became citizens automatically, while habitual residents born in the country could register as citizens during a transitional period. Malawi added the possibility of registration for those who had been citizens of

[4] Rieko Karatani, *Defining British Citizenship: Empire, Commonwealth, and Modern Britain* (Frank Cass 2003) 156–163.

[5] 'Agreement between the government of the United Kingdom, His Highness the Sultan of Zanzibar, the government of Kenya and the government of Zanzibar', October 1963, Cmnd. 2161; 'Exchange of letters between His Highness the Sultan of Zanzibar and the British Resident terminating the 1890 Agreement as respects the dominions of the Sultan not comprised in the Kenya Protectorate', December 1963, Cmnd. 2218. With thanks to Iain Walker for sharing these texts.

[6] Colin Leys and Cranford Pratt, *A New Deal in Central Africa.* (Praeger 1960); JJB Somerville, 'The Central African Federation' (1963) 39 International Affairs 386.

the former Federation of Rhodesia and Nyasaland and who had a 'substantial Malawi connection'.[7] Zambia's new constitution (like that of Lesotho), however, provided for a more expansive attribution of citizenship at independence based purely on birth in the territory before independence, with no requirement for one parent also to have been born there.[8] But the law made no further provision for acquisition of nationality by those with a connection to the other territories of the former Central African Federation. Those born outside each country became citizens, according to the usual terms, if their fathers became citizens under to the other provisions. The (mis)interpretation of these provisions later resulted in several cases brought to the African Commission on Human and Peoples' Rights (see Chapter 5.5).

Zimbabwe, Namibia and South Africa had rather different trajectories, both legally and politically, resulting from their self-governing legal status and white-minority governments. Since its earlier unilateral declaration of independence had never been recognised by Britain, Zimbabwe was the only country of these three that had the same legal pattern as other former British territories, with an independence constitution and matching Zimbabwe Act adopted in the UK in 1979, when it made the transition from Rhodesia to Zimbabwe. However, there was already a thirty-year history in relation to independent regulation of nationality, and the 1979 constitution provided for continuity of citizenship; for those born after the act came into force it re-enacted the citizenship provisions already in existence without major revision (see further, Chapter 7.1).[9]

Although South Africa never accepted the authority of the UN Trusteeship Council, a UN-brokered agreement ultimately led to the independence of Namibia in 1990. The new constitution and citizenship act did not contain explicit transitional provisions, but established a relatively open regime for citizenship with rights based on ordinary residence. Namibia also adopted a specific piece of legislation offering Namibian citizenship to those who would have been Namibian citizens if they or their ancestors had not fled persecution before 1915, reintegrating those who had fled the German genocide of the Herero from 1904 to 1907.[10] In South Africa itself, there was no succession of States as such on the attainment of majority rule in 1994, since there was merely a change in government in an existing State with existing nationality laws. The new government reformed the general citizenship law within two years and also offered a series of immigration amnesties to particular groups of foreigners from the region, including migrant workers and refugees from the Mozambican civil war (Chapter 9.3).

[7] Independence Constitution, ch I, Arts 1, 2 and 3. The status of those of Asian descent in British nationality law who were citizens of the UK and colonies prior to independence is complex, and has been subject to litigation in the UK. See Fransman, Berry and Harvey (n 3) catalogue entry on Zambia.

[8] Independence Constitution, ch II, Art 3. See also Elspeth Guild, 'British Nationality and East African Independence' (1990) 4 Immigration and Nationality Law and Practice 99.

[9] Fransman, Berry and Harvey (n 3) catalogue entry on Zimbabwe.

[10] Namibian Citizenship (Special Conferment) Act No.14 of 1991.

4.3. French Territories

The practice in the French colonies was different. After the collapse of the short-lived 1958 constitution of the French Community, the regulation of nationality became the responsibility of the new fully independent States.[11] According to French law, nationality in the context of the State successions was based on the criterion of domicile, a status based on residence (though with more particular definition in French law). Thus, French nationals domiciled in the newly independent States lost French nationality on the date of transfer of sovereignty. However, in order to avoid the loss of French nationality by those of metropolitan origin, a law of 28 July 1960 modified the 1945 nationality code to permit French nationals originating in metropolitan France and their descendants to keep their French nationality even if they were domiciled in the new State (including those of African origin, but mainly providing for the *métis*)[12]; persons born and domiciled in the new States were also allowed to retain their French nationality under certain conditions (for example, based on service in the French army).[13]

In Algeria, the question of nationality in the context of State succession was of particular sensitivity. Algeria had a unique status among all the European colonies in Africa, given the size of the population of European origin (more than a million people) and the legal status of the territory as an integral part of France. The process of defining who would be entitled to be an Algerian national after independence was the very process of deciding what the Algerian 'nation' would be. Would the new State be race-religion-and-colour-blind, or would it differentiate between different categories of citizen, just as the French had differentiated on the grounds of personal religious status? The texts adopted by the *Front de libération nationale* (FLN) had appealed to those of European descent to integrate into the post-colonial State and promised a non-discriminatory future legal regime. In the March 1962 Evian Accords that ended the civil war it was agreed that the Algerian-born *colons* would have the right to opt for Algerian nationality or to remain in Algeria as foreigners, with a three-year period of permitted dual nationality.

It had initially been proposed that French-born persons resident in Algeria would also automatically become nationals of Algeria at independence; however, this proved unacceptable to the leaders of the liberation struggle, and in the final settlement they were given the right to naturalise, providing they renounced their French nationality, but not the status of nationals of origin. Those Algerians who

[11] Frederick Cooper, *Citizenship between Empire and Nation: Remaking France and French Africa, 1945–1960* (Princeton University Press 2014) 414–428.

[12] Loi No.60-752 du 28 juillet 1960 portant modifications de certaines dispositions du Code de la nationalité, Art 1.

[13] Stanislas Melone, 'La nationalité des personnes physiques', *Encyclopédie juridique de l'Afrique : Vol VI, Droits des personnes et de la famille* (Nouvelles éditions africaines 1982) 88–89; Christian Bruschi, 'La nationalité dans le droit colonial' (1988) 18 Procès : Cahiers d'analyse politique et juridique 29 text with footnote 213; Ruth Donner, *The Regulation of Nationality in International Law* (Transnational Publishers Inc 1994) ch V, Nationality and State Succession, s 3.2.2.

had renounced Muslim personal status to become full French citizens were also Algerians of origin as of right, though they could renounce Algerian nationality and remain French if they so wished. The code also stated that those convicted of 'crimes against the nation' after the date of the Evian Accords would not have a right to nationality; while those participating in the liberation struggle were given a right to opt for Algerian nationality.[14] The great majority of Algerians, of '*statut civil du droit local originaires d'Algérie*' lost their French nationality; although those who wished to were permitted by a French ordinance of 21 July 1962 to retain French nationality if they transferred their domicile to France and made a signed declaration during a transitional period of five years.[15]

In relation to those born after independence, the law included a limited double *jus soli* provision,[16] and was on the face of it non-discriminatory in relation to the role of religion (though it discriminated on the basis of gender). However, the massive departure of those of French civil status in the period between the Evian accords and the referendum of July 1962 left the new government feeling threatened by the concept of three years of dual nationality for people whose loyalty was so suspect. Article 34 of the 1963 *Code de la nationalité*, in the section of the law dealing with evidence and dispute resolution, introduced a critical element of religious identity to the concept of nationality. The article defined 'Algerian' as a person of Muslim religion whose father and father's father was born in Algeria. This definition made clear that neither Christian nor Jewish Algerians would be fully regarded as part of the national community.[17] Even though the status of non-Muslims was less contested in other north African States, most also adopted nationality provisions inspired by more general post-independence efforts to consolidate an Arab nationality and Muslim identity.[18]

There were important variations among the sub-Saharan francophone countries; and in some cases there was a long gap between the end of colonial rule and the adoption of a new nationality law – five years in the case of Dahomey (future Benin) – with a consequent lack of clarity on the status of those born or

[14] Loi, No.63-92 du 27 mars 1983 portant Code de la nationalité algérienne, arts 8-10 and 43. Jacqueline Bendeddouche, *Notion de nationalité et nationalité algérienne* (Société Nationale d'Édition et de Diffusion 1974).

[15] Ordonnance No.62-825 du 21 juillet 1962 relative à certaines dispositions concernant la nationalité française, arts 1-4. The main group targetted with this provision were the *harkis*, those who had fought for the French army during the civil war.

[16] Loi No.63-96 du 27 mars 1963 portant Code de la nationalité algérienne, art 11, provided for nationality to be given to a child born in Algeria of two parents also born in Algeria after the date of independence (that is, unlike the similar provision in most other nationality codes, it would not apply to anyone already alive at the date of independence, and it required for a positive option for nationality rather than a default attribution).

[17] See also circulaire du 9 mai 1963 relative à l'application de la Loi No.63-96 du 27 mars 1963 portant Code de la nationalité algérienne. A French court decision of 1965 in the *tribunal de grande instance*, ruled that because the Algerian nationality code gave nationality of origin only to Muslims, the person concerned – a Jewish Algerian – kept French nationality even though his parents had not obtained full French citizenship before independence. Bendeddouche (n 14) 146.

[18] Parolin (n 1).

resident during this period and on the possible conflict of laws with the French nationality code. Explicit transitional provisions were usually limited to giving the formal right to opt for nationality of the host country to those who had come to the newly independent State from elsewhere in the French African territories, an option that had to be exercised within a limited time and was directed primarily at the educated elite who had served in the civil service across the French territories.[19]

For those born after independence, the new nationality codes mostly followed the general outline and adopted variants of the substantive and procedural provisions of French law applicable at the time, the 1945 nationality code. All countries provided for nationality by descent from a father who was a national, with most (though not all) distinguishing between children born in and out of wedlock, with rights for the child of a national mother and foreign father only if born out of wedlock and not recognised by the father, or only if the father was unknown or stateless. A large majority adopted variants on double *jus soli*, applying equally to those born before or after independence, while some also provided for the automatic attribution of nationality to those born in the country and still resident there at majority and others the right to opt for nationality at that time. In Niger, which also had a provision on double *jus soli*, the law created a presumption that this was fulfilled based simply on habitual residence in the country at independence.[20] Mali's double *jus soli* rule, however, restricted rights based on birth in the territory to those 'of African origin', without providing a definition of what that meant.[21]

In most countries there were transitional rules for certain categories of person to be able to acquire nationality by option on the date of independence; but the main definition of the citizen body was left to the cumulative application of the general double *jus soli* rules. Led by Senegal, the first to adopt a nationality code, many also called on the idea of *possession d'état*, allowing a person who had always been treated as a national to claim formal recognition of that nationality (a concept originally taken from the French Code Napoléon of 1804, where it was applied in the context of family law, and progressively to other spheres).[22] All the francophone countries included provisions in their laws on the means of obtaining proof of or contesting the nationality of a person, conferring this role on the lower level courts.[23]

Côte d'Ivoire, the most highly developed economy of AOF and the recipient of the greatest number of migrant workers to the new cocoa and coffee plantations, adopted somewhat different rules. Unusually, the new nationality code provided for equal rights for men and women in relation to citizenship by descent. It also

[19] Melone (n 13) 86–90; Alexandre Zatzepine, *Le droit de la nationalité des républiques francophones d'Afrique et de Madagascar* (Pichon et Durand-Auzias 1963) 10–31.

[20] Loi No.61-26 déterminant la nationalité nigérienne, Art 7.

[21] Code de la nationalité malienne, Loi No.62-18 AN-RM du 3 février 1962.

[22] Kéba M'Baye, 'L'attribution de la nationalité sénégalaise « jure soli » et l'option de nationalité dans la loi sénégalaise de 7 mars 1961' (1961) 71 Penant 347.

[23] Zatzepine (n 19) 32–75 & 94–109.

did not attribute nationality on the basis of double *jus soli*, but rather, in a provision that was believed at the time to be more liberal, to every person born in Côte d'Ivoire unless both of his or her parents were 'foreigners' (*étrangers*). In a fateful omission, the law did not define what 'foreigner' meant. In addition, those born in the country could acquire nationality 'by declaration' at majority, and those resident in the country at independence could naturalise without further conditions within a limited period. Almost nobody in fact took the steps needed to obtain recognition of nationality under these rules (see further, Chapter 7.4).

Guinea simply copied over the French law virtually verbatim despite its revolutionary rhetoric and despite (or because of) its earlier exit from French nationality. The transitional provisions did not establish rules relating to the attribution of nationality to those who became Guinean at independence; and even the date of entry into force of the new nationality code was not clear.[24] Thanks to its status as a trust territory, Cameroon adopted a nationality code even before it was formally independent; the first French-administered territory to do so.[25] Togo, however, only adopted a law regulating nationality more than a year after the dissolution of the French community.[26] Both followed more or less closely the French model, while emphasising rights based on birth in the territory.[27]

4.4. Others

In the five former Portuguese colonies (known collectively as the *Países Africanos de Língua Oficial Portuguesa*, (PALOP)), most of the new national constitutions and political regimes were given a socialist content when independence was attained following the 1974 collapse of the *Estado Novo* in Portugal. Some countries also voted for rules favouring the grant of nationality to those who had fought against the Portuguese and penalising those who had collaborated with the colonial regime. For example, in Mozambique individuals who had participated in the liberation struggle within the structures of the *Frente de Libertação de Moçambique* (FRELIMO) were given the right to opt for Mozambican nationality, and nationality was excluded for people who had been members of 'colonial-fascist political organisations'.[28] Cape Verde and Guinea Bissau had matching provisions mutually facilitating access to the other's nationality, based on the relationship created by the single party that brought both to independence, the *Partido africano de independência da Guiné e Cabo Verde* (PAIGC), founded by Amilcar Cabral. Generally, transitional measures favoured the automatic attribution of the

[24] Roger Decottignies and Marc de Biéville, *Les nationalités africaines* (A Pedone 1963) 153.
[25] Ordonnance No.59-66 du 26 novembre 1959.
[26] Loi No.61-18 du 25 juillet 1961.
[27] Decottignies and de Biéville (n 24) entries on Cameroon and Togo.
[28] Lei da nacionalidade de 20 de Junho de 1975, Arts 3 and 7.

nationality of the new State: for example, Angola's first nationality law provided that those born in Angola who did not want to maintain Angolan nationality had to declare their renunciation within one year of independence; the other four lusophone countries attributed nationality to a range of categories of person, including based on double *jus soli* and to those domiciled in the country at independence, and also provided for renunciation within one year.[29]

The 1968 independence constitution for the former Spanish colony of Equatorial Guinea provided as one of its transitional provisions that those of African descent born in the country would obtain nationality.[30]

Belgium's hasty abandonment of its central African colony in Congo without putting in place a comprehensive framework to cater for those resident on the territory created problems that still resonate today. Right up to the last minute before independence, Belgian scholars were debating the possibility of creating a 'Congolese nationality' as a sub-category of Belgian nationality, in order to provide clarity on the status of autochthonous Congolese both in Congo and in Belgium, as well as of other 'foreign nationals', including the Rwandan-speaking populations of the east. Independent Congo did not adopt provisions on nationality until 1964, four years after independence (see Chapter 7.5). Rwanda adopted a nationality law in 1963, within one year; but Burundi did not until 1971, nine years after independence.

Italy's colonies in Somalia and Eritrea were conferred to Britain as United Nations trust territories following the Second World War, and eventually were joined to British Somaliland and reunited to Ethiopia (see Chapter 8.1) by referendum at independence. The legacy of their existence as separate colonial territories was to give both a sense of distinct identity that eventually led to their secession from the States to which they had been (re)joined. Libya fell under Allied military administration from 1943 until gaining independence in 1951. A new nationality law provided that a person born before the 1951 constitution was adopted became Libyan if he or she was 'a regular resident of Libya on that date, and had no other nationality or affiliation with a foreign jurisdiction', and was also born in Libya, or born outside of Libya and one of the parents was Libyan-born, or had been resident in Libya for ten years at that date.[31]

The rules on acquisition of nationality at independence were inevitably contentious, given the preceding history. The most visible of those whose status was left in doubt – the Europeans, Asians, Middle-Easterners – were the most immediately

[29] Angola Lei de 10 de novembro de 1975, Article 1; Cabo Verde Decreto-Lei No.71/76 de 24 de julho, Art 1; Guiné Bissau Lei da nacionalidade No.1/76 de 4 de maio, Art 1; Mozambique Lei da nacionalidade de 20 de Junho de 1975, Art 1; Sao Tomé & Príncipe, Lei da nacionalidade de 1 de decembro 1975, Art 1.

[30] 'Con independencia de lo que en su día disponga la Ley de Nacionalidad, se considerarán nacionales guineanos las personas de ascendencia africana que hayan nacido en Guinea Ecuatorial y sus hijos, aunque hayan nacido fuera de ella, siempre que en uno y otro caso vengan poseyendo como tales la nacionalidad guineana.' 1968 Constitution, Disposiciones Transitorias.

[31] Nationality law, no 17 for the year 1954, 25 April 1954, art 1.

affected, and their status as nationals either of the former European colonial powers or in the new States was the subject of many of the early crises over citizenship as well as litigation in courts on both continents. The impact on the less visible – the Africans who migrated within common imperial boundaries, or were brought as forced labour – was in most cases less obvious in the first decades after independence, but has remained a much longer-lasting and more destabilising question for the governance of the States as they have consolidated (or not, as the case may be).

The lack of clarity and inaccessible procedures in the allocation of nationality at independence to the 'non-indigenous' residents of each territory left a dangerous level of confusion and exclusion. Where the ongoing rules for attribution of nationality at birth include generous rights based on birth in the territory these provisions have had relevance for a shorter period of time. However, where the law was or became primarily descent-based, the transitional rules on succession of States have retained a significant role in determining the status of these populations. The next chapter considers the trends in nationality law since independence, including their impact on these populations.

PART III

African Nationality Laws Since Independence

'The Committee … reminds African States that States do not enjoy unfettered discretion in establishing rules for the conferral of their nationality, but must do so in a manner consistent with their international legal obligations.'

— African Committee of Experts on the Rights and Welfare of the Child,
General Comment No.2 on Article 6 of the Charter

5

Trends and Patterns in Nationality Law

The legal framework for nationality established in African States at the date of independence was almost entirely determined by the laws in place at that time in the colonial power that had control over that territory. This was most apparent in the former British territories, where citizenship provisions governing the transition and the initial period after independence were included in the independence constitutions. But even in French, Belgian and Portuguese territories, where rules on nationality were left to the new States to determine for themselves, the laws adopted at independence essentially copied the legal framework of the metropolitan State, if not absolutely all the substantive provisions.

To this extent, the sort of comparative analysis of the development of nationality regimes based on the political traditions of France and Germany disputed between Rogers Brubaker and others[1] is not possible in the African context. Nationality law was inherited with the idea of the 'nation state' itself, rather than built up over centuries from a palimpsest of existing traditions.

Regional comparisons have become more meaningful over time, but there remains a strong degree of path dependency based on these initial frameworks. This continuity is perhaps more in evidence at the procedural level than at the substantive, but is nonetheless present across all legal codes – even in those States which were never formally colonised by an external power (Liberia and Ethiopia), which also drew on American and European examples. There have been amendments in all countries, but often even major changes, such as the removal of rights based on birth in the territory to create a descent-based system, have left basic formulations in place. There has been a complete re-think of the framework in only a minority of countries, which would include Nigeria, Rwanda, South Africa, Swaziland and Uganda – and even there, the underlying concepts of the law are remarkably sticky.

Nonetheless, nationality laws have by no means remained static, and they have been influenced by the same battles over inclusion and exclusion that are seen in

[1] Rogers Brubaker, *Citizenship and Nationhood in France and Germany* (Harvard University Press 1992); Christian Joppke, *Immigration and the Nation-State* (Oxford University Press 1999); Patrick Weil, 'Access to Citizenship: A Comparison of Twenty-Five Nationality Laws' in Thomas Alexander Aleinikoff and Douglas B Klusmeyer (eds), *Citizenship Today: Global Perspectives and Practices* (Carnegie Endowment for International Peace : Migration Policy Institute 2001); Patrick Weil, *Qu'est-ce qu'un Français? Histoire de la nationalité française de la Révolution à nos jours* (Grasset 2002).

other continents. The first set of amendments were clustered around the status of those who immigrated – or were brought – to the country before independence, and the nature of the regime for attribution of citizenship based on birth in the territory. The next set of amendments responded to demands for gender equality in transmission to children from a progressively strengthening women's movement. Last to take off were the adjustments to permit dual nationality, acknowledging the importance of the steadily growing post-independence diaspora – and the reality that many African politicians themselves held two nationalities.

Rules on acquisition of nationality after birth have also been modified, mostly to provide gender equality in acquisition through marriage. Naturalisation based on long residence has seen relatively few substantive changes; perhaps because the procedures are highly discretionary, so very few obtain nationality as adults by this channel.

As of the end of 2017, around half of Africa's States, mostly but not only in the civil law tradition, had laws that gave some rights based on birth in the territory, even if stopping short of a general *jus soli* rule. Seven attributed citizenship at birth based on birth in the territory (at least on paper), of which four had a racial or ethnic restriction; four stated that children born in the territory automatically became nationals at majority; and another eleven that such children could apply for and acquire citizenship at majority as of right. Sixteen established some form of double (or triple) *jus soli*, providing for rights to accrue if multiple generations were born in the territory. However, a substantial proportion had a purely descent-based law leaving a very large number of people dependent on establishing proof of descent from a national of the country of birth or another country to avoid statelessness.[2]

A majority provided for an abandoned infant or, more generously, an older child of unknown parents to be presumed to be a national (though more than a dozen did not). However, despite near-universal ratification of African Charter on the Rights and Welfare of the Child, only a minority of States had adopted the provision (also required by the Convention on the Reduction of Statelessness) that a child born in the territory who is otherwise stateless should have the right to acquire nationality; a slightly larger number provided protections for children of stateless parents.

It can be difficult to follow the routes by which these outcomes were reached through the fog of multiple amendments to the law, especially in those countries where the issue of nationality has been most controversial. Indeed, it can take advanced legal interpretation skills to understand what the law is saying. In some countries, there are conflicting provisions in the constitution and the law, or between different laws, sometimes with important implications; for example,

[2] For more discussion of these provisions, including detailed tables on different modes of acquisition and loss of citizenship, see Bronwen Manby, *Citizenship Law in Africa: A Comparative Study* (3rd edn, Open Society Foundations 2016).

as of 2017 in Burundi, Comoros, Liberia, Mozambique, South Africa, and Togo. In other countries, such as Tanzania, the official interpretation of the law does not follow its literal meaning, leaving an ambiguity that makes the law practically unclassifiable in terms of the regime it creates.

It can also be difficult to understand the underlying causes behind these changes and the extent to which the reasons for which amendments were adopted are shared or differ across the continent. However, there are some overall patterns that are suggestive. This chapter and the next describe, first, the developments in the substantive content of the laws, and then the administration of the law in practice – which may differ significantly. They explore the patterns behind these trends, the commonalities and differences among them, and the possible reasons for divergence and convergence. Finally, I consider the relationship between the formal and informal in determining who belongs. Viewed from a trans-continental level it is possible to see how the norms and procedures established in law create a framework with an impact on State practice that is discernible even through the most extravagant drapings of corruption, lack of due process, and inefficiency.

5.1. Acquisition at Birth: The Balance of Jus Soli and Jus Sanguinis

The initial frameworks for attribution of nationality at birth varied across the continent according to the models provided by the colonial powers. These rules have not converged across the region in the same way as the European laws on which they were based (with the exception of the trend towards gender equality in transmission to children, considered in the next section).[3] Nonetheless, it is possible to see the influence of amendments made in one country on others, especially those within the same legal tradition or sharing the same official language: the power of imitation has been influential in Africa as in Europe.[4] Broadly speaking, the *jus soli* rules based on British precedent were rapidly abandoned, and a descent-based regime is now dominant in both the Commonwealth countries as well as the former Belgian territories (excepting Rwanda). Even where they were left in place, the *jus soli* laws were largely interpreted out of existence. The double *jus soli* rules of AOF and AEF (excepting Côte d'Ivoire), however, have remained in place since they were first adopted, and influential also in France's North African territories. The introduction of provisions that discriminate at birth on the basis of race, ethnicity and religion reflect a direct reaction to colonial-era discrimination

[3] Randall Hansen and Patrick Weil, 'Introduction: Citizenship, Immigration and Nationality: Towards a Convergence in Europe?' in Randall Hansen and Patrick Weil (eds), *Towards a European nationality: citizenship, immigration, and nationality law in the EU* (Palgrave 2001).

[4] Rainer Bauböck and others (eds), *Acquisition and Loss of Nationality: Policies and Trends in 15 European States*, vol 1 (Amsterdam University Press 2006).

in the reverse direction, are the norm in North Africa, and are also scattered across sub-Saharan Africa.

5.1.1. The Commonwealth States

At independence, the Commonwealth countries were universally bequeathed a pure *jus soli* basis for citizenship, incorporated in their initial constitutions, reflecting the long-standing system in the UK codified for the first time in the 1948 Nationality Act, which applied both in the UK and in its colonies (see Chapters 3.1 and 4.2). The transitional provisions placed weight on double *jus soli*, and then provided for *jus soli* attribution of citizenship after independence. A child born in the territory after independence was a citizen from birth as of right, subject to the exception that this did not apply if the father was entitled to diplomatic immunity or was an enemy alien, unless the mother was a citizen.[5] The rather convoluted drafting of these rules created room for varied interpretations of the law. Provision was made for citizenship by descent for those not born in the country, but only if the father was a citizen at the time of the birth, and limited to one generation of transmission to those born outside.

However, citizenship based on birth in the territory was removed across almost all the former British colonies and protectorates and replaced with rules that founded citizenship on the basis only of descent. The concept that citizenship would be acquired based solely on the accident of location of birth was too challenging for very fragile governments with limited legitimacy, control over the territory, and administrative infrastructure. This trend continued throughout the decades since the 1960s (see Table 5.1). Ghana's 1969 Nationality (Amendment) Decree repealed *jus soli* citizenship with retroactive effect to independence; and Kenya's 1985 constitutional amendment did the same, meaning that persons who had been born after independence but whose parents had not acquired citizenship at independence under the transitional provisions then lost their citizenship (see box below, and Chapter 7.3). Amendments to the law in the Seychelles, Mauritius, and Gambia adopted in the 1990s repealed *jus soli* provisions for those born after the amendments took effect.

The removal of *jus soli* rights was in most cases implicitly or explicitly intended to exclude potential citizens of non-African descent. This targeting was made even clearer where provisions were introduced to the law that directly discriminated on grounds of race or ethnicity.

[5] eg: 'Every person born in Botswana on or after 30th September, 1966 shall become a citizen of Botswana at the date of his birth: Provided that a person shall not become a citizen of Botswana by virtue of this section if at the time of his birth (i) neither of his parents is a citizen of Botswana and his father possesses such immunity from suit and legal process as is accorded to the envoy of a foreign sovereign power accredited to Botswana; or (ii) his father is a citizen of a country with which Botswana is at war and the birth occurs in a place then under occupation by that country.' Constitution of Botswana 1966, s 21.

In Sierra Leone, amendments to the law adopted immediately after independence were designed to reduce the political influence of prominent politicians of partial Lebanese descent (see Chapter 7.2). The changes both removed *jus soli* to provide for attribution of citizenship at birth on a *jus sanguinis* basis only through the father, and also introduced the requirement – clearly inspired by the provisions in place in Liberia (see Chapter 3.3) – that the father be of 'negro African descent'. The amendments also established more restrictive rules for the naturalisation of those who were not of 'negro-African descent'. In 1973, the change was partially reversed when a double *jus soli* provision was enacted, similar to the transitional provisions at independence, so that a child born in Sierra Leone to a father or grandfather also born there would acquire nationality, but still with the requirement that the ancestor be 'negro African'.[6] Though gender discrimination in these provisions was removed in 2006 for those born in the country and in 2017 for those born outside, the racial discrimination remained. A proposed draft constitution put forward in 2016 would remove both the racial discrimination and the double *jus soli* provisions and create a descent-based model, with wording drawing on the Kenyan constitution of 2010 (see Chapter 7.2).

Changes in the law in Uganda made the bargain around access to citizenship even more explicit: the original *jus soli* law was repealed in 1967, when the independence constitution was first replaced, but then reinstated 30 years later, with an ethnic limitation. The completely revised 1995 constitution restored a *jus soli* right, but only for a child born in Uganda 'one of whose parents or grandparents is or was a member of any of the indigenous communities existing and residing within the borders of Uganda as at the first day of February, 1926', with a list of such communities provided in a schedule to the constitution. When the 1995 constitution was being negotiated, representatives of Uganda's Asian population argued that they should be recognised as indigenous by this definition. Although several other ethnic groups whose status was also controversial were successful in gaining inclusion – including the Banyarwanda, as well as the Batwa, Lendu, and Karamojong – the Asians were not (Chapter 7.3).

Malawi introduced a racial element to its law in 1966, repealing the citizenship chapter in the independence constitution, and adopting a new Citizenship Act that not only restricted attribution of citizenship at birth to children who had at least one parent who was a citizen, but also required that parent to be 'a person of African race' (unless the child would otherwise be stateless).[7] References to 'African race' were deleted in 1992, though the system for attribution at birth remained descent-based.[8]

[6] An apparent accidental omission in the Sierra Leone law was a provision granting citizenship to those born in the country of one parent who was a citizen, but who did not have a parent or grandparent also born there.

[7] Malawi Citizenship Act No.28 of 1966, ss 4, 5 and 12–15 (provisions left in place by amendments in Acts No. 37 of 1967 and 5 of 1971). Those not 'of African race' could naturalise.

[8] Malawi Citizenship (Amendment) Act 1992 (No. 22 of 1992).

In other cases, however, the amendments to base nationality on ethnic grounds had at the same time an inclusive intention, to create access to citizenship for undocumented populations whose connection to the country could not otherwise be proved, or to members of ethnic groups bisected by colonial borders. This was true to some extent even in Uganda, where some ethnic groups were listed as indigenous, such as the Nubian community, even though their origins lay outside the borders of the colonial State.

In Nigeria, the 1974 Constitution (Amendment) Decree replaced Chapter II of the constitution. The new rules restricted the initial *jus soli* provisions, instead applying the modified double *jus soli* rules that decided who acquired citizenship at independence to those born after independence: a child born in the country would be attributed citizenship only if one parent or grandparent was also born there (subject to some further restrictions).[9] The rules thus echoed those adopted in Sierra Leone the previous year (without the racial restriction). Those born in the country with one parent who was a citizen by registration or naturalisation were also citizens.[10] Those born outside would now only acquire citizenship if *both* parents were citizens.

The 1974 amendments also repealed the initial post-independence citizenship acts, without replacing them – leaving a situation that continues today, in which citizenship is governed solely by the constitution, with no subsidiary legislation to provide detail. The 1979 Constitution adopted by the military regime then in office to govern a restoration of civilian government then completely reformulated the basis for citizenship. The new framework removed all rights based only on birth in the territory after independence, creating a descent-based rule through either parent or any grandparent. The rules on automatic acquisition of citizenship at independence were also revised, requiring membership of a 'community indigenous to Nigeria'; although the law permitted people of any background to naturalise. While clearly exclusionary in some ways, these rules were also designed in part to accommodate cross-border populations whose status in Nigeria was otherwise in doubt – and, in the absence of effective civil registration systems, also to create a more 'instinctive' system for determining entitlement (see Chapter 7.7).

In Swaziland, one of the few African States whose borders bear some relationship to a pre-colonial polity, an ethnic element was introduced in 1992 and remains in place today. Swaziland spent a period of 18 months in 1967–68 as a British 'protected State', with a greater degree of internal self-government than under its former status as a protectorate. The 1967 constitution of the protected State provided for a *jus soli* right to citizenship for anyone born in the territory before or after its adoption. The 1968 constitution of Swaziland as a fully independent country, however, provided a descent-based rule, reflecting the preferences of

[9] There was an exclusion if any parent or grandparent had lost his citizenship by any means (i.e. including by acquiring another nationality), unless one parent was a citizen.

[10] Constitution (Amendment) Decree, No.33 of 1974. See EI Nwogugu, 'Recent Changes in Nigerian Nationality and Citizenship Law' (1976) 25 International and Comparative Law Quarterly 423.

the Swazi king for 'traditional' modes of government (including a ban on political parties). Citizenship was attributed to those born in or outside Swaziland from that date only if the child's father was a citizen of Swaziland at the time of the birth (though existing citizens remained so).[11] In 1974, following a political crisis in which the citizenship of opposition leaders was questioned and the constitution repealed, a new Citizenship Order adopted by the Swazi King removed *jus soli* rights retroactively, to create a purely descent-based system through the father.[12] The 1992 Citizenship Act, which replaced the earlier legislation, included within its provisions the acquisition of citizenship 'by KuKhonta', that is, by customary law through pledge of allegiance to a traditional ruler; the 2005 constitution confirmed a preference in favour of those 'generally regarded as Swazi by descent'.[13] Though other ways of qualifying for citizenship were also possible in theory, in practice those who were not ethnic Swazis often found it difficult to obtain recognition of citizenship. At the same time, the government treated the thousands of ethnic Swazis living across the border in South Africa as indistinguishable from citizens and routinely granted them Swazi documentation.[14]

Nearby Lesotho – similar to Swaziland in many ways as a small, largely ethnically homogenous State with a hereditary monarchy – took a different path, first reducing but then restoring rights based on birth in the territory. The 1966 independence constitution already restricted the *jus soli* right for those born after independence, extending the usual exclusions from automatic acquisition of citizenship based on birth in the territory to a child whose father was not a 'Commonwealth citizen' (a status envisaged by the 1948 British Nationality Act but no longer meaningful), unless the child would otherwise be stateless.[15] These terms were preserved in the 1971 Citizenship Order. However, the 1993 Constitution, which partially repealed the 1971 Citizenship Order, restored *jus soli* citizenship for all, with only the usual exceptions if the father was entitled to diplomatic immunity or an enemy alien. Lesotho is a small, labour-exporting enclave country, with a very large percentage

[11] Laurie Fransman, Adrian Berry and Alison Harvey, *Fransman's British Nationality Law* (3rd edn, Bloomsbury Professional 2011) catalogue entry on Swaziland.

[12] Citizenships Order, King's Order in Council, 22 of 1974, s 6(2), reproduced in *Fransman's British Nationality Law*.

[13] 'A person who has Khontaed, that is to say, has been accepted as a Swazi in accordance with customary law and in respect of whom certificate of Khonta granted by or at the direction of the King is in force, shall be a citizen of Swaziland.' Swaziland Citizenship Act No.14 of 1992, s 5. The Constitution of Swaziland, 2005, Art 42, provides that persons born before the constitution came into effect are citizens 'by operation of law' if either parent is a citizen and also if the person is 'generally regarded as Swazi by descent'. Article 43 of the constitution removed this (not entirely clear) ethnic basis for children born after the constitution came into effect, but entrenched gender discrimination, providing that citizenship is only passed by a father who is a Swazi citizen.

[14] Hugh Macmillan, 'A Nation Divided? The Swazi in Swaziland and the Transvaal, 1865–1986' in Leroy Vail (ed), *The creation of tribalism in Southern Africa* (James Currey 1989); Bureau of Democracy, Human Rights, and Labor, 'Country Reports on Human Rights Practices' (US Department of State various years) entries on Swaziland.

[15] Constitution of Lesotho 1966, Art 25(3).

of its citizens earning a living – and having families – in South Africa. Few children of foreigners born in Lesotho to non-Sotho parents would be interested to claim citizenship there; at the same time, it may be that the *jus soli* provisions ensure relatively uncomplicated access to citizenship for those presenting themselves as Basotho, without the need to provide evidence of the parents' status.

Tanzania is the only other Commonwealth country that has preserved the independence *jus soli* provision in its law almost unaltered.[16] The pan-Africanist commitment of post-independence president Julius Nyerere was expressed in many statements supporting easy access to citizenship, including for refugees from Mozambique as well as former migrant workers on tea and sisal plantations. Although the 1961 Citizenship Act was replaced in 1995, to remove gender discrimination in transmission to children born outside the country, the new law left the basic *jus soli* framework unaltered.[17] Nyerere's rhetoric, however, was never translated into effective procedures that in fact ensured that the law was implemented; and Nyerere's non-racial vision was far from being shared by all his peers.[18] The interpretation of the law came to be that the citizenship regime was based on descent, simply ignoring the exception to the restriction. A guidance note issued by the attorney-general, reportedly based on a reading of the parliamentary debates at the time the 1995 Act was adopted, provided guidance to the immigration department to this effect.[19] The absence of a national identity card, or requirements to prove citizenship to access services, allowed this contradiction to continue without much remark. Yet Tanzania also took the highly unusual step of

[16] When the independence constitution was repealed in 1962 (as Tanganyika became a republic), the citizenship provisions were transposed unaltered into a new law, the Citizenship Act 1961, as created by the Republic of Tanganyika (Consequential, Transitional and Temporary Provisions) Act, No.2 of 1962. This law was extended to Zanzibar when the United Republic of Tanzania was formed in 1964. The Citizenship Act was protected against amendment by less than a 2/3 majority in parliament by both the 1965 Interim Constitution and the 1977 Constitution that is still in effect (as most recently amended 2005).

[17] The 1995 act provided that a person born in Tanzania becomes a citizen at birth, unless 'neither of his parents is or was a citizen of the United Republic and his father possesses the immunity from suit and legal process which is accorded to an envoy of a foreign sovereign power accredited to the United Republic' (s 5(2)(a)).

[18] Bruce Heilman, 'Who Are the Indigenous Tanzanians? Competing Conceptions of Tanzanian Citizenship in the Business Community' (1998) 45 Africa Today 369; Ronald Aminzade, *Race, Nation, and Citizenship in Post-Colonial Africa: The Case of Tanzania* (Cambridge University Press 2013); Charlotte Lee Miller, 'Who Are the 'Permanent Inhabitants' of the State? Citizenship Policies and Border Controls in Tanzania, 1920–1980' (PhD, University of Iowa 2011) http://ir.uiowa.edu/etd/4877.

[19] Section 5 of the 1995 Citizenship Act States '(1) Subject to the provisions of subsection (2), every person born in the United Republic on or after Union Day shall be deemed to have become and to have continued to be a citizen of the United Republic with effect from the date of his birth [...]; (2) A person shall not be deemed to be or to have become a citizen of the United Republic by virtue of this section if, at the time of his birth, (a) neither of his parents is or was a citizen of the United Republic and his father possesses the immunity from suit and legal process which is accorded to an envoy of a foreign sovereign power accredited to the United Republic; or (b) any of his parents is an enemy and the birth occurs in a place then under occupation by the enemy.' The official interpretation of the law is based on a reading that stops after '... neither of his parents is or was a citizen'. Interviews, Department of Immigration Services, Dar es Salaam, July 2016; unpublished letter from the Ministry of Justice and Constitutional Affairs to the Commissioner-General of Immigration, 9 March 2000.

implementing several programmes of mass naturalisation for long-term refugees (Chapter 9.2). It is more or less impossible to categorise the regime in place, given the contrast between the literal meaning of the law and its official application. A draft new constitution proposed in 2014 would formally remove the *jus soli* provision to replace it with a descent-based system; although the official understanding was that this proposal simply codified existing law.[20]

The standard *jus soli* citizenship provisions of Botswana's 1966 constitution were repealed in 1982, and, as in Malawi and Tanzania (and as is the rule for the civil law States), the rules on citizenship were delegated to the law. The 1982 Citizenship Act kept the rights to Botswanan citizenship based on birth in the country, but only if the child did not acquire the father's foreign citizenship at birth. It was amended again in 1984 to establish a purely descent-based rule, through the father. Among the reasons for the change were likely Botswana's status as a refugee host country, especially for those fleeing war in Angola. Gender equality was established in 1995 following a campaign by women's rights organisations and the 1992 decision of the Court of Appeal in the successful litigation by the lawyer Unity Dow, married to an American, to challenge the rules in place since 1984. However, no rights were restored to citizenship based on birth in Botswana, while foreign spouses became subject to the same conditions as any other person applying for naturalisation.[21] The law remained exclusively descent-based for children, with no protection against statelessness even for foundlings.

Zambia, which had provided more expansive transitional provisions for attribution of citizenship at independence, requiring only birth in the territory and not also that of a parent, amended its constitution in 1973 to create a one-party State. In relation to citizenship, the 1973 constitution established a half-way house, granting citizenship at birth if one of the child's parents was a citizen or if the father (only) was an 'established resident' (ordinarily resident at least four years preceding the birth), a similar provision to that in place in Rhodesia at the time. The 1991 constitution adopted on return to multi-party rule provided for continuity of citizenship, but also established a purely descent-based rule for those born after it came into effect, albeit based on gender equality for transmission to children. After more than a decade of repeated constitution-drafting exercises, in which a key issue had been the citizenship requirements for the presidency, and with them the rights of those established in Zambia at independence (see section below), the new constitution of 2016 re-stated this basic principle, although it also created the

[20] Bronwen Manby, 'Tanzanian Constitutional Review Proposes Radical Changes to Citizenship Law' africanarguments.org, 15 April 2014; Bronwen Manby, 'Citizenship and Statelessness in the East African Community' (UNHCR 2018).

[21] Botswana Citizenship (Amendment) Act 1995. See Manby, *Citizenship Law in Africa* (n 2) 69–70; Unity Dow (ed), *The Citizenship Case: The Attorney General of the Republic of Botswana vs. Unity Dow, Court Documents, Judgements, Cases and Materials* (Metlhaetsile Women's Information Centre 1995); Jenny Zetterqvist, 'Refugees in Botswana in the Light of International Law' (Scandinavian Institute of African Studies 1990).

right 'to apply to be registered as a citizen' on attaining majority for a person born in Zambia and ordinarily resident there for at least five years.[22]

The three southern African former 'settler States' of Namibia, South Africa, and Zimbabwe, had pre-existing laws when white minority rule ended that provided rights to citizenship based on birth in the territory, unless the parents were in irregular migration status (see Chapters 3.1 and 4.2). But the trajectory of the three countries was different after majority rule was attained, reflecting the different way in which the transitions took place: whereas the liberation movements that became the governments in Namibia and South Africa reformulated their rules to be more inclusive, and have largely stuck with that framework, Zimbabwe adopted no new framework in 1980, and then moved in the opposite direction.

The constitution negotiated under British auspices for Zimbabwe's transition to democracy continued the citizenship regime introduced after Southern Rhodesia declared UDI in 1963, including restrictions on *jus soli* based on legal residence. This framework was endorsed by the Citizenship Act of 1984. In 1996, however, Zimbabwe removed all rights based on birth in the territory, making this change at the same time that gender discrimination was removed in transmission of citizenship to spouses and children. This change facilitated the denationalisations of the 2000s, though the main tool was rather the manipulation of provisions prohibiting dual citizenship. Amendments to the constitution adopted in 2009 adjusted the rules, but did not restore rights based on birth in Zimbabwe; the new constitution of 2013 made further important changes, including to protect children of unknown parents, but left in place a fundamentally descent-based regime (see Chapter 7.1).

The Namibian constitution of 1990, drafted under UN guidance and thus through a far more inclusive and open process than that in Zimbabwe, aimed at a much greater transformation of the foundation of Namibian society, though it also drew on pre-existing legal frameworks. The citizenship chapter automatically attributes citizenship to children born in Namibia of parents who are 'ordinarily resident', unless the parents are in irregular migration status. Even if the parents are not legally present in the country the child acquires Namibian citizenship if no other citizenship is acquired at birth. Litigation has confirmed these rights; and in 2016 the government backed down from a proposal to overrule a Supreme Court decision upholding the right to Namibian citizenship of a child born in the country to foreign parents who were long-term residents.[23]

The new South African Constitution that entered into force in 1996 abolished previous racial and ethnic distinctions and created a common citizenship with equal rights for all citizens. The 1995 Citizenship Act established gender neutral

[22] Constitution of Zambia (Amendment) Act No.2 of 2016, art 37.

[23] Namibia Constitution 1990, art 4; *De Wilde vs. Minister of Home Affairs*, Supreme Court of Namibia, Case SA 48/2014; Report of the National Council Select Committee on the Namibian Citizenship Bill [B11 of 2016] 3 August 2016; Kaity Cooper and Dianne Hubbard, 'By the Skin of Its Teeth: How Namibia Narrowly Avoided a Constitutional Crisis' citizenshiprightsafrica.org, 7 February 2017.

citizenship by descent, and continued the rule already in place that a child born in South Africa of two parents who were permanent residents acquired citizenship at birth (a more restrictive wording than that in Namibia, being based on a formal immigration status rather than a factual situation).[24] Specific guarantees were included against statelessness, as the constitution established the right to a nationality for every child[25], while the Citizenship Act granted citizenship from birth to a child born in South Africa if 'he or she does not have the citizenship or nationality of any other country, or has no right to such citizenship or nationality'.[26] Amendments adopted in 2010 responded to a xenophobic national mood with restrictions on the attribution of citizenship at birth. A previous automatic right to citizenship if parents held permanent residence was converted into the right to retroactive recognition on application after reaching majority. At the same time, however, a child born in South Africa of two foreign parents without permanent residence status was for the first time given the right to apply to naturalise (a more discretionary process) as a South African at majority. These rights were subject to the child's birth being registered according to the law, a condition not applied to citizenship by descent.[27]

The amendments adopted by former British territories after independence were not, it seems, influenced by developments in British law. Britain itself removed *jus soli* citizenship rights in 1981 (with effect from 1983), which may perhaps have given some encouragement to Kenya's decision to do the same four years later. However, Britain did not remove the rights completely, retaining automatic attribution of citizenship to the children of those 'settled' in the country.[28] This formulation was not copied in any of the amendments adopted after 1981 in other Commonwealth States. Equally, it was only in 1981 that British law was amended to provide a formal protection against statelessness for children of unknown parents; under the previous *jus soli* regime, the presumption of nationality had applied in administrative practice rather than in law. African States had inherited the absence of this protection at independence but only began to introduce presumptions in

[24] South African Citizenship Act 1995, s 2(3). Up to 2010, the Department of Home Affairs in fact granted citizenship from birth to children with only one parent who was a permanent resident. For background, see Jonathan Klaaren, 'Post-Apartheid Citizenship in South Africa' in Thomas Alexander Aleinikoff and Douglas B Klusmeyer (eds), *From Migrants to Citizens: Membership in a Changing World* (Carnegie Endowment for International Peace : Migration Policy Institute 2000).

[25] South African Constitution, 1996, Art 28. See also Raylene Keightley, 'The Child's Right to a Nationality and the Acquisition of Citizenship in South African Law' (1998) 14 South African Journal on Human Rights 411; Jonathan Klaaren, 'Constitutional Citizenship in South Africa' (2010) 8 International Journal of Constitutional Law 94.

[26] South African Citizenship Act 1995, s 2(2).

[27] South African Citizenship Act 1995, as amended to 2010, ss 2(3) and 4. The 2010 amendments came into force on 1 January 2013.

[28] The term 'settled' excluded short term visitors, students, and people in irregular migration status; however, the child of non-'settled' parents who remained in the country until ten years of age could apply to register as a citizen. Access to the various forms of British nationality under the 1981 law as originally adopted, including for stateless children, is outlined in, Charles Blake, 'Citizenship, Law and the State: The British Nationality Act 1981' (1982) 45 Modern Law Review 179.

favour of children with unknown parents with constitutional reforms from the turn of the millennium, responding rather to lobbying by children's rights activists (and UNHCR).[29] Ghana, Kenya, Swaziland, Uganda, Zambia, and Zimbabwe, drawing inspiration also from each other, all added provisions for children of unknown parents to be presumed to be citizens, if when found they are believed to be under the age of 7 or 8 (for the first 5) or 15 (in the case of Zimbabwe).[30] Surprisingly, neither South Africa nor Namibia included such a provision in their post-democracy citizenship acts; an omission which appears accidental rather than deliberate.

In relation to attribution of nationality to those born outside of the country, the Commonwealth countries initially limited transmission to one generation born outside, and only through the father, in line with the British rules that assumed transfer of citizenship based on birth in a new country. Gradually these restrictions were removed – in parallel with the trend to accept dual nationality and reflecting the demands of the increasing diaspora – though a number that had repealed or never had such a limit still applied requirements for parents to register a birth with consular authorities for a child born overseas to acquire recognition of nationality in practice.[31]

Table 5.1 Commonwealth countries removing the right to citizenship based solely on birth in the territory

Country	**Original *jus soli* provision**	**Amendment removing *jus soli* (in chronological order)**
Sierra Leone	1961 Constitution Art 4	1962 Sierra Leone Constitution (Amendment) (No.2) Act[32]
Malawi	1964 Constitution Art 4	1966 Constitution and Citizenship Act
Uganda	1962 Constitution Art 9	1967 Constitution Art 4[33]
Swaziland	1967 Constitution Art 127	1968 Constitution Art 21
Ghana	1957 Ghana Nationality and Citizenship Act	1969 Ghana Nationality (Amendment) Decree (retroactive to 1957)
Nigeria	1960 Constitution Art 10	1979 Constitution Art 23

(continued)

[29] Hague Convention on Certain Questions Relating to the Conflict of Nationality Laws, art 14.

[30] UNHCR recommends that provisions on foundlings should 'apply to all young children who are not yet able to communicate accurately information pertaining to the identity of their parents or their place of birth.' UNHCR, *Guidelines on Statelessness No. 4: Ensuring Every Child's Right to Acquire a Nationality through Articles 1-4 of the 1961 Convention on the Reduction of Statelessness*, HCR/GS/12/04, 21 December 2012, para 58.

[31] Manby, *Citizenship Law in Africa* (n 2). At the end of 2017 restrictions on transmission to children born outside the country for more than one generation were in place in Gambia, Lesotho, Malawi, Mauritius, and Tanzania.

[32] The 1973 Sierra Leone Citizenship Act restored a double *jus soli* element for those of 'negro African descent'.

[33] The 1995 Constitution restored a *jus soli* right, but only for members of 'indigenous communities'.

Table 5.1 *(Continued)*

Country	Original *jus soli* provision	Amendment removing *jus soli* (in chronological order)
Botswana	1966 Constitution Art 21	1982 Constitution Amendment Act
Kenya	1963 Constitution Art 3[34]	1985 Constitution of Kenya (Amendment) Act (retroactive to 1963)
Zambia	1964 Constitution Art 5	1991 Constitution Art 5
Seychelles	1976 Constitution Art.6	1993 Constitution Art 9
Mauritius	1968 Constitution Art 22	1995 Constitution Amendment Act
Gambia	1965 Constitution Art 3	1996 Constitution Art 10
Zimbabwe	1979 Constitution Art 5[35]	1996 Constitution of Zimbabwe Amendment Act
Tanzania	1961 Constitution Art 3[36]	–
Lesotho	1966 Constitution Art 25	–
Namibia	1990 Constitution Art 4[37]	–

5.1.2. Former French Territories

By comparison to the Commonwealth States, the former territories of France have seen much greater stability in their nationality codes. New citizenship laws in the former French colonies were for the most part based on the French civil code, as it had evolved since the Revolution and was applied in France; in its most recent iteration as the nationality code established by *ordonnance* in 1945. Since 1889, the civil code had automatically attributed nationality not only to the child of a citizen born in France, but also to a child born in France of one parent born in France, and to a child born in France of foreign parents, if he or she remained there until majority (though in that case with the option to reject French nationality as an adult).[38] Abandoned infants were to be presumed nationals. The code also incorporated the concept, derived from French family law, of *possession d'état de national*: the recognition (on application to court) of the nationality of those who

[34] Unchanged but renumbered as Art 89 of the 1969 Constitution.

[35] Zimbabwe's initial provisions restricted jus soli citizenship attribution to those whose fathers were 'ordinarily resident' (based on the law in place in Rhodesia since 1972). See ch 7.1 for more detail.

[36] Not applied in practice.

[37] Parents must be legal residents.

[38] From 1851, when double *jus soli* was first introduced, until 1889, a child born in France of a father also born there, had the option to reject the attribution of nationality on attaining majority, while acquisition on the basis of birth on the territory was not automatic but on the basis of declaration. These rules were changed largely to prevent men born in France from avoiding military service. Weil, *Qu'est-ce qu'un Français?* (n 1) ch 2.

had always behaved and been accepted as if they were nationals. The code allowed for naturalisation after a residence period (reduced from 10 years to three years in 1927, and increased again to five years in 1945).

These terms were the basis for most of the new nationality codes of the AOF and AEF territories, as well as the former League of Nations mandates in Togo and Cameroon. The main variation was that some States required an application to acquire nationality at majority rather than attributing nationality automatically at that date to those born in the territory.[39] Chad went beyond the French pattern to provide for pure *jus soli*, and all the rest adopted the double *jus soli* provisions, with the exception of Côte d'Ivoire. Côte d'Ivoire adopted provisions that attributed nationality to children born in the country unless both parents were 'foreigners', a rule that, at the time it was adopted, was understood to be *more* generous than the double *jus soli* regime of its neighbours; although the ambiguity of the wording meant that the rule could later be re-interpreted as more restrictive (see Chapter 7.4).

These rules remained mostly quite stable. Nevertheless, a restriction of rights based on birth in the country was also enacted in some of the former French territories, including Côte d'Ivoire and Niger, which (in 1972 and 1973 respectively) removed the right to opt for nationality at majority for those born in the country of foreign parents, though Niger retained its double *jus soli* rule (never enacted in Côte d'Ivoire). In Côte d'Ivoire, the same amending act even removed presumption of nationality for an abandoned infant, rendering the law the most restrictive in the former AOF territories; Côte d'Ivoire also saw repeated changes to procedural rules to make it more difficult to obtain nationality documents in practice.[40]

A few countries enacted elements of the ethnic or racial preference adopted in some Commonwealth laws. Mali's double *jus soli* rule restricted rights based on birth in the territory to those 'of African origin' (*d'origine africaine*), without providing a definition of what that meant. It was clearly designed to exclude a right to nationality on this basis for those of European and Middle Eastern origin, but presumed (at least initially) in a pan-African spirit to include those of North African descent but 'white' skin colour; it was not clear how it might apply more generally.[41] This original provision was reformulated in 2011 to require rather that the parent also born in Mali should have the nationality of origin of another African country.[42] In Chad, the provision on *possession d'état de Tchadien* was similarly restricted to those of 'African ancestry' (*de souche africain*).[43] Gabon's 1998 nationality code introduced interesting provisions unique in Africa relating

[39] Automatic attribution at majority only in Benin, Burkina Faso, Congo Republic, and Guinea. See Manby, *Citizenship Law in Africa* (n 2).

[40] Cote d'Ivoire Loi No. 72-852 du 21 décembre 1972; Niger Loi No. 73-10 du 27 Février 1973.

[41] Pierre Decheix, 'Le code de la nationalité malienne' (1963) 73 Penant 300; Frederick Cooper, *Citizenship between Empire and Nation: Remaking France and French Africa, 1945–1960* (Princeton University Press 2014) 419.

[42] Code des personnes et de la famille, 2011, art 227.

[43] Ordonnance no.33/PG-INT du 14 août 1962 portant Code de la nationalité tchadienne, art 14.

to children born in the border zones of countries neighbouring Gabon or raised by Gabonese citizens, who can claim Gabonese nationality of origin in certain circumstances.[44]

Madagascar's nationality law never included provisions on double *jus soli* or acquisition of nationality based on birth and residence till majority. This departure from the norm for the AOF and AEF countries was derived from pre-independence French decrees aimed at protecting French nationality from dilution through immigration to Madagascar from (British) Asia. Members of the Karana community of Indo-Pakistani origin in Madagascar continued to face difficulties in being recognised as Malagasy nationals.[45] The only protection against statelessness in the new nationality code for those without a parent who was a national was for children of unknown parents.

In North Africa, all the different States, whatever their colonial-era history, drew on Ottoman, Arab and Muslim traditions to emphasise *jus sanguinis* principles to a greater extent, initially through the father's line, as well as privileging other Arabs or Muslims in access to nationality. French law was also influential in the former French territories, though less dominant than in AOF and AEF.[46]

The nationality law of independent Algeria also reflected the politics of France's ongoing relationship with its former territory (see Chapters 3.2 and 4.3). The 1963

[44] Gabon code de la nationalité, Loi No.37-1998, art 14. This provision is similar to those of several Latin American countries, which have specific provisions in their constitutions aiming to assist in resolving the nationality status of indigenous communities in border areas. Colombia's constitution, for example, provides that 'Members of the indigenous peoples who share border areas' are nationals by adoption (*por adopción*; implying a process equivalent to naturalisation), on the basis of reciprocity with other countries; in addition, dual nationality is allowed and no naturalised citizen is required to renounce another nationality (Constitution 1991, amended 1997, Art 96: 'Son nacionales colombianos: [...] 2. Por adopción: [...] c) Los miembros de pueblos indígenas que comparten territorios fronterizos, con aplicación del principio de reciprocidad según tratados públicos.[...]. » The matching provision in the nationality law has been declared enforceable by the Colombian Constitutional Court: Sentencia C-893/09, Diciembre 2; Bogotá D.C. In Ecuador, the constitution States that citizens by birth include 'Persons belonging to communities, peoples or nations recognized by the State living in border areas.' (Constitution Art 7. « Son ecuatorianas y ecuatorianos por nacimiento: 1. Las personas nacidas en el Ecuador. 2. Las personas nacidas en el extranjero de madre o padre nacidos en el Ecuador; y sus descendientes hasta el tercer grado de consanguinidad. 3. Las personas pertenecientes a comunidades, pueblos o nacionalidades reconocidos por el Ecuador con presencia en las zonas de frontera. »).

[45] Roger Decottignies and Marc de Biéville, *Les nationalités africaines* (A Pedone 1963) 14–25 & 201–210; Caroline McInerney, 'Accessing Malagasy Citizenship: The Nationality Code and Its Impact on the Karana' (2004) 19 Tilburg Law Review 182; Bureau of Democracy, Human Rights, and Labor (n 14) entries on Madagascar.

[46] Gianluca P Parolin, *Citizenship in the Arab World: Kin, Religion and Nation-State* (Amsterdam University Press 2009) 95–100. See also Delphine Perrin, 'Citizenship Struggles in the Maghreb' in Engin F Isin and Peter Nyers (eds), *Routledge Handbook of Global Citizenship Studies* (Routledge 2014); Delphine Perrin, 'Immigration and Citizenship Law in the Maghreb: Turning Aliens into Citizens' (Robert Schuman Centre For Advanced Studies 2011) RSCAS 2011/40; Delphine Perrin, 'Beyond the Borders: Dual Nationality in Western Mediterranean Countries' in I Schäfer and JR Henry (eds), *Mediterranean Policies from Above and from Below* (Nomos 2009); Delphine Perrin, 'Identité et transmission du lien national au Maghreb : Etude comparée des codes de la nationalité' (2007) 3 L'Année du Maghreb 479.

nationality code provided for nationality to be given to a child born in Algeria of two parents also born in Algeria after the date of independence (that is, unlike the similar provision in most other nationality codes in former French territories, it would not apply to anyone already alive at the date of independence, and required both parents to have been born in the territory).[47] The law was on the face of it non-discriminatory in relation to the role of religion, but discriminated on the basis of gender in relation to citizenship by descent. However, in a chapter of the 1963 code dealing with evidence (*preuve*), 'Algerian' was defined, for the purposes of transmission of citizenship by descent, as a person of Muslim religion whose father and father's father were born in Algeria.[48] The provisions neatly reflected France's discrimination against its Muslim Algerian nationals during the period in which Algeria formed part of France. A 1970 *ordonnance* then increased the primacy of descent over birth in the territory, removing the limited double *jus soli* provision in the 1963 nationality code, while retaining the 'triple *jus soli*' element introduced by the provisions on evidence. The law also made naturalisation more difficult, including for women married to Algerian men. In 2005, the law was again amended, this time to reduce gender discrimination in transmission by descent, and by providing that the two generations of people born in the country could be either the male or female line – though they had still to be of Muslim personal status.[49]

The former French protectorates of Tunisia and Morocco adopted a primarily descent-based citizenship regime on gaining independence from France, based on paternal descent, but with elements of *jus soli* drawn from the French tradition. Tunisia's 1956 nationality code attributed nationality through the father, and also provided that a child born of a Tunisian mother (whether born inside or outside the territory) could opt to acquire nationality at majority, as could a child born in Tunisia of foreign parents of whom one was also born there. In 1963, the nationality code was replaced, and the new provisions adopted similar 'triple *jus soli*' rules to those in Algeria, providing for nationality to be acquired based on birth in the country of the child and the father and grandfather.[50] Morocco established a similar though more restrictive pattern. The initial code of 1958 provided for paternal descent, with rights to opt for nationality through the mother at majority only if born in Morocco, and with the right to opt for those born of foreign parents only if both were born in Morocco *after* the entry into force of the code. There was easier access to nationality for the child of a foreign father if the father originated from a country where the majority spoke Arabic or followed the Muslim religion

[47] Loi No.63-96 du 27 mars 1963 portant Code de la nationalité algérienne, art 11.

[48] Code de la nationalité algérienne, art 32.

[49] Ordonnance No.70-86 du 15 décembre 1970, art 32; as amended by Ordonnance No.05-01 du 27 février 2005.

[50] Décret No.34 du 26 janvier 1956 portant Code de la nationalité tunisienne and Décret-Loi No.63-6 du 28 février 1963 portant refonte du Code de la nationalité tunisienne.

(adapting the rules introduced in Egypt in 1929: see chapter 4.1).[51] Modifications adopted in 2007 to reduce gender discrimination did not adjust the basic model.

Mauritania had provisions on nationality at independence similar to the other countries of AOF but later moved closer to the North African States, both politically and legally, exemplified by its departure from the Economic Community of West African States (ECOWAS) in 2000. In 1989–90, the government expelled tens of thousands of people of black African ancestry on the basis that they were not nationals. The nationality code was not amended, however, until 2010, when revisions repealed rights based on double *jus soli* and *possession d'état de mauritanien* to create a pure *jus sanguinis* regime, with protection only for foundlings (see Chapter 7.6).[52]

Those African States with a Belgian, French or Portuguese civil law tradition adopted standard provisions establishing a presumption of nationality for children of unknown parents, based on the rule established by the 1930 Hague Convention that, where parents and location of birth are unknown, a child found in the territory shall be presumed to have been born there of parents holding the nationality of that State. These provisions remained in place, with the sole exception of Côte d'Ivoire, which removed the protection from 1973, at the same time as the right to apply for nationality based on birth and residence until majority was also repealed (see Chapter 7.4).

Many nationality codes based on the French model provide for a child born in the country to be able to acquire nationality on application if still resident there at majority (or after a shorter period of residence). It is very hard to find statistics about access to these procedures, but in general it seems as though they are modes of acquisition that exist primarily on paper and are little used. In Côte d'Ivoire, for example, this option was revoked in 1972 based on anxiety about too easy acquisition of nationality – yet later research found that only two people had accessed this possibility before it was abolished in 1972.[53] In Guinea and Burkina Faso, however, acquisition of citizenship at majority through delayed *jus soli* is automatic under the law, and this right appears to be respected.[54] The difference may be the responsibility of the courts to oversee the issue of such documents in the civil law system, rather than an application to one or other ministry in the executive branch of government.

[51] Dahir no. 1-58-250 du 12 septembre 1958 portant Code de la nationalité marocaine.

[52] Loi. No. 2010-023 du 11 février 2010 abrogeant et remplaçant certaines dispositions de la loi 61-112 du 12 juin 1961 portant Code de la nationalité mauritanienne.

[53] Exposé des motifs, Projet de loi portant dispositions particulières en matière d'acquisition de la nationalité par déclaration (No.2013-653 du 13 septembre 2013).

[54] See, eg, information on the Certificat de nationalité available at the website of the Burkina Faso Justice ministry, stating that a certificate will be issued to persons born in Burkina Faso of foreign parents and resident there for at least five years preceding their majority, based on production of a birth certificate and a certificate of residence and of identity: http://infos-pratiques.justice.gov.bf/certification-de-nationalite/.

5.1.3. Others

Egypt's colonial heritage was more complex than most, influenced by the Ottoman Empire, British and French legal regimes. Citizenship law started from the provisions reflecting ethnic and religious preference adopted on transition from the Ottoman period, and showed a steady progression to more restrictive access. A 1950 nationality law removed a limited double *jus soli* provision included in the 1929 decree-law (providing for a child born in Egypt whose father was also born in Egypt to be Egyptian if the father ethnically belonged to a country whose language was Arabic or religion Muslim). The 1956 nationality law (adopted after the 1952 revolution, the independence of Sudan, and the nationalisation of the Suez Canal) strengthened the requirements for attachment to Egypt, reduced access to citizenship for the children of stateless fathers, and enabled the government to deprive those suspected of disloyalty (notably in relation to support of Israel) of their nationality. The 1958 nationality law of the short-lived United Arab Republic between Egypt and Syria again reinforced ideas of membership in an Arab community; the 1975 nationality law which replaced it in Egypt (the 1958 law had remained in effect until then, just for Egyptians) once again narrowed access to nationality for the children of foreign men as well as extending the residence requirements for naturalisation.[55] Steps to reduce gender discrimination did not affect the general regime.

Sudan, formerly a British-Egyptian condominium, did not follow the Commonwealth model, nor that of Egypt. It provided for citizenship based on descent through the male line for those born after independence in 1956, with no limitations related to religion or language, even after the separation of South Sudan in 2011; this descent-based rule, based on tracing ancestry to a specific start date, has remained in place, though with a limited softening on access to citizenship through the mother in 2005 (see Chapter 8.2).

Libya's first nationality law was adopted in 1954, three years after the establishment of the Kingdom of Libya on the departure of the French and British administrations in control since the expulsion of the Italians in 1942. The new law provided relatively easy access to Libyan nationality for those already resident in the country (without explicit exclusions on racial or ethnic grounds), and on an ongoing basis for those born in the country 'who did not acquire another nationality at birth'; though the procedures made clear that nationality was dependent on the status of the father. Transmission outside the country was explicitly restricted to the children of Libyan fathers.[56] The law remained in place following the coup

[55] Law 160 of 1950, Law 391 of 1956, Law No 82 of 1958 and Law No 26 of 1975. Parolin (n 46) 81–82; Centre for Migration and Refugee Studies (CMRS), 'Africa Citizenship and Discrimination Audit: The Case Study of Egypt, Prepared for the Open Society Justice Initiative' (American University in Cairo 2005).

[56] Nationality law, no. 17 for the year 1954, 25 April 1954.

that brought Mu'ammar Ghadafi to power in 1969. In 1980, in line with Ghadafi's pan-Arab alignment at the time, a Law on Arab Citizenship purported (it is not clear how far it was ever applied) to create access on demand to Libyan citizenship for those of Arab ethnicity or Muslim religion (with the exception of Palestinians, excluded from naturalising elsewhere by the 1963 Casablanca Protocol of the League of Arab States, see introduction to Chapter 9).[57] A new nationality code adopted in 2010, just before the collapse of the Libyan State, established a descent-based regime through the father, but without differential treatment for Arabs or Muslims.[58]

The law of the Republic of Somalia, created in 1960 from the merger of British and Italian Somaliland (Italian Somalia had been restored to Italian administration under UN trusteeship in 1950), established an ethnic-based framework through paternal descent from the outset. An unchanged article of the 1962 citizenship law provides for citizenship to be acquired by any person 'who by origin, language or tradition belongs to the Somali Nation', is living in Somalia (though not necessarily born there), and renounces any other nationality.[59] Somalia is one of the few countries in Africa where such a formulation would be possible, given its relative linguistic and ethnic unity, and clan-based social organisation. Among those potentially excluded by this law were Somalis of Bantu ethnic origin, descendants of those brought to the country as slaves during the period of the Zanzibar Sultanate.[60] Since the disintegration of the Somali State following the fall of the dictatorial government of President Siad Barre in 1991, the practical implications have been limited, but the understanding remains the same.

In the former Belgian territories of central Africa, the influence of Belgian law was evident both in the descent-based model adopted for nationality, and in the fact that final approval of naturalisation in Congo, Rwanda, and Burundi was in all cases given to the legislature and not the executive. Burundi's first nationality code was only adopted in 1971, nine years after independence, following a period of turbulence as the initial monarchical regime was overturned to become a republic.[61] Although the law was replaced in 2000, the new version retained the rules based on *jus sanguinis* through the father (not modified when the 2005 constitution provided for equal rights), with an exception only for children of unknown parents.[62]

Congo (DRC) had its own trajectory in which rights based on ethnic origin were dominant, and is perhaps the clearest case where a failure to sort out

[57] Libya Law No. 17 of 1954 on Nationality and Law No.18 of 1980 on 'Arab nationality'; it also made apostasy from Islam a grounds for deprivation of nationality. See also Parolin (n 46).

[58] Law No. 24 of 2010.

[59] Law No.28 of 22 December 1962 on Somali Citizenship, arts 2 and 3. See also NA Noor Mohammed, 'Chapter 2: Citizenship', *The Legal System of the Somali Democratic Republic* (Michie 1972).

[60] Catherine Besteman, 'Translating Race across Time and Space: The Creation of Somali Bantu Ethnicity' (2012) 19 Identities 285.

[61] Décret-Loi No.1-93 du 10 août 1971 portant code de la nationalité burundaise.

[62] Loi 1/013 du 18 juillet 2000 portant reforme du code de la nationalité.

workable transitional provisions at independence in 1960 has had ongoing serious consequences. This lack of clarity combined with the enormous size of the territory, the absence of effective civil registration or other administrative systems, and above all the presence of large populations of imported labour, to create a perfect storm of disputes around entitlement to nationality. Since nationality provisions were first adopted in 1964, the law has founded nationality on descent, and in addition created the presumption that citizenship is in the first instance acquired through membership of one of the 'tribes' (more recently, 'ethnic groups') established in Congo on a particular date. This date was successively changed from 1908 (in 1964), to 1960 (in 1971, for some only), to 1950 (in 1972, for some only), to 1885 (in 1981, for all), to 1960 (from 2004, for all). Those most explicitly targeted by these shifts were the Kinyarwanda-speaking populations of the east (see Chapter 7.5).[63]

Rwanda's 1963 nationality code was similarly based on paternal descent. But the cataclysmic events of 1994 brought a major effort to rethink the legal framework. The post-genocide nationality law adopted in 2004 and replaced in 2008 comprehensively revised the Belgian-derived model, providing for much more substantial rights based on birth and residence in Rwanda, as well as protections for children of unknown parents or who would otherwise be stateless. In addition, Rwanda introduced a provision in its 2003 constitution, repeated in the 2015 revision, that 'All persons originating from Rwanda and their descendants shall, upon their request, be entitled to Rwandan nationality'.[64] Finally, the 2003 constitution and 2004 nationality code included a measure aimed at facilitating the reintegration of members of Rwandan diaspora who left the country during the post-colonial period of Hutu nationalist government, stating that 'Rwandans or their descendants who were deprived of their nationality between 1st November 1959 and 31 December 1994 by reason of acquisition of foreign nationalities automatically reacquire Rwandan nationality if they return to settle in Rwanda'. This automatic attribution based on residence – which had in fact encouraged the argument that Banyarwanda Congolese were not Congolese, or did not need to be so – was not included in the 2008 code, nor in the 2015 constitution. The 2008 nationality code also made the procedure for people of Rwandan origin to reacquire nationality more difficult, similarly in recognition of the difficulties this provision had created for people of Rwandan ethnicity in Congo.

The lusophone PALOP countries that gained independence in 1975, following the fall of the Portuguese dictatorship, adopted the quite liberal rules on access to citizenship applicable in Portugal at that time, and also drew on the ideology of international socialism that had inspired their liberation movements (a generational contrast to most of the independence leaders of the francophone

[63] Loi No. 04-024 du 12 novembre 2004 relative à la nationalité congolaise.

[64] Constitution of the Republic of Rwanda, 2003, Art 7; Constitution revised 2015, Art 25. This provision was incorporated in the Loi Organique No.29/2004 du 03/12/2004 portant Code de la nationalite rwandaise, art 26, and repeated in Law No. 30/2008 of 25/07/2008 relating to Rwandan nationality, art 22.

and anglophone States, leaving Sékou Touré of Guinea aside).[65] Portugal's nationality regime, relatively constant since the nineteenth century, had favoured double *jus soli* and the automatic attribution of Portuguese nationality to children of foreigners still resident in the territory at majority, subject to a right to refuse this status.[66] These rules were adopted by the new States: rights based on birth and residence were strong, and interpreted to be so. Privileged access to nationality was given to comrades in the struggle (as in Algeria). Gender equality was the norm in attribution to children, reflecting strong socialist influence on the liberation movements.

Both Angola and Guinea Bissau, however, reduced the element of *jus soli* in their laws. Angola first created greater limits in 1984, adjusted in revisions to the law in 1991, 2005 and 2016; though it maintained the right to apply for Angolan nationality for a child born on the territory of unknown or stateless parents, or of parents with unknown nationality.[67] Guinea Bissau removed the more generous provisions in 1992, leaving a descent-based system, but then in 2010 restored stronger protections against statelessness for children born in the country without a nationality.[68]

A detailed nationality law was not adopted in Equatorial Guinea until 1990, relying until then on constitutional provisions established in 1968. The law provided a limited *jus soli* right on application at majority, and gender neutrality.[69] A new law adopted in 2011, largely to permit dual nationality and remove gender discrimination in marriage, also greatly simplified the rules on acquisition at birth, while retaining the right to acquire citizenship based on birth and residence until majority.[70]

Africa's newest States, Eritrea and South Sudan, both adopted descent-based laws, in both cases giving equal rights to men and women to transmit nationality to their children – a decision that was unremarkable in Eritrea, given the Marxist-Leninist orientation and discipline of its liberation movement, but hotly debated among the more ethnically aligned and ideologically diverse membership of the new South Sudanese Parliament. Although the transitional rules on acquisition of Eritrean citizenship at the date of secession appeared at first sight to discriminate on ethnic grounds, the basic qualification applied was that of long-term residence in Eritrea (see Chapter 8.1). The new citizenship law of South Sudan, by contrast, created in opposition to the dominance of the Arab north of Sudan, emphasised membership of an 'indigenous tribal community', though also leaving channels

[65] On the other hand, the matching new Portuguese law adopted at the same time did not avoid statelessness for some of those who previously had full Portuguese citizenship. Rui Manuel Moura Ramos, *Estudos de direito português da nacionalidade* (Coimbra Editora 2013).

[66] Civil code, 1867; Lei da nacionalidade, 1959.

[67] Lei no.2/84 de 7 de fevereiro; Lei No.13/1991 de 11 de maio; Lei No.1/2005 da 1 de julho; Lei No.2/2016 da 15 de abril.

[68] Lei no.2/1992 de 6 de abril; Lei No.6/2010 de 21 de junho.

[69] Ley núm. 8/1990, de fecha 24 de octubre, Reguladora de la Nacionalidad Ecuato-guineana.

[70] Ley no.3/2.011, de fecha 14 de julio, Reguladora de la Nacionalidad Equatoguineana.

open to provide access on the basis of long-term residence or the birth of ancestors in the territory (see Chapter 8.2). The two States they split away from also modified their laws, in Sudan's case specifically to disallow those who had acquired South Sudanese nationality from retaining their Sudanese nationality – even if they were resident in Sudan and had little connection to the South. Ethiopia replaced its 1930 law only in 2003, bringing gender equality but retaining the *jus sanguinis* regime, except for the introduction of protection against statelessness for abandoned infants.

Finally, in Liberia, the 1955 nationality law was replaced in 1973 and a new constitution adopted in 1984, both of which preserved the requirement to be of 'negro descent' first established in the nineteenth century (see Chapter 3.3).[71] However, the law and the constitution contradicted each other in other ways: the 1973 Aliens and Nationality Law provides for *jus soli* rights, but discrimination on the basis of gender for those born outside the country; whereas the 1984 constitution provided for gender equality in transmission by descent, but no rights based on birth in the territory.[72] As in the case of Tanzania, the difference made the legal regime exceptionally difficult to categorise. Reform to the law to permit dual citizenship and remove racial discrimination was under discussion as of late 2017.

Ghana's debates over *jus soli*

Although in most Commonwealth countries the original citizenship provisions were included in the independence constitution, Ghana – the first to gain independence – was an exception, and the Ghana Independence Act 1957 and Ghana (Constitution) Order in Council 1957/277 simply referred the question to national legislation.

The Ghana Nationality and Citizenship Act 1 of 1957 included in its transitional provisions the usual terms contained in later Commonwealth independence constitutions: any citizen of the UK and colonies or British protected person born and resident in Ghana became a citizen of Ghana provided that at least one parent or grandparent was also born in Ghana. Thus, some British protected persons born in Ghana did not become Ghanaian citizens (and so remained British protected persons): notably the

[71] Art 20.1 of the 1973 Aliens and Nationality Law states that citizenship is attributed to 'a person who is a Negro, or Negro descent, born in Liberia and subject to the jurisdiction thereof'. Art 27 of the 1984 constitution (entry into force in January 1986) states that, 'In order to preserve, foster and maintain the positive Liberian culture, values and character, only persons who are Negroes or of Negro descent shall qualify by birth or by naturalization to be citizens of Liberia.' Art 28 provides for the child of a Liberian father or mother to be a citizen, and allows the law to prescribe other qualification criteria (which could, in principle, include birth in the territory).

[72] Constitution of the Republic of Liberia, 1984, 27. See also Jessie Tannenbaum, 'Analysis of the Aliens and Nationality Law of the Republic of Liberia' (American Bar Association Rule of Law Initiative 2009).

community of Lebanese descent, but also those from neighbouring African territories. For those born in the territory after independence, *jus soli* applied (subject only to the usual exceptions relating to the child's father being entitled to diplomatic immunity or an enemy alien, if the mother was not a citizen). Those born outside the country before independence became citizens if at least one parent was born in Ghana; those born outside the country after independence became citizens if the father was a citizen born in the country or a citizen by registration or naturalisation, or if the mother was a citizen by birth. British protected persons ordinarily resident in Ghana for at least five years and who renounced any other nationality could register as citizens, as could women married to a citizen of Ghana. (In 1960, the act was amended by the Constitution (Consequential Provisions) Act (CA8) to take account of the adoption of a new republican constitution, adjusting the relationships with other Commonwealth States.)

The law ran into political difficulties immediately after the Convention People's Party (CPP) government of Kwame Nkrumah took power in 1957, and was challenged by politicians of immigrant descent. The Immigration Act 15 of 1957 and the Deportation Act 19 of 1957 were enacted to 'legalise' the deportations of two prominent leaders of Hausa origin.[73] The acts provided for controls over foreigners, and amendments to the Deportation Act in 1958 and 1959 facilitated the deportations of people involved in opposition politics who were not eligible for automatic citizenship under the transitional provisions. The Aliens Act 160 of 1963 required all foreigners to obtain residence permits, regulating their employment and making them subject to deportation if they did not have the correct papers, and the government also promoted economic advancement of 'indigenous' populations. The position of migrant populations became increasingly precarious.

The Ghana Nationality Act 62 of 1961 repealed the 1957 Act, but in relation to citizenship by birth provided in similar terms that a person born in Ghana after the commencement of the Act was a citizen by birth. Those who were already citizens remained so. The grounds for deprivation of citizenship were widened.

The Ghana Nationality Decree, NLCD 191 of 1967, adopted by the National Liberation Council that had taken power the year before, made the terms relating to the transition to independence significantly more generous: a person born in Ghana who was a citizen of the UK and colonies or British protected person before the date of independence was given citizenship by

[73] Amadu Baba and Othman Lalemie; however, it was claimed that both they and their parents had been born in Ghana. See Akin L Mabogunje, 'Regional Mobility and Resource Development in West Africa' (Centre for Developing-Area Studies, McGill University 1972) 123–124.

birth with no requirement that a parent or grandparent also be born in the country. *Jus soli* was continued for those born after independence.[74]

The Ghana Nationality (Amendment) Decree NLCD 333 of 1969 restored the restrictions of the 1957 Act in relation to those born before independence, requiring a person born in Ghana also to have a parent or grandparent born in Ghana; but removed the *jus soli* rule for those born since independence by adding the requirement that one parent be a citizen wherever the child was born. These changes had retroactive effect and thus took away nationality from many who had acquired citizenship on the basis of the 1967 decree.

The 1969 Constitution, which reinstated a civilian government, simplified the law under the uniform requirement that a person born in or outside Ghana became a citizen of Ghana if at least one parent was a citizen of Ghana at the time of the birth, thus removing *jus soli* acquisition definitively.

Citizenship politics reached their nadir at this date: following the adoption of the Aliens Compliance Order 1969 and other measures, more than 200,000 people were expelled from the country in 1969–1970, most of them migrants from other West African countries.[75]

The Nationality Act 361 of 1971 introduced confusingly different rules for those born before independence, between independence and the entry into force of the 1969 constitution, and after the entry into force of the constitution. A person born in Ghana before independence was a citizen if at least one parent or grandparent was born in Ghana; a person born outside was a citizen if at least one parent was born in Ghana. Those born in or outside of the country since independence and before the entry into force of the 1969 constitution were citizens if at least one parent and also at least one grandparent or great-grandparent were also born in Ghana; except that if the relevant parent or grandparent had 'by any means lost his citizenship of Ghana'. A person born in Ghana was also a citizen by birth if either parent was a citizen by registration or naturalisation; and if born outside Ghana if both parents were citizens by registration or naturalisation. Those born in or outside the country after the entry into the force of the constitution were citizens if either parent was a citizen, restated the provisions of the 1969 constitution.

A court ruling in 1972 on a case brought by two Lebanese born in Ghana of parents born elsewhere who had naturalised under the 1967

[74] Ghana Nationality Decree, NLCD 191 of 1967, Art 1.

[75] Margaret Peil, 'Ghana's Aliens' (1974) 8 International Migration Review 367; Margaret Peil, 'Host Reactions: Aliens in Ghana' in William A Shack and Elliott P Skinner (eds), *Strangers in African Societies* (University of California Press 1979).

decree found that the deprivation of their citizenship through the 1969 amendment was unlawful, on the grounds that the amendment had not specifically divested those who had acquired citizenship under the decree of their rights. Under the 1969 constitution they remained Ghanaian citizens, and 'the new definition of citizenship in the Ghana Nationality Act 1971 (Act 361) is void and of no effect in so far as it seeks to restrict citizenship within narrower limits than those prescribed in the constitution.'[76]

The Ghana Nationality (Amendment) Decree 1972 NRCD 134, adopted by a new military government, the National Redemption Council, was brought in to overrule the court decision and declare that only those qualified as citizens under the 1971 Nationality Act were citizens, and that those who had previously had rights to citizenship no longer did so, except that those particular people who had been awarded citizenship by a court were able to keep it. Those deprived of their citizenship by the 1969 amendment decree were given the right to apply for naturalisation only, on the basis of ten years' residence. Further amendment decrees in 1978 and 1979 deprived named persons of their naturalisation citizenship (many of them Lebanese).[77]

The 1979 Constitution restored more generous provisions. A person born in Ghana after the entry into force of the Constitution was a citizen if at the date of birth either parent or any grandparent was a citizen of Ghana. Those born outside the country were citizens if either parent was a citizen of Ghana.

The 1992 Constitution then extended the grandparent connection to those born outside the country: those born in or outside Ghana since the entry into force of the 1992 constitution (on 7 January 1993) are citizens by birth if either parent or one grandparent was or is a citizen of Ghana at the time of the birth. There are no rights to citizenship based only on birth in the territory, even for children who would otherwise be stateless, though children of unknown parents are presumed to be Ghanaian. In 1996, the constitution was amended to permit dual nationality for the first time, thus potentially allowing for recognition of nationality for many who had been previously refused on the basis of mixed parentage.[78]

The convoluted history of these provisions was summarised in the Citizenship Act 591 of 2000, which preserved the distinctions among people born on different dates.

[76] *Shalabi and Another v. The Attorney-General* [1972] 1 GLR 259–270.

[77] Emmanuel K Akyeampong, 'Race, Identity and Citizenship in Black Africa: The Case of the Lebanese in Ghana' (2006) 76 Africa 297; Ousman Kobo, '"We Are Citizens Too": The Politics of Citizenship in Independent Ghana' (2010) 48 The Journal of Modern African Studies 67.

[78] Constitution of the Republic of Ghana (Amendment) Act 527 of 1996

5.2. Gender Equality

The story in relation to nationality discrimination on the basis of sex is much clearer and more unidirectional than the rules based on descent or location of birth: gender equality is increasingly the norm. At independence in the 1960s, most citizenship laws in Africa discriminated on the basis of gender. Female citizens were unable, or had restricted rights, to transmit their citizenship to their foreign spouses or to their children. In this, the laws reflected the situation in the law of the colonial powers at that time, and indeed globally.

Nonetheless, some early laws did not discriminate in relation to the right of parents to transmit nationality: for example, Chad, which gained independence in 1960, changed its rules between 1961 and 1962 to remove gender discrimination.[79] Côte d'Ivoire's law did not discriminate when first adopted in 1961 (though it introduced discrimination on the basis of birth in or out of wedlock, but not sex, in 1972).[80]

The lusophone States, with their later attainment of independence and socialist leanings, adopted gender equality right from the date of independence in 1975 in respect of transmission of nationality to children and (except Mozambique and São Tomé and Príncipe) to spouses. The revolutionary regime of Thomas Sankara that took power in Burkina Faso (as he renamed Upper Volta) in 1983 also had a strong commitment to gender equality, leading to the adoption of a new family code in 1989 (albeit after he was ousted from power) which enshrined equal rights for men and women in matters of nationality.[81]

A key turning point for the Commonwealth countries came in 1992 with the landmark and well-publicised decision in the *Unity Dow* case in Botswana, where the Court of Appeal upheld a woman's right to pass Botswana citizenship to her spouse and children, and the law was reformed as a result.[82] The decision received widespread publicity,[83] and Dow's own status as an activist ensured that the result was well-diffused among the women's rights networks.

By the end of 2017, discrimination in the grant of nationality to children no longer existed on the face of the nationality law in 42 of Africa's 54 countries. Discrimination in transmission to a spouse had been removed in just under a half.[84] Moreover, Africans polled by Afrobarometer overwhelmingly supported the equal right of men and women to transmit nationality to their children.[85]

[79] Loi No.31-60 du 27 février 1961; Ordonnance No.33 du 14 août 1962.

[80] Loi No.61-415 du 14 décembre 1961, amended by Loi No.72-852 du 21 Décembre 1972.

[81] Code des personnes et de la famille du 31 octobre 1989, Zatu No.AN VII-0013/FP/PRES. See Hilde Nuytinck, 'Les principes du nouveau droit de la famille au Burkina Faso' (1991) 806 Penant 258.

[82] Dow (n 21).

[83] eg, Human Rights Watch, 'Botswana: Second Class Citizens: Discrimination against Women under Botswana's Citizenship Act' (1994).

[84] Manby, *Citizenship Law in Africa* (n 2).

[85] At least 70% support in 29 countries polled between 2011 and 2013. Afrobarometer online data analysis tool, Round 5 (2011/13), 'Right to be citizen: born in country with one non-citizen parent', http://afrobarometer.org/online-data-analysis/analyse-online.

Among the countries that had amended their laws to provide for greater (though not in all cases total) gender equality were, up to the end of 2017: Algeria, Botswana, Burkina Faso, Burundi, Côte d'Ivoire, Djibouti, Egypt, Ethiopia, Gambia, Guinea, Kenya, Lesotho, Libya, Mali, Madagascar, Mauritius, Morocco, Niger, Rwanda, Senegal, Sierra Leone, Sudan, Tunisia, Uganda, and Zimbabwe. Removal of gender discrimination was under discussion in other countries, including Liberia and Togo, and in Benin, where, in September 2014, the Constitutional Court declared four articles of the nationality code to be unconstitutional on the grounds of (quite limited) gender discrimination in relation to a woman's right to transmit nationality to her children and spouse.[86]

There were significant variations in the degree of restriction imposed by those countries that still discriminated on the basis of gender in transmission of nationality to children. In most cases, a woman might transmit nationality to her child if the father was unknown, but in the more extreme cases there were no other rights. At the other end of the spectrum, discrimination was reflected only in the right to non-discretionary repudiation of nationality at majority for the child of a foreign father (where renunciation otherwise required consent).[87] Almost all these distinctions reflected discrimination present in the law of European countries at the time the new States gained independence.

In total, as of the end of 2017 around a dozen countries still discriminated at least to some extent on the grounds of gender in granting nationality rights to children who were either born in their country or born overseas (Benin, Burundi, Guinea, Liberia, Libya, Mauritania, Somalia, Sudan, Swaziland and Togo). Even where the nationality law did not discriminate explicitly on the basis of gender, where there were distinctions between children born in or out of wedlock the family code rules on establishing descent might re-introduce discrimination through these procedures (as in Côte d'Ivoire, where the law was otherwise gender-neutral, but also Benin, Burundi, Cameroon, Gabon, Guinea, Libya, Mali, Mauritania, Niger, Somalia, Sudan, Swaziland, and Togo).[88]

The political context of the reforms on gender equality tended to be different from the debates surrounding the changes made over the same period to access

[86] Décision DCC 14-172, Benin: Cour Constitutionnelle, 16 September 2014.

[87] eg, in Benin: Loi No.65-17 du 23 juin 1965 portant code de la nationalité béninoise, Arts 8, 12, 13 and 18. In the Congo Republic, provisions permitting repudiation apply to any child with one parent (father or mother) who is a foreigner not born in Congo: Code de la nationalité congolaise, 1961, Arts 7-9.

[88] eg, in provisions that are typical, in Madagascar transmission of nationality to a child born in wedlock was until January 2017 restricted to the father; however, a child born in wedlock of a Malagasy mother might claim Malagasy nationality up to the age of majority (21 years), and a child born out of wedlock took the nationality of the mother, or might claim nationality of the father if descent was established. Ordonnance No. 1960-064 portant Code de la nationalité malgache (amended by Loi No. 1961-052; Loi No.1962-005; Ordonnance No.1973-049; and Loi No.1995-021), s 16. These rules were changed to bring gender equality in transmission to children by Loi No.2016-038 of 15 December 2016.

through *jus soli* or *jus sanguinis* – though of course the two themes are closely related.[89] Gender equality in nationality law followed the global trend, and was above all the prize of the women's movement across Africa, drawing inspiration from the UN Convention on the Elimination of All forms of Discrimination Against Women (CEDAW). These reforms were won country by country, legislative reform by legislative reform, often in close communication with continental and global advocacy networks working on the same issues. It is hard to discern any pattern as regards legal tradition, region or cultural background across these changes but the influence of amendments in other African countries was clearly felt. National campaigns for gender equality both drew on continental networks of women's rights activists and influenced the adoption of continental norms that supported their work. In turn, these norms were used by activists in other countries to support their own campaigns. Individual politicians were also important in some cases: in Senegal, for example, gender discrimination was finally removed in 2013 during the tenure of Aminata Touré as justice minister, who made the reform a priority.[90]

As in the rest of the world, gender equality in transmission to children also contributed to the greater tolerance of dual nationality (see Chapter 5.3); but in some cases concessions of gender equality were paired with restrictions on rights to acquire nationality based on birth in the territory. In Mauritius, Zambia, and Zimbabwe, for example, removal of gender discrimination in transmission to children was accompanied by the removal of rights based on birth in the territory.[91]

Despite the trends, gender equality remained controversial. Resistance to the idea of the equal rights of women to transmit nationality to a spouse or child was illustrated most clearly by the terms of the Protocol to the African Charter on Human and Peoples' Rights on the Rights of Women in Africa adopted in 2003.

[89] On gender and citizenship in Africa, see generally: Jennifer C Seely and others, 'Second-Class Citizens? Gender in African Citizenship Law' (2013) 17 Citizenship Studies 429; Ayesha Imam and Evelien Kamminga, *Women in Search of Citizenship: Experiences from West Africa* (KIT Publishers 2012); Charmaine Pereira, 'Understanding Women's Experiences of Citizenship in Nigeria: From Advocacy to Research', *Gender, Economies and Entitlements in Africa* (CODESRIA 2004); Mounira Charrad, 'Unequal Citizenship: Issues of Gender Justice in the Middle East and North Africa' in Maitrayee Mukhopadhyay and Navsharan Singh (eds), *Gender Justice, Citizenship and Development* (Zubaan and International Development Research Centre, 2007); Suad Joseph (ed), *Gender and Citizenship in the Middle East* (1st ed, Syracuse University Press 2000); Sara C Mvududu and Patricia McFadden, *Reconceptualizing the Family in a Changing Southern African Environment* (Women and Law in Southern Africa Research Trust 2001).

[90] Among the networks involved in work on gender equality, including equal nationality rights, have been FEMNET (African Women's Community and Development Network), Solidarity for African Women's Rights (SOAWR), Women and Law in Southern Africa (WLSA), and Women in Law and Development in Africa (WILDAF). For a discussion of a similar dynamic in a related field, see Sally Engle Merry, *Human Rights and Gender Violence: Translating International Law into Local Justice* (University of Chicago Press 2006).

[91] Mauritius Constitution Amendment Act No.23 of 1995 and Citizenship Amendment Act No.24 of 1995; Constitution of Zambia Act No.1 of 1991; Constitution of Zimbabwe Amendment (No.14) Act No.14 of 1996.

The protocol placed strong non-discrimination requirements on States in general, but was weak on citizenship rights, thanks largely to the efforts of the North African States.[92] In marriage, it reflects the terms of the 1957 Convention on the Nationality of Married Women rather than CEDAW, providing only that 'a woman shall have the right to retain her nationality or to acquire the nationality of her husband', while the right to transmit nationality to children is rendered empty by an exception 'where this is contrary to a provision in national legislation or is contrary to national security interests'.[93]

Accordingly, some reforms adopted after the protocol provided only for greater access to nationality for the children of national mothers, rather than total equality. For example, in Sudan reforms adopted in 2005 gave the child of a national mother the right to claim nationality rather than automatic attribution.[94] In Sierra Leone, 2006 reforms still retained gender discrimination in relation to children born outside the country; this was removed only in 2017. In Burundi, the 2005 constitution provided that children of Burundian men or women had the same right to a nationality; but the nationality code of 2000 continued to provide that the status of children born of a Burundian mother is technically the right to acquire citizenship 'by declaration' and automatic attribution of nationality of origin is restricted to those born of a father who is a national.[95] In Swaziland, the 1992 citizenship law conferred a right to Swazi nationality on persons whose mother but not father was a Swazi; but all such persons were required to seek a certificate of naturalisation from the Minister of Home Affairs. The 2005 constitution removed even this right, to State that a child born after the constitution came into force was a citizen only if his or her father was a citizen.[96] The unrecognised State of Somaliland also adopted a citizenship law that discriminated on the basis of gender, providing that citizenship from birth was granted to 'anyone whose father is a descendant of persons who resided in the territory of Somaliland on 26 June 1960 and before.'[97]

In Mali, nationality law was successfully (if partially) reformed in 1995 to create some rights for women in relation to transmission of nationality to their children and spouses. Subsequently, a long campaign for a new family law that would entrench these and other reforms led to the adoption of a progressive new *Code des personnes et de la famille* by the National Assembly; but this law was ultimately vetoed by the president, faced with resistance from the religious

[92] See discussion of the drafting process in Fareda Banda, 'Protocol to the African Charter on the Rights of Women in Africa' in Malcolm D Evans and Rachel Murray (eds), *The African Charter on Human and Peoples' Rights: the system in practice, 1986–2000* (2nd ed, Cambridge University Press 2008).

[93] Protocol to the African Charter on Human and Peoples' Rights on the Rights of Women in Africa, art 6.

[94] Sudan Nationality Act 1994 (as amended 2005), s 4(3).

[95] Constitution of Burundi, 2005, Art 12, Loi No.1-013 du 18 juillet 2000 portant réforme du code de la nationalité burundaise, arts 2, 4 and 5.

[96] Swaziland Citizenship Act 1992. Constitution of the Kingdom of Swaziland, 2005, art 43.

[97] Republic of Somaliland, Citizenship Law, No.22/2002 (unofficial translation).

establishment, and the version that finally became law in December 2011 perpetuated some forms of gender discrimination. The section of the law relating to nationality (which replaced the 1962 nationality code) in both versions removed the remaining explicit gender discrimination in transmission of nationality, but retained discrimination on the basis of birth in or out of wedlock, thus effectively retaining gender discrimination in practice.[98]

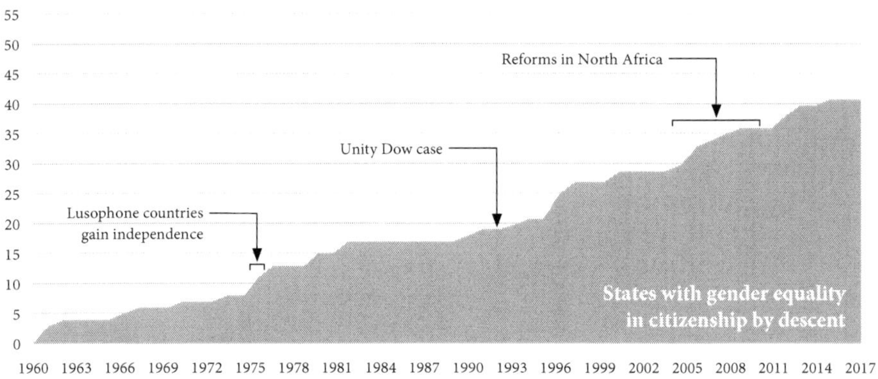

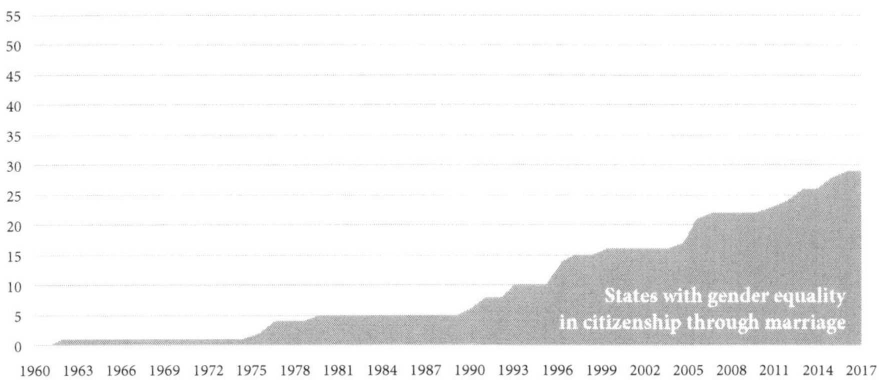

Scoring is based on the tables in Bronwen Manby, *Citizenship Laws in Africa: A Comparative Study* (3rd edition, 2016), updated by the author. States score one for total gender equality, and zero if there is any element of gender discrimination (although the degree of gender discrimination in law varies considerably).

Gender equality in acquisition of nationality by spouses has faced more resistance than in transmission to children. At independence, the anglophone countries

[98] See press releases related to the Code de la famille on the website of the Féderation Internationale des Droits de l'Homme, http://www.fidh.org/fr/afrique/mali/.

adopted the English modified 'dualist' system (so named by Bernard Dutoit in his study of nationality and the married woman around the world), by which marriage in itself had no effect on a person's nationality; however, a woman marrying a citizen could obtain nationality by registration or option (an easier and less discretionary system than naturalisation), usually on condition that she renounced her former nationality.[99] Some francophone countries followed a similar system where the woman could obtain the nationality of her husband by option, upon application submitted within a certain time after marriage.

Algeria, reacting to its colonial history, adopted a completely dualist system, by which marriage gave no additional rights, and a foreign wife or husband had to naturalise in the same way as any other alien. Most francophone countries, however, followed the combined system of the French nationality code of 1945, by which a woman marrying a national automatically acquired the nationality of her husband, but with the ability to refuse this within a certain period of the marriage. Ethiopia's 1930 nationality law (since superseded) and Somalia had a completely unitary system, by which an alien woman marrying a national automatically acquired her husband's nationality with no option to refuse.

In the case of a woman marrying a foreigner, similar variations applied in relation to her ability to retain her nationality of origin, and there was some tolerance of dual nationality if she acquired the nationality of her husband automatically.

By 1990, the absolute dualist system, in which marriage had no effect at all on nationality, was only in place in Algeria and Liberia (where the 1955 law had attributed Liberian – or foreign – nationality to a woman on marriage, but the 1973 law removed all effect of marriage on nationality). However, a system of facilitated naturalisation for spouses had become more common than the system of nationality by registration or declaration (that is, acquisition was made more difficult). Facilitated naturalisation, previously in place only for Sudan and South Africa, had been adopted in Angola, Botswana, Djibouti, Mozambique and Seychelles. At the same time, demands for gender equality had already brought equal rights for spouses in transmission of nationality in Angola, Cape Verde, Djibouti, Ghana, Guinea-Bissau, Namibia and Seychelles; in Burkina Faso, unusually, the reform was to provide that a foreign husband also acquired his wife's nationality automatically.

From that date, often explicitly in response to increasing demands for gender equality in marriage rights – and hence the possibility that foreign men and not just foreign women would obtain nationality on easy terms – the dualist system made a come-back on the African continent, either in modified form, so that nationality was acquired on marriage by a non-discretionary process of declaration

[99] Bernard Dutoit and others, *La nationalité de la femme mariée*, vol II: Afrique (Librairie Droz 1976); Bernard Dutoit and Denis Masmejan, *La nationalité de la femme mariée, Supplément 1976–1990*, vol II: Afrique (Librairie Droz 1991).

or registration, or only on the same basis of discretionary naturalisation as for any other foreigner. In Botswana, in 1995, reforms enacting gender equality also removed any rights in case of marriage. Similarly, as of 2017, marriage in itself provided no rights in Djibouti, DRC, and Liberia. Algeria, however, restored the right to nationality through marriage in 2005 (for either spouse), but only by a process of facilitated naturalisation.[100] Niger's 1984 nationality code provided for the right of a woman married to a Nigerien man to opt for nationality (replacing automatic attribution in the post-independence code), but 2014 reforms bringing gender equality – 15 years after it was introduced for transmission to children – created conditions similar to those for naturalisation.[101] Similar sorts of disquiet in other countries lengthened the period a spouse must wait: in 2010, Namibia amended its constitution to change the period for acquisition of citizenship by marriage from two to ten years.[102]

In Zimbabwe, the ground-breaking *Rattigan* case heard in the Supreme Court in 1995 ruled that a foreign husband should have the same rights of residence in Zimbabwe as a foreign wife. In direct response to the case, the government adopted the 14th amendment to the constitution, which removed, prospectively, all rights to citizenship based on marriage; the amendment also removed gender discrimination in relation to transmission of citizenship to children, but at the same time created greater restrictions on acquisition of nationality based on birth in the territory (see further Chapter 7.1).[103] In 2009, as part of a constitutional amendment allowing for the installation of a government of national unity, gender discrimination was completely removed from the constitution in relation to citizenship by birth and marriage.[104] The 2009 amendments also increased the general period for naturalisation to 10 years, but provided that those married to a citizen could naturalise in five (albeit subject to all the other usual conditions). These changes were confirmed in the 2013 constitution, reducing the period of residence in case of marriage but making acquisition of citizenship still subject to satisfaction of conditions to be established in law (yet to be amended by end 2016).[105]

In Zambia reforms to provide gender equality were enacted in 1996, and, as in Zimbabwe, removed all rights based on marriage. Submissions to a Constitution Review Commission highlighted concerns that acquisition through marriage

[100] Ordonnance No.70-86 du 15 décembre 1970 portant Code de la nationalité algérienne as modified by Ordonnance No. 05-01 du 27 février 2005.

[101] Niger Loi No.2014-60 du 5 novembre 2014.

[102] Namibian Constitution Second Amendment Act 2010 (Act No. 7 of 2010), s 1.

[103] Constitution of Zimbabwe Amendment (No. 14) Act 1996; see also Tandeka C Nkiwane, 'Gender, Citizenship, and Constitutionalism in Zimbabwe: The Fight Against Amendment 14' (2000) 4 Citizenship Studies 325 and ch 7.1.

[104] Constitution of Zimbabwe Amendment (No.19) Act 2009. The Citizenship Act (last amended in 2003) continued to quote the pre-1996 version of the constitution, leading to significant confusion.

[105] Zimbabwe Constitution 2013, art 38.

would make it too easy for people who were not members of the 'indigenous' Zambian population to obtain nationality.[106] The 2016 constitution restored some rights based on marriage, on a gender-equal basis, but at the discretion of the authorities.[107]

In Côte d'Ivoire and the DRC also, anxiety was expressed in constitution- or law-drafting processes about the ease with which foreign men marrying female citizens might acquire nationality. In the DRC, the law provides that an application for citizenship by marriage must be approved by decree of the Council of Ministers and considered by the National Assembly.[108] In Côte d'Ivoire, however, where rules on marriage have changed several times, the most recent version returned to a more open attitude. The 1961 nationality code started from the position of automatic acquisition by a foreign woman of her husband's Ivorian nationality. From 2004, a man could acquire Ivorian citizenship from his wife, but only after a delay of two years; a woman could acquire citizenship from an Ivorian man immediately, by declaration. The current provisions, adopted in 2013, return to the unitary system, but with gender neutrality (as in the case of Burkina Faso), so that either a woman or a man of foreign nationality marrying an Ivorian acquires Ivorian nationality automatically at the time of celebration of the marriage.[109]

Most of the civil law countries specify that marriage (like other civil status events) is only officially recognised if formally registered. In a continent where the majority of marriages are religious or traditional, the impact of this gap may be to exaggerate gender discrimination, and render rights based on marriage available only to a few – there is a lack of research on this point. Only a few countries, including Namibia, Rwanda, South Africa, and Togo, explicitly recognise customary marriages in their nationality or family laws.[110]

[106] Zambia Constitution Review Commission report, 16 June 1995, p.40.

[107] Zambia Constitution 2016, Art 37(2); Zambia Citizenship Act 2016, Art 18.

[108] In DRC, gender discrimination was ultimately removed, though the conditions under which citizenship may be required by marriage are extremely restrictive; Loi No.04/024 du 12 novembre 2004 rélative a la nationalité congolaise, art 19.

[109] Loi No.61-415 du 14 Décembre 1961 portant Code de la nationalité ivoirienne, Art 12, as amended by Loi No.2004-662 du 17 décembre 2004 and Loi No.2013-654 du 13 septembre 2013.

[110] The Namibian constitution, art 4(3)(b), states that for the purposes of citizenship 'a marriage by customary law shall be deemed to be a marriage'. The Niger nationality code, Art 16, provides that marriage may be either the law or custom, but if customary must be evidenced in writing Ordonnance No.84-33 du 23 août 1984, as amended 1988 and 1999. The Rwanda Civil Code, art 3 states: 'In the absence of an applicable legislative provision, the judge decides on the basis of customary law and in the absence of a custom, on the basis of the rules he would make if called on to legislate. He takes inspiration from the solutions set out in doctrinal writing and the decisions of the courts.' The South African Citizenship Act 1994 defines 'marriage' to include a marriage conducted under the Recognition of Customary Marriages Act, No. 120 of 1998. Togo has similar provisions to those in Niger (Ordonnance 78-34, Art 7).

Increasing gender equality in north Africa

All of the countries of north Africa saw a marked turn towards gender equality from the start of the twenty-first century; a notable development by comparison with the Arab countries of the Middle East, where gender discrimination remains entrenched.[111] At independence, these countries all included the standard forms of gender discrimination at that time: nationality was transmitted to a child only through the father, and only a wife acquired nationality through marriage.

Tunisia was the first to remove gender discrimination in transmission to children born in the country, establishing gender equality from 1963; those born abroad were automatically Tunisian only through the father, though they could claim nationality by declaration. Reforms in 1993 and 2002 changed the procedures slightly for those born abroad, but the code remained discriminatory on its face.[112] In 2010, the law was reformed to remove discrimination in the transmission of nationality by descent for those born after it came into effect.[113] In 2014, the new government in Tunisia withdrew its reservations to CEDAW in relation to the transmission of nationality to children;[114] however, gender discrimination in marriage remained in the law. In addition, the 'triple jus soli' provisions attributing nationality to a child born in Tunisia continued to specify that it was the father and grandfather who must also be born there.

The other north African countries all adopted reforms in the new millennium.

In Egypt, a 2004 reform to the 1975 Nationality Law amended the law to provide that children born to Egyptian mothers were Egyptian citizens regardless of their father's status or their place of birth (excepting

[111] For a comparison of North African with Middle Eastern trends, see Zahra Albarazi and Laura van Waas, 'Transformations of Nationality Legislation in North Africa' in Engin F Isin and Peter Nyers (eds), *Routledge Handbook of Global Citizenship Studies* (Routledge 2014); Perrin, 'Citizenship Struggles in the Maghreb' (n 46); Manby, *Citizenship Law in Africa* (n 2).

[112] Loi No.63-7 du 22 avril 1963 ratifiant le décret Loi No.63-6 du 28 février 1963 portant refonte du Code de la nationalité tunisienne, ss 12 and 13; See Souhayma Ben Achour, 'L'étranger et la nationalité tunisienne : Le droit tunisien de la nationalité, est-il discriminatoire ?' (Faculté de droit et des sciences politiques 2005).

[113] Loi No.2010-55 du 1 décembre 2010.

[114] List of participants to CEDAW at the UN treaties website, https://treaties.un.org/pages/ViewDetails.aspx?src=TREATY&mtdsg_no=IV-8&chapter=4&lang=en. See also 'Tunisia: Withdrawal of the declaration with regard to Article 15(4) and of the reservations to Articles 9(2), 16 (c), (d), (f), (g), (h) and 29(1) made upon ratification', UN Document C.N.220.2014.TREATIES-IV.8 (Depositary Notification), 23 April 2014. The decision to withdraw the reservations (Art 9(2) relates to the equal right to transmit nationality to children) was first announced in 2011.

only children of Palestinian fathers).[115] Those born before the changes to the law came into effect (in November 2005) were given the right to apply for their citizenship to be recognised. Despite heavy administrative procedures, by 2006 it was estimated that 17,000 people had obtained citizenship, most of them born of Sudanese or Syrian fathers.[116] In May 2011, following the Egyptian revolution of earlier that year and responding to protests by women, the Ministries of Interior and Foreign Affairs issued a decree allowing Egyptian women married to Palestinian men to transmit their nationality to their children.[117] Applications for nationality rapidly increased, with 893 obtaining documents by late October, of which the vast majority were children of Palestinian fathers.[118] The 2014 constitution confirmed equal rights for men and women to transmit nationality to their children. However, gender discrimination in marriage persists under the 1975 law.

In 2005, Algeria went beyond the example of Tunisia and Egypt, and amended its nationality law to allow an Algerian woman married to a foreigner to transmit Algerian nationality to her children and also to her spouse on equal terms, and also providing that the triple *jus soli* rule was through either maternal or paternal line.[119]

In April 2007, after a long campaign by women's rights organisations, amendments to the Nationality Code came into force in Morocco. The reform finally gave Moroccan women married to foreign men the right to pass Moroccan citizenship to their children (with retroactive effect). However, the law only provides for a foreign woman married to a Moroccan man for five years to be able to acquire marriage by declaration (opposable by the government), and not a foreign man married to a Moroccan woman. In addition, despite other recent reforms, Morocco's family code (known as the

[115] Law No. 154 of 2004 amending some provisions of Law No. 26 of 1975 concerning Egyptian nationality, Official Gazette, Vol. 28, 14 July 2004. The Ministry of Interior also issued Decree No. 12025 of 2004, explaining the process of application for citizenship for those born to Egyptian mothers and non-Egyptian fathers. Al-Waqa'e'Al-Masreya/Government Bulletin, issue 166, 24 July 2004. See also http://www.learningpartnership.org/egypt.

[116] Reem Leila, 'Citizenship costs less,' *Al Ahram Weekly Online*, Issue 806, 3-9 August 2006.

[117] 'Egypt to grant citizenship to kids of Palestinian dads', *Jerusalem Post*, 8 May 2011; 'Post-Revolution, Egypt Establishes the Right of Women Married to Palestinians to Pass Nationality to Children', the Arab Women's Right to Nationality Campaign in Lebanon, 13 May 2011.

[118] Gianluca Parolin, 'New policy on Egyptian citizenship for children of Palestinian fathers', Global Citizenship Observatory, globalcit.eu, 24 November 2011.

[119] Ordonnance No. 05-01 du 27 février 2005 revising Ordonnance No.70-86 du 15 décembre 1970 portant code de la nationalité algérienne. See also Convention on the Rights of the Child, *Consideration of Reports Submitted by States Parties under Article 44 of the Convention: Concluding Observations: Algeria*, CRC/C/15/Add.269, 12 October 2005.

Moudawana) States that a Moroccan Muslim woman cannot marry a non-Muslim man, and the two codes read together indicate that the family code should take preference, with implications for birth in or out of wedlock.[120] Gender discrimination also still affects the provision of the nationality code providing for Moroccan nationality to be given to children born in Morocco of foreign parents who were themselves also born in Morocco. This provision applies in a gender-neutral way only if the *parents* were born after the law came into force; until that time the double *jus soli* rules apply only if their father was born in Morocco, is an Arabic-speaking Muslim, and comes from a country where Arabic-speaking Muslims are in the majority.[121]

Unexpectedly, Libya adopted a new nationality law in 2010, before the fall of Ghaddafi, which also included changes that somewhat reduced gender inequality. In 1998, the Committee on the Rights of the Child considered a report from Libya and expressed the concern that 'decisions related to the acquisition of nationality are only based on the status of the father.'[122] In 2003, the committee noted with approval that Libya was considering adopting a rule that would permit a Libyan mother to transfer her nationality to her children, irrespective of her husband's nationality.[123] But the 2010 law only implemented this promise in the most limited way possible, and left gender discrimination entrenched, so that Libya still gives the automatic right to nationality only to the child of a Libyan father, whether born in country or abroad. Although the law allowed for the grant of nationality to the child of a Libyan mother and foreign father, this is at the discretion of the State, and regulations were required to implement it.[124] Despite the 2010 reforms, virtually every article still enshrined lesser rights for women: these issues were still live in constitutional discussions underway in early 2017.[125]

[120] See Dahir No.1-04-22 du 12 Hija 1424 (3 Fevrier 2004) portant promulgation de la Loi No.70-03 portant Code de la famille, arts 2 and 39; Code de la nationalité marocaine, Loi No.62-06 promulguée par le dahir No.1-07-80 du 23 mars 2007 – 3 rabii I 1428, Art 3. Art 29 of the Code de la famille also forbids a Moroccan man from marrying a woman who is not Muslim, unless she is Christian or Jewish ('*sauf si elle appartient aux gens de la Livre*'). See also Khadija Elmadmad, 'Maroc: La dimension juridique des migrations', *Mediterranean Migration Report 2007–2008* (Euro-Mediterranean Consortium for Applied Research on International Migration, European University Institute 2008).

[121] Code de la nationalité marocaine, art 9.

[122] Committee on the Rights of the Child, *Consideration of Reports Submitted by States Parties under Article 44 of the Convention: Concluding Observations: Libyan Arab Jamahiriya*, CRC/C/15/Add.84, 23 January 1998.

[123] Committee on the Rights of the Child, *Consideration of Reports Submitted by States Parties under Article 44 of the Convention: Concluding Observations: Libyan Arab Jamahiriya*, CRC/C/15/Add.209, 4 July 2003.

[124] Libya Nationality Law No.24 of 2010, Art 3.

[125] 'Libya granted women new constitutional rights – then took them away again', *Al Bawaba*, 1 May 2017.

5.3. Dual Nationality

Rules on dual nationality show a similar unidirectional trend to those on gender equality. Long regarded as anomalous and regrettable in international law, dual nationality is increasingly permitted around the world, and Africa is no exception.[126] Although it is still too early to talk of a norm allowing dual nationality, as some countries remain strongly against, the trend is clear. During the same period as the campaigns for gender equality, a parallel lobbying effort largely from the African diaspora – but also from those advocating gender equality – meant that a large majority of African States allowed dual nationality by the end of 2017, a major change from the situation in the 1960s.

At independence, many African countries took the decision that dual citizenship should not be allowed: they wished to ensure that those who might have a claim to another citizenship – especially those of European, Asian, or Middle Eastern descent – had to choose between the two possible loyalties. Those who did not take the citizenship of the newly independent country were then regarded with suspicion, as a possible 'fifth column' for the former colonial powers and other interests. A person acquiring another nationality automatically lost his or her birth nationality; and renunciation of another nationality was required for naturalisation. In almost all the Commonwealth countries a child with dual nationality from birth had to renounce one or the other at majority; the law in the civil law countries, however, often permitted dual nationality of origin, although a person would automatically lose nationality if they acquired another by voluntary act.

Dual nationality in case of marriage was equally frowned upon. Commonwealth countries required renunciation of foreign nationality before a woman marrying a national could obtain her husband's nationality by registration. Practice in the civil law countries was more varied, but for the most part did not allow dual nationality in the case of marriage. As an exception, however, dual nationality was sometimes allowed in the case of a foreign woman married to a male citizen, or a female citizen married to a foreign man, even where dual nationality was generally not allowed.[127]

Increasingly, however, an African diaspora with roots in individual African countries, in addition to the earlier involuntary diaspora of slavery, has grown to match migrations from Europe and Asia. These 'hyphenated' Africans, with roots both in an African country and a European or American one, have brought

[126] Maarten Vink, René de Groot and Ngo Chun Luk, 'MACIMIDE Global Expatriate Dual Citizenship Dataset'.

[127] As of 1975, Cameroon, Chad, Egypt, Ghana, Kenya, Lesotho, Madagascar, Malawi, Mauritius, Morocco, Nigeria, Sierra Leone, Sudan, Tanzania, Uganda, and Zambia required renunciation of previous nationality in case of acquisition of a new nationality following marriage; but not in the case of Burundi, Gambia, Libya, Mauritania, Rhodesia, Swaziland. Tunisia. By 1990, Gabon, Namibia and Niger allowed dual nationality for married women; Cape Verde, Guinea-Bissau and Zaire had joined those forbidding dual nationality. Dutoit and others (n 100); Dutoit and Masmejan (n 100).

political pressure to bear on their 'home' governments to change the rules on dual citizenship and to concede that people with connections to two different countries need not necessarily be disloyal to either State.[128]

Many African States have either changed their rules to allow dual nationality in more circumstances or are considering such changes. A few countries allowed dual nationality in all circumstances right from the start (including Chad and Gabon), but more than twenty have changed the rules since independence in the 1960s or 70s to liberalise the rules on dual nationality. As of the end of 2017, only ten countries did not allow dual nationality in any circumstances, and even there, amendment of the law was under active discussion (for example, in Liberia and Tanzania).[129]

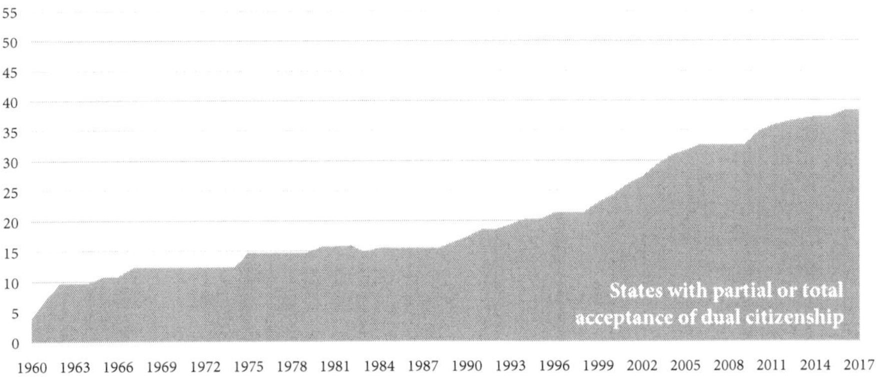

Scoring is based on the tables in Bronwen Manby, *Citizenship Laws in Africa: A Comparative Study* (3rd edition, 2016), updated by the author. States score one for complete openness to dual nationality; 0.75 if dual nationality is allowed in law for citizens from birth but not for others, or if it is allowed with permission or notification; 0.5 if dual nationality is allowed if born with two nationalities, but not if voluntarily acquire another; and 0.25 if dual nationality is allowed only for those who have naturalised.

In a few countries, the constitutions had been changed to allow dual nationality, but the legislation had yet to be updated by 2017, including Comoros, Congo Republic, Gambia, Mozambique, São Tomé & Príncipe, Somalia, and Zimbabwe. In Zimbabwe, for example, a new constitution adopted in 2013 allowed dual citizenship for those holding citizenship from birth, but the Citizenship Act had

[128] Beth Elise Whitaker, 'The Politics of Home: Dual Citizenship and the African Diaspora: Dual Citizenship and the African Diaspora' (2011) 45 International Migration Review 755; Okechukwu C Iheduru, 'African States, Global Migration, and Transformations in Citizenship Politics' (2011) 15 Citizenship Studies 181; George M Bob-Milliar and Gloria Bob-Milliar, 'Mobilizing the African Diaspora for Development: The Politics of Dual Citizenship in Ghana' in Toyin Falola and Kwame Essien (eds), *Pan-Africanism, and the politics of African citizenship and identity* (Routledge 2014).

[129] Manby, *Citizenship Law in Africa* (n 2).

yet to be replaced by the end of 2017 (see Chapter 7.1). The Republic of Sudan (North Sudan) introduced a ban on dual nationality specifically for people who became nationals of the new Republic of South Sudan in 2011, even though dual nationality had been generally allowed since 1993. The new State of South Sudan, however, followed continental trends by adopting a nationality law that permitted dual nationality (see Chapter 8.2).[130] Other countries, including Egypt, Eritrea and South Africa, required permission to hold dual nationality in any circumstances.

Lack of clarity in the drafting of the law, or competing provisions of different laws have seen litigation in countries such as Namibia, where the High Court has been called on to confirm the right in law for citizens from birth (although not naturalised citizens) to hold the citizenship of another country.[131] In practice, interpretation and application of these laws can vary widely, or small differences in wording resulted in different outcomes.

5.4. Naturalisation

All African countries permit, in principle, the acquisition of nationality by naturalisation (in some Commonwealth countries confusingly called registration) on the basis of long term residence and other conditions.[132] Although these rules have been tweaked here and there, they have remained relatively constant, by contrast to the trends noted for European laws[133] – perhaps because accessing them in practice is very difficult.

Nonetheless, there have been changes, mostly to the length of residence required before a person can qualify to naturalise (almost always to extend this period); less often to change the other conditions. As of the end of 2017, more than 20 countries provided for a right to naturalise based on legal residence of

[130] Before the secession of States, the government of the 'New Sudan' as South Sudan, was then known, adopted a Nationality Act that, in addition to discriminating on the basis of gender, also required anyone acquiring 'New Sudanese' nationality by naturalisation to renounce any other nationality. Sudan Nationality Act 2003, Laws of the New Sudan, s 9. The actual law adopted in 2011 following secession reversed this provision.

[131] Manby, *Citizenship Law in Africa* (n 2).

[132] The suggested definition for naturalisation in the Global Citizenship Observatory glossary is: 'Any mode of acquisition after birth of a nationality not previously held by the target person that requires an application by this person or his or her legal agent as well as an act of granting nationality by a public authority.' See http://globalcit.eu/glossary_citizenship_nationality/. In many African countries there is also the possibility of acquiring citizenship by an easier process known in the Commonwealth countries (though not consistently), as 'registration' and in civil law countries as 'declaration' or 'option'. These non- or less-discretionary processes are usually open to spouses of citizens or to persons born in the country and still resident there at majority (and are covered above in relation to the rules applied to children born in the country or in case of marriage). Confusingly, in some Commonwealth countries, such as Kenya and Zambia, law reforms adopted since independence mean that there is only one process, known as registration, and this is discretionary rather than being a purely administrative process (the original meaning of registration in the independence constitutions and laws).

[133] Bauböck and others (n 4).

five years, the most common period in European laws at the date of independence. Some others required ten years; in Chad, Nigeria, Sierra Leone, and Uganda, the period required had been increased to 15 or 20 years. The Central African Republic increased the five-year residence period in the 1961 nationality code to 35 years in 1966, but then repealed this provision, returning to five years in 1984. Equatorial Guinea increased the required residence period from 10 to 40 years in 2011. Other conditions commonly include proof of good health, a clean criminal record, and an intention to remain in the country.[134]

A number of countries provide for preferential access to nationality by naturalisation on the grounds of ethnicity or religion: in North Africa, those of Arab ethnicity and Muslim religion have easier access. Liberia and Sierra Leone, in line with their other provisions based on race, take the position that only those persons 'of Negro descent' may be citizens from birth. Sierra Leone also has more restrictive rules for naturalisation of 'non-Negroes' than 'Negroes,' while Liberia forbids 'non-Negroes' from becoming citizens at all. (Reflecting now-superseded provisions of US law, Liberia's conditions for naturalisation also exclude anarchists and communists from becoming Liberian.) Malawi provides for several categories of person with a close connection to the country with somewhat easier access to naturalisation.[135] This favourable treatment is based on similar provisions that existed for 'Commonwealth citizens' in most anglophone countries at independence, which were extended by Kenya and Tanzania, as well as by Malawi, to people originating in other African countries (see Chapter 4.2). In the other countries, however, the more favourable provisions no longer exist: a connection to the Commonwealth very rapidly came to seem meaningless; while the attractions of pan-Africanism also did not overcome the highly discretionary framing of naturalisation.

Other countries – including Botswana, Egypt, Ethiopia, Ghana and Mauritania – have introduced conditions based on cultural assimilation, in particular knowledge of one of the national languages. Botswana, for example, requires a knowledge of Setswana or another language spoken by a 'tribal community' in Botswana.[136] Until 2003 Ethiopia required a person to 'Know [the] Amharic language perfectly, speaking and writing it fluently'; the 2003 Proclamation on Ethiopian Nationality required only the ability to 'communicate in any one of the languages of the nations/nationalities of the Country.'[137] Ghana requires knowledge of an indigenous Ghanaian language.[138] Egypt, in line with its generally preferential treatment for Arab foreigners, requires an applicant for naturalisation to 'be knowledgeable

[134] Manby, *Citizenship Law in Africa* (n 2).

[135] Malawi Citizenship Act, No.28 of 1966, ss 12-15; until 1992, preference was also given to those 'of African race'.

[136] Citizenship (Amendment) Act 1995, s 5, amending s 12 of the Citizenship Act 1982.

[137] Ethiopian Nationality Law of 1930, s 12; Proclamation No. 378/2003, s 5.

[138] Constitution of the Republic of Ghana, 1992, art 9(2); Ghana Citizenship Act 2000, s 14(e).

in Arabic.'[139] Mauritania redefined the languages required for naturalisation in 2010, removing French and Bambara (mainly spoken in Mali) from the list, clearly with the aim of restricting access for certain categories of person.[140]

There are often distinctions between the rights enjoyed by naturalised citizens as against citizens from birth. Only a few, including Ethiopia, provide that all citizens have equal rights, regardless of how nationality was obtained. In particular, the State may usually deprive a naturalised citizen of his or her nationality much more easily; in many countries it is common for deprivation only to be possible at all in the case of naturalised citizens. Some countries explicitly place restrictions on the role of naturalised citizens in public life.[141]

Naturalisation procedures are usually left almost entirely to the discretion of the executive in both the civil and common law systems. A large number of countries provide that, although reasons must be provided for a decision that the person is not formally qualified to naturalise, a refusal to approve a naturalisation has no reasons attached and the decision cannot be challenged in court.[142] This is true even in the civil law countries where deciding eligibility for nationality of origin is the final decision of the judicial branch (applying the criteria set out in law). Only in Liberia, uniquely in Africa, the Aliens and Nationality Law gives 'exclusive jurisdiction' to naturalise persons as citizens of Liberia to the circuit courts in each county, which are to hear the application in open court.[143] Generally, however, there is no sense that, provided a person fulfils the basic criteria set by the law, the executive's discretion could be constrained by court review.[144]

This difficulty in naturalising is partly a matter of law but even more a matter of practice: the procedures tend to be heavy in bureaucratic requirements, and in the processing. Although the process may appear relatively straightforward, multiple requirements for different paperwork that can make access very difficult or even impossible. Even if explicit fees are relatively low (by no means always the case), the costs for naturalisation may be high, given the multiple documents, many of them from another country, that need to be assembled for an application. One of the most difficult conditions to fulfil can be proof of the person's other nationality: a requirement inherited from the days when it was expected that the person would have to renounce that nationality, but still in place even where dual nationality

[139] Egypt Nationality Act (No. 26 of 1975).

[140] Loi No.2010-023 du 11 février 2010, replacing Art 19 of the nationality code to provide a new list of national languages: Arabic, Pular, Soninké and Wolof (previously Toucouleur, Saracollé, Wolof, Bambara, Hassaniya, Arabic and French. Toucouleur and Pular are effectively the same, and so are Saracollé and Soninké).

[141] See Manby, *Citizenship Law in Africa* (n 2).

[142] Among them, Central African Republic, Comoros, Congo Republic, Côte d'Ivoire, Djibouti, Equatorial Guinea, Guinea, Lesotho, Madagascar, Mali, Mauritania, Niger, Seychelles, Swaziland, Togo, Zambia and Zimbabwe.

[143] Aliens and Nationality Law, 1973, arts 21.1 to 21.5.

[144] For a discussion in the European and North American context, see Christian Joppke, *Citizenship and Immigration* (Polity 2010) 45–47.

is allowed. Many of those who would most want to seek to naturalise in African States are those who are not recognised as having obtained citizenship at birth, but, whether or not they may have a theoretical right to nationality in another country, have no documents recognising that nationality, or evidence of the facts that would enable them to claim it.

In Niger, for example, a person requesting naturalisation on the basis of ten years' residence has to provide both a certificate of nationality from the country of origin (though they are not required to renounce that nationality), and residence permits showing legal residence for ten years. However, among those requesting naturalisation are people born and brought up in the country of parents born elsewhere (who are not eligible for nationality of origin in Niger). These people have never considered obtaining a residence permit (*permis de séjour*); for those from Mali, a bilateral treaty (additional to the ECOWAS regime) means that such a residence permit has not been required for many years. To obtain proof of nationality of one or other or both of their parents' countries they would have to travel to that country to collect all the documentation and go through onerous administrative processes – and then go through another round of procedures in Niger. Even people who were born and grew up in another ECOWAS country and do have evidence of nationality of that country would be unlikely to have a residence permit, since most are not operating in the formal economy and have regarded West Africa as a zone of free movement. ECOWAS abolished the requirement for a residence permit in 2016.[145]

The Tanzanian naturalisation procedure is especially elaborate, involving multiple stages of approval and a total official cost of US$5,000. After filling in the relevant forms, the applicant submits the application at his or her nearest local government area (the ward executive secretary, or *sheha* in Zanzibar). The forms are sent, with an initial recommendation letter, to the district immigration office. At that time, the application process is formally registered, the applicant pays a non-refundable fee of US$1,500, and must also pay for the publication of a notice of intention to apply for naturalisation in two consecutive issues of daily newspapers registered in the Tanzania mainland and in Zanzibar. The applicant is interviewed by the district defence and security committee, and the file is then sent, with a recommendation, to the regional immigration officer. The application is then scrutinised at the regional level, with or without an interview, and forwarded with a recommendation from the regional defence and security committee to the Commissioner General of Immigration Services. The applicant may be interviewed again at national level, and the commissioner general makes a recommendation to the minister of home affairs. For an applicant from Zanzibar, an additional layer of scrutiny comes through the office of the second vice president (representing the islands). The minister makes the final decision, and may

[145] Bronwen Manby, 'Migration, Nationality and Statelessness in West Africa' (UNHCR and IOM 2015).

disregard or overrule recommendations (which may in any event contradict each other), or simply not respond. If the minister approves the application, a further fee of US$3,500 is payable before citizenship is formally granted. Children of the person naturalising are not automatically included and must make a separate application with a separate fee, as must those adopted by an existing national.[146]

It is indicative of the difficulty of naturalisation in practice that there are almost no published statistics about the numbers naturalised in most African countries. Those statistics that are available reveal that the numbers of naturalised persons vary hugely across countries, but are generally low: in Nigeria, for example, only around one or two hundred persons a year, in a population of more than 150 million (see Chapter 7.7). In South Africa, the one country where decisions had been made at an administrative level, numbers naturalised drastically reduced from 2010, and the government proposed reducing access and creating a purely discretionary process (see Chapter 9.3).

Discretion in naturalisation is illustrated by power given by almost all nationality laws for the executive to grant of nationality in case of 'exceptional services' rendered to the country or other similar criteria. In addition, the international trend for small islands to seek revenue through granting 'citizenship by investment' was followed by the Seychelles in amendments to the law made in 2013[147]; Comoros took this to a higher level with its 2008 law on 'economic citizenship'. The law has been invoked mainly for the grant of Comoros nationality documents to stateless persons, known as *Bidoon* (from *bidoon jinsiyya*, 'without nationality'), from the United Arab Emirates (UAE) and Kuwait, whose governments have paid for them to take up this option.[148]

The difficulty of naturalisation means that questions around integration and membership are centred rather on rights acquired at birth, with the exception of some rather rare efforts to provide facilitated naturalisation to specific groups of long-term migrants or former refugees, as in Kenya, Côte d'Ivoire, or Tanzania (see Chapters 7.3, 7.4 and 9.2).

5.5. Loss and Deprivation

The most common provision for automatic loss of birth nationality is in case of acquisition of another, in countries where dual nationality is not allowed. As prohibitions on dual nationality have been removed, automatic loss has of course

[146] Manby, 'Citizenship and Statelessness in the East African Community' (n 20). The fees set by Government Notice (G.N.) No.262 of 3 August 2012 increased the cost of naturalisation from $600.

[147] Seychelles Citizenship Act No. 18 of 1994, amended by Act 11 of 2013.

[148] Loi relative à la citoyenneté économique en Union des Comores, 2008, full text published in *Al Watwan* newspaper, 3 December 2008. The law was passed by 18 to 15 votes in the national assembly. See Atossa Araxia Abrahamian, 'The Bizarre Scheme to Transform a Remote Island into the New Dubai' *The Guardian* (11 November 2015); Atossa Abrahamian, *Cosmopolites: What It Is like to Be a Citizen of the World* (Columbia Global Reports 2015).

also fallen away. Legal provisions allowing deprivation of nationality from birth (of origin, in the civil law terminology) were present in only a minority of African States as of 2017. However, most allowed for the deprivation of nationality acquired by naturalisation, some of them on quite vague and arbitrary grounds. The former British colonies borrowed language from the British precedents and provide for deprivation on the grounds of 'disloyalty' or the 'public good'; while the francophone countries referred to behaviour 'incompatible with the status of a national' or 'prejudicial to the interests of the country'.[149]

These provisions had been relatively stable since independence, though the more recently adopted constitutions had increased due process protections, often informed by a history of arbitrary manipulation of nationality laws. In Kenya, for example, where deprivation had previously been highly discretionary, the 2010 constitution allowed deprivation only if a naturalised citizen (citizenship from birth cannot be revoked) had actually been convicted of a serious crime.[150] Meanwhile, Gambia, Ghana, Liberia, and Rwanda all provided that deprivation could only be carried out by a court, on the government's application.[151] A majority, though not all, provided for judicial oversight of executive decisions to deprive. Some in the Commonwealth tradition, however, specifically excluded court review of any decision relating to nationality.

Africa has seen relatively few amendments specifically expanding deprivation provisions in response to the global threat of terrorism. However, in 2013, the Seychelles inserted a new article to its citizenship law expanding the grounds for deprivation of citizenship if the minister 'is satisfied' that the person has been involved in terrorism, piracy, drugs offences, treason, and other offences, or has acted with disloyalty.[152] In 2010, the South African Citizenship Act was amended to provide for loss of citizenship if a citizen 'engages, under the flag of another country, in a war that the Republic does not support'.[153]

But a review of deprivation provisions has a slightly unreal feel. These procedures are hardly used, so far as one can tell, though statistics are rarely if ever published; indeed, since they mostly apply only to naturalised citizens, and naturalisation is rare, they are not often likely to be applicable. Countries such as Kenya and Nigeria, both facing well-publicised and serious security threats from the Al-Qaeda-affiliated Al-Shabaab and Boko Haram are not known to have deprived any individual of citizenship through the formal procedures of the law

[149] Manby, *Citizenship Law in Africa* (n 2).

[150] Kenya Constitution, 2010, s 17.

[151] Gambia Constitution 1996, Art 13; Ghana Constitution 1992, Art 9, Citizenship Act 2000, Art 18; Liberia Aliens and Nationality Law 1973, Arts 21.53; Rwanda Nationality Law No.30 of 2008, Art 20.

[152] Section 11A of the Citizenship Act No. 18 of 1994, inserted by Act 11 of 2013.

[153] South African Citizenship Act 1996, as amended 2013, Art 6(3). This amendment came into force on 1 January 2013. The 1996 Constitution provides in Art 20 that 'No citizen may be deprived of citizenship.' It is possible that the phrasing of the revised Art 6(3) is designed to avoid this prohibition by providing for automatic loss. See further *Submission on the South African Citizenship Amendment Bill, B 17 - 2010*, Citizenship Rights in Africa Initiative, 6 August 2010.

on deprivation. The only State where deprivations are widely – and increasingly – reported is Egypt: following the installation of the military government led by General Abdel Fattah el-Sisi, nationality was revoked from 800 people in 2014, apparently on national security grounds.[154]

Abuse of nationality law has most often reached the courts in case of refusal to recognise the citizenship of high profile individuals running for the presidency or other political office.[155] In all these cases, the refusal has been based on the assertion that the person had never been a citizen, and thus recognition had been in error, rather than on an attempt to deprive the person of citizenship through the formal procedures.

In Zambia, for example, a newly elected government bent the law in Kafkaesque ways to declare that Kenneth Kaunda, president of the country from 1964 to 1991, was not a citizen and thus could not run for office again; and also to exclude from power the less internationally well known politicians William Banda and John Chinula. In Botswana, the government tried the same strategy against John Modise, after he attempted to establish an opposition party, leaving him in a no-man's land limbo for years (see section below). Chapter 7.4 describes how the courts in Côte d'Ivoire annulled the nationality certificate of former Prime Minister Alassane Ouattara, on grounds that it had been irregularly issued.

These high-profile cases reached the African Commission on Human and Peoples' Rights, which in every case ruled the government was in violation of several articles of the African Charter. Some similar cases have been litigated or protested only at national level. The case of John Akar of Sierra Leone, encompassed within a general suspicion of the role of 'Lebanese' in Sierra Leonean politics, reached the British Privy Council (Chapter 7.2).

Other cases can be found from many countries. In Nigeria, the federal government of President Shehu Shagari in January 1980 arrested and expelled to Chad the majority leader of the opposition-controlled State legislature of the north-eastern State of Borno, Alhaji Shugaba Abdulrahman Darman, alleging that he was Chadian. The Nigerian courts struck down this act as illegal, finding that Shugaba was a Nigerian citizen and that citizens were not liable to be deported from their own countries of nationality.[156]

In Swaziland, the default response to those who criticise the monarchy or organise to challenge the government is to accuse them of not being Swazi. During the lead up to independence in 1968, King Sobhuza and his supporters had

[154] 'Egyptian nationality stripped from 800, including Palestinians', *Egypt Independent*, 29 October 2014; Sonia Farid, 'Stripping Egyptians of citizenship: a new punishment?', *Al Arabiya News*, 23 October 2014.

[155] Beth Elise Whitaker, 'Citizens and Foreigners: Democratization and the Politics of Exclusion in Africa' (2005) 48 African Studies Review 109.

[156] *Shugaba Abdulrahman Darman vs. Federal Minister of Internal Affairs and 3 Others* [1981], 2 Nigerian Constitutional Law Reports 459; Samuel Akanmode, *The Shugaba Affair* (Nigerian Council for National Awareness 1980).

resisted the operation of political parties, already describing them as antithetical to the 'traditional' systems of Swazi government. Parties were formally allowed by the independence constitution, by when an opposition party gained three seats in the 1972 elections, the reaction was immediate. The government first sought to deport one of the new parliamentarians, Bhekindlela Thomas Ngwenya, on the ground he was not a citizen, and on being frustrated by the High Court,[157] rushed through an amendment to the Immigration Act to establish a government-appointed tribunal to decide cases of disputed nationality.[158] The tribunal predictably ruled that Ngwenya was not a citizen of Swaziland. When the Court of Appeal overturned a High Court ruling in favour of the tribunal's decision,[159] the response of the king was to repeal the constitution and ban political parties.

Such tactics may also be used against other critics. In Swaziland, again, one of the many forms of persecution used during the 1990s against Jan Sithole, the vocal general secretary of the Swaziland Federation of Trade Unions (SFTU) was the allegation that he was a 'foreigner', on the basis that his father came from Mozambique. Similar tactics were used against Richard Nxumalo, the SFTU president, who was claimed to be a South African.[160] In Tanzania, the government declared in 2001 that four individuals were not citizens, though giving them the option of applying for naturalisation; the move was interpreted as reprisal for independent media criticism of political and economic developments in Tanzania.[161]

These cases, which could be described as 'arbitrary retroactive non-recognition' of nationality rather than as deprivation (though in international law terms having the same effect), are far from confined to these high-profile individuals, though it is these cases that have reached the courts. For those who are not considering running for public office or challenging the government in other ways, it is through the process of applying for or renewing a national identity card or passport – or when they are arrested and deported – that they find that they are in fact not, or no longer, considered to be citizens.

Governments wishing to 'denationalise' a person simply deny that he or she ever had nationality to start off with, arguing that any nationality documentation previously held was void because it was issued in error. More generally, individuals

[157] *Bhekindlela Thomas Ngwenya v. The Deputy Prime Minister* 1970–76 SLR (HC) 88.

[158] Immigration (Amendment) Act No. 22 of 1972.

[159] *Bhekindlela Thomas Ngwenya v. The Deputy Prime Minister and the Chief Immigration Officer* 1970–76 SLR (HC) 119; *Bhekindlela Thomas Ngwenya v. The Deputy Prime Minister and the Chief Immigration Officer* 1970-76 SLR (CA) 123.

[160] International Labour Organisation, Committee on Freedom of Association, 'Swaziland' (Case No. 1884), 23 May 1996, Report No. 306 *(Vol. LXXX, 1997, Series B, No. 1)* – Complaint against the Government of Swaziland presented by the International Confederation of Free Trade Unions (ICFTU).

[161] 'Tanzania drops envoy to Nigeria over citizenship', *The Guardian*, Dar es Salaam, 5 February 2001. The four were Timothy Bandora (the country's then High Commissioner to Nigeria); Jenerali Ulimwengu (a leading publisher, journalist, media proprietor and chief executive of Habari Media Limited and also a former Tanzanian diplomat and member of parliament, who was born and educated in Tanzania), Anatoli Amani (the leader of the ruling Chama Cha Mapinduzi (CCM) party in the north-western Kagera region), and Mouldine Castico (a former publicity secretary of CCM in Zanzibar).

who are members of groups facing discrimination in access to nationality far more often face the practical impossibility of obtaining official documentation confirming their status than an explicit legal denial or withdrawal of recognition. Thus, key amendments to nationality laws in Africa have not been to increase government powers to deprive, but rather to restrict access to nationality based on birth and residence and to exploit any ambiguity in the rules applied on succession of States at independence.[162]

Zambia: Kenneth Kaunda and others

After 27 years of one party rule following independence, Zambia held multi-party presidential and parliamentary elections on 31 October 1991. The elections were won by the Movement for Multiparty Democracy (MMD), led by Frederick Chiluba. It was one of the first post-cold war transitions on the African continent, much heralded as a model for other countries.

In 1993, the MMD fulfilled a campaign pledge to review the constitution. The Mwanakatwe Commission, named for its chairman John Mwanakatwe, released its report in June 1995, including a contentious recommendation for a constitutional amendment to require that both parents of any presidential candidate should be Zambians by birth.[163] It was clear that this clause was intended to disqualify former president Kenneth Kaunda, whose parents had come from what was then Nyasaland, current Malawi, from standing for the presidency in the 1996 elections on the ticket of the United National Independence Party (UNIP) – the party that he had led during the independence struggle and that had been in power since 1964 until defeated by the MMD. The ruling party pushed the amendment through parliament in 1996.[164]

[162] Bronwen Manby, 'You Can't Lose What You Haven't Got: Citizenship Acquisition and Loss in Africa' in Audrey Macklin and Rainer Bauböck (eds), *The Return of Banishment: Do the New Denationalisation Policies Weaken Citizenship?* (Robert Schuman Centre for Advanced Studies 2015).

[163] The Constitution at the time of independence provided in art 3(1) as follows: '3(1) Every person who, having been born in the former protectorate of Northern Rhodesia, is on 23rd October 1964 a British protected person shall become a citizen of Zambia on 24th October 1964.' Zambia was, indeed, the only former protectorate not requiring that a person also have a parent or grandparent also born in the territory in order to be attributed citizenship at independence. See Elspeth Guild, 'British Nationality and East African Independence' (1990) 4 Immigration and Nationality Law and Practice 99.

[164] Constitution of the Republic of Zambia, 1991, Art 34(3)(b), added by the Constitution (Amendment) Act No. 18 of 1996. The Constitution also provides in Art 7(b) that a person may not be deprived of citizenship except on the grounds that they are the citizen of another country or they have obtained citizenship by fraud. See discussion in Melvin LM Mbao, 'Human Rights and Discrimination: Zambia's Constitutional Amendment, 1996' (1998) 42 Journal of African Law 1.

The opposition Zambia Democratic Congress party unsuccessfully litigated to prevent the adoption of the constitutional amendment.[165] Kaunda was thus not allowed to contest the 1996 elections, which were held in an atmosphere of severe threat to all opposition candidates[166]; in 1997 he was detained for several months during a general crackdown following an alleged coup attempt.

Chiluba's government had already began to use citizenship and immigration law to disable its political opponents. William Steven Banda and John Lyson Chinula – both leading members of the UNIP – were separately deported to Malawi in 1994 under the Immigration and Deportation Act, on the grounds that they were not citizens and were 'likely to be a danger to peace and good order in Zambia'. The Malawian courts declared both deportees not to be Malawian citizens.

In an ironic twist, following the 1996 elections, the dual parentage clause was invoked to challenge in court the re-election of President Fredrick Chiluba. The petitioners alleged that Chiluba's father was not Zambian by birth and therefore Chiluba did not qualify to be elected president of Zambia. This time, the Supreme Court affirmed that citizenship must not be defined in discriminatory terms. It found that, whichever of several proposed biographies was adopted, Chiluba's ancestors came from Northern Rhodesia (what is today Zambia) and his citizenship and eligibility for the presidency could not be questioned, since citizenship was attributed at independence to anyone born in Zambia.[167]

The African Commission on Human and Peoples' Rights eventually ruled against the Zambian government in complaints brought on behalf of Kaunda and Banda and Chinula.[168] Chinula died in Malawi before the Commission concluded its consideration of the case; despite the ruling, the Zambian government did not allow William Banda to return until fresh elections brought the new government of President Levy Mwanawasa, heading the MMD, in 2002. Kaunda's case had been settled following further litigation in Zambia[169] and his citizenship restored.

165 *Zambia Democratic Congress v. Attorney General*, Appeal No. 135/96, SCZ Judgment No. 37 of 1999. The Supreme Court of Zambia ultimately (long after the elections had come and gone) ruled against the petition, declaring that the Zambian parliament had the power to adopt the proposed amendment to the constitution without a referendum.

166 Human Rights Watch, 'Zambia: Elections and Human Rights in the Third Republic' (1996).

167 *Lewanika and Others v Chiluba*, 1998 ZLR 86.

168 Communication 212/98, *Amnesty International v. Zambia* African Commission on Human and Peoples' Rights (2000); Communication 211/98, *Legal Resources Foundation v Zambia*, African Commission on Human and Peoples' Rights (2001).

169 *Mushota and Another v Kaunda and Another* 1997/HN/357 unreported. The judgment was published in the *Times of Zambia* on 1 April 1999. Kaunda lost in the High Court, but the case was appealed to the Supreme Court and settled before it was heard.

Finally, after multiple changes of government and repeated constitutional commissions, a new constitution was adopted under the government of President Edgar Lungu. The 2016 constitution enacted a primarily descent-based framework for citizenship, but with the right to apply for naturalisation based on birth and residence in the country until majority; it also permitted dual citizenship for the first time. In relation to the qualifications for public office, it finally laid the 'Kaunda amendment' to rest, establishing that 'A person qualifies to be nominated as a candidate for election as President if that person – (a) is a citizen by birth or descent…'.[170]

Botswana: The case of John Modise

John Modise was born in South Africa of Batswana parents, prior to the independence of Botswana, and brought up in Botswana. Until 1978, the year that he became a founder and leader of an opposition political party, Modise held Botswana citizenship without problems. In that year, the government of Botswana decided that Modise could not claim citizenship by descent,[171] and the Office of the President declared Modise a prohibited immigrant. His arrest and deportation to South Africa followed soon thereafter, despite efforts to challenge the decision in court.

The South African government did not recognise Modise as a citizen either and he was forced to settle in the then 'homeland' of Bophuthatswana, where he lived for seven years before he was again deported, this time to the no-man's land border zone between Botswana and South Africa where he lived for several months. Modise was finally allowed to re-enter Botswana on humanitarian grounds, but was forced to live on temporary residence permits which were renewed every three months at the discretion of the Ministry of Home Affairs.[172]

The Botswana government was prepared to offer Modise citizenship by naturalisation: however, though citizenship by naturalisation extends nearly all of the same rights as are conferred on citizens by descent, the constitution places limits with regard to the holding of political office. As a naturalised citizen Modise would not be eligible to run for the presidency.

[170] Constitution of Zambia 2016, Pt IV and Art 100.

[171] The government alleged that because Modise was born in the Republic of South Africa and was not a subject of the British Crown at the time of Botswana's independence in 1966, because his father (who had been born in a British Protectorate) was not alive in 1966, and because he had not exercised his right to become a naturalised Botswana citizen by October 1968, he could not be considered a citizen of Botswana.

[172] See African Commission on Human and Peoples' Rights, Communication No. 97/93, *John K. Modise v Botswana* (2000). The judgment in the decision contradicts itself on facts of the case in paras 5 and 91; what is stated here are believed to be the correct facts, based on information from Interights, the plaintiff's representatives.

Citizenship by naturalisation would also not guarantee citizenship of his children, unless it was granted retroactively.

The African Commission ruled in favour of Modise, found Botswana to be in violation of the African Charter on several grounds, and recommended that Botswana grant Modise citizenship.[173] After follow-up from the Commission, the Botswana government agreed in principle to recognise citizenship by birth for Modise, but refused meaningful compensation.[174]

5.6. Making Sense of Legal Amendments

The great diversity of the African continent makes it hard to follow the underlying reasons for the trends observed, especially those that cross the legal traditions. What this book has not done is to seek to correlate developments in citizenship law in a statistical way with developments in regime type; to judge, for example, if more democracy leads to more open or more closed access to citizenship. Though such efforts are interesting,[175] coding of the openness of citizenship law is a complex matter, not reducible to simple binaries between *jus soli* and *jus sanguinis*. Nonetheless, it is possible to discern some patterns amidst the noise.

In the first place, the colonial models set the initial frameworks and continue to have a strong influence on the acquisition of citizenship at birth. In almost all cases, the basic framework of the law remains recognisably within the legal tradition that each State inherited. In particular, the former French and Portuguese territories that adopted a double *jus soli* rule – birth on the territory and one parent also born there gives an automatic right to nationality – have maintained this rule unaltered. The North African States are more varied, but also retain the essential rules established on attaining independence. Similarly, the Central African territories administered by Belgium all adopted a descent-based law after independence, based on the Belgian model. Among them only Rwanda has seen a movement towards granting rights based on birth in the territory.

The Commonwealth States, by contrast, rapidly shed the foundational role of birth right citizenship. A concept with its ideological roots in loyalty to the

[173] *Modise v Botswana*, para 96.

[174] The government reportedly offered Modise P100 000 (around US$21,000 at the contemporary exchange rate) as compensation in 2004 for his 1978 deportation from Botswana in response to the African Commission's ruling, an offer he is said to have rejected. Donny Dithato, 'State in Secret Talks with Modise,' *Mmegi*, 25 August 2004. See also Frans Viljoen and Lirette Louw, 'State Compliance with the Recommendations of the African Commission on Human and Peoples' Rights, 1994–2004' (2007) 101 American Journal of International Law 1.

[175] Graziella Bertocchi and Chiara Strozzi, 'The Evolution of Citizenship: Economic and Institutional Determinants' (2010) 53 The Journal of Law and Economics 95.

feudal ruler of the place of birth had no purchase when the new rulers of African States had so little history behind them, the control over territory was so fragile, civil registrations systems so weak, and the economy often dominated by the descendants of recent immigrants whose loyalty to those new rulers was highly questionable. There is no absolute path-dependency. But legacies of the old rules remained in place and had ongoing impact, including the unfortunate omission of a rule to provide nationality to children of unknown parents (since one had not existed in the British law of 1948), as well as gender discrimination.

Secondly, the character of the different liberation movements, their structure, makeup and ideology, and the nature of the transition to independence also cast an important shadow over at least the first few decades of the new States. The relatively open frameworks of the PALOP countries, Namibia, and South Africa, can in part be attributed to these histories; as can the restructuring of citizenship law in Rwanda. The very different experiences of Algeria or Zimbabwe, for example, created a different dynamic; as did those of South Sudan or Eritrea. Gender equality was among the legacies of the socialist influence in the PALOP States, where women were given equal rights with men from the date of independence in 1975, around 20 years ahead of the major wave of reforms on this point elsewhere.

Thirdly, individual political leaders also made a difference. The most expansive official acceptance of the attribution of nationality based on birth in the territory (and of citizenship in the broader sense of the right to participate) in the first decades after independence was seen in those countries headed by leaders strongly embracing the pan-African ideals, including most notably presidents Julius Nyerere in Tanzania and Félix Houphouët-Boigny in Côte d'Ivoire. Sékou Touré used similar rhetoric in Guinea, which also adopted rules providing very open access to nationality, and with greater gender equality than in most former AOF States. Thomas Sankara's commitment to gender equality was similarly important for Burkina Faso's post-revolution family code adopted in 1989. There are more recent reforms where the will of the president has had a powerful effect: in both Uganda and Rwanda, for example, the personal views of presidents Yoweri Museveni and Paul Kagame seem to have been influential in the reformulation of citizenship laws in 1995 and 2003, respectively. The reforms that finally brought gender equality in Senegal were pushed through by minister of justice Aminata Touré.

Fourthly, organised pressure for reform of the law has had an impact in many cases: by the women's movement for gender equality; by diaspora groups for dual citizenship; and by children's rights organisations for prevention of statelessness among abandoned children. More recent advocacy, by human rights groups and by UNHCR, has begun to have an effect in efforts to reduce statelessness among particular groups (for example, in the case of the Makonde in Kenya, mentioned in Chapter 7.3), but not yet in generally applicable amendments to the law.

Fifthly, the new laws and constitutions adopted since independence have clearly drawn inspiration from legal changes in other African countries, especially those within the same legal tradition. Both statutory reforms and court decisions have been influential. Perhaps most obviously, reforms to ensure gender equality and permit dual nationality have been contagious. Less obviously, perhaps, among Commonwealth States the restrictive interpretation or deletion of provisions granting citizenship based on birth in the territory seem to have encouraged other anglophone countries to do the same. More recently, the trend to introduce protections for children of unknown parents has also spread among the same countries, with similar wordings in many places; as well as the reduction of executive discretion and introduction of greater due process protections. Sierra Leone's 'negro African' preference drew on Liberia's example. This and similar examples of apparent imitation – for example, in the idea of 'indigenous community' in Nigeria and Uganda – would merit further research.

Finally, however, the patterns related to explicit discrimination based on race, ethnicity or religion are hard to frame within one analysis. Some small, ethnically unified States have adopted such rules; others have not. Some large and ethnically diverse States have done so; others have not. Those doing so belong to various legal traditions. It is only in relation to the individual history and politics of each State that the distinctions begin to make sense.

Preferences based on Arab language and Muslim religion in North Africa are easy to understand, as they draw on the ideal of the Muslim *umma*, the heritage of the Ottoman empire and the transitional provisions established as it was dissolved (even as European tutelage continued for some decades), while also reflecting a reaction to the discrimination of the colonial era (especially in Algeria), and the pan-Arab political commitments of the post-independence decades. The Liberian and Sierra Leonean provisions based on 'negro' identity respond to their shared (though quite distinct) history as founded by freed slaves. References to 'African' identity at different times in Chad, Equatorial Guinea, Mali, and Malawi, again suggest an explicit rejection of pre-independence immigration and exploitation and a recognition of the ideal of pan-African solidarity – but it is not clear why these countries adopted such provisions, and not their neighbours. Ethnic preferences in countries such as Rwanda, Somalia, and Swaziland, meanwhile, perhaps come closest to concepts embraced by those European countries with descent-based regimes, since the idea of the nation-State – of a congruence between nation and State – makes sense in those relatively ethnically homogeneous countries in a way that it does not in most of Africa. But Lesotho is a counter-factual where ethnicity plays no legal role; and Rwanda also moved away from the limited ethnic preferences established in 2003 with the law adopted in 2008.

The more complex cases are DRC, Nigeria, and Uganda, now joined by South Sudan. All four countries are much more typical of African States in their multi-ethnic composition than Rwanda, Somalia, or Swaziland, yet all four have reached for ethnic categories as a way of framing citizenship. Despite the lack of any obvious overlap between the boundaries of 'nation' and 'state', a conceptualisation of the State as, perhaps, a coalition of nations, has proved more useable (or at least useful to politicians) in the national context than the idea of an undifferentiated common national citizenship. Decisions on nationality are thus effectively decentralised to the local level for most purposes. To some extent, of course, this is the case in many other States without explicit discrimination in the law: as the next chapter shows, local leaders of one kind or another are often involved in some form of verification of the identity of applicants for nationality documents.

The ethnicity-based provisions adopted by DRC were transparently designed to restrict access to Congolese nationality for the descendants of labourers brought to the country to work on Belgian plantations; although they have also been used to deny citizenship to those of European or Middle Eastern descent. At the same time, it is arguable that the extremely weak administrative infrastructure and even the idea of Congo left behind by the Belgians made an ethnic-based law easier to understand and apply (see Chapter 7.5). A similar case could be made for South Sudan (see Chapter 8.2). The Nigerian and Ugandan provisions are also ambivalent. On the one hand the reference to 'indigenous communities' in the constitutions of both countries (coupled with a list of the approved communities in Uganda) clearly excluded those not encompassed in this term, notably people of non-African descent. But the provisions could also operate to some extent inclusively, depending on context, by permitting local-level decisions on who might be indigenous (see Chapters 7.3 and 7.7). Both provisions were adopted in response to civil wars in which divisions based on ethnic identity had played a major role, and at least in part were attempts to recognise unity in diversity. In application, they have had different effects in different contexts.

In each case where such provisions have been adopted, it is possible to come up with reasons for their deployment related to State consolidation, exclusion of political rivals, or efforts to reduce the influence of other States in domestic politics. Perhaps more interesting is the task of explaining why some African States did *not* reach for the same tools, given the challenges of institution- and nation-building in the post-independence decades.

6

Identification and Registration

Something as simple as an inability to access birth registration or an indefinite delay in obtaining a national identification card upon reaching adulthood, processes regarded as purely administrative, can have consequences just as damaging and permanent as if denationalisation had been enacted in the law or by executive decree. It is the low-level administrative decisions – to register a child's birth or enrol her in school, to issue an identity card or passport, to permit a house to be built or land to be cultivated, and of course to vote – that determine whether someone has access to the rights that go with nationality, and thus for all practical purposes to nationality itself.

Thus, the regulations and *décrets* that provide detailed rules for application of the laws, as well as the internal directives of government departments and the level of training of the officials who implement them, may in practice be at least as important as the constitution or legislation in shaping the understanding of the government officials responsible for issue of identity and other documentation, and thus access to proof of nationality in practice. In practice, due to institutional weaknesses and corruption, the implementation of the law may be much more haphazard than the formal procedures suggest.

6.1. Proof of Nationality: The Civil/ Common Law Divide

The basic administrative frameworks bequeathed by the European powers to their African territories have had great durability; more durability than the substantive provisions of the law. In particular, differences between the civil law and common law systems governing nationality administration have remained mostly intact, without much convergence. At the same time, there have been creative efforts everywhere to adapt or get around these rules.

In the civil law countries, nationality is a responsibility of the ministry of justice. The nationality codes all establish the basic procedures to litigate any question at issue in relation to nationality. In the common law countries, by contrast, nationality is usually the responsibility of the ministry of home affairs or immigration. The courts have a very limited role: Botswana, Lesotho, Malawi, Mauritius, Seychelles, Tanzania, and Zimbabwe explicitly state in their legislation that the decision of the minister on any matter under the nationality law cannot be reviewed in court.[1] (Constitutional provisions may in principle override these exclusions, but not in all cases.) These institutional differences make a major difference to the official approach to nationality administration, which is more firmly situated within the realm of rights in the civil law system, and within executive discretion in the common law countries.

An important illustration of this division is seen in the systems to determine, where it is in doubt, if a person is in fact a national. In the civil law countries, a well-established procedure provides for the ordinary civil tribunals, usually at the level of the *département* or equivalent level of government administration, to make this decision. Judges in these courts are trained in the conditions provided by the nationality law and will issue a certificate of nationality to the person if they are entitled, which constitutes definitive proof of nationality of that person (unless and until it is overturned by another tribunal based on new evidence).

In the common law countries by contrast, there is often no document that is definitive proof of citizenship. Although there may be the theoretical provision for a certificate of nationality in cases of doubt, this is delivered by the executive, and is effectively unknown in practice.[2] Thus, there is no single document that provides conclusive proof of nationality: while the passport has highest status, most people do not have an international passport. Passports in many countries are also explicitly stated to be issued at the discretion of the State, and not to be proof of nationality. In practice, a variety of documents may be accepted as proof of nationality, depending on the circumstances.

Naturalisation is discretionary in all systems, but there are still some general differences between the civil and common law. In the civil law countries it is usually the case that applications for naturalisation are considered by the ministry of justice in the first instance, before being passed to the political authorities (usually the president, sometimes a minister) for decision. Although the final decision is discretionary, any decision that the application does not fulfil the basic criteria must be reasoned. Naturalisations are adopted by decree and published in the official journal. In the common law countries, naturalisation is equally

[1] Botswana Citizenship Act 1998, s 22; Lesotho Citizenship Order 1971, s 26; Malawi Citizenship Act 1966, s 29; Mauritius Citizenship Act 1968, s 17; Seychelles Citizenship Act 1994, s 14; Tanzania Citizenship Act 1995, s 23; Zimbabwe Citizenship Act 1984, s 16.

[2] eg, the Ghana Citizenship Act 2000, provides in its s 20 that: 'The Minister may, on an application made by or on behalf of any person with respect to whose citizenship of Ghana a doubt exists under Part I of this Act, certify that the person is a citizen of Ghana and a certificate issued under this section shall be prima facie evidence that the person was such a citizen at the date indicated in the certificate, but without prejudice to any evidence that he was such a citizen at an earlier date.' There is a similar provision in s 14 of the Gambia Nationality and Citizenship Act, 1965, and in s 24 of the Sierra Leone Citizenship Act 1973; but not in Nigeria. In southern Africa, Botswana, Lesotho, Malawi, Swaziland, Zambia and Zimbabwe also have such provisions, as does Tanzania; however, the laws in Kenya and Uganda have no such provision (though the Uganda Citizenship and Immigration Control Act, 1999 does provide in s 33 for a 'duly certified citizenship certificate' to be proof of nationality it does not establish how to obtain one).

discretionary, but even a decision not to accept an application often need not be reasoned. Neither names nor statistics of those naturalised are generally required to be published. However, the naturalisation certificate is proof of nationality for other purposes, creating more certainty than there often is for citizens from birth.

6.2. Civil Registration

There is also a difference between the civil and common law countries around the importance of civil registration to nationality administration. These differences, however, have tended to reduce over time, especially under the influence of the international emphasis on civil registration as criticial to the recognition of nationality, and a major push in the new millennium to increase birth registration rates.

Even if not required to acquire nationality, birth registration still forms the most conclusive proof of the facts surrounding birth. It establishes in legal terms the place of birth and parental affiliation, which in turn serves as documentary proof underpinning acquisition of the parents' nationality or the nationality of the State where the child is born. The African Charter on the Rights and Welfare of the Child, like the UN Convention on the Rights of the Child, combines the right to birth registration and the right to acquire a nationality within one single article, making this explicit link.[3]

As in the case of the provisions on nationality, the administrative procedures brought into the post-independence era under both systems were based on the pre-independence models applied to Europeans rather than the natives or *indigènes*. Civil registration had only been compulsory for French citizens in the French territories, leading some to question whether elections could be held at all in the newly independent countries, given the lack of a population register.[4] In the British colonies, birth registration was only compulsory for 'Europeans' and 'Asians', meaning that rates were similarly low.

The laws adopted on nationality, however, usually assumed that universal civil registration and other documentation procedures were already in place, including formal work or residence permits, to provide evidence to support recognition or acquisition. This included an assumption that consular services for registration of the births of children born outside the territory were also in place; in many

[3] Art 6, African Charter on the Rights and Welfare of the Child; also African Committee of Experts on the Rights and Welfare of the Child, 'General Comment on Article 6 of the African Charter on the Rights and Welfare of the Child' (2014).

[4] Frederick Cooper, *Citizenship between Empire and Nation: Remaking France and French Africa, 1945–1960* (Princeton University Press 2014) 155; Frederick Cooper, 'Voting, Welfare and Registration: The Strange Fate of the État-Civil in French Africa, 1945–1960' in Keith Breckenridge and Simon Szreter (eds), *Registration and recognition: documenting the person in world history* (Published for the British Academy by Oxford University Press 2012).

cases, registration of births with consular authorities is either required within a certain time period for nationality to be acquired by the child, or birth registration in the other country must be formally transcribed into consular records before it is recognised as valid. This assumption is generally problematic in the African context, and in any context for refugees.[5]

The francophone countries adopted laws at independence that provided, in line with the French civil code, that all facts relevant to nationality (birth, adoption, marriage, divorce, death) had to be proved through civil registration; if not registered at the time, then the standard process is for a lower level tribunal to issue a court judgment (*jugement supplétif*) confirming the facts for the purposes of late entry of the details into the civil registry. Campaigns to improve civil registration and documentation mobilised the existing system of *audience foraines* (mobile hearings away from the court's main seat), to facilitate this process. Usually there was also a family code, governing questions related to descent, adoption, and marriage.

The former British colonies had none of this administrative apparatus. Although most colonies and protectorates had a more-or-less standard-form law on registration of births and deaths that remained in force at independence, the new citizenship acts did not make civil registration a formal requirement for recognition of nationality in most cases.

UNICEF reported as of 2015 that an average of only 44% of births were registered in sub-Saharan Africa; while some (mostly smaller) countries reached rates of 90%, birth registration was below 50% in 18 countries (including Nigeria, Africa's most populous country), and below 10% in Eritrea, Ethiopia, Liberia, Malawi and Somalia.[6]

In most countries, official fees for obtaining registration of birth (whether within the set time limits or by late registration procedures), identity documentation and certificates of nationality are fairly modest. Initial birth registration in particular is usually free, and nominal fees have in some countries been reduced or eliminated altogether with the support of the UN Children's Fund, UNICEF. However, even a fee of a few dollars may put the process out of reach; and almost everywhere additional unofficial charges may be levied, if not by the officials themselves then by intermediaries who play an important role in explaining the system and facilitating acquisition of documents by those who do not know what the procedures are. It may be particularly difficult to obtain late registration of birth for vulnerable children; for example, in case of an orphaned child it may first be necessary to establish both a birth and death certificate for the child's own parents (or at least the father), which can be near-impossible in practice. Those most likely not to be registered at birth are children born out of wedlock, or those

[5] Gábor Gyulai, 'The Long-Overlooked Mystery of Refugee Children's Natioanilty', *The World's Stateless: Children* (Institute on Statelessness and Inclusion 2017).

[6] Statistics available at https://data.unicef.org/topic/child-protection/birth-registration/.

whose parents are foreigners without regular migration status, or whose parents may be nationals but do not hold any form of identification.

In recent years, a central part of the development support for State capacity in Africa has been to strengthen identification systems, including a major initiative to improve civil registration of births and deaths (and significant civil status events in between: marriages, divorces, adoptions, changes of name).[7] This has led to appreciable increases in birth registration rates in particular across many countries.

South Africa is perhaps the most successful example. Following the inauguration of the new post-apartheid government in 1994, there were major strides in improving birth registration rates, both for newborns and through a campaign for late registration (incentivised by State grants available to those looking after children). However, South Africa also demonstrates the limits to a purely technical approach. Anxieties over access to citizenship for the children of foreigners began to make access to birth registration more problematic for some (see Chapter 9.3).

Some States still have extremely low rates of birth registration (see Table 6.1) – in some cases for reasons that can clearly be traced to conflict or lack of State capacity; but elsewhere for reasons of political will.

Table 6.1 Birth registration rates in Africa, 2013[8]

Country	Total	Country	Total	Country	Total
Algeria	99	**Ethiopia**	**7**	**Niger**	**32**
Angola	**36**	Gabon	90	**Nigeria**	**42**
Benin	80	Gambia	53	Rwanda	63
Botswana	72	Ghana	63	STP	75
Burkina Faso	77	**Guinea**	**43**	Senegal	75
Burundi	75	**G. Bissau**	**24**	Seychelles	–
Cameroon	61	Kenya	60	S. Leone	78
Cape Verde	91	**Lesotho**	**45**	**Somalia**	**3**
CAR	61	**Liberia**	**4**	South Africa	95
Chad	**16**	**Libya**	–	**South Sudan**	**35**
Comoros	88	Madagascar	80	Sudan	59
Congo Rep.	91	Malawi	–	Swaziland	50
Côte d'Ivoire	65	Mali	81	**Tanzania**	**16**

(continued)

[7] See the information on the Africa Programme on Accelerated Improvement of Civil Registration and Vital Statistics, at http://www.apai-crvs.org/.

[8] UNICEF, 'Every Child's Birth Right: Inequities and Trends in Birth Registration' (2013). Less than 50% rate in bold.

Table 6.1 *(Continued)*

Country	Total	Country	Total	Country	Total
DRC	**28**	Mauritania	59	Togo	78
Djibouti	92	Mauritius	–	Tunisia	99
Egypt	99	Morocco	94	**Uganda**	**30**
Eq. Guinea	**37**	Mozambique	48	**Zambia**	**14**
Eritrea	–	Namibia	78	**Zimbabwe**	**49**

6.3. Child Protection

The effectiveness of protections aimed at protecting children from statelessness depend on administrative systems to provide them with the documents needed to recognise their nationality. In the case of children of unknown parents, the relevant sections of the nationality code usually need to be backed up by a family code or a specific children's law setting out detailed procedures for birth registration and recognition of nationality.

In the civil law countries, such procedures are long-established. In Senegal, Niger, and Guinea, for example, a system exists to declare an abandoned infant to the State authorities, and the child will then be given a provisional birth certificate and name, which can later be confirmed if no parents are found; and the child will obtain nationality with no further difficulties. In Senegal, however, the nationality code provision is restricted to abandoned new-born infants, excluding children who are found at an older age but are still unable to identify or trace their parents.

The lack of such established procedures have hampered the implementation of some newer law reforms in the Commonwealth countries. In Kenya and Zimbabwe, new constitutions adopted in 2010 and 2013 (respectively) introduced protections for children of unknown parents for the first time. But in both countries officials were left improvising at local level on how to implement this new responsibility, with no formal system in place.[9]

This is also true in some civil law countries: in Niger, the lack of a *Code de la famille* or children's code and the wide variety of customary rules (custom is recognised as a source of law in Niger, but not further defined or codified), means that there is confusion about the validity and consequences of different decisions. In Côte d'Ivoire, where no foundling provision exists, provisional identity documents are sometimes issued to children who are fortunate to come into contact with child services agencies; however, this may not resolve the risk of statelessness when such

[9] Paul Ndlovu, 'RG office urged to give street kids IDs', *The Zimbabwean*, 22 August 2011; 'Good Practices Paper – Action 2: Ensuring that no child is born stateless', UNHCR, March 2017.

children are obliged to acquire identity documents at majority, and questions can be raised if the birth certificate mentions that the parents are unknown.[10]

If a baby or child is likely to be adopted, adoptive parents will usually sort out legal identity and documents; assuming their own country of nationality establishes procedures to do so. In more than a dozen countries, however, the nationality law makes no provision for adopted children.[11] In all countries, children in the 'hard to adopt' category, including disabled children, may be left without documentation of any kind. Some children's homes (such as SOS Children's Villages) ensure that every child has a personal file compiling every aspect of his or her known identity, and that the necessary official documents are acquired, including late birth registration if needed. Other children may not be so lucky even if they are in a children's home. With persistence, most children that are helped will eventually find some documentation; but many never find help, and the closer they are to adulthood the harder it is to resolve their situation.

Ziguinchor, Senegal[12]

Abdoul, aged about 6 or 7, was brought to the attention of *Futur au Présent*, a centre for children in difficulty in Ziguinchor, southern Senegal, by other children who pointed him out as a child who sometimes slept in the streets, and needed medical attention for an injured foot. His father was from Guinea, much older than his mother, who was from Guinea-Bissau; the father had decided to return to Guinea, leaving the child with the mother. The mother had died and he was staying with his uncle, who worked in the market. Abdoul's birth had not been registered, and one of the first actions of the children's centre was to try to get him documented: a birth certificate is necessary for the *juge pour enfants* to give the centre the *ordonnance de garde* that provides legal authority for their custody of any child. It was a huge struggle to find witnesses who could give evidence as to his parentage, given the demands on time to attend court, transport costs etc, but eventually they were able to establish a birth certificate for Abdoul, and he is enrolled in school and doing well. However, Abdoul will not be entitled to Senegalese nationality on majority, since neither of his parents is Senegalese, nor born in Senegal. He has no contact with any family in either Guinea or Guinea Bissau.

[10] Bronwen Manby, 'Migration, Nationality and Statelessness in West Africa' (UNHCR and IOM 2015).

[11] Bronwen Manby, *Citizenship Law in Africa: A Comparative Study* (3rd edn, Open Society Foundations 2016).

[12] Extracted from Manby, 'Migration, Nationality and Statelessness in West Africa' (n 10).

Case study from Lawyers for Human Rights, South Africa[13]

Elizabeth Nthunya was born in Lesotho in 1982. Her mother was a Lesotho citizen, while her father was South African. When she was three years old, she came to stay with her paternal grandmother in South Africa. Over the years, she struggled to register as South African because she does not have a birth record from Lesotho, which is required in terms of the Births and Deaths Registration Act. Lesotho has very low rates of birth registration. Home Affairs told her to go back to Lesotho and find her mother. Eventually she returned to Lesotho for her mother's funeral. She discovered that the clinic where she was born does not have records prior to 1985. She returned to South Africa but Home Affairs still refuses to assist her. Her father and grandmother have since passed away, but she has five South African aunts and uncles willing to testify to her identity.

Elizabeth has a son born in South Africa to a South African father, but Home Affairs will not allow them to register the child's birth because Elizabeth does not have an ID. Thus her son is also unable to access his South African citizenship, even though his father has a valid South African ID document. Elizabeth's case illustrates the generational impact that lack of documentation has on the right to a nationality. Such strict requirements – for a foreign birth certificate and for the mother's ID document – result in a complete block to citizenship for Elizabeth and her son, with consequences on their economic mobility, right to work and education, and their physical and emotional health.

6.4. Identification and Nationality

Despite the differences in legal systems, it is invariably the executive branch of government that makes the first decisions around entitlement to nationality, most often when it comes to issuance of a national identity card or passport.

In the former French and Belgian countries, national identity cards were introduced immediately after independence, following the model of the colonial power. The national identity card is issued not by a court or justice ministry but by the ministry of the interior, even if the procedure to obtain a certificate of nationality from a court is often available in principle in case of doubt. In the common law countries, national identity cards were not generally in place before independence in the protectorates; though 'pass laws' regulating the status of

[13] Extracted from Jessica P George and Rosalind Elphick, 'Statelessness and Nationality in South Africa' (Lawyers for Human Rights 2013).

'natives' in the colonies, applied with particular force in Kenya, South Africa, and Zimbabwe, created the basis for identification systems carried forward into the post-independence era.[14] A requirement to carry a national identity card was later introduced in some other countries of southern Africa; at the time of independence in Zambia.[15] While only a minority of African countries had a national identity card at independence, almost all countries had adopted a requirement to carry one by 2017.

Although a national ID card is usually not formal proof of nationality under the law, it will usually indicate nationality as one of the pieces of information shown on the face of the card. In practice, possession of an identity card may be key to accessing all sorts of other rights restricted to citizens, including not only voting and other political rights, but also health care and education, as well as participation in the formal economy. A national identity card may also be necessary to obtain a passport.

In Kenya, for example, national identity cards have been compulsory for all adult men since 1947 (for all African men since 1915), and all women since 1978. A national identity card is needed for a vast array of purposes, including entering a government building – which would be required to sort out a problem related to lack of identification. Lack of a national identity card means that a person will not be able to perform any role in the formal economy, including obtaining paid employment, opening a bank account, or accessing a loan. An identity card is needed to purchase real property, and may be critical to retaining existing property rights. Counter-terrorism measures mean that an ID document is also needed to purchase a SIM card for a mobile phone. The national identity card of a parent is needed for a child to take school-leaving exams, and a school leaver will need an identity card to progress to tertiary level education. Freedom of movement is severely restricted for those without an ID card, most of all for those who are members of ethnic groups whose documentation is most likely to be challenged. Vetting procedures for members of specific ethnic groups, or people living in certain areas, can make obtaining a card a major obstacle course (see Chapter 7.3).

In some countries, a riot of different kinds of identification has flourished until recent efforts at standardisation. In Sierra Leone, for example, no national system of identification was put in place at independence. Different forms of document served as proof of identity; for many years the annual tax receipt issued by a chief to 'heads of household' was the only identity document valid for travel within the

[14] For the very particular and influential history of South Africa, see Keith Breckenridge, *Biometric State: The Global Politics of Identification and Surveillance in South Africa, 1850 to the Present* (Cambridge University Press 2014).

[15] For southern Africa, see Jonathan Klaaren and Bonaventure Rutinwa, *Towards the Harmonization of Immigration and Refugee Law in SADC* (Idasa 2004) ch 2, Population registration and identification; also Krishna Pidatala and others, 'Identification Systems Analysis Country Assessment: Zambia' (World Bank, Identification for Development Initiative 2016).

country. Other documents were introduced by different agencies during a period of 'hyper-identification' after the end of the civil war.[16]

In others, including Ethiopia and Nigeria, documents issued by local government authorities are essential to proof of identity, in the absence of an equivalent of the civil law system to certify nationality. The Nigerian 'certificate of indigeneity' and the Ethiopian 'kebele ID' are also foundational to proof of nationality – despite the lack of a legal framework for the system (see Chapters 7.7 and 8.1). This situation is replicated somewhat in Togo, which is one of the few francophone countries where a certificate of nationality is issued by the ministry of justice rather than a court. In practice, a certificate of nationality is refused when there is any doubt about a birth registration established by a *jugement supplétif* from a tribunal, the usual form of late registration in the francophone countries; thus the administrative authorities effectively question the decision of the courts. In such cases of doubt the practice is to demand a '*certificat d'origine*' which is awarded on the basis of an enquiry carried out in the district where the person is from; but no legal authority exists for this practice.[17]

National identity card systems are in the process of radical change across the continent. Identity cards are being introduced where they did not previously exist: both ECOWAS and the EAC have adopted decisions that common-form biometric national identity cards shall be adopted among the members of the two regional economic communities, upgrading those identity documents that already exist and introducing them where they do not.[18] Across the continent systems for voter registration are also being upgraded, often with biometric technology, often in parallel with the national identity card system.

These changes are revealing problems with the old systems, and sometimes introducing new ones. In Senegal, for example, the national identity card system was in the process of being digitised during 2014, revealing widespread problems as the system rejected people who applied with the same numbered birth certificate. This was caused by the sale of duplicate or triplicate birth certificates, from the birth registration books made with tear-off slips to issue to parents and for local and national records. Often, the person in possession of such a document would have been completely unaware that the birth certificate was not valid: they had simply followed the understood procedure in paying a fee. Any person who applied for an ID document or certificate of nationality with a number already used would be sent back to court to have the birth certificate cancelled or confirmed by the registrar (*greffier*); if it was invalid, the person would then need a *jugement supplétif* confirming the facts of birth and a new birth certificate; and then

[16] Mariane Ferme, 'Deterritorialized Citizenship and the Resonances of the Sierra Leonean State' in Veena Das and Deborah Poole (eds), *Anthropology in the margins of the State* (School of American Research Press; James Currey 2004).

[17] Manby, 'Migration, Nationality and Statelessness in West Africa' (n 10).

[18] ibid; Bronwen Manby, 'Citizenship and Statelessness in the East African Community' (UNHCR 2018).

a certificate of nationality before getting their final identity document issued. The procedure to obtain a *jugement supplétif* for late registration of birth required the physical presence of five people: the person him or herself, both parents (or their death certificates) and two witnesses. Each stage of this process had fees attached.[19] If the identity card itself was incorrectly issued, the person would need to travel to Dakar to get it sorted out. It could take months to complete the unravelling for those trapped in this situation; or they might never do so. People displaced by the conflict in Casamance faced still more difficult hurdles, since records had sometimes been destroyed, while family members and witnesses might be dispersed across two or three countries.[20]

In countries where national identity cards have not previously existed, different questions arise. Where new systems are adopted without considering the underlying legal and policy frameworks, there can be a risk of generating new forms of exclusion. For example, in Tanzania and Uganda, registration for new national identification systems were carried out in 2014 and 2015, finally implementing legislation that had been adopted some years earlier.[21] Each country had to establish systems to decide who would be eligible for these new cards, establishing local level committees for verification of identity, comprising a mix of security personnel and local government administration.

In both countries, there were allegations of discrimination on the grounds of ethnicity against internal migrants as well as people perceived to be foreign during the roll-out of the new documents. There were also allegations that corruption created a risk that people who were not qualified would obtain recognition as nationals. In Uganda, the law provides an ethnic basis for citizenship (see Chapter 7.3), and the registration was conducted on this basis, including an important role for attestation of membership by traditional leaders. In Tanzania, similarly, newly required national identity cards recording people as citizens were also being approved based on an understanding of descent or ethnicity, despite the apparently *jus soli* based law. Many thousands of applications were referred to the immigration department for verification. In both countries, people who had believed themselves to be citizens, found that they had not been approved for

[19] In Senegal, a certificate of nationality cost CFA2300 in 2014; a national identity card was free, though until recently had cost CFA1000. Birth registration was free if done within the correct time limits, if outside those limits via a *jugement supplétif* the charges had recently been dropped from CFA4,000 to CFA700. To get an *extrait de minute du greffier* confirming that a birth certificate is correct (in case of doubt) cost CFA2500, as did an annulation and reissue of a certificate. Reported 'faciliation fees' paid to intermediaries ranged from a few hundred to a few thousand francs. Interviews Dakar and Ziguinchor, May 2014. The exchange rate at the time was roughly 490 CFA francs to one US dollar.

[20] Manby, 'Migration, Nationality and Statelessness in West Africa' (n 10).

[21] In Tanzania, the Registration and Identification of Persons Act No.11 of 1986; in Uganda, the Citizenship and Immigration Control Act 1999, Pt IV, provided for 'Registration of citizens and issue of national identification numbers and national identity cards.' Uganda adopted a new Registration of Persons Act 2015, consolidating, amending and replacing the existing laws on registration of births and deaths and national identity cards.

their cards. Services that those not issued cards had previously accessed, including health care, were now being denied.[22]

In Botswana, the introduction of a new computerised passport system in 2011 found some who had previously been recognised as Botswanan suddenly denied the right to renew their passports unless they renounced another nationality that they had never claimed (in a manner very similar to what had happened in Zimbabwe, see Chapter 7.1).[23] Meanwhile, Bazezuru descendants of followers of a religious sect who came to Botswana from Zimbabwe in the 1950s, faced what was described as a 'citizenship crisis' in their efforts to acquire Botswanan identity cards and passports.[24] Dual citizenship is not allowed in Botswana, and the authorities administering the identity card system (introduced in 1996) required proof of renunciation of Zimbabwean citizenship before giving them Botswanan documents – though they had never sought Zimbabwean citizenship and, indeed, would have difficulties gaining recognition of Zimbabwean citizenship in order to renounce it. In Botswana, a birth certificate is evidence of citizenship[25], which has meant that, though government ministers urged the community to register all births, the Bazezuru even struggled to obtain this most basic of documents, preventing their children from accessing education. The minister for home affairs promised in 2013 to appoint a task force to deal with the matter, but one year later a member of the community commented:

> We appreciate the minister's intervention even though it did not bring the results we expected. Most of us still cannot get help from immigration and national registration due to the dual citizenship alleged by the officers. Our citizenship remains a mystery despite the fact that our first generation has long passed; we don't know what is expected of us because we were born and bred in Botswana.[26]

In some cases the law has been changed at the same time as new identification systems are introduced, with the specific purpose of preventing some from accessing the new cards. The lobby group *Touche pas à ma nationalité* in Mauritania, for example, accused the government of 'biometric genocide' in its implementation of a new identity card system coupled with amendments to the nationality code

[22] Manby, 'Citizenship and Statelessness in the East African Community' (n 18).

[23] Lawrence Seretse, 'Thousands of Batswana become foreigners overnight', *Mmegi* (Gaborone), 18 November 2011. See also Francis B Nyamnjoh, 'Local Attitudes towards Citizenship and Foreigners in Botswana: An Appraisal of Recent Press Stories' (2002) 28 Journal of Southern African Studies 755.

[24] Members of the same church faced similar problems in Kenya; see ch 7.3.

[25] Children's Act No.8 of 2009, s 12(3): 'A birth certificate issued by the Registrar of Births under [the Births and Deaths Registration Act] shall be proof of the nationality of the child.' Births and Deaths Registration Act, No.48 of 1968, as amended to 1998, s 10(2): 'Every such certificate [of birth, still-birth or death] shall, in all courts of law and public offices within Botswana, be prima facie evidence of the particulars set forth therein.'

[26] Sesupo Rantsimako, 'Bazezuru still in citizenship predicament', *Botswana Gazette*, 6 February 2014; See also, 'Commissioner urges Bazezuru to register', BOPA, 29 February 2012; Sesupo Rantsimako, 'Bazezuru seek clarity on their citizenship', *Botswana Gazette*, 3 October 2012; Goitsemodimo Williams, 'Bazezuru want minister's intervention', *Botswana Daily News*, 9 January 2013.

(see Chapter 7.6). The new national number and biometric identity card introduced by Sudan following the secession of South Sudan combined with reforms to the nationality code to denationalise people living in Sudan who have never considered themselves South Sudanese (see Chapter 8.2).

There have also been some positive initiatives to address problems created by lack of clarity over identification, such as exists in border zones, often facilitated by UNHCR under its Statelessness mandate. For example, UNHCR was engaged in finding legal solutions for children born in the Democratic Republic of Congo of mixed Angolan and Congolese parentage denied recognition as Congolese citizens.[27] UNHCR also assisted the Namibian government to negotiate with the Angolan, Botswanan, South African and Zambian governments to undertake joint identification exercises to document formerly undocumented populations in its border regions. The process started in 2010, and by November 2011, more than 900 persons had been naturalised or officially recognised as Namibian through this process. Among them were around 200 people of Nama and Damara heritage removed in the 1970s by the South African government from the Riemvasmaak area of the Northern Cape to what was then South West Africa, as well as people who fled from Angola to Namibia during the Angolan civil war.[28]

6.5. The Relationship Between the Formal and the Informal

A discussion of the finer distinctions of nationality law and procedure can on occasion feel like an exercise in fiction, not least in the face of the mass expulsions that have convulsed many States since independence: in the more extreme cases it is only at the moment of being expelled that a person discovers that he or she is not considered to be a national.[29]

[27] UN High Commissioner for Refugees, *Africa Newsletter*, third quarter 2006.

[28] Information provided at UNHCR regional meeting on statelessness in Southern Africa, Mbombela, South Africa, 1-3 November 2011. See Bronwen Manby, 'Statelessness in Southern Africa' (UNHCR 2011).

[29] In addition to reporting by human rights groups and decisions of the African Commission on Human and Peoples' Rights, there is a large academic literature on this phenomenon. See, eg, the essays collected in William A Shack and Elliott P Skinner (eds), *Strangers in African Societies* (University of California Press 1979); and Catherine Coquery-Vidrovitch and others (eds), *Etre étranger et migrant en Afrique au XXe siècle: enjeux identitaires et modes d'insertion*, vol 1 (L'Harmattan 2003); also Suzanne Bonzon, 'Les Dahoméens En Afrique de l'Ouest' (1967) 17 Revue française de science politique 718; Margaret Peil, 'The Expulsion of West African Aliens' (1971) 9 Journal of Modern African Studies 205; Lynne Brydon, 'Ghanaian Responses to the Nigerian Expulsions of 1983' (1985) 84 African Affairs 561; Aderanti Adepoju, 'Illegals and Expulsion in Africa: The Nigerian Experience' (1984) 18 International Migration Review 426; Aderanti Adepoju, 'The Politics of International Migration in Post-Colonial Africa' in Robin Cohen (ed), *The Cambridge survey of world migration* (Cambridge Univ Press 1995); Christopher J Gray, 'Cultivating Citizenship through Xenophobia in Gabon, 1960–1995' (1998) 45 Africa Today 389; Steve Tonah, 'The Politics of Exclusion: The Expulsion of Fulbe Pastoralists from

Given that identity card applications are usually vetted in the first instance by quite low-ranking civil servants, often within the police or immigration services, this gives the power to determine someone's right to nationality documents – for practical if not legal purposes – to a person who is in no way trained in nationality law. In this context, decisions on eligibility are often made on the basis of popular understanding rather than the letter of the law. Often, the decisions are discriminatory on the basis of gender or ethnicity, even where such discrimination is not explicit in the law. In Swaziland and Madagascar, for example, persons who are not of Swazi or Malagasy ethnic origin often find it impossible to obtain recognition of citizenship.[30]

A lack of systematic birth registration leaves the responsible government departments considerable discretion in deciding what evidence to accept as to who is a citizen; a discretion exaggerated in a country like Liberia, where less than 10% of children under five are registered.[31] Conflict and displacement mean that even those who may have held documentation at birth have lost their documents; and in some cases archives have been destroyed – as in Côte d'Ivoire or Senegal's Casamance region. A survey conducted by the Danish Refugee Council in May 2013 found that 55% of the internally displaced living in Mopti, Mali, had no documentation (ID card or birth certificate).[32] Without these foundational documents, officials rely on witness testimony to distinguish citizens from non-citizens.

Corruption in nationality administration is widespread, and blurs the boundaries of the law.[33] Many purchase the documents they need in order to survive. In Guinea – where an assessment mission noted that 'the administrative system suffers serious dysfunction, including related to lack of financial, human and material resources, difficulties in managing the various institutions and a generalised corruption'[34] – senior government officials freely admit that nationality

Ghana in 1999/2000' (Max Planck Institute 2002) Working Paper 44; Simon Imbert-Vier, 'Afars, Issas and Djiboutians: Toward a History of Denominations' (2014) 13 Northeast African Studies 123; SA Bezabeh, 'Citizenship and the Logic of Sovereignty in Djibouti' (2011) 110 African Affairs 587.

[30] Bureau of Democracy, Human Rights, and Labor, 'Country Reports on Human Rights Practices' (US Department of State various years) entries on Swaziland and Madagascar.

[31] Augustine Konneh, 'Citizenship at the Margins: Status, Ambiguity, and the Mandingo of Liberia' (1996) 39 African Studies Review 141; Stephen Lubkemann, Deborah H Isser and Philip AZ Banks III, 'Constraint of Customary Justice in Post-Conflict Liberia' in Deborah H Isser (ed), *Customary justice and the rule of law in war-torn societies* (United States Institute of Peace Press 2011); Robtel Neajai Pailey, 'Birthplace, Bloodline and beyond: How "Liberian Citizenship" Is Currently Constructed in Liberia and Abroad' (2016) 20 Citizenship Studies 811.

[32] Cited in *Forced Displacement of and Potential Solutions for IDPs and refugees in the Sahel – Burkina Faso, Chad, Mali, Mauritania & Niger*, UNHCR and Global Program on Forced Displacement of the World Bank, October 2013.

[33] See Bruce Whitehouse, *Migrants and Strangers in an African City: Exile, Dignity, Belonging* (Indiana University Press 2012) for a discussion of these issues among West African immigrants in Brazzaville.

[34] Commissariat Général aux Réfugiés et aux Apatrides (CGRA/Belgique), Office Français de Protection des Réfugiés et Apatrides (OFPRA/France) and Office Fédéral des Migrations (ODM/Suisse), 'Rapport de Mission En République de Guinée 29 Octobre – 19 Novembre 2011' (2012).

documents can be obtained with little if any check on entitlement.[35] While Guinea is perhaps an extreme case, many African countries struggle with the same issues. In Kenya, for example, the Commission on the Administration of Justice established by the 2010 Constitution reported delays, inefficiency and ineffectiveness across the administration of civil registration, identity documents and immigration, as well as 'rampant' corruption.[36] The South African Public Protector has investigated many similar cases.[37]

In the Commonwealth countries, the lack of a document that is conclusive proof of nationality, coupled with the tradition of executive discretion, exacerbates the doubt: a passport or national ID card can be called into question at an administrative and not judicial level, and a person rendered stateless simply by an indefinite delay in processing a renewal application rather than any reasoned decision. Even in the civil law countries where a tribunal can provide proof of nationality in cases of doubt, judges cannot overcome weaknesses in the law itself; and interpretations of the law may sometimes vary across different tribunals. Moreover, the procedures may be quite inaccessible to someone without connections and resources. Many give up, managing as best they can without the documents they are supposed to have, and remaining in the informal sector.

As the remaining chapters of this book explore, however, these weaknesses in the official systems do not render them meaningless. Outside any tribunal or other office for nationality papers will be a queue of people waiting to speak to someone to sort out their case; some of them have been returning to the same spot multiple times over several months or years. There are certain categories of people who are most at risk of not being recognised as citizens where they live: the descendant of migrants or refugees; a member of a minority ethnic or religious group; a person from a nomadic family or border community; a child born out of wedlock, orphaned or separated from his or her parents, or simply the child of a foreign father. For them, documents are both more difficult or costly to obtain, and the consequences of not having them are often more severe than for members of a majority group whose rights to citizenship are instinctively accepted. If they are also unable to show a connection to a State 'of origin' sufficient to obtain proof of nationality there, then their situation is even more precarious.

These challenges are likely to become more acute as identification requirements become ever more pervasive, and the formal restrictions and procedures impact more directly on the status of people who have hitherto navigated through the informal. The strengths and weaknesses of the underlying legal frameworks that this book argues have always been relevant will come to determine access to documents far more absolutely than they have previously done. I return to these arguments in the conclusion.

[35] Manby, 'Migration, Nationality and Statelessness in West Africa' (n 10).

[36] Kenya Commission on Administrative Justice (Office of the Ombudsperson), 'Stateless In Kenya: An Investigation Report on the Crisis of Acquiring Identification Documents in Kenya' (2015).

[37] Investigation reports collected at http://www.pprotect.org/.

The situation of nomads

Amongst those most affected by discrimination that is not apparent on the face of the law but embedded in its administrative details are those belonging to ethnic groups that have traditionally followed a nomadic or pastoralist way of life – a population of many millions in Africa.[38] There is an almost total lack of international law or national precedent relating to the determination of the nationality of those who are not 'habitually resident' in any particular place.[39]

The status of the Sahelian Tuaregs has often been doubtful within the contemporary African States where they have a presence. Tuareg are nomadic inhabitants of the Sahara, spread mainly among Algeria, Libya, Mali and Niger, and speaking a dialect of the Berber language (Tamasheq). Demands for self-determination date back to the 1950s, and there were Tuareg rebellions in Niger and Mali in the 1960s and 1990s.[40] In the countries where they now live, documentation is a critical problem for many Tuaregs, even if they have been resident there many years or generations.

Niger, for example, amended its nationality law in 1973 to remove the right to opt for Nigerien nationality based on birth and residence until majority, so it is only when two generations have been born in Niger that a person is automatically attributed nationality at birth. More recently, there has been a major push to increase birth registration rates through additional tribunal hearings (*audiences foraines*) organised, with the support of UN agencies, to authorise late registration. Many Tuaregs who are long-term

[38] The AU estimates the total population of pastoralists in Africa is estimated at 268 million, or a quarter of the total population (not all of them nomadic). African Union, 'Policy Framework for Pastoralism in Africa: Securing, Protecting and Improving the Lives, Livelihoods and Rights of Pastoralist Communities' (2010). For a discussion of the comparable situation of the Roma in Europe see Henriette Asséo, 'L'invention des « Nomades » en Europe au xx siècle et la nationalisation impossible des Tsiganes' in Gérard Noiriel (ed), *L'identification: genèse d'un travail d'État* (Belin 2007).

[39] There is no treaty-level guidance, and the only State-endorsed document of normative value currently seems to be a rather general Recommendation adopted by the Council of Europe in 1983 that urged Member States to facilitate the recognition of nationality for nomadic populations. The Recommendation suggested the following criteria for consideration in establishing a link on the basis of which nationality should be granted: whether the State is 'the State of birth or origin' of the person concerned or the 'State of origin' of his or her immediate family; whether it is the State of habitual residence or frequent periods of residence of the person (provided the residence is not unlawful); and the presence in the State of members of the person's immediate family. Council of Europe Committee of Ministers Recommendation No. R.(83)1, 22 February 1983. In its guidelines on avoiding statelessness among children, UNHCR recommends that: 'in cases where it is difficult to determine whether an individual is habitually resident in one or another State, for example due to a nomadic way of life, such persons are to be considered as habitual residents in both States.' UNHCR, *Guidelines on Statelessness No. 4*, para 42.

[40] See ch 3.2; Mohand Salah Tari, 'Tuareg: The Tragedy of a Forgotten People' www.amazighworld.org, 2002; Pierre Boilley, *Les Touaregs Kel Adagh: dépendances et révoltes : du Soudan francais au Mali contemporain* (Karthala 2012).

migrants from Mali (over several decades) presented themselves to these hearings, on the understanding that the process to obtain recognition of nationality starts with acquiring a birth certificate. They were bemused that they had been rejected, believing that this showed discrimination against them. Yet the tribunal was simply applying the rules. For someone who is not familiar with the system, it is not at all clear why you can obtain a birth certificate only from the country where you are born, but nationality documents only from the State where you have a claim to nationality, which could be a different country – and what would be the appropriate procedures in each case. Nobody had directed those same people towards an application for naturalisation – which would be initiated at the *mairie* rather than the tribunal; but which would also require proof of another nationality as the basis for acquisition of Nigerien nationality, and thus an almost insurmountable burden of document collection, as well as a discretionary decision by the president. As one Tuareg with Nigerien nationality commented, 'it outrages them' (*ça les révolte*) that so many have no documentation from the Nigerien State – except for a card confirming payment of taxes to the commune over many years – symptomatic of a generalised neglect: 'it is only when Boko Haram comes that they notice us.'[41]

Members of the Fulani (known as Peul in French) ethnic group found across the West African region similarly find themselves treated as presumptively 'foreign'.[42] The Mbororo Fulani sub-group found in Cameroon and as far east as Sudan face similar difficulties: even during the period of British rule in Cameroon there was discussion over whether the Fulani-Mbororo were 'natives' ('a person originating from the area where he is living') for the purpose of 1927 Land and Native Rights Ordinance.[43]

[41] Interviews, in Niamey and Tillaberi, Niger, May 2014. See Manby, 'Migration, Nationality and Statelessness in West Africa' (n 10).

[42] The nomenclature used for this widely dispersed West African ethnic group (itself made up of several sub-groups) is complex: in Commonwealth countries they are usually known as Fula or Fulani; in countries of the Francophonie as Peul. The language may be known as Fulfulde or Pulaar, and those who speak it are sometimes also known as Halpulaar(en). The variations in terminology are complex and not consistently used. For a discussion of the issues, see the thread on 'Names for African peoples & language' on the H-Africa discussion logs for December 2007, available at https://networks.h-net.org/h-africa.

[43] Michaela Pelican, 'Mbororo Claims to Regional Citizenship and Minority Status in North-West Cameroon' (2008) 78 Africa: Journal of the International African Institute 540; Sam Hickey, 'Caught at the Crossroads: Citizenship, Marginality and the Mbororo Fulani in Northwest Cameroon' in Sara Dorman, Daniel Hammett and Paul Nugent (eds), *Making nations, creating strangers: States and citizenship in Africa* (Brill 2007); Nicodemus Fru Awasom, 'From Migrants to Nationals and from Nationals to "Undesirable Elements": The case of the Fulani (Mbororo) in the North West Province of Cameroon' in Catherine Coquery-Vidrovitch and others (eds), *Etre étranger et migrant en Afrique au XXe siècle*, vol 1 (Harmattan 2003); Rogers Tabe Egbe Orock, 'The Indigene-Settler Divide, Modernisation and the Land Question: Indications for Social (Dis) Order in Cameroon' (2005) 14 Nordic Journal of African Studies 68; Manby, 'Citizenship and Statelessness in the East African Community' (n 18).

In the context of clashes over land use, Fulani pastoralists are routinely labelled as foreigners.[44]

In the most extreme cases, Fulani have been caught up in one of the periodic mass expulsions, often in response to clashes over land use rights. For example, in 1982, Sierra Leone expelled Fulani allegedly originating from Guinea; Ghana expelled Fulani pastoralists in 1988–89 and again in 1999–2000.[45] Of the approximately 70,000 people expelled by the Mauritanian government in 1989–1990, the majority were cattle herders of Fulani ethnicity from the Senegal River Valley (though civil servants, military officers and activists from other black African ethnic groups were included; see Chapter 7.6).

Though the Fulani have historically followed a nomadic lifestyle of transhumance with herds of cattle, and many still do so, others are settled for several generations in the same location, or migrate only within the borders of one country, yet still face resistance to the idea that they are nationals of that country. Those who are victims of discrimination on the grounds they have a Fulani last name may eventually be able to establish documentation through payment of bribes, or with the assistance of intermediaries who will vouch for them; others may be able to establish documentation of a country 'of origin' different from that where they currently live. But the poorest and most marginalised members of such communities are highly likely to face significant problems in obtaining the identity documents that serve as proof of nationality in most circumstances.

[44] In Nigeria, eg, see Rasheed Oyewole Olaniyi, 'Bororo Fulani Pastoralists and Yoruba Farmers' Conflicts in the Upper Ogun River, Oyo State Nigeria, 1986–2004' *Journal of Asian and African Studies*, Vol.50, No.2, (2015), pp 239–252; Mohammed Bello Tukur, 'Conflicts between transhumant pastoralist and farmers in Nigeria – the way out: Perspectives on the conflicts between farmers and transhumant pastoralists in Nigeria, 11 June 2013, available at https://pastoralist2.wordpress.com/2013/06/11/conflicts-between-transhumant-pastoralist-and-farmers-in-nigeria-the-way-out/.

[45] Adepoju, 'The Politics of International Migration in Post-Colonial Africa' (n 29); Tonah (n 29).

PART IV

Country Case Studies

Extract from : ***Quel est mon pays ?*** by Yodé et Siro (Côte d'Ivoire)[1]

Quand je suis au Gabon on m'appellee ghanéen ;
Quand je suis au Ghana on m'appellee gabonais.
Au Burkina on dit voilà ivoirien ;
En Côte d'Ivoire voilà burkinabè.

De part et d'autre je suis reconnu mais pas en tant que tel :
Quel est mon pays, le pays de métis ?
Ne regarde pas mon visage pour m'attribuer une nationalité ;
Mon accoutrement pour donner le nom de mon pays.

***

When I am in Gabon they call me Ghanaian;
When I am in Ghana they call me Gabonese.
In Burkina, they say there's an Ivorian;
In Côte d'Ivoire, there's a Burkinabè.

In every place I am recognised but not as what I am:
Which is my country, the country of the mixed?
Don't look at my face to give me a nationality;
Or at my clothes to know the name of my country.

[1] Available at www.youtube.com/watch?v=ok8a5Drvj_Y.

7

Who is a Native?

Across the world it is normal practice for foreigners to be blamed in tough economic times, scapegoated for national setbacks, or targeted for verbal or legal abuse – or worse – by politicians seeking to consolidate support among their own natural constituency. Africa is no exception. Where national cohesion and State institutions are weak, the temptation has proved great to use exhortations against foreigners almost as a form of 'nation-building' in political discourse, uniting a core constituency around the fear of an outside threat.

Incitement of public anger at 'strangers' in the national community was the most easily accessible tool to shore up the shaky authority of new governments struggling to deliver on the promise of independence. Yet at the outset there were also reasonable arguments for the need to ensure that those resident in the new State were loyal and committed to its future; arguments that led to the very common ban on dual nationality in the newly adopted citizenship laws, as well as measures of affirmative action to rebalance colonial distortions of the economy and foster an 'indigenous' middle class of administrators and business people. When such legal measures moved into mass expulsions and other abuses, it was easy to respond that these groups had acquired their privileged position by similar means. But manipulation of nationality law has very often affected much more seriously people who had no connection with colonial abuses, or indeed the descendants of those who were themselves victims of colonial policies, especially of forced recruitment.

This chapter provides some case studies of the more egregious abuses of nationality law for political purposes. Most involve the situation of pre-independence immigrants, including both those from outside the African continent (Asians and Lebanese), and also those who were brought from neighbouring territories as labourers on colonial agricultural and infrastructure projects. New flows of refugee and migrants since independence add additional complexity, especially where it is hard to distinguish them from older arrivals. Several cases illustrate the situation of cross-border communities. Among the most vulnerable are pastoralist nomads (or those belonging to such communities whether or not they are in fact nomadic) whose traditional territory crosses contemporary international borders. Finally, there are the internal migrants, whose often precarious status illustrates the intimate linkages between recognition of citizenship at the local and national levels.

Zimbabwe provides perhaps the clearest example of policies of dispossession dating from the era of colonial and minority rule returning boomerang-like to give their perpetrators' descendants a knock-out blow. Yet those worst affected by the efforts to denationalise the 'former oppressors' have not been white Zimbabwean farmers but rather African migrants from neighbouring countries.

In the East African countries of Kenya and Uganda, unlike in Zimbabwe, virtually all those whites who had acquired land and property during the period of British colonial rule left at independence. Though vast white-owned estates still exist in Kenya, they are few, and resentment in the post-independence era has instead mainly been targeted at the South Asian migrants who came to East Africa at a time when the region and the Indian subcontinent were equally part of the British empire. Asians for the most part did not acquire large landed eStates, but they did achieve an economic success that came to be seen as a threat to the autonomy of the new States. To undercut the political power that relative wealth might have given them, the new States argued that these Asian immigrants should not have the right to be full citizens – and then took action accordingly. But other communities have found themselves with similar problems, including both the Nubian Kenyans who were brought to the country by the British from what is now Sudan; and Somali Kenyans, including those whose territory was incorporated within the borders of the Kenyan State at independence. In Uganda, the Banyarwanda similarly faced a fight to be recognised as legitimate Ugandans.

In West Africa, the Middle Eastern migrants who came to the region under colonial rule played a similar role as the South Asians in East Africa. They have remained a dominant economic force, whose right to nationality is often contested. In Sierra Leone, the law was amended immediately after independence to introduce restrictions on the citizenship of those who were not 'Negro Africans', defined – until 2006 – with reference to the male line only. As in East Africa, however, it is rather the status of African immigrants that has created the greatest challenges.

The instability and civil war that devastated Côte d'Ivoire's once-prosperous economy after 1999, displacing some 750,000 people and causing three million to require humanitarian assistance, was fundamentally rooted in the question of who was a 'real' citizen of the country. As one of those who took up arms stated: 'We needed a war because we needed our identity cards'.[2] Colonial-era cross-border migration, and the failure to create an effective and widely-accepted legal regime for the integration of these people and their descendants as Ivorian citizens, sowed the seeds of today's tensions. More recent migration kept the tensions alive and ready for exploitation by unscrupulous politicians. Each step towards denial of nationality was meticulously spelled out in laws, decrees and circulars.

While Côte d'Ivoire shows the impact of nationality law in one of the most legally formalistic countries in Africa, the post-independence history of the current

[2] 'Côte d'Ivoire: What's in a name? A fight for identity', UN Integrated Regional Information Network (IRIN), 1 November 2005.

Democratic Republic of Congo (DRC) illustrates the negative consequences of the manipulation of nationality law even in a country where the State's reach is far weaker. Congo's *jus sanguinis* citizenship law, with an explicit foundation in ethnicity, rendered hundreds of thousands of people doubtful as to their rights and legal status; and this uncertainty has repeatedly been used as a justification or excuse for taking up arms. The disputed status of the Kinyarwanda-speaking populations of the provinces of North and South Kivu in eastern DRC was at the heart of the conflicts that afflicted the region with devastating consequences from the early 1990s.

The final two case studies here illustrate different problems. In Mauritania, there was no major colonial-era population movement; the identity of the State has been contested rather because a dominant majority wishes to impose its cultural vision of the nation. Denationalisation has been applied by the 'white' Moors to 'black' Africans, both through mass expulsions, and through the more bureaucratic means of registration systems and amendments to the law. Nigeria's extreme diversity is more similar to that of DRC; so, too, is the relative unimportance (to date) of formal identity documents in its conflicts over identity and belonging. Yet, like DRC, Nigeria illustrates the relevance of legal frameworks even in an informalised system, and the inter-dependence of the national and local.

The stories of these crises and conflicts have been partly told in other publications: what this chapter aims to do, however, is show specifically how the application and abuse of the law played an important and sometimes unintended role. Even in quite dysfunctional States, law matters.

7.1. Dual Citizenship, Denationalisation and Disenfranchisement in Zimbabwe

What was then Southern Rhodesia was one of the most favoured destinations for white settlement under the British empire. Profitable commercial farms were rapidly established on the rich land expropriated from its former cultivators, and the colonial government established systems to recruit cheap labour from neighbouring Nyasaland (today's Malawi) and Northern Rhodesia (Zambia), as well as from Portuguese-held Mozambique. The nationality status of the people who came to Zimbabwe during this period (black and white) has remained under question till today.

Zimbabwe's citizenship law has roots that go back well before the attainment of universal suffrage in 1980. Administration of what is now Zimbabwe was chartered by the British crown to Cecil Rhodes' British South Africa Company in 1889. First known as Rhodesia, it became Southern Rhodesia when Northern Rhodesia was also annexed. In 1923, Southern Rhodesia became a British colony, and had a large measure of self-government, though it never became a 'dominion' under the scheme created in 1931. In 1948, it became an 'independent Commonwealth country' along with the former 'dominions' (including South Africa), a new status established by the British Nationality Act of 1948 (see Chapter 3.1). The Southern Rhodesian Citizenship and British Nationality Act 1949, the first nationality law for the territory, was adopted in line with the planned scheme for all the independent Commonwealth countries. It conferred citizenship on a *jus soli* basis, with the standard exceptions relating to those whose fathers had diplomatic status or were enemy aliens and, as a transitional measure, to those who were British subjects by birth, descent, naturalisation or annexation.[3] The same distinctions between the legal status of citizenship and the rights of different categories of citizens within the territory – between 'Europeans' and 'natives' – applied as within South Africa and other settler colonies, as well as the distinction between 'natives' and 'native foreigner' migrant workers. Africans were required to carry passes indicating their status.[4]

The white minority government in Southern Rhodesia successfully argued for a formal link to the protectorates of Nyasaland and Northern Rhodesia, overcoming the protests of the African leaders in those territories, to ease the import of labour for white-owned farms and mines. The 'Central African Federation' was established in 1953, by which time there were already a quarter of a million migrant farmworkers; migrant labour peaked at close to 300,000 in 1956.[5] Southern Rhodesian citizenship was suspended during the period that the Citizenship of Rhodesia and Nyasaland and British Nationality Act was in force; the migrant farmworkers from Northern Rhodesia and Nyasaland did not acquire the merged citizenship, remaining British protected persons (see Chapter 3.1). On the dissolution of the federation in 1963, a new law was adopted, the Citizenship of Southern Rhodesia and British Nationality Act, which provided for continuity of citizenship, and citizenship on a *jus soli* basis going forward, with the standard exceptions.[6]

White Rhodesian resistance to African enfranchisement proved irresolvable within the Commonwealth framework. Southern Rhodesia made its unilateral declaration of independence from Britain in November 1965, known as UDI, announcing that it was now the independent sovereign State of Rhodesia. The citizenship law became significantly more restrictive under the new regime. In 1967, the 1963 Act was amended to create a new exception to exclude from citizenship those born in Rhodesia whose fathers were 'prohibited immigrants' (in line with the South African law in force at the time).[7] A new Citizenship of

[3] Southern Rhodesia Citizenship and British Nationality (No. 13) Act 1949, s 6.

[4] James Muzondidya, 'Zimbabwe for Zimbabweans: Invisible Subject Minorities and the Quest for Justice and Reconciliation in Post-colonial Zimbabwe' in Brian Raftopoulos and Tyrone Savage (eds), *Zimbabwe: injustice and political reconciliation* (Institute for Justice and Reconciliation; Weaver Press 2005); Anusa Daimon, 'Politics of "Othering" and the Struggle for Citizenship in Independent Zimbabwe: Voices from Malawian Descendants' (2014) 44 Africa Insight 137. See ch 7.7 for a discussion of similar categories in Nigeria.

[5] Anusa Daimon, 'ZANU (PF)'s Manipulation of the "Alien" Vote in Zimbabwean Elections: 1980–2013' (2016) 68 South African Historical Journal 112.

[6] Citizenship of Southern Rhodesia and British Nationality (No. 63) Act 1963, ss 4–8.

[7] Citizenship of Rhodesia and British Nationality Amendment (No. 25) Act 1967.

Rhodesia Act adopted in 1970 continued this framework, and a 1972 amendment expanded the exceptions to further restrict transmission of citizenship on the basis of birth in the country for those born after the amendment came into force, requiring the father either to be a citizen or 'ordinarily resident' in Zimbabwe (or the mother if born out of wedlock).[8]

Though new foreign recruitment largely ceased with UDI, the existing workers remained. An end to white minority rule came in 1980 only after a protracted war of liberation, though ultimately negotiated through talks brokered by the British government. At that time, between a quarter and a half of farm workers were of foreign origin (though the majority had been born in Zimbabwe); there were also substantial numbers of workers of foreign descent in the mining and commercial sectors.[9] A new government was elected on the basis of universal suffrage, headed by Robert Mugabe (first as Prime Minister and from 1987 as president) as the leader of the dominant liberation movement, the Zimbabwe African National Union – Patriotic Front (ZANU-PF).

The twists and turns of Zimbabwe's citizenship law since majority rule was attained have shadowed the political history of the country. Rights based on birth in the territory were further restricted, and rules on dual citizenship interpreted to disenfranchise those Zimbabweans who might have a possible claim on some other citizenship – whether or not they actually held that citizenship in fact.

The 1979 Constitution of Zimbabwe provided for continuity of citizenship from previous laws, and carried into the new law restrictions on *jus soli* right to nationality that had first been enacted in 1967 and 1972; now, however, with equal rights for all racial categories.[10] Thus, it limited the transmission of citizenship by birth to children born in the country of a father (or, if out of wedlock, of a mother) who was a citizen or ordinarily resident and legally present in Zimbabwe; while transmission of citizenship to children born outside the country was limited to one generation, through provisions that stated that only a citizen 'otherwise than by descent' could pass on citizenship to a child also born outside the country. In the case of marriage, only the wife of a Zimbabwean citizen had the right to acquire citizenship on that basis, but not the husband.

An additional departure from the standard model in the independence constitutions in British protectorates in Africa was that, as a protection for white interests, the constitution initially allowed dual citizenship.[11] As in the case of constitutional

[8] Citizenship of Rhodesia (No. 11) Act 1970, as amended by Act No.49 of 1972, s 5(1)(c) and (d) (incorporated into the revised edition of the Statutes of Rhodesia 1974, Cap 23). See generally, *Fransman's British Nationality Law*, catalogue entry on Zimbabwe, and the history of citizenship law set out in *Piroro v Registrar General of Citizenship and Others*, Case No.HC 7248/10 [2011] ZWHHC 128.

[9] Amanda Hammar, Brian Raftopoulos and Stig Jensen (eds), *Zimbabwe's Unfinished Business: Rethinking Land, State and Nation in the Context of Crisis* (Weaver 2003); Angus Selby, 'Commercial Farmers and the State: Interest Group Politics and Land Reform in Zimbabwe' (DPhil, Oxford University 2006).

[10] Citizenship of Rhodesia Act, Cap 23, s 5; Constitution of Zimbabwe 1979, art 5.

[11] Constitution of Zimbabwe 1979, art 8.

provisions providing special protections for white Zimbabweans and restricting redistribution of land for the first decade of majority rule, this provision was opposed by ZANU-PF.[12] Unlike the other transitional arrangements, permission to hold dual nationality had no special constitutional protection. ZANU shared the same anxieties about dual loyalties as other newly independent African States, and moved quickly to address this question: in 1983, the constitution was amended to prohibit dual citizenship.[13]

A new citizenship law passed in 1984 confirmed this position and also introduced a comprehensive requirement that Zimbabwean citizens with entitlement to another citizenship declare by the end of 1985 that they had renounced any other citizenship, or automatically lose their Zimbabwean citizenship.[14] Perhaps two-thirds of the up to a quarter of a million white residents left the country during the years immediately after independence, but at least twenty thousand did renounce their entitlement to a foreign citizenship before Zimbabwean officials and kept or obtained Zimbabwean passports as a result; thousands more remained in the country as permanent residents but used foreign passports.[15]

However, when dual citizenship was abolished, many persons of foreign origin with less access to information than the white population typically had – especially farm workers – were considered to have lost their Zimbabwean citizenship because they had failed to sign the prescribed form renouncing their foreign citizenship. In 1990, the government provided a partial response to the excluded status of this group by adding a new provision to the constitution that extended the categories of voters entitled to vote in a presidential or parliamentary election beyond citizens to 'persons who, since 31 December 1985, have been regarded by virtue of a written law as permanently resident in Zimbabwe'.[16] Thus, the government ensured they were not deprived of the franchise as well as their citizenship – no doubt with the hope of obtaining their votes in return. Yet farm workers were still regarded with suspicion by the government, tainted by their association with white farm owners – even though they were amongst the lowest paid groups in

[12] Brian Raftopoulos, 'The State in Crisis: Authoritarian Nationalism, Selective Citizenship and Distortions of Democracy in Zimbabwe' in Amanda Hammar, Brian Raftopoulos and Stig Jensen (eds), *Zimbabwe's Unfinished Business: Rethinking Land, State and Nation in Zimbabwe in the Context of Crisis* (Weaver 2003).

[13] Constitution of Zimbabwe Amendment (No. 3) Act 1983.

[14] Citizenship of Zimbabwe (No. 23) Act 1984, art 9. Art 4 also required naturalising citizens to renounce their other nationality; and art 11 gave extremely wide discretion to the minister to deprive a person of citizenship.

[15] Brian Raftopoulos, 'Nation, Race and History in Zimbabwe' in Sara Dorman, Daniel Hammett and Paul Nugent (eds), *Making nations, creating strangers: States and citizenship in Africa* (Brill 2007); AP Cheater and Rudo Gaidzanwa, 'Transcending the State? Gender and Borderline Constructions of Citizenship in Zimbabwe' in Thomas M Wilson and Hastings Donnan (eds), *Border Identities: Nation and State at International Frontiers* (Cambridge University Press 1998).

[16] Constitution of Zimbabwe (Amendment No.11) Act, No.30 of 1990, inserting art 3(1)(b) to Sch 3 of the constitution.

Zimbabwe.[17] The question of dual citizenship remained live: in 1994, the government introduced, but was forced to abandon, a bill that required those with another citizenship to produce proof of renunciation from the relevant embassy, not just to submit a declaration to the Zimbabwean authorities that they had done so.[18]

Running in parallel with this racially charged debate on dual nationality was a separate (but related) argument over gender discrimination. Under Zimbabwean citizenship law, women did not have the right to pass on citizenship to their non-Zimbabwean husbands, nor to their children by a non-Zimbabwean father. Immigration law also subjected foreign husbands (but not wives) of Zimbabwean citizens to the discretion of the State in terms of their right to reside in Zimbabwe. In 1994, the Supreme Court of Zimbabwe, using its powers to interpret Zimbabwean law in light of international obligations, ruled in the *Rattigan* case that these restrictions violated the constitutional right of Zimbabwean women to freedom of movement.[19]

The government promptly introduced a bill to amend the constitution to enable the restrictions on foreign husbands to be reinstated. Just as in the case of dual citizenship, although the amendment was presented as a law that would only affect 'elite' women bringing husbands from overseas, most of those potentially affected were rural women living in Zimbabwe's border regions. Women's rights activists won a pyrrhic victory over the bill: the government conceded on the gender discrimination point, but the constitutional amendment was resubmitted and passed in a form that subjected any spouse (wife or husband) to a discretionary naturalisation procedure. At the same time, gender discrimination in the transmission of citizenship to children was removed for those born after the amendment came into effect. However, perhaps even more importantly, the previous right to citizenship of the child of a father ordinarily resident and legally present in Zimbabwe was not extended to a child of a mother with that status; instead, citizenship based on birth in Zimbabwe was restricted to children of citizens, removing any rights that came from birth in the territory (and with no protection against statelessness even for foundlings). Citizenship by descent was still limited to one generation born outside the country, as it had been since 1979 (and before).[20] Although existing rights to citizenship were stated to be preserved,

[17] Blair Rutherford, 'Shifting Grounds in Zimbabwe: Citizenship and Farm Workers in the New Politics of Land' in Sara Dorman, Daniel Hammett and Paul Nugent (eds), *Making nations, creating strangers: States and citizenship in Africa* (Brill 2007); Sam Moyo, Blair Rutherford and Dede Amanor-Wilks, 'Land Reform and Changing Social Relations for Farm Workers in Zimbabwe' (2000) 27 Review of African Political Economy 181.

[18] Musiwaro Ndakaripa, 'The State and Contested Citizenship in Zimbabwe, 1980–2011' in Sabelo J Ndlovu-Gatsheni and Finex Ndhlovu (eds), *Nationalism and national projects in Southern Africa: new critical reflections* (Africa Institute of South Africa 2013).

[19] *Rattigan and others v. Chief Immigration Officer, Zimbabwe, and others*, 1995 (2) SA 182 (ZS). See also Simon Coldham, 'Case Note: Devagi Rattigan and Others v Chief Immigration Officer and Others' (1994) 38 Journal of African Law 189.

[20] Constitution of Zimbabwe Amendment (No.14) Act 1996; Welshman Ncube, 'Defending and Protecting Gender Equality and the Family Under a Decidedly Undecided Constitution in

the status of the children of migrants who did not have documentation as citizens was immediately thrown into further doubt.

In 1999, a new opposition movement was formed, the Movement for Democratic Change (MDC), to contest upcoming elections and challenge the long dominance of ZANU-PF. The MDC campaigned against a proposed new constitution put forward by the government, which would have greatly strengthened the executive at the expense of Parliament as well as extending the powers of the government to acquire land compulsorily without compensation. The proposed changes were rejected in a February 2000 referendum. In June 2000, parliamentary elections were held. The MDC won 57 seats, only just short of the 62 seats won by ZANU-PF, and took 77% of the urban vote. ZANU-PF chose to attribute its losses to the MDC in the referendum and elections to the influence and finance of white Zimbabwean citizens considered anti-government, especially the approximately 4,000 white commercial farm owners, as well as the several hundred thousand farm workers and their families. In addition to mobilising violence against the opposition and other measures, steps were taken to amend the criteria for Zimbabwean citizenship, with the transparent aim of disenfranchising these groups.

In May 2000, the government warned whites they would be stripped of their Zimbabwean citizenship if they could not produce foreign documentation showing they had no entitlement to the citizenship of another country. Around 86,000 whites who had allegedly failed to renounce their British citizenship would have to turn in their Zimbabwean passports, a government newspaper advertisement stated; of these, around 30,000 were adults, able to vote.[21] In accordance with this announcement, the registrar-general's office began to refuse to renew the Zimbabwean passports of many whites, arguing they should have renounced any entitlement to foreign nationality to individual foreign governments.[22]

At least two court cases successfully challenged these provisions. In December 2000, the Supreme Court ordered the registrar-general to renew the passport of Robyn Carr because she had complied with the requirements of renunciation under Zimbabwean law by filling in a form of renunciation of citizenship, and the registrar-general had no power to require her to renounce her citizenship under British law.[23] In January 2001, Sterling Purser, an 18-year-old born in Harare in 1982 of a British father was denied a passport on the grounds he had not renounced his British citizenship. Purser challenged the decision, arguing that he had fulfilled the legal requirements to renounce his entitlement to foreign

Zimbabwe' in John Eekelaar and Ronald Thandabantu Nhlapo (eds), *The changing family: international perspectives on the family and family law* (Hart 1998); Tandeka C Nkiwane, 'Gender, Citizenship, and Constitutionalism in Zimbabwe: The Fight Against Amendment 14' (2000) 4 Citizenship Studies 325.

[21] 'Mugabe tries to bar whites from Zim poll', AFP, 13 May 2000.

[22] The registrar-general's office is responsible for maintaining the voters' roll and other aspects of elections, citizenship, passports, births, marriages and deaths, and for national population registration and the system of national identity cards.

[23] 'Court Rules on Zimbabwe Citizenship', AP, 1 December 2000; *Carr v Registrar-General*, 2000 (2) ZLR 433 (S).

citizenship, and the Supreme Court agreed, following its earlier ruling in the *Carr* case. In both cases, the Supreme Court awarded costs against the registrar-general.[24]

In light of these court defeats and the electoral results of 2000, the government increased its powers to revoke citizenship. The Citizenship Amendment Act No 12 of 2001 required a person with foreign citizenship to prove renunciation of the other citizenship under the relevant foreign law, and not only under Zimbabwean law, reviving the proposal from 1994.[25] A six-month deadline was set, expiring on 6 January 2002.

According to the State-owned media, quoting a government official, the amendment was required because '[t]here are concerns that those with dual citizenship are behind efforts to discredit the Government economically and politically by enlisting foreign governments to use diplomatic and other means to topple the ZANU-PF Government.'[26] Information Minister Jonathan Moyo described passports as 'privileges' not rights, and threatened their withdrawal from anyone involved in calls for international sanctions against Zimbabwe.[27]

While lawyers argued that the amendment Act only required those people who actually had documents evidencing dual citizenship to renounce their foreign citizenship (mainly those of European descent), the law came to be applied far more expansively. Registrar-General Tobaiwa Mudede placed an advertisement in a national newspaper stating that even those people with only a claim to foreign citizenship (but who had never sought confirmation of that citizenship in fact) had to renounce that potential citizenship. He repeatedly restated this position.[28] Thus, for example, a person born in Zimbabwe of a father of Malawian descent and a mother of Mozambican origin had to renounce entitlement to Malawian and Mozambican citizenship: something virtually impossible to do. Despite protests from farm workers' organisations at this interpretation of the Act, the registrar-general issued a statement confirming that 'any failure by farm workers to renounce foreign citizenship in the form and manner prescribed by the foreign law will result in loss of Zimbabwean citizenship after 6th January 2002.'[29] Before the 6 January deadline, the Mozambican High Commission in Harare stated that it was overwhelmed with applications for documentary proof that persons of Mozambican descent were not eligible for Mozambican citizenship, and were unable to

[24] 'Registrar-General loses citizenship case', *Daily News*, 17 January 2001.

[25] Citizenship Amendment (No. 12) Act 2001, s 3(c), amending s 9(7) of the Citizenship of Zimbabwe Act, ch 4:01. The amendment act also inserted a provision in art 13 to revoke the citizenship of a person who was absent from the country for five years.

[26] *Sunday Mail*, quoted in the *Zimbabwe Human Rights Bulletin*, Issue 5, Zimbabwe Lawyers for Human Rights, September 2001.

[27] 'Zim threatens to take away critics' passports', *The Star* (Johannesburg), 17 February 2001. Moyo later argued against just this position once he left ZANU-PF to become an independent MP. See Prof Jonathan Moyo, 'Constitutional madness will not save Zanu PF' *NewZimbabwe*.com, 26 August 2005.

[28] As noted by the 'Fourth Report of the Portfolio Committee on Defence and Home Affairs on the Citizenship of Zimbabwe Act', presented to Parliament 13 June 2007.

[29] 'Citizenship law under scrutiny', *Zimbabwe Independent*, 19 October 2001.

supply it.[30] Similarly, those who could not provide sufficient details to the Malawian High Commission in Harare to satisfy the consular officials that they were entitled to Malawian citizenship, were in the paradoxical situation that they could not therefore renounce that citizenship to the satisfaction of the Zimbabwean authorities.[31]

As Mudede confirmed, the vast majority of persons affected by the amendment were farm workers and others born in neighbouring countries or whose parents were born in neighbouring countries.[32] But although the amendment was given some publicity in the urban areas of Zimbabwe, many affected people in the outlying areas remained uninformed until the deadline had passed and their Zimbabwean citizenship had been lost by operation of law. Rectifying the situation was costly and time-consuming; in any event it would not restore citizenship by birth, but only the status of citizen by registration (making deprivation easier in future). In practice, people with ancestry from neighbouring countries came to be allocated 'alien' or 'citizen' identity cards on an almost random basis.[33]

Neither one thing nor the other: Testimony to the Research and Advocacy Unit, Harare[34]

'I was born in Zimbabwe. My mother was Zambian and my father was from Malawi. Both my parents are late now but before they died they both had Zimbabwean birth certificates, Zimbabwean identity documents and Malawian passports. I have a short birth certificate and a Zimbabwean identity document. When my parents were still alive and we were still young they got us Malawian passports and I have always been using a Malawian passport. I took my passport in 1995 and it expired in 2000.

I tried to renew my passport and the people at the Malawian embassy processed it but refused to give it to me when I went to collect it, saying that I needed to renounce my Zimbabwean citizenship before I could get the Malawian passport. To renounce Zimbabwean citizenship I had to prove that I am an alien. Proof that you are an alien is found on the long birth certificate certifying that you are an alien; I have a short birth certificate. The Malawian embassy also asked for a letter from the village headman of the kraal from which my ancestors in Malawi came from as proof that I am of Malawian origin. I do not know anyone in Malawi and I am sure if

[30] 'Zimbabwe loses second citizenship case', *The Star* (Johannesburg), 12 June 2002.

[31] 'Stateless Zimbabwe residents gain citizenship', IRIN, 21 June 2013.

[32] 'Submissions on the interpretation of citizenship laws to the Parliamentary Committee on Defence and Home Affairs', Zimbabwe Lawyers for Human Rights, 7 March 2007.

[33] Daimon (n 4).

[34] Case history from Rumbidzai Dube, 'A Right or a Privilege' (Research and Advocacy Unit 2008).

I were to go there no one would remember me. My home is in Zimbabwe, I was born here, I grew up here and I know no other place as home but this one. I know that I also will not be able to get a Zimbabwean passport if I try because the Registrar-General's office will also require me to renounce Malawian citizenship and I will have to prove my Malawian origin yet again. My father died with an identity card that showed that he was Zimbabwean. To make matters worse, the people at the Malawian embassy treated me badly. They refused to help me at first because I was not speaking to them in the Malawian language. I speak Shona because that is the language I have been speaking since I was born. I had to struggle to speak to them using the little I know of the Malawian language. One man was holding a long list of chiefs and headmen as he asked me where I said my ancestors came from. Other people who were there were turned away for making a mistake in identifying the correct chief or headman. Not having a passport has deprived me of my source of livelihood.

When I had a passport I used to be a cross border trader. I would go to Botswana and do piece meal jobs such as doing people's laundry, ironing and house cleaning. I could actually get enough money to buy all the things I needed to survive. Now my life is miserable. I do not have any money and I struggle just to get food on the table.'

A class action suit challenging the registrar-general's interpretation of the citizenship law was filed with the High Court in October 2001 by Lesley Leventhe Petho. Initially struck out by the High Court, on the grounds that Petho's case was not sufficiently typical to be the basis of a class action (he was born in Zimbabwe, the son of Hungarians who had fled the aftermath of the 1956 uprising) the Supreme Court confirmed the possibility of bringing a class action case in October 2002, providing Petho advertised in national newspapers and on radio to let others in the same plight know he was doing this.[35] The State-run Zimbabwe Broadcasting Corporation then refused to accept his advertisements, and negotiations to have the advertisements run at an affordable price never reached conclusion.

Several other cases were successfully brought in the High Court over the next year. In February 2002, the High Court ruled in a case brought by trade union and opposition leader Morgan Tsvangirai, stating that it could not be assumed that a person had a right to foreign citizenship only because his parents were born elsewhere and that a person could not be required to renounce what they had never possessed, and extending the deadline for renunciations to 6 August 2002.[36]

[35] *Petho v Minister of Home Affairs, Zimbabwe and Another* (07/06/02) [2002] ZWSC 80; *ZWNews*, 9 March 2003.

[36] *Tsvangirai v Registrar General and Others* (HC 12092/01) [2002] ZWHHC 29, 27 February 2002.

In May 2002, the High Court found in favour of Judith Todd, daughter of former Rhodesian Prime Minister Sir Garfield Todd, deposed as head of government when he tried to liberalise Rhodesia's apartheid-style rule, and herself a high-profile opponent of the former white minority regime. In 1998, she had become a shareholder and director of Associated Newspapers of Zimbabwe, publisher of the newly established independent newspaper the *Daily News*. The registrar-general asserted that Judith Todd should lose her citizenship because she had not renounced any claim to citizenship of New Zealand, where her father was born. The court, however, ruled that she was still a Zimbabwean citizen, and ordered the restoration of her passport.[37] She was issued a temporary passport, valid one year, and the government appealed. In June 2002, the High Court also ruled in favour of Ricarudo Manyere, a dancer of Mozambican parentage.[38]

Presidential elections were held in March 2002. In January, the first set of 'notices of objection' issued in terms of section 25 of the Electoral Act were sent to Zimbabwean citizens who had purportedly lost their Zimbabwean citizenship because they had failed to comply with the terms of the 2001 Citizenship Amendment Act. Each notice alleged that the person affected had lost his/her Zimbabwean citizenship and therefore was no longer entitled to remain on the voters' roll. The affected voter was given seven days to appeal to the constituency registrar. Many received these notices even though they had in fact renounced their alleged foreign citizenship and thus remained Zimbabwean citizens. In a large majority of the cases the notices were received after the seven-day deadline, and appeals were met with refusal by the registrar-general's office. Many affected farm labourers and rural dwellers never received the notices at all, and were summarily struck off the voters' roll.[39]

In parallel with the cases dealing with dual citizenship, the courts also ruled on the issue of the rights of permanent residents under the constitutional provision allowing permanent residents to vote. Lawyers argued that those who had supposedly lost their Zimbabwean citizenship under the new rules were nevertheless entitled to remain on the voters' roll, because they remained permanent residents. In January 2002, in another case brought by Morgan Tsvangirai, the High Court ordered the registrar-general to restore this group of persons to the voters' roll.[40] In February, however, the Supreme Court overturned this decision, holding that

[37] *Todd v Registrar General of Citizenship and Another* (HC 55/2002) [2002] ZWHHC 76, 7 May 2002.

[38] *Ricarudo Manyere v Registrar General* (HH 87/02), 27 February 2002, cited in 'Submissions on the interpretation of citizenship laws to the Parliamentary Committee on Defence and Home Affairs', Zimbabwe Lawyers for Human Rights, 7 March 2007; 'Zimbabwe loses second citizenship case', *The Star*, Johannesburg, 12 June 2002.

[39] See generally, Zimbabwe Lawyers for Human Rights, 'The Path to Disenfranchisement: 2002 General Elections', *Pambazuka News*, Issue 58, 21 March 2002; also 'More information on citizenship issues', Zimbabwe Lawyers for Human Rights, 19 April 2002, and other updates issued on citizenship, renunciation and passport issues available at http://archive.kubatana.net.

[40] *Tsvangirai v Registrar General of Elections and Another, Tsvangirai v Registrar General of Elections and Others* (HC 11843/01, HC 12015/01) [2002] ZWHHC 22, 25 January 2002.

citizenship and permanent residence were two separate statuses that could not be held at the same time, and those who had lost their citizenship were therefore not permanent residents by default and not entitled to vote.[41] Other cases in the High Court followed the Supreme Court's ruling.[42] Litigation on these issues was still under way as the presidential election was held on 9–11 March, including a challenge to a new statutory instrument issued on 9 March that changed the rules for disputes over the voters' roll. On the days of polling those people who had obtained orders from the magistrates' courts in favour of their right to be on the voters' roll were nonetheless denied the chance to vote.

Among those disenfranchised by the various legislative amendments was Sir Garfield Todd, who had, somewhat ironically, previously been deprived of his passport by the government of the last Rhodesian Prime Minister, Ian Smith.[43] Paying attention to symmetry, the government also refused to renew the passport of Ian Smith.[44]

In November 2002, the minister of justice published a cabinet-approved notice in the Government Gazette clarifying that renunciation of citizenship would not apply to a potential right to foreign citizenship, but only a to a person who was actually and presently a citizen of a foreign country.[45] Despite this, the registrar-general continued to apply the rule that renunciation applied to potential as well as actual citizenship.[46] Moreover, in February 2003, the Supreme Court – which by 2002 had been augmented by judges known to support the government – considered the government's appeal against the ruling in Judith Todd's case and agreed with the government's interpretation that a potential claim to citizenship had to be renounced, as well as an actual citizenship. It examined New Zealand law and concluded that although Judith Todd had not actively sought New Zealand citizenship at any time in her life, she was nevertheless entitled to it under the foreign law, and therefore should renounce such entitlement. If she did not do so within two days, she would lose Zimbabwean citizenship.[47] Todd attempted to comply with the ruling. The New Zealand authorities responded stating that Todd's application could not be processed as she had never laid claim to New Zealand citizenship.

The High Court, however, continued to rule against the registrar-general on the grounds that individuals had in fact no foreign citizenship to renounce.

[41] *Registrar General of Elections and Others v Tsvangirai* (30/2002) [2002] ZWSC 12, 28 February 2002.

[42] *Peter Jackson and 634 Others v Registrar-General* (HC 2434/02), 7 March 2002 (unreported).

[43] Judith Todd, 'When would-be heroes turn bad', *Mail & Guardian*, Johannesburg, 3 May 2007.

[44] Basildon Peta, 'Zimbabwe strips former PM Smith of his citizenship', *Independent*, London, 28 March 2002.

[45] General Notice 584 of 2002. In June 2007, a parliamentary committee of which MDC members formed a substantial part issued a report supporting the cabinet's 2002 notice. Fourth Report of the Portfolio Committee on Defence and Home Affairs on the Citizenship of Zimbabwe Act, 13 June 2007.

[46] Dube (n 34); Rumbidzai Dube, 'Identity, Citizenship, and the Registrar General: The Politicking of Identity in Zimbabwe' (Research and Advocacy Unit 2012).

[47] *Registrar General of Citizenship v Todd* (58/02/01) [2003] ZWSC 4, 27 February 2003.

In June 2005, the High Court handed down a judgment in favour of lawyer Job Sibanda, whose father was born in Malawi, finding that Sibanda was 'a Zimbabwean citizen with all privileges, duties and obligations attaching such citizenship'.[48] In 2006, the High Court confirmed the right of lawyer Lewis Uriri, born in Zimbabwe of Mozambican parents, to obtain a birth certificate for his son.[49] In January 2007, the High Court ordered the registrar-general to issue a passport to Trevor Ncube, owner of the independent and critical newspapers the *Zimbabwe Independent* and the *Standard*, who had been informed in December 2005 that he had forfeited his Zimbabwean citizenship because he had failed to renounce his Zambian citizenship (his father was allegedly born in Zambia).[50] Ncube's passport was restored to him.

Zimbabwe's neighbours in the Southern African Development Community (SADC) were feeling the impact of this campaign of denationalisation. In Mozambique, UNHCR identified hundreds of stateless individuals who were mainly returnees from Zimbabwe and who did not have recognition of either Mozambican or Zimbabwean citizenship.[51] Malawi was willing to restore citizenship if evidence was available, but the process was expensive and difficult to access; an unknown number of diaspora returnees did not have any citizenship documents.[52] In South Africa, the authorities eventually responded to the crisis by adopting a twelve-month 'special dispensation permit' for Zimbabweans on the basis of the 2002 Immigration Act, granting the right to legally live and work in the country (later extended several times).[53]

Protests from the region led to concessions in favour of descendents of migrant workers. In 2003 the Citizenship of Zimbabwe Act was amended again to allow people who were born in Zimbabwe, but whose parents came to Zimbabwe from another SADC country as farm labourers, mine workers, domestic employees or 'in any other unskilled occupation', to apply for 'confirmation' of their citizenship of Zimbabwe and at the same time sign a form renouncing their foreign citizenship (without the need to obtain any documentation from the other SADC country).[54] Although this should have substantially improved the situation of the many farmworkers who had been rendered stateless, the amendment was published after most of the people concerned had already lost their Zimbabwean citizenship, and

[48] *Job Sibanda v Registrar-General of Citizenship and Others* (HH 3626/02); 'Man born of foreign parents is Zimbabwean – Judge', *Legalbrief Today*, 20 June 2005.

[49] *Lewis Uriri v Registrar General of Citizenship and another* (HH 7128/03); 'Submissions on the interpretation of citizenship laws to the Parliamentary Committee on Defence and Home Affairs', Zimbabwe Lawyers for Human Rights, 7 March 2007.

[50] *Trevor Ncube v Registrar-General* (HH 7316/06), 25 January 2007.

[51] 'Mozambique: UNHCR to Support Registeration of Stateless People', UNHCR, 5 October 2011.

[52] According to information provided at a UNHCR regional Statelessness meeting, 1–3 November 2011, Malawi restored citizenship to 85 persons during the period 2008 to 2011.

[53] Tara Polzer, 'Regularising Zimbabwean Migration to South Africa' (Forced Migration Studies Program University of the Witwatersrand and Consortium for Refugees and Migrants in South Africa 2009).

[54] Citizenship of Zimbabwe Amendment (No. 12) Act 2003, ch 4, art 9A(d).

did not have retroactive effect; while burdensome administrative requirements were imposed, and the attitude of the authorities did not change in practice.[55]

Moreover, in 2005, the Constitution of Zimbabwe Amendment (No. 17) Act finally repealed the constitutional provision allowing permanent residents to vote, removing any remaining ambiguity about the rights of those who were caught in the potential dual citizenship trap.[56] Their problems were extended by a new law to support the 'economic empowerment of indigenous Zimbabweans'.[57] The law entered into force in 2010, with a deadline for disinvestment of September 2011, at which time even the smallest businesses found themselves subject to renewed harassment if they could be alleged to be 'non-indigenous'.[58]

Parliamentary and presidential elections took place in March 2008, though MDC presidential candidate Morgan Tsvangirai withdrew from the second round of the presidential elections, citing State-sponsored violence against the opposition. Mugabe was declared the winner, but agreed to take part in talks mediated by SADC. In September 2008, a two-year power-sharing agreement known as the Global Political Agreement (GPA) was reached, and on 30 January 2009, the MDC formed a unity government with ZANU-PF.[59] Tsvangirai became prime minister, a new position, while Mugabe remained president. A maximum 18-month timetable for the coming into force of a new constitution was established, to be followed by new elections.

The constitutional amendment allowing for the installation of a government of national unity also revised the citizenship provisions.[60] The amendments expanded the law to provide a right to citizenship deriving from grandparents in some circumstances – but did not restore the rights to citizenship based on birth in the country that had existed until 1996 for children born in Zimbabwe of legal residents, confirming a purely descent-based system. The amendment kept the terminology of citizens by birth and by descent, but removed the restriction on transmission of citizenship to children born outside the country, critical for the diaspora who had left the country.[61] However, the language on registration of

[55] Zimamoza Institute, 'Ethnic Cleansing In Zimbabwe: The Origins and Objectives of the Zimamoza Institute' (2007); Daimon (n 5); Daimon (n 4).

[56] Constitution of Zimbabwe Amendment (No.17) Act 2005, s 20(b), repealing schedule 3, article 3(1)(b) of the Constitution on 'Qualifications and disqualifications for voters'. See also, 'Representations on the Bill made by the Zimbabwe Human Rights NGO Forum to the Portfolio Committee on Justice, Legal and Parliamentary Affairs', 4 August 2005.

[57] Indigenisation and Economic Empowerment (No. 14) Act 2007, preamble and s 2.

[58] 'Some are more indigenous than others', IRIN, 14 October 2011.

[59] The MDC had split into two factions by this time; both factions joined the unity government.

[60] Constitution of Zimbabwe Amendment (No. 19) Act 2009. The Citizenship Act (last amended in 2003), however, continued to quote the pre-1996 version of the constitution.

[61] A child born in Zimbabwe was a citizen by birth if either parent was a citizen (of any type), or if any grandparent was a citizen by birth or descent (that is, not if the grandparent was only registered as a citizen). A child born outside Zimbabwe was also a citizen by birth if one of the parents was a citizen (of any type) and 'ordinarily resident' in Zimbabwe or working for the State or an international organisation. A child born outside Zimbabwe was a citizen by descent if either parent or any grandparent was at the time of the birth a citizen 'by birth or descent' or if either parent was a citizen by registration.

births of children born outside the country was amended to require registration '*in Zimbabwe* in accordance with the law relating to the registration of births'; leaving an ambiguity as to whether consular registration would be sufficient.[62] In 2013, the Ministry of Home Affairs announced an effort to stop the issue of fake Zimbabwean birth certificates to those born out of the country, centralising the system in Harare.[63]

The constitutional amendment did not generally prohibit dual citizenship, though it permitted legislation to provide for loss of citizenship by descent or registration (only). The Citizenship Act's existing provisions were not, however, amended, and efforts to prevent those with a *potential* other nationality from claiming citizenship continued. In 2011, a Canadian-based Zimbabwean whose citizenship was denied on the grounds that his father had been born in Mozambique, so that he must renounce Mozambican citizenship, obtained an order confirming he was a citizen and instructing the registrar-general to renew his passport. The High Court ruled that the Citizenship Act's provisions requiring a citizen from birth with dual citizenship to renounce the other citizenship were in breach of the amended constitution.[64] In another case, however, the High Court failed to confirm the Zimbabwean citizenship of a white Zimbabwean and election expert who had acquired South African citizenship after being declared an 'undesirable person' in Zimbabwe in 2005, on the grounds that he had himself acquired the other nationality, rejecting arguments that under the circumstances this was not a 'voluntary act'.[65] The Supreme Court eventually overturned this ruling, deciding that a citizen of Zimbabwe by birth could not lose citizenship and be declared a prohibited immigrant.[66]

Meanwhile, a flurry of government initiatives were taken to crack down on sham marriages, including the extraordinary requirement that a foreign national must produce a 'certificate of no marriage' from the country of origin

[62] As of 2008, birth registration and a birth certificate were free for those born in Zimbabwe, but the parents of a child born in South Africa had to pay a deposit of ZAR110 (around US$15) into the Zimbabwean consulate's bank account, and then US$50 on submitting the required forms for the certificate noting the birth abroad issued by the registrar-general's office in Harare. Dube (n 34); Dube (n 46).

[63] Eugene Majuru. 'Diaspora dual birth certificates scam for children exposed', ZimDiaspora.com, 6 January 2013.

[64] Alex Bell, 'Registrar-General faces court action after refusing Zim man passport', SW Radio Africa, 26 October 2011; *Piroro v Registrar General* 2011(2) ZLR 26 (H); 'Justice Bhunu reserves judgment in the Mudede passport case', Zimbabwe Lawyers for Human Rights (ZLHR), 27 October 2011.

[65] *Whitehead v Registrar-General and others*, HH-349-12, judgment delivered 13 September 2012, noted in Legal Resources Foundation Case Summaries, July–December 2012, available at http://www.lrfzim.com/case-summaries/. The applicant was born in Southern Rhodesia of a naturalised Rhodesian father (born in South Africa) and a mother also born in the country, and had renounced any claim to South African citizenship in 2002. He had acquired South African citizenship after being declared an undesirable person in Zimbabwe in 2005, in order to avoid being stateless.

[66] Silas Nkala, 'Whitehead Wins Citizenship Case', *The Standard*, 15 September 2013.

before marrying in Zimbabwe[67]; a new register of marriage officers, and a ban on 'mass weddings'.[68]

The government of national unity was shaky and often acrimonious, but the coalition finally succeeded in agreeing a new constitution, approved by referendum in March 2013. Citizenship, especially dual citizenship, was a key point of disagreement in these debates. Public opinion polling showed that dual citizenship remained unpopular, but also that 65% of Zimbabweans supported the grant of citizenship based on birth in Zimbabwe.[69] Fresh elections were held in July 2013, with the voters' roll and status of alleged 'aliens' a continuing point of contention. Mugabe was re-elected as president and ZANU-PF gained a two-thirds majority in the parliamentary poll; the MDC rejected the election outcome, unsuccessfully challenged some results in the courts, and boycotted the opening of the new Parliament in September.[70]

The new constitution retained many of the changes on citizenship that had already been made in 2009: the provisions on citizenship by birth and descent were the same, with the distinction between citizens by birth and by descent becoming meaningful only in the context of the provisions on dual citizenship.[71] The constitution was now silent on the question of dual citizenship for citizens by birth, providing only that parliament may make legislation regarding 'the prohibition of dual citizenship in respect of citizens by descent or registration'. The constitution generally preserved the framework introduced in 1996 (and kept in 2009) by which birth in the territory gave no rights to citizenship. It did, however, introduce for the first time a provision protecting children of unknown parents from Statelessness: a child found in Zimbabwe 'who is, or appears to be, less than fifteen years of age, and whose nationality and parents are not known, is presumed to be a Zimbabwean citizen by birth'.[72]

The MDC also ensured that the new constitution included a provision aimed at redressing some of the injustices of the previous decade against persons with a parent who was a citizen of a neighbouring country. A person born in Zimbabwe before the constitution came into force of one parent who was a SADC citizen was recognised as a citizen by birth; though only if the person was 'ordinarily resident in Zimbabwe' when the constitution came into effect (excluding many of those who had left the country as a result of being denied citizenship, or seeking work and income elsewhere).[73]

[67] 'Zimbabwe clamps down on sham marriages', *New Zimbabwe*, 1 February 2012; 'Court blocks MDC-T MP's "sham marriage"' *New Zimbabwe*, 10 March 2012; 'Evelyn Masaiti finally marries her man', *New Zimbabwe*, 29 March 2012.

[68] 'Zimbabwe bans mass weddings', Nehanda Radio, 17 July 2012.

[69] *Eldred v Masunungure and Heather Koga*, 'Zimbabweans' (Mostly) Tolerant Views on Citizenship' (Afrobarometer 2013).

[70] Mmanaledi Mataboge and Takudzwa Munyaka, 'MDC-T resolves to reject Zim election results', *Mail & Guardian* (South Africa), 2 August 2013.

[71] Bronwen Manby, 'Draft Zim Constitution Fails Citizenship Test' www.osisa.org, 11 October 2012.

[72] Constitution of Zimbabwe 2013, ch 3 (ss 35 to 43).

[73] Constitution of Zimbabwe 2013, s 43(2).

Many of those who had been affected by the previous rules began to re-apply for confirmation of Zimbabwean citizenship, including some of the poorest people desperate to reassert their right to be Zimbabwean, and thus be able once again to cross the border freely, establish a bank account, get a job, or rent an official trading site. Yet, despite the removal of the constitutional ban on dual citizenship (at least for citizens from birth), the registrar-general continued to deny passports to those who had acquired another citizenship.[74] Court applications challenged this refusal: in June 2013, the Constitutional Court ruled that Mutumwa Mawere, one of Zimbabwe's richest businessmen, who had obtained South African citizenship, was entitled to be reinstated with Zimbabwean citizenship and a passport without renouncing his other nationality.[75] A year later, the court confirmed the right of a Zimbabwean who had also held South African nationality since birth to reside in Zimbabwe without a residence permit.[76] But, with a new Citizenship Act not yet proposed by the end of 2017, the registrar-general was still left significant latitude to apply the old rules to those seeking identity documents, unless specifically ordered otherwise in an individual case.[77] Voter registration in 2017 in preparation for 2018 elections was once again plagued by the same issues.[78]

Throughout this history, the government of Zimbabwe was careful to follow the forms of the law. The registrar-general insisted that nobody was made Stateless when he refused to issue documents confirming Zimbabwean citizenship, on the grounds that those affected held another citizenship; and for the most part he respected individual court orders against him. While there was certainly much arbitrary decision-making, each effort to disenfranchise those who might vote against the ruling party was set out in the small print of law and regulation. The methods used were those that had been first established through the executive discretion to determine entitlement to nationality given by the British legal model.

7.2. The 'Lebanese' of Sierra Leone

In Sierra Leone, the post-independence government mobilised citizenship law in two main ways: specifically to frustrate the political ambitions of John Akar,

[74] Alex Bell, 'Zim Citizenship Rules in Chaos As Nationals Denied Documentation', SW Radio Africa (London), 22 October 2013; Daimon (n 5).

[75] Violet Gonda, 'Mawere wins landmark dual citizenship case', SW Radio Africa (London), 27 June 2013.

[76] 'Constitutional Court endorses dual citizenship', ZBC, 25 June 2014.

[77] Mthulisi Mathuthu, 'Confusion on Zimbabwe dual citizenship continues', Bulawayo24.com, 8 July 2014; Zvamaida Murwira, 'Scramble for Zim citizenship, Enquiries flood from all over the world, RG's office overwhelmed', *The Herald*, 23 July 2014; 'Citizenship Act Needs Realignment', *The Herald*, 25 July 2014; Mthulisi Mathuthu, 'Government Delays Realignment of Laws', SW Radio Africa (London), 29 July 2014.

[78] Veritas Zimbabwe, 'Election Watch 7-2017 – ZEC Press statement on Voter Registration for Zimbabwean Citizens whose National IDs are Marked "ALIEN"', 4 August 2017; *The Legal Monitor* (special edition on citizenship), Zimbabwe Lawyers for Human Rights, 30 November 2017.

a prominent mixed-race Lebanese-Sierra Leonean, in the immediate aftermath of independence; and more generally to restrict access to political power and economic security of the wealthy community of Lebanese descent. These provisions remained in place at the end of 2017, despite reforms to create gender equality and proposals to remove race discrimination. As a subsidiary point, but in a similar way, legal definitions of membership were also deployed to restrain the reach of the Krio community descended from 'returned' slaves and others of African origin settled in Sierra Leone by the British.

The kernel for the British Colony of Sierra Leone was founded in 1787, when several hundred immigrants, made up largely but not only of London's 'poor blacks' supported by funds from the abolitionist movement, arrived in the territory and established the first new settlement. In 1792, bolstered by the arrival of ex-slaves from Nova Scotia, the settlers established Freetown, and were joined there by other 'returnees' from Jamaica and America. Then, from the date of the abolition of the slave trade by the British Parliament in 1807, the British navy began intercepting slave ships travelling from Africa to the Americas, and landed thousands of freed slaves in Freetown, where a naval base had been established. The territory previously managed by the private Sierra Leone Company was surrendered to the British Crown in the same year. Though contacts both peaceful and military between the Colony and the interior then steadily increased, it was not until 1896 that a British Protectorate was declared over the remaining territory of what is now Sierra Leone.

During the last decade of the nineteenth century, migrants from what are now Syria and Lebanon but was then the Ottoman Empire began arriving in Freetown, which had become a thriving port. By the date of independence, around 3,000 individuals of Middle Eastern descent, known collectively as 'Lebanese', were living within the borders of either the Colony or the Protectorate, among 18,300 estimated to be in West Africa as a whole.[79] Others continued to arrive, especially during the civil war in Lebanon, though many left again during Sierra Leone's own civil war. Many 'Lebanese' resident in Sierra Leone today have parents and grandparents born in Sierra Leone and are highly integrated; at the same time, a strong Lebanese identity is retained by some, through institutions such as the Lebanese International School in Freetown.[80]

The Lebanese in Sierra Leone, as elsewhere in West Africa, are for the most part businesspeople, dominating commerce in the large towns, and the diamond

[79] HL van der Laan, *The Lebanese Traders in Sierra Leone* (Mouton 1975); Neil O Leighton, 'The Political Economy of a Stranger Population: The Lebanese of Sierra Leone' in William A Shack and Elliott P Skinner (eds), *Strangers in African Societies* (University of California Press 1979); Andrew Arsan, *Interlopers of Empire: The Lebanese Diaspora in Colonial French West Africa* (Oxford University Press 2014).

[80] Lina Beydoun, 'The Complexities of Citizenship among Lebanese Immigrants in Sierra Leone' (2013) 3 African Conflict & Peacebuilding Review 112; Michael Humphrey, 'Lebanese Identities: Between Cities, Nations and Trans-Nations' (2004) 26 Arab Studies Quarterly 31; Chris Bierwirth, 'The Lebanese Communities of Côte d'Ivoire' (1999) 98 African Affairs 79.

trade in particular. In the context of the drive to 'Africanise' the economy common to most post-independence African States, resentment of the Lebanese role as middlemen and supporters of the colonial government meant that they were early targets of efforts to reduce their privileged economic position and formalise their status as 'strangers' in the new State. Yet Lebanese money was freely drawn on by political parties to support their own efforts to gain office.

In 1961, the independence constitution of Sierra Leone created a single nationality, without any distinction by race, ethnic group or sex. 'Every person' born in the former colony or protectorate who was a citizen of the UK and colonies or a British protected person on 26 April 1961 became a citizen of Sierra Leone on 27 April 1961, unless neither of his or her parents nor any of his or her grandparents was born in Sierra Leone; those born outside the country became citizens if their father became a citizen under this provision. Others born in the country, but without a parent or grandparent also born there, could apply to register as citizens, a non-discretionary form of naturalisation. In addition to these transitional provisions, the constitution provided for citizenship to be attributed automatically to everyone born in the country after the date of independence (with the standard exception for children of diplomats), and to a child born outside the country to a Sierra Leonean father (himself born in the country).[81] The 1961 constitution also had an extensive bill of rights including a non-discrimination provision (with some exclusions in relation to customary law). Dual citizenship was forbidden for adults, in line with usual African and international practice at that time. Legislation provided details on citizenship by naturalisation and registration and on renunciation and deprivation of citizenship.[82]

Within a year after independence, Sierra Leone's constitutional provisions on citizenship were amended three times to become more restrictive and discriminate against individuals on the basis of race and sex.[83] First, an act deleted the transitional provisions of the constitution providing for non-discretionary registration of those excluded from automatic acquisition of citizenship for lack of a parent or grandparent born in the country.[84] Then, the words 'of negro African descent' were inserted immediately after the words 'every person' in relation both to those

[81] Constitution of Sierra Leone, 1961, ss 1, 2 and 4.

[82] Sierra Leone Nationality and Citizenship (No. 10) Act 1962.

[83] Constitution (Amendment) (No. 11) Act 1962; Constitution (Amendment) (No.2) Act, No.12 of 1962; and Constitution (Amendment) (No.3) Act, No.39 of 1962. The amendments were subsequently consolidated in the Constitution (Consolidation of Amendments) (No. 52) Act 1965.

[84] Whereas s 2(1) of the 1961 Constitution had provided that 'Any person who, but for the proviso to subsection (1) of section 1 of this Constitution [relating to the exclusion from citizenship of those without a parent or grandparent born on the territory] would be a citizen of Sierra Leone by virtue of that subsection *shall be entitled*, upon making an application before the 27th day of April 1963 … to be registered as a citizen of Sierra Leone.' (Emphasis added). This subsection was repealed by the Constitution (Amendment) (No.11) Act 1962, and although the Sierra Leone Nationality and Citizenship (No. 10) Act 1962, dealt generally with registration and naturalisation as a citizen, this particular provision was not re-enacted. All of these amendments were deemed to have come into effect on the date of independence.

who automatically became citizens at independence and those born on the territory after independence, to apply retroactively from the date of independence. At the same time, the restriction on *jus soli* citizenship for those whose father held diplomatic status or was an enemy alien was lifted – so a person of negro African descent born in Sierra Leone would become a citizen, whatever the status of the parents. Finally, the non-discrimination clause that prohibited any law that is 'discriminatory of itself or in its effect', was amended to exclude laws relating to the limitation of citizenship to persons of negro African descent. Individuals who were not of 'negro African descent' but who had acquired citizenship by virtue of the 1961 Constitution were thus stripped of their citizenship of Sierra Leone after less than a year, and many more who should have been able to opt for citizenship by a simple application process had that right taken away. Moving forward, no person born on Sierra Leonean territory not of negro African descent would be a citizen by birth.[85] In these amendments, Sierra Leone was clearly inspired by the tradition in neighbouring Liberia, where the constitution had, since the first version was adopted in 1847, always provided that only a 'Negro' could be a citizen, whatever the other circumstances.[86]

The 1962 constitutional amendments defined 'person of negro African descent' as follows: 'a person whose father and his father's father are or were negroes of African origin', introducing both racial and gender discrimination at one step. Even if a person was born in Sierra Leone of a 'negro African' mother, that person could not qualify for citizenship by birth if that person's father and grandfather were not *both* of negro African descent. The amendments permitted a person whose mother was a negro of African descent could apply to be registered as a citizen, though only on a discretionary basis.[87] However, a registered citizen did not qualify to become a member of the House of Representatives or of any local elected body, unless he or she had been resident in Sierra Leone or served in the army for twenty-five years.[88] Nor did the law provide how registration should be done; the new Citizenship Act did not take account of this further amendment to the constitution.

Subsequent laws restricted the rights of non-citizens to acquire property both in the Western Area (the historic Colony of Sierra Leone, comprising Freetown

[85] In Britain, meanwhile, the 1962 Commonwealth Immigrants Act introduced for the first time restrictions on immigration to Britain for citizens of former colonies. Though not explicitly racial in its language, the new provisions were aimed at non-white immigrants from the newly independent countries of Africa and the Caribbean; the effect was to leave some residents of former British colonies with no right of citizenship in any country.

[86] See chs 4.3 and 5.1.

[87] 'Any person, either of whose parents is a negro of African descent and who would, but for the provisions of subsection (3) [requiring the father and father's father to be negroes of African origin] have been a Sierra Leone citizen, *may* … be registered as a citizen of Sierra Leone, but such person shall not be qualified to become a member of the House of Representatives, or of any District Council or other local authority unless he shall have resided continuously in Sierra Leone for twenty-five years after such registration or shall have served in the civil or regular Armed Services of Sierra Leone for a continuous period of twenty five years'.

[88] Sierra Leone Constitution (Amendment) (No.2) Act, No. 12 of 1962, s 2(b).

and the surrounding area) and in the provinces (though it did not take any right away from those non-citizens who had already purchased property in the Western Area).[89] In 1965 and 1966, the government introduced successive acts restricting non-citizens' ability to own and profit from retail trade; in 1969 a new government widened the scope of restrictions.[90] These new laws – which to a large extent allowed money to be extorted from those affected, rather than preventing businesses operating altogether – were also extended to other Africans resident in Sierra Leone, and not just Lebanese and Europeans; affecting in particular the large community of Fula traders, many originating from neighbouring Guinea.[91] Another act required all non-citizens to register their presence, and gave the government extensive powers to expel non-citizens in the interests of the 'public good'.[92]

These legal changes were motivated not only by resentment of Lebanese and other foreign dominance of the commercial economy, but also by political considerations. In particular, the initial aim was to narrow the set of candidates eligible to contest elections due to be held in 1962, by depriving Lebanese and mixed-race Sierra Leoneans of the political rights conferred by citizenship.

John Joseph Akar, a prominent mixed-race Sierra Leonean with political ambitions, became the best known case of those affected by the changes to citizenship law and the face of efforts to reverse them. Akar's mother was a black Sierra Leonean; his father was of Lebanese origin and thus not 'of negro African descent', though he had never visited Lebanon. When Sierra Leone became independent on 27 April 1961, Akar automatically became a citizen by operation of the constitution, as both he and one of his parents had been born in Sierra Leone. With the 1962 amendments, however, he lost his citizenship by birth; though he did apply for and was granted citizenship by registration. He challenged the amendments in court. In his application, he contended that the true intention of the amendments was to exclude persons not of negro African descent from being elected to the House of Representatives.

This litigation proceeded against a turbulent political background, from which Akar himself was excluded. In 1964, Sir Milton Margai, leader of the Sierra Leone People's Party (SLPP) and the new State's first Prime Minister, died and was succeeded by his brother Sir Albert Margai. In closely contested elections in March 1967, Siaka Stevens, candidate of the All People's Congress (APC), was declared winner over Margai – only to be ousted in a coup within a few hours. A year of military rule by successive groups was ended with a return to civilian rule

[89] The Non-Citizens (Interests in Land) Act of 1966.

[90] Non-Citizens (Restriction of Retail Trade) Act 1965; Non-Citizens (Restriction of Trade and Business) Act 1965; Non-Citizens (Trade and Business) Act 1969. A 1966 Act was repealed the same year.

[91] See Alusine Jalloh, *African Entrepreneurship: Muslim Fula Merchants in Sierra Leone* (Ohio University Center for International Studies 1999) 85–86.

[92] Non-Citizens (Registration, Immigration and Expulsion) Act 1965.

in 1968 under Siaka Stevens. Though further disturbances and attempted coups followed, Stevens retained power for the next 17 years, first as Prime Minister and then, after a republican constitution was adopted in 1971, as President.

Akar's case succeeded in the first hearing in 1967, but the Court of Appeal in Freetown reversed the decision. Akar appealed to the Privy Council in London (then the highest court for Sierra Leone). In 1969 the Privy Council reversed the Court of Appeal and declared that the amendment was of no effect, though on different grounds from the judge at first instance.[93] The victory was short lived. The Siaka Stevens government disregarded the judgment and re-enacted the discriminatory provisions in a completely reworked Citizenship Act adopted in 1973.[94] The 1971 constitution removed the right of appeal to the Privy Council.

The 1973 Citizenship Act granted citizenship by birth to anyone born in Sierra Leone before 19 April 1971, or resident in Sierra Leone on 18 April 1971, provided that his or her father *or* grandfather was born in Sierra Leone and he or she was 'a person of negro African descent'. Those born after 19 April were deemed to be citizens of Sierra Leone by birth, subject to the same conditions. Dual citizenship was excluded. Persons entitled to apply for naturalisation under the 1973 Act were foreign women married to citizens, other persons of negro African descent born in Sierra Leone, and persons of negro African descent continuously resident for a period of not less than eight years.[95] Persons who whose mothers were black Sierra Leonean but whose fathers were not 'negro African' could in principle apply to be naturalised under this provision, though no procedures to do so were initially established. The 1973 Act did not define who was a negro African, relying on the 1971 Interpretation Act, which stated: "negro African descent' used in relation to any person means that his father and paternal grandfather were African negroes', adding some extra confusion by its slight variation from the 1962 constitutional amendment.[96] The presumption was that the phrase meant black African, reducing the essential condition for the acquisition of citizenship to the colour of the person's skin. Thus a black man's children by a Sierra Leonean woman were understood to be citizens by birth wherever they were born.[97] A white or mixed-race man's children by a Sierra Leonean woman could only acquire Sierra Leonean

[93] *Akar v Attorney General*, Sierra Leone Supreme Court, 1967; *Attorney General v Akar*, Court of Appeal Decision, 1968; *Akar v Attorney General*, Privy Council Appeal No.20/68, 30 June 1969. See case notes in JPWB McAuslan, 'John Joseph Akar v Attorney General' (1968) 12 Journal of African Law 89; JPWB McAuslan, 'John Joseph Akar v Attorney General' (1969) 13 Journal of African Law 103. Akar was appointed ambassador for Sierra Leone to the US while the appeal was still pending.

[94] Sierra Leone Citizenship (No. 4) Act 1973. The 1971 Constitution did not include provisions on citizenship, except in that it repeated the exclusion of limitations on citizenship from the non-discrimination article. There was therefore a two year hiatus, before the adoption of new legislation in 1973, in which the citizenship provisions were entirely unclear.

[95] Sierra Leone Citizenship Act 1973, ss 7 and 8.

[96] Interpretation (No. 8) Act 1971.

[97] In fact, by a quirk in the legal drafting, a child born in Sierra Leone who did not have a parent also born there was not, technically, automatically attributed citizenship, even if the parent was a citizen. This error was disregarded.

citizenship by naturalisation. The 1983 Births and Deaths Registration Act reinforced this discrimination by requiring the officer registering a child's birth to include the race of the child's parents in the birth certificate.[98]

In 1974, the constitution was amended to provide greater restrictions on access to public office by naturalised and non-negro-African citizens.[99] Yet further restrictions were enacted in 1976.[100] After a period of 25 years, the restrictions could be lifted; but only by parliamentary resolution passed by a two-thirds majority.

Those without a parent of negro-African descent did not even have a right to naturalise until an amendment to the Citizenship Act came into force in 1977, which allowed for individuals over 21 years of age and without a parent of negro-African descent to apply for naturalisation based on a residence period of 15 years, renunciation of any other citizenship, and other criteria.[101] Those under 21 could apply to naturalise only if one of their parents was already naturalised: the children of naturalised citizens were issued with Sierra Leonean passports, but as soon as the children were 18 years old the Immigration Department required these passports to be returned. Persons of 'negro-African descent' born in Sierra Leone, however, could apply for naturalisation at any time, with no further requirements; and those with a parent of negro-African descent not born in the country could apply for naturalisation after only eight years. The minister was not required to give any reason for the refusal of any application for naturalisation and his decision on any such application could not be challenged in any court.[102] The minister also had very wide powers to revoke the grant of citizenship by naturalisation. A person whose certificate is revoked ceased to be a Sierra Leonean and might be subject to expulsion.[103] Naturalisation became progressively more nearly impossible to obtain.

[98] Act No.11 of 1983. Although the birth certificate was later amended to require the parents' nationality (rather than race) to be stated, 'Lebanese' may be recorded in cases where the parents are of Lebanese origin, even though the *nationality* of the parents is not Lebanese. Jamesina King, 'Africa Discrimination and Citizenship Audit: Sierra Leone' (Open Society Justice Initiative 2005).

[99] Constitution (Amendment) (No. 6) Act 1974.

[100] Sierra Leone Citizenship Amendment (No. 13) Act 1976, s 8(5); Constitution (Consequential Provisions) Act 1976. See also Constitution of Sierra Leone, 1991, art 76(1).

[101] 'Every person of full age and capacity, neither of whose parents is a person of negro African descent who is resident in Sierra Leone and has been continuously so resident for a period of not less than fifteen years may on application being made by him in the manner prescribed, be granted a certificate of naturalization if he satisfies the Minister that he is qualified for naturalization under the provisions set for the in the Third Schedule'. Sierra Leone Citizenship Amendment (No. 13) Act 1976, amending s 8(3) of the principal act. The third schedule and s 9 of the act set out requirements related to a clean criminal record, knowledge of an indigenous Sierra Leonean language, oath of allegiance, and payment of fees.

[102] Sierra Leone Citizenship Act 1973, s 24; see also Lina Beydoun, 'Lebanese Migration to Sierra Leone: Issues of Transnationalism, Gender, Citizenship, and the Construction of a Globalized Identity' (PhD, Wayne State University 2005).

[103] In April 1998, following the restoration of the elected government of President Kabbah, 22 people, mostly Lebanese, were expelled from Sierra Leone because of their activities during the rebel regime. Sierra Leone Web News Archive, available at http://www.sierra-leone.org/Archives/slnews0498.htm.

In 1978, a referendum approved a new constitution that did not include provisions on citizenship, but provided that a two-thirds majority would be needed to change the citizenship law[104]; it also made the country a one-party State. Despite these restrictions, Lebanese commercial interests were central to the increasing corruption and 'privatisation' of the Sierra Leonean State under the Stevens government, and especially to the exploitation of Sierra Leone's important alluvial diamond industry. The trade acts were used rather as a source of revenue for the government than to restrict non-citizens' ability to operate businesses in practice.[105]

These amendments aimed at those who were not 'negro-Africans', were matched by less well known legal interventions over the same period aimed at restricting what was seen as the disproportionate economic and political influence of the educated Krio (Creole) elite, descendants of various groups of freed slaves landed in Freetown in the eighteenth and nineteenth centuries (and estimated to form about 3% of the population today; whereas those of Lebanese descent never came close to 1% of the total). Since they were indisputably of 'negro-African descent', other means had to be found to limit their rights than restrictions on non-citizen property ownership.[106]

The distinction between the Colony and Protectorate of Sierra Leone had existed throughout the period of British rule, creating different legal regimes and different rights and treatment of the residents of each zone, including in relation to taxation: residents of the Colony were British subjects (after 1948, citizens of the UK and colonies), subject to versions of the law applied in the UK; those in the Protectorate were subject to the jurisdiction of the native courts, which – in the standard language also used in other British colonies – applied 'native law and custom, so far as it is not repugnant to natural justice, equity and good conscience',[107] particularly in matters of personal law. Legislation dating from 1927 (and still in force as of 2017) drew a distinction between 'natives' and 'non-natives' in relation to land-owning, aimed at preserving the control of 'tribal authorities' in the interior. A 'non-native' could only acquire a leasehold interest in the land in the Provinces, as the former Protectorate was renamed, subject to the approval of a 'tribal authority'. A 'native' was still subject to tribal authority in the Provinces, but could hold and use land for any period and anywhere, including in the Western

[104] Constitution of Sierra Leone 1978, Art 158: 'The Provisions of the Constitution (Consequential Provisions) Act 1976 of any Act relating to Citizenship shall not be amended, repealed, re-enacted or replaced unless the Bill incorporating such amendment, repeal re-enactment or replacement is supported at the final vote thereupon by the votes of not less than two-thirds of the Members of Parliament.'

[105] See the literature on 'conflict diamonds'; eg, Lansana Gberie, 'Sierra Leone: Diamonds, Corruption and the Lebanese Connection' (Partnership Africa Canada 2002) Occasional Paper 6.

[106] However, it could be possible that the difference in phrasing from the Liberian law (which refers only to 'negro descent') was aimed at the same exclusion?

[107] Native Courts Ordinance 1933, consolidated as Cap.8 Laws of Sierra Leone 1960.

Area, the former Colony of Sierra Leone.[108] 'Non-natives', even if they were living outside the Western Area, were not subject to customary law. These distinctions remained relevant, and were among the resentments that led to the civil war, as the Krio elite dominated politics and the economy; just as the Americo-Liberians did in next door Liberia.

The definition of 'native' went through several contortions during the 1970s, according to the drift of the political tides at any one moment. At the date of independence:

> "native" means any person who is a member of a race, tribe or community settled in Sierra Leone (or the territories adjacent thereto) other than a race, tribe or community —
>
> (a) which is of European or Asiatic origin; or
> (b) whose principal place of settlement is in the Colony
>
> "non-native" means any person other than a native.[109]

This definition was retained in legislation passed in 1961 and 1965 (with the substitution of Western Area for Colony, in line with new terminology).[110] The exclusion from 'native-ness' of any 'race, tribe or community' whose principal place of settlement was in the Western Area encompassed the Krio; and in 1971, a new law added a reference to American origin to the list in subparagraph (a), taking in any with ancestors who had been slaves in the US.[111]

The legislation regulating land holding in the provinces was also amended in 1972 to provide a specific definition of 'non-native' in the context of land ownership in the former Protectorate. Henceforward, a 'non-native', rather than simply being 'any person other than a native' as generally applied, was for the purposes of land ownership in the Provinces 'any person not entitled under customary law to rights in land in a Province'.[112]

The Sierra Leone Citizenship Act of 1973 then re-amended the definition, removing the question of settlement in the Western Area, though retaining the American connection and also introducing a citizenship requirement.[113] The 1976

[108] The Protectorate Land Ordinance 1927, as amended, Cap.122 Laws of Sierra Leone 1960. See also Ade Renner-Thomas, *Land Tenure in Sierra Leone: The Law, Dualism and the Making of a Land Policy* (AuthorHouse 2010).

[109] Interpretation Ordinance 1945, as amended, consolidated as Cap.1 Laws of Sierra Leone 1960.

[110] Interpretation (No. 46) Act 1961; Interpretation (No. 7) Act 1965.

[111] '"native" means any person who is a member of a race, tribe or community settled in Sierra Leone (or the territories adjacent thereto) other than a race, tribe or community – (a) which is of European or Asiatic or American origin; or (b) whose principal place of settlement is in the Western Area.' Interpretation (No. 8) Act 1971.

[112] Laws (Adaptation) (No. 29) Act 1972, amending the Provinces Land Act Cap.122 (as renamed, consequent on independence).

[113] '"native" means a citizen of Sierra Leone who is a member of a race, tribe or community settled in Sierra Leone, other than a race, tribe or community which is of European or Asiatic or American origin or of mixed European and Asiatic American origin.' Sierra Leone Citizenship (No. 4) Act 1973, s 29(3), amending the Interpretation Act 1971. There is no 'or' between Asiatic American in the final phrase in the version of the act published in the official gazette.

amendments to the Citizenship Act reintroduced the exclusion for those settled in the Western Area and set the definition which is still in force as follows:

> "native" means a citizen of Sierra Leone who is a member of a race, tribe or community settled in Sierra Leone, other than a race, tribe or community –
>
> (a) which is of European or Asiatic or American origin; or
>
> (b) whose principal place of settlement is the Western Area.[114]

These word-games would in principle permit restrictions not only on the activities of Krio from the Western Area but also on other groups persistently regarded as not citizens, such as the Fula merchants seen as migrants from neighbouring Guinea rather than 'settled' in Sierra Leone. Siaka Stevens was of course playing politics with these changes, aiming to mobilise the frustrations of the ethnic groups in the north and east of Sierra Leone against the SLPP. The legal adjustments were paired with the mobilisation of violence to ensure the consolidation of power.

Siaka Stevens retired from office in 1985, and installed Joseph Saidu Momoh as his successor. Pulled by the tide of reform that swept across Africa with the end of the cold war, Momoh instituted a constitutional review process. A new constitution was adopted in 1991 that provided for multi-party elections but did not address the citizenship questions, endorsing the discrimination established in the citizenship acts.[115]

In March 1991, fighters from a group calling itself the Revolutionary United Front (RUF) launched a rebellion from a base in Liberia. The outbreak of the war brought fresh instability to Sierra Leone's central politics. In 1992, Momoh was overthrown in a military coup by Captain Valentine Strasser, whose National Provisional Ruling Council (NPRC) was in turn overthrown in 1996 by his deputy. A short-lived elected civilian regime under Ahmad Tejan Kabbah, heading the SLPP, was again removed by coup; to be reinstated in March 1998 through a regional intervention by West African troops. Only in 1999 was a peace agreement signed, and only in 2002, following the deployment of a large UN peacekeeping force, was the conflict finally declared over. Elections held the same year returned President Kabbah's SLPP to office for a second term; peacefully succeeded in 2007 by an APC administration under President Ernest Bai Koroma.

When the NPRC took power, it launched a process to reform the 1991 constitution, with the professed aim of addressing the corruption of APC rule. Ahmed Tejan Kabbah, Solomon Berewa, and Banda Thomas (subsequently president, vice-president and minister of internal affairs, respectively) were all members of

[114] Sierra Leone Citizenship (Amendment) (No. 13) Act 1976, s 3, re-amending the Interpretation Act 1971. For a discussion of unsuccessful attempts to unify a definition of 'native' in British southern and eastern Africa in the 1930s, and the differing weights given to descent and culture, see Christopher Joon-Hai Lee, 'The 'Native' Undefined: Colonial Categories, Ango-African Status and the Politics of Kinship in British Central Africa, 1929–38' (2005) 46 Journal of African History 455.

[115] The provisions of the non-discrimination clause in the 1991 constitution are stated not to apply to laws affecting non-citizens, registered or naturalised citizens, and laws limiting rights to citizenship. Constitution of Sierra Leone 1991, art 27(4).

the National Advisory Council appointed to lead the review process. The draft new constitution published in 1994 proposed removing citizenship discrimination based on race or ethnicity and granting citizenship by birth to any person born to parents who were ordinarily resident in Sierra Leone for a continuous period of 15 years, thus retaining rights based on birth in the country. It also provided equal rights to naturalise, due process protections for the revocation of citizenship (by naturalisation only), and excluded naturalised citizens from only the very highest offices of State.[116] These reforms were never implemented, as governments came and went and civil war wracked the country during the 1990s.

With the restoration of a civilian government in 2002, there were some steps towards repealing the discriminatory provisions. The 2004 report of the Truth and Reconciliation Commission established after the war recommended the removal of racial and gender discrimination in citizenship provisions.[117] In October 2006, a law was adopted to amend the 1973 citizenship act to remove gender discrimination in citizenship by descent. Dual citizenship was also permitted for the first time. But attribution of citizenship at birth and the rules on acquisition through naturalisation still discriminated on the basis of 'negro-African descent'.[118] The Law Reform Commission put forward proposals for a more thorough-going reform of citizenship law: the draft of a new Citizenship Act presented to the government in 2007 would finally do away with the racial and gender provisions of the existing law.[119]

Naturalisation remained controversial, and extremely hard to access – though it was alleged by the APC that the NPRC military government had carried out 'mass naturalisation', especially of Chinese and Korean nationals.[120] No naturalisations were carried out under the SLPP government in office between 1996 and 2007; there was reportedly a total of only about 115 naturalised citizens in Sierra Leone in 2005, almost all of Lebanese descent.[121] Only in 2013 did President Koroma carry out the first officially reported naturalisations in perhaps two decades, conferring nationality on British journalist Mark Doyle and around 20 others.[122] Nonetheless, despite the continued racial basis of the law and popular sentiment opposing Lebanese participation in politics, both President Kabbah and President Koroma appointed ministers of partial Lebanese ancestry.[123] Lebanese money

[116] King (n 98).

[117] Sierra Leone Truth and Reconcilation Commission, 'Report of the Sierra Leone Truth and Reconciliation Commission, Vol.2' (2004) 133.

[118] Sierra Leone Citizenship (Amendment) (No. 11) Act 2006. In 2004, the 1969 Non-citizens (Trade and Business) Act was repealed, freeing up foreign-owned business, though not addressing the underlying question of who is a foreigner. Article 20, Investment Promotion Act, 2004.

[119] Draft Sierra Leone Citizenship Bill, dated 22 November 2007.

[120] 'Immigration unveils Naturalization and Citizenship Application Forms', *Awoko*, 4 May 2011.

[121] According to the Immigration Department in Sierra Leone, cited in King, *Report on Sierra Leone*.

[122] 'Mark Doyle Subscribes to the oath of allegiance as Sierra Leonean', Sierra Leone presidency, 5 November 2013; '"We Expect You To Be Good Citizens" – President Koroma Admonishes', Sierra Leone presidency, 11 September 2013, at http://www.statehouse.gov.sl/.

[123] eg, Joe Blell, deputy minister of defence under President Kabbah, and John Saad, Minister of Housing and Infrastructural Development under President Koroma. 'President Kabbah's Sixth Cabinet

remained important for the funding of political parties, even as their membership of the State remained questionable.

In 2011, the UN Human Rights Council adopted a decision on the Universal Periodic Review of Sierra Leone which included a recommendation that the government should 'Urgently address, the anomaly – accepted by the Government – regarding citizenship status for residents of non-African descent'.[124] In July 2013, President Koroma launched a fresh constitutional review process; the draft constitution published by the Constitutional Review Committee (CRC) in February 2016 and officially presented to the president in February 2017 proposed removing this restriction. At the same time, however, the draft would have removed the double *jus soli* rights derived from the birth of a parent or grand-parent in the 1973 law (as amended 2006), creating a purely descent-based law – with language that clearly owed much to the Kenyan constitution of 2010.[125] In July 2017, the existing Citizenship Act was amended to remove the final vestiges of gender discrimination in relation to children born abroad.[126] But the government's official response to the CRC proposals on citizenship was that any further changes should be made by legislation and not in a new constitution.[127]

The debates over citizenship in Sierra Leone for many years centred on the status of the 'Lebanese', a community facing much resentment for its dominance of the economy – especially the diamond trade, viewed as having fuelled the civil war. Other forms of legal discrimination built on British law precedents primarily affected the Krio community, indisputably 'negro African' but nonetheless resented as a corrupt elite by many in the former protectorate. Both sets of restrictions were undeniably founded on real economic injustice; but they were mobilised in large part for purely political aims rather than genuine redistribution of power and wealth. At grass roots level, the weakness and dysfunction of the Sierra Leonean State, and the lack of systematic requirement for identity documents, made the law less relevant; and other forms of ethnic distinction were equally visible as the country descended into civil war. The reestablishment of a stable civilian government anxious to document its citizens created the prospect of resolving these

and Deputy Ministers, May 2002–September 2007', Sierra Leone Web, at http://www.sierra-leone.org/cabinet-kabbah6.html; 'Calibre of Koroma's Cabinet is Impressive So Far', *Awareness Times*, 9 October 2007.

[124] Report of the Working Group on the Universal Periodic Review: Sierra Leone, A/HRC/18/10, 11 July 2011, endorsed by Human Rights Council Decision 18/108, Outcome of the Universal Periodic Review: Sierra Leone, A/HRC/DEC/18/108, 18 October 2011; see also Addendum: Views on conclusions and/or recommendations, voluntary commitments and replies presented by the State under review, A/HRC/18/10/Add.1, 13 September 2011.

[125] Constitutional Review Committee, 'Abridged Draft Report' (2016). It seems that the implications of this move were not fully understood by the CRC: the proposed removal of racial discrimination was controversial, with much media commentary, but the other reforms less debated. Interview, member of Constitutional Review Committee, December 2016; Umaru Fofana, 'Challenging Sierra Leone's racist citizenship law', *PoliticoSL*, 9 March 2016.

[126] Sierra Leone Citizenship Amendment Act 2017.

[127] 'Govt. betrays CRC's efforts on dual citizenship', *Awoko* (Freetown), 19 January 2018.

issues. Yet the proposal of a new constitution that would remove rights based on birth in Sierra Leone as the foundation for citizenship created risks that problems arising from the same wording in Kenya – explored in the next chapter – could be replicated in Sierra Leone.

Lila's story[128]

'In 2002, Lila, a second-generation Lebanese woman born in Sierra Leone, who had become a naturalised citizen in 1990, applied for a new passport. Her application was denied because, after scrutiny, the Immigration Office found that she had naturalised 'illegally' when she was over the age limit of 21. She could not, however, have obtained naturalisation before the age of 21, because she had to wait for her father to take the Oath [of allegiance]. To qualify for a new passport, she had to take the Oath herself, but the President at the time had suspended the process of naturalisation. On the surface, Immigration Officers seemed concerned about implementing Immigration Laws, but underlying that façade was a hidden message: By showing that the law cannot be used to facilitate renewal of the passport, the bribe expected is higher than would be if the law had applied. An Officer suggest that Lila change her birth certificate to make the 'nationality' of one of her parents Sierra Leonean, ie of Negro African descent. This way, she could obtain citizenship based on the amended [law] that states that one of her parents should be Sierra Leonean at her birth. After bribing the staff, she then took her falsified birth certificate to immigration, bribed the Immigration Officer and received a new passport.'

7.3. 'Asians' and other 'others' in Kenya and Uganda

The post-independence crises over the status of people of Asian descent in Kenya and Uganda were among the most widely covered political developments in Africa in the international English language media; thanks in large part to concerns in Britain over the possible 'mass influx' of those rejected by the East African countries but carrying different categories of British passport. There were commonalities between these anxieties and those in Sierra Leone over the status of 'Lebanese', given the dominance of Asians in the economy. However, the later legal trajectory of the East African countries was shaped as much by concerns over the status of African migrants as it was by the role of those originating from outside

[128] Lila's story extracted from Beydoun (n 102).

the continent. In Kenya, questions around entitlement to citizenship became pervasive, a continuation of identification and security concerns established in the colonial era. Uganda created a more welcoming framework for inclusion of 'stranger' groups, with a radical reworking of the basis of citizenship, but its decision to do so on the basis of ethnicity created new difficulties for some. In both cases, the legal frameworks established during the colonial era continued to have strong influence on the contemporary debate.

Asian migration to East Africa began many centuries ago, as trading links across the Indian Ocean developed among communities in the littoral zones of Africa, Arabia, and South and South-East Asia. This contact was accelerated and brought into the interior of the continent, first by Arab slave traders and then more permanently under British colonial rule. Thousands of people from the Indian subcontinent were either imported to work as indentured labour on the railways, or came as traders and businessmen following the economic opportunities those railways brought.

The relative privilege and economic success of these immigrants in the colonial economy meant that their status was highly sensitive in both Kenya and Uganda during the transition to independence. Initially it was in Kenya in particular that the loyalty of the Asian population was in question; not just because of their greater numbers, but also because the status of (most of) the territory as a colony rather than a protectorate meant that not only Kenyans of British descent but also most Kenyan Asians (as well as Africans) had the status of citizens of the UK and colonies rather than British protected persons, giving them full right of abode in Britain.[129] They retained this status after independence (unless they renounced British citizenship to become Kenyan), though with already reduced rights to enter Britain from 1962 – until the UK changed the law in 1968 (see Chapter 4.2).

The constitutions of both countries applied the same transitional rules for acquiring citizenship at independence: a person who had been born in Kenya or Uganda of at least one parent who was also born in the country, and who was on the date of independence either a citizen of the UK and colonies or a British protected person automatically became a citizen of the newly independent State. In addition, a person born outside the country was automatically a citizen if his or her father became a citizen according to these rules. Various categories of people who did not fulfil these conditions but who were either British protected persons or citizens of the UK and colonies, or citizens of other African countries, had the right to apply for citizenship by registration during a two-year period – a non-discretionary

[129] Daniel DC Don Nanjira, *The Status of Aliens in East Africa: Asians and Europeans in Tanzania, Uganda, and Kenya* (Praeger 1976); Dharam P Ghai and Yash P Ghai, 'Asians in East Africa: Problems and Prospects' (1965) 3 The Journal of Modern African Studies 35; YP Ghai, 'The Kenya Council of State and the African Affairs Board of the Central African Federation: An Experiment in the Protection of Minorities' (1963) 12 International and Comparative Law Quarterly 1089; Donald Rothchild, 'Kenya's Minorities and the African Crisis over Citizenship' (1968) 9 Race & Class 421.

process.[130] Approximately 20,000 people applied to register as Kenyan during the two-year transitional period, most of them South Asian, out of an estimated 230,000 eligible.[131] Those born after independence would acquire citizenship by the fact of birth in the territory – with the usual exceptions for the children of diplomats or enemy aliens. Dual citizenship was uniformly prohibited for adults, in line with the standard model in the newly independent Commonwealth countries of Africa.

Both during the independence negotiations and immediately after the adoption of the new constitutions, discontent over the economically advantaged position of Asian immigrants to Kenya and Uganda led to agitation for changes in the law. The 1963 Kenya Citizenship Act mainly reiterated the constitutional provisions with regards to citizenship. Roughly half of Kenya's Asian population automatically became citizens on this basis (provided they could prove the relevant facts). However, section 3, on registration of citizens, introduced a requirement not present in the constitution that an applicant to be registered as a citizen had to satisfy the minister that he was of 'African descent'.[132] These measures were clearly aimed at Kenyans of Asian descent: the 45,000 people of European descent also resident in Kenya at the time were equally excluded by the new requirements, but it was (rightly) assumed that most would relocate to Britain, which would permit them to retain or reacquire its citizenship.[133]

In Uganda, meanwhile, the requirements of the 1962 independence constitution were implemented by the Uganda Citizenship Act.[134] During the parliamentary proceedings for the adoption of the Act, Asian members of Parliament argued unsuccessfully for an easier registration process and restrictions on the revocation of citizenship acquired through registration. By 1967, only around 11,000 of the just under 25,000 applicants for registration made within the two-year time limit had been granted citizenship.[135] As of 1969, the Asian population recorded in

[130] Constitution of Kenya, 1963, arts 1–12; Constitution of Uganda 1962, arts 7–12. In 1969 a new constitution was adopted in Kenya that consolidated other amendments that had greatly strengthened executive power; on citizenship, however, it renumbered but otherwise repeated unaltered the provisions of the 1963 constitution. The addition in the Kenyan constitution of citizens of other African States to the preferential access through registration was not repeated in the Ugandan constitution, but included in the Uganda Citizenship Act of 1962, s 4.

[131] The estimated 1965 population was 185,000 people of Asian descent, and 42,000 Europeans: Rothchild (n 129). Figures for eligible Africans not given.

[132] In addition, the person had to show that either 'he was born, and one of his parents was born, in a country to which this section applies', or that 'he has been resident for a period of not less than ten years in a country to which this section applies and he is not a citizen of an independent State on the Continent of Africa.' The minister could declare the countries to which the section applied (essentially on the basis of reciprocity); the provision was rooted in a commitment to African (rather than Commonwealth) solidarity, in an era before all African States were independent. Kenya Citizenship Act 1963, s 3(1)(b)(ii).

[133] Rieko Karatani, *Defining British Citizenship: Empire, Commonwealth, and Modern Britain* (Frank Cass 2003) 154–163.

[134] Uganda Citizenship Ordinance (No. 63 of 1962); renamed as the Uganda Citizenship Act, Cap.65.

[135] John Jean Barya, 'Reconstituting Ugandan Citizenship under the 1995 Constitution: A Conflict of Nationalism, Chauvinism and Ethnicity' (Centre for Basic Research 2000) 55.

Uganda was just under 75,000 (less than 1% of the total population of 9.5 million); of which 26,657 were Ugandan citizens (more than 11,000 of them under 11 years old); 36,593 remained British protected persons (the majority) or citizens of the UK and colonies; 8,890 were Indian citizens; and 1,768 Kenyan citizens. The total non-citizen population in the country was more than 500,000, mainly Kenyans and Tanzanians.[136]

A 1964 attempted military coup led to the suspension of the constitution by Prime Minister Milton Obote, the deposition of the Buganda King, the Kabaka, from the role of head of State, and the adoption of a republican constitution in 1966 which created an executive presidency. A 1967 constitution further strengthened executive powers. The short-lived 1966 constitution left the citizenship regime unaltered, but the 1967 constitution removed the *jus soli* citizenship rights included in the standard Commonwealth independence constitution. At the same time, it extended the right to derive citizenship on the basis of descent from a single grandparent as well as a parent, and removed gender discrimination for citizenship by descent (though not in marriage). Dual nationality remained prohibited.[137]

As in Sierra Leone, both Uganda and Kenya also took measures to promote the 'Africanisation' of the economy, perceived to be too dominated by businesses owned by Kenyans of European and Asian descent. Each country passed Trade Licensing Acts during the 1960s to restrict the operations of non-African owned businesses.

In Kenya, these measures led to a case before the Kenyan High Court in 1968 which considered the concept of 'African descent' under the Citizenship Act in order to decide if non-Africans could be deprived of property rights.[138] The plaintiffs were individuals of Asian descent who had been given notices to quit the stalls they rented from the Nairobi city council. They had applied for citizenship by registration and were awaiting the results. The court found that the quit notices were void – but not that the policy was unconstitutional in itself, on the grounds that the constitutional protection against discrimination did not apply to non-citizens.[139]

[136] Vishnu D Sharma and F Wooldridge, 'Some Legal Questions Arising from the Expulsion of the Ugandan Asians' (1974) 23 International and Comparative Law Quarterly 397; James S Read, 'Some Legal Aspects of the Expulsion' in Michael Twaddle (ed), *Expulsion of a Minority: Essays on Ugandan Asians* (Athlone Press 1975); KC Kotecha, 'The Shortchanged: Uganda Citizenship Laws and How They Were Applied to Its Asian Minority' (1975) 9 The International Lawyer 1.

[137] Constitution of the Republic of Uganda, 1967, arts 4 and 6; see also Uganda Constitutional Review Commission report, 1995. Although either parent could be a citizen in the first instance for transmission by descent to those born outside the country, this was not the case if the father had also been born outside. Citizenship by marriage was restricted to women marrying Ugandan men.

[138] *Madhwa and Others v City Council of Nairobi* [1967) LLR 5986, [1968] E.A 406; see also Alan H Smith, 'Prevention of Discrimination under Kenyan Law' (1971) 20 International and Comparative Law Quarterly 136.

[139] The Council argued that its resolution was not racially discriminatory since the term African should be taken to mean not a person whose forefathers were born in Africa but rather a citizen of any country on the continent of Africa, without regard to race. The judge rejected this line of argument on the grounds that the provisions on citizenship did not extend automatically to citizens of other countries in Africa, except as listed in the Citizenship Act. In a somewhat similar case heard before the

Effectively, the Court accepted that the State's delay in processing applications for citizenship, and introduction of discriminatory criteria not mentioned in the constitution, justified its actions against the very same group of people.

In Uganda, similar initial steps to reduce the disproportionate Asian dominance of the economy rapidly escalated into more drastic measures, following a period of increasing political instability which culminated in the seizure of power by President Idi Amin in early 1971. He led a reign of terror in which perhaps up to half a million Ugandans died, only terminated by Tanzanian military intervention in 1979 in response to Amin's seizure of Tanzanian territory.

Amin stated his ambition to return the Asian-controlled businesses to 'black Ugandans', on the grounds that the Asians were 'sabotaging Uganda's economy and encouraging corruption'.[140] In December 1971, Amin announced that 12,000 outstanding applications to register for Ugandan citizenship would be cancelled, but could be resubmitted. On 4 August 1972, he demanded that the British government take over responsibility for the Asian Ugandans and ensure their removal from Uganda within three months. Successive decrees cancelled all entry permits and certificates of residence issued to persons of Asian origin; these initially required that the persons involved be citizens or subjects of the UK, India, Pakistan, and Bangladesh, but from October 1972 the requirement that the person hold another nationality was removed. Although the decrees did not technically apply to those holding Ugandan citizenship, a process of 'verification' of citizenship by registration reduced the numbers of those recognised as Ugandan – all of whom had been required to renounce another nationality in order to obtain citizenship.[141] Most Asians and many other foreigners left the country. The consequential movement of East African Asians to the UK, meanwhile, led to new legislation applying immigration controls restricting their entry to Britain (ultimately successfully challenged under the European Convention on Human Rights).[142]

The status of the Ugandan and Kenyan Asians gradually became a less politically sensitive problem (though still controversial) – in part because so many left.

Kenya High Court in 1968, *Fernandes v Kericho Licensing Court*, the question of citizenship arose once again. The plaintiff was of Indian origin and was denied renewal of a liquor licence on the basis that he was not a citizen. The court found in favour of the plaintiff, on the grounds that under the relevant law (Liquor Licensing Act, Laws of Kenya, Cap.121) the liquor court had power to refuse to renew the applicant's licence only if he was suffering from one of the six disqualifications set out in the Act, and lack of citizenship was not one of them.

[140] See, eg, Mahmood Mamdani, 'The Ugandan Asian Expulsion: Twenty Years After' (1993) 6 Journal of Refugee Studies 265.

[141] Immigration (Cancellation of Entry Permits and Certificates of Residence) Decree (No. 17 of 1972), 9 August 1972; Immigration (Cancellation of Entry Permits and Certificates of Residence) (Amendment) Decree (No. 30 of 1972), 25 October 1972. See Read, 'Some Legal Aspects of the Expulsion'.

[142] Commonwealth Immigration Act 1968, Immigration Act 1971; *East African Asians v UK – Application 4403/70* [1973] ECHR 2, 14 December 1973; see Richard Plender, 'The Exodus of Asians from East and Central Africa Some Comparative and International Law Aspects' (1971) 19 American Journal of Comparative Law 287.

In 1983, a new government in Uganda reversed the policies of the Amin era, passing legislation to return confiscated property and encouraging the return of the Asian community and other foreigners and investors to Uganda,[143] though the process was not a simple one and there was much controversy over ownership of the property formerly held by Asians.[144] The issues of loyalty and belonging remained live, but the immediate concerns over the status of those with a claim on another citizenship were diluted by the dawn of the twenty-first century. First Uganda (in 2005) and then Kenya (in 2010) changed the law to allow dual nationality, though in both cases with significant conditions attached.[145]

Nevertheless, the question of who qualified to be a citizen of either country remained in contention, increasingly with a greater impact on people of African descent. At this point, the trajectories of the two countries diverged, partly by deliberate political decision, but also based on the frameworks for governance of access to and proof of citizenship that each had inherited. In Uganda, an explicitly ethnic definition of citizenship was adopted in 1995, which excluded both Asians and other groups not listed within the constitution, but which otherwise operated in a fairly inclusive way. Until 2015, Uganda had no requirement to carry a national identity card, and access to services was not restricted on the basis of citizenship. In Kenya, the colonial heritage of 'native registration' and pass-books continued to shed a long shadow over citizenship administration. In both countries, the question of integration of refugees created major challenges, especially difficult to overcome in Kenya.

7.3.1. Kenya

Kenya's history relating to registration of persons dates back to the origins of the State as one of the main 'settler colonies' of the British Empire where control of the 'native' population was a requirement for expropriation and exploitation of

[143] Uganda Expropriated Properties Act, Laws of Uganda, 2000, ch 87, transferred the properties and businesses of Asians that had been acquired or expropriated during the military regime to the Ministry of Finance and ensured their return to former owners or their lawful disposal by government.

[144] The issue led to many court cases. In *Kayondo v Asian Property Custodian Board* (HCCS No. 345 of 1981), the presiding judge stated that the seizure of businesses and other properties by the military government from Asians was unconstitutional. On appeal (HCB No. 17 of 1982), however, it was held that the takeover of the property amounted to nationalisation and therefore was not a violation of the constitution. Some cases relating to ownership of formerly Asian held properties took years to resolve; others continue to be fought out in the courts. Judgments of the Ugandan courts available at http://www.ulii.org/ (search for eg 'custodian' since most cases named the Property Custodian Board as defendant). See also Mamdani (n 140).

[145] Constitution (Amendment) Act 2005, Art 6, amending Art 15 of the 1995 Constitution; Uganda Citizenship and Immigration Control (Amendment) (No. 5) Act 2009, s 9, replacing s 19 of the principal act (also creating significant limitations on dual citizenship). Constitution of Kenya 2010, art 16 permits dual nationality for citizens from birth; Kenya Citizenship and Immigration (No. 12) Act 2011 (Cap.172) repeats this provision in s 8 and does not require a person naturalising as a Kenyan to renounce another citizenship (s 13).

land by the European immigrants. The British colonial government in Kenya first enacted a Native Registration Ordinance in 1915, aimed at facilitating recruitment of labour. From 1921, every African male over 16 had to carry a passbook known as a 'kipande' confirming his registration under the Act.

In 1947, the Native Registration Ordinance was replaced by the Registration of Persons Ordinance, which applied to all males over the age of 16; following independence the ordinance was incorporated into the new laws of Kenya as the Registration of Persons Act; women were included within the registration requirements from 1978; and the age of compulsory registration for all citizens was raised to 18 years in 1980. Section 5 of the Act required people to declare their 'race or tribe' in order to obtain an ID card; at least from time of the 1969 census, which listed 42 'tribes' for the purposes of recording population, persons of African ethnicity not belonging to one of these 'tribes', or whose 'tribal' allegiance was not clear, would face difficulties obtaining an identity card.[146] Section 8 of the Act empowered any registration official to require a person to furnish any 'documentary or other evidence of the truth' of any information provided.[147] In border areas and in urban neighbourhoods known to host people of foreign or border-region origin, additional 'vetting committees' were established from representatives of different relevant government departments and security agencies, with elders from the community as advisers, to verify identity before a card would be issued.

From 1974, the Kenyan government also required non-citizens to register as aliens and to carry an 'alien card';[148] the distinction between citizen and alien thus became more significant, especially for those from other East African countries who had previously been able to live in Kenya without explicit documentation. Some registered as aliens; others preferred to leave the situation ambiguous, believing or presenting themselves to be Kenyan.

In 1985, President Daniel arap Moi rushed through Parliament an amendment to the constitution to remove rights to citizenship based on birth in Kenya and put in place a purely descent-based system, with retroactive effect to the date of independence.[149] Despite the arguably illegal nature of such retroactivity – stated to be necessary because the provision was 'incompatible with government policy' and had been 'misinterpreted' to attribute citizenship to people born in Kenya – there was no legal challenge to the amendment. In practice, rights based on birth in Kenya had already been ignored by the immigration department.[150]

[146] Samantha Balaton-Chrimes, 'Statelessness, Identity Cards and Citizenship as Status in the Case of the Nubians of Kenya' (2014) 18 Citizenship Studies 15. The date at which the '42 tribes' were first listed, nor the legal instrument by which they came to be applied to registration of persons, is not clear in the literature; nor to the Chief Registrar in the National Registration Bureau as of 2016.

[147] Interviews, Nairobi, June 2016.

[148] Aliens Restriction (No. 5) Act 1973, Cap.173.

[149] Constitution of Kenya Amendment (No. 6) Act 1985.

[150] Ramnik Shah, 'Britain and Kenya's Citizenship Law: A Conflict of Laws?' (1992) 6 Tolley's Immigration & Nationality Law & Practice 120; Ramnik Shah, 'Kenya's Citizenship Laws Revisited' (2012) 26 Journal of Immigration Asylum and Nationality Law 269.

The change to the law was adopted three years after one-party rule was put in place, and just one year following the massacre of thousands of civilians at Wagalla in the Somali-dominated north east;[151] among the objectives was presumably the further restriction of the rights of those who might oppose Moi's increasingly dictatorial rule.

The impact of the constitutional amendment was to render the State succession provisions in the independence constitution immediately far more relevant: proof of Kenyan citizenship at birth would now depend on showing that a parent had acquired citizenship automatically or by registration at independence (or subsequently by registration or naturalisation). Naturalisation remained highly discretionary and hardly accessed in practice, while judicial oversight of the executive in determining eligibility for citizenship was specifically excluded.

Among those affected were of course Kenyan Asians, including (a relatively small number of) children born in Kenya whose parents were British overseas citizens (BOCs) of Asian ethnicity, but who from 1983 were no longer eligible for any form of British nationality.[152] However, the impact of the amendment went much wider, preventing many migrant communities from gaining any access to Kenyan citizenship. Those worst affected were the descendants of those who had settled in Kenya before or soon after independence, who had also lost any connection to the country 'of origin'.

Kenyan Nubians became the best-known representatives of these excluded groups.[153] The Nubians were conscripted into the British army from what is now Sudan, at the time administered jointly by Britain and Egypt. They became known as the King's African Rifles, or as *askaris* (the Arabic/Swahili word for soldier or guard), during the British expeditions of colonisation in East Africa and in both world wars. When they were demobilised in Kenya they were not given any meaningful compensation or benefits, although many were allocated small plots of land for farming in a place known as Kibera ('forest' in the Nubian language), near Nairobi. They held a somewhat ambiguous status during the colonial period, with

[151] On the Wagalla massacre, the most serious atrocity of Kenya's post-independence history, see *Report of the Truth, Justice and Reconciliation Commission*, Volume IV, 2013, paras 75-88; Thuo Kinyanjui, 'Remembering Wagalla Massacre 30 Years Later', Kenya National Commission on Human Rights, 14 February 2014.

[152] The status of BOC was created in a major reform of the UK law in 1981 (entered into force 1983), and originally encompassed around 1.5 million people with some connection to the British empire; it is not transmissible to the next generation. Laurie Fransman, Adrian Berry and Alison Harvey, *Fransman's British Nationality Law* (3rd edn, Bloomsbury Professional 2011) s 11.1.3.

[153] The Nubian situation has received much attention: Maurice Odhiambo Makoloo, 'Kenya: Minorities, Indigenous Peoples and Ethnic Diversity' (Minority Rights Group International/ CEMIRIDE 2005); Douglas H Johnson, 'Tribe or Nationality? The Sudanese Diaspora and the Kenyan Nubis' (2009) 3 Journal of Eastern African Studies 112; Adam Hussein Adam, 'Kenyan Nubians: Standing up to Statelessness' (2009) 32 Forced Migration Review; Samantha Balaton-Chrimes, 'The Nubians of Kenya and the Emancipatory Potential of Collective Recognition' (2011) 32 Australasian Review of African Studies 12; Samantha Balaton-Chrimes, 'Indigeneity and Kenya's Nubians: Seeking Equality in Difference or Sameness?' (2013) 51 Journal of Modern African Studies 331; Balaton-Chrimes, 'Statelessness, Identity Cards and Citizenship as Status in the Case of the Nubians of Kenya' (n 146).

somewhat more privileges than the 'native' Kenyans, yet without the security of land tenure that would guarantee their future.[154] A request by some for repatriation to Sudan was refused by the British authorities, and at Kenya's independence in 1963 they remained where they had been settled. Kibera became an enormous informal settlement, gradually incorporated into Nairobi, which the Kenyan authorities insisted was government land. In 2003, representatives of the Nubian community brought a case to the Kenyan courts seeking confirmation of their citizenship and the right to be issued with relevant official documents.[155] After more than three years of blocked progress at national level on procedural grounds, the Nubians took their case to the human rights bodies of the African Union, gaining two favourable judgments.[156] Gradually the status of the Nubians improved, and the community as a whole was recognised as Kenyan, though residents of Kibera remained subject to the additional vetting procedures applied in border regions. In 2017, President Kenyatta recognised the legal title of the Nubian community to a large part of Kibera, as recommended by the African Commission on Human and Peoples' Rights.[157]

Less well known groups completely without recognition of Kenyan citizenship were scattered around the country.[158] Among them were the Makonde, a community of a few thousand descendants of migrant workers recruited from Mozambique during the 1950s to work on sisal plantations in what became Kwale County near Mombasa. This group had not automatically become Kenyan under the transitional provisions on independence since few were born in the country and none of parents also born in the country. Although most would have been eligible to register as citizens through the transitional provisions at independence, as originating from another African country, they did not do so, whether because of the cost, or because they expected to return to Mozambique, or because they did not hear of the requirement. Descendants of Rwandan workers on tea plantations faced the same issues. Also left high and dry were several hundreds of people of Zimbabwean and other southern African descent, followers of the Gospel of God Church who came as missionaries in the 1960s.[159] Members of this community were issued different forms of permit at different times, but the alien cards issued from 1974 expired in 2007 and were not replaced. The Zimbabwean High

[154] Samantha Balaton-Chrimes, 'The Nubians of Kenya: Citizenship in the Gaps and Margins' in Emma Hunter (ed), *Citizenship, belonging, and political community in Africa: dialogues between past and present* (Ohio University Press 2016).

[155] High Court civil case no. 256 of 2003, Nairobi.

[156] *The Nubian Community v Kenya*, Communication 317/06, African Commission on Human and Peoples' Rights; *Institute for Human Rights and Development in Africa and Open Society Justice Initiative on behalf of Children of Nubian Descent in Kenya v Kenya*, Communication 002/2009, African Committee of Experts on the Rights and Welfare of the Child.

[157] April Zhu, 'Kenya: A home to call your own – even if it is a slum', IRIN, 14 December 2017.

[158] Bronwen Manby, 'Citizenship and Statelessness in the East African Community' (UNHCR 2018).

[159] Founded in 1932 by a Zimbabwean, Father Johane Masowe, born in what was then Southern Rhodesia in 1914.

Commission in Kenya refused applications by the second generation descendants of the original migrants for Zimbabwean papers: under Southern Rhodesian and then Zimbabwean law citizenship did not transmit to the second generation born outside of the country.[160]

The largest group of doubtful citizenship in Kenya were, however, those of Somali ethnicity, whose long-term marginal status within the Kenyan State was exacerbated by the impact of the 'global war on terror'. Among the modalities of exclusion was the strict control exercised over their access to national identity cards.

During the British colonial era, the Northern Frontier District of Kenya comprised of six sub-districts: three where the residents were mainly of Somali ethnicity (Mandera, Wajir, and Garissa) and three dominated by other pastoralist groups (Moyale, Marsabit, and Isiolo). Somalia became independent before Kenya, and Somali politicians appealed to the British colonial authorities to grant sovereignty over the Northern Frontier District to Somalia or to allow a referendum. A commission was appointed to consider the future of the region and reported that the vast majority of the population favoured secession. Nevertheless, it was decided that the Northern Frontier District would remain in Kenya: the three Somali districts – where secession was supported almost unanimously – became the North Eastern Province of Kenya. The other three districts joined the Eastern Province.[161]

Protests at the imposition of Kenyan sovereignty rapidly became violent. On becoming president, Jomo Kenyatta almost immediately declared a state of emergency in the North Eastern Province, later extended to the neighbouring districts of Isiolo, Marsabit, Tana River, and Lamu.[162] The Preservation of Public Security Act and other laws restricted free movement.[163] The region became increasingly militarised, with several security force massacres in addition to that at Wagalla.

[160] Although this absolute rule changed with the adoption of the 2013 Constitution, transmission of citizenship is subject to registration of the birth of a child in Zimbabwe: Constitution of Zimbabwe, 2013, Art 37. The Citizenship of Zimbabwe Act (Cap.4:01, No.23 of 1984) was last amended in 2003, and had yet to be amended by end 2017, still providing for transmission of citizenship by descent to be limited to the first generation born outside the country (S 6).

[161] Following the adoption of the 2010 constitution, Kenya is now divided into 47 counties. The three former districts of North Eastern Province – Mandera, Wajir, and Garissa – are now counties in their own right.

[162] See Truth, Justice & Reconciliation Commission of Kenya, 'Final Report Vol. IIA' (2013) ch 3; Ben Rawlence, *'Bring the Gun Or You'll Die': Torture, Rape, and Other Serious Human Rights Violations by Kenyan Security Forces in the Mandera Triangle* (Human Rights Watch 2009).

[163] Preservation of Public Security Act, Cap. 57 (introduced by Act No. 2 of 1960, and amended by L.N. 2/1964, Act No. 18 of 1966, and L.N. 766/1963), s 4(2)(b). Other laws included the Outlying Districts Act and the Special Districts (Administration) Act. Regulations were set out for the North-Eastern Province and contiguous districts, allowing for the control of movement of specified ethnic nationalities or into 'prohibited zones'. Special regulations were set out for the North-Eastern Province and contiguous districts, allowing for the control of movement of specified ethnic nationalities or into 'prohibited zones'. Legal notices No. 264 of 1966 and No. 185 of 1967; The Public Security (Control of Movement) Regulations, L.N.43, 1967. Under the 1963 constitution, protections for freedom of movement did not apply to restrictions imposed 'for interests of defence, public safety, public order, public

Somali irredentism (in Kenya and Ethiopia) was also fuelled by support and recruitment from President Siad Barre's Somalia.

In 1989, the Office of the President ordered a comprehensive screening process for all Somali-Kenyans, on the pretext of incursions across the border for ivory poaching, and allegations that Somali businessmen had illegally acquired Kenyan citizenship.[164] Ethnic Somali Kenyans aged 18 and over were required to go to one of 51 centres in towns across the country and 'furnish such documentary or other evidence of the truth of their registration between the 13th November 1989 and 4th December 1989'. Rift Valley Provincial Commissioner Yusuf Haji headed the screening taskforce, made up of Somali-Kenyan public officers. The crackdown was also linked to intra-Somali clan politics and competition for business, as the process was led by prominent members of the Ogaden clan, above all Yusuf Haji himself.

The screening process took place before panels of elders who questioned applicants on their family history, lineage, and knowledge of Kenya. Those successful were issued with pink identity booklets, to be carried along with the regular Kenyan identity card. The Task Force submitted to the Registrar a list of persons whose registration records were cancelled. Many who failed the exercise were detained and deported. In North Eastern Province, police conducted door-to-door searches for suspected aliens, looting and assaulting people as they went. Thousands fled to Uganda.[165] Many whose Kenyan citizenship was not in doubt had their documents confiscated and not returned as a result of this screening. These included, for example, several dozen members of the Galje'el Somali community resident in the Tana River area, north of Mombasa, whose own troubles owed as much to local competition for land use rights as national politics.[166]

The 1989 screening process was abandoned after some weeks, amidst international protest. The emergency measures imposed in the 1960s were then relaxed in the 1990s, with the return of multi-party democracy to Kenya in 1991 after several decades of single-party rule.[167]

At around the same time, however, Kenya came to host hundreds of thousands of refugees from Somalia, entering the country after the collapse of the Somali

morality, public health or the protection or control of nomadic peoples', provided they were 'reasonably justifiable in a democratic society': 1963 Constitution, art 25(3)(b). The provision was re-enacted as art 81(3)(b) of the 1969 constitution and remained in effect until 2010.

[164] Legal Notice No.5320, Kenya Government Gazette 10 November 1989.

[165] See generally, Human Rights Watch, 'Screening of Ethnic Somalis: The Cruel Consequences of Kenya's Passbook System' (1990); Emma Lochery, 'Rendering Difference Visible: The Kenyan State and Its Somali Citizens' (2012) 111 African Affairs 615; Gianluca Iazzolino, 'A Safe Haven for Somalis in Uganda?' (Rift Valley Institute 2014).

[166] Alamin Mazrui, 'Banditry and the Politics of Citizenship: The Case of the Galje'el of Tana River' (Muslims for Human Rights (MUHURI), 1999); Truth, Justice & Reconciliation Commission of Kenya (n 162) paras 66–70.

[167] Lochery (n 165). The Statute Law (Repeals and Miscellaneous Amendments) (No. 10) Act 1997 repealed the Outlying Districts Act and the Special Districts (Administration) Act; it also amended the Preservation of Public Security Act 1966 to remove the provisions relating to detention of persons, but the other provisions remained in force, including those relating to control of free movement.

State. This new crisis immediately undermined any chance of a relaxation of attitudes towards the north-east; measures of control continued to centre on access to national identity cards, and to reference the 1989 screening. A 2008 letter addressed to a member of the Galje'el community stated that an application for an identity card could not be processed 'because the holder was declared to be non-Kenyan by the … Task Force of 1989.'[168]

Coastal Muslims faced similar, though less acute, issues with documentation, whose particular form also had roots in the colonial era. The coastal strip of Kenya – up to and including Lamu, the northernmost district – had a separate legal status under colonial rule. While most of Kenya was a colony, this ten-mile-wide ribbon of territory was formally conceded to Britain by the Sultan of Zanzibar by treaty in the late nineteenth century and was governed as a protectorate, notionally remaining under the Sultan's administration for internal matters.

The status of the coastal strip was, like that of the Northern Frontier District, highly contested during the negotiations leading to independence, with coastal leaders arguing for the strip to return to the control of the Zanzibar government (initially an independent State before merging with Tanganyika to become Tanzania), and inland leaders mobilising strongly held feelings of resentment at historical 'Arab' domination and slave raids to argue that it should become part of Kenya. Another commission was appointed, recommending that the strip be included within Kenya, with guarantees of respect for Muslim law and religion and for existing land titles in the coastal region. This was implemented by an agreement between President Jomo Kenyatta and the sultan and prime minister of Zanzibar that conceded sovereignty to Kenya. Resentment at failures to respect the terms of this agreement led to the periodic resurgence of demands for coastal independence or autonomy.[169]

Among the coastal communities whose Kenyan citizenship was disputed were families with close connections to Pemba, the northern of the Zanzibari islands, with centuries-long connections to the nearby Kenyan coast.[170] In an even more complex situation were people of Comorian descent in Kenya, mainly drawn from the Comorian community in Zanzibar. Their status under British rule in Kenya was already somewhat ambiguous, because of the status of Comoros as French territory. Although some merged into the general Swahili population of the coast, others remained likely to be considered non-citizens by the Kenyan immigration authorities.[171]

[168] Letter from National Registration Bureau, 28 March 2008, cited in Adam Hussein Adam, 'Making of Stateless People – The Kenyan Style', 2008 (on file with author).

[169] Justin Willis and George Gona, 'Pwani C Kenya? Memory, Documents and Secessionist Politics in Coastal Kenya' (2013) 112 African Affairs 48.

[170] Wanja Munaita and June Munala, 'Identity and Articulations of Belonging: A Background Study on the Pemba of Coastal Kenya' (UNHCR 2016).

[171] Gillian Marie Shepherd, 'The Comorians in Kenya: The Establishment and Loss of an Economic Niche' (PhD, London School of Economics 1982).

In 2001, there were demonstrations in Mombasa after a press release was issued by the district registrar of births and deaths that, in case of late registration, Asians and Arabs now had to apply for birth and death certificates in Nairobi.[172] The directive requiring this vetting procedure was then asserted to have been in place since 1997 and to apply to all 'Kenyans of foreign extraction', rather than only Asians and Arabs; the minister denied any discrimination. The government backed down, but reinstated the controls following the 9/11 attacks later that year.[173] In early 2005, the minister for immigration announced on the radio that any late (ie, longer than six months after birth) registration of births in the coastal areas would have to be vetted by the central government.[174] In 2007, the National Registration Bureau (NRB) issued a circular to chiefs on requirements for issue of national identity cards that revived the requirements for 'Asians and Arabs' to produce parents and grandparents birth certificates as proof of citizenship'.[175]

These histories were among the factors feeding into a decades-long struggle by pro-democracy activists for constitutional reform to address the over-centralisation of power in the Kenya State. Multiple constitution-drafting processes dating from the 1990s were finally given impetus by international intervention in response to a crisis of violence following the December 2007 elections, and the implausible support for President Mwai Kibaki's re-election by the Supreme Court, forcing the creation of a temporary government of national unity. A new constitution was finally adopted by referendum in 2010.

The reformed constitutional provisions on citizenship were influenced by lobbying from the women's and children's rights movements, and by Kenyan diaspora groups, as well as by those protesting the long history of discrimination in access to Kenyan citizenship documents. A constitutional review commission that reported in 2002 had heard repeated complaints from those ethnic groups subjected to additional vetting before they could get identity cards or passports, or exercise the right to vote.[176] The Kenya National Human Rights Commission (established by statute in 2002) and national human rights groups had done the same; while complaints to the African regional human rights bodies lodged during

[172] The requirement in relation to 'Asians' had a certain logic, given that obligatory registration of births in the Kenyan colony had applied to children of 'Asiatic origin or descent' (as well as Europeans) from 1928 – meaning that it could be reasonably presumed that most 'Asians' born in the colony (though not the protectorate) would have access to such documents. However, the provision relating to 'Arabs' had no such basis.

[173] 'Kenya: Imams Meet Over Rule On Immigrants', Daily Nation (Nairobi), 31 May 2001; Kenya National Assembly Official Record (Hansard), 13 June 2001, pp.1098–1099; 'Christian churches burnt down in Kenya', BBC, 27 September 2001.

[174] 'Kenya: National registration process leaves minorities on the edge of Statelessness', *Bulletin*, Refugees International, 23 May 2008.

[175] Circular dated 12 March 2007.

[176] Constitution of Kenya Review Commission, 'The People's Choice: The Report of the Constitution of Kenya Review Commission' (2002).

the constitution-drafting process had ensured these issues were also in the international spotlight.[177]

Security concerns, however, were pulling in the opposite direction, dating especially from the 1998 bombing of the US embassy in Nairobi. There were repeated calls for non-citizens (that is, in practice those without national identity cards) to be deported, and police crackdowns in the Somali-dominated Nairobi neighbourhood of Eastleigh.[178]

The new citizenship chapter reflected these opposing currents. It ended gender discrimination under the law in relation to a woman's ability to pass her nationality to her child or spouse, allowed Kenyans to hold dual citizenship under some circumstances, and restricted the grounds on which nationality might be revoked.[179] For the first time, the law provided that a child of unknown parents found in Kenya would be presumed to be Kenyan, though even this standard protection was politically controversial in Kenya's ethnically charged politics – with allegations that it would be used to bring Somali children into the country to claim Kenyan citizenship.[180] But the fundamental basis of citizenship in descent did not change: no rights were included based on birth in the country, even for those who would otherwise be stateless.[181]

The constitution also provided for the first time that every Kenyan citizen was entitled to 'a Kenyan passport and any document of registration or identification issued by the State to citizens', thus including an identity card.[182] This article, reinforced in new citizenship legislation,[183] responded directly to the contested nature

[177] Kenya National Commission on Human Rights, 'An Identity Crisis? Study on the Issuance of National Identity Cards in Kenya' (2007); Kenya National Commission on Human Rights, 'Out of the Shadows: Towards Ensuring the Rights of Stateless Persons and Persons at Risk of Statelessness in Kenya' (2010); see also the NGO report Kenya Human Rights Commission, 'Foreigners at Home: The Dilemma of Citizenship in Northern Kenya' (2009). The Kenyan Nubian Children's Case was lodged before the African Committee of Experts on the Rights and Welfare of the Child in 2009; and another case concerning discrimination against the Nubians before the African Commission on Human and Peoples' Rights in 2006; both were decided after the 2010 constitution was adopted, but the arguments before the continental bodies shone light onto the Nubian situation.

[178] See, eg, Amnesty International, 'Kenya: The Government must respect the rights of refugees under international law', 17 August 2005.

[179] Constitution of Kenya 2010, ch III.

[180] UNHCR, *Good Practices Paper – Action 2: Ensuring that no child is born Stateless*, 20 March 2017, case study on Kenya.

[181] Constitution of Kenya, 2010, ch 3, Art 14(4). For detailed commentary on the deficiencies of the draft text of the constitution, see 'Comments on the Citizenship Provisions of the Draft Kenyan Constitution' 18 March 2010, and 'Submission to the Task Force on Citizenship and Related Provisions of the Constitution' 13 April 2011, both by Citizenship Rights in Africa Initiative, available at the website http://citizenshiprightsafrica.org/.

[182] Constitution of Kenya 2010, Art 12(1)(b).

[183] Citizenship and Immigration Act 2011, S 22, states: '(1) Every citizen is entitled to the rights, privileges and benefits and is subject to the limitations provided for or permitted by the Constitution or any other written law including […] (g) the entitlement to any document of registration or identification issued by the State to citizens including – (i) a birth certificate; (ii) a certificate of registration (iii) a passport; (iv) a national identification card; and (v) a voter's card, where applicable.'

of access to identity documents in Kenya. The new provisions strengthened due process protections, requiring reasons to be given and explicitly confirming the right to challenge decisions in the High Court (a proposal to establish a dedicated 'Kenya Citizens and Foreign Nationals Management Appeals Tribunal' was not, however, included in the final version of the act).

Although activists were disappointed at the lack of protection for stateless persons included in the constitution, the Citizenship and Immigration Act of 2011 established temporary measures for the integration of people who had not been incorporated into the body of citizens on succession of States at independence. It provided that:

> A person who does not have an enforceable claim to the citizenship of any recognized State and has been living in Kenya for a continuous period since 12th December, 1963, shall be deemed to have been lawfully resident and may, on application, in the prescribed manner be eligible to be registered as a citizen of Kenya ...[184]

Similar provisions applied to 'a person who has voluntarily migrated into Kenya before 12 December 1963' (the date of independence) who 'does not hold a passport or an identification document of any other country'.[185] The registration in either case was subject to conditions similar to those for naturalisation, including a clean criminal record, and knowledge of Swahili or another 'local dialect'. The application must be made within five years of the entry into force of the Act (expiring at the end of August 2016),[186] with the possibility of extension for a further three years. Descendants of those eligible to register as citizens under these provisions are equally eligible, if born in Kenya.[187]

At the same time, the constitution put in place institutions that highlighted the extent of existing problems and assisted the political momentum for action. The 2013 report of the Truth Justice and Reconciliation Commission, which examined historical abuses dating back to independence, recorded 'evidence demonstrating that communities in North Eastern and Upper Eastern regions of the country and Muslims in general have suffered discrimination for decades in relation to their right to citizenship and associated identity documents.' Moreover, 'Even Somalis

[184] Kenya Citizenship and Immigration (No. 12) Act 2011, s 15.

[185] Amendments adopted in 2012 allowed the Cabinet Secretary, 'for sufficient reason', to waive the requirements that applicants do not hold documentation from any other country and had arrived in the country before 1963, if they satisfy the other conditions. Citizenship and Immigration Act of 2011, sections 15, 16 and 17, as amended by the Statute Law (Miscellaneous Amendments) Act No.12 of 2012.

[186] Citizenship and Immigration Act 2011, s 16. The two sections are headed 'Stateless persons' and 'migrants'. Although the definitions section of the act defines 'Stateless person' as 'a person who is not recognized as a citizen by any State under the operation of the laws of any State', in accordance with the definition in the 1954 Convention relating to the Status of Stateless Persons, s 15 of the act on 'Stateless persons', refers rather to a person who 'does not have an enforceable claim to the citizenship of any recognized State'. It is not clear therefore how the courts will interpret the legislation. Nor is it clear what the distinction is with a person eligible under s 16, who 'does not hold a passport or an identification document of any other country'.

[187] Ibid., s 17.

who have for decades lived outside Northern Kenya face similar challenges of accessing national identity cards.'[188] In 2015, the newly established Commission on the Administration of Justice reported serious problems across the administration of civil registration, identity documents and immigration, including 'rampant' corruption.[189]

This new legal and institutional regime began to have impacts on government practice. In 2011, the High Court found that the requirements to produce religious certificates and for parents' and grandparents' birth certificates for 'Asians and Arabs' were unconstitutional, and ordered the NRB to cease applying these rules.[190] The circular was withdrawn.[191] In a constitutional petition heard on the Galje'el Somali case in 2013, the High Court ordered that, given that the State had not contested the fact that the applicants were citizens, they had a right to national identity cards.[192] The NRB issued cards to the two named plaintiffs in the case in accordance with the court order. Representatives of the NRB visited the community in 2015, to confirm the current status of others whose cards had been confiscated, and their descendants (though as of 2017 no further action had been taken).[193] In 2016, a court ruled that a child born out of wedlock had the right to a birth certificate with the father's name recorded, protecting the child's right to citizenship in some cases.[194] Under donor pressure, there were also efforts by the NRB to ensure greater access to identity documents in the counties of the former North Eastern Province, especially to facilitate cash transfers as part of the national Hunger Safety Net Programme.[195] Some legal authority for the existence of the controversial vetting committees was finally established.[196]

[188] TJRC Report, Vol. IIC, ch 3. The TJRC also reported the conclusions of a committee appointed in 2007 by President Mwai Kibaki to look into concerns of the Muslim community, which made robust findings and recommendations on discriminatory practices in the issue of national identity cards and passports. The report of the committee was not officially published, but a leaked copy of the report, dated 31 March 2008, forms an appendix to ch 3 of the TJRC Report Vol. IIC.

[189] Kenya Commission on Administrative Justice (Office of the Ombudsperson), *Stateless In Kenya: An Investigation Report on the Crisis of Acquiring Identification Documents in Kenya*, 2015.

[190] *MUHURI and Another v. Registrar of Persons and others*, Constitutional Petition No.1 of 2011, High Court at Mombasa, 18 February 2011.

[191] Interview, National Registration Bureau, Nairobi, 2 June 2016.

[192] *Hersi Hassan Gutale & Another v. Attorney General & Another*, High Court at Nairobi (Nairobi Law Courts) Constitutional Petition 50 of 2011, 21 January 2013. A court challenge under the former constitution had been rejected: *Hersi Hassan Gutale and Abdullahi Mohammed Ahmed v Principal Registrar of Persons & Attorney General*, Nairobi HC Misc. Application No. 774 of 2004.

[193] Interviews, Tana River, June 2016.

[194] *LNW v Attorney General and Another*, Constitutional Petition No 484 of 2014, High Court of Kenya at Nairobi, 26 May 2016.

[195] Managed by the National Drought Management Authority (NDMA) under the Ministry of Devolution, with financial support from DFID and Australian Aid. See 'ID Registration for Safety Net Cash Transfers: HSNP experience in facilitating national ID card registration', 23 June 2015; data available at http://hsnp.or.ke/index.php/dashboards/at-a-glance.

[196] Security Laws Amendment Act 2014, s 23, amending the Registration of Persons Act, s 8 provided for 'identification committees … to assist in the authentication of information furnished by a parent or guardian'.

The registration provisions for stateless persons in the 2011 Citizenship Act languished unused, however, until the combined effect of advocacy from UNHCR and other international agencies, as well as national civil society and constitutional bodies, and the prospect of a new election, led the government of President Uhuru Kenyatta to act just as the initial five-year period was expiring. Following a report on their situation published by UNHCR in early 2015, the NRB led an investigation by a government task force, which recommended to the cabinet that they should be registered as Kenyan.[197] In 2016, following a protest march at the lack of any action in their case from the Makonde settlements near Mombasa to State House, Nairobi, President Uhuru Kenyatta extended the registration period by two years,[198] and promised the community registration as Kenyan citizens.[199] Individual registration of the Makonde was commenced immediately, and around 1,000 adults and 500 children had been registered as Kenyan citizens by the end of 2016.[200] Press reports announced the Makonde as the '43rd tribe'; swiftly followed by Kenyatta's (presumed to be election-related) pronouncement that Asians were officially recognised as the '44th tribe' – statements of political if not legal significance.[201]

Despite these reforms and developments, the foundation of Kenyan identification and citizenship administration in colonial systems of population control remained for the most part unshaken – and buttressed by ongoing security concerns. In 2013, following the Westgate shopping mall terrorist attack in which at least 67 people were killed, there were calls for the expulsion of all Somalis in Kenya and the closure of the Dadaab refugee camp; arbitrary arrests of many Somalis followed, as well as dismissals of immigration officials for issuing 'Kenyan identity documents to illegal immigrants, thereby endangering national security'.[202] In late 2014, a controversial new security law amended already stringent provisions in the Public Order Act, the Prevention of Terrorism Act and other legislation.[203]

[197] *Integrated, But Undocumented: A study into the nationality status of the Makonde community in Kenya*, UNHCR Representation in Kenya, in partnership with Haki Centre, Kenya Human Rights Commission, Haki Africa, Open Society Initiative for Eastern Africa, February 2015. Interview with NRB director, June 2015.

[198] Legal Notice 178, The Kenya Citizenship and Immigration Act: Extension of Time, 4 October 2016.

[199] Wanja Lisa Munaita, 'Kenya's Stateless Makonde people finally obtain papers', UNHCR, 27 October 2016; Diana Gichengo, 'The Arduous Journey of the Makonde to Kenyan Citizenship', Citizenship Rights Africa website, 9 November 2016 at http://citizenshiprightsafrica.org/region/kenya/.

[200] Wanja Munaita, 'Mission to coordinate, monitor and support the registration of the Makonde of Kenya in Kwale and Kilifi Counties', UNHCR, November 2016; Manby, 'Citizenship and Statelessness in the East African Community' (n 158).

[201] Alloys Musyoka, 'Big read: Kenya's 43rd tribe: Makonde's long journey to identity', *The Star* (Nairobi), 7 February 2017; Zarina Patel and Jill Ghai, 'Big Read: A tribe, a nation, a people – or just Kenyans?', *The Star* (Nairobi), 14 August 2017. The list of census enumeration codes had changed in 2009, to more than double the number of ethnic groups and sub-groups, including the Nubians for the first time. Samantha Balaton-Chrimes, 'Counting as Citizens: Recognition of the Nubians in the 2009 Kenyan Census' (2011) 10 Ethnopolitics 205.

[202] 'Kenya Calls for Somalis to Leave World's Largest Refugee Camp', *AllAfrica.com*, 26 October 2013.

[203] The Refugees Act was also amended to restrict the 'permitted number of refugees and asylum seekers in Kenya' to 150,000 people. The Security Laws (Amendment) Act 2014, ss 18, 25 and 75–84.

Proposed new legislation was put forward in 2014 to replace both the Registration of Persons Act and the Births and Deaths Registration Act – though it remained undebated by Parliament by 2018. The Bill would in principle improve some aspects of the legislation but still placed the burden on any person applying for an identity card to prove that he or she is a Kenyan citizen. It retained existing provisions that allowed for 'any person or class of persons in any particular area of Kenya to attend before the registrar at such dates as may be specified in the notice for the purpose of registration under the provisions of this Act', the basis of the Yusuf Haji task force procedures. It did not provide any rules on membership or rules of procedure of vetting committees nor on appeals from the decisions of such committees. Nor did the Bill finally provide rules on what constituted proof of Kenyan citizenship: neither in the sense of the evidence needed to show that a person is entitled to an identity card; nor in the sense that a national identity card was stated to be proof of citizenship itself until overturned by a court.[204] The executive discretion of the colonial State had been eroded, but not yet subjected to effective control.

7.3.2. Uganda

The development of citizenship law and practice in Uganda followed a very different route from Kenya after the early commonalities around the status of Asians had passed. To some extent, these differences could be traced back to the very different experience of Uganda as a British territory, when it had been governed as a protectorate under the fiction of indirect rule, and far less land had been expropriated for white farms, with accordingly less need for control of 'native' movement and labour.

In particular, the Kingdom of Buganda in the south of the country had played a central role in colonial administration until independence. British policy towards the ethnic groups of northern Uganda was to treat them mainly as a reservoir for labour and especially for recruitment into the army. The independence constitution of 1962 had granted full federal status to the Buganda Kingdom and semi-federal status to a number of other southern kingdoms (Ankole, Bunyoro, and Toro). Disputes over the relative power of central government and traditional authorities had been one of the main causes of the collapse of the first post-independence government, and the same issues dominated politics again following the fall of Amin. Like Amin, Obote also mobilised both ethnic divisions and xenophobia in support of his cause, but not only (or mainly) against those of Asian

See also 'Kenya Security Bill Tramples Basic Rights: Lawmakers Should Reject Amendments', Human Rights Watch and Amnesty International, 14 December 2014.

[204] Registration and Identification of Persons Bill 2014, Kenya Gazette Supplement No. 153 (Senate Bills No. 39); Kenya Human Rights Commission, *Memorandum on the Registration and Identification of Persons Bill, 2014.*

descent: the first Obote government expelled Kenyan Luo and other East African workers in 1970;[205] the second Obote government drove out many Banyarwanda in 1982–83.[206]

In 1985, Obote was deposed for the second time by a combination of rebel forces, among which Yoweri Museveni's National Resistance Army (NRA) became the final victor. Museveni was installed as President in early 1986 and immediately announced that political party activity would be suspended during a transition period, except within the framework of his renamed National Resistance Movement (NRM). In 1989, he appointed a Constitutional Commission, known as the Odoki Commission after its chair Justice Ben Odoki, to lead the process of drafting a new constitution for Uganda.

The Odoki Commission conducted an impressive campaign to reach out to the Ugandan public and get views on a new constitutional order. A constituent assembly then debated the proposed draft, in which the future political system was one of the most controversial issues. NRM influence ensured that the constitution finally adopted in September 1995 essentially endorsed the existing severe restrictions on political party activity.

In relation to the qualifications for citizenship, while the status of those of Asian descent had dominated the drafting of the 1962 and 1967 Constitutions, the 1994–5 constitutional debate focused on the status of African immigrants and refugees. The debates were taking place in the immediate aftermath of the Rwandan genocide and subsequent defeat of government forces by the Rwandan Patriotic Army (RPA), leading to the installation of RPA commander Paul Kagame as Rwandan President. Kagame himself and many of his RPA soldiers had been resident in Uganda for many years, fighting with Museveni's NRA against the government. The status of the 'Rwandese Tutsi' who had come to Uganda as refugees was thus particularly controversial, and many Ugandans opposed the recognition of the 'Banyarwanda' as citizens – even though part of Rwanda had been ceded to Britain by Germany in 1910, meaning that some of Rwandan ethnicity were long established in Uganda at independence. However, it was a minority that sought a more restrictive position; many Ugandans wanted citizenship to be defined to include all people who had been in Uganda for a long period of time and wished to obtain citizenship.[207]

The 1995 Constitution introduced an explicit ethnic definition of Ugandan citizenship for the first time, while also restoring rights based on birth in Uganda removed in 1967. It provided for a right to citizenship by birth for two categories: first, based on a *jus soli* rule for every person born in Uganda, 'one of whose parents

[205] Ali Mazrui, 'Casualties of an Underdeveloped Class Structure: The Expulsion of Luo Workers and Asian Bourgeoisie from Uganda' in William A Shack and Elliott P Skinner (eds), *Strangers in African Societies* (University of California Press 1979).

[206] Mahmood Mamdani, *When Victims Become Killers: Colonialism, Nativism, and the Genocide in Rwanda* (Princeton Univ Press 2002) 160.

[207] Barya (n 135); Odoki Commission, 'Report of the Uganda Constitutional Commission' (1993).

or grandparents is or was a member of any of the indigenous communities existing and residing within the borders of Uganda as at the first day of February, 1926'; and secondly, for every person born in or outside Uganda one of whose parents or grandparents was a citizen of Uganda by birth.[208] Both categories, the former explicitly, the latter by implication, privileged the ethnic groups historically resident in Uganda, making it difficult for those from 'non-indigenous' ethnic groups to obtain Ugandan citizenship, and to transmit it to their children.[209] A schedule listing the 'indigenous communities' of Uganda generated some of the hottest debate as the constitution was adopted; Asians argued unsuccessfully that they should be regarded as an indigenous group. Fifty-six groups were eventually included, among them the Banyarwanda, as well as other cross-border ethnic groups such as the Batwa, Lendu and Karamojong.[210]

The 1995 constitutional provisions also reaffirmed the earlier position denying dual citizenship. Although there were submissions both for and against the issue of dual citizenship made to the Odoki Commission, it recommended, on a statistical assessment of the views submitted to it, that dual citizenship be rejected.[211] The Citizenship and Immigration Control Act adopted in 1999 confirmed these rules, and also established a new Citizenship and Immigration Board to decide on citizenship matters, reducing the discretionary power of the minister.[212]

A new Constitutional Review Commission (CRC) was set up from 2001 to 2003, in which the most contentious discussion was over the extension of the presidential term limit. The commission re-examined the provisions on citizenship, and noted that the majority view was that only people who were descendants of indigenous communities of Uganda should be recognised as citizens and therefore some communities, such as the Banyarwanda, should be excluded.[213] Once again, the majority of responses submitted to the CRC were against dual citizenship, though the Ugandan government's submissions to the CRC argued that it was necessary to allow dual citizenship both for indigenous Ugandans living abroad and for potential foreign investors. The CRC ultimately recommended that Parliament should allow dual citizenship, and the government position was reaffirmed in a white paper responding to the CRC report.[214]

In 2005 legislation was finally passed to amend the constitution, based on these recommendations. A further nine 'indigenous communities' were added to the list

[208] Constitution of the Republic of Uganda 1995, art 10.

[209] Another article provided for those born in Uganda to obtain citizenship by registration on application, if they had been living in Uganda since 1962 and had no parent or grandparent with diplomatic status or who had been a refugee. Constitution of the Republic of Uganda 1995, art 12.

[210] Constitution of the Republic of Uganda 1995, third schedule; Uganda Constitution (Amendment) Act 2005.

[211] Odoki Commission (n 207).

[212] Uganda Citizenship and Immigration Control (No. 3) Act 1999.

[213] Uganda Constitutional Review Commission report, 10 December 2003, p 157.

[214] 'Government white paper on (1) The report of the commission of enquiry (2) Government proposals not addressed by the report of the commission of inquiry,' para 1.11(f), available at www.cmi.no/pdf/?file=/uganda/doc/government-whitepaper.pdf.

of those with presumptive citizenship; the Banyarwanda, protected by Museveni, were allowed to retain their status. The amendments also permitted both Ugandans and non-Ugandans to acquire dual citizenship, but with many conditions attached. The Act mandated that Parliament prescribe the offices of State that those with dual citizenship would be disqualified from holding.[215] It took four years for Parliament to pass amendments to the Citizenship Act, which set out the detailed rules for citizenship applications, as well as a long list of official positions that could not be held by dual citizens, including the presidency, Prime Minister, ministers, and senior positions in the armed forces, intelligence services and police. The requirements for those naturalising as Ugandan who wished to retain another nationality were also drastically increased.[216] The Citizenship and Immigration Board proposed in 1999 was finally established in 2007, the delay leading to backlogs of applications for restoration of citizenship by dual nationals.[217]

Although controversial, the rights based on birth in Uganda provided significant protection against statelessness, for those who could claim to be members of an 'indigenous community'. For this reason, the Nubian community in Uganda, for example, included in the list in schedule 3 of the constitution, did not have the same problems in relation to citizenship as the Nubians in Kenya – even though they were still subject to significant discrimination in different spheres.

But the ethnically-based approach also increased the risk of statelessness for members of other communities not listed in the constitution. Among these groups were the Ugandan Somalis, including descendants of pre-independence immigrants from British Somaliland, whose special status was acknowledged, but subject to proof of descent from a person who would have automatically become Ugandan at independence. The Maragoli, related to the Luhya of Kenya and resident within the Bunyoro Kingdom, began to face difficulties only with the introduction of a new national identity card from 2014. The ethnic basis for citizenship did not fully protect even members of those groups who were listed. For example, the Kuku ethnic group, listed in the constitution but mainly found in South Sudan, faced difficulties in obtaining Ugandan passports.[218]

The legal framework also placed significant obstacles to the acquisition of citizenship, and for similar reasons as in Kenya: Uganda hosted hundreds of thousands of long-term refugees, whose potential voting power could upset local if not national power balances. Both the 1995 constitution and 1999 Citizenship and Immigration Control Act required 20 years' residence in the country before a

[215] Uganda Constitution (Amendment) Act 2005, Pt III, ss 5 to 8, amending arts 14 to 17 of the 1995 Constitution.

[216] Uganda Citizenship and Immigration Control (Amendment) (No. 5) Act 2009, introducing ss 19A to E in the original Act. See also Felix Osike and Mary Karugaba, 'Rules set for dual citizens,' *New Vision* (Kampala), 18 August 2008; Henry Mukasa and Catherine Bekunda, 'Parliament passes dual citizenship law' *New Vision*, 17 May 2009.

[217] 'Let sanity begin at immigration,' *The Monitor*, Kampala, 12 November 2007.

[218] Manby, 'Citizenship and Statelessness in the East African Community' (n 158).

person could naturalise, an unusually long period, and other conditions apply.[219] Although children born in Uganda to non-citizens could apply for registration as citizens, children of refugee parents or those who did not themselves 'legally and voluntarily' immigrate to Uganda, perhaps the most likely category to need this right, were explicitly excluded.[220] In 2006 a new Refugees Act was passed to replace the tellingly-named 1960 Control of Alien Refugees Act, and instituted a significantly more generous management regime for refugees. Whereas the former legislation had excluded any period spent in Uganda from counting as residence for the purposes of naturalisation, the new Act stated that 'the Constitution and any other law in force in Uganda shall apply to the naturalisation of a recognised refugee'.[221] In practice, remaining ambiguities allowed Ugandan officials to continue to interpret the law to mean that refugees could not naturalise. Forms and procedures used as of 2011 still referred to the long-repealed 1964 Citizenship Act.[222] A Constitutional Court decision in 2015 denied a petition that the provisions relating to registration should be interpreted to include refugees, but expressed its opinion that refugees would be eligible for naturalisation (while not ruling specifically on that question).[223]

At the time of the judgment, almost 500,000 refugees were resident in Uganda (with new outflows from South Sudan doubling that number by 2017). Some long-term refugees had been present in the country for more than fifty years, including Tutsi Rwandese who fled to Uganda in various episodes from 1959 to 1973, and Congolese who fled after the 1964 defeat of the Lumumbist rebels.[224] Around 60,000 had been present in the country at least 20 years, the baseline for naturalisation, including Sudanese refugees from before the 2005 Comprehensive Peace Agreement that led to the secession of South Sudan, and both Rwandan and Congolese refugees from the mid-1990s fleeing the genocide in Rwanda and

[219] Constitution of Uganda 1995, Art 12(2)(b) and (c); Uganda Citizenship and Immigration Control Act 1999, as amended 2009, ss 14(2)(b), 15(5)(a) and 16.

[220] Constitution of Uganda, Art 12(1)(a)(ii); Uganda Citizenship and Immigration Control Act 1999, s 14(1)(a)(ii).

[221] Control of Alien Refugees Act 1960, Art 18; Refugees Act 2006, s 45; see also Refugee Law Project, 'Critique of the Refugees Act (2006)' (2006); Samuel G Walker, 'From Refugee to Citizen? Obstacles to the Naturalisation of Refugees in Uganda' (Refugee Law Project 2011). Uganda's Control of Alien Refugees Act, adopted in 1960, was originally an ordinance of the Protectorate government that provided specifically for the refugees (mostly Tutsi) – from Rwanda, Burundi, and what is now DRC – who fled to Uganda during 1959 and 1960.

[222] Walker (n 221). Article 14 of the Citizenship and Immigration Control Act 1999, as amended 2009, provides for various categories of person to be registered as a citizen on application, including a person born in Uganda who has lived continuously in Uganda since 1962 unless neither parent nor any grandparent had diplomatic status or was a refugee; and a person who has legally and voluntarily migrated to and has been living in Uganda for at least ten years. The 'legal and voluntary' caveat does not apply to naturalisations under Art 16; but in that case twenty years' residence is required.

[223] Judgment in Constitutional Petition No.34 of 2010, delivered 6 October 2015.

[224] Charles Celestin Bafaki Rweyunga, 'Local Integration as a Durable Solution for Protracted Refugees in Uganda: A Case Study of the Lumumbist Congolese Refugees at Kyaka 2 Refugee Settlement', Makerere University LLM Dissertation, 2014.

the regional conflicts that followed.[225] Although Uganda did not apply the 'ceased circumstances' clause for Rwandan refugees as recommended in 2013, the status of approximately 15,000 Rwandan refugees in Uganda also become more vulnerable; yet they were unwilling to return, on various grounds.[226]

At the same time, questions of citizenship could remain quite ambiguous in Uganda, by comparison with Kenya, thanks to the lack of a national identification system like that inherited in Kenya from the colonial era. Although Uganda had been subjected to similar types of control over the 'native' population, with requirements to carry passes imposed for the purposes of controlling movement and ensuring tax collection, these measures never penetrated as deeply as in Kenya, and they were abandoned on independence. The 1999 citizenship law allowed for the issue of ID cards, but this power was not immediately invoked.[227] Only from 2013, against the background of a push from the East African Community to standardise identification documents, was registration for a national identity card finally rolled out.

There were allegations of discrimination in this process on the grounds of ethnicity against internal migrants as well as people perceived to be foreign. Yet, by contrast to the situation in Kenya, the mass registration process allowed for the possibility of registering (though not naturalising) eligible people *as citizens*, as well as registration for the purposes of issuing an identity card.[228] From January 2016, population registration moved onto a more regular footing, with the entry into force of new legislation, the Registration of Persons Act 2015, and the establishment of a new agency, the National Identification and Registration Authority (NIRA) to be responsible for its implementation. As of 2017, it was not yet clear now this would work in practice and whether the more open procedures would remain in place.

The Ugandan case forms an interesting contrast to the separate development of citizenship in Kenya. On the one hand, both Uganda and Kenya made a clean break from the substantive basis of citizenship inherited from the British in the independence constitution as governments struggled, in good or bad faith, to manage the tensions of post-colonial nation-building. But the ways in which this break was made also differed radically from each other: Uganda established an explicit basis of citizenship in ethnicity while restoring rights based on birth in Uganda for those groups; Kenya eliminated rights based on birth in the country altogether, and with retroactive effect, thus greatly increasing the importance

[225] Interview, office of the Prime Minister, 3 August 2016.

[226] See generally, Marshall Godfrey Alenyo, 'International Refugee Law and the Right to Nationality: Legal Responses to the Rwandan Refugee Crisis in Uganda', LLM Dissertation, University College Cork, October 2014.

[227] Citizenship and Immigration Control Act 1999, Pt IV, provided for 'Registration of citizens and issue of national identification numbers and national identity cards.'

[228] Brief to Parliament on the On-Going Mass Registration of Citizens Exercise under the National Security Information System (NSIS) Project, by The Hon. Minister of Internal Affairs, 29th July 2014. See Manby, 'Citizenship and Statelessness in the East African Community' (n 158).

of historical proof of acquisition of citizenship at independence and, paradoxically, also increasing the importance of ethnicity. Yet even as they made these changes, both countries reflected a continuity of legal forms established during the colonial period: Uganda with the emphasis on devolution of power and membership of ethnic communities; Kenya with the mobilisation of the security State to police the boundaries of citizenship and free movement through requirements for identification.

7.4. Côte d'Ivoire's War of Conjunctions: The 'and' and the 'or'

Historical explanations for the crisis of ethnic identification in Côte d'Ivoire reach back far into the past, to the 1930s and the population movements imposed by the then colonial power France. At independence, the status of these migrants and their children was left unclear, though initially uncontested by the post-independence leadership. It was only later that the impact of the lack of clarity was felt, leaving open the door to legal manipulation by a xenophobic government.

The French assessed the rich and well-watered land of Côte d'Ivoire, first created as a colony in 1893, to be ideal for agricultural development, especially coffee and cocoa cultivation, but underpopulated. Meanwhile, the much drier savannah zone to the north known by the French as Haute Volta (Upper Volta; future Burkina Faso), under military governorship when first created as an administrative district in 1919, had a high population density. The obvious answer was to move the 'surplus' labour south.[229]

In 1933 France modified the administrative borders within AOF, including between Côte d'Ivoire and Upper Volta. The new zone of Haute Côte d'Ivoire brought together three quarters of the territory of Haute Volta and the northern parts of Côte d'Ivoire. A program of forced movement of agricultural workers to plantations further south was instituted and, as part of this process, the French established by decree a number of 'colonial villages' in central Côte d'Ivoire, where recruits from Haute Volta were housed in new settlements that took on the names of the towns of origin of the workers further north.[230] Forced labour was ended

[229] There is a vast literature on migration and the question of identity in Côte d'Ivoire. In addition to the works cited specifically below, see in particular: Sylvie Bredeloup, 'La Côte d'Ivoire ou l'étrange destin de l'étranger' (2003) 19 Revue européenne des migrations internationales 85; Bruno Losch (ed), 'Dossier: Côte d'Ivoire, La Tentation Ethnonationaliste' (2000) 78 Politique africaine; Daouda Gary-Tounkara, *Migrants Soudanais-Maliens et Conscience Ivoirienne: Les Étrangers En Côte d'Ivoire, 1903–1980* (Harmattan 2008); Richard Banégas and Ruth Marshall-Fratani, 'Côte d'Ivoire: Negotiating Identity and Citizenship' in Morten Bøås and Kevin C Dunn (eds), *African guerrillas: raging against the machine* (Lynne Rienner Publishers, Inc 2007).

[230] By 1934, three colonial villages were established in the area surrounding Zuénoula that were named Ouagadougou, Kaya, and Koudougou; and four villages around the Ivorian town of

in 1946, by which time around 420,000 migrants had been registered,[231] and the Haute Côte territory was re-divided between Côte d'Ivoire and Haute Volta in 1947; but the policy of encouraging migration continued. A private labour recruiting consortium known as the *Syndicat inter-professionel pour l'acheminement de la main-d'oeuvre* (SIAMO) worked in conjunction with the French West African labour inspectorate (*Inspection du travail de l'AOF*) that had been created in 1932.[232] By independence in 1960 SIAMO had imported more than 250,000 workers.[233] Many others had migrated voluntarily – from Haute Volta, but also from Mali, Guinea, and other parts of AOF – to take up cocoa and coffee farming in their own right on land ceded by southern Ivorian ethnic groups. The majority of the migrants were Muslims from the Malinké ethno-linguistic group, itself a sub-group of the Mandé, though other groups were also represented.[234]

The development of the cocoa and coffee economy also promoted internal migration within the territory, especially by the east-central Baoulé, related to the Akan of Ghana. Though some cocoa and coffee was grown in the southern parts of their territory, Baoulé themselves were internal migrants to the main areas of cultivation in the south east and south west. As in the case of the migrants from Upper Volta, many of these became established as farmers in their own right. Independence leader Félix Houphouët-Boigny, himself a Baoulé, first came to political prominence as leader of the *Syndicat agricole africain* (SAA), defending the interests of small-scale African farmers against European domination of the plantation economy, and protesting the use of forced labour.[235]

The French administration also made use of many Dahomeyans and Senegalese in the Ivorian civil service, given their earlier exposure to western education; as early as the 1930s there was an *Association de défense des intérêts des autochtones de Côte d'Ivoire* protesting this tendency. In October 1958, less than a month after the referendum on the constitution of the *Communauté française* that gave

Bouaflé: Koudougou, Garango, Koupéla, and Fankodogo. Chikouna Cissé, *Migrations et mise en valeur de la Basse Côte d'Ivoire, 1920–1960* (L'Harmattan 2013) 120–123.

[231] Statistics on historical migrant numbers from the Institut national de la statistique, 'Recensement Général de La Population et de l'Habitat, 1988 : Tome 2, Répartition Spatiale de La Population et Migrations, Analyse Des Résultats Définitifs' (République de la Côte d'Ivoire 1992). (Hereafter Recensement Général, vol 2, 1988.)

[232] Vincent Bonnecase, 'Les étrangers et la terre en Côte d'Ivoire à l'époque coloniale' (Institut de Recherche pour le Développement (IRD) 2001) 2.

[233] Recensement Général, vol 2, 1988 (n 231).

[234] The ethnic make-up of the migrants was of course more complex: among the Burkinabè, a large percentage were Mossi from Burkina Faso's central plateau, not one of the Mandé groups; many Mossi are also not Muslim. Among the northern ethnic groups in current Côte d'Ivoire are also the Senoufo, whose members include those who follow Muslim, Christian or traditional religions. For a good summary of autochthonous and migrant ethnic groups, the fluidity of the definitions, and the different pre-colonial political and membership arrangements within each group, see Mike McGovern, *Making War in Côte d'Ivoire* (University of Chicago Press 2011) ch 1.

[235] Jean-Pierre Dozon, 'L'étranger et l'allochtone en Cote d'Ivoire' in Bernard Contamin and Harris Memel-Fotê (eds), *Le modèle ivoirien en questions: crises, ajustements, recompositions* (Editions Karthala : Editions de l'ORSTOM 1997).

internal self-government to Côte d'Ivoire and other French territories, popular riots forced around seventeen thousand Dahomeyans, Togolese and others to leave the country.[236]

The transitional provisions adopted at the time of the dissolution of French West Africa completely failed to provide a clear definition of who became 'Ivorian of origin' on the date of independence. As was the case across AOF, the independence constitution of Côte d'Ivoire adopted in 1960 left the details of nationality law to be determined by legislation, leaving a gap that created ambiguity, nowhere more than in Côte d'Ivoire. In 1961, Article 6 of the new Ivorian nationality code gave 'nationality of origin' to every person born in Côte d'Ivoire unless both of his or her parents were foreigners (*étrangers*).[237] Those born outside Côte d'Ivoire would be Ivorian if they had one Ivorian parent (unusually for the era, with no gender discrimination).[238] A child born in Côte d'Ivoire of foreign parents and resident there for at least five years could, however, acquire nationality 'by declaration' on majority; this applied equally to those born before or after independence, but was dependent on the birth being formally registered.[239] In addition, as a transitional provision, those who had their permanent residence in Côte d'Ivoire before independence could also be naturalised as citizens without further requirements if they applied within one year.[240] Otherwise, a regular naturalisation process was

[236] Herschelle Sullivan Challenor, 'Strangers as Colonial Intermediaries: The Dahomeyans in Francophone Africa' in William A Shack and Elliott P Skinner (eds), *Strangers in African Societies* (University of California Press 1979); Alain Tirefort, 'L'affaire « Daho-Togo »: Une fièvre de xenophobie en Côte d'Ivoire' in Catherine Coquery-Vidrovitch and others (eds), *Etre étranger et migrant en Afrique au XXe siècle*, vol 1 (L'Harmattan 2003); Joseph-Roger de Benoist, 'Pogrom contre les Dahomeens et les Togolais en Cote d'Ivoire en octobre 1958' in Catherine Coquery-Vidrovitch and others (eds), *Etre étranger et migrant en Afrique au XXe siècle*, vol 1 (Harmattan 2003).

[237] Article 6 of the Code de la nationalité 1961, stated in its original form under 'nationality of origin' that: « Est ivoirien tout individu né en Côte d'Ivoire, sauf si les deux parents sont étrangers ». After 1972, this article was amended to impose a discrimination based on birth in or outside marriage, stating that the following persons are 'ivorian of origin' : «1- L'enfant légitime ou légitimé, né en Côte d'Ivoire, sauf si ces deux parents sont étrangers; 2- L'enfant né hors mariage, en Côte d'Ivoire, sauf si sa filiation est légalement établie à l'égard de ses deux parents étrangers ou d'un seul parent également étranger. »

[238] Article 7, Code de la nationalité 1961 : « Est ivoirien, l'individu né hors de Cote d'Ivoire d'un parent ivoirien ». The difference between the wording of Arts 6 and 7 is puzzling. However, Art 7 appears to requires proof that one parent is Ivorian, while Art 6 requires proof that both parents are foreigners. That is, not only that they do not have Ivorian nationality, but that they do have nationality elsewhere: which would mean that children of unknown or stateless parents (and also parents whose nationality was unknown) would be Ivorian based on birth in the territory. This would also make sense of the drafting of Art 9 of the 1961 Nationality Code, which created a presumption of birth on Ivorian soil for abandoned children of unknown parents found in Côte d'Ivoire, but not also a presumption that at least one parent was Ivorian. See discussions on the 1961 Ivorian code in Alexandre Zatzepine, *Le droit de la nationalité des républiques francophones d'Afrique et de Madagascar* (Pichon et Durand-Auzias 1963); Roger Decottignies and Marc de Biéville, *Les nationalités africaines* (A Pedone 1963).

[239] Articles 17–23 Code de la nationalité 1961. The requirement for birth registration, « to the exclusion of all other forms of proof » was introduced by the National Assembly, « in order to avoid abuses ». Procès-verbal de la séance du mercredi 8 novembre 1961, Commission des Affaires Générales et Institutionnelles, Assemblée Nationale.

[240] Article 105, Code de la nationalité 1961.

set up in law, providing for discretionary grant of nationality to those who fulfilled a range of conditions, including five years' legal residence, but also satisfactory health and police reports and other hurdles.[241] A final article, introduced by the National Assembly, provided that all those established in the territory who did not acquire Ivorian nationality could remain in the territory and continue to benefit from all their acquired rights (though not the right to vote or be elected).[242]

The convoluted language on acquisition of nationality of origin, drafted in a way that at first sight appeared to be – and was indeed understood to be – founded on *jus soli* rights based on birth in the territory,[243] plus the lack of a definition of *étranger*, meant that in many cases it was more or less impossible to know if a person's parents were 'foreign' under the law and therefore if further action was needed or not. All those living in French West Africa had previously had French nationality, and a large number of people had been forcibly brought to Côte d'Ivoire by the French. It would be possible to argue that none of those who made up the population of the country at independence were 'foreigners', unless they had the nationality of a country that had not previously been under French control. Equally, it could be the case that all those attributed the nationality of another country were not Ivorian. If they knew of the new law's provisions at all, many potentially affected may have assumed that if they had come from another formerly French territory then they were not 'foreign'; or that there was no need to make a choice of nationalities, given their continued right to stay in Côte d'Ivoire if already established in the country. The law included no definition that created clarity on the attribution of Ivorian nationality by operation of law on those who might potentially have the claim on the nationality of one of the other newly created States. As a matter of fact, not a single person applied for naturalisation during the one-year transitional period, while the right of option was only accessed by two people before it was abolished in 1972.[244]

For some years these drafting ambiguities were not significant. While ensuring that no ethnic group was completely left out in his management of the political chessboard, President Houphouët-Boigny and his *Parti Démocratique de la Côte d'Ivoire* (PDCI) were also politically allied with northerners and migrants to Côte d'Ivoire, as well as internal migrants, including the Baoulé, who shared many of the same interests. In the context of a strong post-independence economic boom, the PDCI continued to encourage economic migration from neighbouring

[241] Articles 25–32, Code de la nationalité 1961.

[242] Article 106, Code de la nationalité 1961 ; Procès-verbal de la séance du mercredi 8 novembre 1961.

[243] Exposé des motifs de la Loi de 1961 portant Code de la nationalité ivoirienne, présenté par le Président de la République (« l'art 6 consacre comme principe de la nationalité d'origine, le premier critère, à savoir la naissance sur le sol »); see also Procès-verbal de la séance du mercredi 8 novembre 1961, and Procès-verbal de la séance du mercredi 24 novembre 1961. All three texts reproduced in the *Recueil des textes législatifs et réglementaires relatifs au droit de la nationalité ivoirienne*, prepared by the Ministry of Justice of Cote d'Ivoire with UNHCR support, 2014.

[244] Exposé des motifs, Projet de loi portant dispositions particulières en matière d'acquisition de la nationalité par déclaration (No.2013-653 du 13 septembre 2013).

African States, as well as from north to south of the country, and adopted an expansionary attitude towards both the pre-independence and more recent migrants, without ever directly addressing the question of citizenship. In December 1965, Houphouët-Boigny even proposed granting regional and reciprocal citizenship rights to nationals of neighbouring countries,[245] a proposal defeated by parliament in a rare moment of independence from the executive, and abandoned by Houphouët-Boigny with the lamentation that Ivorians 'suffered from an inferiority complex' in relation to their neighbours.[246] In the interests of building electoral support in the north and centre of the country, as well as satisfying a need for labour to increase export earnings from commercial crops of coffee and cocoa in plantations in the south, Houphouët-Boigny promoted both the migration-friendly policy that 'the land belongs to those who work it' (*la terre appartient à celui qui la met en valeur*),[247] and the liberal grant of identification documents and political rights. From 1980, the electoral law provided that non-Ivorians of African origin would be allowed to register and vote in national elections.[248]

Tensions related to migration were already evident: as early as 1970, a Bété uprising in the south-western plantation country briefly declared an independent State, whose demands included the departure of migrants. The uprising was brutally suppressed.[249]

In 1972 the nationality code was amended to 'correct the too great liberalism' of the existing law by removing the right of those born in the country of foreign parents to opt at majority for Ivorian nationality; as well as introducing distinctions between those born in or out of wedlock, with the requirement

[245] The States involved were Benin, Niger, and Burkina Faso (and later Togo), members of the *Conseil de l'Entente* created in 1959 by Houphouët-Boigny as a counterbalance to Senegal's union with Mali during the final phases of the French Community; Houphouët-Boigny's initial proposal for reciprocal citizenship rights reached across the former French territories in Africa, but was reduced in scope and then abandoned, faced with resistance from other States. For a discussion of this initiative, see Henri-Michel Yéré, 'Double Nationalité and Its Discontents in Ivory Coast, 1963–66' in Emma Hunter (ed), *Citizenship, belonging, and political community in Africa: dialogues between past and present* (Ohio University Press 2016).

[246] Quoted in Suzanne Bonzon, 'Les Dahoméens En Afrique de l'Ouest' (1967) 17 Revue française de science politique 718.

[247] Widely cited, though with some variants in phrasing; see, eg, Alfred Babo, 'The Crisis of Public Policies in Côte d'Ivoire: Land Law and the Nationality Trap in Tabou's Rural Communities' (2013) 83 Africa 100.

[248] Article 57 of Loi No.80–1039 du 1er Septembre 1980 relative à l'élection des députés à l'Assemblée nationale: « Pour les élections de 1980, pourront prendre part au vote les non-ivoiriens d'origine africaine inscrits sur les listes électorales ». See also Loi. No.80-1038 portant modification des articles 10 et 29 de la Constitution; (however, Art 5 of the 1960 constitution still reserved the right to vote to 'Ivorian nationals'). This decision was in line with the ECOWAS discussions on establishing a 'community citizenship', though not implemented in other countries, nor required by the Protocol on the Definition of Community Citizen adopted by ECOWAS in 1982. See also Reynald Blion and Sylvie Bredeloup, 'La Côte d'Ivoire dans les stratégies migratoires des burkinabès et des sénégalais' in Bernard Contamin, Harris Memel-Fotê and Groupement interdisciplinaire en sciences sociales, Côte d'Ivoire (eds), *Le modèle ivoirien en questions: crises, ajustements, recompositions* (Editions Karthala : Editions de l'ORSTOM 1997); Epiphane Zoro-Bi, *Juge en Côte d'Ivoire: désarmer la violence* (Karthala 2004) 81.

[249] For an account of this revolt, see McGovern (n 234).

to establish descent by the formal process of law. Even the right to nationality for an abandoned infant found in Côte d'Ivoire was repealed.[250] Since the original law had, unlike the other AOF countries, not provided for double *jus soli*, birth in the country now provided no rights to nationality in any circumstances. Foreign nationals of whatever origin could in theory still acquire Ivorian citizenship by naturalisation in the normal way,[251] but this discretionary process was only readily accessible to those working in the formal economy, with full proof of legal residence and a range of other documentation (nonetheless, thanks to Côte d'Ivoire's highly legalistic approach to identification of citizens, the process was accessed far more readily than in, for example, Congo).[252] Although, for the most part, an ideology of welcome to fellow-Africans was accepted by the host populations, who saw that increasing prosperity depended on their labour,[253] a lack of clarity over the status of the newcomers created the conditions for future problems.

By 1988, the national census showed a population of foreign origin of more than three million (half of them of Burkinabè origin), forming just over 28% of a total population of 10.8 million; up from 17.5% in 1965. At least 45% of these 'foreigners' had been born in the country and more than 60% of the remainder had been resident for more than five years and thus theoretically eligible to naturalise.[254] Yet only just over 51,000 people were identified as naturalised Ivorian nationals.[255] Ten years later, the 1998 population census indicated that of the approximately 15 million inhabitants of the country just over a quarter were

[250] Cote d'Ivoire Loi No. 72-852 du 21 décembre 1972 ; quote on the need to « corriger le trop grand libéralisme » from the Exposé des motifs. The law deleted the second paragraph of the original Art 9 that provided for children of unknown parents to be presumed born in Cote d'Ivoire (and, thus, Ivorian, on the basis that *étranger* did not include an unknown parent). The first paragraph, requiring all facts related to birth and descent to be proved by civil registration procedures, remained in place. There was no explanation for the removal of the provision on children of unknown parents in the exposé des motifs for the 1972 law.

[251] Articles 25–26 of Loi No. 61-415 du 14 décembre 1961 portant Code de la nationalité ivoirienne, modifiée par Loi No. 72-852 du 21 décembre 1972.

[252] Following the change of government in 2011, the Ministry of Justice conducted at least two comprehensive surveys of the archives of the Official Journal, where decrees of naturalisation are published. The first review estimated that at 31 December 2012, 32,819 individuals had been naturalised since 1962 by the signing of 7,121 decrees. These numbers did not include minor children who would have acquired subsidiary Ivorian nationality through the naturalisation of their parents. Another review conducted by the Ministry of Justice in 2013 concluded that 14,793 naturalisation decrees had been signed concerning 92,760 beneficiaries, over the same period. The discrepancies may have been the result of different counting techniques with respect to inclusion of subsidiary acquisition of Ivorian nationality by spouses and minor children. Adjami, 'Statelessness and Nationality in Côte d'Ivoire', based on internal report of the Ivorian Ministry of Justice to UNHCR submitted in February 2012.

[253] Ousmane Dembélé, 'La construction économique et politique de la catégorie 'étranger' en Côte d'Ivoire' in Marc Le Pape and Claudine Vidal (eds), *Côte d'Ivoire: l'année terrible, 1999–2000* (Karthala 2002).

[254] Recensement Général, vol 2, 1988 (n 231).

[255] Institut national de la statistique, 'Recensement Général de La Population et de l'Habitat, 1988 : Tome 3, Caractéristiques Socio-Culturelles et Économiques de La Population,' (République de la Côte d'Ivoire 1992), table 2.3.

non-citizens; once again almost half of them had been born in the country, and 88,714 were identified as naturalised.[256]

By the late 1980s, the *modèle ivoirien*, supposedly an exception to instability in the West African region, was in crisis.[257] Large falls in the global price of cocoa and coffee were twinned with increasing pressure on land in the southern plantation territories. State guarantees of prices paid to producers were no longer sustainable, and a structural adjustment programme forced retrenchment of the public workforce and an end to regulated prices, including reform of the *Comité de gestion de la filière café-cacao* responsible for marketing coffee and cocoa on the international markets (and an important source of funds for the PDCI).[258] With the changes in eastern Europe and the end of one-party regimes elsewhere in Africa, the PDCI was also forced to concede a return to multi-party democracy; a transition took place just as economic recession was exacerbating, in the classic way, popular resentment against immigrants. Long-standing but previously suppressed tensions came to the fore and were exploited for political purposes by the opposition to the PDCI. In the 1990 elections, the main opposition party, the *Front populaire ivoirien* (FPI) led by Laurent Gbagbo (a Bété from the south-west, the area most affected by in-migration, who also had close links to the French Socialist Party) mobilised around a campaign that accused the PDCI of favouring foreigners.

Houphouët-Boigny died in 1993. His successor as PDCI leader and president, Henri Konan Bédié, also a Baoulé, abandoned the PDCI's unofficial allegiance with migrant groups (internal and from outside the country), and canvassed a new political definition of the concept of *ivoirité* ('Ivorian-ness'). A group of PDCI intellectuals devised a manifesto promoting a highly restrictive interpretation of Ivorian citizenship, limiting it to those whose parents were *both* members of one of the 'autochthonous' ethnic groups of Côte d'Ivoire.[259] This new interpretation, creating an anthropological definition of nationality in the absence of a satisfactory legal one,[260] effectively defined those whose forebears had migrated before

[256] Georges Photios Tapinos, 'La population étrangère' in Georges Photios Tapinos, Philippe Hugon and Patrice Vimard (eds), *La Côte d'Ivoire à l'aube du XXIe siècle: défis démographiques et développement durable* (Karthala 2001). According to UN estimates, however, international migrants (persons born abroad and foreign nationals) formed 15% of the population in 1990, dropping to 12.5% in 2010, with total population increasing from 12.6 million to 19 million over the same period. 'Trends in International Migrant Stock: The 2013 Revision' (UN Department of Economic and Social Affairs 2013) POP/DB/MIG/Stock/Rev.2013.

[257] Bernard Contamin and Harris Memel-Fotê (eds), *Le modèle ivoirien en questions: crises, ajustements, recompositions* (Editions Karthala : Editions de l'ORSTOM 1997).

[258] The role of the *filière* 'slush fund' in Ivorian politics, and the failure of privatisation to create a transparent and accountable system is discussed in McGovern (n 234) ch 5.

[259] 'L'ivoirité, ou l'esprit du nouveau contrat social du Président H. K. Bédié', 1996, published by the Cellule Universitaire de Recherche et de Diffusion des Idées et Actions Politiques du Président Henri Konan Bédié (CURDIPHE), extracted in *Politique africaine* No.78, June 2000 : 'L'individu qui revendique son ivoirité est supposé avoir pour pays la Côte d'Ivoire, né de parents ivoiriens appartenant à l'une des ethnies autochtones de la Côte d'Ivoire'.

[260] Epiphane Zoro-Bi, 'Je suis un Sidibé de Tiémélékro : L'acquisition de la nationalité ivoirienne à titre originaire : Critère juridique ou critère anthropologique?' in Jean-Bernard Ouédraogo and Ebrima Sall (eds), *Frontières de la citoyenneté et violence politique en Côte d'Ivoire* (Codesria 2008).

independence as foreigners (including those who had moved or been moved when the Ivorian borders encompassed a much larger territory); and, by extension, those who were their ethnic kin but had always lived within the borders of Côte d'Ivoire. Eventually these unofficial documents became official policy, as the National Economic and Social Council described the 'tolerable threshold' of immigration as being 'long overstepped'.[261] Those with 'foreign' names by these interpretations, known pejoratively as 'Dioula' (derived from the Malinké word for trader), or with one parent who was a foreigner, faced ever-increasing difficulties in obtaining the identity cards and certificates of nationality necessary to claim their other rights, especially to vote and to hold land. Bédié also strengthened programmes for the *ivoirisation* of the workforce – a *Ministère du travail et de l'ivoirisation des cadres* was established as early as 1978, but had originally been aimed at French and other foreign personnel in senior civil service positions – turning the programme, some said, into an agenda of *baoulisation*.[262]

From 1990, a new law required all foreigners, including citizens of the Member States of the Economic Community of West African States (ECOWAS), to obtain and carry as proof of identity a *carte de séjour*, a type of residence permit.[263] However, the general law on identity cards adopted after independence remained in force, and only required production of a birth certificate to get an ID card, with formal proof of nationality needed only at the discretion of the administrative official.[264] In 1998, a new law on identification was adopted, stating that Ivorian nationals would be identified inside the country by the national identity card, and distinguishing among ECOWAS and non-ECOWAS nationals for residence permits;[265] a new decree created more onerous requirements for applications, including that a certificate of nationality be submitted in all cases.[266]

[261] Rapport du Conseil économique et social (octobre 1998) « Immigration en Côte d'Ivoire: le seuil du tolérable est largement dépassé », republished in *Politique africaine*, No.78, 2000.

[262] Dembélé (n 253); Jean-Pierre Dozon, 'La Côte d'Ivoire Entre Démocratie, Nationalisme et Ethnonationalisme' 78 Politique africaine 45; Arnim Langer, 'Horizontal Inequalities and Violent Conflict: Côte d'Ivoire Country Paper' (UNDP Human Development Report Office 2005) 2005/32.

[263] Loi No. 90-437 du 29 mai 1990 relative à l'entrée et au séjour des étrangers en Côte d'Ivoire. See also Mirna Adjami, 'Statelessness and Nationality in Côte d'Ivoire' (UNHCR 2016) Annex III.

[264] Loi No. 62-64 du 20 février 1962 portant institution de la Carte Nationale d'Identité ; Décret No. 67-86 du 10 mars 1967, fixant les modalités d'application de la Loi No. 62-64 du 20 février 1962, modifiée par Décret No. 71-63 du 6 février 1971 ; Circulaire No. 1138 du 13 juin 1962. A temporary substitute for an identity card was created, under Décret No.94-348 du 22 juin 1994, which allowed witness evidence to be submitted to obtain an *attestation administrative d'identité* valid only for the 1995 elections.

[265] Loi No. 98-448 du 4 août relative à l'identification des Personnes et au Séjour des Etrangers en Côte d'Ivoire. Art.1: 'L'identification des ivoiriens âgés de plus de 16 ans s'établit à l'intérieur du territoire national par la Carte nationale d'identité.'

[266] Décret No. 98-471 du 12 août 1998 modifiant et complétant le décret No. 67-h86 du 10 mars 1967 fixant les modalités d'application de la Loi No. 62-64 du 20 février 1962 instituant une carte nationale d'identité. All persons submitting a first-time request to obtain an Ivorian ID card were required to submit as documentary proof not only a copy of a birth certificate or *jugement supplétif*, but also a certificate of residence, a certificate of nationality, and copies of the national ID cards of at least one of the person's parents or a copy of a parent's decree of naturalisation. The 1998 changes, however, were

The emphasis on *ivoirité* was designed both to undercut the FPI's ethno-nationalist demands and to exclude Bédié's strongest opponent for the presidency, Alassane Dramane Ouattara, a Muslim from the north of Côte d'Ivoire. Ouattara had been Prime Minister under Houphouët-Boigny (1990–1993) but left the PDCI on Boigny's death to become the leader of a new opposition party, the *Rassemblement des Républicains* (RDR), which drew heavily on support from the largely Muslim north. Bédié accused Ouattara of not being a native Ivorian citizen, since one or both parents were in fact from Burkina Faso, an assertion Ouattara himself strenuously denied.[267] The fact that Ouattara had spent most of his professional life outside the country working for the World Bank and International Monetary Fund, and was responsible for the application of austerity programmes in Côte d'Ivoire as elsewhere in Africa, did not help his case.

Under the independence constitution and the electoral law in effect until the death of Houphouët-Boigny, the holders of the highest national offices – president of the republic and president or vice-president of the National Assembly – had, simply, to be Ivorian citizens. Bédié's administration changed the electoral law in December 1994 to require a person running for these offices to be 'Ivorian by birth' (*ivoirien de naissance*), of two parents also Ivorian by birth, and never to have held another nationality. The same requirements were adopted with regards to the eligibility requirements to be a candidate for member of Parliament.[268] The term *ivoirien de naissance* did not exist in the nationality law; moreover, since Ivorian nationality had not existed before 1960 and to be eligible for president a person had to be a minimum of 45 years old, it was hard to know what this amendment meant as a matter of law. Nonetheless, the requirement was clearly aimed at Ouattara, and he did not stand for president in the 1995 elections, which were won by Bédié. The 1995 electoral law also restricted the right to vote to citizens alone, a reversion to the pre-1980 position that immediately greatly increased the importance of citizenship to long-term migrants. During 1999, the government instituted a judicial investigation into Ouattara's nationality certificate, and it was annulled by a court on 27 October 1999 on the grounds of irregularity in its issue. Protests and riots followed, for which several RDR politicians were convicted under laws allowing organisers of demonstrations to be held responsible for violence. In November 1999, an arrest warrant for Ouattara was issued while he was staying abroad, on the grounds of alleged use of forged documents to support his eligibility to run in the elections in October 2000.

never implemented because all identification operations were suspended with the military coup led by General Robert Guéï on 24 December 1999.

[267] Ouattara's account of his origins, as given at a 2001 national reconciliation forum, is quoted extensively in Francis Akindès, 'The Roots of the Military-Political Crises in Côte d'Ivoire' (Nordiska Afrikainstitutet 2004) Research Report 128 37–39.

[268] Loi No. 94-642 du 13 décembre 1994 du 13 décembre 1994 portant Code Électoral, Articles 3, 49–50, and 77–78 ; Décret no 94-662 du 21 décembre 1994 déterminant les modalités d'établissement, de révision et de refonte de la liste électorale.

The changes in the law brought to the fore the lack of legal clarity on who in fact was a 'foreigner', especially for those whose ancestors arrived in the country before independence. Questions about the status of the descendants of the migrants from the 1930s settled in the 'colonial villages', some of whom were prominent people, did lead to an effort to resolve their particular situation. In 1995, Bédié signed a decree accepting the requests for naturalisation presented by 'persons of original Burkinabè nationality of the villages of Garango, Koudougou, Koupela, Tenkodogo, in Bouaflé Department, and the villages of Kaya, Koudougou, Ouagadougou, in Zuénoula Department.'[269] A list of the 8,133 individuals affected was attached. Despite this apparent resolution of the situation for at least one group of people, those named still struggled to obtain national ID cards and nationality certificates; and their children, who should under the law have been automatically Ivorian, were often not recognised as such.[270] The decision to naturalise these individuals as a group was still controversial 20 years later, when many of those listed in the decree, and their descendants, still had no documentation of nationality.[271]

Bédié's administration also changed the land law to introduce a system of written evidence of title to land rather than the unregistered systems of tenure that had existed up to then.[272] Since the pre-colonial period, the dominant system in the south of the country had been the customary law system known in French as the *tutorat*, in which 'autochthonous' landholders ceded the use of land for cocoa and coffee plantations in exchange for a range of cultural and economic obligations, including payment in labour and cash. Prior to the promulgation of the new law in 1998, existing legislation only recognised land transactions carried out in the presence of a notary. Customary law had not historically provided for absolute individual title to land, but there was an increasing ambiguity as to the nature of the rights ceded, following the rhetoric of Houphouët-Boigny and as a cash economy became more dominant. Local communities had developed a range of systems for the regulation of land use by 'strangers' to the area, including written documentation and adjudication by traditional courts or village councils. The 1998 law – backed by opposition as well as government members of the national assembly – did not recognise the validity of these hybrid systems, instead opting for a 're-traditionalisation' of land tenure, reasserting the overriding claims of the

[269] Décret No. 95-805 du 26 septembre 1995.

[270] Adjami (n 263) s 2.2.

[271] See, eg, « Lutte contre l'apatridie : 8.133 postulants a la nationalité ivoirienne obtiennent leur naturalisation » Government of Cote d'Ivoire, 4 March 2013; and « Bradage massif de la nationalité ivoirienne: Ouattara se sert de Bédié, grosse colère au PDCI », *IvoireBusiness.net*, 13 March 2013.

[272] Loi No. 98-750 du 23 décembre 1998 relative au Domaine foncier rural. See also Jean-Pierre Chauveau, 'Question Foncière et Construction Nationale En Côte d'Ivoire' (2000) 78 Politique africaine 94; Jean-Pierre Chauveau, 'La loi ivoirienne de 1998 sur le domaine foncier rural et l'agriculture de plantation villageoise: Une mise en perspective historique et sociologique' (2002) 2002/1 Land Reform: Land Settlement and Cooperatives (FAO) 62; Barbara McCallin and Marzia Montemurro, 'Whose Land Is This? Land Disputes and Forced Displacement in the Western Forest Area of Côte d'Ivoire' (Norwegian Refugee Council Internal Displacement Monitoring Centre 2009).

'autochthonous' southern populations to the land since ceded on various terms to 'stranger' farmers. The law provided for the transformation of customary rights into formalised individual private ownership over a period of ten years. Rights of land users not suitable for transfer into exclusive title had no status under the new law, making the ambiguous status of many existing rights immediately more critical. Most controversially of all, the 1998 land law provided that only the State, public entities and Ivorian nationals (*personnes physiques ivoiriennes*) had rights to own land in rural areas (except for existing owners of formal title deeds, which covered less than 2% of the land, largely in urban areas); other users could only hold a long-term lease.[273]

The surface intention of the amended law was positive – to provide greater security of tenure for customary rights holders – and the changes were supported by the World Bank and other development partners since they appeared to provide a more 'modern' market in land. However, the law also responded to the increasingly xenophobic national mood, and provided a basis for attacks on northern and foreign migrants farming in their own right or working on others' land in the south and west of the country. During September 1999, perhaps up to 20,000 people, mainly Burkinabè migrants and northerners, were expelled from their land and villages in the south-west without any intervention to protect them by the police, administrative or political authorities.[274] Similar incidents continued into 2000.

It was against this background that General Robert Guéï, Bédié's retired chief of army (a Yacouba from the far west of the country) led Côte d'Ivoire's first coup d'état on 24 December 1999. Initially, it seemed that the new regime would roll back some of the political exclusion of the previous five years. Guéï formed a broad-based administration which included ministers from leading opposition parties, including the RDR and the FPI. He pledged to clean up corruption, rewrite the constitution, and hold fresh elections. These stated ambitions were, however, soon diverted. The manipulation of identification intensified rather than decreased. In 2000, Guéï issued a decree creating a highly discretionary model for issuing national ID cards, foreseen as a two-year temporary measure. According to this decree, in place of the normal requirements for obtaining a national ID card, Ivorians should go to their 'village of birth or origin' to obtain a national ID card on the basis of an interview with a verification committee rather than the

[273] A decade later, the African Commission on Human and Peoples' Rights found both the restrictive provisions on standing for election as president and the 1998 land law to be in violation of non-discrimination provisions of the African Charter on Human and Peoples' Rights: Communication No.246/02, *Mouvement ivoirien des droits humains (MIDH) v Côte d'Ivoire* (2008); Communication No.262/02, *Mouvement ivoirien des droits humains (MIDH) v. Côte d'Ivoire* (2008).

[274] Babo (n 247). The south-west territory of the Bétés had been integrated rather later than the Agni south-east into the cocoa growing economy, and had seen particularly rapid alienation of land in favour of Dioula or immigrants. For a detailed historical treatment of this issue, see Jean-Pierre Chauveau and Jean-Pierre Dozon, 'Au cœur des ethnies ivoiriennes : L'Etat, l'économie de plantation et les ethnies en Côte d'Ivoire' in Emmanuel Terray (ed), *L'Etat contemporain en Afrique* (L'Harmattan 1987).

presentation of documents. Although this appeared to be a relaxation of normal provisions, it effectively instituted a period of entirely discretionary issue of identification documents.[275]

In late July 2000, a flawed referendum was held to approve a new constitution which, among other things, inserted into the constitution itself the requirements of Bédié's electoral laws that candidates for the presidency must be 'Ivorian by origin', born to a father *and* a mother who were themselves both Ivorian by origin.[276] Although the phrasing *ivoirien d'origine* could be argued to be simply a paraphrase of the nationality code's reference to 'nationality of origin' as opposed to 'nationality by acquisition' (by marriage, naturalisation etc), the provision effectively implied a new constitutional concept of *ivoirité*. The nationality code stated that an individual had Ivorian 'nationality of origin' if born to one parent who is a citizen; and it still did so after the 2000 constitution was adopted. Yet the anchoring of the right to run for elected office in a requirement to prove 'Ivorian-ness of origin' by both paternal and maternal lineage enshrined in law the arguments of the proponents of *ivoirité* that to be Ivorian required something deeper than birth in the territory of a citizen parent. Rather, it confirmed the idea already in popular circulation of a pure ancestry connected to Ivorian soil 'from time immemorial'. A revised electoral code adopted in August endorsed these eligibility criteria for the presidential office in Côte d'Ivoire.[277] though it eased the eligibility criteria for parliamentary candidates.[278] Following the referendum, the government of General Guéï led an 'identification campaign' during which many who had previously believed themselves to be Ivorian were designated foreigners.[279]

[275] Décret No. 2000-419 du 31 mai 2000 fixant les modalités d'application de la Loi No. 62-64 du 20 février 1962 instituant la carte nationale d'identité. According to this decree, the normal requirements for obtaining a national ID card as most recently defined in 1998 (Decree 98-471) were suspended. Instead Ivorians could go to their 'village of birth or origin' to obtain a national ID card. Those individuals who did not possess the required documents relating to the birth and nationality of their parents, could present whatever documents they actually held and appear with two witnesses before a mobile team (*équipe itinérante*), including a magistrate and various other officials, advised by the local chiefs and notables. This mobile team could issue an identity card and certificate of nationality. General Guéï also signed two ordinances that allowed as a temporary measure for individuals to present informal administrative certificates or receipts issued by local municipalities in place of identification through documents otherwise required by law. Ordonnance No.2000-504 du 26 juillet 2000 instituant une attestation administrative d'identité tenant lieu de carte de résident; Ordonnance No.2000-502 du 26 juillet 2000 instituant une attestation administrative d'identité.

[276] Article 35, Constitution of Côte d'Ivoire, 2000 : « Le Président de la République … doit être ivoirien d'origine, né de père et mère eux-mêmes ivoiriens d'origine. Il doit n'avoir jamais renoncé à la nationalité ivoirienne. Il ne doit être jamais prévalu d'une autre nationalité. » The significance of the change in language from *ivoirien de naissance* in the 1994 electoral code to *ivoirien d'origine* in the new constitution was not clear, but did bring the law into closer line with the nationality code.

[277] Article 48, Loi No. 2000-514 du 1er Août 2000 portant Code Electorale.

[278] Article 71 requires that candidates for the National Assembly be at least 25 years old, be 'Ivorian by birth' « *Ivoirien de naissance* » and have never renounced Ivorian nationality.

[279] Ruth Marshall-Fratani, 'The War of 'Who Is Who': Autochthony, Nationalism and Citizenship in the Ivorian Crisis' in Sara Dorman, Daniel Hammett and Paul Nugent (eds), *Making nations, creating strangers: States and citizenship in Africa* (Brill 2007).

With the new constitution and electoral code in place, presidential and parliamentary elections were held in October and December 2000. On 6 October, the Supreme Court, which had been dissolved and reconstituted following the 24 December coup and was widely believed to have been hand-picked by Guéï himself, disqualified 14 of the 19 presidential candidates, including Ouattara and Bédié.[280] Nonetheless, the coup leaders did not obtain the 'right' result. After early results showed Laurent Gbagbo leading in the 22 October presidential polls, General Guéï dissolved the National Electoral Commission and proclaimed himself the winner. Massive popular protests were met with a violent response, but Guéï ultimately fled the capital and Gbagbo declared himself president. Ouattara's RDR demanded fresh elections, leading to further fighting characterised by religious and ethnic divides, as security forces and civilians supporting President Gbagbo clashed with the mostly Muslim northerners who formed the core of support for the RDR. President Gbagbo imposed a curfew and state of emergency; amongst other atrocities, around sixty RDR supporters were killed by security forces in the 'charnier du Youpougon' on 29 October.[281] On 30 November 2000, the Constitutional Council barred Ouattara from standing in the parliamentary elections scheduled for 10 December, again because of questions about his citizenship.[282] Nonetheless, the parliamentary election went ahead, boycotted by the RDR. The FPI won a slight majority, with 96 seats, followed by the former ruling party, the PDCI, which won 94 seats.[283]

In March 2001, local elections were held, which the RDR contested, winning more constituencies than any other party. President Gbagbo immediately instituted a new process of national identification, claiming that most of those on the electoral roll were not citizens and therefore not eligible to vote.[284] By the time of departmental elections in July 2002, some 20% of potential voters had not obtained their new registration cards; others attempting to register found themselves given a foreign resident's card in place of a national identity document. When individuals attempted to register in their place of residence, they faced demands based on the new rules for identity documents that they return to their 'village of origin' to establish their identity. The director of the newly established *Office Nationale d'Identification* (ONI)[285] publicly endorsed these demands, stating that 'whoever

[280] Cour Suprême, Chambre constitutionnelle, Liste définitive des candidats à l'élection du Président de la République du 22 octobre 2000, Arrêt No.E 0001-2000 du 6 octobre 2000.

[281] Human Rights Watch, 'The New Racism: The Political Manipulation of Ethnicity in Côte d'Ivoire' (2001).

[282] Conseil constitutionnel, Arrêt No.E 10-2000 du 30 novembre 2000 relatif aux 227 requêtes en contestation d'éligibilité des députés à l'Assemblée nationale.

[283] See results posted on African Elections website, http://africanelections.tripod.com/ci.html.

[284] Loi No. 2002–03 du 3 janvier 2002 also reinstated the use of the term *cartes de séjour* as the standard terminology for all residence permits to be acquired by all foreigners, including ECOWAS citizens; in relation to nationals however, Décret No.2002-331 du 13 juin 2002 removed the compulsory requirement established by the 1998 decree that an applicant for a national identity card had to have a nationality certificate.

[285] Established by Décret No.2001-103 du 15 février 2001.

claims to be Ivorian must have a village. Whoever has done everything to forget the name of his village or who is incapable of showing he belongs to a village is a person without bearings and is so dangerous that we must ask him where he comes from'.[286] This was not just rhetoric, but a policy operationalised by the decree of two years earlier. Nonetheless, Alassane Ouattara himself, the most high profile victim of these efforts and the subject of considerable international support, was issued a new certificate of nationality by the brave judge of a tribunal in June 2002.[287]

Testimony of Abdou Houabou Bah[288]

'My name is Abdou Houabou Bah. I was born in Bouaké, Republic of Côte d'Ivoire, on 27 April 1961. My parents are of Guinean origin, themselves born in Côte d'Ivoire. I am the last in a family of seven children, all born in Côte d'Ivoire.

I went to school in Bouaké at the Military Camp School for my primary school, then college and high school in Bouaké, where I got my Baccalaureate A1 in 1985, after a break of four years due to the distractions of adolescence. After that, I moved to the University of Abidjan Faculty of Law, where I obtained my degree in private law in 1990 and my masters in public law in 1991.

I note that since my birth, I had always and exclusively held Ivorian nationality, until it was contested in 2001, under the circumstances which I will summarize briefly.

In short, after my completion of the competition for entry to the magistracy in 1998 – the training lasted two years, that is to say, from January 1999 to December 2000 – I was unpleasantly surprised to find, during the assignment of magistrates to their courts in September 2001, that my nationality was doubtful, because my name was foreign sounding. They asked me to prove that I was really Ivorian; I fulfilled all that was asked. But, despite my efforts, the then authorities (the Laurent Gbagbo regime) found that the papers of my mother (illiterate, of mixed Ivorian and Guinean descent), were not regular. This is the source of all my problems that continue to this day.

[286] *Notre Voie* 28 July 2002, cited in Marshall-Fratani (n 279).

[287] Zoro-Bi (n 248).

[288] Testimony of Abdou Houabou Bah to the African Commission on Human and Peoples' Rights, March 2011, French original in possession of and English translation by the author.

As previously stated, I finished my training at the magistrates' college, where I obtained my diploma to practice as a magistrate. But, from 18 September 2001, the day assignments to positions were made, to date, I have tried everything but not succeeded. That includes judicial, administrative, and human approaches.

When it comes down to it, since I live in in a xenophobic or 'Ivoritarian' regime, my efforts were unlikely to succeed. On reading my case, you will perhaps not be surprised to know why we had the rebellion in Côte d'Ivoire that lasts to this day.

I did not choose my parents nor the place of my birth. It has been nearly a decade since I have lived in a state of quasi-unemployment caused by power-hungry politicians and administrators who are zealots and careerists.

I do not wish to write a book about my life, but if the story of my experience of denial of citizenship can be used to help rectify the situation, then I remain ready to tell you of my painful journey.'

In August 2002, facing pressure from the EU and other international actors, President Gbagbo announced a government of national reconciliation, with representation of the four principal political parties in his cabinet. However, an attempt to demobilise many of the soldiers who had been brought into the army by General Guéï led to a rebellion by some of those affected. Calling themselves the *Mouvement patriotique de la Côte d'Ivoire* (MPCI), they launched an attempted coup d'état on 19 September 2002. Though they failed to topple the central government, the rebels took control of the northern Ivorian town of Korhogo and the central town of Bouaké, engaging in fierce fighting with government soldiers. A short-lived ceasefire from mid-October gave way to further fighting in which the mid-west cocoa capital of Daloa saw heavy combat. The south-west also burst into conflict between and among autochthonous and immigrant groups; many immigrants or northerners were driven out. MPCI leader Guillaume Soro emphasised the foundation of the war in the right to nationality: 'Give us our identity cards and we hand over our Kalashnikovs'.[289]

The French government swiftly intervened with military force, launching *Operation Licorne* in September 2002 to reinforce troops already based in Côte d'Ivoire. Though controversial, because seen as self-interested and (in the first instance) hostile to Gbagbo's government, the intervention eventually helped to establish an often misnamed 'zone of confidence' in the main areas of tension.[290]

[289] Quoted in Christian Bouquet, « La crise ivoirienne par les cartes », *Géoconfluences*, 4 June 2007, available at http://geoconfluences.ens-lsh.fr/doc/etpays/Afsubsah/AfsubsahDoc5.htm.

[290] Pierre Weiss, 'L'Opération Licorne en Côte d'Ivoire : Banc d'essai de la nouvelle politique française de sécurité en Afrique' (2004) V Annuaire français de relations internationales.

The French were soon joined by West African soldiers mandated by ECOWAS, and from early 2003, the joint forces were authorised to act to re-establish security by the United Nations Security Council[291]; a year later, a UN peace keeping force was established, supported by French troops operating under their own command.[292] Active fighting gradually gave way to a de facto partition of the country into two separate zones, controlled by the government of Gbagbo in the largely Christian south (including the south-west, retaken by government forces), and by the rebel 'New Forces'[293] led by Soro in the Muslim north.

The French also instituted a succession of peace negotiations and agreements that attempted to find a permanent solution to the conflict, variously under the auspices of the French government, ECOWAS, the African Union and the United Nations. Throughout these negotiations and in successive agreements, the question of citizenship as well as of land ownership was central. In January 2003, the Linas-Marcoussis agreement signed in France by all major political parties failed to end active hostilities in Côte d'Ivoire, but set the framework followed in subsequent talks (Accra I, II, III; Pretoria I, II).[294] Amongst other provisions aiming at the formation of a new government with jurisdiction over all the territory of Côte d'Ivoire it established the principle of a general revision of citizenship law, including that the conditions for eligibility to senior public offices should be that candidates hold Ivorian citizenship and a father *or* – not *and* – a mother who held Ivorian nationality of origin. On that basis and under pressure from South Africa's then president Thabo Mbeki, who played a role in facilitating talks, President Gbagbo confirmed in April 2005 that all signatories of the Marcoussis agreement (which included Ouattara) would be able to run for office in the next presidential elections.[295]

Economic interests affected by the war also intervened to ensure some changes to the 1998 land law in relation to the rights of non-citizens. Amendments adopted in August 2004 recognised the rights of those non-citizens who could prove legal title to land dating before the 1998 land law, including the right to pass title to others; though with the requirement that these rights only took effect if the owners were specifically listed in a decree of the Council of Ministers.[296] Only a handful in the formal sector actually benefited from this legislation; the vast majority of non-citizen land holders, or land-holders without national identity cards, were still left with no secure tenure.[297]

[291] Resolution 1464 (2003), Adopted by the Security Council at its 4700th meeting, 4 February 2003.

[292] Resolution 1528 (2004), Adopted by the Security Council at its 4918th meeting, 27 February 2004.

[293] Formed by an amalgamation in March 2003 of the MPCI with the *Mouvement Populaire Ivoirien du Grand Ouest* (MPIGO) and the *Mouvement pour la Justice et la Paix* (MJP), both based in the south-west.

[294] Accord de Linas-Marcoussis, 24 January 2003, Annex « Programme du gouvernement de réconciliation ».

[295] 'La présidentielle envisagée par Gbagbo pour fin 2007', *L'Humanité*, 8 August 2007.

[296] Loi No. 2004-412 du 14 août 2004 portant amendement de la Loi No.98-750 du 23 décembre 1998 relative au Foncier Rural (amending Art 26).

[297] McCallin and Montemurro (n 272).

Two laws adopted in late 2004 in application of the agreement at Linas-Marcoussis revised the nationality code and established temporary special naturalisation procedures that on the face of it partially addressed some of the nationality problems. The revisions to the nationality code made it possible for the first time for a man marrying an Ivorian woman to acquire Ivorian nationality, rather than having to naturalise by the procedures applicable to any foreigner.[298] In addition, the amendments introduced explicit restrictions on the exercise of public office by naturalised citizens.[299]

The law creating temporary special naturalisation procedures applied to all those who had been allowed to claim nationality from 1961 either during the transitional period of one year or until the procedures for acquisition by declaration were repealed by the amendments to the nationality code in 1972 (that is, those aged under 21 at the date of independence and born in Côte d'Ivoire of foreign parents, those born in Côte d'Ivoire of foreign parents between 1960 and 1973, and those who habitually lived in Côte d'Ivoire before independence). The law established that people in these categories could, during a limited period, apply for naturalisation with written evidence in the form of an original birth certificate or a *jugement supplétif*, a form of late certification of birth from a tribunal. In addition, an applicant was required to provide proof of renunciation of nationality of origin – something difficult or impossible to do, for those who had lost any connection to the country of their parents' birth – as well as proof of residence and a criminal record check.[300] At the same time, restrictions on 'foreign' participation in the formal workforce were also strengthened, and the law on identification of foreigners was again adjusted.[301] The law on special naturalisation procedures was modified twice by presidential decisions in 2005 clarifying and redefining the categories of people to which it applied and adjusting the procedures for application.[302]

[298] Loi No. 2004-662 modifiant et complétant la loi 61-415 portant Code de la nationalité. Under the 1961 nationality code as in force to that date, a foreign woman marrying an Ivorian man had automatically acquired nationality on marriage; the amendments changed this rule to a right for the woman to opt for Ivorian nationality at the time of marriage; but for a man marrying an Ivorian woman only to be able to do so after a two-year delay. Presidential decisions 2005-03/PR of 15 July 2005 and 2005-09/PR of 29 August 2005 reduced and then removed the discrimination based on sex, and made it possible for either a man or a woman marrying an Ivorian national to acquire nationality by option at the time of marriage.

[299] Loi No.2004-662 initially amended the provisions on loss of nationality to provide for automatic loss of nationality if a person exercised office in a foreign country; presidential decision 2005-03 restored the previous situation, where loss would be dependent on government action to deprive the person by decree.

[300] Loi No.2004-663 du 17 décembre 2004 portant dispositions spéciales en matière de naturalisation. See also Habibou Bangré, 'Côte d'Ivoire : révision du code de la nationalité et de la naturalisation ; Les amendements apportent des progrès mitigés', Afrik.com, 21 December 2004.

[301] Arrêté No.1437 du 19 février 2004 portant modification de l'arrêté No.4810 du 21 avril 1997 relatif à la réglementation du recrutement et des frais de visa du contrat de travail des personnels non ivoiriennes ; Loi No.2004-303 du 3 mai 2004 portant modification de la Loi No.2002-03 relative à l'identification des personnes et au séjour des étrangers en Côte d'Ivoire.

[302] Décision no. 2005-04/PR du 15 juillet 2005 and Décision no.2005-10/PR du 27 décembre 2005.

The implementing decree was only finally adopted by the Council of Ministers in May 2006, starting an initial one-year period for those who wished to apply for naturalisation under its provisions.[303]

The government then implemented a programme of late registration of birth through special hearings by departmental tribunals travelling away from their usual seat (*audiences foraines*).[304] A birth certificate is an essential first step to gaining recognition of nationality through a certificate of nationality or national identity card, as well as for applying for naturalisation under the special procedures. The civil war had caused birth registration rates to fall from 72% in 2000 to 58% by 2006,[305] and the process aimed to provide those who had not been registered at birth with a *jugement supplétif*, that is, with court approval for late registration of birth (as provided for in the civil status law[306]). Applying for recognition of nationality was a second step of the process. The special identification process was repeatedly postponed by Gbagbo and interrupted by his supporters: in July–August 2006 the FPI's *Jeunes patriotes* (Young Patriots) militia responded to a party leadership call to arms and brought the hearings to a halt by staging violent demonstrations and attacking foreigners and opposition party organisers.[307] As a result of these issues, in the end, not a single naturalisation was actually approved as a result of these special measures.[308]

While this process was still blocked, Gbagbo and Soro finally signed an agreement in March 2007 in Ouagadougou, creating a government of national reconciliation. Gbagbo was to be President and Soro Prime Minister. Further measures agreed for the reunification of the country included the redeployment of administrative authorities throughout the country, the demobilisation of militias, the disarmament of former combatants, the organisation of fresh democratic elections within one year; and first of all, a process of identification of the population, with renewed *audiences foraines*, the reconstitution of civil registries damaged in

[303] Décret No.2006-76 du 31 mai 2006 portant modalités d'application de la Loi No.2004-663 du 17 décembre 2004, which again re-adjusted the precise definition of those who were eligible to benefit, to bring the law precisely into line with the original provisions in the 1961 nationality code, repealed in 1972.

[304] A 2004 decree had tasked the ONI with the mission of modernizing the civil registration system and organizing such mobile court hearings. Article 13, Décret No. 2004-28 du 15 janvier 2004 portant modification du décret No. 2001-103 du 15 février 2001 portant création de l'Office Nationale d'Identification.

[305] *Every Child's Birth Right: Inequities and trends in birth registration*, UNICEF, 2013.

[306] Loi No.64-374 du 07 octobre 1964, sur l'état civil telle que modifiée par les lois no.83-799 du 02 août 1983 et no.99-691 du 14 décembre 1999. This system of *jugement supplétifs* (or *déclaratifs*) is the standard procedure in the francophone countries.

[307] See, eg, « Abidjan paralysée par les Jeunes Patriotes hostiles aux audiences foraines », IRIN, 19 July 2006. Also *Situation des droits de l'homme en Côte d'Ivoire: Rapport No.6, mai-juin-juillet-août 2006*, Mission des Nations Unies en Côte d'Ivoire ; *Rapport du Président de la Commission sur la situation en Côte d'Ivoire*, African Union Peace and Security Council, PSC/AHG/3(LXIV), 64th meeting, 17 October 2006.

[308] Explanatory memorandum for Law No.2013-653 du 13 septembre 2013.

the crisis, a new identity card system and a new electoral register.[309] A 'Flame of peace ceremony' was held in Bouaké, in central Côte d'Ivoire, on 30 July 2007, to symbolise the end of the war and the beginning of the reconciliation process.

The Ouagadougou Accord provisions on identification were implemented through the adoption of a decree providing new procedures under the 1962 law requiring all nationals to hold an identity card. Under this decree there were two ways of obtaining an ID card: either by 'ordinary identification' or by registering to vote. To obtain a card by 'ordinary identification' it was required for the first time that a person must produce not just a birth certificate, but also a certificate of nationality; but those who were registered to vote needed only produce a birth certificate to get a card – and a certificate of nationality was not needed in order to be entered on the voters roll.[310] The requirement for ECOWAS nationals to hold a *carte de séjour* was repealed.[311]

The identification process resumed, with modified procedures,[312] and by mid-May 2008, when it was declared completed after time extensions, the *audiences foraines* had issued more than 600,000 *jugements supplétifs*.[313] Following an extension, the UN reported that 750,000 people had received late registration of birth by 25 September 2008; even so, the numbers were lower than they might have been, since the central administration had yet to be re-established in many parts of the north of the country.[314] However, the 'ordinary identification' process was not yet re-instituted, with the focus on the second form of identification, based on the voters' roll.

Inevitably, there were also extended delays and confusion over the process of voter identification and registration – in which the rights of those with contested nationality (who would be expected to vote against Gbagbo) was the principal issue at stake. The 2000 electoral code remained in force, as modified in 2008 to provide for 'elections to exit the crisis'.[315] Voters were 'Ivorian nationals and those

[309] Accord Politique de Ouagadougou, March 2007. Chapter I of the OPA was headed 'General identification of the population'; ch II was on the electoral roll. Reproduced in UN Security Council document S/2007/144, 13 March 2007.

[310] Décret No. 2007-647 du 20 décembre 2007 portant conditions d'établissement, d'obtention et de forme de la Carte Nationale d'Identité, arts 4 and 5.

[311] Ordonnance No.2007-604 du 8 novembre 2007 portant suppresion de la Carte de Séjour.

[312] Décision No.2007-14/PR du 21 septembre 2007 portant Dispositions spéciales en matière d'audiences foraines.

[313] See statement of the Ministry of Justice and Human Rights on the mobile court process at www.audiencesforaines.gouv.ci/faq4.php; *Seventeenth Progress Report of the Secretary-General on the United Nations Operation in Côte d'Ivoire*, UN Security Council Document S/2008/451, 10 July 2008.

[314] *Eighteenth Progress Report of the Secretary-General on the United Nations Operation in Côte d'Ivoire*, UN Security Council Document S/2008/645, 13 October 2008; In addition, 250,000 civil registry entries had been reconstituted; *Rapport Final : Election Présidentielle 31 octobre–28 novembre 2010*, Mission d'Observation Electorale de l'Union Européenne, 25 January 2011.

[315] Ordonnance no.2008-133 du 14 avril 2008 portant ajustements au Code Electoral pour les élections législatives de sortie de crise ; Décision no. 2008-15/PR du 14 avril 2008 portant modalités spéciales d'ajustements au Code Electoral.

who had acquired nationality by naturalisation or marriage'.[316] The criteria to stand for president or for the national assembly established in 2000 remained in place. Elections were repeatedly postponed, as the protagonists argued over the identification of those eligible to vote.

Responsibility for the voter identification process, officially launched in September 2008, was split between five entities, led by the Independent Electoral Commission (*Commission électorale indépendante*, CEI) and the National Commission for Supervision of Identification (*Commission nationale de supervision de l'identification*), highly disorganised, accompanied by intimidation and violence, and lacking a clear framework for operations. In late 2009, two electoral lists were published after many delays and 'cross-checking' of lists: the 'white list' of 5.3 million people who were in principle accepted for the electoral roll; and the 'grey list' with an additional 1.1 million 'doubtful' cases of people who were required to show further proof of their right to vote, that is, of their nationality. Militants from the *Jeunes patriotes* sought the removal of many other names on the 'white list'; Gbagbo himself did not miss an opportunity to emphasise the distinction between Ivorians and foreigners throughout the campaign; and dissolved and reconstituted the CEI in February 2010.[317] A new 'provisional electoral list' was published in July 2010, after further additions and deletions, and the final definitive list of 6 September 2010 numbered 5.7 million people. Although accepted by the UN as credible, it was rather the product of agreement between the parties than a verified process. The full final list was never distributed to voting stations, while the nationality status of 601,322 persons who remained on the grey list was never clarified.[318]

Presidential elections were finally held in two rounds in October and November 2010. Given the context in which they were held, challenges to the validity of the results were hardly surprising; but victory for Ouattara against all the odds and without the benefits of incumbency was more unexpected. On 1 December, the CEI announced that Ouattara had taken 54.1% in the run-off vote, with 45.9% to Gbagbo. On 3 December, however, the Constitutional Council ruled that the results announced by the CEI were invalid in seven northern constituencies supportive of Ouattara, and that Gbagbo had won with 51.45% of the vote. By the end of 2010, the country was back in full scale crisis.[319] Both presidential candidates began appointing a government, and Côte d'Ivoire was suspended from both ECOWAS and the African Union, which urged Gbagbo 'to respect the

[316] « Sont électeurs les nationaux ivoiriens de deux sexes et les personnes ayant acquis la nationalité ivoirienne soit par naturalisation soit par mariage ».

[317] See International Crisis Group, 'Côte d'Ivoire: Ensuring Credible Elections' (2008); International Crisis Group, 'Côte d'Ivoire: What's Needed to End the Crisis' (2009); International Crisis Group, 'Côte d'Ivoire: Securing the Electoral Process' (2010).

[318] Numbers on the different lists taken from *Rapport Final*, Mission d'Observation Electorale de l'Union Européenne; also Adjami (n 263).

[319] International Crisis Group, 'Côte d'Ivoire: Finally Escaping the Crisis?' (2010); International Crisis Group, 'Côte d'Ivoire: Is War the Only Option?' (2011); Human Rights Watch, 'That Land Is My Family's Wealth: Addressing Land Dispossession after Côte d'Ivoire's Post-Election Conflict' (2013).

results of the election and to facilitate, without delay, the transfer of power to the President-Elect, in the best interests of Côte d'Ivoire, the region and Africa as a whole.'[320] At least 1,000 people were killed in renewed conflict over the next five months.[321]

Ultimately, a military offensive from the Ouattara side led to the arrest of Laurent Gbagbo in Abidjan, facilitated by French and UN support. On 21 May 2011, Alassane Ouattara was finally inaugurated as President.[322] Legislative elections were held on 11 December 2011,[323] the first since 2000, just two weeks after Gbagbo's transfer to the International Criminal Court in The Hague. The elections were boycotted by Gbagbo's party, the FPI, and on a turnout of only around one third of those on the electoral register established the previous year, the RDR and PDCI took 122 and 76 seats each, with the remainder of the 255 seats going to smaller parties and independents.[324]

Among the many critical issues for the new administration and legislature to address, including national reconciliation, measures of accountability for war crimes, and the reconstruction of the economy, was the continued crisis over nationality and identification. Even before a new National Assembly was in place, President Ouattara adopted an ordinance in September 2011 to facilitate the late registration of births that had taken place since 2002.[325] A new law adopted in 2013 further extended the deadlines, allowing late registration up to the end of July 2014.[326] After some consultation and study of the existing procedures, in October 2013 the Council of Ministers authorised the ONI to start the process for 'ordinary identification' provided for under the Ouagadougou Political Accord and resume the issuing of identity cards, based on the requirement that a person have a certificate of nationality.[327]

The new legislature also adopted two new laws on nationality: as in 2004, one modified the nationality code, and the other provided temporary special procedures. The law amending the nationality code made acquisition of nationality

[320] Communique of the 252nd Meeting of the Peace and Security Council of the African Union (AU), on the situation in Côte d'Ivoire. 9 December 2010.

[321] 'Death toll in Ivorian post-election violence surpassed 1,000 – UN', UN News Centre, 26 May 2011.

[322] Amnesty International, 'They Looked at His Identity Card and Shot Him Dead: Six Months of Post-Electoral Violence in Côte d'Ivoire' (2011) AFR 31/002/2011.

[323] Also governed by the 2000 electoral code, with further modifications for the 2011 legislative elections. Ordonnance No. 2011-352 du 24 octobre 2011; Ordonnance No. 2011-382 du 10 novembre 2011.

[324] Results as posted at http://africanelections.tripod.com/ci.html#2011_National_Assembly_Election.

[325] Ordonnance No. 2011-258 du 28 septembre 2011 relative à l'Enregistrement des naissances et des décès survenus durant la crise.

[326] Loi No.2013-35 du 25 janvier 2013 portant modification de l'article 2 de l'Ordonnance No. 2011-258 du 28 septembre 2011 relative à l'Enregistrement des naissances et des décès survenus durant la crise.

[327] Projet de Communiqué du Conseil des Ministres du Mercredi 02//10/2013 ; in 2014 a decree was adopted to establish a new framework for the regular issuing of identity cards : Décret No. 2014-319 du 4 juin 2014 portant conditions d'établissement, d'obtention et de forme de la Carte nationale d'identité. See Adjami (n 263) s 4.2.2 and Annex III.

on marriage once again automatic (rather than requiring an option), but now automatic for either a man or a woman marrying an Ivorian national (rather than only a woman marrying an Ivorian man, as it had been at independence).[328] The temporary special procedures provided for a streamlined process of acquisition of nationality by the same category of people as the 2004 law; that is, those who could have benefited from the transitional provision on naturalisation for those habitually resident in 1961, and for those born in the territory before January 1973 and still resident as adults.[329] But the law and its implementing decree made the procedures to access nationality significantly easier than the 2004 special procedures, which had reached nobody at all.[330] Declaration forms were distributed by the Ministry of Justice to the relevant tribunals of first instance, as well as to the offices of the administration. At the same time, the National Assembly also adopted a law approving Côte d'Ivoire's accession to the two Statelessness conventions.[331] By the end of 2014, approximately 60,000 declarations requesting nationality had been submitted, though none yet officially approved.[332] By January 2016, 123,810 people had made applications; only 11,762 nationality certificates were issued by 30 November 2016, and roll-out remained slow.[333]

The apparent limited reach of these measures emphasised the complexity of the situation. The temporary procedures only addressed the situation of those born before 1973, and the procedural requirements for applicants to hold existing documents excluded many from applying. The main provisions of the nationality law on the acquisition of nationality of origin for those born in Côte d'Ivoire remained highly restrictive, and no revision to this law was on the table by end 2017. The challenges of nationality and Statelessness were far from resolved.

The crisis of nationality in Côte d'Ivoire was, as in Zimbabwe, framed throughout by laws and regulations. The highly legalistic State places great weight on the formalities of paperwork. Though the sharpest end of discrimination was violence depending little on law, the lack of the correct identity documents placed Ivorians without recognition of nationality at risk throughout the crisis, whether this was the risk of dismissal from their employment, 'taxation' at roadblocks, or expulsion from land that they had cultivated for many years. At the bottom of this

[328] Loi No.2013-654 du 13 septembre 2013. Although the automatic acquisition can be problematic (eg, if the other country does not allow dual nationality), it does mean that a person does not have to be aware that a positive step must be taken in order to acquire nationality.

[329] Loi No.2013-653 du 13 septembre 2013. However, with some confusion on the categories (especially the application to descendants of those initially entitled) created by different wording in the law, its implementing decree and an interministerial circular. See Adjami (n 263) Annex II.

[330] Loi No.2013-653 du 13 septembre 2013, and its explanatory memorandum; Décret No.2013-848. The law providing for non-discretionary acquisition of nationality by declaration (if the conditions were met) rather than the highly discretionary naturalisation envisaged in the normal framework of the nationality code. The declaration procedure also meant that the person acquiring nationality was not subject to the limitation of political rights placed on those who have naturalised.

[331] Loi No.2013-647 du 13 septembre 2013 and Loi No.2013-649 du 13 septembre 2013 authorising the president to ratify the 1954 and 1961 Conventions.

[332] Information from UNHCR Côte d'Ivoire, email 2 February 2015.

[333] Adjami (n 263).

manipulated legalism, lay the uncertainty about who became Ivorian at independence, and the failure of the nationality code to grant any rights based on birth in Côte d'Ivoire even for the second and third generations.

A stateless victim of internal trafficking in Côte d'Ivoire[334]

Ibrahima was born in 1981 in Abengourou in the east of Côte d'Ivoire. He doesn't know his parents, but he grew up among the community of Burkinabè origin living there and speaks Mooré. At six years old, he was taken away from the family where he was living by an 'aunt', and taken to Bapleu in the west of Côte d'Ivoire.

The 'aunt' left him with a man who subsequently entrusted him to another man, for whom he worked for seven years on a cocoa plantation, until he was 14 years old. At that age, he went back to see the first man, an important business person in Bapleu, asking to be reunited with his family; but, instead, he was threatened and worked a further seven years. In 2012, Ibrahima travelled alone to Abengourou to look for his parents, using as an identity document a Burkinabè consular card lent to him by the father of the young man it had belonged to, now deceased. He stayed three months in Abengourou, but failed to find his parents, and returned to Bapleu. According to the information he obtained from the chief of the Burkinabè community in Abengourou, it was believed that Ibrahima's mother was Burkinabè, but nobody knew the real identity of the father, or had any information about the current whereabouts of his mother. The 'aunt' who had taken him away had essentially stolen the boy and sold him for his labour; but she had since died.

Ibrahima tried to obtain a genuine Burkinabè consular card, on the basis of the information he had found out about his origins, but the Burkinabè consular authorities refused to give him one because he had no documentary proof of his birth or parentage.

7.5. The Banyarwanda of Eastern Democratic Republic of Congo

The two Congo wars, from 1996 to 1997 and from 1998 to 2003, involved most of the neighbouring countries and some further afield,[335] killed perhaps hundreds

[334] Interview by Mirna Adjami, Duékué, July 2014. Name has been changed.

[335] Amongst those whose troops became directly involved were Angola, Burundi, Chad, Namibia, Rwanda, Uganda, and Zimbabwe.

of thousands of people in direct violence, may have indirectly caused the deaths of more than five million, and displaced millions more – hundreds of thousands of them across international borders.[336] Civil war in the east has continued virtually unabated since then, at varying levels of intensity. In all this conflict, the question of who belongs to Congo and when they arrived has been one of the central issues, laying open the arguments that had already seen successive laws set the 'date of origin' for Congolese citizenship variously at 1885, 1908, 1950, and 1960. The argument over the provisions in national laws on who is an indigenous (*autochtone*) Congolese linked comparatively local disputes over land and other resources to national and regional wars.

The dysfunctionality of the Congolese State makes it easy to claim that the law was of little relevance in these conflicts. Yet with hindsight it is precisely in the failure to establish any rational legal regime for the transition to independence that the origins of the longevity of disputes over belonging can be seen. At the very minimum, nationality law reforms created important signals to local administrators of the expectations of national government in different political eras in relation to allocation of resources (above all, land). More generally, from the 1990s they created the framework within which eligibility to vote and determine the country's future were established.

The DRC, with a population estimated, in the absence of any census for several decades, to be around 60 million,[337] comprises several hundred ethnic groups: it is one of the most diverse countries in Africa. In North and South Kivu, among the most troubled provinces in relation to questions of nationality, the majority ethnic groups are the 'indigenous' (*autochtone*) Nande (North Kivu), Bashi and Barega (South Kivu), with substantial minority populations made up of other 'indigenes', including Batwa ('pygmy') groups, and many speakers of Kinyarwanda, the language of Rwanda. Known collectively as Banyarwanda, they are mainly Hutu, with a minority Tutsi. While Tutsi are traditionally regarded as pastoralists, and Hutu and the 'indigenous' groups have been cultivators, most have always raised cattle when they can. As in many parts of Africa, disputes over land ownership and use both among and between pastoralists and cultivators have often been the trigger for wider conflict.

[336] The International Rescue Committee conducted surveys of 'excess mortality' in DRC, and estimated that during the period 1998 to 2007 there were 5.4 million excess deaths attributable to the war, more than 2 million of them after the formal end of the war in 2002: International Rescue Committee, 'Mortality in the Democratic Republic of Congo: An Ongoing Crisis' (2007). However, these figures were considered an exaggeration by other surveys: see Human Security Report Project, 'Human Security Report 2009/2010: The Causes of Peace and The Shrinking Costs of War' (Simon Fraser University 2010) ch 3. In 2003, the UN Special Rapporteur on the DRC reported 2.7 million displaced persons: United Nations, 'Interim Report of the Special Rapporteur on the Situation of Human Rights in the Democratic Republic of the Congo, UN Doc. A/58/534' (2003). The UN High Commissioner for Refugees reported more than 600,000 refugees from DRC in neighbouring countries in 1996, reducing to 200,000 by 2005: *2005 UNHCR Statistical Yearbook Country Data Sheet: Dem. Rep. of the Congo.*

[337] Population Division of the Department of Economic and Social Affairs, *World Population Prospects: The 2006 Revision*, United Nations, 2007. A new census was planned for 2015, but postponed till after elections could be held.

The origins of the Banyarwanda in DRC are diverse and much argued-over. Some Congolese argue that there are in fact no indigenous Banyarwanda in Congo. However, parts of the territory that is now DRC were prior to colonisation subject to the Rwandan King and already occupied by rwandophone populations. These people (the Banyabwisha) became *de facto* Congolese citizens in February 1885, with the recognition of the Belgian King Leopold II's 'private' Congo Free State by the Berlin Conference. In 1908 the Congo Free State was taken over by the Belgian government and became a colony of the Belgian State. In a 1910 agreement between Germany, Belgium and Britain, new borders were established, ceding some parts of what had been Congo Free State territory to the German colony of Rwanda, and other portions to the British colony of Uganda. Following the First World War, the German colonies of Rwanda and Burundi (whose language and ethnic make-up is close to that of Rwanda) were mandated to Belgium by the League of Nations in 1922, and in 1925 Belgium annexed them under the name Ruanda-Urundi to the Belgian Congo (following the Second World War, these mandated territories became instead trust territories under the aegis of the United Nations).[338]

The Belgian colonial administration then established a policy of organised transplantation of tens of thousands of Banyarwanda, both Hutu and Tutsi, from the already densely-populated and famine-prone Rwanda and Burundi to districts in what is now North Kivu in eastern Congo (especially Masisi and Rutshuru). These *transplantés*, brought by the *Mission d'immigration des Banyarwanda* (MIB) in place from 1937 to the mid-1950s, formed a source of labour (often forced) for agricultural plantations of coffee and other export crops and for mines established by the colonial authorities. Large tracts of land were expropriated by the *Comité national du Kivu* both for these purposes and for national parks, a process deeply resented by local populations. In Masisi, an accord for the cession of around 350 square kilometres was signed with the Bahunde chief.[339] Many others migrated independently of this programme; estimates of the total number of immigrants by the time of the dissolution of the MIB ranged up to several hundred thousand, making them a very significant proportion of the population, a majority in places such as Masisi. At the same time, the colonial authorities opposed the expansion of 'Tutsi' pastoralist modes of production: cattle-keeping was closely regulated, and – as a deliberate act to distinguish eastern Congo from the contemporary Tutsi hegemony in Rwanda – the colonial authorities appointed Hutu leaders as chiefs for their administrative purposes.[340]

One sub-group of the Banyarwanda today in DRC are for the most part descendants of Tutsi pastoralists who migrated to the area around Mulenge in what is now the province of South Kivu from Rwanda, Burundi and Tanzania; mainly

[338] Discussed in Susan Pedersen, *The Guardians: The League of Nations and the Crisis of Empire* (Oxford University Press 2015).

[339] Jean-Pierre Pabanel, 'La question de la nationalité au Kivu' (1991) 41 Politique africaine 32.

[340] Jean-Claude Willame, *Banyarwanda et Banyamulenge: Violences Ethniques et Gestion de l'identitaire Au Kivu* (Institut africain-CEDAF ; L'Harmattan 1997).

in the eighteenth and nineteenth centuries, but some of them perhaps earlier (when 'Tutsi' may indeed have had no meaning as a category). From the 1970s, this group began to use the term 'Banyamulenge' (people of Mulenge) to describe themselves. This was both part of a conscious effort by their leaders to affirm a separate identity from other South Kivu ethnic groups in the battle to increase their influence in regional and national politics, and also to distinguish themselves as *autochtones* from other, more recently arrived, Banyarwanda. From the mid-1990s, the term Banyamulenge often came to be used to mean 'Congolese Tutsi' in general.[341]

Since independence, the Kivu provinces[342] have also taken in other Banyarwanda economic migrants as well as refugees fleeing violence in Rwanda and Burundi. In 1959, thousands of Tutsi fled to Congo during the pre-independence Hutu uprising against the prior Belgian-supported Tutsi dominance in Rwanda; and more refugees arrived in further outbreaks of violence in the early 1960s, 1973 (from Rwanda), in 1972 and 1978 (from Burundi), and in the early 1990s (from both Rwanda and Burundi), before the major influx – of hundreds of thousands – following the Rwandan genocide of Tutsi by extremist Hutu that began in April 1994. All those fleeing Rwanda after independence were Tutsi until July 1994, when Tutsi-led RPA rebel forces advancing from Uganda overthrew the Hutu extremist Rwandan government and ended the genocide. The ethnicity of those crossing the border then changed, and western television screens became filled with startling images of massed Hutu refugees flooding into DRC; provoking an immediate relief effort where the genocide itself had notably failed to receive the attention it deserved.

The first law that governed nationality in Congo was an 1892 decree of King Leopold.[343] The law was broadly drafted as part of an effort to recruit as many as possible to come under the jurisdiction of the Congo Free State – where they could contribute their labour to the colonial project. By contrast to Belgium's descent-based law, the decree provided that Congolese nationality was obtained by 'birth on the territory of the State of Congolese parents' as well as by naturalisation, by presumption of law and by option.[344] The decree provided that children born on the territory of parents who were legally unknown or Stateless were presumed

[341] ibid 76–99; Koen Vlassenroot, 'Citizenship, Identity Formation & Conflict in South Kivu: The Case of the Banyamulenge' (2002) 29 Review of African Political Economy 499; Judith Verweijen and Koen Vlassenroot, 'Armed Mobilisation and the Nexus of Territory, Identity, and Authority: The Contested Territorial Aspirations of the Banyamulenge in Eastern DR Congo' (2015) 33 Journal of Contemporary African Studies 191.

[342] Except for a couple of years from 1962, when many new provinces were briefly established, there was only one Kivu Province until 1987, when it was split into North and South Kivu and Maniema.

[343] A comprehensive history of the legal changes related to nationality is set out in Célestin Nguya-Ndila Malengana, *Nationalité et citoyenneté au Congo-Kinshasa: le cas du Kivu* (L'Harmattan 2001). See also Francis M Deng, 'Ethnic marginalisation as statelessness: Lessons from the Great Lakes region of Africa' in T Alexander Aleinikoff and Douglas Klusmeyer (eds) *Citizenship Today: Global Perspectives and Practices* (Washington DC, Carnegie Endowment for International Peace, 2001).

[344] « La nationalité congolaise s'acquiert : par la naissance sur le territoire de l'Etat de parents congolais, par la naturalisation, par la présomption de la loi, et par l'option », Art 1, Décret du 27 décembre 1892 sur la nationalité Congolaise, reproduced in full in ibid.

Congolese, as were foundlings.[345] Those born on the territory of foreign parents could opt for Congolese nationality at majority, and were presumed to have done so if resident on the territory for the three previous years.[346] Naturalisation was possible by application; in practice the Belgian authorities treated those from the neighbouring colonies of *Afrique équatoriale française* or Angola as Congolese after residence in Congo for more than five years. While the provisions related to unknown parents and foundlings had their origins in Belgian law at the time, the provision on children of Stateless parents was an innovation for Congo. Another royal decree of 1904 provided that any *indigène congolais* residing in the territory remained Congolese and subject to Congolese law even if he or she claimed to have acquired another nationality; a Congolese leaving the territory and in possession of another nationality must indicate that this is the case, or the obligations of Congolese nationality would remain in place.[347]

From 1908, the date of the transformation of the Congo Free State into the Belgian Congo, Congolese nationality no longer existed and the Congolese became Belgian nationals, though deprived of the civil and political rights accorded to the white residents of the colony. The decree of 1892 remained in force for the purposes of determining nationality of those resident in the territory. As in other European colonies, residents of the Belgian Congo were firmly divided into categories, according to race and civil status.[348]

Among these categories, the *transplantés* and other immigrants from Ruanda-Urundi had a unique status. The League of Nations mandates established over the former German territories specifically prohibited the grant of nationality *en masse* to the populations of the mandated territory by the relevant European power (though individual naturalisation was possible).[349] The immigrants from the Ruanda-Urundi territories in Congo were in fact arguably Stateless, since they had lost German nationality (in which case their children born in Congo would acquire Belgian Congolese nationality); but Belgium could not grant them

[345] « Est congolais l'enfant né sur le sol de l'Etat de parents légalement inconnus ou sans nationalité déterminée. L'enfant trouvé sur ce sol congolais est présumé, jusqu'à preuve contraire, né sur ce sol. L'enfant naturel dont la filiation est établie pendant sa minorité, suit la condition de son père si la reconnaissance par ses auteurs résulte d'un seul et même acte ; sinon il suit la condition de celui de ses parents qui le premier l'a reconnu. » Décret sur la nationalité Congolaise, Art 4.

[346] « L'enfant né sur le sol de l'Etat, d'un étranger, peut, dans l'année qui suit l'époque de sa majorité, requérir la qualité de Congolais par une déclaration expresse de son intention à cet égard. Si l'enfant a été domicilié au Congo durant l'année qui suit l'époque de sa majorité et pendant les trois années précédentes l'intention d'acquérir la qualité de Congolais est présumée exister à la fin de ce terme, sauf déclaration contraire de volonté. » Décret sur la nationalité Congolaise, Art 5.

[347] Nguya-Ndila Malengana (n 343) 58–59.

[348] Article 6 of the 1892 decree provided that full civil rights were enjoyed by those who had naturalised as Congolese; those whose birth or other recognition of civil status had been registered by the authorities; those who were married before the civil authorities; and those 'who had obtained from the authorities recognition of their entry into the registers of the civilised population' ('qui auront obtenu de l'autorité publique leur immatriculation aux registres de la population civilisée').

[349] Resolution on the Nationality of B and C Mandated Territories, Council of the League of Nations, 22 April 1923; Paul Weis, *Nationality and Statelessness in International Law* (2nd edn, Brill 1979) 20–25.

nationality as a group. They were given identity cards of a different type from the rest of the Congolese population; whereas immigrants from other neighbouring countries were given the same cards as Congolese.[350]

The lack of a new and more comprehensive law on access to Belgian nationality for those outside Belgium created real confusion on who in fact qualified to be Congolese/Belgian (exacerbated by the absence of consistency in whether those concerned were called Congolese or Belgian in other laws). The possibility of adopting a law that would formally recreate 'Congolese nationality' as a type of Belgian nationality, and who exactly would qualify for it, was under debate among Belgian scholars right up to the moment when the question became irrelevant.[351] The status of the Banyarwanda of eastern Congo was therefore already unclear and controversial during the lead-up to independence of what became the Republic of Congo in 1960. Unlike the situation in the French and British colonies, there was no considered period of handover (however short, and however inadequately managed by the colonial powers); rather, the Belgians retreated precipitately, as disturbances broke out in both Congo and Ruanda-Urundi, without negotiating or even imposing a legal framework to govern the transition.

In 1959, the governor-general of Congo had adopted an ordinance permitting those from Ruanda-Urundi to vote and stand for office for newly created local government structures, on the same conditions as 'Congolese', if they had been resident for ten years in Congo.[352] This left unclear the nationality of those concerned. The immigrant Rwandans protested the ten-year requirement; but other ethnic groups objected to any extension of the right to vote to these new arrivals, whose presence would change the balance of power among other political players. The 1960 'Brussels Round Table' that negotiated the terms of independence was held just months after the arrival of tens of thousands of Tutsi refugees from the pre-independence violence in Rwanda, thus making their status key to the political balance of power. Resolution No. 2 of the Round Table adopted in February 1960 ultimately left the determination of nationality of Congo's 'inhabitants' to the law; meaning that the existing law – the 1892 decree on nationality – would remain in force for the meantime.[353] A law on elections adopted the following

[350] Nguya-Ndila Malengana (n 343) 68–73; Stanislas Melone, 'La nationalité des personnes physiques', *Encyclopédie juridique de l'Afrique : Vol VI, Droits des personnes et de la famille* (Nouvelles éditions africaines 1982) 84–85.

[351] André Durieux, *Nationalité et Citoyenneté* (Académie Royale des Sciences Coloniales 1959); Maurice Verstraete, *La Nationalité Congolaise* (Académie Royale des Sciences d'Outre-Mer 1959).

[352] Ordonnance legislative No.25/554 du 6 novembre 1959, cited in Nguya-Ndila Malengana (n 343) 79.

[353] « Le Congo, dans ses frontières actuelles, constitue à partir du 30 juin prochain, un Etat indépendant dont les habitants auront aux conditions que la loi déterminera une même nationalité sur le territoire duquel ils pourront se déplacer et s'établir librement et où les marchandises aussi pourront circuler sans entrave ». Résolution No.2 relative à l'organisation de l'Etat du Congo. The *loi fondamentale* (as the interim constitution of the new State was called) of 19 May 1960 stated that all laws in effect at that date remained in force until changed.

month provided again, separately from the question of nationality, that Rwandan immigrants resident for ten years would be able to vote but not stand for office in forthcoming national elections.[354]

Article 6 of the 'Luluabourg Constitution' of 1964 – the first constitution of the new State and the first legal determination of nationality – declared to be 'Congolese as of 30 June 1960 all persons one of whose ancestors was or had been a member of a tribe or part of a tribe established in the Congo before 18 October 1908',[355] the date on which the Belgian Congo was created. This position, which radically changed the previous framework, was confirmed in the decret-loi of 18 September 1965, which also provided for naturalisation and loss of nationality (not dealt with in the constitution). The décret-loi also finally abrogated the 1892 decree, while providing for its own entry into force to date back to the date of independence.[356] No reference was made to those who had migrated prior to independence (and their descendants) and who had a status recognised by the previous law.[357]

The Banyarwanda (and others) who had migrated to Congo after 1908 were thus not citizens of the new State; which left their status as citizens of any State uncertain, since there was no possibility for most of returning to their country of origin. Arguments that the presence of *some* Banyarwanda on Congolese territory before 1908 meant that all could claim citizenship were not accepted. At the same time, the decision to adopt an ethnic framework for citizenship created an immediate and long-lasting ambiguity over the status of several hundred thousand people who had no effective proof of their pre-1908 origins.

In the years after independence there were outbreaks of violence in eastern Congo and elsewhere, as the political structures and coherence of the fragile new State came under immediate stress. The southern provinces of Katanga and Kasai began secessionist struggles. The 1963 division (reversed in 1965) of existing provinces into smaller units heightened indigene-settler divides all over the country. In Kivu, it took the form of resentment of the Banyarwanda who opposed the creation of a North Kivu province, rather wishing the Banyarwanda majority

[354] Loi du 23 mars 1960 (« Art.1 : Pour être électeur pour la Chambre des Représentants, il faut répondre aux conditions suivantes : 1. être de statut congolais, ou être né de mère congolaise, ou être ressortissant du Ruanda-Urundi résidant au Congo depuis dix ans au moins .... Art.10 Sont éligibles ... des personnes qui 1. sont de statut congolais ou sont nées de mères congolaises ... »). Cited in Nguya-Ndila Malengana (n 343) 80–81. See also Isidore Ndaywel è Nziem, 'La nationalité congolaise à l'épreuve du séisme des Grands Lacs' in Pamphile Mabiala Mantuba-Ngoma (ed), *La Nouvelle Histoire du Congo : Mélanges euroafricains offerts à Frans Bontinck*, vols 65–66–67 (L'Harmattan 2004).

[355] « Il existe une seule nationalité congolaise. Elle est attribuée, à la date du 30 juin 1960, à toute personne dont un ascendant est ou a été membre d'une tribu ou d'une partie de tribu établie sur le territoire du Congo avant le 8 octobre 1908. » Constitution of 1 August 1964, Art 6.

[356] Décret-loi du 18 septembre 1965.

[357] In principle the descendants of the *transplantés* born on the territory were citizens under the 1892 decree, since they would either have acquired nationality on a *jus soli* basis as the children of Stateless parents; or by presumption within a year of majority as the children of foreign parents if born on the territory and resident for three years previously.

territories to be attached to a proposed Central Kivu territory.[358] A period of national instability and civil war followed, ended in November 1965 by a Belgian and US-backed coup putting Joseph-Désiré Mobutu in power. During this period, a rebellion led by Pierre Mulele, formerly a minister in the cabinet of murdered Prime Minister Patrice Lumumba, broke out in Kivu and Orientale provinces in 1964. The Mulelist rebels espoused a variant of communist philosophy, though support for their cause from the dominant Bashi ethnic groups in South Kivu was based rather on personal and ethnic alliances than on ideology; the Banyamulenge sided with the Congolese National Army to crush the revolt.

In North Kivu, meanwhile, politicians of the 'indigenous' ethnic groups mobilised supporters by labelling as foreigners even those Banyarwanda who could trace their ancestry to the Congolese side of the colonial borders from before 1908. From 1963 to 1965, fighting known as the 'Kanyarwanda war' pitted the Banyarwanda (Tutsi and Hutu) of the newly created North Kivu against the indigenous Nande, Hunde and Nyanga as each group agitated for creation of new districts where they would be in control. Not insignificantly, the Kanyarwanda war centred on Masisi, the location of the largest number of Banyarwanda *transplantés*. Even before the war broke out, Banyarwanda were accused of obtaining fake Congolese identity documents in order to participate in the planned referendum that would vote on the creation of the new provinces; meantime, indigenous Hunde lost no time in replacing Banyarwanda in all notable administrative positions. In October 1965, the North Kivu authorities adopted a '*résolution-loi*' directed at the expulsion of all Banyarwanda for 'collusion with the rebels'; various Banyarwanda leaders were arrested and transferred to Leopoldville (the future Kinshasa).[359] The nationality provisions of the constitution of 1964 and décret-loi of 1965 were drafted amidst these disturbances, before the assumption of power by Mobutu, and played their own role in heightening tensions.

Following Mobutu's accession to power and the end of active hostilities, a commission of inquiry was then sent by the central government to Kivu province to inquire into the vexed question of the nationality of the Banyarwanda. The Tewen Commission presented its report in October 1966, and classed the Banyarwanda of the Kivus into four categories, of which only members of the first were considered Congolese: (1) those who freely immigrated from the seventeenth century and were present on the territory as of 1885; (2) fugitives from famine and political disturbances in Rwanda who arrived between then and around 1918; (3) the *transplantés* brought by the Belgians as labour; (4) the refugees of 1959

[358] Willame (n 340) 48.

[359] Willame (n 340); Frank van Acker, 'La « Pembenisation » du Haut-Kivu : Opportunisme et droits fonciers revisités' (1999) 1998–1999 L'Afrique des grands lacs Annuaire 201; Stephen Jackson, 'Sons of Which Soil? The Language and Politics of Autochthony in Eastern D.R. Congo' (2006) 49 African Studies Review 95; Angele N Makombo, 'Civil Conflict in the Great Lakes Region: The Issue of Nationality of the Banyarwanda in the Democratic Republic of the Congo' (1997) 5 African Yearbook of International Law 49.

following the deposition of the Rwandan king during the independence of Rwanda (of which others went to Tanzania or Uganda).[360] This interpretation became the dominant official view on those who were entitled to be Congolese (albeit with some variation on dates of origin between 1885 and 1908).

A new constitution was adopted in 1967 that stated that the law would provide for nationality, leaving in place the rules of the 1964 constitution and the décret-loi of 1965 (1974 and 1978 revisions did not affect these provisions).[361] However, under the influence of powerful individuals close to Mobutu, including Barthélémy Bisengimana (a Tutsi from North Kivu appointed to be director of the president's office from 1969 and thus a figure of power in the government), laws were adopted to favour the position of the Banyarwanda.[362] Mobutu's party, the *Mouvement Populaire de la Révolution* (MPR), created in 1967 and effectively merged with State structures, recognised the Banyarwanda of Masisi, stated to make up '85 percent of the inhabitants of the region', as citizens of right, and confirmed their chief as the administrative authority of their territory – perhaps more significantly for day-to-day life.[363]

An ordinance-law adopted in 1971 by Mobutu specifically addressed the situation of persons originating from Rwanda and Burundi, providing that if they were established in Congo before 30 June 1960 they had Congolese nationality.[364] In 1972, a general nationality law voted by Parliament soon after the change of the country's name to Zaire first reaffirmed the basic principle of the 1964 constitution based on date of arrival before 1908, but, after hearing from Bisengimana on the decision of the MPR, provided an exception for persons originating from Rwanda or Burundi who had taken up residence before 1 January 1950.[365] Although the 1972 law would in principle exclude the Tutsi refugees of 1959, no subsidiary legislation implementing the 1972 law was adopted. These highly controversial laws

[360] Nguya-Ndila Malengana (n 343) 40–41.

[361] Constitution du 24 juin 1967, Art 46 : « La loi fixe les règles concernant [...] La nationalité, l'état et la capacité des personnes, les régimes matrimoniaux, les successions et les libéralités ; ... » Art 49 : « La loi électorale, la loi sur la nationalité et les lois auxquelles la présente Constitution confère le caractère de lois organiques ne sont adoptées par l'Assemblée nationale qu'à la majorité absolue de ses membres. Elles sont modifiées dans les mêmes conditions. »

[362] Willame (n 340) 53–55.

[363] Nguya-Ndila Malengana (n 343) 96–98, quoting the minutes of a meeting of the Bureau politique of the MPR, 29 July 1970 and Bisengimana's address to parliament.

[364] « Les personnes originaire du Ruanda-Urundi établies au Congo à la date du 30 juin 1960 sont réputées avoir acquis la nationalité congolaise à la date susdite. » Ordonnance-Loi No.71-020 du 26 mars 1971 rélative à l'acquisition de la nationalité congolaise par les personnes originaires du Ruanda-Urundi établies au Congo au 30 juin 1960, seul article.

[365] Loi No.72-002 du 5 janvier 1972 relative à la nationalité zaïroise : Article 1 : « Il existe une nationalité zaïroise. Sont zaïrois ... à la date de 30 juin 1960 toute personne dont un des ascendants est ou a été membre d'une des tribus établies sur le territoire de la République du Zaïre dans ses limites du 15 novembre 1908 et telle que modifiées par les conventions ultérieures. » Art 15 : « Les personnes originaires du Ruanda-Urundi qui étaient établies dans la province du Kivu avant le 1er janvier 1950 et qui on continué à résider depuis lors dans la République du Zaïre jusqu'à l'entrée en vigueur de la présente loi on acquis la nationalité zaïroise à la date du 30 juin 1960. »

thus aimed to give citizenship by origin to those Banyarwanda who had arrived in the country after 1908 and up to the date of independence. In theory, the incorporation of the Banyarwanda into the citizen body by this process would completely change the balance of political power in North Kivu: in Masisi, according to the 1970 census, out of a total population in the Masisi district of 273,920, 193,428 were 'foreigners'.[366] In practice, all still faced difficulties in gaining national identity cards or being allowed to run for office.[367]

At the same time, Bisengimana favoured his ethnic group in official appointments, using the process of 'zairianisation' of the civil service and economy for this purpose. An equally controversial land law was adopted in 1973 and used to benefit Tutsi elites at the expense of more traditional forms of land-holding: most of the colonial-era plantations in the Kivus confiscated from Europeans then ended up in Banyarwanda hands. The increasing corruption of the State meant that national identity cards were easily available for those who could buy them, even if they did not fulfil the provisions of the newly generous law. It was during this period that the question of the status of the Banyarwanda in general and Tutsi in particular, and their access to land, was elevated from a regional preoccupation to an issue of general national concern.[368]

Bisengimana fell from power in February 1977, perhaps after one too many accusations of personal benefit from his activities. The nationality question immediately returned to the table, with a series of memoranda and counter-memoranda addressed to Mobutu as head of State. A commission of inquiry was appointed to look into the issues, composed of members of the central committee of the MPR. In 1981, a new nationality code was adopted by the Zairian Parliament which reversed the changes of the 1970s, and created the most exclusionary rules yet implemented. Law No.2 of 29 June 1981 provided nationality only for 'any person one of whose ancestors was a member of one of those tribes established in the territory of the Republic of Zaire as defined by its frontiers of 1 August 1885', the date on which the borders of the Congo Free State were officially recognised.[369] This law took the date at which an ethnic group could claim to be 'indigenous' back to its furthest yet; though it did allow for the first time a Congolese woman married to a foreigner to transmit her nationality to her child. The law also provided that

[366] Willame (n 340) 54, citing 1970 census figures quoted in Léon de Saint Moulin Atlas des collectivités du Zaire, Kinshasa : Presse universitaire du Zaire, 1976.

[367] Verweijen and Vlassenroot (n 341).

[368] The 1973 *Loi foncière* – which is still in force – greatly enhanced State control over land and thus allowed for award of land to favoured individuals for political reasons; van Acker (n 359); Stanislas Bucyalimwe Mararo, 'Land, Power, and Ethnic Conflict in Masisi (Congo-Kinshasa), 1940s–1994' (1997) 30 International Journal of African Historical Studies 503; José Mvuezolo Bazonzi, 'Crise identitaire et lutte de leadership dans la région des grands lacs : Lecture des principaux conflits fonciers et armés du Kivu 1900–2005' in Bahru Zewde (ed), *Society, State, and Identity in African history* (Forum for Social Studies 2008).

[369] 'Est zaïrois … à la date du 30 juin 1960 toute personne dont un des ascendants est ou a été membre d'une des tribus établies sur le territoire de la République du Zaïre dans ses limites du 1er août 1885, telle que modifiées pas les conventions subséquentes ». Loi No.81-002 du 29 juin 1981, art 4.

the grant of nationality could be only individual and not collective (thus cancelling the provisions of the law of 1972 relating to the Banyarwanda), and that those naturalised were subjected to significant constraints in relation to the holding of political office for a period of 15 years. Individual naturalisation had in any event been rarely granted: only 28 cases could be traced in the period 1973 to 1993 by Célestin Nguya-Ndila Malengana in his comprehensive consideration of nationality issues in Congo.[370] In implementation of the law, a 1982 ordinance explicitly annulled the certificates of nationality issued under the law of 1972, leaving these people stateless unless they applied for naturalisation; it made use of such a certificate punishable by six months of penal servitude.[371]

Although some of the Banyarwanda could trace the arrival of their ancestors to a date preceding 1885, proof was difficult to establish and in practice they were treated as denationalised: they were prevented from participating in local elections during the 1980s, and many were expelled.[372] At the same time, however, a Banyarwanda elite still held wealth and land amassed from official patronage during the 1970s, an economic dominance that continued to fuel resentment of their position and enabled them to get past the rules that supposedly now applied. It was alleged that powerful individuals from or even based in Rwanda acquired land and used the local Banyarwanda or imported Rwandans as labour; many were alleged to have documents showing nationality of both countries, despite the ban on dual nationality. Local elections scheduled for 1987, then postponed to 1989, were never held in North Kivu, due to the impossibility of identifying who was entitled to vote and violence attending efforts to do so.[373]

During the early 1990s, the regime of Joseph-Désiré Mobutu weakened under international pressure and the end of US support to his government with the end of the Cold War; he was forced to agree to the creation of a 'sovereign national conference' (*Conférence nationale souveraine*, (CNS)) to debate the future structures of government in what was still Zaire. The prospect of elections and new political arrangements encouraged ethnic mobilisation to control political space, using the language of autochthony where it was useful, or simple political deal-making where it was not: alliances formed and reformed in different locations according to local politics. A 1991 population census to identify and register citizens in advance of anticipated elections contributed to the raising of tensions, since the voting power of the Banyarwanda, if recognised as nationals, would have a significant effect on the electoral outcomes.[374]

[370] Nguya-Ndila Malengana (n 343) 112.

[371] Ordonnance No.82-061 of 15 May 1981, cited in ibid 99–100.

[372] Uganda also displaced a large number of Banyarwanda in the early 1980s, including some 40,000 people who claimed Ugandan citizenship and 31,000 people registered with UNHCR as refugees, forcing most of them to seek refuge in Rwanda. See Bonaventure Rutinwa, 'The End of Asylum? The Changing Nature of Refugee Policies in Africa' (2002) 21 Refugee Survey Quarterly 12, 6.

[373] Willame (n 340); Pabanel (n 339).

[374] Stanislas Bucyalimwe Mararo, 'La guerre des chiffres: Une constante dans la politique au Nord-Kivu' (2000) 1999–2000 L'Afrique des Grands Lacs Annuaire 225; United Nations, 'Democratic Republic of

Ultimately, Banyarwanda were largely excluded from the sovereign national conference itself, as a *Commission de verification et de validation des mandats de la CNS* refused to recognise delegates decided to be representing 'foreigners'[375]; a stipulation that delegates should be 'indigenous' also affected other ethnic groups straddled between provinces within Zaire's borders (such as 'Kasaians' in Shaba Province). A sub-commission of the national conference adopted a report proposing four categories of Banyarwanda – *autochtones* (from before 1885), *transplantés*, refugees, and *clandestins* (undocumented immigrants) – with only the first entitled to citizenship.[376] The final text adopted by the CNS on nationality was more moderate, however, recommending an approach that 'preserved the integrative vocation of the Congolese State' while 'avoiding the creation of statelessness that would put our country among the ranks of human rights violators'.[377]

As these debates were going on in Kinshasa, the politics of Rwanda and Burundi impacted dramatically and negatively on the situation in the east. The Uganda-based Rwandan Patriotic Front (RPF) began its military campaign to overthrow the Hutu-controlled and discriminatory Rwandan government in 1990, and also organised and recruited among the Congolese Tutsi. Meanwhile, the Rwandan government similarly formed links with and supported Hutu groupings within Congo's eastern provinces. In October 1993, a Tutsi-led coup in Burundi accompanied by massacres sent thousands of Hutu refugees across the borders.

In March 1993, the already tense situation escalated from occasional confrontations into generalised violence in North Kivu. Electoral arithmetic, coupled with tensions over land use, had generated a coalition of 'indigenous' groups (led by the largest, the Nande) against the Hutu, especially in Masisi, where Hutu were the majority. The 'Masisi war', in which the provincial authorities encouraged attacks on Hutu in the region and Hutu militia responded, began a process of 'ethnic cleansing' that continued thereafter, with previously mixed-ethnicity communities becoming exclusively Hutu, Nande, Hunde, Nyanga, Tutsi and so on. But the configuration of ethnic conflict was not fixed. In some areas, the Tutsi fought with the Nande; in others they formed part of a general Banyarwanda group; in others Hutu (describing themselves as *autochtones*) attacked Tutsi, in yet others they were outside the local conflict. In the short term, the Masisi war caused political damage

the Congo, 1993–2003: Report of the Mapping Exercise Documenting the Most Serious Violations of Human Rights and International Humanitarian Law Committed within the Territory of the Democratic Republic of the Congo between March 1993 and June 2003' (UN Office of the High Commissioner for Human Rights 2010) paras 151–155.

[375] Willame (n 340) 62–63.

[376] Jackson (n 359).

[377] 'La question délicate de la nationalité à été abordée avec les précautions qui s'imposent pour à la fois concilier le souci de préserver au Congo sa vocation de pays intégrateur, métissé sans ostracisme outrancier d'aucune sorte, et celui de faire respecter les lois nationales en matière d'immigration, de résidence ou de naturalisation, tout en évitant de plonger des catégories de citoyens dans l'apatridie qui mettrait notre pays au banc des pays violateurs des droits de l'homme ». Final report of the *travaux* of the conference, cited in Willame (n 340) 63.

to the Nande, as Governor Jean-Pierre Kalumbo Mbogho, a Nande, was removed from office in July 1993; to the profit of the Tutsi.[378]

Hostilities had hardly begun to die down under efforts to negotiate peace, symbolised by the arrival of Mobutu in the region with his presidential guard in July 1993, when, from April 1994, the Rwandan civil war and genocide spilled over into Zaire. Rwandan Hutu extremists murdered nearly one million Rwandan Tutsi and Hutu who opposed the policy, in a government-organised campaign of violence that was unleashed just as negotiations to end the increasingly powerful RPF rebellion had seemed to reach a conclusion. First Rwandan Tutsis, and then, following the military success in Rwanda of the Tutsi-dominated RPF, several hundred thousand Hutus, including both innocent civilians and perpetrators of the genocide, fled across the border and were housed in refugee camps placed largely among local Hutu communities.

Hutu militia joined forces with ex-Rwandan army soldiers to continue their violence against Zairian Tutsi, and divisions between Zairian Tutsi and Hutu were stirred into renewed violence. Zairian government forces either stood by or actively assisted the Hutu militia in this violence against Tutsi, including by providing weapons and participating in killings; official comments supported 'indigenous' groups in efforts to expel all Banyarwanda. Tens of thousands of Tutsi people moved from Congo to Rwanda during late 1994 and 1995, mainly chased from their lands in the Masisi area, and their cattle stolen or killed.[379]

On 28 April 1995, the transitional Parliament (*le Haut Conseil de la République – Parlement de transition*) adopted a 'resolution on nationality' describing all Banyarwanda, including groups such as the Banyamulenge and Banyabwisha who claimed autochthony, as foreigners 'who have acquired Zairian nationality fraudulently'. The resolution included a list of people to be arrested and expelled, the cancellation of any sale or transfer of assets, the replacement of existing governors and commanders with new officials, and the removal of all 'Rwandan and Burundian refugees and immigrants', as well as other foreigners, from all administrative posts.[380] This resolution led to a challenge in the Supreme Court by two members of the transitional Parliament, Mutiri Muyongo and Kalegamire Nyirimigabo, requesting that it set aside a decision to exclude them on grounds of

[378] Stanislas Bucyalimwe Mararo, 'Le Nord-Kivu au cœur de la crise congolaise' (2002) 2001–2002 L'Afrique des Grands Lacs Annuaire 153; United Nations, 'DRC: Report of the Mapping Exercise' (n 374) paras 153–158.

[379] Human Rights Watch, 'Forced to Flee: Violence Against the Tutsis in Zaire' (1996), citing UNHCR figures for those fleeing to Rwanda; United Nations, 'DRC: Report of the Mapping Exercise' (n 374) paras 162, 182, 191–2.

[380] '[L]'annulation de tout acte de vente, d'acquisition ou d'attribution de titres fonciers ou immobiliers au bénéfice des immigrés et transplantés ayant acquis frauduleusement la nationalité zairoise ainsi que tout acte de nomination de réfugiés et immigrés rwandais et burundais dans les fonctions publiques'. Le Haut Conseil de la Republique – Parlement de Transition, 'Résolution sur la nationalité', Kinshasa, 28 April 1995, cited in Nguya-Ndila Malengana (n 343) 101; and in Stephen Jackson, 'Of 'Doubtful Nationality': Political Manipulation of Citizenship in the D. R. Congo' (2007) 11 Citizenship Studies 481. See also 'Briefing on the conflict in South Kivu', IRIN, 10 July 1996.

doubt about their nationality. The court annulled the decision of the transitional Parliament on both procedural and substantive grounds, ruling that the Congolese nationality of the two parliamentarians was sufficiently proved by the certificates of nationality or identity cards that they had obtained from the Ministry of the Interior; though it declined to award any damages.[381]

Those without the status of parliamentarians were not so fortunate. In South Kivu, the district commissioner of Uvira ordered in September 1995 an inventory of all property and land owned by the Banyamulenge. Evictions of South Kivu Banyamulenge from their homes became common, as were deportations to Rwanda or Burundi, escalating during 1996. Ultimatums were issued for the Banyamulenge to leave the country, and slogans adopted supporting ethnic cleansing: '*Opération rendre les rwandais au Rwanda*'; '*Bukavu et Uvira villes propres*'.[382] In early September, 'indigenous' ethnic militia, supported by government soldiers, began attacking Banyamulenge villages, killing and raping, and forcing survivors to flee. On 8 October 1996 the deputy governor of South Kivu decreed that all Banyamulenge must relocate to temporary camps within a week. On 31 October, the transitional Parliament announced the expulsion of Rwandan, Burundian and Ugandan nationals. Scores of Banyamulenge were arrested and reports of executions and disappearances were widespread. Violence against Tutsi escalated throughout the eastern regions and many fled to Rwanda; guards at the border confiscated and destroyed their Zairian identity cards.[383]

From mid-1996, the new RPF government in Rwanda began a decisive intervention, in response to the threat from Hutu militia and ex-Rwandan army forces in eastern Congo. The first infiltrations of trained forces from Rwanda began around July. Then, in mid-October, the Rwandan government played the key role in the creation of the ill-matched alliance of four disparate groups (including both the South Kivu Banyamulenge and other, 'indigenous' ethnic militia), the *Alliance*

[381] Mabanga Monga Mabanga, 'Le Contentieux Constitutionnel Congolais' (Editions Universitaires Africaines 1999) 56–58. The 1965 and 1972 nationality laws required that evidence of Congolese nationality must include 'proof of all the conditions established by the law.' However, a court could also take into account 'weighty, precise and corroborating presumptions' (*présomptions graves, précises et concordantes*) as evidence of nationality, drawing inferences from known to unknown facts. This provision was not included in later versions of the law (neither that of 1981, which set the date of ethnic qualification for citizenship as 1885, nor its replacement of 2004), which state only that evidence of nationality is provided by an official certificate of nationality supplied by the correct State authority.

[382] 'Operation return the Rwandans to Rwanda'; 'Bukavu and Uvira clean cities': from 'Declaration de la communauté banyamulenge à la conference sur la paix, la sécurité et le développement au Nord et au Sud Kivu', January 2008 (copy obtained by author).

[383] For the sequence of events, see Human Rights Watch, 'Rearming with Impunity: International Support for the Perpetrators of the Rwandan Genocide' (1995); Human Rights Watch, 'Forced to Flee' (n 379); Human Rights Watch, 'Zaire: Attacked By All Sides' (1997); Human Rights Watch, 'Zaire: Transition, War and Human Rights' (1997); Human Rights Watch, 'What Kabila Is Hiding: Civilian Killings and Impunity in Congo' (1997); Human Rights Watch, 'Transition and Human Rights Violations in Congo' (1997); United Nations, 'DRC: Report of the Mapping Exercise' (n 374) paras 178–188.

des Forces démocratiques pour la libération du Congo-Zaïre (AFDL).[384] This became the catalyst for a regional war in which the AFDL rebels, led by Laurent-Désiré Kabila, a former Lumumbist originally from Katanga, were backed by both Rwanda and Uganda, whose troops crossed the border into Zaire in late 1996. By late 1996, a large percentage of the Hutu refugees had been driven back into Rwanda; AFDL soldiers were responsible for extensive and systematic massacres of refugees in this process. Thousands were killed and many more died in the forests.[385] The rebels eventually ousted President Mobutu from power in May 1997 and installed Kabila as president in Kinshasa; as well as instituting their own administration in much of the east. The country was renamed the Democratic Republic of Congo.

Kabila's support among the Banyamulenge was effectively ended in August 1998 when, amidst increasing discontent in Kinshasa at foreign control of many posts, he decided to expel Rwandese and Ugandan contingents from his army. A new and even more deadly war broke out in the east, in which a new rebel group, the *Rassemblement congolais pour la démocratie* (RCD), with the active backing of Rwanda, stated that it championed the cause of the Banyamulenge and Congolese Tutsi more generally. Uganda, meanwhile, armed the *Mouvement de liberation congolais* (MLC), headed by Jean-Pierre Bemba (later indicted by the International Criminal Court for war crimes in the Central African Republic). Among the disputed objectives of the RCD during the war (and in the negotiations that ended it) was the establishment of the specific administrative territory of Minembwe, where Banyamulenge would be in the majority.[386] Rwanda itself again sent troops across the border, again justifying its presence in DRC as self-defence, as well as part of an effort to protect the Banyamulenge communities.[387]

[384] For a detailed account, see Jason K Stearns, *Dancing in the Glory of Monsters: The Collapse of the Congo and the Great War of Africa* (PublicAffairs 2011); see also Willame (n 340) 93–94; Human Rights Watch, 'What Kabila Is Hiding: Civilian Killings and Impunity in Congo' (n 383).

[385] Human Rights Watch, 'What Kabila Is Hiding: Civilian Killings and Impunity in Congo' (n 383); United Nations, 'Report on the Situation of Human Rights in Zaire by the Special Rapporteur, Mr. Robert Garretón, in Accordance with Commission Resolution 1996/77, UN Doc. E/CN.4/1997/6/Add.1' (United Nations 1996) E/CN.4/1997/6/Add.1; Emmanuel Lubala Mugisho, 'La Situation Politique Au Kivu: Vers Une Dualisation de La Societé' [1998] L'Afrique des Grands Lacs Annuaire 1997–98 307; Jean-Claude Willame, 'Kivu : La Poudrière', in Colette Braeckman et al *Kabila prend le pouvoir* (Groupe de recherche et d'information sur la paix et la sécurité (GRIP) 1998); United Nations, 'DRC: Report of the Mapping Exercise' (n 374) paras 191–243 ch IIB.

[386] The territory was in fact created by a departmental *arrêté* (No.001/MJ/DAT/MB/ROUTE/1999) in September 1999, though of shortlived and contested legal validity. Verweijen and Vlassenroot (n 341); Paul-Robain Namegabe Rugarabura, 'Traditional Chieftaincy and Decentralisation in the Democratic Republic of Congo: Opportunities and Challenges' (PhD, Libera Università Internazionale degli Studi Sociali 2008); International Crisis Group, 'Understanding Conflict in Eastern Congo (I): The Ruzizi Plain' (2013).

[387] In early 2002, RCD-Goma officer Patrick Masunzu rejected the rebel movement's authority and took many supporters with him, causing a split in the Banyamulenge community. RCD-Goma troops tried unsuccessfully to suppress Masunzu's group. Rwandan government soldiers then joined in attacking the Banyamulenge, a people whose security had once been a pretext for the Rwandan army presence in Congo. See Human Rights Watch, *World Report 2003: Democratic Republic of Congo*, New York, 2003.

Kabila armed both 'Mai-Mai' and Congolese Hutu militia in response to the Rwandan army's supply of weapons to the RCD. Angola and Zimbabwe supported Kabila's government.[388]

In 1999, the nationality law of 1981 was restated in order to replace the name Zaire with that of Congo, while reaffirming the presumption that nationals were members of those tribes established in the territory in 1885.[389]

For the Tutsi Banyarwanda in eastern Congo or in Kinshasa, including the Banyamulenge, the consequence of these events and legal changes was that – whatever the reality for each individual and despite the claims to autochthony of the Banyamulenge in particular – they were presumed by the Zairian/Congolese government and many of its people to be supporters of the Rwandan invaders and of the armed groups that the Rwandans were backing. Illegal extraction of Congo's resources by foreign interests – whether Rwandan, Ugandan or from further afield – increased the general resentment of 'non-indigenous' involvement in the region. Hate speech leaflets multiplied, denouncing Banyarwanda invaders and their puppets who allegedly sought to assert the domination of central African Tutsi (or Banyarwanda in general; the categories slip).[390] In 1998, hate speech was particularly virulent: among other official statements, Foreign Minister Abdulaiye Yerodia Ndombasi publicly asserted that Tutsi were 'vermin' worthy of 'extermination', allegedly leading directly to massacres of those targeted.[391]

After the assassination of Laurent-Désiré Kabila in January 2001, his son Joseph took over power and quickly began steps to end the war. Peace meetings were held in Lusaka, Zambia and Sun City, South Africa, culminating in a 'global and all-inclusive agreement on the transition in the DRC' signed on 17 December 2002.[392] The transitional constitution negotiated at Sun City provided that 'The ethnic groups and nationalities whose representatives and territories made up what became the Congo at independence should enjoy equal rights and equal protection

[388] Human Rights Watch, 'Rearming with Impunity' (n 383); Human Rights Watch, 'Forced to Flee' (n 379); United Nations, 'DRC: Report of the Mapping Exercise' (n 374) paras 308–358.

[389] Décret-Loi No.197 du 29 janvier 1999.

[390] United Nations, 'DRC: Report of the Mapping Exercise' (n 374) paras 189–191, 312–318; Stearns, *Dancing in the Glory of Monsters* (n 384). The discredited colonial-era 'Hamitic hypothesis' in which 'Nilotic' pastoralist invaders were said to have dispossessed Bantu cultivators throughout much of east and central Africa, still has much currency in the discourse of difference today, despite the lack of evidence to support it. For a discussion, see Edith R Sanders, 'The Hamitic Hypothesis; Its Origin and Functions in Time Perspective' (1969) 10 Journal of African History 521; Jan Vansina, *Paths in the Rainforests: Toward a History of Political Tradition in Equatorial Africa* (James Currey 1990).

[391] Prosecutors in Belgium issued an international arrest warrant for Yerodia in 2000 in connection with these Statements, accusing him of breaches of the Geneva Conventions and crimes against humanity (in 2002 the International Court of Justice ruled that Belgium had violated international law in issuing the warrant against a serving minister). Pieter HF Bekker, 'World Court Orders Belgium to Cancel an Arrest Warrant Issued Against the Congolese Foreign Minister' (American Society of International Law 2002) ASIL Insights; United Nations, 'DRC: Report of the Mapping Exercise' (n 374) para 313.

[392] Accord global et inclusif sur la transition en République Démocratique du Congo, 17 December 2002. Article 2(D)(2)(e) delegated questions of nationality to the Senate and National Assembly.

of the law as citizens.'[393] Regional efforts to secure peace through the 'Great Lakes Pact' among all Congo's neighbours also recognised the central importance of nationality among the causes of the conflict.[394]

Nonetheless, violence continued in North and South Kivu provinces, and between the supposedly newly integrated armed forces (*Forces armées de la République démocratique du Congo*, FARDC) and dissidents who refused to accept the settlement.[395] During 2004, thousands of settlers from Rwanda crossed the border into DRC with Rwandan military support, and cleared land for farming in the Virunga National Park, a UNESCO World Heritage Site.[396] Oil exploration also heated up in the region following the signing of the memoranda of understanding between Heritage Oil and the Congolese and Uganda governments in 2002, creating higher stakes for control of territory.[397]

In November 2004, a new nationality law was finally adopted, after heated debate in the transitional Parliament. This law followed the transitional constitution to return the foundation date for nationality to 1960, as it had been in the decree of 1971 (at that date only for those from Rwanda and Burundi). The law still founded Congolese nationality on ethnicity, rather than on birth, residence or other objective criteria, giving nationality by origin to 'every person belonging to the ethnic groups and nationalities of which the individuals and territory formed what became Congo at independence.'[398] No further guidance was given on which ethnic groups were included in this description. In a major departure

[393] Constitution de la Transition, 5 April 2003, art 14.

[394] The 2004 Dar es Salaam Declaration on Peace, Security, Democracy and Development in the Great Lakes Region committed States to 'adopt a common approach for the ratification and implementation of the UN Conventions on Statelessness, harmonise related national laws and standards, and provide refugees and displaced persons with identification documents enabling them to have access to basic services and exercise their rights.' The original signatories to a later Pact on Security, Stability and Development for the Great Lakes Region, adopted in December 2006, were Angola, Burundi, Central African Republic, Congo, DRC, Kenya, Rwanda, Sudan, Tanzania, Uganda and Zambia; in 2012, the new State of South Sudan joined the pact. See Internal Displacement Monitoring Centre and International Refugee Rights Initiative, 'The Great Lakes Pact and the Rights of Displaced People: A Guide for Civil Society' (2008).

[395] After the entry into force in 2002 of the treaty establishing an International Criminal Court, the Kabila government referred the situation in the DRC to the ICC; several cases are under investigation from Ituri Province, north of the Kivus, in relation to atrocities committed by different ethnic militia (including Tutsi militia) as well as the army, and arrest warrants issued.

[396] Stefan Lovgren, '"Gorillas in the Mist" Park Slashed by Squatters', *National Geographic News*, 12 July 2004; Finbarr O'Reilly, 'Mountain gorilla region under threat', *The Scotsman*, 23 August 2004; see also Christian Nellemann, Ian Redmond and Johannes Refisch (eds), *The Last Stand of the Gorilla: Environmental Crime and Conflict in the Congo Basin. A Rapid Response Assessment* (UN Environment Programme & GRID-Arendal 2010).

[397] International Crisis Group, 'Black Gold in the Congo: Threat to Stability or Development Opportunity?' (2012).

[398] « Est Congolais d'origine toute personne appartenant aux groupes ethniques et nationalités dont les personnes et le territoire constituaient ce qui est devenu le Congo (présentement la République Démocratique du Congo) a l'indépendance. » Loi No.04/024 du 12 novembre 2004 relative a la nationalité congolaise, art 6. The upper house of Parliament (the Senate) did not approve this critical article; under the transitional constitution the views of the lower house took precedence.

from the framework in place since 1964, however, the law also provided that a person could apply for recognition of nationality based on birth in Congo and residence until majority. Implementing regulations, however, made acquisition on this basis subject to the effective discretion of the minister (with appeal only to the President and then the Supreme Court).[399] Naturalisation was possible under the law, but extraordinarily difficult in practice, requiring a raft of supporting documents and entirely discretionary. The law excluded from naturalisation people guilty of economic crimes or who had worked for the profit of a foreign State – common accusations against the Banyarwanda.[400] Dual nationality remained prohibited.[401]

A law on electoral registration, meanwhile, provided for a range of different forms of proof of nationality, including, in the absence of any form of documentation, the testimony of five witnesses who had already been registered and were resident for at least five years in one constituency.[402] It was this law that had immediate practical impact. A referendum in December 2005 based on the voters' roll established by these rules overwhelmingly approved a new constitution, which came into force in 2006. Article 10 again recognised members of ethnic groups who were present in the territory of the State at the time of independence in 1960 as nationals of origin of the DRC.[403]

Elections held in 2006 confirmed the political eclipse of the Tutsi-dominated RCD-Goma: from being one of the four political forces governing the country during the transition period, it was wiped out electorally and fell to having virtually no political significance at the national level. The Banyamulenge demand for

[399] Loi No.04/024 du 12 novembre 2004 relative a la nationalité congolaise, arts 21, 34 & 35 ; Arrêté ministériel No.261/CAB/MIN/J/2006 du 04 juillet 2006 portant certaines mesures d'exécution de la Loi No.04/024 du 12 novembre 2004 relative à la nationalité congolaise. The supporting documents for an application based on birth and residence until majority include proof of election of domicile and habitual residence in the DRC and a birth certificate.

[400] Loi No.04/024 du 12 novembre 2004 relative a la nationalité congolaise, art 22. The supporting documents for naturalisation additionally include a certificate of competence in one of the Congolese languages, as well as of good conduct, clean criminal record, good health, sufficient means and other matters.

[401] In early 2007 the newly elected National Assembly hastily adopted a resolution purporting to bring in a six-month moratorium on the enforcement of the provision to itself, after it emerged that a large number of politically important (and non-Banyarwanda) members of the Assembly in fact held two passports. A special committee was appointed to propose a solution to the problem – which remained hanging in the air with no formal decision. « Un moratoire accordé aux personnes concernées par la double nationalité », Agence Congolaise de Presse, 13 February 2007.

[402] Loi No.04/028 du 24 decembre 2004 portant Identification et enrôlement des électeurs en République Démocratique du Congo, art 10 : « Pour justifier l'identité et l'âge de l'électeur, sera prise en considération l'une des pièces ci-après: le certificat de nationalité ou l'attestation tenant lieu de certificat de nationalité; la carte d'identité pour citoyen; le passeport national; le permis de conduire national sécurisé; le livret de pension congolais délivré par l'Institut National de Sécurité Sociale ou par toute autre institution congolaise légalement reconnue en tenant lieu; la carte d'élève ou d'étudiant; la carte de service. A défaut de l'une ou l'autre de ces pièces, sera pris en considération le témoignage fait devant le bureau du Centre d'Inscription par cinq témoins déjà inscrits sur la liste des électeurs du même Centre d'Inscription et résidant depuis 5 ans au moins dans le ressort du centre d'inscription. »

[403] Constitution de la République démocratique du Congo, 2006. The new constitution did not repeat the term 'nationalités' from the 2004 law. Exclusions of naturalised citizens from public office – which had been extremely broad – were restricted to only the very highest posts.

Minembwe to be a territory of its own for the elections was denied.[404] In May 2006, during the election campaign, Abdoulaye Yerodia, by then one of Congo's four Vice-Presidents in the transitional government and a supporter of presidential candidate Joseph Kabila, once again verbally attacked Congolese Tutsi at a rally in Goma, saying they should leave the country. In August 2007, hundreds of people rioted and attacked UN staff in the town of Moba, Katanga province, after rumours of the return to their homes of displaced Banyamulenge.[405]

The east returned to war, as a new Tutsi-led rebel movement formed under the name *Congrès national pour la défense du peuple* (CNDP) fought both the new Congolese army, and a predominantly Rwandan Hutu group, known as the *Forces démocratiques de liberation du Rwanda* (FDLR).[406] At January 2008 peace talks in Goma, provincial capital of North Kivu, the status of the Congolese Tutsi and the return of Congolese Tutsi refugees from Rwanda remained one of the most difficult issues to resolve: Tutsi representatives at the talks complained of continued daily discrimination against their community, including exclusion from public office;[407] while 'indigenous' groups made clear that they regarded them all as immigrants, without a real claim on the land, and possibly working on behalf of the Rwandan government. Later the same year, CNDP forces with Rwandan backing once again went on the offensive, killing thousands, displacing hundreds of thousands, and threatening to overwhelm the UN forces protecting Goma.

At the end of 2008, the political landscape changed dramatically in eastern Congo with a new and unexpected alliance between the governments in Kinshasa and Kigali; which, however, brought a further deterioration of the situation in the Kivus, with increased killings and displacement. President Kabila struck a deal with Rwandan President Paul Kagame, allowing Rwandan soldiers to enter eastern Congo for several weeks of joint military operations with the Congolese army against the FDLR.[408] On 23 March 2009, the CNDP signed an agreement with the Kinshasa government providing for the integration of its supporters into national political and security structures. A CNDP-dominated administration in North Kivu established military control over lucrative mining zones, as well as the key farming and cattle areas of Rutshuru and Masisi.[409]

[404] Verweijen and Vlassenroot (n 341).

[405] 'DR Congo: Refugees urge resumption of repatriation to Moba; UNHCR waits', UNHCR, 8 Oct 2007.

[406] Human Rights Watch, 'Renewed Crisis in North Kivu' (2007).

[407] « Déclaration de la communauté banyamulenge à la conférence sur la paix, la sécurité et le développement au Nord et au Sud Kivu », January 2008.

[408] Negotiations between Rwandan and Congolese officials began from October 2008, and led to the preparation of a joint military plan to disarm the FDLR endorsed by the foreign ministers of both countries at a public ceremony in Goma on 5 December, though the text and details of the plan remained confidential. Negotiations for the implementation of the plan continued over the following weeks. At the same time, Rwanda arrested Laurent Nkunda, the leader of the CNDP, who was indicted for crimes in Congo and had previously enjoyed Rwandan support. See International Crisis Group, 'Five Priorities for a Peacebuilding Strategy' (2009).

[409] Jason Stearns, *North Kivu: The Background to Conflict in North Kivu Province of Eastern Congo* (Rift Valley Institute 2012); Jason Stearns, *From CNDP to M23: The Evolution of an Armed Movement in Eastern Congo* (Rift Valley Institute 2012); International Crisis Group, 'A Comprehensive Strategy to Disarm the FDLR' (2009).

In the renewed fighting, the constant remained, the cross-border themes of citizenship and belonging. The 23 March agreement had placed an emphasis on the return of refugees and displaced persons, but this process had been – inevitably – highly controversial, and there was a total failure to agree any operationalisable procedure to decide who was or was not a Congolese national. In early 2010, a tripartite agreement was signed between UNHCR and the governments of DRC and Rwanda for the repatriation of tens of thousands of Congolese refugees who fled to Rwanda during the 1990s: at that time, UNHCR reported that there were 55,000 Congolese refugees living in Rwanda and 69,800 Rwandan refugees in the Kivus. Local committees were supposed to be established to regulate the process, but 'spontaneous' returns soon caused disruption. In early 2011, the governor and provincial assembly of North Kivu raised the alarm over the identification of Banyarwanda 'returning' in an unplanned manner to Lubero and Rutshuru; in July the CNDP imposed the resettlement of 2,400 families from Rwanda in Masisi. UNHCR, meanwhile, had not repatriated a single Congolese refugee from Rwanda to the DRC, because of ongoing insecurity but above all 'the impossibility of identifying with any degree of certainty the individuals whom the Rwandan authorities present as refugees.'[410]

In November 2011, presidential and legislative elections were held as scheduled. Hate speech was rife once again, despite the commitments of all major political parties to a code of conduct forbidding incitement to violence.[411] There were also many allegations that the CNDP was forcing people in Kivu to vote for Kabila and its own candidates, as well as registering Rwandans.[412] Voter registration remained the effective system for determining nationality, important to allow the holder to travel in the region; indeed, the voter registration cards were explicitly stated to function as temporary national identity cards.[413] International observers reported widespread irregularities, though Kabila's dubious victory in the presidential elections was confirmed by the Supreme Court. The elections in Masisi, North Kivu, were among several constituencies annulled by the election commission on grounds of fraud, but the elections were not re-held in those locations.[414]

The flawed elections did nothing to cement peace. Under international pressure, in April 2012, the Congolese authorities finally ordered the arrest of CNDP leader Bosco Ntaganda, indicted by the ICC in 2006. Ntaganda promptly mutinied from the army to create the M23 rebel movement – referring to the peace

[410] International Crisis Group, 'Eastern Congo: Why Stabilisation Failed' (2012).

[411] 'DR Congo: Candidates Should Not Incite Violence', Human Rights Watch, 28 October 2011.

[412] 'Letter Dated 12 October 2012 from the Group of Experts on the Democratic Republic of the Congo Addressed to the Chair of the Security Council Committee Established Pursuant to Resolution 1533 (2004) Concerning the Democratic Republic of the Congo', UN Doc. S/2012/843; Carter Center, 'Presidential and Legislative Elections in the Democratic Republic of the Congo November 28, 2011' (2012).

[413] International Crisis Group, 'DRC: The Electoral Process Seen from the East' (2011).

[414] Carter Center (n 412); International Crisis Group, 'Eastern Congo: Why Stabilisation Failed' (n 410).

agreement between the government and the CNDP of 23 March 2009 – and joined with other suspected war criminals to create the new force. The UN's revelation of Rwandan support for M23 heightened tensions between Rwanda and DRC,[415] while also bringing the first serious Western condemnation of the Rwandan role in the Congolese war and the suspension of some aid, including by the UK.[416] Threats and attacks on Banyarwanda communities escalated.[417] At the end of 2012, Goma, capital of North Kivu, fell to the M23 rebels.

The latest crisis provoked a renewed international effort to try to resolve the regional conflict: on 24 February 2013, meeting in Addis Ababa under UN auspices, the governments of Congo, Rwanda, Uganda and other signatories of the Great Lakes pact, and the Southern Africa Development Community (SADC), signed a framework agreement for peace, security and cooperation.[418] By the end of the year, M23 had suffered a comprehensive military defeat by the Congolese army, as Rwanda finally withdrew its support. M23 'renounced its rebellion' and committed itself to pursue its objectives through the 'Kampala dialogue' facilitated by the International Conference on the Great Lakes Region (ICGLR), established in 2004. It was promised that M23 members would be included in national structures responsible for refugee issues[419] – but no proposal for identification and verification of nationality was yet on the table. Banyarwanda Congolese refugees who had fled to Rwanda remained trapped in limbo between the two countries.[420] A 2017 declaration and plan of action adopted by the ICGLR for the eradication of statelessness in the region recognised the centrality of the problem, but also lacked detailed implementation provisions.[421]

The fateful lack of agreement on the terms of incorporation of the transplanted Rwandans and Burundians in Congo on the departure of the Belgians cast a long shadow. Of course, the size, diversity and weakness of the Congolese State, the outflows of refugees and military interventions from its eastern neighbours, and the ongoing competition for land and resources previously subject to expropriation by the colonisers, meant that establishing a stable polity was never going to be easy. But the particular form of the conflict in eastern Congo has been intimately tied to the failure to establish a legal and procedural framework that is both seen as

[415] 'Letter Dated 26 June 2012, from the Chair of the Security Council Committee Established Pursuant to Resolution 1533 (2004) Concerning the Democratic Republic of Congo Addressed to the President of the Security Council', UN Doc. S/2012/348/Add.1 (United Nations 2012).

[416] 'UK stops £21m aid payment to Rwanda', BBC News, 30 November 2012.

[417] International Crisis Group, 'Eastern Congo: Why Stabilisation Failed' (n 410).

[418] David Zounmenou and Naomi Kok, 'Peace, Security and Cooperation Framework for the DRC: Hopes and Challenges'. David Zounmenou and Naomi Kok, 'Peace, Security and Cooperation Framework for the DRC: Hopes and Challenges', Institute for Security Studies (South Africa), 8 March 2013 available at https://issafrica.org/iss-today/peace-security-and-cooperation-framework-for-the-drc-hopes-and-challenges.

[419] Declaration of Commitments by the Movement of March 23 at the Conclusion of the Kampala Dialogue, 12 December 2013.

[420] Manby, 'Citizenship and Statelessness in the East African Community' (n 158).

[421] Declaration and Plan of Action of the International Conference on the Great Lakes Region (ICGLR) on the Eradication of Statelessness, October 2017.

legitimate and implemented in such a way that it can make non-arbitrary distinctions between citizens and strangers. The politics of ethnicity that led to conflict depended not only on concepts of primordial belonging drawn from deep in the social imaginary, or the deliberate aggravation of such conflict by neighbouring powers, or a war over natural resources, or local competition for land, but also from laws and institutions recognising legal membership of the community at both national and sub-national levels of the Congolese State. The foundation of the law in ethnicity, shaped itself by politics, has created ethnic identity as a legal category, with profound reciprocal influence on the political realm.

7.6. Mauritania's Efforts to Enforce a 'Nation-State'

The crisis of nationality in Mauritania is different in character from the previous case studies in this chapter. In Zimbabwe, Sierra Leone, Kenya, Uganda, Côte d'Ivoire or DRC those most obviously affected by post-independence difficulties in relation to citizenship were the large groups of pre-independence migrants, whether forced or voluntary. In Mauritania, by contrast, the basic demography is more similar to European countries with 'national minorities': a colonially-imposed border followed the Senegal river, dividing communities that had previously been unified by its resources. Migration across the river has been a constant, including by transhumant pastoralists circulating among the territories of what are now Senegal, Mali and Mauritania, but there was no historical mass transplantation of labour as in Côte d'Ivoire or DRC. Manipulation of nationality law has rather been one tool used to reinforce the dominance of the Arabic-speaking 70% of the population over minorities speaking other languages.

The territory that today forms Mauritania, to the south of both the French and Spanish protectorates in what are now Morocco and Western Sahara, and previously a dependency of the Moroccan Kingdom, was gradually conquered by the French during the European expansion into sub-Saharan Africa in the nineteenth century, and eventually formed part of *Afrique occidentale française*.

The country is inhabited by three principal groups: people speaking Hassaniya Arabic and of mixed Berber-Arab ancestry (collectively known as Beydanes or White Moors[422]); those of dark skin colour who also speak Arabic (a group known as Haratines, descended from former slaves to the Berber-Arabs, many still in servile roles); and dark-skinned people speaking a range of other languages who belong to sub-Saharan African ethnic groups who mostly live in the south of the country, along the Senegal river valley (especially the pastoralist Fulani/Peul, but also Wolof, Soninké and Bambara, both herders and cultivators). During the colonial era, blacks who led a more settled life were able to take greater advantage of

[422] Beydane means 'white' in Hassaniya Arabic; Moor derives from the Roman name for the people of the western North African region.

educational opportunities and came to dominate the lower levels of the administrative structure; although, by contrast with other AOF countries, the French also relied on the traditional emirs of the Beydanes to manage the territory, in a system more similar to the British 'indirect rule'.[423] Since independence, political and economic power has been in the hands of the Beydanes, and governments that have committed some of the most egregious manipulation of access to nationality in the continent.

In 1958, Mauritania gained semi-autonomy, along with other AOF territories, as part of the short-lived *Communauté française*, and, like the other AOF countries, gained its full independence in 1960. Mauritania adopted a nationality law the year following independence, which entered into force on 13 June 1961 (as in many former French territories, there was a gap between independence and the first nationality law that created room for ambiguity on who became a national of the new State). The transitional provisions of the law allowed any person habitually resident in Mauritania who did not fulfil the general criteria to opt for Mauritanian nationality, but did not attribute nationality automatically based on residence. Generally, the law provided for nationality to be attributed by paternal descent (with rights to the mother's nationality if the father was stateless or of unknown nationality) and on the basis of double *jus soli*. All facts relating to place of birth and parentage had to be established on the basis of the civil register; but the conditions for double *jus soli* were presumed fulfilled on the basis of *possession d'état*, of long-standing treatment as a national – though the criteria were not defined, facilitating later discrimination.[424]

The first President, Moctar Ould Daddah, quickly established a one-party authoritarian government and was re-elected, unopposed, in 1966, 1971, and 1976. From the mid-1970s, the government inaugurated a policy of Arabisation: Arabic replaced French as the official language and other measures were taken to identify the State as Arab.[425] This policy was continued by President Maaouya Ould Sid'Ahmed Taya who seized power in 1984 (and was himself displaced by a coup in 2005). In 2000, Mauritania left ECOWAS and aligned itself more closely with the North African Arab Maghreb Union. Mauritanians whose mother tongue was not Arabic protested at these measures and political tensions rose. Economic tensions also increased over control of the fertile land of the Senegal river valley. A 1983 reformulation of the land law that had included the apparently innocuous statement that 'the land belongs to the whole nation and any Mauritanian can

[423] Francis de Chassey, *Mauritanie 1900–1975: Acteurs économiques, politiques, idéologiques et éducatifs dans la formation d'une société sous-développée* (Editions Harmattan 1978); Christopher Harrison, *France and Islam in West Africa, 1860–1960* (Cambridge University Press 2003); Christian Santoir, 'Le conflit mauritano-sénégalais : la genèse : le cas des Peul de la haute vallée du Sénégal' (1990) 26 Cahiers des Sciences Humaines 553.

[424] Loi No.61-112 du 12 juin 1961 portant Code de la nationalité mauritanienne ; see also Zatzepine (n 238) 22–23.

[425] Ambroise Queffélec and Bah Ould Zein, 'La 'Longue Marche' de l'arabisation en Mauritanie' (2001) 15 Le français en Afrique.

become an owner without discrimination in conformity with the law', opened up the redistribution of land in the valley.[426] Pressure on land was also increased by immigration from Senegal, across the river border.

In 1989–1990 the Mauritanian government expelled tens of thousands of people, claiming that they were of foreign nationality illegally present in the country. The expulsions followed a dispute over grazing rights in the Senegal river valley, which erupted into communal violence in the capitals of Dakar and Nouakchott. Under international pressure to prevent further bloodshed, Mauritania and Senegal each agreed to repatriate the other's citizens. The Mauritanian government seized the repatriation process as an opportunity to purge many black Mauritanian citizens from the administration and territory: ultimately 60–65,000 were expelled to Senegal and 10–15,000 to Mali, while a few others fled to Chad.[427]

Most of those expelled were pastoralists and peasant farmers, but the policy also targeted soldiers, civil servants and senior executives. Many expellees were black Mauritanian government employees suspected of opposing the Arabisation policy. These events began a 'campaign of terror' in which the Mauritanian army occupied its side of the Senegal river valley: several hundred villages were entirely emptied of their largely Fulani inhabitants before being renamed and taken over by Moors (as landowners) and Haratines (as labourers) – some of them from among those expelled from Senegal during the 'repatriation' process. Others who were not themselves physically expelled fled the country to escape massacres and political persecution which continued throughout 1989 and over the next two years. In late 1990 and early 1991 several hundred political detainees were tortured and killed.[428]

Among those expelled, there were no doubt some who held Senegalese or Malian nationality documents and others whose fathers had been nationals of those countries (and thus were entitled themselves to that nationality); the role of Senegal as the capital of French West Africa, as well as the nature of the pastoralist lifestyle, meant that many Mauritanians had links in Senegal. However, the great majority had previously been recognised as Mauritanians and had no entitlement to another nationality, even if they had family ties across the river. Mauritanian identity documents were systematically confiscated and destroyed in the course of the expulsions.

From 1994, after a détente with Senegal, the Mauritanian government invited the deportees to return, and approximately 30,000 refugees did go back between 1994 and 1997. Some later left again for exile because they could not get back their

[426] Ordonnance No.83-127 du 5 juin 1983 portant réorganisation foncière et domaniale, Art.1 : 'La terre appartient à la nation, et tout Mauritanien, sans discrimination d'aucune sorte, peut, en se conformant à la loi, en devenir propriétaire, pour partie.'

[427] Human Rights Watch, 'Mauritania's Campaign of Terror: State-Sponsored Repression of Black Africans' (1994); David Stone, 'Enhancing Livelihood Security among Mauritanian Refugees in Northern Senegal: A Case Study' (UNHCR 2005).

[428] Human Rights Watch, 'Mauritania's Campaign of Terror' (n 427). See also Human Rights Watch, *World Report 1989* and *1990*.

lost properties, regain their jobs, or obtain national identity cards to replace those destroyed during the deportation in 1989.[429] By the mid-1990s, when it ceased providing material assistance to the refugees in Senegal, UNHCR stated there were 25,000 people who had not repatriated from Senegal and Mali, though other estimates were 45,000 to 60,000.[430]

In 2000, the African Commission on Human and Peoples' Rights found that the expellees had been arbitrarily deprived of their nationality, were entitled to return to Mauritania, and should have their identity documents and property restored, and that they and other victims should also receive compensation for the harm done.[431] Although this decision was not immediately implemented, donor pressure for the government to fulfil its international obligations was heightened. Prospects for the repatriation and restoration of citizenship to the deportees improved following a coup d'état in 2005, initiating a period of democratic opening that resulted in the election of a new government in April 2007. Freshly elected President Sidi Mohamed Ould Cheikh Abdallahi announced that the government intended to repatriate, restore to citizenship, and compensate the refugees.[432] A tripartite agreement between Senegal, Mauritania, and UNHCR was signed in October 2007.[433] Mauritania undertook to restore the citizenship rights of the refugees, return their properties, and reinstate former civil servants. The programme started in January 2008, by the end of July, more than 4,500 people had returned, and the entire process of repatriation was expected to take 18 months.[434] But on 6 August the government was overthrown in a fresh military coup, throwing the repatriation process into doubt.[435]

After a resumption, the process was suspended again from December 2010 for one year, when the Mauritanian government decided that the issue of all national identity documents would be put on hold as the national population register was replaced with a new biometric version; a move portrayed as a benign effort to increase State capacity.[436] On 6 September 2010, Mauritania signed a contract with

[429] Marion Fresia, 'De l'exil au retour : le rapatriement des Mauritaniens réfugiés au Sénégal en perspective' (2008) 3 (Migrations et Sénégal) REVUE Asylon(s) www.reseau-terra.eu/article710.html.

[430] 'Global Review of Statelessness: Africa', in Maureen Lynch, 'Lives on Hold: The Human Cost of Statelessness' (Refugees International 2005) 29. Human Rights Committee, 'Concluding observations of the Human Rights Committee: Mali', CCPR/CO/77/MLI, 16 April 2003.

[431] African Commission on Human and Peoples' Rights, Communications 54/91, 61/91, 98/93, 164-196/97 and 210/98, *Malawi African Association and others v Mauritania* (2000).

[432] 'Refugees cautiously optimistic about new initiative', IRIN, 10 July 2007; Kissy Agyeman, 'Exiled Mauritanians Begin Tentative Retreat Back to Homeland after 18 Years', Global Insight Daily Analysis, 11 July 2007.

[433] Tripartite Accord: UNHCR and the governments of Senegal and Mauritania, November 2007; 'Tripartite agreement on return of Mauritanian refugees', UNHCR Briefing Notes, 13 November 2007.

[434] 'Thousands of Mauritanians to Return Home From Senegal With Help of UN Agency', UN News Service, 13 November 2007; 'Is Mauritania ready for its refugees?' IRIN, 16 November 2007.

[435] *Briefing paper on the return of expelled Mauritanians to the Islamic Republic of Mauritania following the August 6, 2008 coup*, Institute for Human Rights and Development in Africa, October 2008.

[436] 'Mauritania: a single integrated system', at the website of MORPHO, no date (approx. July 2010).

the France-based biometric identity company Morpho, for the wholesale redesign and reissue of national identity cards, passports and other documents.[437]

In advance of the new identification process, the government introduced legal reforms to make it more difficult for undocumented persons to gain recognition of their nationality. The 2010 amendments reduced gender discrimination in nationality by descent (though not completely removing it), but at the same time removed all rights based on birth in Mauritania (including both double *jus soli* and the right to opt based on birth and residence till majority). The only exception to the now purely descent-based regime was the existing protection for foundlings. At the same time, the language-requirement for a person to naturalise was redefined to remove from the list both French and Bambara (spoken among the groups living in the east, towards Mali). The law also amended the standard provision that facts relating to birth and parentage must be established by an entry in the civil registry to remove the possibility of late registration by court judgment, and the presumption that the conditions for double *jus soli* were presumed to have been fulfilled if a person was in *possession d'état de mauritanien*.[438] These changes would undoubtedly make it more difficult for returnees to establish their Mauritanian nationality; but also generally for those without documented Mauritanian ancestry back to independence – that is, primarily those in poor and rural communities, including the Haratines as well as the returning refugees and other non-arabophones.

Discrimination during the census process and in the issue of new identity cards led to the creation of a protest movement, *Touche pas à ma nationalité*, which called for the adoption of a 'neutral and representative census system to create a reliable civil status registry in a coordinated legal framework'.[439] The movement accused the authorities of 'biometric genocide' in the roll-out of the new documents.[440] Demonstrations against the delays in restoring papers to those who had already been repatriated led to violent clashes with police in Nouakchott in late 2011.[441]

[437] 'Morpho participe au renouvellement du système d'état civil mauritanien', Morpho, 6 September 2010.

[438] Loi. No. 2010-023 du 11 février 2010 abrogeant et remplaçant certaines dispositions de la loi 61-112 du 12 juin 1961 portant Code de la nationalité mauritanienne, especially deletion of art 9 and amendments to arts 13, 19 and 58.

[439] 'L'adoption d'un système de recensement neutre et représentatif pour un état-civil fiable dans un cadre juridique concerté. Memorandum sur le recensement en cours : Recensement a vocation d'etat-civil ou volonté dépuration ethnique?' Touche pas à ma nationalité, 16 October 2011.

[440] '"Génocide biométrique des Negro-mauritaniens": Une saisine de TPMN devant les instances juridiques internationales', *L'Authentique* (Mauritania), 3 July 2014; see also Office français de protection des réfugiés et apatrides (OFPRA), 'Mauritanie : Informations sur le mouvement "Touche pas à ma nationalité" qui s'oppose au recensement tel qu'il est conduit actuellement', 23 April 2014.

[441] 'Répression violente du mouvement "Touche pas à ma nationalité"', FIDH and AMDH, 28 September 2011; Sebastian Kohn, 'Fear and Statelessness in Mauritania', Open Society Justice Initiative, 3 October 2011; 'Black Mauritanians in 'Racist' Census Protest', AFP, 24 September 2011; 'Police Arrest 56 in Mauritania Over Census Protests', AFP, 30 September 2011; 'Police Disperse Mauritanian Blacks in 'Racist' Protest', AFP, 28 November 2011.

Eventually repatriation from Senegal was resumed, and more than 24,000 refugees had returned under the voluntary repatriation agreement by March 2012, when the programme was declared completed.[442] However, many still faced difficulties in re-establishing their Mauritanian nationality, as the Mauritanian government insisted on evaluating eligibility on a case by case basis. Although the government stated that 90% of the 24,000 who returned under the voluntary repatriation agreement had received identity documentation, refugee representatives in Senegal asserted that only 8,000 had recovered Mauritanian documents as of mid-2014 (leaving some with the paper approving their voluntary repatriation as their only identity document); and even fewer had recovered land and other property.[443] Several hundred of the repatriated Mauritanians staged a march from the Senegal Valley to Nouakchott in May 2014 to protest their situation.[444]

At that date, Senegal still hosted some 13,700 Mauritanian refugees, and Mali more than 12,000, of whom some 8,000 had expressed the wish to return home.[445] Those who opted to stay in Senegal still retained refugee status, since the ceased circumstances clause had not been invoked. The refugees were eligible for naturalisation under Senegalese law, and the Senegalese authorities repeatedly confirmed that naturalisation was available; however, representatives of the Mauritanian community in Senegal stated that they did not wish for naturalisation, but either resettlement in a third country or repatriation to Mauritania with full restoration of nationality, property and other rights. In the long run, it seemed likely that, while those who themselves fled the persecution in Mauritania would continue to reject the options available, the descendants of the refugees who had stayed in Senegal would blend into the Senegalese population: by contrast to refugees in East Africa, under the double *jus soli* rule, the grandchildren of those who fled would be automatically attributed nationality under the law.[446]

The nationality status of those who returned to Mauritania was more precarious. A process to re-issue national identity cards portrayed as purely technical and an important step to strengthen civil administration (for which it was likely supported by development assistance from France, Mauritania's largest donor), had been instrumentalised to achieve more exclusionary aims. Yet the authorities had carefully followed the forms of the law, meaning that the discrimination

[442] UNHCR, 'Stratégie d'intégration locale et moyens de subsistance des refugies Mauritaniens au Sénégal', 2011; 'UNHCR completes repatriation of more than 24,000 Mauritanians', UNHCR, 27 March 2012.

[443] Interviews, Dakar, May 2014; Information from UNHCR Nouakchott, August 2014.

[444] 'Répression à Nouakchott d'une marche des rapatriés mauritaniens du Sénégal', APA 5 May 2014; 'Société : Régler les problèmes des ex-réfugiés mauritaniens au Sénégal', PANA 12 May 2014; 'Le gouvernement mauritanien s'engage à régler les problèmes des réfugiés rapatriés', PANA, 21 May 2014.

[445] UNHCR, '2014 regional operations profile: West Africa' and '2014 country operations profiles', Mauritania and Mali.

[446] Interviews with Senegalese officials, representatives of the Mauritanian refugee community, and human rights activists, Dakar, May 2014.

involved in screening out those who were unable to claim the new cards could be portrayed as a process to ensure the integrity of the identification system.

7.7. 'Indigeneity' in Nigeria: The Links Between Local and National

On the surface, the challenges that have surrounded the management of nationality in Nigeria are unique. Nigeria is a huge and highly diverse country; it was not, however, subjected to the same forms of land expropriation and import of labour as Congo, Côte d'Ivoire, Kenya, or Zimbabwe. While there were small populations of non-African origin living in Nigeria at independence, they were not sufficiently economically dominant to cause major disquiet.

Nonetheless, the challenge of managing diversity is common across these cases. Many of the same ambiguities existed as in other countries over who became Nigerian at independence, and who was therefore later entitled to citizenship. Nigeria, like Uganda, ultimately adopted an ethnically-based foundation for citizenship in an effort to accommodate these complexities. However, in place of the highly legalistic and procedural approach both to identification and to official manipulation of the criteria for recognition of nationality that was adopted in Côte d'Ivoire, for example, Nigeria's citizenship management was delegated in large part to the local level, and ungoverned by statute. The defects of this system, and the similarities with other countries, are likely to become more apparent with the introduction of a national identity card, and the prospective that the exercise of many other rights will depend on holding a card confirming national citizenship, and not just a local identity.

Nigeria's four constitutions since independence in 1960[447] have all grappled with the problem of creating an appropriate framework to manage the tensions between the different parts of the country, and among the three largest ethnic groups and the several hundred others. They have not yet established a clear legal and procedural framework to determine questions of citizenship and rights at different levels of the federation. Lacking such legal scaffolding Nigeria's identification system has evolved organically to depend on authentication by a local government authority rather than a federal agency. Although this system is without specific legal authority, it reflects a requirement for membership of an 'indigenous community' as the foundation of citizenship that was established in the national constitution in 1979, and also harks back to colonial categories.

The territory of what is now Nigeria is made up of what were initially three separate units under British control: the Colony of Lagos in the south west; the Protectorate of Southern Nigeria (the rest of the southern half of the country);

[447] These were adopted in 1960, 1963, 1979 and 1999. A 1989 constitution never came into force.

and the Protectorate of Northern Nigeria.[448] From 1914, when the Protectorate of Northern Nigeria was joined to the south for administrative purposes, the entire territory was known as the Colony and Protectorate of Nigeria. The protectorates were shortly divided for administrative purposes into three regions: Northern, Western and Eastern, each dominated by one major ethnic group, the Hausa-Fulani,[449] Yoruba and Igbo, respectively.

The Colony of Lagos was ceded to the British crown in 1861, thus becoming part of the 'crown's dominions', and the inhabitants British subjects. Those born in the colony after that date also became British subjects, with the same status as those born in Britain for the purposes of their rights in Britain or to British protection abroad. Inhabitants of the protectorates had the lesser status of British protected persons, but from 1914 could naturalise locally as British subjects within the Colony of Lagos under certain conditions. From 1948, British subjects in the Colony of Lagos became citizens of the UK and colonies, in line with the 1948 British Nationality Act; those born in a protectorate continued to hold the now statutorily established status of British protected persons (see Chapter 3.1).

As in other British territories, rights in colonial Nigeria depended on distinctions between 'natives' and 'non-natives', as well as the distinction between British protected persons and citizens of the UK and colonies. The authoritative law on these categories was the 1939 Interpretation Act, which created two categories of 'native'. A 'native of Nigeria' was 'any person whose parents were members of any tribe or tribes indigenous to Nigeria and the descendants of such persons, and includes persons one of whose parents was a member of such tribe.' A 'native foreigner' was a 'person (not being a native of Nigeria), whose parents are members of a tribe or tribes indigenous to some parts of Africa and the descendants of such person, and shall include any person any of whose parents is a member of such tribe'. A 'non-native' was someone who was neither a native of Nigeria nor a native foreigner.[450] Rights under other laws depended on membership of one of these groups. The definitions were based on ethnic identity and did not allow for assimilation of others into the idea of 'native' of a particular place, nor did they create any definition of the length of time needed before a tribe could be considered as 'indigenous'.

The different categories of 'native' meant that there was potentially much legal confusion about who became Nigerian in 1960, as they blurred the distinctions between British nationals (whether citizens of the UK and colonies or British protected persons) and aliens in the pre-independence era. A native foreigner

[448] Added to these were (part of) the western section of the German colony of Kamerun, mandated to Britain by the League of Nations in 1922.

[449] A complex ethnonym, used only in Nigeria: Technically two ethnic groups, the Hausa being the sedentary population conquered during the 19th century by Fulani pastoralists who went on to establish the emirates in the north of what is now Nigeria – and to speak Hausa rather than Fulfulde (see also ch 6, fn 42).

[450] Interpretation Ordinance No.27 of 1939.

could be a citizen of the UK and colonies (a child of Ghanaian parents born in Lagos); whereas a native of Nigeria could be an alien (a child born in Dahomey (Benin) of a Yoruba mother who was a British protected person and a Yoruba father who was a French subject). At national level, therefore, those who became Nigerian by operation of law on 1 October 1960 were not necessarily 'natives of Nigeria'; and not all 'natives of Nigeria' qualified as citizens.[451] Under a legal regime where dual nationality was not allowed at independence, neither by Nigeria nor its neighbours, and most people had no documentation of nationality, the status of many thousands of people was potentially in question.

The transitional provisions in the independence constitution for the assignment of nationality followed the standard template for Commonwealth countries, providing for the attribution of citizenship by operation of law to those born in the territory before independence who were British protected persons or citizens of the UK and colonies, provided that one parent or grandparent was also born there; and for those born outside the territory before independence to acquire citizenship if their father qualified under these rules. Those born after the entry into force of the new constitution obtained Nigerian nationality on a *jus soli* basis (based purely on birth on the territory, with standard exceptions for children of fathers who were diplomats, if the mother was not a citizen). In principle, this rule should have erased the confusion about who became Nigerian in 1960 within a generation. Those born outside the country acquired citizenship on the basis of their father's citizenship.

As in the other Commonwealth States, those who were born in Nigeria before independence but did not have a parent or grandparent also born there could register as citizens during a transitional period (a non-discretionary grant, on application, if the facts were proved), as could some other categories with connections to Nigeria or another Commonwealth countries. Those who did not qualify under any of these provisions could naturalise at any time after independence, a discretionary process, based on long residence and fulfilment of other conditions. The Nigerian Citizenship Act 1960 and the Nigerian Citizenship Act 1961 provided greater detail on procedures for registering or naturalising as a citizen and for loss of citizenship.[452]

The 1963 constitution made no significant changes to the provisions on citizenship,[453] but in 1974 an amendment decree adopted by the military government replaced chapter II of the constitution and repealed the Citizenship Acts of 1960 and 1961. The new provisions effectively applied the rules that attributed citizenship automatically at independence to those born afterwards. Instead of an absolute *jus soli* regime, a person born in Nigeria after independence would automatically be a citizen from birth only if one parent or grandparent was also born

[451] Arthur VJ Nylander, *The Nationality and Citizenship Laws of Nigeria* (University of Lagos 1973) 2–4.

[452] See generally, Nylander (n 451); Fransman, Berry and Harvey (n 152) catalogue entry on Nigeria; KC Okoli, 'Nigerian Citizenship Law: A Current Perspective' (1990) 34 Journal of African Law 27.

[453] The 1960 independence constitution chapter on citizenship was reproduced with minor amendments in the 1963 republican constitution, and was unaffected by the suspension of certain provisions following the 1966 military coup.

there.[454] Those born in the country with one parent who was a citizen by registration or naturalisation were also citizens; those born outside only if *both* parents were citizens of any category.[455] There was no statement preserving the rights of those who were already citizens, and the implication was that the amendments applied retroactively.

The 1979 Constitution adopted by the military government led by General Olusegun Obasanjo to govern a transition to civilian rule then fundamentally altered this scheme. The new regime both introduced an ethnic dimension to citizenship, and moved away from rights based on birth in the territory (over two or three generations) towards a descent-based rule, dating from the situation in 1960. Chapter III of the 1979 Constitution established the basic rule that a person became a citizen at independence if he or she was born in the country and either parent or any grandparent 'belongs or belonged to a community indigenous to Nigeria'; at the same time it retained the rule that citizenship was only acquired on this basis if one parent or grandparent was also born in Nigeria. For those born in Nigeria after independence, citizenship was now granted based on descent from a parent or grandparent who was a citizen; those born outside acquired citizenship automatically if one parent was a citizen.

The new wording echoed back to the colonial definition of 'native', and was grappling with the same problem: the reality that pre-existing polities overlapped Nigeria's borders. In the colonial world, the more important distinction was between British and French (or other European) nationals; the 1979 constitution was in many ways an effort rather to provide potential recognition as Nigerian to those whose status was otherwise unclear, but who were born and had ancestry and ethnic kin in Nigeria.

Section 268 also provided that anyone who had acquired citizenship 'by birth, naturalisation or registration' under previous constitutions remained a citizen. That is, those born in Nigeria between 1960 and 1979 who had acquired citizenship based on the rules established in 1974 (with retroactive effect) remained citizens, and therefore also their children. It was not clear how this provision on continuity of citizenship meshed (if at all) with that adding the requirement for membership of an indigenous community in relation to those who became citizens at independence.

These provisions were repeated largely unaltered in the 1999 constitution that is still in force, again adopted by a military regime to apply after elections established a new civilian government. Article 25(1) states that:

> The following persons are citizens of Nigeria by birth – namely:
>
> a) every person born in Nigeria before the date of independence, either of whose parents or any of whose grandparents belongs or belonged to a community

[454] There was an exclusion if any parent or grandparent had lost his citizenship by any means (ie including by acquiring another nationality), unless one parent was a citizen.

[455] Constitution (Amendment) Decree, No.33 of 1974. See EI Nwogugu, 'Recent Changes in Nigerian Nationality and Citizenship Law' (1976) 25 International and Comparative Law Quarterly 423.

indigenous to Nigeria; Provided that a person shall not become a citizen of Nigeria by virtue of this section if neither of his parents nor any of his grandparents was born in Nigeria.

b) every person born in Nigeria after the date of independence either of whose parents or any of whose grandparents is a citizen of Nigeria; and

c) every person born outside Nigeria either of whose parents is a citizen of Nigeria.

In addition, as in 1979, Article 309 of the 1999 Constitution States that those who were already citizens under earlier constitutions remain citizens of Nigeria. The legal history thus remains theoretically relevant in deciding if someone is a Nigerian citizen, especially in relation to Articles 25(1)(b) and (c). There is no definition of 'community indigenous to Nigeria', nor any list of ethnic or other groups who count as indigenous.

The 1999 constitution also makes provision for a woman married to a Nigerian man to acquire citizenship by registration (but not a foreign man married to a Nigerian woman); for naturalisation on the basis of 15 years' residence in the country (a very long period by African and international standards) and other conditions; and for deprivation of citizenship on various grounds. In practice, according to press reports, it seems that only around 100–150 people register or naturalise as Nigerian each year.[456] There are no statistics published on citizenship deprivation. The one significant change made in 1999 was that the prohibition on dual citizenship was removed for those who held Nigerian and another citizenship from birth; however, those wishing to naturalise as Nigerian were required to renounce any other naturalised citizenship.[457] Provisions relating to renunciation of citizenship were also added.

Unusually, instead of providing for additional rules on citizenship to be set out in legislation, both the 1979 and 1999 constitutions rather delegated authority to the president to make regulations. No regulations have ever been promulgated, leaving a lack of detail that allows for a high degree of executive discretion in implementing the constitutional framework. In particular, the absence of prescribed procedures, when combined with the absence of a definition of 'community indigenous to Nigeria', whether under the colonial regime or the 1979 and 1999 constitutions, means that there is great uncertainty about which groups would be included within that term.

At the same time as changing the citizenship regime, the 1979 constitution introduced the concept of 'federal character'. The 'Fundamental Objectives and Directive Principles of State Policy' set out in Chapter II of the constitution established the idea that, in order to promote national unity, government positions at national level should be shared equitably among those coming from the different units that make up Nigeria's federal system, and similarly at State and local government level.

[456] Bronwen Manby, 'Migration, Nationality and Statelessness in West Africa' (UNHCR and IOM 2015).

[457] Constitution of the Republic of Nigeria, 1979, art 23; Constitution of the Republic of Nigeria, 1999, art 25.

These requirements were repeated in the 1999 constitution.[458] The constitutional bill of rights excluded appointments to State office from otherwise comprehensive non-discrimination provisions.[459] The three original regions established in 1960 had by this time become 36 States; while the 301 local government areas created in 1976 as part of a comprehensive reform led by the military government became 774 (plus two sub-divisions of the Federal Capital Territory, Abuja).

The idea of federal character reinforced the concept of 'indigenous community' referred to in Chapter III on citizenship. For example, the president is required to 'appoint at least one minister from each State, who shall be an indigene of the State'.[460] The membership of the executive of any registered political party must also 'reflect the federal character of Nigeria', meaning that the members must 'belong to' at least two-thirds of the States in Nigeria;[461] the interpretation section then provides that 'belong to', 'when used with reference to a person in a State refers to a person either of whose parents or any of whose grandparents was a member of a community indigenous to that State'.[462]

In 1996, the military government led by General Sani Abacha, established a Federal Character Commission with the responsibility to elaborate, monitor and enforce these constitutional provisions.[463] Among the Commission's functions

[458] Constitution, 1979, art 14; repeated verbatim in the 1999 Constitution, 1999, art 14: '(3) The composition of the Government of the Federation or any of its agencies and the conduct of its affairs shall be carried out in such manner as to reflect the federal character of Nigeria and the need to promote national unity, and also to command national loyalty thereby ensuring that there shall be no predominance of persons from a few States or from a few ethnic or other sectional groups in that government or in any of its agencies. (4) The composition of the Government of a State, a local government council, or any of the agencies of such government or council, and the conduct of its affairs shall be carried out in such manner as to recognise the diversity of the peoples within its area of authority and the need to promote a sense of belonging and loyalty among all the peoples of the Federation.'

[459] '(1) A citizen of Nigeria of a particular community, ethnic group, place of origin, sex, religion or political opinion shall not, by reason only that he is such a person:- (a) be subjected either expressly by, or in the practical application of, any law in force in Nigeria or any executive or administrative action of the government, to disabilities or restrictions to which citizens of Nigeria of other communities, ethnic groups, places of origin, sex, religion or political opinions are not made subject; or (b) be accorded either expressly by, or in the practical application of, any law in force in Nigeria or any such executive or administrative action, any privilege or advantage that is not accorded to citizens of Nigeria of other communities, ethnic groups, places of origin, sex, religion or political opinions. (2) No citizen of Nigeria shall be subjected to any disability or deprivation merely by reason of the circumstances of his birth. (3) Nothing in subsection (1) of this section shall invalidate any law by reason only that the law imposes restrictions with respect to the appointment of any person to any office under the State or as a member of the armed forces of the Federation or member of the Nigeria Police Forces or to an office in the service of a body, corporate established directly by any law in force in Nigeria.' Constitution 1999, art 42.

[460] Constitution of the Federal Republic of Nigeria 1999, art 147(3).

[461] Constitution 1999, art 223(2)(b). The membership of the executive of any registered political party must 'belong to different States not being less in number than two-thirds of all the States of the Federation and the Federal Capital Territory, Abuja.'

[462] Constitution 1999, art 318(1). The only section in which the phrase 'belong to' is used is s 223 on political parties.

[463] The 1999 constitution included the Federal Character Commission (FCC) in its list of 'certain federal executive bodies' (Constitution 1999, art 153), but the decree has not been revised since the restoration of civilian rule.

were to work out 'an equitable formula' for distribution of posts and other benefits, as a system 'for redressing the problems of imbalances and reducing the fear of relative deprivation and marginalisation in the Nigerian system of federalism as it obtains in the public and private sectors'.[464]

The Commission adopted Guiding Principles and Formulae for the Distribution of all Cadres of Posts in 1997.[465] The principles included a definition of 'indigene' at each level of government, which effectively leaves it up to each local government to determine who qualifies, though it clearly prohibits claims of 'dual indigeneship':

> 10. (1) An indigene of a local Government means a person:
>
> i. either of whose parents or any of whose grandparents was or is an indigene of the local Government concerned; or
>
> ii. Who is accepted as an indigene by the Local Government:
>
> Provided that no person shall lay claim on more than one Local Government.

Mirroring rules provided for those who could claim to be an indigene of a State or the Federal Capital Territory.[466] The rules offered no permission for a person to change the local government where he or she is an 'indigene', although the discretion given to local governments created some space for flexibility. However, it was clearly stated that women could not change their status on marriage.[467]

The rules established by the 1979 and 1999 constitutions, combined with the interpretative principles adopted by the Federal Character Commission laid the foundation for a regime in which a 'certificate of indigeneity', issued by the chair of a person's local government area 'of origin', is required for many official and unofficial purposes. In the absence of any statutory authority, the criteria applied are variable across local government authorities; but in general there is no ability to 'naturalise' based on birth or residence.[468]

Being labelled as a 'non-indigene' has serious consequences that have been extensively discussed by activists and scholars.[469] No requirements related to

[464] Federal Character Commission Decree, No.34 of 1996, s 4(1)(a) and (d).

[465] Guiding Principles and Formulae for the Distribution of all Cadres of Posts, Pt III, s 3, SI 23 of 1997, available at www.federalcharacter.gov.ng/index.php/about-us/guiding-principles/principles.

[466] Guiding Principles and Formulae for the Distribution of all Cadres of Posts, Pt II, ss 10: '(2) An indigene of a State shall be a person who is an indigene of one Local Government in that State; Provided that no person shall claim to more than one State or to a State and the Federal Capital Territory. (3) An indigene of the Federal Capital Territory: (a) is a Nigerian citizen, other than by naturalization, who cannot lay claim to any State of the Federation; or (b) is a person born in the Federal Capital Territory and whose descendants lived in the area now constituting the Federal Capital Territory before 26 February, 1976 and has continued to reside in the Federal Capital Territory after that date.'

[467] 'A married woman shall continue to lay claim to her State of origin for the purpose of implementation of the Federal Character formulae at the national level.' Ibid. Section 11.

[468] Nigeria Research Network, 'Indigeneity, Belonging, & Religious Freedom in Nigeria: Citizens' Views from the Street' (University of Oxford/Development Research and Project Centre Kano 2014) Policy Brief 5; V Adefemi Isumonah, 'The Ethnic Language of Rights and the Nigerian Political Community' in Emma Hunter (ed), *Citizenship, belonging, and political community in Africa: Dialogues between past and present* (Ohio University Press 2016); David Ehrhardt, 'Indigeneship, Bureaucratic Discretion, and Institutional Change in Northern Nigeria' (2017) 116 African Affairs 462.

[469] For further discussion of the indigene-settler question in Nigeria and efforts to resolve it, see: Chidi Anselm Odinkalu, 'Natives, Subjects, and Wannabes: Internal Citizenship Problems in Post-Colonial

ethnicity or indigeneity are placed by the law on the general right to run for election or hold a public office in any State in the federation. Yet many States refuse to employ non-indigenes in their civil services; non-indigenes are charged higher fees at State universities and are usually not eligible for academic scholarships; non-indigenes may have difficulty in accessing any number of other government services, including police protection in case of ethnic violence. A non-indigene may vote, but will find it very hard to run for office in the area where he or she is resident. Despite the expressed intent to create a consociational system for the integration of minority groups, the consequences in practice have often been rather to exacerbate conflict between 'indigenes' and 'settlers', or to exclude some individuals from recognition as indigenes of any part of Nigeria.

Efforts to establish a national identification system have, by contrast, faltered. The first effort to establish a national identification system in Nigeria dates from the period immediately before the 1979 elections. A presidential decree of General Olusegun Obasanjo proposed the issue of identity cards to all Nigerians over 18.[470] This law was never implemented, though its use was proposed for the verification of voter identity in the 2003 elections, the first to be held by a civilian government (once again headed by Olusegun Obasanjo) after military rule was again ended in 1999.[471]

In 2007, the 1979 law was repealed and replaced by the National Identity Management Commission (NIMC) Act, though NIMC began issuing its first ID cards only in 2014. The identity cards issued are required to include a range of information, including a unique identification number and an indication of 'whether or not the person is a citizen of Nigeria', with reference to the constitutional provisions. The Act does not specify what information must be provided to the Commission for a card to be issued.[472] Section 15 of the NIMC Act states that one of the purposes of the database of registered persons will be to 'facilitate the provision of a convenient method for individuals who have been issued with the

Africa' in Rhoda E Howard-Hassmann and Margaret Walton-Roberts (eds), *The Human Right to Citizenship: A slippery concept* (University of Pennsylvania Press 2015); Uchenna Emelonye (ed), *Nigeria: Peace Building through Integration and Citizenship* (International Development Law Organization 2011); Daniel C Bach, 'Federalism, Indigeneity and Ethnicity in Nigeria' in Larry Jay Diamond, AHM Kirk-Greene and Oyeleye Oyediran (eds), *Transition without end: Nigerian politics and civil society under Babangida* (Lynne Rienner Publishers 1997); Ijeoma Nwachukwu, 'The Challenge of Local Citizenship for Human Rights in Nigeria' (2005) 13 African Journal of International and Comparative Law 235; Olufemi Taiwo, 'Of Citizens and Citizenship' in Okon Akiba (ed), *Constitutionalism and society in Africa* (Ashgate 2004); Laurent Fourchard, 'Bureaucrats and Indigenes: Producing and Bypassing Certificates of Origin in Nigeria' (2015) 85 Africa: The Journal of the International African Institute 37.

[470] National Civic Registration Decree No.51 of 1979, later amended and then integrated as an act in the consolidated laws of Nigeria 1990.

[471] A US$214m contract was issued to Sagem for production of a database, but the project was abandoned amidst allegations that non-Nigerians had allegedly been able to obtain the cards, reportedly leaving the database of more than 60m entries in the control of Sagem in France. 'Government Clears Misconceptions Over National Identity Card Scheme', *Daily Trust*, 18 March 2003; Leke Salaudeen, 'Database stalls National ID card issuance', *The Nation*, 4 December 2007.

[472] National Identity Management Commission (No. 23) Act 2007, ss 5, 14, 15, 18 and 19, also s 33 on interpretation.

Multi-purpose Identity Cards to provide proof of facts entered about themselves in the Database to other persons who reasonably require such proof.' From 2018, access to a range of government services was to depend on presentation of the card.

The new biometric identification system was asserted to be the solution to many problems, from economic empowerment to national security.[473] But roll-out was slow, and plagued by allegations of mismanagement and corruption, and delays in actually issuing the cards.[474] Fourteen million people were enrolled from 2012 to 2016, doubling to 28 million issued by the end of 2017 (compared to a voters' roll of just under 70 million for the 2015 elections), and the intention was that all Nigerians would carry one by 2019.[475] In the meantime, existing systems of identification – primarily the certificate of indigeneity – remained in use.

With the repeated creation of new States and local government areas, Nigerians were indigenes of ever smaller units of territory. At the same time, internal migration within Nigeria is the norm: a survey by the National Population Commission in 2010 found that from 10–45% of the population of every State was made up of migrants.[476] An indeterminate but presumably large number of Nigerians came to be in the situation where they could claim indigeneity in no State of the federation. Provisions originally intended in good faith to address the challenges of maintaining equitable distribution of benefits in a highly diverse society have become diverted from their original purpose. The ambiguity of what it meant to be an 'indigene' or to 'belong to' a political unit of the federal system was at the heart of these problems.

The question of indigeneity also has implications for Nigerian citizenship itself, creating a quite radical legal uncertainty over who is entitled. Since no law establishes another document to do so, and since indigeneity must be proved to obtain any number of official documents, the proof of the right to be Nigerian is effectively a certificate of indigeneity: among the documents for which a certificate of indigeneity is required are passports, the highest status proof of citizenship that exists, as well as the new national ID card.[477]

A range of Nigerian civil society organisations, including the Citizens' Forum for Constitutional Reform, lobbied for years for an end to the official and unofficial

[473] 'MasterCard-Branded National eID Card Launched in Nigeria', Mastercard press release, Abuja, Nigeria 28 August 2014; Colin Freeman, 'Put every Nigerian on biometric database to fight Boko Haram: Government minister says national register is only way to fight terror gangs', *The Telegraph*, 30 January 2015.

[474] Nicholas Ibekwe, 'Over N121 billion wasted, Nigeria's troubled National ID Card project in fresh controversy' *Premium Times*, 27 May 2015; Latifat Opoola, 'The Long, Long Wait for National Identity Cards, *Daily Trust* (Abuja), 11 March 2017.

[475] NIMC enrolment statistics available at www.nimc.gov.ng/enrolstats2012_2016/; 'Committee Proposes 3 Years To Issue 180m National ID Cards', *Leadership* (Abuja), 2 August 2017; 'NIMC enrols over 28m Nigerians and Legal Residents', National Identity Management Commission, 10 January 2018.

[476] Nigeria National Population Commission, 'Internal Migration Survey in Nigeria' (2010).

[477] Interview, Nigerian Immigration Service, Abuja, July 2014; Immigration Regulations 2017; NIMC website, www.nimc.gov.ng/how-to-enrol-adults/.

policies of discrimination based on indigeneity, including drafting specific constitutional amendments to ensure this result. In 2004, a group of Nigerian senators sponsored a Residency Rights Bill that would have prohibited discrimination against non-indigenes who had lived and paid taxes in their State of residence for at least five years (with an exception related only to 'traditional heritage'; such matters as chieftaincy titles).[478] The Bill was never adopted, and lapsed with the election of a new National Assembly in 2007.

In 2014, President Goodluck Jonathan established a 'National Conference' of 500 delegates drawn from different interest groups and different parts of the country, producing a 10,000-page report with recommendations on the structure of the federal system and the way in which power and resources are devolved. The sub-committee on 'citizenship, immigration and related matters' recommended the removal of gender discrimination in transmission of citizenship by marriage, noted the 'overwhelming need to liberalise the path to naturalised citizenship', and lamented the lack of definition of indigene and the discrimination related to internal migrants that resulted from the constitutional provisions.[479]

The costs of the emphasis on 'indigeneity' for ordinary citizens were dramatically highlighted by moves, in the context of the terrorist threat from Boko Haram, from governors of some south-eastern States, including Imo and Abia, to register all 'non-indigenes' resident in their States. Various northern lobby groups then threatened to expel southerners in return, and bills were submitted to several northern State assemblies for the registration of southerners. The National Council of State held an emergency meeting in July 2014 in response to these threats, which discussed the questions of discrimination around indigeneship more widely and acknowledged, under the long shadow of the Biafran war, that the threat of registration and deportation 'was capable of disrupting the unity of the country'.[480] In 2017, these questions were again at the top of the political agenda, with an escalation of herder-farmer violence, and as the ruling All Progressives Congress (APC) established a committee on restructuring headed by the Governor of Kaduna State, Nasiru el-Rufai, which held hearings around the country.

The Nigerian systems for identification based on 'indigeneity' are unusual, but not as unique as they might seem on first sight. The certificate of indigeneity is a version of practices that are common throughout the continent, where vetting committees made up of representatives of local institutions are often requested to certify that an individual belongs to a particular community. What is perhaps more remarkable is the extent to which the problems of such a system are by now widely acknowledged at the political level. If these debates result in a redefinition of

[478] Human Rights Watch, 'They Do Not Own This Place: Government Discrimination against Non-Indigenes in Nigeria' (2006) 63; for other suggestions, see Adimbola O Adesoji and Akin Alao, 'Indigeneship and Citizenship in Nigeria: Myth and Reality' (2009) 2 Journal of Pan African Studies 151.

[479] 'The National Conference: Final Draft Conference Report' (Government of Nigeria 2014), s 5.2.2.

[480] Mohammed Abubakar, 'Nigeria: Council of State Halts Registration of Non-Indigenes, Illegal Relocation', *The Guardian* (Abuja), 31 July 2014.

indigeneity based on place of birth and residence, as has been repeatedly proposed, they would effectively return Nigeria from a descent-based citizenship regime to one that recognises other connections. If such reforms were also recognised in a new citizenship act, it would also be the first effort to create a system for the recognition of citizenship that paid real attention to the nature of belonging at local level, linking the local to the national. In the meantime, Nigeria provides another example of the unintended consequences of legal reform, where the language of 'indigeneity', intended at least in some respects to be inclusive, has become steadily more divisive and the cause of significant discontent and unrest.

8

State Successions Since Independence

State succession, the transfer of sovereignty over a territory, creates well-recognised challenges in relation to determination of the legal membership of the successor States. Whether in the context of decolonisation in Africa, the break-up of federal territories, or the secession of a part of a State to form its own new country, the transfer of legal authority creates multiple opportunities for people caught between different rules to find themselves stateless.[1] It was recognition of the impact of the breakup of the Soviet Union and Federal Republic of Yugoslavia on the nationality of the populations of those territories that led to the development of the International Law Commission's Articles on Nationality of Natural Persons in Relation to the Succession of States, adopted in 1999 (see Chapter 1.2); but the same questions have arisen in similar circumstances around the world.

Africa's colonial history, like that of other zones of former empires, has made the rules governing State succession on transition to independence particularly sensitive. Many of the most notorious cases of individuals or groups deprived of nationality relate to the status of those who were recognised as colonial subjects but whose presence is resented today, to the inhabitants of regions whose borders were altered during the colonial period, or to the determination of where someone belongs whose parents came from another part of a common colonial territory and who migrated as part of colonial policy.

The case studies of Chapter 7 frequently revolved around the rules governing nationality at the succession of States: the content of these laws were central to the status of the 'Dioula' in Côte d'Ivoire or the Banyarwanda in eastern DRC; their implementation (or lack of it) to the position of Asians in East Africa or Lebanese in West Africa. There are many other issues at stake of course, most importantly questions of political power and economic resources, especially access to land; but the problematic nature (or lack) of transitional provisions on nationality in some countries, and their openness to wilful misinterpretation in others, mean that the interpretation of the law at State succession has been a key tool in national politics around the nature of belonging.

[1] Ruth Donner, *The Regulation of Nationality in International Law* (Transnational Publishers Inc 1994) ch V (Nationality and State succession); Paul Weis, *Nationality and Statelessness in International Law* (2nd edn, Brill 1979) ch 11 (Effect of territorial transfers on nationality); Laura van Waas, *Nationality Matters: Statelessness under International Law* (Intersentia 2008) ch VI (Addressing Statelessness in the Context of State Succession).

This chapter considers more recent cases of State succession, long after the departure of the European colonial powers. They illustrate that the rules governing transitions in State authority remain critical: deeply political even when they seem most tediously technical; and with the potential to cause problems long after the rules were first adopted.

The most damaging example so far in the post-colonial history of the continent has been around the secession of Eritrea from Ethiopia, itself never colonised. In 1998, former comrades in arms against the Derg dictatorship over Ethiopia's central government, who had together successfully overthrown that regime and then, to the world's admiration, peacefully managed the process of creating a new State of Eritrea along Ethiopia's northern border, decided to turn their guns on each other instead. The brutal war that followed between the Ethiopian and Eritrean armies, fought out in an arid mountainous version of World War I trenches, devastated the lives of tens of thousands: not only the soldiers who were killed and injured and their families; but of all those who became instant suspected traitors in the land of their birth. Those of Eritrean origin in Ethiopia continued to face challenges to their citizenship two decades after the war.

In the two Sudans, the issue of citizenship lurks to destabilise both halves of the former single country. The determination of successive governments of Sudan to impose a vision of the State as Arab and Muslim was a major driver of the two long civil wars that afflicted the country after independence in 1956. Nonetheless, the idea of Sudanese nationality in itself had not been questioned until the final secession of the south to form a new Republic of South Sudan in 2011. The failure of the parties to agree a definition and a joint mechanism to adjudicate cases in doubt left many former citizens of the united Sudan for the first time at risk of denial of their rights as continuing citizens of the Republic of Sudan; and some at risk of statelessness, excluded from both the successor States. The government of Sudan enacted specific legislative amendments, coupled with a new national identification system, that ensured the exclusion of those of South Sudanese origin.

The transfer of territory between existing States creates similar problems. In 2002, the International Court of Justice (ICJ) handed down a judgment that awarded the Bakassi peninsula bordering Nigeria and Cameroon to Cameroon. Fifteen years later, no constitutional or legislative provisions had been adopted in either country to provide clarity on the nationality status of those affected by the judgment. Both those remaining in what is now Cameroon and those who moved to Nigeria were left without any practical way of establishing nationality in either country. Similar problems affected smaller numbers of people in other cases relating to disputed frontiers between territories formerly administered as part of AOF, where boundary determination had never been a priority during the colonial period.

The ICJ – following recognised principles of international law – notably fails either to take into account the wishes of the inhabitants of these territories in relation to their nationality or to make any ruling on the steps that should be taken to ensure that those affected have a recognised nationality after the transfer of territory. Reading the decisions is to delve back into the imagination of colonial map-making, where zones marked 'terra nullius' were claimed by distant sovereigns as if no human being already lived and worked the land. Political agreements negotiated in the wake of these decisions have also failed to take seriously the question of access to and confirmation of nationality, leaving much to potentially arbitrary decision-making by junior officials responsible for identity documents.

8.1. Eritrea/Ethiopia: State Succession and Mass Expulsion

Ethiopia remained independent under the rule of the Amharic emperors throughout the period of European colonial government in Africa, though its external borders were established by the conquest of neighbouring territories by the Italians, French and British. It was thus the first sub-Saharan African country to have its own nationality law, adopted in 1930 (see Chapter 2).

Though Ethiopia was never formally colonised, the territory of Eritrea was an Italian colony from the late nineteenth century till 1941, when British troops advancing from Sudan defeated the Italians during World War II. Following a period of British military administration, the United Nations adopted a resolution in 1950 designating Eritrea an autonomous unit federated to Ethiopia. In 1962, Ethiopian Emperor Haile Selassie unilaterally annexed Eritrea and declared it a province of Ethiopia; residents of Eritrea without another nationality were declared to be Ethiopian nationals. The Eritrean People's Liberation Front (EPLF) was established to resist Ethiopian rule; following the 1974 overthrow of the emperor by the brutal military government known as the Derg, the EPLF joined other regionally based armed groups in the alliance against the new regime known as the Ethiopian Peoples' Revolutionary Democratic Front (EPRDF).

In 1991, the EPRDF finally defeated the Derg, and the new Ethiopian transitional government immediately approved a referendum on the status of Eritrea, as had been promised within the alliance. All individuals identifying themselves as Eritrean, including those living within the borders of what would become Ethiopia, were allowed to register and vote, provided they obtained an 'identification card' issued by the Eritrean provisional government. More than 1.1 million people registered; including more than 300,000 outside the territory, 60,000 of whom were in Ethiopia. The referendum was held in 1993 under UN supervision; the vote was 99% in favour of independence, and a new State was formed. The two governments agreed that 'until such time that the citizens of one of the sides residing in the other's territory are fully identified and until the issue of citizenship is settled in both countries, the traditional right of citizens of one side to live in the other's territory shall be respected.'[2]

In Eritrea, the Nationality Proclamation of 1992, on the basis of which eligibility to register in the independence referendum was determined, provided that Eritrean nationals are those born of a father or mother 'of Eritrean origin'. Though at first sight an ethnic criterion, the law defined 'Eritrean origin' to mean (descent from) a person who was resident in Eritrea in 1933.[3] Those who entered and resided in Eritrea between 1934 and 1951 were also entitled to a certificate of nationality on application. Any person who arrived in Eritrea in 1952 or later – including Ethiopians – had to apply for naturalisation in the same way as any other foreigner, showing a ten-year residence in Eritrea before 1974, or a twenty-year residence thereafter, and renounce any other nationality. Barred from acquiring nationality were those who had 'committed anti-people acts during the liberation struggle of the Eritrean people'.[4] In practice, those who were recognised as obtaining Eritrean nationality in 1993 included many people of mixed ancestry.

Ethiopia, meanwhile, adopted a new constitution in 1994 that provided a right to a nationality for all children and granted Ethiopian citizenship to 'any woman or man either of whose parents is an Ethiopian citizen', in principle creating gender neutrality. While silent on dual citizenship, the constitution further stated that 'no Ethiopian citizen shall be deprived of his or her Ethiopian citizenship against his or her will', and that marriage of an Ethiopian, male or female, to a foreigner does not result in the loss of Ethiopian nationality unless he or she chooses to take the nationality of his or her spouse.[5] The statute law in force, however, remained the gender discriminatory Ethiopian Nationality Law of 1930, which also stated that any Ethiopian citizen who acquired another nationality would automatically lose his or her Ethiopian citizenship.[6] Nonetheless, as late as 1996, Ethiopia agreed with Eritrea that Eritrean-Ethiopians should choose between their two possible nationalities, rather than automatically losing their existing status.[7]

[2] 'Agreement on Security and Other Related Matters between the Ministries of Internal Affairs of the governments of Ethiopia and Eritrea', Addis Ababa, 13 May 1994, art 2.3. Cited in Human Rights Watch, 'The Horn of Africa War: Mass Expulsions and the Nationality Issue (June 1998-April 2002)' (2003). See also (from the Eritrean perspective) Natalie S Klein, 'Report on the Deportation of Eritreans and Ethiopians of Eritrean Origin from Ethiopia, June – August 1998' (Embassy of Eritrea 1999).

[3] Eritrean Nationality Proclamation (No. 21/1992). A 1933 Italian colonial decree had defined as Eritrean 'subjects' all persons (with the exception of Italian 'citizens'), residing in the country as at that date.

[4] Eritrean Nationality Proclamation No.21/1992, arts 2–4.

[5] Constitution of the Federal Democratic Republic of Ethiopia, 8 December 1994, arts 6, 25, 33, 35 and 26. Article 6 provides that: '(1) Any person of either sex shall be an Ethiopian national where both or either parent is Ethiopian. (2) Foreign nationals may acquire Ethiopian nationality. (3) Particulars relating to nationality shall be determined by law.'

[6] Ethiopian Nationality Law, 1930, art 33(1). The 2003 Proclamation on Ethiopian Nationality removed the gender discrimination, but still prohibits dual nationality.

[7] Agreed minutes of the Fourth Ethio-Eritrean Joint High Commission Meeting, 18–19 August 1996, cited in Human Rights Watch (n 2).

The 1994 constitution declares the State to be a 'Federal Democratic Republic', and gives significant powers to nine regional States, as well as the right of self-government to each of 'the Nations, Nationalities and Peoples of Ethiopia'.[8] The power of self-determination has only been used once (the constitution was adopted after Eritrea was already independent), to create a separate administrative zone for the Siltie in the Southern Nations and Nationalities Region, following a referendum in 2001.[9]

After the initial harmony between the government of Eritrea and their former colleagues, tensions between the two governments began to develop, especially on trade (newly landlocked Ethiopia relied heavily on access to the sea through Eritrea's Red Sea ports of Massawa and Assab) and agreement of the border between them. In 1998, war erupted over the formal demarcation of the route of that border. Fighting continued over the following two years at varying levels of intensity, until repeated attempts to negotiate a truce eventually culminated in a comprehensive peace agreement in December 2000.

At the outbreak of the war, there were still around half a million people of Eritrean origin living in Ethiopia, including approximately 200,000 living in the Tigray border region. An estimated 100,000 Ethiopians were living in Eritrea.

In June 1998, approximately one month after the war began, Ethiopia issued a policy statement that the '550,000 Eritreans residing in Ethiopia' could continue to live and work in the country, although politically active individuals were ordered to leave the country and those in 'sensitive' jobs were told to take a mandatory leave of one month.[10] Despite this reassurance, the very next day saw the first wave of arrests and expulsions of prominent individuals of Eritrean origin, including those working for intergovernmental organisations based in Addis Ababa, and dismissals of those in government jobs. As the arrests and expulsions continued into 1999 and 2000, those affected were increasingly ordinary people with no particular status to attract the authorities' attention. Almost all those expelled from urban areas were detained in harsh conditions, often for weeks, before being transported in bus convoys on a several-day journey to the border. Rural people affected by the campaign were ordered to leave, and usually had to travel on foot, without their personal possessions. Ultimately, the Ethiopian authorities arrested, detained and deported some 75,000 people of Eritrean origin.

In July 1999, the Ethiopian authorities issued a press release stating that the Ethiopians of Eritrean origin who had registered to vote in the 1993 referendum

[8] Article 39(5) defines a 'Nation, Nationality or People', without distinction among the terms, as 'a group of people who have or share a large measure of a common culture or similar customs, mutual intelligibility of language, belief in a common or related identities, a common psychological make-up, and who inhabit an identifiable predominantly contiguous territory.'

[9] Lahra Smith, 'Voting for an Ethnic Identity: Procedural and Institutional Responses to Ethnic Conflict in Ethiopia' (2007) 45 Journal of Modern African Studies 565; see also Lahra Smith, *Making Citizens in Africa: Ethnicity, Gender, and National Identity in Ethiopia* (Cambridge University Press 2013).

[10] *Ethiopian Herald* of 13 June 1998, cited in Human Rights Watch (n 2).

on Eritrea's independence had thus assumed Eritrean citizenship; though that was clearly not the interpretation that any party had put on the process at the time.[11] A month later all those who had registered for the referendum were required to register for alien residence permits with the Security, Immigration and Refugee Affairs Authority, to be renewed every six months. Business licences for these individuals were revoked, and assets frozen.

During the first phase of the conflict, there was no official Eritrean policy of expulsion of Ethiopians, and many were in fact prevented from leaving by denial of the required exit visas. As the war continued, Eritrea's policy became more hostile. From August 1998 to January 1999, during a period of relative calm in the war, around 21,000 Ethiopians left Eritrea with the assistance of the International Committee of the Red Cross (ICRC). The Eritrean authorities claimed the departures were voluntary, though some intimidation was nonetheless reported by those concerned. In July 1999, Ethiopia asserted that some 41,000 of its citizens had been deported from Eritrea. A major Ethiopian offensive in May 2000 caused perhaps one third of Eritrea's three million people to flee their homes. In early June 2000, Ethiopian citizens living in Asmara were told to register with the authorities 'in preparation for repatriation'. Soon after, the Eritrean government admitted holding 7,500 Ethiopian nationals in detention pending deportation, and started expelling batches of several hundred across the border. Property was also confiscated, affecting especially the large Ethiopian community in the port city of Assab. Figures collated by the ICRC and UN ultimately indicated that around 70,000 people were expelled or repatriated from Eritrea to Ethiopia, just less than the mirroring figure, despite the Eritrean government continuing to deny it had any policy of expulsion.[12] Individuals of Ethiopian descent still living in Eritrea who had not sought nationality by the time the war broke out in 1998 were considered aliens, dealt with according to the normal rules applicable to citizens of other countries living in Eritrea.

In 2004, the Claims Commission established under the December 2000 peace agreement adjudicated on the nationality of the citizens of Ethiopia and Eritrea after the splitting of the two countries in 1993. Ethiopia had tried to justify the de-nationalisations and forced population transfers during the war by arguing that those Ethiopians who registered as Eritreans for the referendum in 1993 had thereby lost their nationality. Eritrea argued that they could not have done so because there was no Eritrea in existence at that point. The Claims Commission found that, under the 'unusual transitional circumstances' around the creation of Eritrea, those who qualified to participate in the referendum in fact acquired dual nationality.[13] The outbreak of the war did not of itself suspend this

[11] 'Eritrea's baseless accusations', Ethiopia Office of Government Spokesperson, 9 July 1999.

[12] Human Rights Watch (n 2).

[13] Award of the Eritrea-Ethiopia Claims Commission in *Partial Award (Civilian Claims: Eritrea's Claims 15, 16, 23 & 27–32)*, 44 ILM 601 (2005) (award of 17 December 2004) at para 51, available at the website of the Permanent Court of Arbitration, which acted as registry for the process. 'Taking into

dual nationality, and Ethiopia's action in denying nationality of the dual nationals had been arbitrary and unlawful.[14]

This was not the interpretation of the Ethiopian government, however. Those of Eritrean descent who were not expelled and remained in Ethiopia (an estimated 150,000) were not considered Ethiopians, even if they had made no move to acquire Eritrean or any other nationality, and had not registered to vote in the referendum. They were excluded from exercising citizenship rights such as voting, faced lack of access to employment and education, and remained potentially subject to deportation. A 2002 law which bestowed special rights and privileges on 'foreign nationals of Ethiopian origin', singled out Eritreans who had forfeited Ethiopian nationality and expressly excluded them from enjoying the new rights and privileges.[15]

In 2003, however, Ethiopia adopted a comprehensive reform to the nationality law that should have significantly improved the situation. The 2003 Proclamation on Ethiopian Nationality removed gender discrimination in transmission to spouses and children and eased restrictions on naturalisation, allowing those with Ethiopian mothers and fathers of Eritrean origin to claim citizenship.[16] The immigration authorities also adopted an internal directive on the residence status of Eritrean nationals living in Ethiopia.[17]

Many people of Eritrean origin and others living in Ethiopia were able to reacquire citizenship under the new proclamation, especially those of mixed descent. But problems were still reported in obtaining national identification cards, including delays of several years and interrogation by immigration officials. An Ethiopian of Eritrean descent interviewed in early 2008 observed that 'the gap between law and implementation is like the space between the sun and the moon, and no one knows how to close it'.[18] Among those affected by these issues were individuals who had been expelled from Ethiopia to Eritrea in 1998, but had since then fled Eritrea's highly repressive government and returned to Ethiopia. Though it should have been possible for them to require Ethiopian citizenship under the law, none of

account the unusual transitional circumstances associated with the creation of the new State of Eritrea and both Parties' conduct before and after the 1993 Referendum, the Commission concludes that those who qualified to participate in the Referendum in fact acquired dual nationality. They became citizens of the new State of Eritrea pursuant to Eritrea's Proclamation No. 21/1/1992, but at the same time, Ethiopia continued to regard them as its own nationals.'

[14] See also Sean D Murphy, Won Kidane and Thomas R Snider, *Litigating War: Arbitration of Civil Injury by the Eritrea-Ethiopia Claims Commission* (Oxford University Press 2013) 311–319.

[15] Proclamation to Provide Foreign Nationals of Ethiopian Origin with Certain Rights to be Exercised in their Country of Origin (270/2002), 5 February 2002.

[16] Proclamation 378/2003 on Ethiopian Nationality, ss 3, 5, 6 and 18.

[17] Directive issued to determine the residence status of Eritrean nationals residing in Ethiopia, 2004.

[18] Maureen Lynch and Katherine Southwick, 'Ethiopia-Eritrea: Stalemate Takes Toll on Eritreans and Ethiopians of Eritrean Origin' (Refugees International 2008). This report also noted that travel between Eritrea and Ethiopia was prohibited, there was no interstate phone system, and Ethiopians had reportedly been jailed for communicating with friends and relatives in Eritrea via the internet. At the same time, Ethiopia did accept refugees fleeing political repression and military conscription in Eritrea; a camp on the border housed almost 18,000 people as of early 2008. See also Katherine Southwick, 'Ethiopia-Eritrea: Statelessness and State Succession' (2009) 32 (Statelessness) Forced Migration Review 15.

those who applied to the Security, Immigration and Refugee Affairs Authority to exercise this right were successful, with the rejection being based on the grounds that they were a 'security threat'.[19] Ethiopians of Eritrean origin in other countries were also unable to reacquire Ethiopian documents.[20]

The identity document of most importance for those of mixed parentage or Eritrean origin in obtaining recognition of Ethiopian citizenship is often the local level 'kebele ID'. As in Nigeria, the process of recognition as a citizen depends on first obtaining a document issued by one of more than 16,000 'kebeles', the lowest-level units of government. The kebele ID has its roots in the socialist-inspired Derg period of revolutionary government, and is still closely controlled by the ruling party in Ethiopia, the EPRDF (Ethiopian People's Revolutionary Democratic Front). The award of kebele IDs also draws on the frameworks set by the constitutions of the nine regional States for membership of that State or sub-unit. Minority groups are explicitly classified as 'indigenous' or 'non-indigenous' in some regional constitutions, while the distinction is made in practice in others. In some cases, a degree of autonomy is given to minorities through the three-tier system of local government within each regional State (the zone or 'nationality administration', wereda and kebele).[21] Every neighbourhood has a kebele office, and one of the main responsibilities of these offices is to issue kebele IDs. The kebele card is required for virtually all identification purposes: to register a SIM card, open a financial account, travel internally, stay in a hotel, obtain a birth, death or marriage certificate or a passport, and to enrol to vote. The process is not standardised, but depends on the officials' personal knowledge of the applicant and witness testimony.

In the context of the 1998–2000 war with Eritrea, the kebele identification system was mobilised as a means of control of political opposition, and to facilitate the denationalisation and deportation of suspected Eritreans.[22] People of Eritrean descent may still struggle to be classified as indigenous in any of the nine States (as do members of groups that were forcibly moved during the Derg era, and minorities that are dispersed across geography).[23]

[19] Amsale Getnet Aberra, 'Ethiopians in Limbo: from Statelessness to being a refugee in one's own country', ECADF Ethiopian News, 14 February 2014.

[20] See, eg, Louise Thomas, 'Refugees and Asylum Seekers from Mixed Eritrean-Ethiopian Families in Cairo' (FMRS, American University in Cairo 2006).

[21] On ethnic federalism in Ethiopia, see Paul H Brietzke, 'Ethiopia's 'Leap in the Dark': Federalism and Self-Determination in the New Constitution' (1995) 39 Journal of African Law 19; Jon Abbink, 'Ethnicity and Constitutionalism in Contemporary Ethiopia' (1997) 41 Journal of African Law 159; Christophe Van der Beken, 'Ethiopia: Constitutional Protection of Ethnic Minorities at the Regional Level' (2007) 20 Afrika Focus 105; Yonatan Tesfaye Fessha and Christophe Van der Beken, 'Ethnic Federalism and Internal Minorities: The Legal Protection of Internal Minorities in Ethiopia' (2013) 21 African Journal of International and Comparative Law 32; Solomon M Gofie, 'The State and the 'Peoples': Citizenship and the Future of Political Community in Ethiopia' in Emma Hunter (ed), *Citizenship, belonging, and political community in Africa: Dialogues between past and present* (Ohio University Press 2016).

[22] Magnus Treiber, 'The Kebele System in Ethiopia', Southern Refugee Legal Aid Network, 2011.

[23] Assefa Fiseha, 'Ethiopia's Experiment in Accommodating Diversity: 20 Years' Balance Sheet' (2012) 22 Regional & Federal Studies 435.

Perhaps no legal provisions would have helped to mitigate the impact of the Ethiopia-Eritrea war on those with potential claims to nationality in both countries. However, after immediate hostilities had died down, it is evident that pressure on Ethiopia in particular did bring some improvement in the detail of nationality law and administration that benefitted many in a practical way. The exclusively descent-based nationality law, however, means that only deliberate efforts to provide nationality to those of Eritrean origin will integrate these or other 'stranger' populations in the long term. Moreover, while the federal structure had ambitions to empower previously neglected ethnic groups, the lack of a formal legal system for internal 'naturalisation' has – as in Nigeria – created a class of people who are not regarded as having full rights in the region in which they live, even though they are Ethiopian citizens.

An Egyptian-Sudanese-Ethiopian-Eritrean stateless woman in Egypt[24]

'Mary was born and raised in Sudan. Her father, who was a Sudanese Christian of Egyptian heritage, abandoned the family when she was eleven. Mary's mother was of mixed Ethiopian-Eritrean origin and had never formally elected a nationality after Eritrea's secession. Mary never possessed a birth certificate or any formal identity documents. When she tried to acquire documents by formally applying for Sudanese nationality her request was denied as she was unable to produce any evidence of her father's nationality. She was denied Ethiopian nationality after the Ethiopian Embassy determined her mother to be Eritrean, and denied Eritrean nationality as she was unable to fulfil the evidence requirements. Mary is therefore Stateless. She has no legal right to reside in any country and is thus at risk of immigration-related detention. She is unable to enrol in public education facilities or take up legal employment, and is therefore forced to risk taking up potentially exploitative, informal work. Mary's application for refugee status in Egypt was denied, as she had no well-founded fear of persecution.'

8.2. Sudan and South Sudan

A British-Egyptian condominium was imposed over Sudan from 1899 to 1956, following the defeat of the Mahdist nationalist and Islamic State created in rebellion against Ottoman-Egyptian rule in the 1880s. The condominium was headed

[24] 'Case study 3' from Eirwen-Jane Pierrot, 'A Responsibility to Protect: UNHCR and Statelessness in Egypt' (UNHCR 2013).

by a governor-general theoretically appointed by the Egyptian khedive with British consent, but under effective British control. Egyptian independence from the Ottoman Empire in 1922 led to the withdrawal of Egyptian troops from Sudan, although the condominium continued (as did the presence of British troops in Egypt). From 1924 onwards, Sudan was governed as two separate provinces, kept administratively quite segregated, with controls on movement between them. The Arabic language and Islam were dominant in the north; in the south, the British permitted Christian missionaries to operate, but failed to develop any educated cadre of southern Sudanese. From the mid-1940s, as a degree of self-government was given to Sudan, and a legislative assembly and executive council were established in 1948, the south began to be integrated into the central government's administrative and political structures – in which southern politicians complained of marginalisation.[25]

In 1948, the British-Egyptian condominium adopted a Definition of Sudanese Ordinance to codify the question of who fell under their jurisdiction. The Ordinance defined as Sudanese 'every person of no nationality [thus excluding British, Egyptian and other existing recognised nationalities] who … is domiciled in Sudan and (i) has been so domiciled since 31 December 1897, or else whose ancestors in the direct male line since that date have all been so domiciled' or who is the wife or widow of such a person.[26] This pattern of referring to a date of original residence remains encoded in Sudanese law today (though the reference date has changed).

The 1952 Egyptian revolution led to the abrogation of the condominium treaty with Britain, followed by an Anglo-Egyptian agreement for a process leading to Sudanese self-government; Sudanese nationalists in turn unilaterally declared their own independence in late 1955. The proposed self-government statute was hastily adopted as the Transitional Constitution of 1956.

A year later, the Definition of Sudanese Ordinance was replaced with the first real citizenship law, the Sudan Nationality Act 1957, which, amended several times[27], remained in effect until 1993. The 1957 Act provided that a person was Sudanese if he (sic) was born in Sudan or his father was born in Sudan and he or his direct male ancestors had been resident in Sudan since 31 December 1897, prior to the defeat of the Mahdist forces. Naturalisation was possible based on a ten-year residence period and other conditions, including adequate knowledge of

[25] Douglas H Johnson, 'The Southern Sudan' (Minority Rights Group 1988) 78.

[26] Definition of 'Sudanese' Ordinance, 15 July 1948, Laws of the Sudan 1956, Vol.1, Title 1, sub-title 5. For the purposes of British nationality law, Sudan was simply a foreign country, with no protectorate or other status giving the British government extra-territorial jurisdiction over British subjects (although some condominium passport holders were treated as British protected persons, this was as a matter of royal prerogative rather than statutory right). Laurie Fransman, Adrian Berry and Alison Harvey, *Fransman's British Nationality Law* (3rd edn, Bloomsbury Professional 2011), catalogue entry on Sudan.

[27] In 1959, 1970, 1972, 1963, 1970, 1972, 1973 and 1974.

Arabic and renunciation of any other nationality; a child born after the Act came into effect was a citizen if his or her father was a citizen; and a woman married to a Sudanese man could naturalise based on two years' residence.[28] The provisions of the law thus emphasised male line descent, but based on a starting point of place of birth rather than the ethnic origin of an ancestor.

Even before the ink was dry on Sudan's declaration of independence, southern army officers rebelled against the Khartoum government. Though the mutinies were quickly suppressed, they marked the start of a civil war that took off for real in the early 1960s (after southern demands for a federal system were decisively rejected by Khartoum in 1958), and continued to 1972. A period of military rule from 1958 to 1965 gave way to an unstable series of civilian governments dominated by divisions over the nature of the State, including proposals for the creation of a more Islamic system of government. In 1969 a military coup brought Col. Gaafar Nimeiri to power, proposing a socialist secular State. Initially harsh political repression softened somewhat, and in 1972 the Addis Ababa peace agreement temporarily ended the civil war, with the grant of a degree of autonomy to the south, enshrined in a new 1973 constitution for Sudan. The 1957 Nationality Act was also amended to change the date of origin for residence in Sudan to 1 January 1924, when Sudan was reorganised administratively into two provinces by the British; thus creating an understanding of nationality at least somewhat based on a political recognition of South Sudan.

In 1983, the war was reignited as the Nimeiri government responded to pressure from the Muslim opposition parties by abandoning its former socialist and liberal allies and adopting a policy of Islamicisation, including the adoption of *shari'a* law in the north, as well as the splitting of the southern region into three, revoking its autonomous powers. Nimeiri was overthrown by another coup in 1985, succeeded by a series of elected civilian governments under Prime Minister Sadiq el-Mahdi of the Umma party, which agreed to suspend the application of *shari'a* law and entered into negotiations to end the renewed civil war. In 1989 a new coup d'état brought Omar al-Bashir to power. The new government suspended political parties and re-introduced the *shari'a* laws. In 1993, the military council was replaced by an appointed Transitional National Assembly (TNA), made up of members of the National Islamic Front (NIF), founded in the 1960s by Dr. Hassan al-Turabi; Bashir became President of the new government.

In 1993, Bashir's military government replaced the 1957 Nationality Act with a new law, adopted as a provisional decree; the 1993 decree was amended by the Transitional National Assembly in 1994 and then re-enacted into law.[29]

[28] Sudanese Nationality Act 1957, s 5(1) and s 9. A two-year residence in Sudan was required, although the President of the Republic, upon the recommendation of the Minister of Interior, was entitled to exempt alien women married to Sudanese nationals from the residence requirement.

[29] Provisional Decree No. 19 (or 18; both numbers are used) of 18 August 1993, amended and approved by Transitional National Resolution No.59 of 3 May 1994, and signed into law by the president on 17 May 1994.

Despite the initiatives to Islamicise Sudan in other ways, the new nationality law of 1993 introduced no requirement of Arab ethnicity or Muslim religion. Indeed, its structure was very similar to the 1957 law in relation to the grant of nationality by birth, providing that a person born before the Act came into effect was a national from birth if he or his father was born in Sudan and he or his paternal ancestors were resident in Sudan since 1924. The changes made to the 1957 Act were relatively liberal, limiting the grounds on which citizenship could be taken away by the executive, reducing the period required for a resident in Sudan to become a naturalised Sudanese citizen from ten years to five years, and removing the requirement for knowledge of Arabic to naturalise, as well as removing the prohibition on dual citizenship.[30] The amendments made before the 1993 provisional decree became the 1994 Act included a change to the applicable date for a claim to nationality by birth based on domicile of a male ancestor from 1924 to 1 January 1956, the date of independence, a date that would make significantly more people eligible for Sudanese nationality.[31] The 1994 Act removed adopted children from the definition of children; this was the only provision overtly relating to government adherence to Islamic legal principles, which do not recognise adoption in its modern form.[32] The amendments also added back in some of the grounds for depriving a person of (naturalised) citizenship, including 'an act or words outside Sudan showing his non-allegiance or hatred of Sudan.'[33]

Throughout all these changes, there was surprisingly little dispute over who was a Sudanese.[34] Although the various laws setting out the rules for citizenship of Sudan were discriminatory on the basis of gender, by paternal descent, the legal definition of a citizen was founded on the idea of birth and residence in the country rather than race, ethnicity or religion. The vision of a 'New Sudan' articulated by John Garang, the leader of the Sudan Peoples' Liberation Movement (SPLM) from 1983, was also of a 'just and united democratic secular multiracial, multicultural, multi-lingual and multi-religious Sudan'.[35]

[30] Sudanese Nationality Law 1993, ss 4, 7, 10, and 11. According to some interviewed by the author, these changes were made to facilitate naturalisation of international Islamists who took up residence in Sudan during the 1990s.

[31] Sub-section 4 (b) (ii) of the 1994 Act.

[32] Nasredeen Abdulbari, 'Citizenship Rules in Sudan and Post-Secession Problems' (2011) 55 Journal of African Law 157.

[33] Section 11(1)(d).

[34] Abdulbari, 'Citizenship Rules in Sudan and Post-Secession Problems' (n 32), quoting Alex de Waal; for general background on questions of citizenship in Sudan, see also Nasredeen Abdulbari, 'Identities and Citizenship in Sudan: Governing Constitutional Principles' (2013) 13 African Human Rights Law Journal 383; Amir Idris, 'Rethinking Identity, Citizenship, and Violence in Sudan' (2012) 44 International Journal of Middle East Studies 324; Jennifer Smith and Joel R Charny, 'Sudan: Preventing Violence and Statelessness as the Referendum Approaches' (Refugees International 2010); Ahmad A Sikainga, 'Citizenship and Identity in Post-Secession Northern Sudan' (2011) 86 Bulletin of the Association of Concerned Africa Scholars 11; Elena Vezzadini, 'Genealogies of Racial Relations: The Independence of South Sudan, Citizenship and the Racial State in the Modern History of Sudan' (2011) 86 Bulletin of the Association of Concerned Africa Scholars 30.

[35] Quoted in Christopher Zambakari, 'Sudan and South Sudan: Identity, Citizenship, and Democracy in Plural Societies' (2015) 19 Citizenship Studies 69.

In 1998, a new constitution for the whole of Sudan was adopted, following a process that allowed for some public debate, though the final draft was closely edited by the executive. The TNA became an elected National Assembly, and the NIF created the National Congress Party (NCP), headed by President Bashir, as its formal political arm and the only legally recognised party in the country. In relation to the right to nationality, the constitution represented a step towards a more inclusive idea of citizenship, in particular by removing gender discrimination at least in principle. Article 22 provided that 'Everyone born of a Sudanese mother or father has the inalienable right to Sudanese nationality, its duties and obligations. Everyone who has lived in Sudan during their youth or who has been resident in Sudan for several years has the right to Sudanese nationality in accordance with the law.' This commitment to gender equality, was not, however, translated into an amended version of the 1994 nationality law, which continued to discriminate on the basis of gender.

The civil war continued with brutal effects, exacerbated by efforts to exploit oil deposits discovered in the south. Peace negotiations resumed in 2002 and finally brought the war to an end in 2005, with the adoption in Kenya first of the Machakos Protocol, outlining the terms of a peace treaty, and subsequently a detailed Comprehensive Peace Agreement (CPA). The CPA provided for a five-year transition period, during which the south would have a degree of autonomy, followed by a referendum on independence. Meantime, however, a further rebellion had broken out in 2003 in Darfur, in the west of northern Sudan.

In 2003, the SPLM had already adopted a Nationality Act as one of the laws of the New Sudan, applied in the areas under its control. The Act moved to an ethnic definition of belonging, proposing that citizenship be attributed on the basis of membership of one of the 'tribes of the New Sudan', as well as on 'uninterrupted domicile'; like the existing Sudanese law, it discriminated on the basis of gender.[36] This formulation proved influential on subsequent texts for South Sudan.

The CPA provided that 'the people of South Sudan have the right to self-determination'. This right was also enshrined in the interim constitutions for Sudan and Southern Sudan that followed the peace agreement. But who were 'the people of South Sudan'? The Interim Constitution for Southern Sudan and the legislation establishing the eligibility for individuals to vote in the referendum on

[36] The Act provided that a person born before 2003, the date of the entry into force of the Act, was a New Sudan national by descent if he or she was or his/her parents or his/her grand and great grandparents were born in the New Sudan provided that he or she belonged to one of the 'tribes of the New Sudan'. A person could also be a New Sudan national by descent if he or she, at the time of coming into force of the new Nationality Act, was domiciled since April 1994 and his or her ancestors in the direct male line had all been domiciled in the New Sudan. Alternatively, a person could be a New Sudan national by descent if he or she had acquired and maintained the status of a New Sudan national by uninterrupted domicile. In addition, persons born after the ratification of the New Sudan Nationality Act would be also New Sudan nationals by descent if their fathers were New Sudan nationals by naturalization at the time of their birth. The Act provided that deserted infants or of unknown parents would be presumed nationals by descent until the contrary was proved.

the independence of South Sudan provided two parallel definitions, one based on ethnicity, thus permitting 'southerners' resident in the north – whether displaced by the war, or employees in the Sudanese State or economy – or in other countries to vote; the other on residence, thus allowing those (many fewer in number) 'northerners' resident in the south to be heard also. The choice of a dominant ethnicity-based definition, echoing the 'New Sudan' law of 2003, then shaped the trajectory of debates over 'who belongs where' over the years to come.

The Interim Constitution for Southern Sudan provided that:

> For purposes of the referendum ... a Southern Sudanese is:
>
> (a) any person whose either parent or grandparent is or was a member of any of the indigenous communities existing in Southern Sudan before or on January 1, 1956; or whose ancestry can be traced through agnatic or male line to any one of the ethnic communities of Southern Sudan; or
>
> (b) any person who has been permanently residing or whose mother and/or father or any grandparent have been permanently residing in Southern Sudan as of January 1, 1956 ....[37]

The Southern Sudan Referendum Act 2009 repeated these provisions in very similar language, but removed the reference to agnatic (patrilineal) descent, providing for voting rights through either parent or any grandparent.[38] There was no definition of 'indigenous community'.

In relation to Sudanese citizenship itself during the transitional period, the Interim National Constitution of Sudan 2005 repeated the gender-neutral rules of the 1998 constitution for the transmission of citizenship to children, and continued to allow dual nationality, delegating rules on naturalisation to legislation.[39] The 1994 nationality law was also amended in 2005, in response to the CPA and the adoption of the Interim National Constitution, and for the first time gave the child of a Sudanese woman and foreign father the right to apply for nationality (although not the automatic conferral of nationality by operation of law, as for the child of a Sudanese father).[40]

[37] Interim Constitution of Southern Sudan, 2005, Art 9. Although other wording was similar, the proposal in the 2003 law of the 'New Sudan' for the date of origin to be 1994 was not taken forward.

[38] 'The voter shall meet the following conditions: 1) be born to parents both or one of them belonging to one of the indigenous communities that settled in Southern Sudan on or before the 1st of January 1956, or whose ancestry is traceable to one of the ethnic communities in Southern Sudan; or, 2) be a permanent resident, without interruption, or any of whose parents or grandparents are residing permanently, without interruption, in Southern Sudan since the 1st of January 1956; 3) have reached 18 years of age; 4) be of sound mind; 5) be registered in the Referendum Register'. Southern Sudan Referendum Act, 2009, section 25, unofficial translation.

[39] Interim National Constitution of Sudan, 2005, Art 7: (1) Citizenship shall be the basis for equal rights and duties for all Sudanese; (2) Every person born to a Sudanese mother or father shall have an inalienable right to enjoy Sudanese nationality and citizenship; (3) The law shall regulate citizenship and naturalization; no naturalized Sudanese shall be deprived of his/her acquired citizenship except in accordance with the law; (4) A Sudanese national may acquire the nationality of another country as shall be regulated by law.

[40] The 2005 amendment added sub-s (3) to s 4 of the Nationality Act, to provide that: 'A person born to a mother who is a Sudanese by birth shall be eligible for the Sudanese nationality by birth provided

The long and complex history of the territory known as Abyei, which at different times had been administratively positioned on either side of the north-south line between northern and southern Sudan, meant that the Abyei Area was accorded 'special administrative status' by a protocol to the CPA.[41] The Abyei Protocol and the Abyei Area Referendum Act 2009 provided for a separate referendum for the Abyei area, to determine whether it should remain a special administrative region of north Sudan or become part of South Sudan. As for the other referendum, those eligible to vote were defined partly by ethnicity and partly by residence:

> (a) Members of the Ngok Dinka Community;
> (b) Other Sudanese residing in Abyei Area in accordance with the criteria of residency, as may be determined by the Commission according to section 14(1) of this Act [establishing the powers of the Abyei Area Referendum Commission]; ...[42]

The Ngok Dinka are members of the large southern Sudanese Dinka ethnic group that has historically dominated the SPLM. In relation to (b), the people whose 'residence' was most controversial for the purposes of the Abyei referendum were the mainly pastoralist Misseriya Arabs, who traditionally migrate to Abyei for a part of every year, though the home base ('*dar*') for most is in North Sudan. The Sudanese government argued that the Misseriya were residents of Abyei for the purposes of the referendum; but their status was disputed by the SPLM and the Ngok Dinka.[43]

The question of how existing Sudanese nationals would be allocated to the citizenship of either Sudan or South Sudan was supposed to have been resolved in negotiations between the NCP and SPLM in advance of the main referendum on South Sudanese independence, which took place on 9 January 2011; or, at the

that he or she submits an application to become a Sudanese national by birth'. Note that the available English translation of the 1994 law is based on an incorrect version in Arabic that had an critical omission in s 4(2), stating that 'a person born after the ratification of this act shall become a citizen by birth at the time of his birth'. The official Arabic version makes clear that the father must be a citizen.

[41] Protocol on the resolution of Abyei conflict, Kenya, 26 May 2004.

[42] Abyei Area Referendum Act 2009, s 24. As for the referendum on the status of the rest of South Sudan, the other criteria are '(c) Not less than 18 years of age; (d) Of sound mind; (e) Registered in the Referendum Register.'

[43] An Abyei Boundary Commission made up of experts nominated by both sides had been established by the Abyei Protocol, tasked by the parties with the responsibility of evaluating historical and conflicting claims to the land and demarcating a border between the groups. The final report of the Commission was completed in July 2005, but was rejected by the government of Sudan. In 2008, the government of Sudan and the SPLM referred the dispute to the Permanent Court of Arbitration (PCA) in The Hague. In 2009, the tribunal ruled that the best way of determining borders of the Abyei Area was in a 'predominantly tribal manner' – rather than a 'predominantly territorial approach' based on the 1905 provincial boundary, which could split the Ngok Dinka community, depending on the outcome of the referendum. The boundaries it decided were thus defined primarily by the area of 'permanent habitation' of the Ngok Dinka. In this approach, the tribunal notably departed from the *uti possedetis* rule applied by the International Court of Justice in settling border disputes. Government of Sudan / The Sudan People's Liberation Movement/Army (Abyei Arbitration), Final Award, 22 July 2009, especially paras 595–596.

latest, before the 9 July 2011 official independence of South Sudan.[44] However, the parties failed to reach any agreement. The legal drafting issues were quite technical, but fundamentally the problem was lack of political will; and closely linked to other blockages about the sharing of oil revenue and the national debt, and the status of the Abyei region.

While negotiations were supposed to resume post-independence, both States moved separately to introduce laws and procedures on nationality. South Sudan adopted a new constitution and nationality law; and Sudan adopted amendments to the existing Sudan Nationality Act 1994, providing for withdrawal of Sudanese nationality from those who had acquired the nationality of South Sudan.

The Transitional Constitution of South Sudan, adopted in 2011 pending the appointment of a commission to draft a final constitution, contained no transitional provisions on nationality, but echoed the wording of the 1998 and 2005 constitutions of Sudan that 'Every person born to a South Sudanese mother or father shall have an inalienable right to enjoy South Sudanese citizenship and nationality' (departing from the SPLM's previous position to provide for a gender-neutral descent-based citizenship regime).[45] The constitution also explicitly permitted dual nationality.[46]

Article 8 of the new South Sudanese Nationality Act, adopted in June 2011, just before the secession of South Sudan, drew on the 'New Sudan' model of 2003 and the referendum criteria to provide that:

> An individual will be considered a South Sudanese national if such person meets any of the following requirements:
>
> (a) Any parents, grandparents or great grandparents on the male or female line were born in South Sudan;
> (b) Such person belongs to one of the indigenous tribal communities of South Sudan;
> (c) Such person, at the time this bill came into force, has been domiciled in South Sudan since 1.1.1956; or
> (d) Such person has acquired and maintained the status of a South Sudanese national by an uninterrupted domicile.

[44] Extensive suggestions on language and procedures to resolve the question of nationality of those who might have a claim to belong to either State were made by advisers, including the author, working with UNHCR and the AU High Level Implementation Panel (AUHIP) led by former president Thabo Mbeki of South Africa.

[45] There had been heavy resistance to the idea of gender equality in a citizenship law for the new State, but under international pressure, the leaders of the SPLM were obliged to accept – initially in the terms of the Southern Sudan Referendum Act – that they could not justify a male-line legal regime.

[46] Transitional Constitution of the Republic of South Sudan, Art 45: (1) Every person born to a South Sudanese mother or father shall have an inalienable right to enjoy South Sudanese citizenship and nationality. (2) Citizenship is the basis of equal rights and duties for all South Sudanese. (3) Every citizen shall enjoy all the rights guaranteed by this Constitution. (4) The law shall regulate citizenship and naturalisation; no naturalised citizen shall be deprived of his or her acquired citizenship except in accordance with the law. (5) A South Sudanese national may acquire the nationality of another country as shall be prescribed by law. (6) A non-South Sudanese may acquire the nationality of South Sudan by naturalisation as shall be prescribed by law.

The law also provided for possibility of acquiring citizenship by naturalisation based on ten years' residence (longer than the five years applied in the north since 1993) and other conditions.

The ethnic definition of citizenship in the second paragraph held the same ambiguities as similar formulations in Uganda, DRC or Nigeria (see Chapter 7, 7.3, 7.5 and 7.7). While the approach perhaps provided an instinctively understandable framework that could be operated through non-formal governance systems, it was not clear which groups in fact formed the 'indigenous tribal communities of South Sudan'. In practice, as the new law began to be implemented through the issue of documents, the usual categories faced challenges: non-dominant ethnic groups, especially those also present in neighbouring countries (including Sudan), the descendants of immigrants from other parts of Africa, and those of mixed parentage. Nonetheless, by adding other criteria based on residence and birth on the territory, the law did provide potential avenues for those with a strong link to South Sudan to get recognition of South Sudanese nationality.[47]

More immediately problematic was the failure of the new law to make any distinction between people who were habitually resident in South Sudan on the date of independence and those resident abroad. The law simply conferred nationality automatically on all, without any requirement to opt or apply for recognition, even for those resident for many years in another country who held another nationality.

The broad attribution of nationality by South Sudan was not only potentially in conflict with international norms prohibiting the en masse conferral of nationality on residents of neighbouring States,[48] but also immediately created the threat of denationalisation for those 'South Sudanese' resident in the North. On 19 July 2011, the National Assembly of the Republic of Sudan adopted amendments to the Sudan Nationality Act 1994, which removed the right to dual nationality – but only for those with a claim to South Sudanese nationality. New section 10(2) provided that 'An individual will automatically lose his Sudanese nationality if he has obtained, de jure or de facto, the nationality of South Sudan.' A minor child of an affected parent would also lose his or her nationality.

An additional Article 16 was also added, which stated that: 'Without prejudice to Article 10(2), the president may reinstate nationality to any individual who has lost his/ her nationality … when s/he applies for it.' But the law provided no process to allow a person to argue that he or she had not obtained the nationality

[47] Mike Sanderson, 'Key Threats of Statelessness in the Post-Secession Sudanese and South Sudanese Nationality Regimes' (2014) 19 Tilburg Law Review 236; Bronwen Manby, 'Citizenship and Statelessness in the East African Community' (UNHCR 2018).

[48] See Recommendation 11 of the *Bolzano/Bozen Recommendations on National Minorities in Inter-State Relations* adopted by the OSCE in June 2008; also Enrico Milano, 'The Conferral of Citizenship En Masse by Kin-States: Creeping Annexation or Responsibility to Protect?' in Francesco Palermo and Natalie Sabanadze (eds), *National Minorities in Inter-State Relations* (Martinus Nijhoff Publishers 2011); Myres S McDougal, Harold D Lasswell and Lung-chu Chen, 'Nationality and Human Rights: The Protection of the Individual in External Arenas' (1974) 83 Yale Law Journal 900, 918–922.

of South Sudan (or even to renounce any such right in order to remain a citizen of the Republic of Sudan).[49]

The paradox was that the broad terms of the South Sudanese law allowed Khartoum to argue that a very large number of people (in principle anyone with one great-grandparent born in South Sudan) had automatically lost their Sudanese nationality.[50]

The government of Sudan stated that southerners resident in the north must 'regularize their status' in Sudan by 8 April 2012, nine months after the date of the 9 July 2011 referendum, or be dealt with as foreigners. Southerners resident in the north then began to be dismissed from employment in the civil service and in the private sector, while their children were refused registration in school and treatment in public health clinics.[51] Under the Interim National Constitution of Sudan 2005 (which remained in force), the right to property is only protected for citizens,[52] and people of southern origin faced difficulties in buying or selling immovable property – hindering their ability to remain in Sudan, and also to realise funds to relocate to South Sudan, should they wish. Khartoum State announced that it was establishing evacuation camps for moving 'foreigners who live illegally in Khartoum', while the popular committees at neighbourhood level were instructed to draw up lists of foreign residents and report violators.[53] Faced with this situation, several hundred thousand people of southern origin had already headed south since the date of the referendum, on their own or with the assistance of the UN; tens of thousands of others who had made the first steps to returning, selling their homes and many of their possessions, found themselves stuck in temporary camps without the means to continue their journey.

On 10 April 2012, the Ministry of the Interior of South Sudan issued its own press release announcing that, 'in response to procedures issued by the Government of the Republic of the Sudan concerning the status of South Sudanese in the Republic of Sudan', 'all nationals of the Republic of Sudan are declared foreigners as of 9th April 2012', and that those entering South Sudan would require visas.[54]

[49] The residence period for naturalisation in Art 7 was also increased to ten years (in line with the new law in the South, and returning it to the period required in the 1957 law), and required to be 'lawful and continuous'.

[50] In similar circumstances, however, the Eritrea-Ethiopia Claims Commission, set up by the comprehensive peace agreement of December 2000 that ended the war between the two countries, found that individuals became dual national, even though Ethiopian law did not allow dual nationality: see ch 8.1.

[51] 'Sudan's split takes shape of exclusion as Khartoum fires southerners in private sector', *The Niles*, 7 July 2011; 'South-bound but stranded in Sudan', UNHCR, 16 January 2012; 'Sudan – South Sudan: Southerners running out of options', IRIN, 16 February 2012.

[52] 'Every citizen shall have the right to acquire or own property as regulated by law.' Interim National Constitution of Sudan, 2005, Art 43 (1).

[53] 'Camps to Evacuate Illegal Foreigners in Khartoum State', *Al Sudani*, 1 February 2012; Al-Sahafa, 23 February 2012.

[54] 'Status of Sudanese Nationals in the Republic of South Sudan', Press Release, Ministry of the Interior, Republic of South Sudan, 10 April 2012.

In the wake of the secession, Khartoum adopted a new civil registration law and biometric national identity card. In principle, this was a welcome step to improve birth registration and documentation of citizens. In practice, the process of application for the new ID cards appeared to be designed in part as a mechanism to deprive southerners in the north of their status there.[55] As early as January 2012, an Arabic language daily newspaper reported that the Khartoum North Court had sentenced a man and woman with a Sudanese father and South Sudanese mother who had sought to obtain identity cards to one month imprisonment and a fine for providing incorrect information regarding their nationality, on the grounds that they were no longer entitled to Sudanese documents since they had become South Sudanese.[56]

In September 2012, the two Presidents finally signed a long-awaited 'Framework Agreement on the Status of Nationals of the Other State and Related Matters'. The agreement, one of eight protocols to a general cooperation agreement between north and south, was modelled on a similar 2004 agreement between Sudan and Egypt known as the 'four freedoms' agreement and provided for nationals of each State to have freedom of residence, movement, economic activity, and ownership of property in either State. But the agreement did not address the determination of citizenship itself.[57] No further progress was made before the breakdown of the South Sudanese government in late 2013 put an end to all further negotiations between the two sides. More than 300,000 people of southern Sudanese origin who were long-term residents in Sudan were assessed by UNHCR to be at risk of statelessness; tens of thousands of those newly displaced from the fighting in the South came to join them, now as refugees rather than as internally displaced.[58]

The Khartoum government's denationalisation of those it considered southern Sudanese continued. The new national identity card was denied to many thousands of people completely assimilated in Sudan and considering themselves Sudanese, but descended from cross-border or southern ethnic groups. As of the end of 2014, there were almost 35,000 people still living in camps for presumed southern Sudanese in the greater Khartoum area; and even with the assistance of UNHCR, fewer than 450 had been able to obtain confirmation of South Sudanese nationality.[59] The Constitutional Court refused to strike down the 2011 amendments to the nationality law as unconstitutional, in cases brought before it concerning individuals with one Sudanese parent.[60] A complaint against Sudan

[55] Munzoul AM Assal, 'Struggles of Citizenship in Sudan' in Engin F Isin and Peter Nyers (eds), *Routledge Handbook of Global Citizenship Studies* (Routledge 2014).

[56] *Al Intibaha*, 4 January 2012.

[57] Framework Agreement on the Status of Nationals of the Other State and Related Matters between The Republic of the Sudan and The Republic of South Sudan, Addis Ababa, 27 September 2012.

[58] 2014 UNHCR Country Operations Profile – Sudan; 'Number of South Sudanese refugees in Sudan set to double', UNHCR, 24 July 2014.

[59] Draft report, *Nationality and Statelessness in Sudan following the Secession of South Sudan*, Human Rights Centre, University of Khartoum, 2016, on file with author.

[60] *Iman Hasan Benjamin v. Sudan Government, Sudan Constitutional Court*, Ref. 150/2012, Judgement of 3 July 2014; *Mazin Adil Ali Deng and others vs. Ministry of Interior and Ministry of Justice*,

was lodged before the African Committee of Experts on the Rights and Welfare of the Child in one of these cases.[61] Although, perhaps reflecting this attention, a 2017 decision did order the restoration of citizenship to a person with a mother of South Sudanese origin, the law itself remained unamended.[62]

Meanwhile, thanks to ongoing deep political disagreements between the negotiating parties, the Abyei Area Referendum Commission was never set up, despite further proposals from the Mbeki-chaired AUHIP on the final status of the territory and the criteria to determine who should be eligible to vote.[63] In October 2013, as the chance for a formally approved referendum retreated, Ngok Dinka leaders held a 'community referendum', in which the result was announced to be 99.9% in favour of union with South Sudan. The UN and the African Union expressed concern at 'unilateral actions'.[64] Both the governments of Sudan and South Sudan also condemned the vote, for their own reasons – largely to do with resolving ongoing disagreements over the flow of oil from the South through the territory of Sudan to the Red Sea.[65] Officials of the Republic of Sudan issued public statements to the effect that the Ngok Dinka of Abyei would continue to be treated as Sudanese citizens;[66] but the amendments to the Sudan Nationality Act did not explicitly protect the citizenship rights of the Ngok Dinka. SPLM leaders from Abyei, meanwhile, criticised as 'shameful' the idea that the Ngok Dinka might not be South Sudanese citizens.[67]

As in the case of the Ethiopia-Eritrea split, fundamental political differences between North and South meant that no framework agreement could be reached to provide an orderly system to sort those with a claim to both nationalities into groups with clear rights to documents from one or the other (or both). The extreme weakness of the inherited legal and administrative systems in South Sudan, and the

Sudan Constitutional Court, Judgement of 23 August 2016; see Nasredeen Abdulbari, 'Sudan: A Commentary on Mazin Adil Ali Deng and Others v. Ministry of Interior and Ministry of Justice' citizenshiprightsafrica.org, 16 November 2016.

[61] *African Centre of Justice and Peace Studies (ACJPS) and People's Legal Aid Centre (PLACE) v. Government of Sudan*, Communication 005/Com/001/2015.

[62] 'Sudanese nationality returned to South Sudanese by court order,' *Dabanga Sudan*, 11 July 2017.

[63] AU High Level Implementation Panel for Sudan (AUHIP), Proposal on the Final Status of the Abyei Area, 21 September 2012, paras 26-28: '26. The residents of the Abyei Area shall be eligible to vote in the Referendum. The residents of the Abyei Area are: a. members of the Ngok Dinka community; and, b. other Sudanese residing in the Abyei Area. 27. The criterion for qualifying under Paragraph 26(b) shall be permanent abode within the Abyei Area. 28. The Abyei Area Referendum Commission (AARC) shall compile the voters roll based on the criterion identified.' See also Interim Report of the African Union High-Level Implementation Panel on the Matters Detailed in the 24 April 2012 Communiqué of the Peace and Security Council, AU Peace and Security Council, PSC/PR/2(CCCXXXIX), 24 October 2012.

[64] 'Abyei: Security Council 'gravely concerned' about highly volatile situation' UN News Centre, 26 October 2013; AU Peace and Security Council Communique, PSC/PR/COMM.(CDIII), 26 October 2013.

[65] 'What they're saying about Abyei', IRIN, 1 November 2013.

[66] Hassan Berkia, 'Ngok Dinka citizenship falls through cracks of post-split Sudan', *The Niles*, 8 August 2011.

[67] Luka Biong Deng, 'Are Ngok Dinka of Abyei South Sudanese?' *Sudan Tribune*, 1 March 2013.

nature and ethnic organisation of the long-running civil war against the Sudanese government always meant that ethnic understandings of citizenship were likely to be dominant in the laws of the new State, and that legal rules were likely to be strongly influenced as well as subsumed by popular understandings of belonging. However, in Sudan itself the law continued to have important effects, and the newly ethnic understanding of the law had serious impacts on many tens of thousands of people. As in Zimbabwe, the government chose to manipulate the rules on dual nationality to achieve this result. It was through instrumentalisation of the law and its detailed application in the re-issue of national identity cards that it was able to exclude those with a possible loyalty to the breakaway State.

8.3. The Bakassi Peninsula

State succession need not result in the creation of a new State, but also occurs with transfer of territory between two existing States. The challenges related to nationality can be equally acute; yet they are largely ignored in the court decisions and agreements resolving such border disputes.

The resource-rich Bakassi peninsula lies on the boundary between what are now Nigeria and Cameroon, but was previously the British Protectorate of Southern Nigeria and what was first German Kamerun and subsequently known as the Southern Cameroons, mandated to Britain by the League of Nations after the First World War. The precise delimitation of the boundary in the peninsula zone had not been important, since the mandated territory was administered from Nigeria. At independence, the Southern Cameroons voted in a referendum to join Cameroon, the former French-mandated part of German Kamerun, while the Northern Cameroons voted to join Nigeria. While the Bakassi peninsula continued to be administered from Nigeria (and is listed as one of 774 local government areas in the 1999 Constitution), Cameroon contested ownership, and by the early 1990s the dispute had escalated into confrontations between the military forces of the two States.

In 1994, Cameroon referred the dispute over the Bakassi peninsula, as well as territory further north towards Lake Chad on the border with the former Northern Cameroons, to the International Court of Justice. The ICJ issued its final judgment in the case in 2002, and granted sovereignty over the peninsula and other territory to Cameroon.[68] In accordance with established international law, the court case did not consider the wishes of the people living in the territory affected (who had largely considered themselves Nigerians), but rather the historical exercise

[68] *Land and Maritime Boundary between Cameroon and Nigeria (Cameroon v Nigeria: Equatorial Guinea intervening)*, ICJ Judgement of 10 October 2002. For a detailed history of the dispute, the court case and its aftermath, see Hilary V Lukong, *The Cameroon-Nigeria Border Dispute: Management and Resolution, 1981–2011* (Langaa Research & Publishing Common Initiative Group 2011).

of sovereignty over the territory.[69] Nor did the Court rule on the nationality of those living in the transferred territory; in accordance with international norms which base nationality in case of succession of States on habitual residence, it was presumed that Bakassi residents would become Cameroonian.[70] The number of people affected was also disputed between Cameroon and Nigeria, but was alleged by Nigeria to be more than 150,000 people.[71]

Nigeria rejected the judgment, stating that 'For Nigeria, it is not a matter of oil or natural resources on land or in coastal waters, it is a matter of the welfare and well-being of her people on their land.'[72] UN Secretary General Kofi Annan facilitated the establishment of a Cameroon-Nigeria Mixed Commission to negotiate implementation of the judgment. In 2006, a bilateral agreement was reached at Greentree, New York, between the two countries, by which Cameroon guaranteed fundamental rights and freedoms to Nigerian nationals living in the peninsula; and in particular promised not to force Nigerian nationals living in the Bakassi Peninsula to leave the zone nor to change their nationality.[73] The territory was formally handed over to Cameroon on 14 August 2008, though a Nigerian presence remained during a five-year transitional period. The understanding was that at the end of the transitional period, Bakassi residents could become Cameroonian with the right to Cameroonian identity documents; but could also remain Nigerian with resident alien status in Cameroon, or leave Bakassi and resettle in Nigeria.[74] But the legal authority to enable these outcomes on either side of the border was left unclear; and neither the ICJ judgment nor the

[69] 'The Court finds that the evidence before it indicates that the small population of Bakassi already present in the early 1960s grew with the influx from Nigeria in 1968 as a result of the civil war in that country. Gradually sizeable centres of population were established. The Parties are in disagreement as to the total number of Nigerian nationals living in the peninsula today, but it is clear that it has grown considerably from the modest numbers reported in the 1953 and 1963 population censuses. Nor is there any reason to doubt the Efik and Effiat toponomy of the settlements, or their relationships with Nigeria. But these facts of themselves do not establish Nigerian title over Bakassi territory; nor can they serve as an element in a claim for historical consolidation of title, for reasons already given by the Court.' Ibid. para 221.

[70] ILC, *Articles on Nationality of Natural Persons in relation to the Succession of States*, art 5.

[71] Statement of Mrs. Nella Andem-Ewa, Attorney-General of Cross River State, to the ICJ, 28 February 2002.

[72] Statement of the Federal Government of Nigeria on the Judgement of the International Court of Justice at The Hague (Cameroon v Nigeria, Equatorial Guinea intervening), 23 October 2002.

[73] Article 3(2) states that 'Cameroon shall: a) Not force Nigerian nationals living in the Bakassi Peninsula to leave the zone or to change their nationality …'. See also, Alain Didier Olinga, *L'accord de Greentree du 12 juin 2006 relatif à la presqu'île de Bakassi* (Harmattan 2009); Kevin Ngang, 'Understanding the Bakassi Conflict: A Showcase of Conflict Prevention in Practice' (European University Centre for Peace Studies (EPU) 2007) 04/07. There was no similar agreement in relation to the populations living in the disputed border area towards Lake Chad whose territory was allocated to Cameroon; similar problems may exist in relation to the recognition of the nationality of those living there, but there has been much less attention drawn to them (even before the current insecurity in the region).

[74] 'Bakassi – more than one place, more than one problem', IRIN, 13 November 2007; *Le temps des realisations*: *Bulletin mensuel bilingue d'informations No.14*, Special Edition on Bakassi, Government of Cameroon, August/September 2013.

Greentree Agreement made any provision to ensure the resolution and ongoing monitoring of these issues.

Within Cameroon, at the end of the transitional period on 14 August 2013, Nigerians had to apply either for a residence permit or for Cameroonian citizenship if they wished to remain.[75] Without special dispensation, Bakassi residents would first require a Nigerian passport to acquire residence permits as aliens.[76] In addition, under the Cameroonian system, a birth certificate would be required to obtain any official papers of this type, which very few Bakassi residents hold. While the Cameroonian government gave assurances to the ICJ that the Bakassi residents would be made as welcome as other Nigerians in Cameroon,[77] the situation of those who were living where they had always lived was significantly different from those who had moved to Cameroon for other purposes.[78] Without national identity documents, Bakassi residents faced difficulties with freedom of movement inside Cameroon, especially given that there were ongoing security concerns over the territory. They were taxed and otherwise treated as foreigners by the Cameroonian authorities.[79]

Meanwhile, several thousands of Bakassi residents relocated to the other side of the Nigerian border. The Cross Rivers government purported to carve out a new local government area for the Bakassi displaced – though it had no constitutional authority to do so – and granted or facilitated some humanitarian assistance.[80] UNHCR took steps to rent land for those displaced to occupy, but their conditions remained very poor.[81]

At the federal level, no agency took charge of resolving the situation of the displaced Bakassi, and there was no effort to adopt the legal and procedural

[75] 'Le Cameroun retrouve la plénitude de sa souveraineté sur la presqu'île de Bakassi », Présidence de la République du Cameroun, 14 August 2013; 'Bakassi residents to pay tax under Cameroon sovereignty', BBC News, 15 August 2013; 'Press statement on Bakassi Peninsula Developments', SC/11094 AFR/2680, UN Security Council, 15 August 2013.

[76] There is an argument that Bakassi residents could be considered as being in *possession d'état d'originaires de Cameroun occidental*. Article 45 of the 1968 Cameroon nationality code provides that a person will be considered as holding this status if one of his or her parents was born in Western Cameroon (ie former Southern Cameroons), even if the person him or herself was not born there. Since the ICJ has held that Bakassi was in fact in Western Cameroon, the nationality would change with the transfer of territory; reinforcing the usual presumption in relation to nationality and succession of States. The Greentree Agreement, however, contradicts this presumption, which is only a presumption and not a binding rule.

[77] *Cameroon v. Nigeria*, ICJ Judgement of 10 October 2002, para 317.

[78] See generally, Fongot Kini-Yen Kinni, *Bakassi or the Politics of Exclusion and Occupation?* (Langaa Research & Publishing Common Initiative Group 2013).

[79] 'We're now Stateless, Bakassi Indigenes cry out', *Vanguard* (Abuja), 10 June 2017; '97 Nigerians Feared Killed in Bakassi By Gendarmes', *Guardian* (Abuja), 7 July 2017.

[80] The National Commission for Refugees, Migrants and Internally Displaced Persons was reported by the Cross River State government to have distributed relief supplies to more than 1,500 households in two local government areas in the State. 'Bakassi, Akpabuyo Refugees Get Relief from Refugees Commission' Cross Rivers State government, 29 July 2013.

[81] Lanre Arotimi, 'The Many Plights of Bakassi Returnees', *Leadership*, 26 April 2015; 'Bakassi returnees ask for permanent resettlement', *Premium Times*, 28 June 2015.

provisions to document their Nigerian citizenship.[82] They were denied the right to vote in various elections, since the locations where they were registered no longer exist; there was litigation by the Independent National Electoral Commission on this point.[83] In February 2014, Nigerian Attorney General of the Federation and Minister of Justice Mohammed Adoke, speaking at the opening of the 32nd Session of the Mixed Commission, stated that those affected by the judgment who wished to be Nigerian should simply 'apply for Nigerian citizenship' implying that they needed to naturalise, rather than obtain recognition of ongoing nationality from birth.[84]

In the case of the Bakassi peninsula it seems that there was a complete lack of serious attention to the means of resolving the nationality status of those living there, not only from the ICJ, but also the UN and others mediating the resolution to the stand-off between Nigeria and Cameroon. No substantive point of disagreement was reported preventing the establishment of procedures to create an effective way for confirmation of continuing Nigerian nationality or acquisition of Cameroonian nationality. Instead, the Greentree Agreement was satisfied with broad statements of principle with no mechanism for their implementation or attention to the best solutions for those affected.

8.4. The Tebu and the 'Aouzou strip' between Chad and Libya

The Tebu (also Tubu or Tabu and other spellings in English) are an ethnic group (or a collection of related smaller groups) speaking a language of the diverse Nilo-Saharan language family and following a semi-nomadic lifestyle in what is now southern Libya, northern Chad and northeastern Niger. They were known for their resistance to French colonial encroachments. Following the independence of all the countries concerned, they also played a sometimes controversial role in the politics of the region, as Tebu politician Goukouni Oueddei became president

[82] The nationality status of Bakassi residents was complicated by their status as former residents of what had now been decided was part of the Southern Cameroons: special provisions on the nationality of the residents of the Northern Cameroons were introduced into the Federal Constitution of 1960 by the Nigeria Constitution First Amendment Act of 1961, following the referendum which led to the Northern Cameroons becoming part of Nigeria. There would in principle be the need for an explicit constitutional amendment to provide similarly for the Nigerian nationality of residents of the Southern Cameroons – that is, natives of Bakassi – who moved to Nigeria. See annotated text of the legislation in Arthur VJ Nylander, *The Nationality and Citizenship Laws of Nigeria* (University of Lagos 1973).

[83] Chidi Anselm Odinkalu, 'Stateless in Bakassi: How a Changed Border Left Inhabitants Adrift' Open Society Foundations, 2 April 2012, available at www.opensocietyfoundations.org/voices/stateless-bakassi-how-changed-border-left-inhabitants-adrift; Jude Okwe, 'INEC – Bakassi May Not Participate in 2015 Elections', *This Day* (Abuja), 4 April 2014; interview with Chidi Anselm Odinkalu, chair Nigerian National Human Rights Commission, July 2014.

[84] Dele Ogbodo, 'Greentree Agreement: FG Advises Bakassi Indigenes to Apply for Nigerian Citizenship', *This Day*, 3 February 2014

of Chad between 1979 and 1982, with Libyan backing against the French-backed Hissène Habré (also a Tebu, from another branch).[85]

During the 1970s, Libya under Colonel Gaddafi invaded what became known as the 'Aouzou Strip', a uranium-rich region contested between Chad and Libya. Libya registered the inhabitants of the strip as its nationals and issued them with documents; many Tebu who were resident in other parts of Libya and had previously held documents issued by other local administrative authorities came to hold papers issued from Aouzou.[86] After President Oueddei was overthrown by Habré in a 1982 coup, there were several years of conflict over the Aouzou strip, ended on 31 August 1989 with the signature in Algiers of a framework agreement (*accord-cadre*) on the peaceful settlement of the dispute. But without a definitive outcome, the two countries jointly referred the dispute to the ICJ in September 1990. In its 1994 judgment, the ICJ awarded the territory to Chad, on the basis of a 'Treaty of Friendship and Good Neighbourliness' concluded by the French Republic and the Kingdom of Libya in 1955. After further talks, an agreement was signed on 4 April 1994 establishing the practical modalities for the implementation of the judgment.[87]

Despite Gaddafi's support for the Tebu in Chad, Arabisation policies in Libya meant that they were also not accepted by his government as fully Libyan, and after the handover of the Aouzou strip to Chad they were further ostracised. In 1996, a decree declared that 'Those who carry the ID of that area [Aouzou] are considered as foreigners and all come under the jurisdiction of the law relating to foreigners'.[88] Around 7,000 people were affected; some among them were also imprisoned.[89] In December 2007, the Libyan government issued a directive that the Tebu were not Libyans but Chadians. Local authorities barred Tebu from access to ration books, education and health care services, and refused to renew or extend passports and identity cards to members of this minority, or to register births of Tebu children. In November 2008, up to 33 people died in Kufra, during five days of fighting between the official security forces and the Tebu, and the local government continued to evict Tebu people from their residential areas.[90] In his final months in power Gaddafi reportedly annulled the 1996 decree, and recognised holders of documents issued from Aouzou as nationals once again.[91] After the fall

[85] For historical context, see Jérôme Tubiana and Claudio Gramizzi, 'Tubu Trouble: State and Statelessness in the Chad–Sudan–Libya Triangle' (Small Arms Survey 2017).

[86] Laura van Waas, 'The Stateless Tebu of Libya?' (Tilburg Law School 2013).

[87] *Territorial Dispute (Libyan Arab Jamahiriya/Chad)*, ICJ Judgment of 3 February 1994. See also information on the United Nations Aouzou Strip Observer Group, available at www.un.org/en/peacekeeping/missions/past/unasog.htm.

[88] Decree No.13(1485), cited in van Waas (n 86) 6–7.

[89] Tubiana and Gramizzi (n 85) 104.

[90] *Summary prepared by the Office of the High Commissioner for Human Rights in accordance with paragraph 15 (c) of the annex to Human rights Council resolution 5/1: Libyan Arab Jamahiriya*, A/HRC/WG.6/9/LBY/3, 15 July 2010 (summary of submissions from nine organisations, including the Society for Threatened Peoples, for Libya's Universal Periodic Review).

[91] van Waas (n 86) 8.

of the Libyan regime, the Tebu were seen as pro-Gaddafi foreigners.[92] In 2012, the Carter Center reported that the district court in Kufra had removed 1,085 names from the voters' list on the basis that they were inhabitants of the Aouzou area, and thus not Libyan nationals[93]; while 'in Murzuq, an area said to be currently controlled by the minority Tubu community, a large percentage of the population do not have documents.'[94] The transitional Libyan government of Prime Minster Zeidan in place from 2012 to 2014 began implementing a new national identification scheme; in August 2013 the body managing the process announced that it had cancelled one million 'fake' IDs including those held by alleged Chadian Tuareg and Tebu. In October, Tebu and Tuareg protesters blockaded oil fields to demand the regularisation of their citizenship status. The Geneva-based Small Arms Survey noted that 'In the absence of a clear approach to the citizenship issue, this process risks stripping substantial numbers of people of their rights.'[95]

Although the situation of the Tebu community in Libya was not directly caused by the decision of the ICJ on the Aouzou strip – other non-Arab minorities in Libya faced not dissimilar discrimination – it exemplifies the lack of certainty that remains for many ethnic groups found in remote border areas that were never clearly delineated during the colonial period, nor provided for at the time when sovereignty was transferred, and whose nationality status is not considered when territory changes hands. The Libyan authorities, having issued the Tebu with documents from the Aouzou administrative zone, then failed to recognise the holders as Libyan once the zone was handed to Chad, even if they had their main residence elsewhere in Libya. In the context of the breakdown of central authority in Libya, the disputed status of the Tebu and other minorities as Libyan nationals is one of many threats to national and regional security, as they claim their own right to participate in determining the future of the State.

8.5. Other ICJ Rulings in Border Disputes

The Bakassi Peninsula case, and to a lesser extent the ruling on the Aouzou strip, illustrate the curious lack of interest of international law in the views or best interests of the people living in a disputed territory when it comes to deciding on sovereignty. According to its statute, the Court applies the following sources of law, more or less in order of precedence: international conventions, international

[92] International Crisis Group, 'Popular Protest in North Africa and the Middle East (V): Making Sense of Libya' (2011); Jamestown Foundation, 'Arab-Tubu Clashes in Southern Libya's Sabha Oasis' (2012) 10 Terrorism Monitor; Asylum Research Consultancy, 'Libya Country Report, Commissioned by the Office of the United Nations High Commissioner for Refugees (UNHCR), Division of International Protection' (UNHCR 2013).

[93] 'Carter Center Congratulates Libyans for Holding Historic Elections', 9 July 2012.

[94] 'Libyan minority rights at a crossroads', IRIN, 24 May 2012.

[95] Wolfram Lacher, 'Libya's Fractious South and Regional Instability' (Small Arms Survey 2014).

custom, 'the general principles of law recognized by civilized nations', and finally and subsidiarily, 'judicial decisions and the teachings of the most highly qualified publicists of the various nations'. If agreed by the parties, the Court may also decide a case under general principles of equity.[96]

Claims to territory at the court have been based on grounds categorised by scholars in various ways, starting from effective control of the land in question, but including historical and cultural links, as well as natural lines of geography.[97] In its jurisprudence, the Court has developed its interpretation of the applicable sources of law to these claims. In disputes over post-colonial boundaries in Africa and elsewhere it has favoured the principle of *uti possidetis*, the doctrine that, absent separate agreement, territory remains with the possessor; and thus that the independent States must respect the boundaries set by the former colonial powers. Effective control over the territory is a subsidiary criterion, and other links, including language or economic patterns, are even less significant. The result has been an often futile effort to seek the precise delimitations of colonial boundaries – when in reality these were never precisely established. But in addition, the decisions have tended to disregard not only the wishes of the people living in the territory at issue in relation to sovereignty over the land, but also the need for any ruling or monitoring mechanism related to the recognition of their future nationality and other rights, wherever sovereignty is decided to lie.

In some of its more recent judgments in Africa, the Court has expressed some disquiet over this outcome; but it has taken no concrete steps to address the problems arising.

In a judgment from 1986 adjudicating a frontier dispute between Burkina Faso and Mali, the ICJ noted the difficulty of 'ascertain[ing] where the frontier lay in 1932 in a region of Africa little known at the time and largely inhabited by nomads, in which transport and communications were very sketchy.'[98] While affirming the principle of *uti possedetis*, the Court noted that:

> At first sight this principle conflicts outright with another one, the right of peoples to self-determination. In fact, however, the maintenance of the territorial status quo in Africa is often seen as the wisest course, to preserve what has been achieved by peoples who have struggled for their independence and to avoid a disruption which would deprive the continent of the gains achieved by much sacrifice.[99]

The Court emphasised the 1964 decision of the OAU to respect colonial borders, and focused on the delimitation and exercise of administrative power during the colonial period (and the dissolution in 1932 and reconstitution in 1947 of the French colony of Upper Volta), without considering any evidence related to the

[96] Statute of the International Court of Justice, 26 June 1945, Art 38.

[97] Andrew F Burghardt, 'The Bases of Territorial Claims' (1973) 63 Geographical Review 225; Brian Sumner, 'Territorial Disputes at the International Court of Justice' (2004) 53 Duke Law Journal 1779. Sumner considers several of the ICJ cases noted here.

[98] *Frontier Dispute (Burkina Faso/Mali)*, ICJ Judgment of 22 December 1986, paragraph 64.

[99] Ibid., paragraph 25.

wishes of those living in the territory affected. Their nationality was presumed to be allocated with the territory itself.

In southern Africa, the ICJ has ruled on a dispute between Namibia and Botswana on the ownership of an island in the Chobe river forming the boundary between the two States along the southern border of the Caprivi Strip – itself one of the more ludicrous examples of colonial-era border determination.[100] Although there was acknowledgement that the territory was occupied by members of the Masubia ethnic group originating from the Namibian side of the border, this aspect was, according to the usual precedents, found by the majority to be irrelevant to the ultimate decision to award the island to Botswana.[101]

The consequences of the lack of attention paid to the population affected (whatever way the decision on territory goes) can be seen in the dispute between Benin and Niger over ownership of 25 islands along a 150km stretch of the River Niger where it forms the border between the two countries. The largest island, Lété, is 'fertile, with rich pastures, and is permanently inhabited; according to information supplied by Niger, its population numbered some 2,000 in the year 2000'.[102] The islands had been disputed between the two countries from the early days of independence, a conflict that provided the spark leading to the expulsion of some 16,000 Dahomeyans (Beninois) from Niger in late 1963 and early 1964.[103] The two countries jointly referred the dispute to the Court in 2002. In its 2005 decision the ICJ awarded Niger sovereignty over 16 of the islands, including Lété, the remainder going to Benin. The judgment contained no commentary or ruling on the nationality status of the populations currently living in or using the resources of the islands.[104]

The two groups affected by the decision were, first, the Fulani nomads who had traditionally moved from one country to the other with their livestock, many of whom had no nationality documentation from either of the countries (but who had paid taxes to both); and, secondly, the fishermen and agriculturalists who lived on the islands for some or all of the year. One of the islands allocated to Benin, the *Ile aux oiseaux*, is occupied temporarily during the dry season – but the inhabitants relocate to one side of the river or the other (Niger or Benin) when the island is flooded. The semi-nomadic nature of the populations makes their documentation difficult since they have no settled residence; many have no identity papers, and no access to public services. A community that had moved to Benin when Lété island (allocated to Niger) was flooded in 2012, were accommodated in a village in Karimama commune – tellingly named

[100] *Case concerning Kasikili/Sedudu Island (Botswana/Namibia)*, ICJ Judgment of 13 December 1999.

[101] Three minority judgments disagreed; but not on the basis of the wishes of the people using the island.

[102] *Frontier Dispute (Benin/Niger)*, ICJ Judgment of 12 July 2005, paragraph 19.

[103] Suzanne Bonzon, 'Les Dahoméens En Afrique de l'Ouest' (1967) 17 Revue française de science politique 718.

[104] See also, 'Benin-Niger: International Court rules that main disputed island belongs to Niger not Benin', IRIN, 12 July 2005.

Sabon Gari ('strangers' quarter') – but Beninois nationality had not been offered or confirmed; and a large percentage also had no birth registration. One of them commented: 'Because no country recognises us, we live as if we were in prison'; without documents they are subjected to extortion from the security forces of both countries.[105]

In another dispute affecting two former territories of French West Africa, Burkina Faso and Niger referred disputes over their border to the ICJ in 2010, after several decades of failed attempts to finalise the line between their two States. In 2013, the Court handed down its decision, showing a new concern over the people affected by the decision, at least at the level of rhetoric. The judgment expressed the wish that 'each Party, in exercising its authority over the portion of the territory under its sovereignty, should have due regard to the needs of the populations concerned, in particular those of the nomadic or semi-nomadic populations, and to the necessity to overcome difficulties that may arise for them because of the frontier.'[106] In a separate opinion, Judge Cançado Trindade welcomed the common concern expressed by Burkina Faso and Niger for the local populations (on both sides of their border and constantly moving across it), extending his focus from the territory alone to its inhabitants.[107] But there was no specific ruling or expression of views on the nationality of those affected by the judgment; it being presumed that nationality would transfer with the transfer of territory. There has been no further bilateral agreement or national action to confirm the nationality of those affected.

Other border disputes rumble on across Africa on without referral to the ICJ and without resolution of the status of those living in the affected territory. The consequences can be severe for those affected.

[105] Information and interview from UNHCR mission to the region, May 2014.
[106] *Frontier Dispute (Burkina Faso/Niger)*, ICJ Judgment of 16 April 2013, paragraph 112.
[107] *Frontier Dispute (Burkina Faso/Niger)*, Opinion of Judge Cançado Trindade.

9

Access to Citizenship for Refugees

The influx and long-term presence of large populations of refugees creates particular challenges for the politics of access to nationality. Although not as significant for the citizenship crises described in Chapter 7 as the presence of substantial numbers of descendants of pre-independence migrants, a major inflow of refugees after independence was among the factors complicating or exacerbating several of these cases, especially in Kenya, Uganda, and Congo.

Two main areas of study arise: first, the influence of refugee inflows on nationality regimes in the country of refuge generally, including the rules both for naturalisation and for acquisition of nationality based on birth in the territory; and secondly, the impact of refugees' access to nationality in the country of refuge on their broader integration and participation in society. Not for nothing did the plight of refugees lead Hannah Arendt to articulate citizenship as the right to have rights.

The official international law position is that naturalisation of refugees should be facilitated,[1] although the African refugee convention, notably, did not endorse the same principle.[2] On paper, African nationality laws usually permit refugees to naturalise. In practice, naturalisation is often out of reach. Some countries even specifically exclude periods of residence as a refugee from the qualifying period of residence for acquisition of citizenship: in Uganda, for example, this was a deliberate choice aimed at preventing refugees from acquiring citizenship (see Chapter 7.3). However, these amendments are rare; perhaps because in all countries naturalisation is generally difficult to obtain, not only for refugees (Chapter 5.4). The high fees applicable and discretionary decision-making have, it seems, been sufficient to assuage political anxieties about access to citizenship for large numbers of new arrivals.

In relation to the rules on acquisition by children, the impact of refugee inflows on national attitudes to foreigners appears to have been the underlying reason behind some amendments to restrict attribution of citizenship based on birth in the territory. For example, the removal of *jus soli* rules in Botswana may have been influenced by the inflows of Angolan refugees (see Chapter 5.1.1). Amendments to South Africa's Citizenship Act in 2010 reflect similar concerns, though retaining

[1] Convention relating to the Status of Refugees, 1951, Art 54.
[2] Convention Governing the Specific Aspects of Refugee Problems in Africa, 1969.

the principle of eventual access to citizenship for children born in the country; as do the adoption and interpretation of Tanzania's 1995 citizenship law (see below). These connections would merit further research.[3]

This chapter, however, concentrates on the impact of access to nationality, or the lack of it, on refugees themselves and their descendants; especially where formal refugee status has been ended on the grounds that it is now safe for those who fled to return. The nationality status of refugees themselves is always ambiguous, caught as they are between a notional nationality and a temporary protection status. For the children of refugees born in exile, the notional nationality of origin is often quite meaningless.[4]

The two best-known populations of stateless refugees in Africa are in North Africa: the Palestinians, among whom the largest group is in Egypt; and the Sahrawis, mainly in Algeria. Their situation is not really paralleled elsewhere in the continent, tied as it is to high-level political questions around the potential existence of a Palestinian or Sahrawi State. Yet their stark experience of statelessness certainly does illustrate similar impacts on other long-term refugees.

Palestinian refugees are excluded from the possibility of obtaining citizenship in most Middle Eastern and North African countries. A 1959 decision of the Arab League, enshrined in the 1963 Casablanca Protocol for the treatment of Palestinians in Arab States, established the principle that the Palestinian diaspora should not be given citizenship in other Arab countries, as a way of preserving their identity and political cause.[5] Around 70,000 Palestinian refugees live in Egypt. Unlike other refugees, they are to some extent integrated into Egyptian society and have preferential treatment with regards to accessing work; and with a reform to remove gender discrimination (see Chapter 5.2), children of mixed marriages are now recognised as Egyptian.[6] Most, however, retain their long-term non-citizen status, at the margins of society, obliged to renew their papers every six months.

Like the Palestinians, Western Saharan refugees in Algeria are trapped in a citizenship black hole, thanks to a failure to resolve the fundamental questions of State existence that first led to their flight; though unlike the Palestinians they do at least have the possibility in principle of returning to Western Sahara. Since the end

[3] For a preliminary effort to correlate refugee flows with popular attitudes to acquisition of citizenship in Africa, see Yang-Yang Zhou, 'How Refugees Affect Conceptions of Citizenship in Africa' (Social Science Research Network 2017) SSRN Scholarly Paper ID 2454409 https://papers.ssrn.com/abstract=2454409.

[4] Gábor Gyulai, 'The Long-Overlooked Mystery of Refugee Children's Natioanilty', *The World's Stateless: Children* (Institute on Statelessness and Inclusion 2017).

[5] League of Arab States Decree, No.1547 of 1959; Protocol for the Treatment of Palestinians in Arab States (Casablanca Protocol), League of Arab States, 11 September 1965.

[6] See generally: Oroub El-Abed, 'The Palestinians in Egypt: An Investigation of Livelihoods and Coping Strategies' (Forced Migration Refugee Studies Program, The American University in Cairo 2003); Oroub El-Abed, 'The Forgotten Palestinians: How Palestinian Refugees Survive in Egypt' (2004) 20 Forced Migration Review 29; Oroub El-Abed, 'Palestinian Refugees of Egypt: What Exit Options Are Left for Them?' (2005) 22 Refuge 15.

of Spanish colonial control in 1976, the status of Western Sahara has been disputed between the Kingdom of Morocco and the Polisario Front[7] independence movement, which proclaimed the existence of the Sahrawi Arab Democratic Republic (SADR) the day after Spain's withdrawal. While this dispute has remained unresolved, with Morocco in occupation of the territory, more than 150,000 Western Saharans, known as Sahrawis, have lived as refugees in camps in southern Algeria, near Tindouf.[8] The Algerian government issues short-term passports for travel to those who apply through the SADR bureaucracy in the camps – for reasons of medical treatment, family unification, and so on – to countries that do not recognise the SADR. But these are only travel documents and do not imply recognition of the refugees as Algerian citizens.[9] Their socio-economic status is bleak.

For the Palestinians and Sahrawis, the regularisation of their citizenship status goes way beyond any question of reforms to the rules and procedures established in nationality laws, requiring rather a political resolution to the reasons for their exile – or an abandonment of their cause. Their statelessness is fundamentally tied to the demand for a specific State. In other cases, in sub-Saharan Africa, however, where long-term refugees are now effectively settled in the country of refuge, there is somewhat more scope to make changes that could materially improve both their legal status and therefore also their social and political situation.

In most African countries, where UNHCR plays a major role in administering refugee camps and assistance, registered refugees often receive both a UN document and a document issued by a national refugee agency recognising their refugee status. For those refugees who return home within a few years such documentation is usually sufficient to provide them both with a legal status in their country of refuge, and with proof of nationality on return. For those who remain long term in the country of refuge, such documents may ensure only limited freedom of movement and ability to integrate into society or contribute to the economy – but they do at least (usually) provide the most basic protections against detention and deportation.

There is much research highlighting the complex nature of feelings of belonging and the possibilities of local integration for refugees, and the relevance (or not) of official paperwork for these trajectories.[10] In Tanzania, for example,

[7] The Frente Popular para la Liberación de Saguia el-Hamra y de Río de Oro (Frente POLISARIO), named after the two former Spanish provinces making up the territory.

[8] Tony Hodges, *Western Sahara: The Roots of a Desert War* (L Hill 1983); Pablo San Martin, 'Nationalism, Identity and Citizenship in the Western Sahara' (2005) 10 Journal of North African Studies 565; Human Rights Watch, 'Human Rights in Western Sahara and in the Tindouf Refugee Camps' (2008).

[9] In 2007, the Spanish Supreme Court ruled in favour of a Sahrawi refugee who had applied to be recognised as stateless by the Spanish authorities, even though she had travelled to Spain on an Algerian passport granted to enable her to seek medical treatment seven years earlier. Case of Ms. Khadijatou Bourkari Dafa, Recurso Casacion Num: 10503/2003.

[10] For a summary of a series of related reports on the issue, see International Refugee Rights Initiative, 'The Role of Citizenship in Addressing Refugee Crises in Africa's Great Lakes Region' (2014); also Lucy Hovil, *Refugees, Conflict and the Search for Belonging* (Springer 2016).

Liisa Malkki highlighted the difference between those Burundian refugees living in refugee camps, or settlements that had previously been camps, who remained relatively isolated from the rest of Tanzanian society, perceived by themselves and others as 'refugees'; and those who had moved to nearby towns, who effectively dissolved into the local population, resolving problems of documentation in various ways.[11] Among Angolan refugees in Zambia, those settled in rural areas became largely indistinguishable from the local populations whose language they shared, and many acquired national identity cards enabling them to function in Zambian society; questions of formal citizenship were of more interest to officials than they were to the people concerned.[12] Nevertheless, some refugees may desire to retain the principal identity and nationality of their country of origin, even over the very long term; though this is less likely to be true of their children.[13]

The details of legal status and access to citizenship can nonetheless be critical for any individual, especially for those whose status as refugee or citizen is contested. In Kenya, for example, the citizenship status of Somali Kenyans has been constantly under question, dating back even before the arrival of several hundred thousand Somali refugees in the 1990s (see Chapter 7.3.1). The details of legal status and access to citizenship become immediately more important from the moment that refugee status is no longer recognised, and the protection and permissions provided by that status removed. In recent years, increasing requirements for identification for both nationals and refugees have also raised the stakes on access to documentation confirming legal presence in the country. It is now harder, for example, for refugees who have crossed an international border but remain within communities speaking the same language to merge into those communities.

UNHCR estimated in 2004 that there were approximately 2.3 million people living in sub-Saharan Africa in a protracted refugee situation, a term applied to those who have been in exile for more than five years.[14] Under pressure both from donor governments to UNHCR and from some of the countries of origin of the refugees, this study was the basis for efforts to resolve some of these protracted situations by invoking the 'ceased circumstances clause' from the 1951 Refugee Convention. If the situation in the country of origin has changed sufficiently to make return possible, there is a process for a statement to be made by UNHCR

[11] Liisa H Malkki, *Purity and Exile: Violence, Memory, and National Cosmology among Hutu Refugees in Tanzania* (University of Chicago Press 1995).

[12] Oliver Bakewell, 'Repatriation and Self-Settled Refugees in Zambia: Bringing Solutions to the Wrong Problems' (2000) 13 Journal of Refugee Studies 356.

[13] Jennifer Byrne, 'Should I Stay or Should I Go? National Identity and Attitudes Towards Local Integration Among Liberian Refugees in Ghana' (2013) 32 Refugee Survey Quarterly 50.

[14] Protracted Refugee Situations, Executive Committee of the High Commissioner's Programme, EC/54/SC/CRP.14, 10 June 2004; See also, Conclusion on Protracted Refugee Situations, No. 109 (LXI) – 2009, EXCOM Conclusions; Alexandra Fielden, 'Local Integration: An Under-reported Solution to Protracted Refugee Situations' (UNHCR 2008) Research Paper 158; Jeff Crisp, 'No Solutions in Sight: The Problem of Protracted Refugee Situations in Africa' (2003) 22 Refugee Survey Quarterly 114.

that, as a group, refugees from that country no longer have a well-founded fear of being persecuted (though individuals may rebut the presumption).[15]

The ceased circumstances clause has been invoked four times in Africa, relating to the situations in Sierra Leone (at the end of 2008), Angola and Liberia (in 2012) and Rwanda (in 2013). It is for each host country to decide whether to apply this decision. Once this happens, the refugees then in principle have the same status (and requirements to regularise their status) as any other foreigner. UNHCR typically enters into agreements with the countries of refuge and origin on measures for the voluntary repatriation or local integration of the former refugees; or for individual exemption from the ceased circumstances clause on the grounds of a need for continued international protection. Resettlement in a third country is highly unlikely to be available at the moment the ceased circumstances clause is invoked.

Local integration, based on the grant of a new status enabling a person to remain in the country of current residence, often depends on confirmation of nationality from the country to which it is now deemed safe to return. This has been particularly problematic in the case of former Rwandan refugees, for whom the invocation of the ceased circumstances clause was highly controversial; many who failed in a claim for further protection remained reluctant to approach their consular authorities.[16]

In other cases, returnees to a country that they have left decades before, or even those internally displaced who never crossed an international border, may equally struggle to re-establish recognition of citizenship in their country of origin. This has been the case for some returning Angolan refugees;[17] and also for those feeling ethno-religious political violence in the Central African Republic.[18]

The three case studies below highlight the situation of long-term refugees or former refugees in three very different contexts, the differing State response to those situations, and the influence and relevance of formal legal procedures for the refugees affected.

[15] 'The Cessation Clauses: Guidelines on their Application', UNHCR, Geneva, April 1999.

[16] 'Implementation of the Comprehensive Strategy for the Rwandan Refugee Situation, including UNHCR's recommendations on the Applicability of the 'ceased circumstances' Cessation Clauses', UNHCR, 31 December 2011; *Rwanda: Cessation of Refugee Status is Unwarranted: Memorandum of Fact and Law*, FAHAMU, 22 September 2011; Barbara Harrell-Bond and Guillaume Cliche-Rivard, 'Rwandan refugees face no choice but repatriation', OpenDemocracy.Net. 10 May 2012; 'No consensus on implementation of cessation clause for Rwandan refugees' IRIN, 12 July 2013. See also, Lindsey N Kingston, 'Bringing Rwandan Refugees "Home": The Cessation Clause, Statelessness, and Forced Repatriation' (2017) 29 International Journal of Refugee Law 417.

[17] Jeff Crisp, José Riera and Raquel Freitas, 'Evaluation of UNHCR's Returnee Reintegration Programme in Angola' (UNHCR 2008); Jean-Michel Mabeko-Tali, '« Congolenses », « Congoleses », « Zairenses » : L'immigration centr-africaine et la problématique identitaire angolaise' in Catherine Coquery-Vidrovitch and others (eds), *Etre étranger et migrant en Afrique au XXe siècle: enjeux identitaires et modes d'insertion*, vol 1 (Harmattan 2003); Human Rights Watch, 'Struggling through Peace: Return and Resettlement in Angola' (2003).

[18] Bronwen Manby, 'Migration, Nationality and Statelessness in West Africa' (UNHCR and IOM 2015).

Firstly, the situation of former Liberian and Sierra Leonean refugees in West Africa, especially in Guinea. Although questions of identity and belonging remain complex, it is clear that access to identity documents, ideally identity documents confirming nationality in the place of residence, are of critical importance to the life chances of those who have not returned home. Yet local integration was only conceived of in terms of residence permits, not naturalisation. The decision of the Liberian authorities to reject long-term UNHCR registration as evidence of Liberian citizenship has been particularly harsh for those affected. There are lessons for future processes of the same kind.

Secondly, the highly unusual programme of refugee naturalisation carried out by the Tanzanian government. Although some other countries have provided a long-term residence status or naturalisation to former refugees, Tanzania's programme has been by far the most generous. Zambia, for example, adopted a local integration strategy in 2014 offering permanent residence to 10,000 Angolans and 4,000 Rwandans; but despite residence in the country over some decades this status would only create eligibility for naturalisation after another ten years.[19] Under the new constitution adopted in 2016, children of refugees born in Zambia would have the right to apply for citizenship at majority.[20] Tanzania has adopted successive programmes of naturalisation, and in 2007 offered facilitated naturalisation to 160,000 long-term Burundian refugees. Though the process faced significant hiccoughs along the way, while the ambiguities of Tanzania's citizenship law created further challenges, it is a remarkable example.

Finally, a study of refugee status in South Africa, and the access of refugees to South African citizenship, whether by naturalisation or through the birth of their children in the territory. The promise of the constitution adopted in the heady first days of the transition to full democracy in 1994 remains embedded in the citizenship rules – but anxieties are clearly visible in their adjustment and application in practice, with impacts on former Angolan refugees, among others.

In all of these cases, the self-perception of the refugees or former refugees of their nationality and identity varies, both between groups and within each group. The importance of documented citizenship also varies by context, depending on the importance of documents generally in the national legal environment, and the political and popular attitudes to the status of refugees. However, the more an individual comes into contact with formal State structures, and the more interactions with the State depend on identification, the more the possibility of access to recognised citizenship is likely to become important – for the refugees themselves but above all for their children; and for the State itself.

[19] For further information, see Strategic Framework for the Local Integration of Former Refugees in Zambia, January 2014; 'Field evaluation of local integration of former refugees in Zambia' US Department of State, April 2014; 'Zambia, UNHRC launch local integration strategy framework', PANA, 30 April 2014; Arthur Simuchoba, 'How Did Zambia Become the Continent-Leader in Refugee Integration?', *African Arguments*, 17 June 2014 http://africanarguments.org/2014/06/17/zambia-continent-leader-in-refugee-integration-by-arthur-simuchoba/.

[20] Constitution of Zambia, 2016, art 37.

9.1. Former Liberian and Sierra Leonean Refugees in Guinea

The situation of former refugees in Guinea is the most difficult among these three cases, with failures by several governments and UNHCR to resolve the status of those who no longer held refugee status but did not wish to return 'home'. The ceased circumstances clause was invoked for Sierra Leonean refugees at the end of 2008. At that time, the vast majority of the hundreds of thousands of refugees who had at one time fled the civil war had already returned home, with or without the assistance of UNCHR. The total number of remaining Sierra Leonean refugees worldwide was estimated at 43,000, the great majority in neighbouring countries.[21] At the time the ceased circumstances clause came into effect for Liberia, on 30 June 2012, almost 67,000 Liberian refugees were still registered with UNHCR in nine West African countries, with the largest populations in Côte d'Ivoire (23,650), Ghana (11,295), Guinea (9,972), and Sierra Leone (8,046).[22]

Guinea, home to a large number of this remaining caseload from both countries, is representative of their situation. Several thousand Sierra Leonean and Liberian refugees applied for continued international protection.[23] Many hoped that resettlement in a third country might still be possible; but if not, that they would be granted an ongoing status enabling them to remain in Guinea.[24] In the case of those who opted for repatriation or local integration, UNHCR negotiated with the governments of Sierra Leone and Liberia to issue either travel documents allowing the former to return home, or passports on the basis of which the latter could obtain a residence permit in the country of asylum.[25]

The Guinean government established a system to review the applications for exemption from the ceased circumstances clause on the basis of the need for continued protection, which were first considered by officials, and then appealed to a three-person panel of magistrates. While the Liberian group had some legal assistance, supported by UNHCR, the Sierra Leoneans had no advice at all. The overwhelming majority of requests for continued protection were rejected, with no reasons for the rejection. Others among both the Sierra Leoneans and the Liberians simply did not engage with the process at all, rejecting the two options on offer and holding out for resettlement, and/or not understanding the need to

[21] 'Applicability of Ceased Circumstances Cessation Clause to Refugees from Sierra Leone', UNHCR, 2 June 2008.

[22] 'Protracted refugee situations in Liberia and Angola to finally end', UNHCR, 29 June 2012.

[23] Among all the Liberians in West African countries, around 13% (6,172 individuals) applied for exemption from the cessation clause. Information from UNHCR, June 2014.

[24] For the attitudes of those in the camps, see Lacey Andrews Gale, 'The Invisible Refugee Camp: Durable Solutions for Boreah "Residuals" in Guinea" (2008) 21 Journal of Refugee Studies 537.

[25] Strangely, therefore, the criteria for determination of nationality were more stringent for those seeking local integration outside Liberia or Sierra Leone (who required a passport) than for those seeking to return home (on the basis of a simple one-way travel document).

apply in order to have an official status of some kind. During 2013, a group of around 200 former Sierra Leonean refugees protested first at the UNHCR office and then at an encampment for several weeks outside the US Embassy in Conakry, in both cases eventually being dispersed by police and gendarmes, with some injured as a result. Some refugees remaining in the former refugee camps were completely unaware of this process, apparently cut off from all contact with the Guinean administration.[26] In addition to the former refugees, there were people who had never applied for refugee status though they left Sierra Leone or Liberia because of the wars, and who were not therefore included within the processes surrounding the invocation of the ceased circumstances clause; IOM did facilitate the acquisition of documents from their home country for some in this category.[27]

The Liberian government sent missions to the various countries to verify the Liberian citizenship of those seeking these documents. Typically, the applicants were asked questions about their town of origin, customs of their ethnic group, and other knowledge of Liberia. It seemed, from lists submitted to UNHCR, that just under 10% of the original applicants for Liberian passports (around 1,000 individuals) who had been registered as refugees for decades by UNHCR and mostly claimed birth in Liberia of parents also born there, had been rejected as non-Liberian by the vetting missions (coded red on the lists), but on very unclear criteria.[28]

Among those rejected were individuals who had spent a long time out of the country, having left as children, and who no longer spoke Liberian English or any national language fluently. Given that only 5% of births are registered in Liberia, official proof of birth in the country (which should, under the law, automatically give Liberian citizenship provided the child is 'negro African') is rare.[29] With no knowledge of the villages they came from and no documentation to prove a connection to Liberia, a registration with UNHCR as a Liberian refugee apparently did not confirm their Liberian nationality. For those never registered as refugees, the evidence of a Liberian connection was even more difficult to show. For example, among those rejected were Liberian women who had children with Guinean soldiers who were part of the ECOWAS peacekeeping forces in Liberia and had returned with them to Guinea, only to be rejected by the families of those soldiers, 'and now they cannot find their way home.' Others included non-Liberians married to Liberian citizens, who would under Liberian law be required to naturalise formally to obtain Liberian citizenship; and at least one person who

[26] 'Rapport de mission à Kissidougou du 2 au 6 juin 2013', Commission nationale pour l'intégration et le suivi des réfugiés (CNISR), Conakry, 2013; interviews, Conakry, June 2014.

[27] Telephone interview, IOM Accra, July 2014.

[28] Interviews & internal memos, UNHCR, 2014.

[29] For those born abroad, although the constitution provides that a child of a Liberian father or mother is Liberian, the nationality law only grants nationality to those whose fathers are nationals, and they must take an oath of allegiance before they are 23. Liberia Constitution Art 28; Aliens and Nationality Law, Art § 20.1(b).

held a voter's card in another country (in this case, Nigeria), which under Liberian law results in automatic loss of Liberian nationality.[30]

Altogether perhaps a number in the low thousands of former Sierra Leonean and Liberian refugees remained in Guinea with no legal status as of 2014.[31] They had neither Guinean documents, nor any documents proving nationality of their home country, nor any continuing refugee status. Their lack of valid documentation meant they had no access to health care and their children were not in school; the assistance that UNHCR used to provide had ended and as non-nationals they could not access Guinean public health facilities or schools. Without Guinean papers, they were also subject to constant extortion by police, which severely curtailed their freedom of movement. Even the most menial jobs were difficult to access. At the same time, if they 'returned' to Sierra Leone or Liberia many would struggle to be recognised as nationals, as the 'red-coding' of Liberians indicated. Guinea had no process to provide a status to stateless persons.

Even if not technically stateless (if the passport of the country of origin was issued), the very point of choosing local integration among the options offered was to establish links to what was a new home. These former refugees had many reasons for not wishing to return to their country of origin (or that of their parents), and their real need was for recognition of Guinean nationality – which the Guinean nationality code should theoretically have permitted by naturalisation. Without a Guinean identity document they faced serious daily challenges in accessing public services, or simply in moving about, even at a local level. The lack of access to naturalisation had real impacts on their lives.

Guinea, however, has one of the most open nationality laws in Africa. In this, it reflects the legacy of the pan-Africanist and socialist politics of the first post-independence president, Sékou Touré. Though highly repressive, Touré did also invest in 'nation-building' in a way that few other African governments did apart from Tanzania.[32] The revised nationality code adopted in 1983, the year before Touré's death, and still in force, provides for automatic acquisition of nationality at majority by a person born in the country, as well as the rule of double *jus soli* (the second generation born in the country acquires nationality automatically at birth).[33] The children of refugees born in Guinea would, under the law, in due course become Guinean.

Nonetheless, the long-term status of the former refugees in Guinea would depend on the willingness of the courts and the Guinean State to apply the law. In common with other nationality codes based on the French model, that right would in principle depend on the registration of the child's birth. Since UNHCR

[30] Information from the CNISR and UNHCR, July 2014.

[31] According to UNHCR and CNISR unofficial estimates – but no audit had been done to determine the numbers.

[32] Mike McGovern, *A Socialist Peace? Explaining the Absence of War in an African Country* (University of Chicago Press 2017).

[33] Code Civil, 1983 (as amended to 1996), Titre III.

had ceased facilitating registration with the end of refugee status, many children were not being registered: Guinea's overall birth registration rate was under 50% in 2013.

Other countries of West Africa also provided little realistic chance of naturalisation for these refugees. In Ghana as of 2014, UNHCR had no information that any refugee or former refugee had been able to naturalise. Even the far less numerous former Rwandan refugees faced difficulties: in Niger, for example, a group of Rwandan refugees had already submitted naturalisation requests even before the ceased circumstances clause was invoked, with no success; an application lapses and must be resubmitted if no reply has been received within a year. The exception, ironically enough, appeared to be Liberia, which offered to naturalise several thousand Sierra Leonean former refugees based on long residence in the country.[34]

A former Sierra Leonean refugee in Guinea[35]

'I was born in Freetown in 1970, both my parents were Sierra Leonean. I was a news presenter and I was declared wanted when the rebels attacked. I left Freetown in March 1999 and came to Guinea by the boat. We were met by the Red Cross and I have been here since then. I was given a document by the Red Cross in 1999, and then an *attestation de réfugié* when they snapped [photographed] me in 2005, which enabled me to go to hospital and also to travel around Guinea. In 2008 they told me there were three options – return to Sierra Leone, stay in Guinea or further international protection. I chose further international protection. Then they gave me an appointment and an interview but I was rejected. I appealed, but that was also rejected. They gave me no reasons for the rejection but they said the refugee status was removed. They gave me another slip that gave me just one year more of refugee status. They told me that from 1 January 2010 I could no longer be a refugee. There are too many problems in this country. They will not give me a job as a foreigner, even a cleaning job – there is too much discrimination. My brother went home to Freetown, but he was killed there. I am with an Ivorian woman who is also a refugee; she came here in 2006. She recently gave birth to my son, just three weeks ago, but they would not see her at the hospital. We went there at midnight and said we were refugees and they said 'we have no place for you people', so we went home and she gave birth there. We have not registered the birth of the baby – you have to have the hospital slip to be able to register a baby, that

[34] See generally, Manby, 'Migration, Nationality and Statelessness in West Africa' (n 18).
[35] Interviewed in Conakry, June 2014.

is how it works. Without the slip you cannot go to the commune. I have no documents to prove my nationality so that we can get a birth certificate saying the child is Sierra Leonean.'

9.2. Tanzania: A Unique Offer of Citizenship to Refugees

The case of Tanzania provides a major contrast. Tanzania is one of the African countries that has made the most positive efforts to grant citizenship to refugees, especially the hundreds of thousands of refugees it has received from Rwanda and Burundi over the years, dating back to the 1960s. But Tanzania also supplies a warning that provisions in the nationality law may not necessarily be applied according to their literal reading.

The situation is complex. Official policy towards refugees has gone through marked swings, with failings in the implementation of policy commitments and periodic mass expulsions at times of political tension. Although the independence constitution provisions attributing citizenship to a child born in the country were preserved in the 1995 Citizenship Act, the understanding by some was that the new law had departed from that rule. Officials came to interpret the confusingly drafted exceptions relating to the child of a father with diplomatic status (if the mother was not a citizen) to require that one parent must be a citizen.[36] There exists an unpublished interpretation of this law by the attorney general, which reportedly draws on parliamentary debates at the time of adoption to State that the law will be applied as a purely descent-based system. Unlike in the civil law countries, the judicial branch has no role in interpreting the law: indeed, legislation explicitly provides that the decision of the minister on citizenship matters is final, and cannot be reviewed in court.[37]

An unease around definitions of citizenship similar to that in Kenya and Uganda at the time of independence was also reflected in repeated official discussions of how to determine who was an 'indigenous Tanzanian' in the context of efforts to reduce the dominance of the economy by people of Arab and Indian ethnicity,

[36] Tanzanian Citizenship Act 1995, Arts 5–9 and second sch. Article 5 provides: '(1) Subject to the provisions of subsection (2), every person born in the United Republic on or after Union Day shall be deemed to have become and to have continued to be a citizen of the United Republic with effect from the date of his birth […]. (2) A person shall not be deemed to be or to have become a citizen of the United Republic by virtue of this section if at the time of his birth: (a) neither of his parents is or was a citizen of the United Republic and his father possesses the immunity from suit and legal process which is accorded to an envoy of a foreign sovereign power accredited to the United Republic; or (b) any of his parents is an enemy and the and the birth occurs in a place then under occupation by the enemy.'

[37] Tanzania Citizenship Act 1995, s 23.

as well as tussles over the definition of 'Zanzibari' and the status of people of Comorian descent.[38] Major inflows of refugees from central Africa encouraged the identification of 'indigenous' populations with the Tanzanian State, in opposition to the newcomers; an impact felt even where the cultural and linguistic characteristics of those coming across the border were very close to the populations on the Tanzanian side.[39] Dual citizenship remained prohibited for adults as of the end of 2017, requiring (in principle) an option for either citizenship at majority for those of mixed parentage.

At the same time, however, Tanzania's history on identification and citizenship was, with exceptions, relatively open and unpoliticised by comparison with its neighbours in the East African Community. The original pan-African vision and rhetoric of President Julius Nyerere still had a hold on the State administration and the popular imagination. Many of those descended from pre-independence migrants or refugees from the pre-independence war in Mozambique considered that public statements by Nyerere and others that they were to be considered as citizens indicate that in fact they became citizens. But no legal procedures were ever completed to that effect.

In 1980, refugees who had fled the immediate pre- and post-independence violence in Rwanda and Burundi were given the right to apply for Tanzanian citizenship on a group basis in which normal application procedures and fees were waived. Once the naturalisation process was said to be complete, former refugee camps became normal Tanzanian villages, theoretically integrated into State structures. Certificates of naturalisation were, however, slow to be issued, and years later many former refugees were still waiting for their documents.[40] Yet in a context where national identification procedures were not stringent, acquisition of a party membership card, for example, could be sufficient to operate for normal purposes, and many blended into the national population.[41]

The large influxes of refugees to Tanzania from both Rwanda and Burundi in the mid-1990s put a strain on the policy and practice of integration. Already there had been expulsions of Burundians from Tanzania in 1987 and 1991, as militarisation of the refugee camps created genuine security concerns. In 1993, several

[38] Bruce Heilman, 'Who Are the Indigenous Tanzanians? Competing Conceptions of Tanzanian Citizenship in the Business Community' (1998) 45 Africa Today 369; Ned Bertz, 'Educating the Nation: Race and Nationalism in Tanzanian Schools' in Sara Dorman, Daniel Hammett and Paul Nugent (eds), *Making nations, creating strangers: States and citizenship in Africa* (Brill 2007); Iain Walker, 'Comorians and Hadramis in the Western Indian Ocean: Diasporic Practices in a Comparative Context' (2012) 38 Social Dynamics 435; Iain Walker, 'Identity and Citizenship among the Comorians of Zanzibar, 1886–1963' in Abdul Sheriff and Enseng Ho (eds), *The Indian Ocean: Oceanic connections and the creation of new societies* (Hurst & Company 2014); Bronwen Manby, 'Citizenship and Statelessness in the East African Community' (UNHCR 2018).

[39] Loren B Landau, *The Humanitarian Hangover: Displacement, Aid, and Transformation in Western Tanzania* (Wits University Press 2008).

[40] Charles P Gasarasi, 'The Mass Naturalization and Further Integration of Rwandese Refugees in Tanzania: Process, Problems and Prospects' (1990) 3 Journal of Refugee Studies 88.

[41] Malkki (n 11).

hundred thousand Hutu Burundians fled an upsurge of violence in October of that year. In 1994, hundreds of thousands of Rwandans crossed the border during the genocide and civil war: as in Congo, first of Tutsi and then Hutu ethnicity.

The various crises brought an end to the historical open-door policy. In late 1996, just as Rwandan refugees were driven back to their country from DRC, the Tanzanian army also forced several hundred thousand Rwandan refugees back across the border. Though most were recent arrivals, some had been resident in Tanzania since the 1960s. The Rwandan border remained closed until 1998, though Tanzania still accepted refugees from DRC and Burundi (as of 2008, perhaps 25,000 Rwandan refugees from the 1994 outflow still remained in Tanzania).[42] In late 1997, the government ordered the army to round up all foreigners living outside refugee camps; this time the bulk of those affected were Burundian, and included many born in Tanzania.[43] At the same time, the legal framework was reviewed. The adoption of a new Citizenship Act and Immigration Act in 1995, and in 1998, a new Refugee Act, marked a tightening in official policy towards refugees and migrants. The Refugee Act incorporated the UN and OAU refugee definitions into national law, but required refugees to live in designated sites. Five years later, in 2003, a National Refugee Policy was adopted, which continued to cast 'local settlement' as a temporary solution. Officials continued intermittent campaigns to arrest and expel Rwandan refugees, justifying their actions based on threats to local security and the absences of sufficient international support.[44]

Nevertheless, the integration of long-term refugees remained a live debate. In June 2003 the government announced that it would look favourably upon the request for Tanzanian citizenship from Somali refugees of Bantu ethnicity, who had fled persecution and denial of citizenship by the Siad Barre regime in Somalia, and the civil war that followed his fall from power. In May 2005, citizenship was granted to the first 182 of around 3,000 Somalis living in Chogo settlement in the north-eastern part of Tanzania.[45]

Then in 2007, Tanzania offered naturalisation to refugees resident in the country since they had fled an upsurge in violence in Burundi in 1972, and their descendants; of those eligible, 80% or 162,000 people, expressed their desire to remain in Tanzania, and the remaining 20% were to receive assistance with repatriation from March 2008. The European Commission, announcing support for the processing

[42] Bonaventure Rutinwa, 'The Tanzanian Government's Response to the Rwandan Emergency' (1996) 9 Journal of Refugee Studies 291; Human Rights Watch, 'In the Name of Security: Forced Round-Ups of Refugees in Tanzania' (1999); Charles P Gasarasi, 'The Question of the Recent Expulsion of Rwandans from Tanzania' (2008) 1 Journal of African Conflicts and Peace Studies 111.

[43] International Crisis Group, 'Burundian Refugees in Tanzania: The Key Factor to the Burundi Peace Process' (1999).

[44] Gasarasi (n 42).

[45] 'Somalia-Tanzania: Government grants Somali refugees citizenship', IRIN 20 June 2005; UNHCR, 'Finding a Home on Ancestral Land: Somali Bantu Refugees Gaining Citizenship in Tanzania' (United Nations 2010).

of the applications in August 2008, described the decision as 'a unique and unprecedented act of generosity and humanity.'[46] The process was not without its own issues: among them the exclusion of more recent refugees from Burundi, disagreements over the status of those born in Tanzania (some of whom according to the principles of Tanzania's *jus soli* law should on paper have had the right citizenship from birth) or married to Tanzanians, and problems with documentation of their existing status. Because dual nationality was not permitted, those wishing to naturalise had to renounce their Burundian nationality, with no possibility of retaining refugee status without naturalising. There was a demand, driven by concerns over the political impact of the new voters, that refugees relocate from their existing settlements to other parts of Tanzania as a condition for receiving their certificates. The naturalisation procedure was then stalled.

The precarious status of those considered non-citizens, when faced with national political developments, was dramatically highlighted in September 2013, while the naturalisation process was still incomplete. President Kikwete launched 'Operation Kimbunga' to expel 'illegal immigrants' living in Tanzania without a permit. The government later stated that a total of approximately 35,000 migrants had been forcibly expelled by the end of the operation; according to IOM, around 65,000 left altogether, including those who were not expelled but left because they feared deportation.[47] Among those expelled, some claimed Tanzanian citizenship, and others were rejected as citizens by the immigration officials of the countries to which they were expelled on the grounds that they were either Tanzanian or from another State.[48] The fact that most Tanzanians had no identification documents, given that a national identity card was only introduced after this episode, while rates of birth registration were amongst the lowest in Africa (less than 20%), meant that the ambiguity over the legal status of those expelled could be profound. Although most were admitted and resettled in the countries to which they were expelled, others were left stranded in countries where they had no connections; some returned to Tanzania once the campaign was over.[49]

In late 2014, the government resumed the process of issuing naturalisation certificates to the registered Burundian refugees whose applications had been accepted.[50] As of April 2016, 151,019 naturalisation certificates had been distributed and 6,620 applications had been submitted on behalf of children of those naturalised. UNHCR had assisted 1,850 to appeal a refusal, while more than 8,000

[46] 'EU funds naturalisation of Burundians,' *Daily News* (Dar es Salaam), 19 August 2008; UNHCR, Global Report 2007.

[47] 'IOM Tanzania launches migrant registration exercise in Kigoma', 2 December 2014; further information from IOM office in Dar es Salaam.

[48] See, eg, 'Expelled immigrants stranded as 'countries of origin' deny their citizenship', *The East African*, 21 September 2013.

[49] Interview, Office of the Prime Minister, Uganda, 3 August 2016.

[50] 'Tanzania Grants Citizenship to 162,000 Burundian Refugees in Historic Decision', UNHCR, 17 October 2014.

cases were still pending, and over 22,000 Burundian refugees from the 1972 case load in the Kigoma Region had not accessed the process.[51]

The case of Tanzania shows how difficult it may be to provide for naturalisation and local integration in a context where new refugee flows and political considerations disrupt efforts to normalise the situation of long-term settled refugee populations. National politics and anxieties linked to the electoral cycle led to criticism of official policy of naturalisation believed to be aimed at bolstering votes for the ruling party.[52] Tanzania's expulsion of refugees and those perceived to be irregular migrants was also affected by regional politics, not only in relation to the internal crises of its neighbours, but also its positioning in the most important regional political and economic institution, the East African Community. Whereas the expulsion of Rwandan refugees in the early 2000s appeared linked to opposition to Rwanda joining the EAC, those in 2012 and 2013 somehow tracked the closer alliances being formed between Kenya, Uganda, and Rwanda, to the exclusion of Tanzania. Individual refugees were thus caught up in wider regional issues.[53]

Yet Tanzania also shows that naturalisation and local integration is possible, given the political will, even for very substantial populations of refugees. The pan-Africanist outlook established in the Nyerere era continued to carry weight, even though the resistance to that rhetoric also established legal blockages for those who thought they had already become Tanzanian through his welcome. The naturalisation programme remains a remarkable example.

9.3. South Africa: The Dream Deferred

The last of these three case studies on the status of refugees is set in South Africa, a context that is very different from either Guinea or Tanzania. Refugees and asylum seekers are largely urban dwellers, and there are no camps; and with the exception of the long-standing Mozambican population, most have arrived as

[51] UNHCR, *Tanzania: Mpanda Operational Update*, Special Edition for April 2016. These processes have been quite extensively documented: see 'Going Home or Staying Home? Ending Displacement for Burundian Refugees in Tanzania' (International Refugee Rights Initiative 2008); 'Resisting Repatriation: Burundian Refugees Struggling to Stay in Tanzania' (International Refugee Rights Initiative 2012); '"I Can't Be a Citizen If I Am Still a Refugee": Former Burundian Refugees Struggle to Assert Their New Tanzanian Citizenship' (International Refugee Rights Initiative 2013); 'From Refugee to Returnee to Asylum Seeker: Burundian Refugees Struggle to Find Protection in the Great Lakes Region' (International Refugee Rights Initiative 2013).

[52] James Milner, 'Can Global Refugee Policy Leverage Durable Solutions? Lessons from Tanzania's Naturalization of Burundian Refugees' (2014) 27 Journal of Refugee Studies 553; Development and Training Services, Inc, 'Field Evaluation of Local Integration of Former Refugees in Tanzania: Field Visit Report – Final' (US Department of State 2014).

[53] Giles Muhame, 'Rwanda, Tanzania Tensions Threaten Regional Integration', *Chimpreports* (East African news service), 20 August 2013; Dismas Nkunda, 'Tanzania must learn to be a good neighbour', *The Observer* (Kampala), 15 September 2013.

individuals rather than fleeing violence en masse. The legal framework is also very different, and, with the greater functionality of State institutions, more immediately relevant for the ability of an individual to negotiate a place in society.

On South Africa's 1994 transition to a full democracy based on universal suffrage, among the many areas of reform were the legal regimes for citizenship, immigration and refugee status. The new constitution provided for the right to a nationality, and for children who were otherwise stateless to acquire citizenship based on birth in South Africa. A new Citizenship Act operationalised these commitments, continuing the previous rule that a child of parents who were permanent residents born in South Africa acquired citizenship automatically, and creating a framework for naturalisation.[54]

In the first five-year administration of the new regime, a series of immigration amnesties was also offered to particular groups of foreigners from the region: contract mine workers (1995); a broader category of people from countries of the Southern African Development Community who had lived in South Africa for at least five years and had economic or family ties in the country (1996); and finally Mozambican refugees displaced by the civil war in that country (1999). An estimated 1 to 1.5 million people became eligible for South African permanent residence (and thus in principle subsequently citizenship) through these measures. However, only 51,000 applications were received from miners, and just over 200,000 from other SADC nationals.[55]

Other laws created new regimes to distinguish refugees and other migrants, and established a bureaucratic apparatus to deal with applications for refugee status. They also provided for a transfer of status from refugee to permanent residence and then naturalised citizenship. After five years of continuous residence in South Africa from the date that asylum was granted, the Immigration Act allowed for the granting of permanent residence to a refugee, if the Standing Committee for Refugee Affairs provided a certificate that he or she would remain a refugee indefinitely (a significant barrier).[56] Five years after that, a permanent resident could in principle apply for citizenship by the usual rules under the Citizenship Act. The Immigration Act also allowed the minister for home affairs discretion to grant persons permanent residence.[57]

[54] South African Citizenship (No. 88) Act 1995.

[55] Jonathan Crush and Vincent Williams (eds), *The New South Africans? Immigration Amnesties and Their Aftermath* (IDASA 1999); Human Rights Watch, 'Prohibited Persons: Abuse of Undocumented Migrants, Asylum-Seekers, and Refugees in South Africa' (1998); Bronwyn Harris, 'A Foreign Experience: Violence, Crime and Xenophobia during South Africa's Transition' (Centre for the Study of Violence and Reconciliation 2001) 5; Tara Polzer, 'Local Government and Migration Management in Border Areas – Challenges and Opportunities for Public Service Provision' (Forced Migration Studies Programme, University of the Witwatersrand 2007).

[56] Immigration Act (No. 13) 2002, s 27(d), read with the Refugees Act (No. 130) 1998, s 27(c).

[57] While not much used, there was some successful litigation in this area. On 7 March 2008 the High Court handed down judgment in the Transvaal Provincial Division in the matter of *Kamelia Tcherveniakova v The Minister of Home Affairs and Others* granting the applicant along with her husband

The system struggled to cope as immigration to South Africa greatly increased. National human rights organisations reported ever more serious worries about xenophobia among the native South African population toward incomers.[58] In May and June 2008, attacks on foreigners surged in a wave of violence across major urban centres, leaving more than 60 dead and displacing tens of thousands.[59] Tangled up with the resentment and competition for resources that led to violence was the strong sense of ordinary, poor, South Africans that they had been excluded from the great wealth of the country, despite the transition of 1994, and often overtaken by the newcomers. More than a quarter of South Africans stated that they wanted a total ban on immigration.[60]

The 1996 Citizenship Act had made the rights to citizenship founded on birth in South Africa explicitly subject to the child's birth being registered in accordance with the Births and Deaths Registration Act (which citizenship based on descent was not).[61] Access to birth registration thus became key to access to citizenship. South African birth registration rates dramatically increased after 1994: from less than 25% of under-fives registered in 1998, to 50% in 2001, 72% in 2005, 92% by 2009, and 95% in 2012.[62] However, even children with one South African parent could face difficulties in gaining recognition of citizenship. Home Affairs regulations prevented a father from registering a child out of wedlock without the

and minor child an exemption for permanent residence in terms of s 31(2) (b) of the Immigration Act, based on their individual circumstances to remain in South Africa. The applicant came to South Africa from Bulgaria in 1996, prior to there being a legislative framework to deal with asylum seekers and refugees. In 2003, after the refugee status of the applicant and her family was denied, they brought an application for exemption to the minister, which was only finalised in November 2006. In awarding permanent residence, the court took into account the length of time taken for the process to be finalised in accordance with just administrative action. Communication from Lawyers for Human Rights, who brought the case, 14 May 2008.

[58] Anthony de V Minnaar, Mike Hough and Chris Paul De Kock, *Who Goes There? Perspectives on Clandestine Migration and Illegal Aliens in Southern Africa* (HSRC Publishers 1996); Loren B Landau, 'The Laws of (In)Hospitality: Black Africans in South Africa' (University of the Witwatersrand 2004) 7; Francis B Nyamnjoh, *Insiders and Outsiders: Citizenship and Xenophobia in Contemporary Southern Africa* (Zed Books 2006); John O Oucho and Jonathan Crush, 'Contra Free Movement: South Africa and the SADC Migration Protocols' (2001) 48 Africa Today 139.

[59] Jonny Steinberg, 'South Africa's Xenophobic Eruption' (Institute of Security Studies 2008) ISS Paper 169; Jean Pierre Misago, Loren B Landau and Tamlyn Monson, 'Towards Tolerance, Law, and Dignity: Addressing Violence against Foreign Nationals in South Africa' (International Organisation for Migration 2009).

[60] 'Citizenship, Violence and Xenophobia in South Africa: Perceptions from South African Communities' (Human Sciences Research Council 2008); Daniel Hammett, 'Requiring Respect: Searching for Non-Racialism in Post-Apartheid South Africa' (2012) 39 Politikon 71; Francis B Nyamnjoh, 'From Bounded to Flexible Citizenship: Lessons from Africa' (2007) 11 Citizenship Studies 73.

[61] eg, though the Citizenship Act provides that citizenship is granted to a child born on the territory who would otherwise be Stateless, this right is conditional on birth being documented through a birth certificate. South African Citizenship Act 1995, as amended to 2010, s 2(2). Rights based on descent are not stated to be based on this condition.

[62] Statistics South Africa, 'The Coverage and Quality of Birth Registration Data in South Africa: 1998–2005, Report No. 06-03-01' (2007). Figures for 2009 and 2013 from UNICEF.

mother's consent and presence to acknowledge paternity, leaving children abandoned by their mothers at risk of statelessness.[63] Amendments to the Citizenship Act adopted in 2010 tightened rules on attribution of citizenship to the children of permanent residents. Children of non-citizens began to be issued birth certificates in a different format, creating problems in accessing public services.[64] In September 2014, the government announced that late registration of birth would become significantly more difficult at the end of 2015, alleging that it had created an avenue for foreigners 'who do not deserve South African citizenship being able to bribe their way onto the NPR [National Population Register]'.[65] Those most likely not to be registered in time were children whose parents could not produce a passport or South African identity card.[66] Despite the various provisions for the reduction of statelessness in the law, many individuals seemed to fall through the cracks, mostly those in the usual vulnerable groups.[67] The government refused to recognise the South African citizenship of a child born in the country of Cuban parents who could not in law transmit their nationality to their child born abroad.[68]

Naturalisation rates also fell dramatically in response to the xenophobic national mood, from figures in the range of 10-30,000 each year for the decade after 2001, to 6,000 in 2010–11 and 1,600 in 2011–12 – when the Department of

[63] In a 2011 report, the Public Protector found that the Department of Home Affairs' failure to register the birth of a child with a South African father and non-South African mother was 'procedurally and substantively flawed' and in violation of the constitution; in another case the High Court ordered that the details of the South African father be entered on the birth certificate for a child born out of wedlock to a non-South African mother and the child declared to be a South African citizen. *Report on an investigation into allegations of failure to register the birth of a child and the naturalisation of the mother by the Northern Cape Department of Home Affairs*, Report No.38 of 2011, Public Protector of South Africa; *Steven Sikhumbuzo Moyo and another v Minister Home Affairs*, North Gauteng High Court case number 44424/09.

[64] From 2010, children of permanent residents began to be given handwritten 'foreigner' birth certificates rather than computerised certificates with a national ID number. Information presented by Lawyers for Human Rights at UNHCR regional statelessness meeting 1-3 November 2011.

[65] 'Gigaba blames crooked priests in immigration fraud', SAPA, 28 September 2014. See also, 'Gigaba blames crooked priests in immigration fraud', SAPA, 28 September 2014; 'Arrest of ID Syndicate Welcomed', Parliament of South Africa Portfolio Committee on Home Affairs 1 December 2014; '16 Days: Stateless in South Africa', 4 December 2014, at Realising Rights blog, https://realisingrights.wordpress.com/2014/12/04/16-days-Stateless-in-south-africa/.

[66] *Towards Universal Birth Registration in South Africa: A Briefing Paper*, Lawyers for Human Rights, Pretoria, 2011.

[67] Jessica P George and Rosalind Elphick, 'Statelessness and Nationality in South Africa' (Lawyers for Human Rights 2013); 'Childhood Statelessness in South Africa' (Lawyers for Human Rights (South Africa) and Institute on Statelessness and Inclusion 2016).

[68] 'High Court recognises child as Stateless and declares her to be a SA citizen', Lawyers for Human Rights (Pretoria), 8 July 2014; Order of court in *DGLR and KMRG v The Minister of Home Affairs and others* (unreported), 3 July 2014; Liesl Muller, 'South African Courts Confirm the Right to Nationality of a Stateless Child – 20 Year Old Legal Principle Protecting Stateless Children Is Finally Implemented' www.statelessness.eu, 13 September 2016.

Home Affairs stopped publishing its statistics.[69] The 2010 amendments also made naturalisation more difficult to access, requiring a person to show that the country of their other nationality permitted dual nationality or that it had been renounced, posing problems especially for refugees and stateless persons.[70] Policy papers on migration published in 2016 and 2017 proposed that 'granting of citizenship should be considered as being exceptional and requiring an executive decision of the minister', moving away from an administrative process based on fulfilment of set criteria.[71]

The refugee processing system was also overwhelmed, as both refugees and others accessed the system in the absence of any other method of obtaining a temporary residence permit. By 2012, around 65,000 people had been granted refugee status in South Africa; but there was a backlog of almost a quarter of a million people who had applied for asylum. By 2014, this had risen to more than 112,000 recognised refugees and more than 460,000 asylum seekers.[72] Even acknowledged refugees struggled to gain the identity documents that should follow, necessary to enable a semi-normal life to be established. Twenty years after the regularisation process at the transition to democratic government, the status of permanent residence rather than citizenship, and a lack of any papers for some, still created vulnerabilities among the former Mozambican refugees.[73]

Among those affected by the tightening of citizenship policy were approximately 2,000 Angolan refugees still resident on cessation of their refugee status in April 2013. Many had been in the country for close to two decades, with children born in South Africa and a significant level of integration in the local economy and society, using South African languages at home.[74] The Department of Home

[69] According to figures published in the Department of Home Affairs Annual Reports, the numbers of people naturalised each year were:

2001/02	2003/04	2004/05	2005/06	2006/07	2007/08	2008/09	2009/10	2010/11	2011/12
14,108	20,648	18,107	19,888	24,671	9,346	32,627	37,522	6,102	1,603

The 2002/03 Annual Report is not on the website (nor are earlier years) and the 2012–13, 2013–14 and 2014–15 Annual Reports did not contain this statistic. See www.dha.gov.za/index.php/about-us/annual-reports; Bronwen Manby, *Citizenship Law in Africa: A Comparative Study* (3rd edn, Open Society Foundations 2016).

[70] eg, from Congo. Email communication, Lawyers for Human Rights, 4 November 2014.

[71] Green Paper on International Migration for South Africa, Department of Home Affairs, 24 June 2016; White Paper on International Migration for South Africa, Department of Home Affairs, July 2017.

[72] UN High Commissioner for Refugees, *Statistical Yearbooks* for the relevant years (annexes, table 1). By 2015, UNHCR reported over 121,000 recognised refugees, and more than a million asylum seekers; however, the methodology for the number of asylum seekers was challenged, and a figure of roughly half proposed. See Richard Stupart, 'Is South Africa home to more than a million asylum seekers? The numbers don't add up', *Africa Check*, 15 August 2016.

[73] Enid J Schatz, 'Reframing Vulnerability: Mozambican Refugees' Access to State-Funded Pensions in Rural South Africa' (2009) 24 Journal of Cross-Cultural Gerontology 241.

[74] Julia Sloth-Nielsen and Denise Ackermann, 'Foreign Children in Care in the Western Cape Province' (Scalabrini Centre 2015).

Affairs did not, however, offer naturalisation to this group, at first issuing only two-year temporary residence permits.[75] When these expired in 2015, a year of negotiations and litigation by the Scalabrini Centre of Cape Town culminated in a court order that the Department of Home Affairs should consider applications for permanent residence from the former refugees. In the meantime, the Centre received reports of affected refugees losing their jobs, having problems accessing their bank accounts, and being scared to leave their homes due to their lack of documentation.[76] In July 2017, rights equivalent to permanent residence were granted to some 1,200 of the ex-refugees (just over 70% of those who applied), but only for four years – with a lack of clarity about their ultimate access to citizenship or that of their children, or the status of those refused.[77]

Many States have responded to increased immigration and refugee flows by making access to citizenship more difficult; South Africa is one of the clearest examples of this trend in Africa. The consequences for those without an alternative status are serious, in an environment where paperwork is very important to be able to function. As in other countries, however, it is unlikely for such a position to remain tenable if large numbers of people who have, as a matter of fact, made their homes in South Africa are permanently excluded. Indeed, even as hostility to immigration was increasing, 59% of South Africans expressed the view that a person born in South Africa of two foreign parents should have a right to citizenship.[78]

[75] 'Statement on the Angolan cessation clause: former refugees from Angola face deportation as temporary permits expire', Lawyers for Human Rights, 17 September 2015.

[76] 'Loss of refugee status leaves many Angolans undocumented in South Africa', IRIN, 10 September 2013; Sergio Carciotto, 'Angolan Refugees in South Africa: Alternatives to Permanent Repatriation?' (2016) 2 African Human Mobility Review 262.

[77] 'Angolan ex-refugees given chance to apply for residency in South Africa', Legal Resources Centre (South Africa), 21 November 2016; 'Home Affairs grants residency to majority of Angolan former refugees', Scalabrini Centre (Cape Town), 10 July 2017.

[78] Afrobarometer online data analysis tool, Round 5 (2011/13), 'Right to be citizen: born in country with two non-citizen parents', http://afrobarometer.org/online-data-analysis/analyse-online.

PART V

Conclusions

10

The Importance of Nationality Law in Africa

It may be true that the law cannot make a man love me, but it can keep him from lynching me, and I think that's pretty important.

– Martin Luther King, Jr.[1]

Citizenship is not just a legal concept but also a profoundly political question of self-definition, periodically the focus of controversy anywhere in the world. The history of Africa has exaggerated these controversies. The carving up of the continent by European powers, without respect for pre-existing political boundaries and institutions; the temporary creation of large zones of free movement; the forced recruitment of labour from one region to another; the adjustment of borders and jurisdictions among the colonial powers, followed by an often troubled and hasty transition to independence and re-imposition of smaller political units; not to mention ongoing irredentist demands for new States (some of them successful), have all made membership a fraught affair. There are libraries of books on these problems, their fundamental causes, and proposals for their resolution.

But to what extent does formal legal citizenship play a role in these difficulties; and thus to what extent does citizenship law reform provide a possible route out of them? African politicians have manipulated and mobilised ethnic identity to devastating effect without any recourse to citizenship law (Rwanda); countries with blameless citizenship laws have also seen crises in which ethnic divisions have played a dominant role (Chad, Angola); other countries have seen identity-based violence that owes nothing to membership of the national polity, but rather a lower-level administrative-political unit (Nigeria); the African Union has a major strand of programming around 'managing diversity' coming out of the surveys of governance carried out by the African Peer Review Mechanism (APRM), yet analysis of these surveys does not find it necessary to mention citizenship laws.[2] Often, the law is poorly understood even by those supposed to implement it.

This chapter attempts to draw out some of the lessons from the preceding case studies that indicate why citizenship laws may merit further consideration in

[1] Speech at Western Michigan University, 18 December 1963.

[2] 'Diversity Management in Africa: Findings from the African Peer Review Mechanism and a Framework for Analysis and Policy-Making' (UNECA 2011).

these discussions. They are put forward tentatively: an analysis of the continents' laws combined with a few country studies cannot begin to put forward a cast-iron case around the significance of citizenship law in Africa. But they attempt to highlight some of the findings and conclusions that it may be interesting to explore further, including: the common patterns and continuities (or discontinuities) across the continent; the influence of international law on these changes; the very deliberate instrumentalisation of citizenship law by some governments; the extent to which the initial framework of citizenship law has had an independent impact on national politics, even when this was not the intention when the laws were adopted; the role of nationality law reforms in promoting integration rather than exclusion; the degree to which tolerance of undetermined nationality can provide a buffer against the worst impacts of exclusionary laws; and finally, the daily and increasing importance of nationality documentation and administrative systems to even the most marginalised.

My conclusion is to agree with Catherine Boone, framing an argument around ethnic politics, that ethnic identity is not so much an 'essentially pre-political or non-political' preference or ideology, but 'better understood as a juridical status, or a state-recognised or even state-imposed political identity, which operates through state processes.'[3] Her own focus is on the impact of land tenure regimes as constitutive of ethnic identity. This book has considered another aspect of juridical status, that of legal citizenship at the national level, and its impact on both national and local identities and politics. I argue that the interaction between membership in both the ethnic or 'primordial' and in the national sense is at least partly shaped – at both levels – by the law.

10.1. Categories of the Excluded and Commonalities with other Regions

Those communities within Africa whose members have found that their legal right to belong to the national community is contested are generally of five main types.

Firstly, descendants of people who migrated, or were forced to move, during the colonial period, when administrative borders among territories of one colonial power were open. This set divides in turn into two main sub-categories: those whose ancestors came from outside the continent (from Europe, Asia or the Middle East); and – less well advertised, but far more numerous – those whose ancestors came from elsewhere in Africa (farmworkers in Zimbabwe, tenant farmers on cocoa plantations in Côte d'Ivoire, Nubian soldiers in Kenya, and many others).

[3] Catherine Boone, *Property and Political Order in Africa: Land Rights and the Structure of Politics* (Cambridge University Press 2014) 317; see also Catherine Boone, 'Land Regimes and the Structure of Politics: Patterns of Land-Related Conflict' (2013) 83 Africa 188.

Most African States that were formerly part of the British, French, and Portuguese empires relied on rules of double *jus soli* to determine nationality at independence. These provisions aimed to exclude (especially non-African) recent arrivals from automatic attribution of citizenship; though a further right to opt for nationality was often provided to some. Where double *jus soli* rules or stronger rights based on location of birth remained in place, the exclusionary effect disappeared over time in relation to pre-independence migrants; but in the British territories where the absolute *jus soli* rule initially applied after independence was repealed, and in the States that adopted laws relying on descent from the outset, the transitional rules (or lack of them) created exclusions that continue till today.

Secondly, ethnic groups whose pre-colonial boundaries cross modern borders, so those speaking the same language now find themselves in two (or more) different States. Among these groups are pastoralists whose nomadic lifestyle takes them across multiple borders.

Thirdly, post-independence migrants and refugees (and their children) in African States face the same challenges of integration (legal and cultural) into the national polity as in other parts of the world in this era of globalisation.

Fourthly, the creation of new States and border changes since independence have left many thousands stranded between two countries without recognition in either.

Fifthly, scattered throughout the continent and not belonging to any recognised 'community', there are those vulnerable children who cannot in law or fact gain recognition of nationality: those with foreign fathers who are affected by gender discrimination in the law, those born out of wedlock, child workers or trafficked children (even within one country), children of mothers with mental disability or illness or who have been raped in war; and those separated from their parents, because they are orphans, by conflict, or as child labour. Even more vulnerable are children of unknown parents – especially, but not only in countries where the law establishes no presumption of nationality in their case. Unlike the other groups at risk of statelessness because of ethnic, racial, or religious discrimination in nationality laws, these children are not necessarily identifiable as a group. Though being a member of a marginalised ethnic group certainly increases the risk to a child who is at the margins of the marginalised, children from any part of society may find themselves in this category, where the law and its implementation do not provide them with a secure legal identity at birth.

Sometimes these categories overlap: in eastern Congo, some of the ancestors of the Banyarwanda were always in the territory of modern-day DRC, and a contemporary international border has cut through a historical polity; others came as forced or voluntary labour on Belgian plantations; added to these are massive outflows of refugees fleeing pre- and post-independence violence in Rwanda and Burundi, and those in search of fertile unoccupied land. There are all too many children separated from their parents and communities or born of rape. Weaknesses of State administration means that all Congolese face challenges in documenting their identity, and conflict has even destroyed those records that exist, especially in the east.

These categories are not fundamentally different from those in other continents, though the particular modalities of exclusion have varied. The underlying reasons for exclusion are also similar, including the impact both of mass migration (forced or voluntary) and of State succession. For example, among those whose status is challenged in other regions have been stateless Russian speakers in the Baltic States or the Meshketian Turks forcibly moved within the Soviet Union; members of the ethnically Cambodian Khmer Krom who live in Vietnam; the descendants of Haitian sugar workers in the Dominican Republic; the children of Balkan Roma refugees born in Italy; Bihari Urdu speakers in Bangladesh; and vulnerable children in any continent.

What is perhaps different in Africa is the difficulty of understanding the scale of the problem, and the blurred edges of belonging, when so many people are undocumented and thus in effect of undetermined nationality, not fitting neatly into binaries of citizen or non-citizen. By contrast, for example, to the rules applied later in the century on the break-up of the Soviet Union, Czechoslovakia, and Yugoslavia, the determination of who belonged where in Africa at decolonisation was based on a much less well-documented existing status. Even in new States that had some foundation in pre-colonial polities (such as Rwanda, Swaziland, or Lesotho), there were no administrative records on which to base continuity of nationality bridging the colonial period.

Along with this confusion, the brutal history of the continent has given a particular inflection to many of the same issues.

Finally, therefore, we can say that states where there was major expropriation of land and forced population transfer during the colonial period have seen the greatest challenges around nationality and belonging. They have also seen the most adjustments to their nationality regimes in relation to acquisition of nationality at birth and through location of birth – though the legal changes adopted to respond to these issues vary widely. Some of these countries were subject to detailed examination in Chapter 7.

The exceptions to this final rule (to date) are Namibia and South Africa. The relative size and wealth of the historical immigrant population of those two countries has combined with the history of the liberation struggle and negotiated achievement of majority rule to shift controversies over their place in the political economy into other fields of law.

10.2. Patterns, Continuities, and Discontinuities in the Law

The categories left at risk of statelessness are also shaped by the same legal frameworks as in other continents. The nationality laws and institutional architecture adopted in African States at independence closely modelled those of the outgoing colonial powers. Even where new laws were drafted from scratch – as in the case of Ethiopia or Liberia – external models played an important role in shaping the language and concepts used. This book has tracked the changes that have been made to the law in response both to efforts to exclude certain individuals and communities, and to resolve disputes over the right to belong following campaigns by various interest groups or in the context of peace settlements at the end of conflict.

The only two clear trends in nationality law that show the same directionality across the continent are those that are also shared with other continents: towards greater gender equality, and towards greater acceptance of dual nationality. In relation to the basic legal regime governing acquisition of nationality at birth (based on descent or location of birth), it is harder to see clear patterns shared across the different legal systems, though a move towards descent-based regimes overall.

More generally, the legal regime bequeathed by the colonial power had and has continued to have a dominant impact on the rules for attribution of nationality at birth. There was thus a striking similarity of legal regimes at independence among States with the same colonial heritage; with perhaps half a dozen basic types across the continent. This heritage has continued to be highly influential, even in the reverse sense that the Commonwealth countries have collectively almost all repealed their initial *jus soli* provisions. Yet *both* the double *jus soli* provisions of the former French and Portuguese colonies *and* the descent-based Arab and Belgian models have been more stable. The adoption of descent-based regimes in the Commonwealth States often constituted a deliberate effort to reduce access to citizenship for the 'non-African' population. At the same time, these changes created a set of rules that were more easily comprehensible in the popular imagination, as well as possible to implement in very fragile States with weak civil registration systems, where even the borders of the State were often unclear. Remarkably, however, the idea that the second generation born in the territory should automatically acquire nationality at birth has been completely acceptable in those States – with otherwise similar characteristics to the Commonwealth or Belgian territories – where the double *jus soli* regime happened to be adopted from the French tradition. The popular imagination appears to be quite flexible.

As argued in Chapter 5.6, however, the legal heritage is by no means the only variable. Post-independence governments with a socialist outlook tended to adopt more open nationality laws and reject discrimination based on sex; while individual political leaders committed to pan-Africanism have also made a difference to the tenor of nationality policy. From the 'demand' side, organised pressure from national and international sources has often brought nationality law reform: from the women's movement, diaspora groups, children's rights organisations, human rights groups more generally, and UN agencies, especially UNHCR. Reforms have often been contagious, especially between countries of the same official language, as pressure groups and politicians have drawn inspiration from legal changes in other African countries. This contagion also applies to some of the rules that have limited access, including the introduction of discrimination based on race, religion, and ethnicity. It is harder to isolate consistent reasons to explain why some States have adopted such rules and others have not, as both small and ethnically homogeneous and large and ethnically diverse States have at different times reached for the same tools.

It is striking that there have been relatively few amendments to the rules on naturalisation, and no clear direction in those changes that have been made. Transitional rules adopted at independence to provide preferential access to nationality to some categories of person with specific types of connection have for the most part lapsed, but the provisions on naturalisation open to all on the basis of long-term residence have remained fairly static. By contrast with European countries, which have reviewed naturalisation rules and created or amended citizenship tests as they have debated the means of integrating new migrants, African States have not given these questions significant legislative attention. Although some have introduced language or cultural requirements, such amendments as have been made have mainly related to period of residence (with changes in both directions, though usually to require more years). Efforts to create greater congruence between cultural 'nationhood' and republican or liberal 'citizenship' have focused rather on attribution of nationality at birth, most obviously in those countries that have incorporated explicit language discriminating on the basis of race, ethnicity or religion. Rules on naturalisation have in all countries remained highly discretionary and within the control of the executive, usually the head of State; the numbers naturalising are correspondingly low. The exceptions relate to rather rare initiatives to integrate large groups, such as the Rwandan and Burundian refugees in Tanzania, or the special procedures adopted in Côte d'Ivoire by the new government following the civil war.

The procedural rules on nationality have shown even more continuity based on the pre-colonial heritage; including continuity in rules around identification and proof of nationality. The Commonwealth States reflect an unfortunate legacy of excessive executive control over the domain of nationality, with no role for the courts. Countries such as Kenya demonstrate the long shadow cast by procedures put in in place by Britain to control the 'native' population. In the former French and Belgian territories by contrast, nationality belongs to the ministry of justice rather than the ministry of the interior, and the courts have the final say on who is a national from birth. This difference in procedures does not cast a magical spell of due process over nationality administration in the civil law countries; but it does make an appreciable difference to the level of discretion that can be applied.

10.3. The Influence of International Law

Without a review of the records of parliamentary debates on legislation it is hard to know what direct influence international and African legal standards have had on these trends. Nonetheless it seems reasonable to propose that their influence has increased. For the first few decades of independence, there is little sense that international, continental and sub-continental standards had any effect on nationality law reforms – in line with the general understanding of the time that determination of nationality was within the complete discretion of the sovereign State. In recent years, however, there has been increasing reference to international law, as well as to decisions of the African regional human rights bodies, in debates around nationality law reform. For example, the introduction of protections for children of unknown parents in the Commonwealth countries where this was absent was influenced by campaigns by child rights groups founding their arguments on international law; similarly, the push for gender equality was firmly grounded in the CEDAW standards (despite the rear-guard action of the North African States which meant that the Protocol on the Rights of Women in Africa adopted in 2003 continued to permit discrimination; see Chapter 1.2).

Decisions of the African Commission on Human and Peoples' Rights in relation to the prominent cases of denial of nationality to politicians also received high profile coverage in discussions around reforms at national level in countries such as Zambia and Côte d'Ivoire – though it is hard to disentangle different contributing factors. The decision of the African Committee of Experts on the Rights and Welfare of the Child in the case of the Kenyan Nubian children was also part of a broad set of advocacy efforts that had significant impacts in improving the recognition of the Nubians as Kenyan (Chapters 1.2 and 7.3.1).

More recently, the efforts of UNHCR have led to greatly increased accessions by African States to the Convention relating to the Status of Stateless Persons and the Conventions on the Reduction of Statelessness. In West Africa, regional and national declarations and plans of action to prevent and reduce statelessness reference these treaties front and centre in the reforms and activities they propose. Similar documents adopted by International Conference on the Great Lakes Region, with UNHCR support, are also evidence of a political recognition of the damage that lack of access to citizenship has caused. The draft Protocol to the African Charter on Human and Peoples Rights on the right to a nationality and the eradication of statelessness adopted by the African Commission on Human and Peoples' Rights in 2015 would radically strengthen rights to 'belong', if endorsed by the political institutions of the AU. The impact of this increased normative effort at continental level is too soon to tell.

African States have responded in the past to international debates on the adoption of new normative frameworks relevant to questions of citizenship and belonging in a way that suggests an understanding that they could have an influence at national level. For example, during the UN process leading to the adoption in September 2007 of the UN Declaration on the Rights of Indigenous Peoples, the African Union expressed strong concerns about the potential of the declaration to 'create tensions amongst ethnic groups and instability within sovereign states'.[4]

[4] 'Draft Aide Memoire : African Group : United Nations Declaration on the Rights of Indigenous People' (2006); see generally on these debates, Felix Mukwiza Ndahinda, *Indigenousness in Africa: A Contested Legal Framework for Empowerment of 'marginalized' Communities* (TMC Asser Press 2011).

A number of African communities had already organised around an identification as 'indigenous', including not only the forest-dwelling Batwa ('Pygmy') populations of Central Africa or the traditionally hunter-gatherer Khoi-san ('Bushmen') of southern Africa, more closely fitting the international understanding of the concept, but also nomadic pastoralists across the Sahel and East Africa, and the Movement for the Survival of the Ogoni People (MOSOP) in the Niger Delta of Nigeria (whom nobody had previously thought of as 'indigenous' in the international sense). The AU Assembly requested an advisory opinion on the issues from the African Commission on Human and Peoples' Rights, which endorsed the Declaration's ambition to reduce discrimination against marginalised groups, but came to the conclusion that 'any African can legitimately consider him/herself as indigene to the Continent'.[5] On this basis – that the Declaration would not create hierarchies of ethnic groups based on 'who was here first' – and faced with international pressure on the issues, most African States eventually agreed to sign the Declaration, with abstentions only from Burundi, Kenya and Nigeria. But the discussion certainly revealed that States believed that the Declaration might later be invoked with the aim of impacting their national laws.

10.4. The Instrumentalisation of Nationality Laws

When it comes to the application of the law in practice, the most obvious political role of nationality law has been its instrumentalisation by politicians. Denial of (proof of) nationality has been a tool used above all against political opponents and those who are believed to be their supporters. Many other scholars have focused on the connection between the flaring of identity-based conflict and the widespread (re)introduction of multiparty elections following the end of the Cold War (see Chapter 1.4). This book concentrates rather on the manipulation of the law as a specific tool within that process: politicians did not only use inflammatory rhetoric, mobilisation of ethnic militias, and manipulation of the electoral process to achieve these ends; they used the laws on citizenship.

The political utility of instrumentalising citizenship law is most obvious in the case of individuals whom the government in power considers to be troublesome. The most notorious cases in Africa where citizenship law has been abused to sideline high profile politicians are those of Kenneth Kaunda in Zambia and Alassane Ouattara in Côte d'Ivoire – a former President and a former Prime Minister – who were both denied the right to run for office again on the grounds that their citizenship had been recognised in error. Other less well known cases encompass not only politicians, but union leaders, journalists and academics whose opinions and activities have troubled the government of the day. Denial of nationality is an

[5] African Commission on Human and Peoples' Rights, 'Advisory Opinion on the United Nations Declaration on the Rights of Indigenous Peoples.' (African Union 2007).

especially powerful tool, because it puts the person outside the realm of those who have a right to share in the State's resources and to participate in the State's political institutions; and as a presumed non-citizen, a significantly reduced ability to access the courts. Above all, it can be used to remove the person from the country, out of reach of political ambitions: most dramatically in the case of John Modise, who was deprived of nationality when he became a candidate for the Botswanan presidency. Perhaps most usefully for those invoking them, creative interpretation of nationality provisions can achieve all of these things while appearing to respect the forms of the rule of law (Chapter 5.5).

It is striking the extent to which broader efforts to undermine actual or potential political opponents have used amendments to the law around acquisition of nationality at birth to achieve that aim, or imaginative reinterpretation of the rules on State succession, rather than any formal invocation of the powers of deprivation. In this, the newly independent States learned well the lessons taught by the former colonial powers. In some countries, the pre-colonial history almost guaranteed that the independence leaders would flip over the discrimination the 'natives' previously faced, as part of the process of sealing their own legitimacy. In the phase immediately after independence, denial of access to or recognition of nationality was a way of clipping the wings of those whose economic and political power had been unfairly increased by the colonial regime.

Algeria is perhaps the paradigm example. During the colonial period, only around ten thousand of five million Muslim Algerians had achieved full French citizenship rights, and at the cost of renouncing their Muslim personal status. Jewish Algerians, meanwhile, were admitted to French citizenship *en bloc*, with the same status as immigrants to Algeria from metropolitan France. As the liberation war ended and independence approached, the mass exodus of the *pieds noirs* confirmed the suspicion of the new government that the former masters could not be trusted with equal legal status in the new era. The new nationality code, though non-discriminatory at first glance, defined 'Algerian' as a person of Muslim religion whose father and father's father was born in Algeria; later changes to the law reinforced this understanding, removing an already limited double *jus soli* provision. The law was the tool to ensure that neither Christian nor Jewish Algerians would be fully regarded as part of the new national community (Chapters 3.2 and 4.3).

In Côte d'Ivoire, the nationality law was never amended to create explicit discriminatory provisions, but amendments to the constitution, to the electoral code, to the laws on identification and civil registration, and to the implementing decrees for the nationality law itself, were diligently enacted to achieve particular effects. Even during the decade of crisis after 2000, each successive requirement for proof of citizenship was carefully set out in a new presidential order, decree or *arrêté* (Chapter 7.4). In (North) Sudan, the exclusion of presumed South Sudanese from ongoing citizenship following the division of the country in 2011 was enabled by very specific amendments to the citizenship law, combined with the roll-out of new identification systems (Chapter 8.2). Even in the Democratic Republic of Congo, a far less legalistic State – a far less State-like State – amendments to the law were important markers for the relative inclusion or exclusion of the Banyarwanda at any one historical moment. Implementing regulations have kept access difficult even where surface changes appeared to liberalise the law (Chapter 7.5). In Rwanda, the nationality law did not discriminate, but the ethnicity-specific identity cards first introduced by the Belgians played a notorious role in the 1994 genocide.[6]

In Zimbabwe, it was the provisions on dual nationality that became a tool of disenfranchisement. The incoming government in 1980 had been forced to accept the possibility of dual nationality in the new law that would come into effect on majority rule, alone among all the Commonwealth countries whose independence constitutions were negotiated in this way. This was changed before long, but the prohibition on dual citizenship was implemented in a straightforward manner to start off with. When the government's hold on power started to look shaky at the turn of the millennium, a 'legal' method was found to shore up its control – and also to bolster support among 'indigenous' Zimbabweans – by applying highly formalist interpretations to foreign laws in relation to the attribution of nationality to children born outside those countries. Potential voters for the first opposition party to challenge the independence leadership's hegemony could be made to vanish at the stroke of the registrar-general's pen. At each step, detailed changes to the citizenship law marked repeated efforts to close loopholes exposed in court (Chapter 7.1).

The expulsion of Ugandan Asians by Idi Amin, meanwhile, was not a simple matter of force, intimidation and arbitrariness (though it was all those things): it depended on changes to the law, the issue of new decrees, the cancellation of residence permits, and a process of 'verification' that those who had chosen to be Ugandan had correctly completed the formalities. In this way, the supposedly non-discretionary right of those born and resident in the territory at independence to register as citizens was 'legally' undermined (Chapter 7.3). In Sierra Leone and Liberia, the law was modified or designed from the outset to restrict access to citizenship for 'non-Africans', aimed – similarly to the case of Uganda – at the economically powerful communities of Lebanese and European descent, ensuring that they could not have access to political power. In Sierra Leone, one of the main targets was John Akar, a half-Lebanese active opponent of the first post-independence government (Chapter 7.2). In Mauritania, amendments to the law in 2010 were designed to make it significantly harder for those of black African ancestry to obtain recognition of Mauritanian nationality (Chapter 7.6).

In all these cases, there was much going on that was outside the framework of the law; but changes in the law have been and remain a key enabling factor for systematic policies of exclusion, even in States where formal institutions are quite weak.

[6] Timothy Longman, 'Identity Cards, Ethnic Self-Perception and Genocide in Rwanda' in Jane Caplan and John Torpey (eds), *Documenting Individual Identity: The Development of State Practices in the Modern World* (Princeton University Press 2001).

10.5. The Unintended Consequences of the Initial Frameworks for Nationality Law

It is more challenging to make the case that nationality law itself is an independent variable that has had an effect beyond the deliberate intentions of those who drafted it. Yet there is evidence that this is the case. For example, let us take a comparison between two francophone West African countries for an indication of how provisions in the law can make a difference in their own right: Côte d'Ivoire, the subject of extended treatment in this book (Chapter 7.4); and Senegal, as a counter-example. Though both fall within the same French legal tradition in terms of the way the laws and procedures were drafted, the substantive differences in the law were significant, and in unexpected ways. The law helps to frame an understanding of what is 'normal'; in Africa as elsewhere.

In Senegal, the nationality code provided and provides in its first article that any person born in Senegal (before or after independence) of one parent also born there is Senegalese (no further conditions); and that a person who has always been treated as Senegalese (is in *possession d'état de sénégalais*) is regarded as fulfilling this requirement and can go to court to obtain a certificate of nationality in case of any doubt.[7] Initially, and until 2013, the law discriminated on the basis of sex: only the child of a Senegalese father was Senegalese by descent, while only a man could transmit nationality to his spouse.

By contrast, in Côte d'Ivoire, the law gave 'nationality of origin' to every person born in Côte d'Ivoire unless both of his or her parents were foreigners (*étrangers*). There was, however, no definition of *étranger*, and a great deal of uncertainty about whom that term encompassed, given the incorporation of a large part of what is now Burkina Faso into Côte d'Ivoire for some of the colonial period and the fact that prior to independence most immigrants to Côte d'Ivoire were French nationals (and thus arguably not 'foreign'). There was no discrimination on the basis of sex in relation to transmission of nationality by descent, though discrimination on the basis of birth in or out of wedlock was introduced in 1973 (requiring additional proof of descent if out of wedlock). The gaps in the Ivorian law created a lack of clarity on who was Ivorian and who was not, that both built up resentment against those 'of doubtful nationality', and also created the possibility of suddenly denying rights to people who had been born and brought up in the country, and who had

[7] Loi No. 61-70 du 7 mars 1961 déterminant la nationalité sénégalaise, Article premier: « Est Sénégalais tout individu né au Sénégal d'un ascendant au premier degré qui y est lui-même né. Est censé remplir ces deux conditions celui qui a sa résidence habituelle sur le territoire de la République du Sénégal et qui a eu de tout temps la possession d'état de Sénégalais. La possession d'état dans le sens du paragraphe précédent consiste dans le fait pour celui qui s'en prévaut: 1°) De s'être continuellement et publiquement comporté comme un Sénégalais; 2°) D'avoir été continuellement et publiquement traité comme tel par la population et les autorités sénégalaises. » Foundlings and children of parents who are stateless or of unknown nationality are also Senegalese; though gender discrimination applied to the children of Senegalese mothers. Ibid. Articles 3 and 5. Gender discrimination was removed in 2013.

since independence been treated as Ivorian. Ultimately, those excluded in this way took to arms to defend their position.

Both in Senegal and in Côte d'Ivoire transitional provisions at independence created an additional right to opt for nationality to various categories of person during a transitional period.[8] While these provisions were accessed by some of the elites, and *fonctionnaires* who had roles within the French administration, many of those who could in theory have used these rights to register as nationals of the new States would have been completely unaware of their existence or importance. Very few did so in practice. These non-automatic provisions were not at all effective to provide for a largely illiterate population whose understanding of what was at stake would have been close to zero. In terms of impact on subsequent politics, they can be discounted.

But which differences explain the different trajectories of the two countries in terms of national identity? Côte d'Ivoire already had a large immigrant population at independence, so that the omission of the double *jus soli* rule could be argued to be the result rather than the cause of problems of integration. However, contemporary commentators at independence regarded the Ivorian code as being fundamentally *more* liberal than the double *jus soli* principle, and foresaw no such problems, even though they noted definitional issues.[9] This interpretation drew support from the pan-Africanist rhetoric and immigration-supportive policies of Félix Houphouët-Boigny that provided extremely liberal access for foreigners to the rights of Ivorian nationals. But the very lack of clarity on who was or was not a foreigner was part of the reason or opportunity for a serious backlash to these policies from the 1990s, the removal of any rights not based on descent, and highly discriminatory application of the existing law.

Senegal, which had been the administrative centre of AOF, also had a large immigrant stock: many had come from across the region for training and higher education; as well as labour for plantations in the Senegal river valley and the building of the Dakar-Bamako railroad. Many refugees fled to Senegal from Guinea during the repressive years of Sékou Touré's rule, and from Guinea-Bissau during that country's war of independence in the early 1970s. Yet the UN figures for foreigners as a percentage of the population were 1.6% for Senegal in 2010, against 12.5% for Côte d'Ivoire.[10] In Côte d'Ivoire itself, the decennial census indicated

[8] eg, in Senegal, Arts 28–31. Article 29 : 'Peut opter pour la nationalité sénégalaise: 1°) Toute personne originaire de l'un des Etats issus des anciens groupes de territoires d'Afrique occidentale française et d'Afrique équatoriale francaise, du Togo, du Cameroun et de Madagascar qui, à la date d'entrée en vigueur de la présente loi, a sa résidence habituelle au Sénégal;(Loi du 7 mars 1961). 2°) Toute personne mariée à une Sénégalaise depuis 5 ans. La même option est ouverte aux originaires des territoires limitrophes du Sénégal.'

[9] Decottignies and de Biéville, *Les nationalités africaines*, pp.178–181 ; Zatzepine, *Le droit de la nationalité*, pp.12–13 and 39–41. Also Procès-verbal de la séance du mercredi 8 novembre 1961, Commission des Affaires Générales et Institutionnelles, Assemblée Nationale.

[10] 'Trends in International Migrant Stock: The 2013 Revision' (UN Department of Economic and Social Affairs 2013) POP/DB/MIG/Stock/Rev.2013, table 3. The notes to the tables indicate that the

that the 'foreign' population formed more than one-quarter of all residents – yet almost half of those had been born in the country (see Chapter 7.4). Despite its own separatist movement in southern Casamance, Senegal has been one of the most stable African countries since the 1960s; nor is there the sense of a subterranean issue ready for exploitation in bad economic times.

As of 2013, 77% of Senegalese believed that a person born in the country of two non-citizen parents should have the right to nationality; 79% of Ivorians thought such a person should not.[11] It is surely plausible that at least one of the significant variables in this difference was the influence of the existing law and its implementation on popular attitudes.

Is Mali a counter-factual to this comparison? Mali's nationality law has since independence provided for the double *jus soli* rule, and for a person born in Mali to be able to opt for Malian nationality if still resident there at majority; yet Mali has also seen repeated rebellions from its Tuareg population in the vast northern regions, a rebellion that from 2011 has threatened the very existence of the State. There are many other variables at play here, including the threat to livelihoods from drought and desertification, and the collapse of the Libyan State to the north. But it is also the case that the double *jus soli* rule, devised in Europe among settled populations, does not work to integrate those following a nomadic lifestyle: the rule depends on two generations being born in the country before nationality is automatic. Moreover, the French civil code system required registration of birth to prove the facts related to nationality (something not accessible to the vast majority of Tuaregs), or rather costly alternative systems of proof through witness testimony to a court hearing. The initial version of the double jus soli rule in Mali also required the two generations to be 'of African origin': this obviously excluded those of European or Lebanese descent, but it was not clear how it applied to those of mixed race or, indeed, the (relatively fair-skinned) Tuareg (see Chapter 5.1.2). There is research to be done into the impact on the Malian conflict of the interpretation of these restrictions over time.

The clearest example of later problems being generated by a failure to create a comprehensive and clear legal transition at independence itself is perhaps that of the Democratic Republic of Congo (Chapter 7.5). In Congo, the extreme predatory nature of the colonial State and the rapidity and unplanned nature of the Belgian departure meant that there was no proper clarification of the legal status of those tens, probably hundreds, of thousands of people of Rwandan or Burundian origin imported to the country as labour on the plantations established for export crops. There was no detailed agreement on nationality and only a hastily adopted law on who could vote in the independence elections. The citizenship status of the

data sources for Côte d'Ivoire encompass both foreign-born persons and foreign nationals; whereas those for Senegal include only foreign-born persons and refugees recorded by UNHCR. Even so, the UN figure is roughly half the percentage reported by the Ivorian census.

[11] Afrobarometer online data analysis tool, Round 5 (2011/13), 'Right to be citizen: born in country with two non-citizen parents', http://afrobarometer.org/online-data-analysis/analyse-online.

Banyarwanda brought to Congo by the Belgians was complicated by the fact that Ruanda-Urundi had been mandated to Belgian administration by the League of Nations, and thus Belgium was expressly disallowed from conferring its nationality on the inhabitants of those territories (who, when brought to Congo, were therefore given different identity cards from the existing populations and other immigrants). Yet their children could also be argued to have obtained nationality automatically on a *jus soli* basis under an expansive 1892 law aimed at bringing as many as possible within Belgian jurisdiction; though Belgium itself had a descent-based law. The uncertainty surrounding their status during the panicky simultaneous withdrawal of Belgium from Congo, Rwanda and Burundi, amid an outbreak of violence in Rwanda that drove refugees into Congo at the critical moment of independence, left the issue open as a running sore in DRC till today.

The decision of the Belgian administration in the Congo to allow all Banyarwanda to vote in pre-independence elections, thus implying – without resolving in law – that they held the nationality of the soon-to-be-recognised State, did not address the concerns of those who might hope to hold positions of authority in that new State as to who would have the right to hold them to account. In the absence of any sensible regulation of this point, the new State then adopted ethnic identity as the basis for recognition of membership, requiring an ancestor who 'was or had been a member of a tribe or part of a tribe established in the Congo'. This focus on 'tribe' (later 'ethnic group' or 'nationality'), meant that forever afterwards the political discussion was necessarily about the date of arrival of some pristine forebear, rather than more practical questions about documentation of place of birth and parentage or length of residence of specific individuals. Again, there are many other variables – above all the rules on land ownership and usage, and the role of Congo's neighbours in the conflict – but the impact of the League of Nations mandate and the failure to create a reasonable framework for attribution of nationality at independence appear to have had the unintended consequence of making it impossible for the Banyarwanda simply to disappear into the Congolese population, as many other colonial-era immigrants did.

10.6. The Impact of Changes in Nationality Laws

It is perhaps even harder to determine the big picture impact of the amendments to nationality laws since independence on national cohesion; especially those that have been undertaken to expand rather than restrict access to nationality. But the trajectories of some countries are suggestive. The impact on individuals who have benefited from liberalisation of access is easier to document.

Ghana, whose political economy is in many ways similar to that of Côte d'Ivoire – mining and plantation-based, dependent on migrants from the north of the country and neighbouring States – at one time looked as though it might follow the same self-destructive path as its neighbour (see box in Chapter 5). The transitional provisions of the 1957 Ghana Nationality and Citizenship Act adopted the framework that became standard for other West African Commonwealth countries gaining independence, attributing citizenship automatically at the date of independence to those born in the country also had a parent or grandparent born in the country (East Africa restricted this to only a parent), and providing the right to register as citizens to many of those who did not qualify for automatic citizenship; *jus soli* was initially enacted for those born on the territory moving forward. Within a year or two of independence, politicians amended the citizenship laws to limit *jus soli* access to citizenship for those born after independence, and to facilitate deportations (aimed at 'foreigners' involved in opposition parties). Soon after, all 'aliens' were required to obtain residence permits, the government adopted official policies to promote economic advancement of 'indigenous' businesses, and by the late 1960s the position of migrant populations had become precarious: more than 200,000 people were expelled from the country in 1969–1970, most of them migrants from other West African countries.

But the policy changed. Politicians started to mobilise the votes of the descendants of foreign migrants, rather than to incite violence against them; the 'stranger' populations themselves organised to engage in politics, and were permitted to do so. The 1979 constitution relaxed the citizenship provisions to expand the category of persons automatically attributed nationality to those with a grandparent as well as a parent who is or was a citizen; and since 1996 Ghana has accepted dual citizenship, meaning that those who are also potentially nationals of another West African State can no longer ipso facto be presumed not to be Ghanaian.

Ghana is certainly not free of ethnic tensions, nor from politicians seeking to use an appeal to xenophobia, and nor is its law as inclusive as it might be (since there are no rights based on birth in Ghana). Perhaps, also, some may argue that it's just a question of timing: Ghana had a flare-up of its identity crisis earlier than Côte d'Ivoire, and that is all; the same issues could return in both countries. But it seems plausible to suggest that at least part of the contrast with Côte d'Ivoire is explained by the initial framework and later decisions to change the citizenship law: not just changes in political rhetoric, but changes in law. Ghana's very early abandonment of *jus soli* citizenship as politically unacceptable forced the discussion on what rules on belonging would, in fact, obtain consensus support. Meanwhile, the vagueness of the original formula in Côte d'Ivoire created an inclusive environment for many years, but meant that there was a dangerous level of ambiguity when the combined effects of commodity price falls and structural adjustment began to bite in the 1990s. This argument on the difference made by State institutions is supported by the illuminating research of Lauren MacLean on informal institutions and citizenship across the Ghana-Côte d'Ivoire border.[12] Though she does not address the content of citizenship laws directly, similar ethnographic research would surely reveal similarly interesting contrasts on questions related

[12] Lauren M MacLean, *Informal Institutions and Citizenship in Rural Africa: Risk and Reciprocity in Ghana and Côte d'Ivoire* (Cambridge University Press 2010).

to nationality law and identification. There is a 30% differential between Ghana and Côte d'Ivoire in support for the right to citizenship for a person born in the country of two non-citizen parents; not quite as large as that between Senegal and Côte d'Ivoire, but still substantial.[13]

Nigeria is an interesting example of infrastructure that has built up around citizenship and identification in the *absence* of formal law – but which is still fundamentally framed by legal scaffolding. Since 1974, the rules on citizenship in Nigeria have been found only in the constitution, with no implementing law; and since 1979, the constitution has provided for a presumption of citizenship founded in the concept of belonging to a 'community indigenous to Nigeria' (though also for naturalisation and for the children of naturalised citizens to be attributed citizenship at birth regardless of ethnicity). Part of the ambition of this reform was inclusive, to provide access to Nigerian citizenship for members of those ethnic groups divided by colonial borders. The simultaneous introduction of the concept of 'federal character' requiring an equitable distribution of government posts across the country, also had inclusive intentions. But in the absence of further statutory definition, these two concepts have combined to create a requirement of proof of 'indigeneity' for any official transaction, including a national passport. The decision on who qualifies as an 'indigene' of a particular area is both entirely decentralised to that area, without any legislative guidance, and also determinative of the national body of citizens (see Chapter 7.7). This may well create an openness in some cases (since it allows some to 'naturalise' at local level), but it also creates the potential to exacerbate the ethnification of competition over resources that many have been highlighted. Nigeria is also by some way the country with the weakest popular identification with national (rather than ethnic) identity among those surveyed by Afrobarometer – followed by Uganda, which also has an ethnic definition of citizenship.[14]

The importance of changes in the law can perhaps also be discerned where amendments have not taken place. In Côte d'Ivoire and Tanzania in particular, the pan-Africanist rhetoric of the post-independence leaders, Presidents Houphouët-Boigny and Nyerere, created a political welcome for immigrants, which many considered sufficient to accredit them as nationals. The lack of legal and procedural steps to put the rhetoric into practice became important much later, when the political welcome was no longer guaranteed.

The removal of gender discrimination in the great majority of African countries has enabled many thousands to obtain recognition of nationality that they

[13] Afrobarometer online data analysis tool, Round 5 (2011/13), 'Right to be citizen: born in country with two non-citizen parents', http://afrobarometer.org/online-data-analysis/analyse-online.

[14] Only 5% in Nigeria and 12% in Uganda stated to pollsters that they felt only Nigerian or Ugandan (compared to 62% in both South Africa and Tanzania; 66% in Guinea; and 71% in Burundi); though in both countries a substantial majority (60 and 69%) stated that they identified equally with both ethnic group and country. In all countries less than 10% stated that they identified only with their ethnic group. Afrobarometer online data analysis tool, Round 5 (2011/13), 'Ethnic or national identity', http://afrobarometer.org/online-data-analysis/analyse-online.

previously did not have; but because the impact of such changes is more diffuse these changes have had less obvious impact on political dynamics. Governments also keep no statistics on how many have therefore gained access to nationality who could not previously do so. But an end to gender discrimination has very important effects on the rights of individuals. Law reform may seem far from the day to day concerns of ordinary people, and respect in practice can remain a struggle, but these changes represent real gains in the daily lives of women; an insight well-understood by feminist legal scholars and activists.[15] Those opposed to equal rights have come to the same conclusion: in Mali, for example, gains in nationality law reform have been compromised in other legal battles (Chapter 5.2).

In many cases, the jury is still out on the influence of legal reforms, both for lack of full implementation of changes to the substantive law and for lack of research. Kenya's 2010 constitution created the possibility of improved access to nationality for some historically excluded groups, including both the children of unknown parents and the descendants of those who migrated to Kenya before independence who had never been documented, as well as for the children of Kenyan mothers born abroad. Only at the end of 2016 were the first efforts made to register qualifying individuals under these rules (Chapter 7.3).

Perhaps the strongest evidence of the relevance of nationality law and identity documentation to politics in the minds of the protagonists themselves is the appearance of such questions at the top of the list of questions to be resolved in peace agreements. This is true not only of the obvious cases such as the 2003 Linas-Marcoussis Accord and 2007 Ouagadougou Political Agreement between the Ivorian political opponents; the 2002 peace agreements and 2003 transitional constitution for the DRC; the adoption of a new constitution in Zimbabwe; or the end of the apartheid regime in South Africa. It is also true of less prominent agreements such as the August 2006 Togolese Global Political Accord (also signed in Ouagadougou) which envisaged the issue of identity cards along with electoral cards.[16] Citizenship also features in unsuccessful attempts to reach agreement: it was one of the five issues preventing an amicable settlement of the Sudan-South Sudan separation (Chapter 8.2).

[15] See, eg, Fareda Banda, *Women, Law and Human Rights: An African Perspective* (Hart Pub 2005); Kafui Adjamagbo-Johnson, 'Les Lois, Une Expression « officielle » Des Rapports de Genre' in Thérèse Locoh and Koffi N'Guessan (eds), *Genre, population et développement en Afrique de l'Ouest* (ENSEA, FNUAP 1999); Celestine Nyamu-Musembi, 'Addressing Formal and Substantive Citizenship: Gender Justice in Sub-Saharan Africa' in Maitrayee Mukhopadhyay and Navsharan Singh (eds), *Gender justice, citizenship and development* (Zubaan, an imprint of Kali for Women; International Development Research Centre 2007). See also the research and publications of Women and Law in Southern Africa (WLSA) or Women in Law and Development in Africa (WILDAF). For a critique of such 'legal centralism', see Ambreena S Manji, 'Imagining Women's "Legal World": Towards a Feminist Theory of Legal Pluralism in Africa' (1999) 8 Social & Legal Studies 435.

[16] Clause 1.2.5 Accord Politique Global, Ouagadougou, 20 August 2006.

10.7. Marginal Citizens: The Buffer Zone

The Nigerian case is illustrative of the reasons why nationality laws may not have received as much attention as perhaps they deserve. When a very large percentage of the population have no document attesting to their nationality, and no identification document is required by law, or where the rules for gaining access to documents are largely informalised, the difference between those who are nationals and those who are not is less obvious.

One characteristic of the policy debates around citizenship and statelessness in non-African contexts is that it is usually assumed that a State knows who is its national and who is not; that the line between citizen and alien is clear – even if there is also an intermediate category of legal resident, while naturalised citizenship may be a less secure status, and there may be some anomalous cases at the margins (for whom the category of Stateless person has been created).[17] There are major debates in citizenship studies about the citizenship behaviours of undocumented migrants in Europe or North America, and the ways in which the undocumented seek to create participatory spaces and exert rights within the civic space of the countries where they now live.[18] Even texts that seek to move away from 'binary categories of 'legal' and 'illegal', 'documented' and 'undocumented' assume that the categorisation at least is for the most part known both by the authorities and the individuals affected.[19]

In most if not all African countries, however, there is a large number of people whose legal status is simply not clear, even though they have never moved from where they and their parents were born and grew up, believe themselves to be nationals, and may, in fact, be nationals. It is only when an application is made for paperwork at the lowest administrative levels – a national identity card or other document, even a birth certificate – that a person may first become aware that his or her nationality is seen as doubtful. This lack of clarity is not just because the law is being misapplied or implemented in a discriminatory way or muddied by corruption (though all may be true), but inherent in the legal and administrative framework of the citizenship law. While this category of 'marginal citizens' exists in other regions around the world, the number of people with an unclear status, often marginal in geography but also marginal in terms of participation in the broader rights of citizenship, may be highest in the African continent.

[17] Bronwen Manby, 'The Human Right to Citizenship: A Slippery Concept by Rhoda E. Howard-Hassmann and Margaret Walton-Roberts (Review)' (2016) 38 Human Rights Quarterly 526.

[18] eg, Parts I and II in Engin F Isin and Peter Nyers (eds), *Routledge Handbook of Global Citizenship Studies* (Routledge 2014); Anne McNevin, 'Undocumented Citizens? Shifting Grounds of Citizenship in Los Angeles' in Peter Nyers and Kim Rygiel (eds), *Citizenship, migrant activism and the politics of movement* (Routledge 2012); Mae M Ngai, *Impossible Subjects: Illegal Aliens and the Making of Modern America* (Princeton University Press 2014).

[19] Roberto G Gonzales and Nando Sigona, 'Mapping the Soft Borders of Citizenship: An Introduction' in Roberto G Gonzales and Nando Sigona (eds), *Within and beyond citizenship: borders, membership and belonging* (Routledge 2017).

Lack of documentation is in part just one symptom of more general weaknesses in the State. A very large number of people in Africa have no documents because they don't see the point of having documents, and because they are costly in time and money to obtain. The first point of need is often when a child should enter school or needs to take an exam, but if schools are inaccessible or worthless, then what need for birth registration? If you remain entirely in the informal sector, a peasant farmer or transhumant pastoralist, then identity documents are not always required; if the police demand money when you cross a border or an internal checkpoint whether or not you have the right documents, then a passport or identity card does not serve even its most basic use of proving your right to be present or to travel. If your strongest allegiance is not to a State but rather to an ethnic group, why obtain documents of such little emotional value? If, in addition, obtaining documentation requires a journey to the nearest administrative centre, a long wait to be seen, a mixture of official and unofficial fees, and several days' lost income, the cost-benefit analysis looks untempting.

Thus, many people exist in a blurred zone in relation to legal nationality. It may be the case that some members of a community have some (but not all) documents related to nationality where they live (just a birth certificate, just an electoral card – but were rejected or never applied for a national ID card or passport); whereas some were never registered at birth and applications for all other documents have been rejected; some have obtained documents by paying bribes to intermediaries; and others have travelled to a different 'home' country to obtain documents there because they cannot get them where they currently live (or because they prefer to keep that affiliation). Equally, there are many who are, under the law, undoubtedly citizens, but they cannot prove it to the satisfaction of administrative requirements based on European models that assumed universal birth registration and movement of labour within a formal economy. This is especially the case because the detailed rules on nationality and its procedural requirements in neighbouring States can vary according to the colonial luck of the draw in ways that have little local resonance and must seem very perplexing to those on the ground.

This lack of clarity complicates the debate and leaves dangerous loopholes for the politically unscrupulous, since it is always possible for a government or political party to claim that there is no problem in principle with the right to nationality of a particular individual or group, while denying access to citizenship in practice through the deployment of administrative obstacles. Or for a politician to say that of course second generation children born in the country have the right to nationality under the law – but to assert at the same time that the documents members of a particular ethnic group produce to show this is the case have been fraudulently acquired.

But the lack of clarity also provides a grey zone that creates a protection against the impacts of the worst citizenship laws. If it is possible to acquire whatever identity document is needed through a combination of connections and cash then under some circumstances (especially of shared language and culture) a population of foreigners will over time simply dissolve into the existing body of citizens.

This effect should not be exaggerated. The informal does not always trump the formal requirements even in weak States; and in some countries and some circumstances rarely if ever does so.

10.8. The Importance of Recognised Nationality and the Impact of Statelessness

High profile cases such as those of Kaunda and Ouattara, and the targeting of those of European descent in Zimbabwe or Algeria, Asians in Uganda, or Lebanese in Sierra Leone, have encouraged a view that challenges related to denial of formal legal citizenship in Africa are fundamentally a problem of the elites, divorced from 'ordinary people'.

Similarly, the campaigns in many countries to amend the law to allow dual nationality have come from the diasporas of African countries now living in Europe or North America, rather than from those with a parent from a neighbouring country. Thus the tenor of those opposing the increasing liberalisation of rules on dual nationality is that those who are impacted by restrictions on dual nationality are individuals with political ambitions, international businessmen and the super-rich of probably dubious moral and social worth, and members of the increasingly numerous African diaspora who betrayed their own country to gain access to new passports but want the best of both worlds and wield their economic power to get it.[20]

For ordinary people, the argument goes, nationality is – except in extreme cases of manipulation of the law, and in States with relatively strong formal institutions, such as Côte d'Ivoire or Zimbabwe – an abstract concept of little relevance to day-to-day life; if indeed it is a concept recognised at all by those living in a peasant or pastoralist economy far from the reach of the modern State. Both officials and those nationals whose own membership of the State is unproblematic will frequently say that Nigerians or South Sudanese or Angolans or Senegalese 'know who they are' at the level of ethnic group, and so there is no real problem with legal categories. Alternatively, it is argued that individuals can assert rights of citizenship by their actions and even gain recognition of legal national citizenship through local acceptance of their status, even if of immigrant origin.

[20] For just one example, quotes from discussion in the Constituent Assembly debating a new constitution for Tanzania: 'Mr Louis Majaliwa proposed total deletion of dual citizenship in the constitution, saying "They (Tanzanians in Diaspora) insulted us and we don't need them either."' Masato Masato, 'Kadhi Court, Union, Citizenship Debate Rock CA', *Tanzania Daily News*, 10 September 2014. 'Dr Mary Mwanjelwa said single citizenship was the key indicator of a person's trust, patriotism and obedience to their country. "The issue here should not be dual citizenship but why people denounced their Tanzanian nationality in the first place".' Masato Masato, 'Katiba Debate Nears Finishing Line', *Tanzania Daily News*, 11 September 2014. The same discussion takes place in other countries yet to legalise dual citizenship.

At the same time, there are genuine concerns about the unwanted imposition of nationality and its requirements of registration and documentation. There may be very good reasons for not wanting to be recognised as a citizen of a particular State, or of any State at all. These have always existed, and indeed frame some of the oldest rules established by national citizenship laws, such as a ban on the capacity of a man to renounce citizenship during the period in which he could be called for military service. People living in the margins of the States who receive little benefit from public services, and only feel the weight of taxation or security harassment, may have good reason not to seek official recognition of their membership of that polity. Contemporary concerns around data protection, privacy, and ever-strengthening capabilities for surveillance create other reasons to opt out. The very meaning of nationality as a legal status is arguably empty when it is of a failed State such as Somalia or the Central African Republic.

But this is an underestimate of the extent to which lack of nationality impacts all but the most isolated communities – and, even more, the degree to which a lack of documents proving nationality is due to the provisions of the law (or lack of them) rather than simple prejudice, corruption, or administrative ineptitude at the level of the individual civil servants responsible for processing applications.

Most obviously, identity documents and proof of nationality are needed for those crossing borders or internal checkpoints. There is testimony in every human rights report investigating a national state of emergency anywhere in the world about the arbitrary use of identity documents in selecting individuals for 'taxation' or, in the worst case, death. Africa is no exception. Some of this relates, of course, to the name shown on the card and what it says about ethnicity or religion; but it is not only so. The distinction between national and foreigner recorded on a card may be just as relevant. Even in less critical moments, the lack of a national identity document can be an excuse for any State official to extract money or refuse access to rights. An identity document was the most immediate need expressed in a survey of 172 migrants by UNHCR and IOM in 2013 in Niger and Togo – 60% mentioning documentation as a more urgent requirement than transport, food, health care, shelter and other needs.[21]

Identification documents are, as others have noted, a tool of empowerment as well as of control, and also much-understudied as a basis for the consolidation or fragmentation of identities.[22] The laws on which the identity documents are based – especially the citizenship laws, but also related laws such as those on national identity cards or civil registration – are perhaps even more understudied by scholars (especially, of course, by those outside the legal field).

[21] Silvère Konan and Harouna Mounkaila, 'Migrants en détresse: Analyse de situation et cadre de protection: Le cas du Niger et du Togo' (UNHCR and IOM 2013).

[22] Edward Higgs, *The Information State in England: The Central Collection of Information on Citizens since 1500* (Palgrave Macmillan 2004); Jane Caplan and John Torpey (eds), *Documenting Individual Identity: The Development of State Practices in the Modern World* (Princeton University Press 2001); Keith Breckenridge and Simon Szreter (eds), *Registration and Recognition: Documenting the Person in World History* (Published for the British Academy by Oxford University Press 2012).

The narratives throughout this book show just how important citizenship law is for 'ordinary people' as they seek to access services and opportunities in even the most dysfunctional of States. For Sierra Leonean and Liberian former refugees in Guinea (Chapter 9.1), Nubian and Somali Kenyans (Chapter 7.3), people of South Sudanese origin denied Sudanese nationality (Chapter 8.2), Tuareg or Fulani nomads (or ex-nomads) in West Africa (box in Chapter 6.5), those affected by changes in borders (Chapter 8.5), and many others, inability to access nationality documents has daily consequences for themselves and their children.

Gender discrimination, whether enshrined in law or simply the norm in practice, ensures that those affected are not confined to particular geographies and members of specific ethnic groups, but spread throughout the population among the descendants of those who have rejected primordial attachments by 'marrying out' (Chapter 5.2). Again, this is not just a question of elite women with non-African husbands – though, thanks to their means, these are the cases that have mostly reached the courts – but just as much of the 'market women' crossing African borders on foot on a daily basis.[23] Perhaps worst affected are children separated from their parents, or whose parents are dead or unknown.

Everywhere across Africa, offices issuing identity cards are besieged with people trying to obtain proof that they belong. It is paradoxically often easier to register to vote than it is to obtain whatever document is required for national identity – even though voting is supposed to be restricted to nationals. Those who do not qualify find that many paths are blocked: that they are unable to get a position in the civil service (from school teacher to customs official to magistrate) or a job in the formal economy, to open a bank account, to buy a mobile phone or real property; or, of course, to organise politically and stand for office. For a young child, recognition of nationality may not be needed to access public services – childhood immunisations, primary school education and the like – but just as soon as there is question of government scholarships or fee-waivers for secondary school or university, or purchase of land, or travel within or without the country, papers proving nationality start to become necessary.

It is of course possible to cross a border or exist in a remote rural area or live in an urban slum without paperwork, and it is certainly possible to resolve some problems of paperwork with money[24]; but only so much can be achieved through bribing officials. Those applying the law are in the end charged with policing the boundaries of the system and ensuring that those who do not qualify do not get

[23] AP Cheater and Rudo Gaidzanwa, 'Transcending the State? Gender and Borderline Constructions of Citizenship in Zimbabwe' in Thomas M Wilson and Hastings Donnan (eds), *Border Identities: Nation and State at International Frontiers* (Cambridge University Press 1998); AP Cheater and RB Gaidzanwa, 'Citizenship in Neo-Patrilineal States: Gender and Mobility in Southern Africa' (1996) 22 Journal of Southern African Studies 189; Rudo Gaidzanwa, 'Citizenship, Nationality, Gender, and Class in Southern Africa' (1993) 18 Alternatives: Global, Local, Political 39.

[24] For a discussion of this issue in the Asian context, see Kamal Sadiq, *Paper Citizens: How Illegal Immigrants Acquire Citizenship in Developing Countries* (Oxford University Press 2009).

papers. If officials transgress too far beyond the limits of the law, they are likely in most places eventually to be found out. In particular, they may face difficulties if they go beyond simply taking money as an unofficial fee to issue a document that should be free, to supplying documents to those who are not nationals within the law. Money may not be enough to overcome the risk of exposure in situations where such questions are critical; and many officials either want to do their job properly or have limits to the extent to which they will bend the rules, even for money (certainly, the amounts of money that poor people have to offer). This is true especially in the civil law system where the final adjudicators on nationality matters are judges; but it is also true of ordinary police officers, consular officials, and immigration ministry clerks.

Corruption in nationality administration may, paradoxically, both ease problems of statelessness and create them. The ability to 'negotiate' the acquisition of a birth certificate, identity card or whatever document has local currency may enable a person to function effectively for most purposes. However, the sense that the system is not reliable may also mean that the mere possession of documents will not convince others that the person concerned is indeed a 'real' national, even if they fulfil all the conditions for nationality from birth or have completed all the procedures for naturalisation. If documents are known to be obtained corruptly, they are mistrusted; and, if a person becomes prominent in some way – or is faced with hostile armed men at a roadblock in a moment of national crisis – will not be believed as proof of nationality. In any event, if a document is revealed as a fraud, those who obtained them will have to start again. Even in South Africa, a far more functional State than many, corruption at the Department of Home Affairs has meant that official documents are not trusted as proof that a person has in fact the right to be in South Africa, or to be South African (Chapter 9.3).

So people take the measures they need to exist, and a situation of doubtful nationality may simply mean the payment of a bigger bribe to obtain the documents required or to pass without documents, but the more difficult it becomes to get round such problems, the greater the level of exclusion. At the extreme ends of such practices, individuals find themselves dismissed from their jobs or driven from their homes; or just left in limbo, unable to progress with their plans for their lives.

Of course, this is not just a matter of legal drafting and State capacity; access to nationality goes to the heart of political and economic power. Recognition as a national (or member of a sub-national unit) is tied up with access to property, especially land, and with economic power more generally, as well as the right to vote and participate in public affairs. In times of economic and political insecurity, the 'stranger' is always likely to be suspect. Politicians around the world have found other means than citizenship law to stir up identity-based violence. Yet law matters, even in some of the most dysfunctional States; and it matters more the greater the State's level of functionality – and for positive reasons of access to services and the political space reserved to citizens, not just because the State's ability to exert control over those who have papers is stronger.

11

An Agenda for Research and Reform

What makes the Nation is the common will to live together. Generally this common will derives from history and from being neighbours – not necessarily good neighbours. Now the history of the last sixty years has brought us together in the former Afrique occidentale française.... We cannot swim back against this stream of history without the risk of drowning.

– Léopold Sédar Senghor[1]

The superficial similarity of nationality laws in Africa, even between the different legal traditions, disguises endlessly varied underlying traditions and concepts of membership and belonging at local levels. The underlying variations have, to date, generally received more attention from scholars than the similarities and differences in law: the law determining rights to national citizenship has often seemed essentially irrelevant to the identity conflicts that have played out since those nationalities were invented. In this book I join the recent voices that have argued that the modern State, despite its frequent dysfunctionality, is nonetheless deeply implicated in the lives of even the poorest and most remote Africans. I also argue that questions of identity, just as much as competition over land, are thus not beyond the reach of the State and national law.

Specifically, the legal rules on who is or is not entitled to documentation that is proof of nationality have a very significant impact on the life chances of millions of people. Often, this impact will not result in any obvious ripple effect, where those impacted are the weakest in society – the orphans, the children born out of wedlock, the disabled – and these impacts are otherwise equally spread among social groups. Alternatively, an attack on an obviously privileged group – as in the expulsion of the Ugandan Asians or denationalisation of whites in Zimbabwe – may have an obvious political utility, even if there are economic costs. But where a particular group with nowhere else to go faces systematic exclusion, the impact can ultimately threaten the very stability of the State.

There is, however, much less detailed ethnographic study of the impact of nationality laws and related identification documentation in particular circumstances than there is of other factors, such as the importance of different land

[1] *Nation et voie africaine du socialisme*, 1961; as quoted in John D Hargreaves, *West Africa: The Former French States* (Prentice-Hall 1967) 3.

regimes or the role of competitive elections. There is even less research on lack of recognised nationality as a cause of migration, criminal activity or motivation to join a rebel movement. Politicians and the public anywhere in the world often blame undocumented migrants for crime, provoking detailed research that exonerates such migrants from that charge; but the deliberate or accidental 'undocumenting' of a person as a cause of migration, crime, or conflict is relatively unstudied, outside the most egregious cases.

I would not, of course, argue that reform of citizenship and identification laws alone would address all the questions around membership and belonging: there are many other variables that have been factors in individual exclusion and group conflict in Africa (or elsewhere). I make the more modest case that there are legal provisions that can be adopted that will significantly help individuals currently excluded from nationality; more ambitiously, that such reforms may also make a contribution to the broader effort to ground the stability of African States and to create a consensus on who has the right to belong and participate in those States. The relevance of legal definitions and nationality law to questions of autochthony could benefit from more research. The analysis must of course go beyond the law as it is written to examine the law as it is applied: law on its own does not produce any outcomes, which depend on the manner of implementation by State officials.

There is a temptation to regard African States as unique in the difficulty of such issues. It may be true that the violence of Africa's introduction to its European colonisers, the irrationality of many of the borders created for African States, and the abruptness of the departure of the colonial powers create particular challenges. Yet it is also the case that borders everywhere have been established by war, that post-imperial hangovers have given every continent headaches, and that contemporary migration threatens the equilibrium of even those States whose citizenship rules seem most stable. Eugen Weber reminds us that the creation of a common French identity was a surprisingly recent effort,[2] while T.H. Marshall's classic work on the development of citizenship rights highlights property qualifications necessary to vote and thus to become a 'citizen' that are perhaps not so different from the issues in Côte d'Ivoire (and many other African countries) over whether those who are tenants on others' land should have the right to participate in the national (and local) polity.[3]

The current international legal framework – while improving – is often unhelpful to address these questions as they manifest on the ground. Nationality law was originally developed for the convenience of States, not for the empowerment and inclusion of residents in their territory. Moreover, despite inroads on

[2] Eugen Weber, *Peasants into Frenchmen: The Modernization of Rural France; 1870 – 1914* (Stanford Univ Press 2007); see also Patrick Weil, *Qu'est-ce qu'un Français? Histoire de la nationalité française de la Révolution à nos jours* (Grasset 2002).

[3] TH Marshall, *Citizenship and Social Class and Other Essays* (Cambridge University Press 1950).

State discretion, international law has a lingering tolerance towards the highly restrictive criteria and arbitrary decision-making processes that are regularly applied to persons wishing to adopt the nationality of a new country, and their children. Developing the international regime may assist States to frame their own national laws in ways that are more helpful, and national advocates to put pressure on their own governments to adopt such reforms. The application of stronger international rules for the grant of nationality, historically considered mainly from the point of view of conflict of laws *between* States, may also be a way of reducing friction *within* States.

What, therefore, is a useful conceptualisation of the core content of nationality and its legal foundations if not the ascriptive one of the colonisers? History and experience is the only possible place to start. At the African level, this idea already has a deep hold on popular consciousness: the heritage of the great pan-Africanists is embedded in a shared sense of Africanness across the continent.[4] The transformation of the OAU into the African Union has brought further discussion of the promotion of freedom of movement, and even the recognition in principle of an African citizenship; but the most notable thinking has gone into the economics rather than politics of integration. Some individual thinkers and independence leaders, Senghor and Nyerere among them, also put serious thought into the creation of a national identity within the borders that had been inherited.[5] But there has been much less intellectual work around the adoption of practical rules for deciding who is a national and how to give recognition of that identity, within the context of the borders of today's States. The project of pan-Africanism (erratic as its progress has been) has often not been matched by equal projects of imagination at the level of political units that actually exist; nor even by efforts to harmonise nationality laws that would facilitate the legal recognition of a pan-African identity.

The common criteria for such laws are not hard to imagine, based as they are on rules that are already in currency: birth and residence of that person, and the birth and residence of his or her parents, grandparents, children or spouse; as well as similar connections to former political units that have been reconfigured to make up the State now in existence. That is, what the International Law Commission in the context of State succession calls an 'appropriate connection' to the State, or, in the words of the Nottebohm case, links such as 'the habitual residence of the individual concerned but also the centre of his interests, his family ties, his participation in public life, attachment shown by him for a given country and inculcated in his children, etc' (see Chapter 1.2).[6] As the African Commission

[4] Toyin Falola and Kwame Essien (eds), *Pan-Africanism, and the Politics of African Citizenship and Identity* (Routledge 2014); Paul G Adogamhe, 'Pan-Africanism Revisited: Vision and Reality of African Unity and Development' (2008) 2 African Integration Review 1.

[5] For a recent perspective, see, eg, Marie-Aude Fouéré, 'Julius Nyerere, Ujamaa, and Political Morality in Contemporary Tanzania' (2014) 57 African Studies Review 1.

[6] Nottebohm Case, (ch 1, n 32) p.22.

on Human and Peoples' Rights stated in the Kenneth Kaunda case, in relation to the status of pre-independence migrants:

> the movement of people in what had been the Central African Federation (now the States of Malawi, Zambia and Zimbabwe)[7] was free and … by Zambia's own admission, all such residents were, upon application, granted the citizenship of Zambia at independence. Rights which have been enjoyed for over 30 years cannot be lightly taken away. To suggest that an indigenous Zambian is one who was born and whose parents were born in what came (later) to be known as the sovereign territory of the State of Zambia may be arbitrary and its application of retrospectivity cannot be justifiable according to the Charter.[8]

Many millions of people in Africa live in a country that is not the one where they were born, and many millions more in a country that is not the one where their parents were born. Most of them have their origins in another African country; many have established new lives and intend to remain indefinitely in the 'new' country, which may be the country of their birth; others are nomadic pastoralists. Despite this, it is very difficult to acquire the nationality of any country through naturalisation; and a number of African countries provide almost no possibility for the descendants of migrants to obtain the nationality of the country where they were born, even over multiple generations.

I conclude by suggesting some key problems that could and should be addressed by law reform, and end with a note of warning that these questions around legal definitions of citizenship and the procedures to apply them are rapidly going to become more critical. Concerns around national security and migration, but also the increasing capacity of (some) States to deliver benefits for their citizens, are combining with the availability of cheap biometric technology to create a perfect storm around nationality and identification, in Africa as elsewhere.

11.1. Pathways to Citizenship

The limited legitimacy and institutional strength of African States has favoured (though not universally) the descent-based framing of nationality – against even the pre-colonial traditions of African polities. Paradoxically, this trend has been most pronounced in many of the countries that inherited the pure *jus soli* rules in the Commonwealth countries from British law, and in reaction to those very rules. The outcome has been that there are many millions of people who have no strong connection to another State who cannot obtain recognition of the nationality of the State where they were born and now live; in some cases even after several generations.

The question for the State and its politicians (and not only in Africa) is to draft the legal provisions that allow these alleged 'strangers' to become 'natives' in a way

[7] On the Central African Federation, see chs 3.1 and 4.2.

[8] *Legal Resources Foundation v Zambia*, African Commission on Human and Peoples' Rights, Communication 211/98 (2001), para 71.

that neither leaves people vulnerable to perpetual exclusion nor creates a backlash among populations that see themselves as the hosts. The rules on membership must have the consensus support of the existing recognised body of citizens, creating conditions for admission that are both rigorous enough not to be seen as an open-door policy, and accessible enough that those who wish to be recognised as members of a State are not condemned to a decades-long or multi-generational limbo. The idea of mutual consent to citizenship, dating back to the early citizenship debates in Europe, still has relevance. In finding this balance, the countries with a pure descent-based system can learn from those francophone states that both adopted and retained rights based on birth and residence in the territory, and provided judicial oversight of decisions on eligibility.[9]

Two continental movements have shown the power of persistent lobbying in changing the law related to nationality – but also in changing the minds of others in the national community on the nature of the problem: the campaigns for an end to gender discrimination, and for dual nationality to be permitted. There are also similar campaigns in individual States and the beginnings of a movement at continental level around rights based on place of birth and residence – both in a State, and within sub-national units – in addition to those based on descent. These arguments focus on the provisions of the law as a way of escaping from an understanding of membership based on ascription and perception. Just as in the case of the campaign to remove gender discrimination, law reform cannot immediately resolve questions of discrimination in broader society, but it can provide real relief for people who are currently denied recognition by the State, and potentially influence societal perceptions in the longer run.

Of course, the development of an inclusive national citizenship (in its fullest sense) must go well beyond legal formalism to the everyday building of trust in institutions, and will depend also on the 'acts of citizenship' that in themselves create the fact of belonging.[10] But debates over law reform can also create the space to engage with these wider questions.

11.2. Resolving the Question of Theoretical other Nationalities

African States have recognised the principle that a child born in a country who does not acquire another nationality at birth should acquire the nationality of the

[9] See Bronwen Manby, *Citizenship Law in Africa: A Comparative Study* (3rd edn, Open Society Foundations 2016) for detailed recommendations; the solutions proposed resemble in many respects those put forward by Rainer Bauböck and others (eds), *Acquisition and Loss of Nationality: Policies and Trends in 15 European States*, vol 1 (Amsterdam University Press 2006) in the European context.

[10] Engin F Isin and Greg Marc Nielsen (eds), *Acts of Citizenship* (Zed Books 2008); Peter Nyers and Kim Rygiel (eds), *Citizenship, Migrant Activism and the Politics of Movement* (Routledge 2012).

State where he or she is born. The African Charter on the Rights and Welfare of the Child, which contains this provision, is almost universally ratified in Africa. In theory, therefore, statelessness would be eradicated within a generation. In practice, the framing of the African Children's Charter around the requirement to prove the lack of another nationality, based on the similar provision in the UN Convention on the Reduction of Statelessness, renders this protection very limited. It is hard to prove a negative.

The view of most African States has been that the attribution of nationality by other States to the children of their nationals born abroad means that those children should not also be attributed any rights to nationality on the basis of the location of their birth. Yet, given weaknesses in nationality and consular administration, including birth registration, a very large proportion of the children of migrants will not, in fact, ever acquire documents recognising the nationality of a foreign parent. Some would be able to acquire that recognition on application; but many would not, even more so with succeeding generations.

Moreover, this interpretation has decreasing sense, now that a large majority of African States allow dual nationality for a person who has held two nationalities from birth (even if they forbid it for those who naturalise or for those who *voluntarily* acquire another nationality). Though the move to relax rules on dual nationality has been driven largely by diaspora Africans, and remains controversial in many countries, it responds also to the lack of legitimacy of African borders, as they cut through members of the same linguistic or other community, and the reality of intra-continental migration.

Advocacy for reform at national and continental level will need to address this question of potential nationality, and the establishment of procedures to resolve it. All over the world where there are large stateless populations, the assertion by the State concerned is that these populations are not stateless, but from somewhere else: this is just as true in Africa. Adjudication mechanisms are needed.

11.3. The Situation of Nomads

The modern State system is peculiarly ill-adapted to accommodate people whose lifestyle is not sedentary. The entire system of international and most domestic law on citizenship (and other) issues has grown up around the idea that individuals have their 'home' in one fixed place and that States have a sovereign right to know where that place is. Modern lifestyles in the rich world challenge this assumption, with the super-rich and their multiple homes and multiple citizenships – or even the visiting professor who splits her time between two universities, or the child of migrant parents who carries two or three passports.[11] While these individuals

[11] Atossa Abrahamian, *Cosmopolites: What It Is like to Be a Citizen of the World* (Columbia Global Reports 2015).

may garner little sympathy for any problems of uncertain identity, those least accommodated by the fundamental framework of nationality law are members of traditionally nomadic populations, including pastoralist groups whose seasonal grazing routes cross national borders.

Pastoralist groups have, of course, also resisted inclusion in the State, occupying the 'shatter zones' between States and evading the obligations of tribute and conformity imposed by the colonial and post-colonial State alike.[12] Alternatively, they have sought autonomy through negotiation with the colonial powers (see the arguments made to France for creation of a Sahelian State, Chapter 3.2); or by simple armed rebellion. Many of these communities have lived, in effect, outside the legal framework of citizenship and its attendant rights and responsibilities. While they may be envied for this so long as it is their choice, many find that statelessness is an unwelcome condition once they need to have contact with the authorities claiming territorial control of the places they earn their livelihoods.

As we progress into the twenty-first century a strategy of State-avoidance is ever harder to sustain. Lack of identification as a national of one or another State through which they pass (or of all) cripples those who follow a pastoralist lifestyle – as well as individuals belonging to ethnic groups perceived to be pastoralist who have never herded a cow in their lives. In West Africa, the Tuareg, Fulani (Peul), Mbororo and other groups have consistently faced problems in recognition as nationals across the Sahel region (Chapter 6.5). The status of the Misseriya in Abyei has been one of the major problems in resolving the status of that territory (Chapter 8.2). Other communities dependent on a hunter-gatherer lifestyle face the same questions.

There have been some State efforts to address issues related to cross-border pastoralism, with bilateral and multi-lateral agreements to facilitate cross-border movement, especially in West Africa, under the aegis of ECOWAS, and a policy adopted by the African Union itself.[13] However, these documents do not address the issue of nationality of the pastoralists themselves – and are focused on facilitating the conflict-free movement of the livestock rather than the people concerned.

There is also an almost total lack of international law or national precedent relating to the determination of the nationality of those who are not 'habitually resident' in any particular place.[14] Nor is there any international law framework

[12] Compare the southeast Asian experience explored in James C Scott, *The Art of Not Being Governed: An Anarchist History of Upland Southeast Asia* (Yale University Press 2009).

[13] ECOWAS, 'Réglementation de La Transhumance Entre Les États Membres de La CEDEAO, Décision A/DEC.5/10/98'; African Union, 'Policy Framework for Pastoralism in Africa: Securing, Protecting and Improving the Lives, Livelihoods and Rights of Pastoralist Communities' (2010). See also Mohamadou Abdoul, 'Policy Frameworks for Cross-Border Transhumance' (Concordis 2011) 5.

[14] The only exception is a rather general Recommendation adopted by the Council of Europe in 1983 that urged Member States to facilitate the recognition of nationality for nomadic populations. The Recommendation suggested the following criteria for consideration in establishing a link on the basis of which nationality should be granted: whether the State is 'the state of birth or origin' of the person concerned or the 'state of origin' of his or her immediate family; whether it is the State of habitual

around the rights of pastoralists more generally. In the absence of such a framework, nomadic pastoralist populations in Africa have often found a space to voice their concerns within the framework of the international debate around the rights of 'indigenous peoples'; although their particular situations vary greatly and often do not fit easily into the same pattern as that of aboriginal populations in other continents.[15] The terminology around indigenous peoples sits uneasily in Africa – where the division between 'natives' and 'settlers' is far more often between different populations of African origin than between those of African origin and recent immigrants from Europe or other continents – and African States have indeed objected to UN recognition of particular rights for the 'indigenous'.[16]

The African Commission on Human and Peoples' Rights has sought to escape these difficulties by expanding the definition of who is 'indigenous' beyond the international usage, and have included some pastoralist groups within that definition;[17] although the principal decision of the Commission of the Commission referring to the concept relates rather to the forest-dwelling Endorois of Kenya.[18]

The very large and longstanding literature on nomadic and seasonal migratory pastoralism in Africa, rarely deals with the rights of pastoralists to a nationality, though problems with identity papers or possession of multiple passports may be mentioned in passing.[19] There is a lack of research around the meaning and utility of nationality and identification documents for nomadic populations, and the systems that would work to provide them with access to the rights and services they need, while satisfying States' needs for some level of knowledge over who is

residence or frequent periods of residence of the person (provided the residence is not unlawful); and the presence in the State of members of the person's immediate family. Council of Europe Committee of Ministers Recommendation No. R. (83)1, 22 February 1983.

[15] Dorothy Louise Hodgson, *Being Maasai, Becoming Indigenous: Postcolonial Politics in a Neoliberal World* (Indiana University Press 2011).

[16] eg, in response to the draft UN Declaration on the Rights of Indigenous Peoples the African Group protested that endorsement of rights based on indigenousness could 'create tensions amongst ethnic groups and instability within sovereign states'. 'Draft Aide Memoire : African Group : United Nations Declaration on the Rights of Indigenous People' (2006); see generally on these debates, Felix Mukwiza Ndahinda, *Indigenousness in Africa: A Contested Legal Framework for Empowerment of 'marginalized' Communities* (TMC Asser Press 2011). The Declaration was eventually adopted in 2007 by a majority of 144 States in favour, 4 votes against (Australia, Canada, New Zealand and the US) and 11 abstentions (Azerbaijan, Bangladesh, Bhutan, Burundi, Colombia, Georgia, Kenya, Nigeria, Russian Federation, Samoa, and Ukraine).

[17] African Commission on Human and Peoples' Rights, 'Advisory Opinion on the United Nations Declaration on the Rights of Indigenous Peoples.' (African Union 2007); African Commission on Human and Peoples' Rights, 'Reports of the African Commission's Working Group on Indigenous Populations/Communities' (various) www.achpr.org/mechanisms/indigenous-populations/. The draft Protocol to the African Charter on Human and Peoples' Rights on the Specific Aspects of the Right to a Nationality and the Eradication of Statelessness in Africa adopted by the African Commission in July 2015 contained an article suggesting the sorts of connections that states should accept to recognise the nationality of nomadic populations.

[18] For a discussion, see Gabrielle Lynch, 'Becoming Indigenous in the Pursuit of Justice: The African Commission on Human and Peoples' Rights and the Endorois' (2012) 111 African Affairs 24.

[19] eg: John Markakis, 'Pastoralism on the Margin' (Minority Rights Group International 2004); Ekuru Aukot, 'Am I Stateless Because I Am a Nomad?' (2009) 32 (Statelessness) Forced Migration Review 18.

entitled to those goods. It may well be that the modern territorial State is simply not how many members of nomadic groups chiefly imagine their identity; but as a matter of fact they need documents to be able to operate, and the current system is not working well for either nomads or the States where they live.

11.4. Bringing Naturalisation in from the Arbitrary Cold

African States have struggled to make effective the European-bequeathed systems devised to enable a person to change nationality through naturalisation. These systems not only radically clash with the experience during the colonial period, when nationality and local tribal identity were matters of attribution and not of choice, but are also quite poorly adapted to the context where centralised State apparatuses have limited legitimacy.

The process of bringing naturalisation procedures within the frame of human rights, legitimate expectation and due process has not begun in African States (with some very few and limited exceptions). These constraints are also limited elsewhere.[20] Executive discretion is almost complete in the grant of nationality by naturalisation in Africa: and in a very large number of countries naturalisation is within the personal gift of the president, guaranteeing that it is inaccessible and politicised (Chapter 5.4). South Africa, the one country with an administrative decision-making process, has moved towards more discretionary access. Yet this situation has received comparatively little attention from the human rights movement.

Figures on the numbers of persons naturalised are rarely published. In the civil law States, naturalisation is usually accomplished by presidential decree, and these decrees will be published in the official journal of the State, which at least in theory are available for public consultation (not all countries publish their official journal regularly); in the common law countries, the only source of information may be a press release or interview. However, it seems clear that very few are naturalised in any country in the normal run of events. There have been few efforts to facilitate access for communities who have not been able to access these procedures.

The impact of these weaknesses, especially in States that found their law on descent, is that large numbers of people who have lost all connection with an ancestral State 'of origin' nonetheless have no access to recognised citizenship where they now live. Yet the ways in which naturalisation works in practice are little studied, outside the few exceptional programmes, such as those implemented in Tanzania and Côte d'Ivoire; nor the ways in which naturalisation might be better arranged.

[20] For a discussion in the European and North American context, see Christian Joppke, *Citizenship and Immigration* (Polity 2010) 45–47.

11.5. The Role of Decentralised Decision-Making

As has been widely noted, an opening of the political system in African States has often led to increased ethnic conflict, leading to discussions on the need for sequencing of institution-building and electoral competition.[21] Decentralisation and devolution have exacerbated the trend to emphasise autochthony and the prior rights of the 'native' at local levels, calling into question the very notion of citizenship at the national level.[22]

For most people, the broader citizenship rights associated with legal status are exercised at the local level. This includes not only the political rights to vote and participate, but also access to schools and hospitals, or even equal protection of the law in all its manifestations. Perhaps most importantly, national and local citizenship rights may be intertwined when it comes to access to and secure tenure over land. Here, too, there is scope for comparative analysis of the ways in which land law and citizenship law have interacted in different African countries, and the implications for political stability and possible efforts at law reform.

To date, there has not yet been a serious effort to advocate for formal written rules for belonging at the sub-national level that both recognise the reality of regions and localities that may have greater popular meaning than the 'nation-state', but also avoid over-reliance on 'instinctive' definitions tending to 'blood and soil', and create the possibility for a person to change his or her place of belonging in a way that recognises internal mobility.

Interesting to explore in this context may be the different experiences of the local identity documents that are almost a form of 'decentralised naturalisation' in the cases of Nigeria or Ethiopia. Problematic as these examples often are in practice, as much commentary has warned (see notes to Chapters 7.7 and 8.1), the underlying ideas and conditions would merit more study, not just in their own right but in comparative context, and in their possible application more broadly to the question of national citizenship in African States (in both the legal and broader participatory senses).

There are few international precedents for decentralisation of the grant of nationality, the most notable example being naturalisation at the cantonal level in Switzerland, based on the unique confederal features of the Swiss constitution. The Swiss model has been heavily criticised for permitting discrimination and arbitrary decision-making.[23] However, rather than simply rejecting the role of

[21] Jack L Snyder, *From Voting to Violence: Democratization and Nationalist Conflict* (Norton 2000); Edward D Mansfield and Jack L Snyder, *Electing to Fight: Why Emerging Democracies Go to War* (MIT Press 2007).

[22] Jean-François Bayart, Peter Geschiere and Francis Nyamnjoh, 'Autochtonie, démocratie et citoyenneté en Afrique' (2001) 10 Critique internationale 177; Peter Geschiere, *The Perils of Belonging: Autochthony, Citizenship, and Exclusion in Africa and Europe* (University of Chicago Press 2009).

[23] In Switzerland the cantons naturalise individuals, but all the other cantons of the federation then recognise that person as a Swiss national. See Alberto Achermann and others, 'Country Report on Switzerland' (European University Institute 2010) RSCAS/EUDO-CIT-CR 2010/25; Nicole

sub-national government out of hand, there is reason to consider the possibilities of better regulation of such systems, with protections against discrimination and a right to appeal.

11.6. The Importance of Subsidiary Legislation and Administrative Procedures

The devil is in the detail when it comes to implementation of nationality law. The top-level statements in the constitution and individual statutes only become truly effective once instructions have percolated down to all the officials responsible for administering the law.

Kenya's 2010 constitution, for example, provides for foundlings to be presumed to be Kenyan and for stateless persons to acquire Kenyan citizenship by registration; but, without implementing regulations and administrative directives, the processes remained largely ineffective five years later. With the law alone, a thoughtful magistrate, or a claimant with a lawyer, can still make a difference for the person before the court, but not for all those who should be entitled. In the francophone countries where treaties are stated by the constitution or nationality code to have direct effect, it is still rare for those treaties to be invoked before a magistrate and applied in the interests of the person affected. Conflicts between the law and constitution in countries such as Liberia, Togo or Burundi, create administrative paralysis where officials choose the more conservative option, even if the constitution is supposed to override it.

But the detailed rules on application of the law are far from irrelevant even where States are weak. A great deal can be achieved simply by adopting secondary legislation that reduces the absolute discretion of junior officials, as well as by updating forms and instructions given to officials to reflect the law itself. Even without a sudden miraculous strengthening of administrative capacity, these top-level efforts create avenues for appeal from arbitrary decisions and points of engagement for civil society organisations and paralegals working at the local level.

There is a need to understand more about the differences in impact on individual applicants of the differences in systems; especially between the Commonwealth countries where nationality administration is executive-dominated but perhaps more flexible, and the civil law system where the courts have a much stronger oversight role, but procedures can become too rigid. Both civil and common law

Wichmann, 'Reforming the Swiss Citizenship Act: Mission Impossible' (Swiss Forum for Migration Studies, University of Neuchatel 2013) SFM Discussion Paper 29; Jens Hainmueller and Dominik Hangartner, 'Who Gets a Swiss Passport? A Natural Experiment in Immigrant Discrimination' (2013) 107 American Political Science Review 159.

systems could benefit from a review of the forms of evidence of the connection to that State that shows entitlement to nationality: a refugee returning home may have (for example) a primary school enrolment card as the sole document of identity connected to that State; but officials recognising that person's nationality may have no or little discretion to accept it as proof of his or her connection. Nomadic pastoralists may lack many or all of the documents that the settled community are expected to have. The continental push to strengthen civil registration is important; but the civil law requirement that all facts are proved through civil registration creates unnecessarily layers of bureaucracy in resolving some cases. How can provisions that provide a right to nationality based on birth and residence in the territory be made effective?

Perhaps most urgently, what is the impact of new requirements for national identification being introduced throughout the continent on those undocumented but perfectly good citizens who have managed to get by so far – but who will struggle when it comes to providing the specific documents that are asked for as proof of nationality as the new systems are introduced?

11.7. 'Legal identity' and New Technologies in Africa

In September 2015, the UN General Assembly adopted the Sustainable Development Goals (SDGs), an ambitious set of objectives for international development to replace and expand upon the 15-year-old Millennium Development Goals (MDGs) adopted in 2000.[24] Goal 16 was one of the broadest: 'Promote peaceful and inclusive societies for sustainable development, provide access to justice for all and build effective, accountable and inclusive institutions at all levels'. Each Goal had a set of more detailed targets: Target 16.9 required that States should, by 2030, 'provide legal identity for all, including birth registration'.

There was relative clarity on the meaning of the target for birth registration (though some argument about the metrics for measuring progress), but a great deal of confusion around the meaning of 'legal identity' more generally and how it related to or differed from either birth registration or nationality.

The proposed indicator to measure progress towards Target 16.9 was the percentage of children under five whose births have been registered, a statistic already collected in many countries through surveys conducted by UNICEF.[25] There was no indicator proposed for other forms of recognition of legal identity beyond birth registration, nor consensus on what success in achieving the broader target would look like. Indeed, 'legal identity' is not a term that has any definition

[24] See the Sustainable Development knowledge platform at https://sustainabledevelopment.un.org/sdgs for further information.

[25] See SDG indicators, available at http://unstats.un.org/sdgs/. Birth registration data is also collected through the global Demographic and Health Survey (DHS) program, funded by the US government.

in international law, although international development agencies have been discussing questions around proof of legal identity for some years.[26]

The World Bank's 2016 *World Development Report* (WDR), considering the development benefits of digital technologies, recommended that the best way to achieve the SDG legal identity target is 'through digital identity systems, central registries storing personal data in digital form and credentials that rely on digital, rather than physical, mechanisms to authenticate the identity of their holder.'[27] Although the WDR also emphasises the importance of strengthening the 'analog foundations of the digital revolution', it suggests that low-income countries may leapfrog the paper-based stage, and move straight to digital identification.[28] Among those that have hitched a ride on the concept of legal identity are the big biometric technology companies, seeing the SDG Target as an endorsement of their own products.[29] There are some overblown claims about the ability of the new systems to eliminate doubts over the identification of citizens and foreigners, in contexts where such uncertainties had nothing to do with authentication of the person holding an identity card, and everything to do with law and politics.[30]

In practice, identification systems across Africa are rapidly being upgraded. National security is behind part of this effort; but also the increasing capability of some States to deliver real benefits to their citizens, and the same concerns shared by States in other regions of the world to restrict access to services to those who are supposed to be entitled to them, largely nationals. Governments are increasingly linking access to services such as health and education to possession of an approved form of identification. There are major efforts to improve birth registration, and civil registration more generally, sponsored by UN agencies working with the African Union.[31] National identity cards have been introduced where they did not previously exist, or converted to biometric versions where they did. In 2016, the West Africa region resolved on the introduction of a new standard form biometric card in all ECOWAS countries, including in the countries that had never had an identity card before. The EAC followed suit.

[26] Bronwen Manby, 'Legal Identity for All and Childhood Statelessness' in Laura van Waas and Amal De Chickera (eds), *The World's Stateless* (Institute on Statelessness and Inclusion 2017); see also, Caroline Vandenabeele and Christine Veloso Lao, 'Legal Identity for Inclusive Development' (Asian Development Bank 2007); Mia Harbitz and Bettina Boekle, 'Democratic Governance, Citizenship, and Legal Identity: Linking Theoretical Discussion and Operational Reality' (Inter-American Development Bank 2009).

[27] Chapter 3: Delivering Services (spotlight on digital identity), in World Bank, *World Development Report 2016: Digital Dividends* (2016) 94–97.

[28] Ibid; see also Alan Gelb and Julia Clark, 'Identification for Development: The Biometrics Revolution' (Center for Global Development 2013) Working Paper 315.

[29] Anne Bouverot, CEO, Morpho (Safran), 'Women and their right to identity', Morpho, 8 March 2016, available at www.morpho.com/en/media/women-and-their-right-identity-20160308; Justin Lee, 'Morpho identity management platform integrating civil registries and vital statistics', *Biometric Update*, 19 November 2015.

[30] eg, 'Côte d'Ivoire: La fin d'un conflit grâce à la biométrie', Morpho, 2014.

[31] Information on the Africa Programme on Accelerated Improvement of Civil Registration and Vital Statistics available at www.apai-crvs.org/.

There is some awareness among development actors of the need for law reform to accompany this drive to digitisation in the field of data protection and privacy.[32] But there is almost no focus on the need to resolve underlying questions of who, in fact, is a national.[33] The danger is that a roll-out in Africa of much more stringent requirements for documentation will simply remove access to all the coping strategies that have previously been deployed, and close the buffer zone in which those of undetermined citizenship gave operated. In Mauritania, the movement *Touche Pas à Ma Nationalité* accuses the government of 'biometric genocide' in its combined project of amendments to the nationality law and rolling out of a new national identity card (Chapter 7.6). Analysis of the impact of nationality law provisions and proposals for their reform are likely to become rapidly more important.

The push to increase documentation of legal identity, especially efforts focused on civil registration, has the potential both to increase State capacity to respond to human needs, and to increase the ability of individuals to assert their rights. The implementation of biometric identity systems for particular purposes could, with the right legal framework, also assist to build up a record of transactions that would enable a person to establish their rights in other contexts. However, given that identity card applications are usually treated in the first instance by quite low-ranking civil servants, the roll-out of new identification systems gives the power to determine someone's right to proof of nationality – for practical if not legal purposes – to a person who is almost certainly not trained in nationality law. Although complaints mechanisms may exist within the identity card management system or through the courts for those whose applications are wrongfully rejected, they are often quite inaccessible unless the person has connections or legal assistance. The person behind the application is left in indefinite limbo.

So we end up with a paradox: documentation of legal identity and nationality are coming to be seen as a right, even as an additional public service, that the State must deliver; yet the process of delivering documentation can in fact exacerbate the exclusion of some even as it increases inclusion for others.

Unlike, for example, water – or even primary health care services – in order to 'deliver' nationality you need to define what it is. You can't start with the elements a State can currently afford and create infrastructure for (communal taps, basic immunisations) and fill in the rest later (water and sanitation in every house, treatment for all common diseases, sophisticated surgery). The strengthening of identification systems that allow a person to show who he or she is for a particular and self-contained purpose as a person, rather than as a national, may be useful

[32] eg, Mariana Dahan, 'Identification for Development (ID4D) Integration Approach Study' (World Bank 2015).

[33] The question of statelessness and identification systems is briefly discussed, especially in the context of the Dominican Republic, in Gelb and Clark (n 28). However, studies on national identification systems in Africa commissioned by the World Bank largely ignore this point. See www.worldbank.org/en/programs/id4d.

in its own right. But the introduction of new 'foundational' national identification systems for adults and more pervasive requirements for proof of identity, without first addressing gaps in the legal framework for nationality, risks making the problem of lack of legal identity worse rather than better. Indeed, it risks creating stateless persons where previously there were only undocumented ones; and exacerbating identity-based conflict rather than reducing it.

11.8. Future Directions: Nationality in National and Continental Law

For Samson, Georges, and Lisa, the cousins from Sierra Leone, Guinea, and Liberia who introduced this book, it might be not at all obvious which country is obliged to recognise them as its own. The same is true of many millions of others in Africa.

The two strongest existing trends in nationality laws should help at least to create more routes to resolve these challenges. Increased gender equality in nationality laws will continue the work of opening up access to citizenship for the many hundreds of thousands of residents of African countries with a father originating from another country. Increased tolerance of dual nationality has to date been analysed mainly in relation to those who have acquired or have a claim to another non-African nationality; it is to be expected that litigation and political argument, disputes over voter registration and the like, will extend the reach more effectively to those with a claim to another African nationality, recognising them as part of the body politic. The impact of these changes and their detailed implementation deserve more attention from both scholars and activists.

It is more challenging to predict the trends in relation to access to nationality based on birth or long-term residence in a territory. So far, the trend has mainly – though not uniformly – been in the opposite direction (Chapter 5.1). Conflicts over the relationship between 'settlers' and 'natives', in the countries highlighted in this book and many others, does not encourage optimism. However, there may be more openness to extension of access than it appears. Public opinion polling by Afrobarometer in 29 countries in 2011–13 found that almost everywhere a majority supported the grant of citizenship to the child born in the country of two foreign parents, with an average of 59% in favour. The major exception was Côte d'Ivoire (for reasons analysed in Chapter 7.4), where only 21% supported such rights. Even among the Commonwealth countries that had moved from rights based on birth in the territory to adopt descent-based regimes, only Botswana had support of less than 50%. The highest levels of support (more than 75%) were in Cape Verde, Mozambique, and Namibia, States with the strongest existing *jus soli* rights, as well as Senegal.[34] The efforts to strengthen the continental normative framework also

[34] Afrobarometer online data analysis tool, Round 5 (2011/13), 'Right to be citizen: born in country with two non-citizen parents', http://afrobarometer.org/online-data-analysis/analyse-online.

suggest a recognition of the deep challenges created by existing law and practice, and at least a partially open stance to nationality law reform.

The rapid introduction of new identification regimes could tip the balance different ways. There is a risk that the push for new forms of identification will provide new opportunities to manipulate the application of existing rules and exclude those whose membership of the body politic is contested. But the new systems could also focus attention on the need for law reform and for procedural measures to include the previously excluded (who in practice have nowhere else to go). If the latter, more optimistic, outcome is achieved, the process of debating a new law or policy becomes itself an important exercise in public (and politician) education – even if there are many setbacks along the way. A law, once adopted, continues to shape attitudes; it is itself a contribution to the process of 'imagining' the national community.[35]

[35] Benedict Anderson, *Imagined Communities: Reflections on the Origin and Spread of Nationalism* (2nd edn, Verso 1983).

BIBLIOGRAPHY

Abbink J, 'Ethnicity and Constitutionalism in Contemporary Ethiopia' (1997) 41 *Journal of African Law* 159.

Abdoul M, 'Sudan Border Management and Security: Policy Frameworks for Cross-Border Transhumance' (London, Concordis International, 2011).

Abdulbari N, 'Citizenship Rules in Sudan and Post-Secession Problems' (2011) 55 *Journal of African Law* 157.

——, 'Identities and Citizenship in Sudan: Governing Constitutional Principles' (2013) 13 *African Human Rights Law Journal* 383.

——, 'Sudan: A Commentary on Mazin Adil Ali Deng and Others v. Ministry of Interior and Ministry of Justice': citizenshiprightsafrica.org, 16 November 2016.

Abrahamian AA, *Cosmopolites: What It Is like to Be a Citizen of the World* (New York, Columbia Global Reports, 2015).

——, 'The Bizarre Scheme to Transform a Remote Island into the New Dubai' *The Guardian* (11 November 2015).

Achermann A and others, 'Country Report on Switzerland' (Fiesole, European University Institute, 2010).

Adam AH, 'Kenyan Nubians: Standing up to Statelessness' (2009) 32 *Forced Migration Review* 19.

Adejumobi S, 'Citizenship, Rights and the Problem of Conflicts and Civil Wars in Africa' (2001) 23 *Human Rights Quarterly* 148.

——, 'Identity, Citizenship and Conflict: The African Experience' in W Alade Fawole and Charles Ukeje (eds), *The Crisis of the State and Regionalism in West Africa: Identity, Citizenship and Conflict* (Dakar, CODESRIA, 2005).

Adepoju A, 'Illegals and Expulsion in Africa: The Nigerian Experience' (1984) 18 *International Migration Review* 426.

——, 'The Politics of International Migration in Post-Colonial Africa' in Robin Cohen (ed), *The Cambridge Survey of World Migration* (Cambridge, Cambridge University Press, 1995).

Adesoji AO and Alao A, 'Indigeneship and Citizenship in Nigeria: Myth and Reality' (2009) 2 *Journal of Pan African Studies* 151.

Adjamagbo-Johnson K, 'Les lois, une expression « officielle » des rapports de genre' in Thérèse Locoh and Koffi N'Guessan (eds), *Genre, population et développement en Afrique de l'Ouest* (Abidjan, Ecole Nationale Supérieure de Statistique et d'Economie Appliquée (ENSEA) and UN Population Fund, 1999).

Adjami M, 'Statelessness and Nationality in Côte d'Ivoire' (Geneva, UNHCR, 2016).

Adogamhe PG, 'Pan-Africanism Revisited: Vision and Reality of African Unity and Development' (2008) 2 *African Integration Review* 1.

African Commission on Human and Peoples' Rights, 'The Right to Nationality in Africa' (Banjul, 2014).

African Committee of Experts on the Rights and Welfare of the Child, 'General Comment on Article 6 of the African Charter on the Rights and Welfare of the Child' (Addis Ababa, 2014).

African Union, 'Policy Framework for Pastoralism in Africa: Securing, Protecting and Improving the Lives, Livelihoods and Rights of Pastoralist Communities' (Addis Ababa, 2010).

Akanmode S, *The Shugaba Affair* (Lagos, Nigerian Council for National Awareness, 1980).

Akindès F, 'The Roots of the Military-Political Crises in Côte d'Ivoire' (Uppsala, Nordiska Afrikainstitutet, 2004).

Akyeampong EK, 'Race, Identity and Citizenship in Black Africa: The Case of the Lebanese in Ghana' (2006) 76 *Africa* 297.
Albarazi Z and van Waas L, 'Transformations of Nationality Legislation in North Africa' in Engin F Isin and Peter Nyers (eds), *Routledge Handbook of Global Citizenship Studies* (Abingdon, Routledge, 2014).
Aleinikoff TA and Klusmeyer DB (eds), *Citizenship Policies for an Age of Migration* (Washington DC, Carnegie Endowment for International Peace and Migration Policy Institute, 2002).
Aminzade R, *Race, Nation, and Citizenship in Post-Colonial Africa: The Case of Tanzania* (Cambridge, Cambridge University Press, 2013).
Amnesty International, 'They Looked at His Identity Card and Shot Him Dead: Six Months of Post-Electoral Violence in Côte d'Ivoire' (London, 2011).
Anderson B, *Imagined Communities: Reflections on the Origin and Spread of Nationalism* 2nd edn (London, Verso, 1983).
Anderson BJ, 'The Restoration of The South African Citizenship Act: An Exercise in Statutory Obfuscation' (1993) 9 *Connecticut Journal of International Law* 295.
Appadurai A, *Modernity at Large: Cultural Dimensions of Globalization* (Minneapolis, University of Minnesota Press, 1996).
Arendt H, *The Origins of Totalitarianism* (New York, Meridian, 1958).
Arsan A, *Interlopers of Empire: The Lebanese Diaspora in Colonial French West Africa* (Oxford, Oxford University Press, 2014).
Assal MAM, 'Nationality and Citizenship Questions in Sudan after the Southern Sudan Referendum Vote' (Oslo, Christian Michelsen Institute, 2011).
——, 'Struggles of Citizenship in Sudan' in Engin F Isin and Peter Nyers (eds), *Routledge Handbook of Global Citizenship Studies* (Abingdon, Routledge, 2014).
Asséo H, 'L'invention des « Nomades » en Europe au xx siècle et la nationalisation impossible des Tsiganes' in Gérard Noiriel (ed), *L'identification: Genèse d'un travail d'État* (Paris, Belin, 2007).
Asylum Research Consultancy, 'Libya Country Report, Commissioned by the Office of the United Nations High Commissioner for Refugees (UNHCR), Division of International Protection' (Geneva, UNHCR, 2013).
Aukot E, 'Am I Stateless Because I Am a Nomad?' (2009) 32 *Forced Migration Review* 18.
Austen RA, *Trans-Saharan Africa in World History* (Oxford, Oxford University Press, 2010).
Ayittey GBN, *Indigenous African Institutions* (Irvington-on-Hudson NY, Transnational Publishers, 1991).
Babo A, 'The Crisis of Public Policies in Côte d'Ivoire: Land Law and the Nationality Trap in Tabou's Rural Communities' (2013) 83 *Africa* 100.
Bach DC, 'Federalism, Indigeneity and Ethnicity in Nigeria' in Larry Jay Diamond, AHM Kirk-Greene and Oyeleye Oyediran (eds), *Transition Without End: Nigerian politics and civil society under Babangida* (Boulder CO, Lynne Rienner Publishers, 1997).
Bakewell O, 'Repatriation and Self-Settled Refugees in Zambia: Bringing Solutions to the Wrong Problems' (2000) 13 *Journal of Refugee Studies* 356.
Balaton-Chrimes S, 'Counting as Citizens: Recognition of the Nubians in the 2009 Kenyan Census' (2011) 10 *Ethnopolitics* 205.
——, 'The Nubians of Kenya and the Emancipatory Potential of Collective Recognition' (2011) 32 *Australasian Review of African Studies* 12.
——, 'Indigeneity and Kenya's Nubians: Seeking Equality in Difference or Sameness?' (2013) 51 *Journal of Modern African Studies* 331.
——, 'Statelessness, Identity Cards and Citizenship as Status in the Case of the Nubians of Kenya' (2014) 18 *Citizenship Studies* 15.
——, 'The Nubians of Kenya: Citizenship in the Gaps and Margins' in Emma Hunter (ed), *Citizenship, Belonging, and Political Community in Africa: Dialogues between Past and Present* (Athens OH, Ohio University Press, 2016).

Banda F, *Women, Law and Human Rights: An African Perspective* (Hart Publishing, 2005).
——, 'Protocol to the African Charter on the Rights of Women in Africa' in Malcolm D Evans and Rachel Murray (eds), *The African Charter on Human and Peoples' Rights: The System in Practice, 1986–2000* 2nd edn (Cambridge, Cambridge University Press, 2008).
Banégas R and Marshall-Fratani R, 'Côte d'Ivoire: Negotiating Identity and Citizenship' in Morten Bøås and Kevin C Dunn (eds), *African Guerrillas: Raging Against the Machine* (Boulder CO, Lynne Rienner Publishers, 2007).
Barya JJ, 'Reconstituting Ugandan Citizenship under the 1995 Constitution: A Conflict of Nationalism, Chauvinism and Ethnicity' (Kampala, Centre for Basic Research, 2000).
Bauböck R, 'Expansive Citizenship—Voting beyond Territory and Membership' (2005) 38 *PS: Political Science & Politics* 683.
—— (ed), *Migration and Citizenship : Legal Status, Rights and Political Participation* (Amsterdam, Amsterdam University Press, 2006).
——, 'Political Membership and Democratic Boundaries' in Ayelet Shachar and others (eds), *The Oxford Handbook of Citizenship* (Oxford, Oxford University Press, 2017).
Bauböck R, Ersbøll E, Groenendijk K and Waldrauch H (eds), *Acquisition and Loss of Nationality: Policies and Trends in 15 European States*, vol 1 (Amsterdam, Amsterdam University Press, 2006).
Bauböck R and Rundell JF, *Blurred Boundaries: Migration, Ethnicity, Citizenship* (Aldershot, Ashgate, 1998).
Bayart J-F, Ellis S and Hibou B, *The Criminalization of the State in Africa* (Oxford, International African Institute in association with James Currey, 1999).
Bayart J-F and Geschiere P, '"J'étais là avant": Problématiques politiques de l'autochtonie' (2001) 10 *Critique internationale* 126.
Bayart J-F, Geschiere P and Nyamnjoh F, 'Autochtonie, démocratie et citoyenneté en Afrique' (2001) 10 *Critique internationale* 177.
Bazonzi JM, 'Crise identitaire et lutte de leadership dans la région des grands lacs : Lecture des principaux conflits fonciers et armés du Kivu 1900–2005' in Bahru Zewde (ed), *Society, State, and Identity in African History* (Addis Ababa, Forum for Social Studies, 2008).
Bekker PHF, 'World Court Orders Belgium to Cancel an Arrest Warrant Issued Against the Congolese Foreign Minister' (2002) 7 *ASIL Insights*; asil.org.
Ben Achour S, 'L'étranger et la nationalité tunisienne : Le droit tunisien de la nationalité, est-il discriminatoire ?' (Tunis, Faculté de droit et des sciences politiques, 2005).
Bendeddouche J, *Notion de nationalité et nationalité algérienne* (Algiers, Société Nationale d'Édition et de Diffusion, 1974).
Benhabib S, *The Rights of Others* (Cambridge, Cambridge University Press, 2004).
Benhabib S and Resnik J (eds), *Migrations and Mobilities: Citizenship, Borders, and Gender* (New York, NYU Press, 2009).
Benoist J-R de, *La balkanisation de l'Afrique occidentale française* (Dakar, Nouvelles éditions africaines, 1979).
——, *Afrique occidentale française de 1944 à 1960* (Dakar, Nouvelles éditions africaines, 1982).
——, 'Pogrom contre les dahoméens et les togolais en Côte d'Ivoire en octobre 1958' in Catherine Coquery-Vidrovitch and others (eds), *Etre étranger et migrant en Afrique au XXe siècle*, vol 1 (Paris, L'Harmattan, 2003).
Bertocchi G and Strozzi C, 'The Evolution of Citizenship: Economic and Institutional Determinants' (2010) 53 *Journal of Law and Economics* 95.
Bertz N, 'Educating the Nation: Race and Nationalism in Tanzanian Schools' in Sara Dorman, Daniel Hammett and Paul Nugent (eds), *Making Nations, Creating Strangers: States and Citizenship in Africa* (Leiden, Brill, 2007).
Besteman C, 'Translating Race across Time and Space: The Creation of Somali Bantu Ethnicity' (2012) 19 *Identities* 285.
Beydoun L, 'Lebanese Migration to Sierra Leone: Issues of Transnationalism, Gender, Citizenship, and the Construction of a Globalized Identity' (PhD, Wayne State University, 2005).

——, 'The Complexities of Citizenship among Lebanese Immigrants in Sierra Leone' (2013) 3 *African Conflict & Peacebuilding Review* 112.

Bezabeh SA, 'Citizenship and the Logic of Sovereignty in Djibouti' (2011) 110 *African Affairs* 587.

Bierwirth C, 'The Lebanese Communities of Côte d'Ivoire' (1999) 98 *African Affairs* 79.

Blackman JL, 'State Successions and Statelessness: The Emerging Right to an Effective Nationality under International Law' (1997) 19 *Michigan Journal of International Law* 1141.

Blake C, 'Citizenship, Law and the State: The British Nationality Act 1981' (1982) 45 *Modern Law Review* 179.

Blion R and Bredeloup S, 'La Côte d'Ivoire dans les stratégies migratoires des burkinabès et des sénégalais' in Bernard Contamin, Harris Memel-Fotê and Groupement interdisciplinaire en sciences sociales, Côte d'Ivoire (eds), *Le modèle ivoirien en questions: crises, ajustements, recompositions* (Paris, Editions Karthala and Editions de l'ORSTOM, 1997).

Blitz B, 'Statelessness, Protection and Equality' (Refugee Studies Centre, 2009).

Blitz B and Lynch M, 'Statelessness and the Benefits of Citizenship: A Comparative Study' (Geneva Academy of International Humanitarian Law and Human Rights, 2009).

Blitz BK and others, *The Cost of Statelessness: A Livelihoods Analysis of Four Countries* (Edward Elgar Publishing Limited, 2011).

Bøås M and Dunn K, *Politics of Origin in Africa: Autochthony, Citizenship and Conflict* (Zed Books, 2013).

Bob-Milliar GM and Bob-Milliar G, 'Mobilizing the African Diaspora for Development: The Politics of Dual Citizenship in Ghana' in Toyin Falola and Kwame Essien (eds), *Pan-Africanism, and the Politics of African Citizenship and Identity* (Abingdon, Routledge, 2014).

Boilley P, *Les Touaregs Kel Adagh: dépendances et révoltes : du Soudan francais au Mali contemporain* (Paris, Karthala, 2012).

Boll AM, *Multiple Nationality and International Law* (Leiden, Martinus Nijhoff Publishers, 2007).

Bonnecase V, 'Les étrangers et la terre en Côte d'Ivoire à l'époque coloniale' (Montpellier, Institut de Recherche pour le Développement, 2001).

Bonzon S, 'Les dahoméens en Afrique de l'Ouest' (1967) 17 *Revue française de science politique* 718.

Boone C, 'Land Regimes and the Structure of Politics: Patterns of Land-Related Conflict' (2013) 83 *Africa* 188.

——, *Property and Political Order in Africa: Land Rights and the Structure of Politics* (Cambridge, Cambridge University Press, 2014).

Borella F, *L'évolution politique et juridique de l'Union française depuis 1946* (Paris, Librairie générale de droit et de jurisprudence, 1958).

Bosniak LS, *The Citizen and the Alien: Dilemmas of Contemporary Membership* (Princeton, Princeton University Press, 2006).

Breckenridge K, *Biometric State: The Global Politics of Identification and Surveillance in South Africa, 1850 to the Present* (Cambridge, Cambridge University Press, 2014).

Breckenridge K and Szreter S (eds), *Registration and Recognition: Documenting the Person in World History* (Published for the British Academy by Oxford, Oxford University Press, 2012).

Bredeloup S, 'La Côte d'Ivoire ou l'étrange destin de l'étranger' (2003) 19 *Revue européenne des migrations internationales* 85.

Brietzke PH, 'Ethiopia's "Leap in the Dark": Federalism and Self-Determination in the New Constitution' (1995) 39 *Journal of African Law* 19.

Brownlie I, 'The Relations of Nationality in Public International Law' (1963) 39 *British Yearbook of International Law* 284.

Brubaker R, *Citizenship and Nationhood in France and Germany* (Cambridge MA, Harvard University Press, 1992).

Bruschi C, 'La nationalité dans le droit colonial' (1988) 18 *Procès: Cahiers d'analyse politique et juridique* 29.

Brydon L, 'Ghanaian Responses to the Nigerian Expulsions of 1983' (1985) 84 *African Affairs* 561.

Bucyalimwe Mararo S, 'Land, Power, and Ethnic Conflict in Masisi (Congo-Kinshasa), 1940s–1994' (1997) 30 *International Journal of African Historical Studies* 503.

——, 'La guerre des chiffres: Une constante dans la politique au Nord-Kivu' (2000) *L'Afrique des Grands Lacs: Annuaire 1999–2000* 225.

——, 'Le Nord-Kivu au cœur de la crise congolaise' (2002) *L'Afrique des Grands Lacs: Annuaire 2001–2002* 153.

Bureau of Democracy, Human Rights, and Labor, 'Country Reports on Human Rights Practices' (Washington DC, US Department of State various years).

Burghardt AF, 'The Bases of Territorial Claims' (1973) 63 *Geographical Review* 225.

Byrne J, 'Should I Stay or Should I Go? National Identity and Attitudes Towards Local Integration Among Liberian Refugees in Ghana' (2013) 32 *Refugee Survey Quarterly* 50.

Caplan J and Torpey J (eds), *Documenting Individual Identity: The Development of State Practices in the Modern World* (Princeton, Princeton University Press, 2001).

Carciotto S, 'Angolan Refugees in South Africa: Alternatives to Permanent Repatriation?' (2016) 2 *African Human Mobility Review* 362.

Carter Center, 'Presidential and Legislative Elections in the Democratic Republic of the Congo November 28, 2011' (Atlanta GA, Carter Center, 2012).

Castles S and Davidson A, *Citizenship and Migration: Globalization and the Politics of Belonging* (Basingstoke, Palgrave Macmillan, 2000).

Centre for Migration and Refugee Studies, 'Africa Citizenship and Discrimination Audit: The Case Study of Egypt, Prepared for the Open Society Justice Initiative' (American University in Cairo, 2005).

Ceuppens B and Geschiere P, 'Autochthony: Local or Global? New Modes in the Struggle over Citizenship and Belonging in Africa and Europe' (2005) 34 *Annual Review of Anthropology* 385.

Chabal P, *Power in Africa: An Essay in Interpretation* (Basingstoke, Palgrave Macmillan, 1993).

——, *Africa: The Politics of Suffering and Smiling* (London, Zed Books, 2009).

Chabal P and Daloz J-P, *Africa Works: Disorder as Political Instrument* (Oxford, International African Institute in association with James Currey, 1999).

Challenor HS, 'Strangers as Colonial Intermediaries: The Dahomeyans in Francophone Africa' in William A Shack and Elliott P Skinner (eds), *Strangers in African Societies* (Berkeley, University of California Press, 1979).

Chan JMM, 'The Right to a Nationality as a Human Right: The Current Trend Towards Recognition' (1991) 12 *Human Rights Law Journal* 1.

Chanock M, *Law, Custom, and Social Order: The Colonial Experience in Malawi and Zambia* (Portsmouth NH, Heinemann, 1998).

Charrad M, 'Unequal Citizenship: Issues of Gender Justice in the Middle East and North Africa' in Maitrayee Mukhopadhyay and Navsharan Singh (eds), *Gender Justice, Citizenship and Development* (Delhi and Ottawa: Zubaan and International Development Research Centre).

Chauveau J-P, 'Question Foncière et Construction Nationale En Côte d'Ivoire' (2000) 78 *Politique africaine* 94.

——, 'La loi ivoirienne de 1998 sur le domaine foncier rural et l'agriculture de plantation villageoise: Une mise en perspective historique et sociologique' (2002) *Journal of Land Reform, Land Settlement and Cooperatives* (UN Food and Agriculture Organisation) 62.

Chauveau J-P and Dozon J-P, 'Au cœur des ethnies ivoiriennes : L'Etat, l'économie de plantation et les ethnies en Côte d'Ivoire' in Emmanuel Terray (ed), *L'Etat contemporain en Afrique* (Paris, L'Harmattan, 1987).

Chauveau J-P and Richards P, 'West African Insurgencies in Agrarian Perspective: Côte d'Ivoire and Sierra Leone Compared' (2008) 8 *Journal of Agrarian Change* 515.

Cheater AP and Gaidzanwa R, 'Transcending the State? Gender and Borderline Constructions of Citizenship in Zimbabwe' in Thomas M Wilson and Hastings Donnan (eds), *Border Identities: Nation and State at International Frontiers* (Cambridge, Cambridge University Press, 1998).

Cheater AP and Gaidzanwa RB, 'Citizenship in Neo-Patrilineal States: Gender and Mobility in Southern Africa' (1996) 22 *Journal of Southern African Studies* 189.

Cissé C, *Migrations et mise en valeur de la Basse Côte d'Ivoire, 1920–1960* (Paris, L'Harmattan, 2013).

Coldham S, 'Case Note: Devagi Rattigan and Others v. Chief Immigration Officer and Others' (1994) 38 *Journal of African Law* 189.

Commissariat Général aux Réfugiés et aux Apatrides (CGRA/Belgique), Office Français de Protection des Réfugiés et Apatrides (OFPRA/France) and Office Fédéral des Migrations (ODM/Suisse), 'Rapport de Mission En République de Guinée 29 Octobre–19 Novembre 2011' (Brussels, Paris and Bern, 2012).

Constitution of Kenya Review Commission, 'The People's Choice: The Report of the Constitution of Kenya Review Commission' (Nairobi, 2002).

Constitutional Review Committee, Sierra Leone, 'Abridged Draft Report' (Freetown, 2016).

Contamin B and Memel-Fotê H (eds), *Le modèle ivoirien en questions: crises, ajustements, recompositions* (Paris, Editions Karthala and Editions de l'ORSTOM, 1997).

Cooper F, 'The Politics of Citizenship in Colonial and Postcolonial Africa' (2005) 16 *Studia Africana* 14.

——, 'Voting, Welfare and Registration: The Strange Fate of the État-Civil in French Africa, 1945–1960' in Keith Breckenridge and Simon Szreter (eds), *Registration and Recognition: Documenting the Person in World History* (Oxford, Published for the British Academy by Oxford University Press, 2012).

——, *Citizenship between Empire and Nation: Remaking France and French Africa, 1945–1960* (Princeton, Princeton University Press, 2014).

Cooper K and Hubbard D, 'By the Skin of Its Teeth: How Namibia Narrowly Avoided a Constitutional Crisis'; citizenshiprightsafrica.org, 7 February 2017.

Coquery-Vidrovitch C, 'Nationalité et citoyenneté en Afrique occidentale français: Originaires et citoyens dans le Sénégal colonial' (2001) 42 *Journal of African History* 285.

Coquery-Vidrovitch C, Georg O, Mande I, and Rajaonah F (eds), *Etre étranger et migrant en Afrique au XXe siècle: enjeux identitaires et modes d'insertion*, vol 1 (Paris, L'Harmattan, 2003).

Costamagna F, 'Statelessness in the Context of State Succession: An Appraisal under International Law' in Alessandra Annoni and Serena Forlati (eds), *The Changing Role of Nationality in International Law* (Abingdon, Routledge, 2013).

Crisp J, 'No Solutions in Sight: The Problem of Protracted Refugee Situations in Africa' (2003) 22 *Refugee Survey Quarterly* 114.

Crisp J, Riera J and Freitas R, 'Evaluation of UNHCR's Returnee Reintegration Programme in Angola' (Geneva, UNHCR, 2008).

Crush J and Williams V (eds), *The New South Africans? Immigration Amnesties and Their Aftermath* (Cape Town, IDASA, 1999).

Cutolo A and Geschiere P, 'Populations, citoyennetés et territoires: Autochtonie et gouvernementalité en Afrique' (2008) 112 *Politique africaine* 5.

da Ponte B, 'The Last to Leave, Portuguese Colonialism in Africa' (London, International Defence and Aid Fund, 1974).

Dahan M, 'Identification for Development (ID4D) Integration Approach Study' (World Bank, 2015).

Daimon A, 'Politics of "Othering" and the Struggle for Citizenship in Independent Zimbabwe: Voices from Malawian Descendants' (2014) 44 *Africa Insight* 137.

——, 'ZANU (PF)'s Manipulation of the "Alien" Vote in Zimbabwean Elections: 1980–2013' (2016) 68 *South African Historical Journal* 112.

de Chassey F, *Mauritanie 1900–1975: Acteurs économiques, politiques, idéologiques et éducatifs dans la formation d'une société sous-développée* (Paris, L'Harmattan, 1978).

de Chickera A, *Unravelling Anomaly: Detention, Discrimination and the Protection Needs of Stateless Persons* (London, Equal Rights Trust, 2010).

de Dominicis F, *Commento alla legge sulla Cittadinanza Italiana del 13 giugno 1912* (Turin, Unione tipografico–Editrice torinese, 1916).

de Donno F, '*La Razza Ario-Mediterranea*: Ideas of Race and Citizenship in Colonial and Fascist Italy, 1885–1941' (2006) 8 *Interventions* 394.

de Frouville O, 'Affaire Ahmadou Sadio Diallo (République de Guinée c. République démocratique du Congo). Exceptions préliminaires: Le roman inachevé de la protection diplomatique' (2007) 53 *Annuaire français de droit international* 291.

de Groot G-R, 'Preventing Statelessness among Children: Interpreting Articles 1–4 of the 1961 Convention on the Reduction of Statelessness and Relevant International Human Rights Norms' (Geneva, UNHCR, 2011).

de Groot G-R and Vonk OW, *International Standards on Nationality Law: Texts, Cases and Materials* (Oisterwijk, Wolf Legal Publishers, 2015).

de Vattel E, *The Law of Nations, Or, Principles of the Law of Nature Applied to the Conduct and Affairs of Nations and Sovereigns* (London, 1797).

Decheix P, 'Le code de la nationalité malienne' (1963) 73 *Penant* 300.

Decottignies R and de Biéville M, *Les nationalités africaines* (Paris, A Pedone, 1963).

Dembélé O, 'La construction économique et politique de la catégorie "étranger" en Côte d'Ivoire' in Marc Le Pape and Claudine Vidal (eds), *Côte d'Ivoire: l'année terrible, 1999–2000* (Paris, Karthala, 2002).

Deng FM, 'Ethnic Marginalisation as Statelessness: Lessons from the Great Lakes Region of Africa' in T Alexander Aleinikoff and Douglas Klusmeyer (eds) *Citizenship Today: Global Perspectives and Practices* (Washington DC, Carnegie Endowment for International Peace, 2001).

Development and Training Services, Inc, 'Field Evaluation of Local Integration of Former Refugees in Tanzania: Field Visit Report – Final' (Washington DC, US Department of State, 2014).

Doek JE, 'The CRC and the Right to Acquire and to Preserve a Nationality' (2006) 25 *Refugee Survey Quarterly* 26.

Don Nanjira DDC, *The Status of Aliens in East Africa: Asians and Europeans in Tanzania, Uganda, and Kenya* (New York, Praeger, 1976).

Donner R, *The Regulation of Nationality in International Law* (Irvington-on-Hudson NY, Transnational Publishers Inc, 1994).

Dorman S, Hammett D and Nugent P (eds), *Making Nations, Creating Strangers: States and Citizenship in Africa* (Leiden, Brill, 2007).

Dow U (ed), *The Citizenship Case: The Attorney General of the Republic of Botswana vs. Unity Dow, Court Documents, Judgements, Cases and Materials* (Gaborone, Metlhaetsile Women's Information Centre, 1995).

Dowden R, 'The State of the African State: The Past, Present and Future of the Nation State in Africa' (2004) 11 *IPPR Progressive Review* 138.

Dozon J-P, 'L'étranger et l'allochtone en Cote d'Ivoire' in Bernard Contamin and Harris Memel-Fotê (eds), *Le modèle ivoirien en questions: crises, ajustements, recompositions* (Paris, Editions Karthala and Editions de l'ORSTOM, 1997).

——, 'La Côte d'Ivoire Entre Démocratie, Nationalisme et Ethnonationalisme' 78 *Politique africaine* 45.

Dube R, 'A Right or a Privilege' (Harare, Research and Advocacy Unit, 2008).

——, 'Identity, Citizenship, and the Registrar General: The Politicking of Identity in Zimbabwe' (Harare, Research and Advocacy Unit, 2012).

Durieux A, 'Essai sur le statut des indigènes portugais de la Guinée, de l'Angola et du Mozambique' (Brussels, Académie Royale des Sciences Coloniales, 1955).

——, *Nationalité et Citoyenneté* (Brussels, Académie Royale des Sciences Coloniales, 1959).

Dutoit B and others, *La nationalité de la femme mariée*, vol II: Afrique (Geneva, Librairie Droz, 1976).

Dutoit B and Masmejan D, *La nationalité de la femme mariée, Supplément 1976–1990*, vol II: Afrique (Geneva, Librairie Droz, 1991).

Earnest D, 'Noncitizen Voting Rights: A Survey of an Emerging Democratic Norm' (Conference paper presented to American Political Science Association, 2003).

Egbe Orock RT, 'The Indigene-Settler Divide, Modernisation and the Land Question: Indications for Social (Dis) Order in Cameroon' (2005) 14 *Nordic Journal of African Studies* 68.

Ehrhardt D, 'Indigeneship, Bureaucratic Discretion, and Institutional Change in Northern Nigeria' (2017) 116 *African Affairs* 462.

Ekeh PP, 'Colonialism and the Two Publics in Africa: A Theoretical Statement' (1975) 17 *Comparative Studies in Society and History* 91.

El-Abed O, 'The Palestinians in Egypt: An Investigation of Livelihoods and Coping Strategies' (Cairo, Forced Migration Refugee Studies Program, The American University in Cairo 2003).

——, 'The Forgotten Palestinians: How Palestinian Refugees Survive in Egypt' (2004) 20 *Forced Migration Review* 29.

——, 'Palestinian Refugees of Egypt: What Exit Options Are Left for Them?' (2005) 22 *Refuge* 15.

Elmadmad K, 'Maroc: La dimension juridique des migrations', in *Mediterranean Migration Report 2007–2008* (Fiesole, Euro-Mediterranean Consortium for Applied Research on International Migration, European University Institute, 2008).

Emelonye U (ed), *Nigeria: Peace Building through Integration and Citizenship* (Rome, International Development Law Organization, 2011).

Englebert P, *State Legitimacy and Development in Africa* (Boulder CO, Lynne Rienner Publishers, 2000).

Faist T and Kivisto P (eds), *Dual Citizenship in Global Perspective: From Unitary to Multiple Citizenship* (Basingstoke, Palgrave Macmillan, 2007).

Falola T and Essien K (eds), *Pan-Africanism, and the Politics of African Citizenship and Identity* (Abingdon, Routledge, 2014).

Ferme M, 'Deterritorialized Citizenship and the Resonances of the Sierra Leonean State' in Veena Das and Deborah Poole (eds), *Anthropology in the margins of the state* (Santa Fe NM and Oxford, School of American Research Press and James Currey, 2004).

Fessha YT and Van der Beken C, 'Ethnic Federalism and Internal Minorities: The Legal Protection of Internal Minorities in Ethiopia' (2013) 21 *African Journal of International and Comparative Law* 32.

Fielden A, 'Local Integration: An Under-reported Solution to Protracted Refugee Situations' (Geneva, UNHCR, 2008).

Fischer G, 'L'indépendance de la Guinée et les accords franco-guinéens' (1958) 4 *Annuaire français de droit international* 711.

Fiseha A, 'Ethiopia's Experiment in Accommodating Diversity: 20 Years' Balance Sheet' (2012) 22 *Regional & Federal Studies* 435.

Forlati S, 'Nationality as a Human Right' in Alessandra Annoni and Serena Forlati (eds), *The Changing Role of Nationality in International Law* (Abingdon, Routledge, 2013).

Fouéré M-A, 'Julius Nyerere, Ujamaa, and Political Morality in Contemporary Tanzania' (2014) 57 *African Studies Review* 1.

Fourchard L, 'Bureaucrats and Indigenes: Producing and Bypassing Certificates of Origin in Nigeria' (2015) 85 *Africa* 37.

Fransman L, Berry A and Harvey A, *Fransman's British Nationality Law* 3rd edn (Oxford, Bloomsbury Professional, 2011).

Fresia M, 'De l'exil au retour : le rapatriement des Mauritaniens réfugiés au Sénégal en perspective' (2008) 3 *REVUE Asylon(s)*; reseau-terra.eu.

Fru Awasom N, 'From Migrants to Nationals and from Nationals to "Undesirable Elements": The case of the Fulani (Mbororo) in the North West Province of Cameroon' in Catherine Coquery-Vidrovitch and others (eds), *Etre étranger et migrant en Afrique au XXe siècle*, vol 1 (Paris, L'Harmattan, 2003).

Gaidzanwa R, 'Citizenship, Nationality, Gender, and Class in Southern Africa' (1993) 18 *Alternatives: Global, Local, Political* 39.

Gale LA, 'The Invisible Refugee Camp: Durable Solutions for Boreah "Residuals" in Guinea' (2008) 21 *Journal of Refugee Studies* 537.

Gans C, 'Citizenship and Nationhood' in Ayelet Shachar and others (eds), *The Oxford Handbook of Citizenship* (Oxford, Oxford University Press, 2017).

Gary-Tounkara D, *Migrants Soudanais-Maliens et Conscience Ivoirienne: Les Étrangers En Côte d'Ivoire, 1903–1980* (Paris, L'Harmattan, 2008).

Gasarasi CP, 'The Mass Naturalization and Further Integration of Rwandese Refugees in Tanzania: Process, Problems and Prospects' (1990) 3 *Journal of Refugee Studies* 88.

——, 'The Question of the Recent Expulsion of Rwandans from Tanzania' (2008) 1 *Journal of African Conflicts and Peace Studies* 111.
Gberie L, 'Sierra Leone: Diamonds, Corruption and the Lebanese Connection' (Ottawa, Partnership Africa Canada, 2002).
Gelb A and Clark J, 'Identification for Development: The Biometrics Revolution' (Center for Global Development, 2013).
Genova JE, 'Constructing Identity in Post-War France: Citizenship, Nationality, and the Lamine Guèye Law, 1946–1953' (2004) 26 *International History Review* 56.
George JP and Elphick R, 'Statelessness and Nationality in South Africa' (Pretoria, Lawyers for Human Rights, 2013).
Geschiere P, 'Autochthony and Citizenship: New Modes in the Struggle over Belonging and Exclusion in Africa' (2005) 32 *Forum for Development Studies* 371.
——, *The Perils of Belonging: Autochthony, Citizenship, and Exclusion in Africa and Europe* (Chicago, University of Chicago Press, 2009).
Geschiere P and Jackson S, 'Autochthony and the Crisis of Citizenship: Democratization, Decentralization, and the Politics of Belonging' (2006) 49 *African Studies Review* 1.
Ghai DP and Ghai YP, 'Asians in East Africa: Problems and Prospects' (1965) 3 *Journal of Modern African Studies* 35.
Ghai YP, 'The Kenya Council of State and the African Affairs Board of the Central African Federation: An Experiment in the Protection of Minorities' (1963) 12 *International and Comparative Law Quarterly* 1089.
Gofie SM, 'The State and the "Peoples": Citizenship and the Future of Political Community in Ethiopia' in Emma Hunter (ed), *Citizenship, Belonging, and Political Community in Africa: Dialogues between Past and Present* (Athens OH, Ohio University Press, 2016).
Gohin O, 'La citoyenneté dans l'outre-mer français' (2002) 101 *Revue française d'administration publique* 69.
Goldston JA, 'Holes in the Rights Framework: Racial Discrimination, Citizenship, and the Rights of Noncitizens' (2006) 20 *Ethics & International Affairs* 321.
Gonidec PF, 'Note sur la nationalité et citoyennetés dans la Communauté' (1959) 5 *Annuaire français de droit international* 748.
——, 'La nationalité dans les Etats de la Communauté et dans les Etats "marginaux"' (1961) 7 *Annuaire français de droit international* 814.
Gonzales RG and Sigona N, 'Mapping the Soft Borders of Citizenship: An Introduction' in Roberto G Gonzales and Nando Sigona (eds), *Within and Beyond Citizenship: Borders, Membership and Belonging* (Abingdon, Routledge, 2017).
Goodwin-Gill GS, 'Convention Relating to the Status of Stateless Persons' (UN Audiovisual Library of International Law, 2010); legal.un.org.
Gorman D, 'Wider and Wider Still?: Racial Politics, Intra-Imperial Immigration and the Absence of an Imperial Citizenship in the British Empire' (2002) 3 *Journal of Colonialism and Colonial History* 1.
——, *Imperial Citizenship: Empire and the Question of Belonging* (Manchester, Manchester University Press, 2006).
Gould E, 'British Nationality and East African Independence' (1990) 4 *Immigration and Nationality Law and Practice* 99.
Gray CJ, 'Cultivating Citizenship through Xenophobia in Gabon, 1960–1995' (1998) 45 *Africa Today* 389.
Green E, 'On the Size and Shape of African States' (2012) 56 *International Studies Quarterly* 229.
Gyulai G, 'The Long-Overlooked Mystery of Refugee Children's Natioanilty', *The World's Stateless: Children* (Tilburg, Institute on Statelessness and Inclusion, 2017).
Hainmueller J and Hangartner D, 'Who Gets a Swiss Passport? A Natural Experiment in Immigrant Discrimination' (2013) 107 *American Political Science Review* 159.
Halisi CRD, Kaiser PJ and Ndegwa SN, 'Guest Editors' Introduction: The Multiple Meanings of Citizenship: Rights, Identity, and Social Justice in Africa' (1998) 45 *Africa Today* 337.

Hall BS, *A History of Race in Muslim West Africa, 1600–1960* (Cambridge, Cambridge University Press, 2011).
Hammar A, Raftopoulos B and Jensen S (eds), *Zimbabwe's Unfinished Business: Rethinking Land, State and Nation in the Context of Crisis* (Harare, Weaver Press, 2003).
Hammett D, 'Requiring Respect: Searching for Non-Racialism in Post-Apartheid South Africa' (2012) 39 *Politikon* 71.
Hansen R, 'The Politics of Citizenship in 1940s Britain: The British Nationality Act' (1999) 10 *Twentieth Century British History* 67.
Hansen R and Weil P, 'Introduction: Citizenship, Immigration and Nationality: Towards a Convergence in Europe?' in Randall Hansen and Patrick Weil (eds), *Towards a European Nationality: Citizenship, Immigration, and Nationality Law in the EU* (Basingstoke, Palgrave, 2001).
Harbitz M and Boekle B, 'Democratic Governance, Citizenship, and Legal Identity: Linking Theoretical Discussion and Operational Reality' (Washington DC, Inter-American Development Bank, 2009).
Hargreaves JD, *West Africa: The Former French States* (Englewood Cliffs NJ, Prentice-Hall, 1967).
Harpaz Y and Mateos P, 'Strategic Citizenship: Negotiating Membership in the Age of Dual Nationality' (2018) 44 *Journal of Ethnic and Migration Studies* 1.
Harris B, 'A Foreign Experience: Violence, Crime and Xenophobia during South Africa's Transition' (Johannesburg, Centre for the Study of Violence and Reconciliation, 2001).
Harrison C, *France and Islam in West Africa, 1860–1960* (Cambridge, Cambridge University Press, 2003).
Harvey A, 'The "De Facto" Statelessness Debate' (2010) 24 *Immigration, Asylum and Nationality Law* 257.
Heilman B, 'Who Are the Indigenous Tanzanians? Competing Conceptions of Tanzanian Citizenship in the Business Community' (1998) 45 *Africa Today* 369.
Herbst J, 'The Role of Citizenship Laws in Multiethnic Societies: Evidence from Africa' in Richard A Joseph (ed), *State, Conflict, and Democracy in Africa* (Boulder CO, Lynne Rienner Publishers, 1999).
——, *States and Power in Africa: Comparative Lessons in Authority and Control* (Princeton, Princeton University Press, 2001).
Hickey S, 'Caught at the Crossroads: Citizenship, Marginality and the Mbororo Fulani in Northwest Cameroon' in Sara Dorman, Daniel Hammett and Paul Nugent (eds), *Making Nations, Creating Strangers: States and Citizenship in Africa* (Leiden, Brill, 2007).
Higgs E, *The Information State in England: The Central Collection of Information on Citizens since 1500* (Basingstoke, Palgrave Macmillan, 2004).
Hodges T, *Western Sahara: The Roots of a Desert War* (Westport CT, Lawrence Hill, 1983).
Hodgson DL, *Being Maasai, Becoming Indigenous: Postcolonial Politics in a Neoliberal World* (Bloomington, Indiana University Press, 2011).
Hovil L, *Refugees, Conflict and the Search for Belonging* (Berlin, Springer, 2016).
Howard-Hassmann RE and Walton-Roberts M (eds), *The Human Right to Citizenship: A Slippery Concept* (Philadelphia, University of Pennsylvania Press, 2015).
Human Rights Watch, 'Screening of Ethnic Somalis: The Cruel Consequences of Kenya's Passbook System' (New York, 1990).
——, 'Mauritania's Campaign of Terror: State-Sponsored Repression of Black Africans' (1994).
——, 'Botswana: Second Class Citizens: Discrimination against Women under Botswana's Citizenship Act' (1994).
——, 'Rearming with Impunity: International Support for the Perpetrators of the Rwandan Genocide' (1995).
——, 'Forced to Flee: Violence Against the Tutsis in Zaire' (1996).
——, 'Zambia: Elections and Human Rights in the Third Republic' (1996).
——, 'Zaire: Attacked By All Sides' (1997).
——, 'Zaire: Transition, War and Human Rights' (1997).
——, 'What Kabila Is Hiding: Civilian Killings and Impunity in Congo' (1997).

——, 'Transition and Human Rights Violations in Congo' (1997).
——, 'Prohibited Persons: Abuse of Undocumented Migrants, Asylum-Seekers, and Refugees in South Africa' (1998).
——, 'In the Name of Security: Forced Round-Ups of Refugees in Tanzania' (1999).
——, 'The New Racism: The Political Manipulation of Ethnicity in Côte d'Ivoire' (2001).
——, 'The Horn of Africa War: Mass Expulsions and the Nationality Issue (June 1998-April 2002)' (2003).
——, 'Struggling through Peace: Return and Resettlement in Angola' (2003).
——, 'They Do Not Own This Place: Government Discrimination against Non-Indigenes in Nigeria' (2006).
——, 'Renewed Crisis in North Kivu' (2007).
——, 'Bring the Gun Or You'll Die': Torture, Rape, and Other Serious Human Rights Violations by Kenyan Security Forces in the Mandera Triangle' (2009).
——, 'Human Rights in Western Sahara and in the Tindouf Refugee Camps' (2008).
——, 'That Land Is My Family's Wealth: Addressing Land Dispossession after Côte d'Ivoire's Post-Election Conflict' (2013).
Human Sciences Research Council, 'Citizenship, Violence and Xenophobia in South Africa: Perceptions from South African Communities' (Pretoria, Human Sciences Research Council, 2008).
Human Security Report Project, 'Human Security Report 2009/2010: The Causes of Peace and The Shrinking Costs of War' (British Columbia, Simon Fraser University, 2010).
Humphrey M, 'Lebanese Identities: Between Cities, Nations and Trans-Nations' (2004) 26 *Arab Studies Quarterly* 31.
Hunter E, 'Dutiful Subjects, Patriotic Citizens, and the Concept of "Good Citizenship" in Twentieth Century Tanzania' (2013) 56 *Historical Journal* 257.
—— (ed), *Citizenship, Belonging, and Political Community in Africa: Dialogues between Past and Present* (Athens OH, Ohio University Press, 2016).
Iazzolino G, 'A Safe Haven for Somalis in Uganda?' (Nairobi, Rift Valley Institute, 2014).
Idris A, 'Rethinking Identity, Citizenship, and Violence in Sudan' (2012) 44 *International Journal of Middle East Studies* 324.
Iheduru OC, 'African States, Global Migration, and Transformations in Citizenship Politics' (2011) 15 *Citizenship Studies* 181.
Imam A and Kamminga E, *Women in Search of Citizenship: Experiences from West Africa* (Amsterdam, KIT Publishers, 2012).
Imbert-Vier S, 'Afars, Issas … and Djiboutians: Toward a History of Denominations' (2014) 13 *Northeast African Studies* 123.
Institut national de la statistique, 'Recensement Général de la Population et de l'Habitat, 1988 : Tome 2, Répartition Spatiale de la Population et Migrations, Analyse des résultats définitifs' (Abidjan, République de la Côte d'Ivoire, 1992).
——, 'Recensement Général de la Population et de l'Habitat, 1988 : Tome 3, Caractéristiques socio-culturelles et économiques de la population' (Abidjan, République de la Côte d'Ivoire, 1992).
Internal Displacement Monitoring Centre and International Refugee Rights Initiative, 'The Great Lakes Pact and the Rights of Displaced People: A Guide for Civil Society' (Oslo and Kampala, 2008).
International Crisis Group, 'Burundian Refugees in Tanzania: The Key Factor to the Burundi Peace Process' (Brussels, 1999).
——, 'Côte d'Ivoire: Ensuring Credible Elections' (2008).
——, 'Five Priorities for a Peacebuilding Strategy' (2009).
——, 'A Comprehensive Strategy to Disarm the FDLR' (2009).
——, 'Côte d'Ivoire: What's Needed to End the Crisis' (2009).
——, 'Côte d'Ivoire: Securing the Electoral Process' (2010).
——, 'Côte d'Ivoire: Finally Escaping the Crisis?' (2010).
——, 'Côte d'Ivoire: Is War the Only Option?' (2011).
——, 'Popular Protest in North Africa and the Middle East (V): Making Sense of Libya' (2011).

——, 'DRC: The Electoral Process Seen from the East' (2011).
——, 'Black Gold in the Congo: Threat to Stability or Development Opportunity?' (2012).
——, 'Eastern Congo: Why Stabilisation Failed' (2012).
——, 'Understanding Conflict in Eastern Congo (I): The Ruzizi Plain' (2013).
International Law Commission, 'First Report on State Succession and Its Impact on the Nationality of Natural and Legal Persons, by Mr. Vaclav Mikulka, Special Rapporteur' UN Doc. A/CN.4/467 (Geneva, United Nations 1995).
——, 'Second Report on State Succession and Its Impact on the Nationality of Natural and Legal Persons, by Mr. Vaclav Mikulka, Special Rapporteur' UN Doc. A/CN.4/474 and Corr.1 and 2 (Geneva, United Nations, 1996).
——, 'Third Report on State Succession and Its Impact on the Nationality of Natural and Legal Persons, by Mr. Vaclav Mikulka, Special Rapporteur' UN Doc. A/CN.4/480 and Add.1 (Geneva, United Nations, 1997).
——, 'Articles on Nationality of Natural Persons in Relation to the Succession of States, with Commentaries, 1999' (Geneva, United Nations, 2000).
International Refugee Rights Initiative, 'Going Home or Staying Home? Ending Displacement for Burundian Refugees in Tanzania' (Kampala, 2008).
——, 'Resisting Repatriation: Burundian Refugees Struggling to Stay in Tanzania' (2012)
——, 'From Refugee to Returnee to Asylum Seeker: Burundian Refugees Struggle to Find Protection in the Great Lakes Region' (2013).
——, '"I Can't Be a Citizen If I Am Still a Refugee": Former Burundian Refugees Struggle to Assert Their New Tanzanian Citizenship' (2013).
——, 'The Role of Citizenship in Addressing Refugee Crises in Africa's Great Lakes Region' (2014).
International Rescue Committee, 'Mortality in the Democratic Republic of Congo: An Ongoing Crisis' (Washington DC, 2007).
Ishemo S, 'Forced Labour and Migration in Portugal's African Colonies' in Robin Cohen (ed), *The Cambridge Survey of World Migration* (Cambridge, Cambridge University Press, 1995).
Isin EF and Nielsen GM (eds), *Acts of Citizenship* (London, Zed Books, 2008).
Isin EF and Nyers P (eds), *Routledge Handbook of Global Citizenship Studies* (Abingdon, Routledge, 2014).
Isumonah VA, 'Migration, Land Tenure, Citizenship and Communal Conflicts in Africa' (2003) 9 *Nationalism and Ethnic Politics* 1.
——, 'The Ethnic Language of Rights and the Nigerian Political Community' in Emma Hunter (ed), *Citizenship, Belonging, and Political Community in Africa: Dialogues between Past and Present* (Athens OH, Ohio University Press, 2016).
Jackson S, 'Sons of Which Soil? The Language and Politics of Autochthony in Eastern D.R. Congo' (2006) 49 *African Studies Review* 95.
——, 'Of "Doubtful Nationality": Political Manipulation of Citizenship in the D. R. Congo' (2007) 11 *Citizenship Studies* 481.
Jalloh A, *African Entrepreneurship: Muslim Fula Merchants in Sierra Leone* (Athens OH, Ohio University Center for International Studies, 1999).
Jamestown Foundation, 'Arab-Tubu Clashes in Southern Libya's Sabha Oasis' (Washington DC, Jamestown Foundation, 2012); jamestown.org, 6 April 2012.
Jembere A, *An Introduction to the Legal History of Ethiopia: 1434–1974* (Münster, Lit Verlag, 2000).
Johnson DH, 'The Southern Sudan' (London, Minority Rights Group International, 1988).
——, 'Tribe or Nationality? The Sudanese Diaspora and the Kenyan Nubis' (2009) 3 *Journal of Eastern African Studies* 112.
Joppke C, *Immigration and the Nation-State* (Oxford, Oxford University Press, 1999).
——, *Citizenship and Immigration* (Polity, 2010).
Joseph S (ed), *Gender and Citizenship in the Middle East* 1st edn (Syracuse NY, Syracuse University Press, 2000).
Julien C-A, *L'Afrique du Nord en marche: Algérie, Tunesie, Maroc, 1830–1952* (Paris, Omnibus, 2002).

Karatani R, *Defining British Citizenship: Empire, Commonwealth, and Modern Britain* (London, Frank Cass, 2003).

Kastoryano R, 'Citizenship, Nationhood, and Non-Territoriality: Transnational Participation in Europe' (2005) 38 *PS: Political Science & Politics* 693.

Keese A, *Living with Ambiguity: Integrating an African Elite in French and Portuguese Africa, 1930–61* (Stuttgart, Franz Steiner, 2007).

Keightley R, 'The Child's Right to a Nationality and the Acquisition of Citizenship in South African Law' (1998) 14 *South African Journal on Human Rights* 411.

Keller EJ, *Identity, Citizenship, and Political Conflict in Africa* (Bloomington and Indianapolis, Indiana University Press, 2014).

Kenya Commission on Administrative Justice (Office of the Ombudsperson), 'Stateless In Kenya: An Investigation Report on the Crisis of Acquiring Identification Documents in Kenya' (Nairobi, 2015).

Kenya Human Rights Commission, 'Foreigners at Home: The Dilemma of Citizenship in Northern Kenya' (Nairobi, 2009).

Kenya National Commission on Human Rights, 'An Identity Crisis? Study on the Issuance of National Identity Cards in Kenya' (Nairobi, 2007).

——, 'Out of the Shadows: Towards Ensuring the Rights of Stateless Persons and Persons at Risk of Statelessness in Kenya' (Nairobi, 2010).

Kesby A, *The Right to Have Rights: Citizenship, Humanity, and International Law* (Oxford, Oxford University Press, 2012).

Khadiagala GM, 'Boundaries in Eastern Africa' (2010) 4 *Journal of Eastern African Studies* 266.

King J, 'Africa Discrimination and Citizenship Audit: Sierra Leone' (New York, Open Society Justice Initiative, 2005).

Kingston LN, 'Bringing Rwandan Refugees "Home": The Cessation Clause, Statelessness, and Forced Repatriation' (2017) 29 *International Journal of Refugee Law* 417.

Kini-Yen Kinni F, *Bakassi or the Politics of Exclusion and Occupation?* (Cameroon, Langaa Research & Publishing Common Initiative Group, 2013).

Klaaren J, 'Post-Apartheid Citizenship in South Africa' in Thomas Alexander Aleinikoff and Douglas B Klusmeyer (eds), *From Migrants to Citizens: Membership in a Changing World* (Washington DC, Carnegie Endowment for International Peace and Migration Policy Institute, 2000).

——, 'Constitutional Citizenship in South Africa' (2010) 8 *International Journal of Constitutional Law* 94.

Klaaren J and Rutinwa B, *Towards the Harmonization of Immigration and Refugee Law in SADC* (Cape Town, IDASA, 2004).

Klein NS, 'Report on the Deportation of Eritreans and Ethiopians of Eritrean Origin from Ethiopia, June–August 1998' (Washington DC, Embassy of Eritrea to the United States, 1999).

Knop K and Chinkin C, 'Remembering Chrystal MacMillan: Women's Equality and Nationality in International Law' (2001) 22 *Michigan Journal of International Law* 523.

Kobo O, '"We Are Citizens Too": The Politics of Citizenship in Independent Ghana' (2010) 48 *Journal of Modern African Studies* 67.

Konan S and Mounkaila H, 'Migrants en détresse: Analyse de situation et cadre de protection: Le cas du Niger et du Togo' (Geneva, UNHCR and IOM, 2013).

Konneh A, 'Citizenship at the Margins: Status, Ambiguity, and the Mandingo of Liberia' (1996) 39 *African Studies Review* 141.

Kotecha KC, 'The Shortchanged: Uganda Citizenship Laws and How They Were Applied to Its Asian Minority' (1975) 9 *The International Lawyer* 1.

Kuba R and Lentz C (eds), *Land and the Politics of Belonging in West Africa* (Leiden, Brill, 2006).

Kymlicka W, *Multicultural Citizenship* (Oxford, Oxford University Press, 1996).

Lacher W, 'Libya's Fractious South and Regional Instability' (Geneva, Small Arms Survey, 2014).

Lampué P, 'L'étendue d'application du statut personnel des autochtones dans les territoires français d'outre-mer' (1957) 7 *Civilisations* 1.

Landau LB, 'The Laws of (In)Hospitality: Black Africans in South Africa' (Johannesburg, Forced Migration Studies Programme, University of the Witwatersrand, 2004).

——, *The Humanitarian Hangover: Displacement, Aid, and Transformation in Western Tanzania* (Johannesburg, Wits University Press, 2008).

Langer A, 'Horizontal Inequalities and Violent Conflict: Côte d'Ivoire Country Paper' (New York, UNDP Human Development Report Office, 2005).

Lawyers for Human Rights, 'Towards Universal Birth Registration in South Africa: A Briefing Paper' (Pretoria, 2011).

——, 'Childhood Statelessness in South Africa' (Pretoria, Lawyers for Human Rights and Institute on Statelessness and Inclusion, 2016).

Lee CJ-H, 'The "Native" Undefined: Colonial Categories, Ango-African Status and the Politics of Kinship in British Central Africa, 1929–38' (2005) *Journal of African History* 455.

Leighton NO, 'The Political Economy of a Stranger Population: The Lebanese of Sierra Leone' in William A Shack and Elliott P Skinner (eds), *Strangers in African Societies* (Berkeley, University of California Press, 1979).

Lewis MD, 'One Hundred Million Frenchmen: The "Assimilation" Theory in French Colonial Policy' (1962) 4 *Comparative Studies in Society and History* 129.

Leys C and Pratt C, *A New Deal in Central Africa* (New York, Praeger, 1960).

Liauzu C, *Histoire des migrations en Méditerranée occidentale* (Brussels, Editions Complexe, 1996).

Lochery E, 'Rendering Difference Visible: The Kenyan State and its Somali Citizens' (2012) 111 *African Affairs* 615.

Longman T, 'Identity Cards, Ethnic Self-Perception and Genocide in Rwanda' in Jane Caplan and John Torpey (eds), *Documenting Individual Identity: The Development of State Practices in the Modern World* (Princeton, Princeton University Press, 2001).

Lonsdale J, 'Unhelpful Pasts and a Provisional Present' in Emma Hunter (ed), *Citizenship, Belonging, and Political Community in Africa: Dialogues between Past and Present* (Athens OH, Ohio University Press, 2016).

Losch B (ed), 'Dossier: Côte d'Ivoire, la tentation ethnonationaliste' (2000) 78 *Politique africaine* 5.

Lubala Mugisho E, 'La situation politique au Kivu: Vers une dualisation de la société' (1998) *L'Afrique des Grands Lacs: Annuaire 1997–98* 307.

Lubkemann S, Isser DH and Banks III, PAZ, 'Constraint of Customary Justice in Post-Conflict Liberia' in Deborah H Isser (ed), *Customary Justice and the Rule of Law in War-Torn Societies* (Washington DC, United States Institute of Peace, 2011).

Lukong HV, *The Cameroon-Nigeria Border Dispute: Management and Resolution, 1981–2011* (Cameroon, Langaa Research & Publishing Common Initiative Group, 2011).

Lynch G, 'Becoming Indigenous in the Pursuit of Justice: The African Commission on Human and Peoples' Rights and the Endorois' (2012) 111 *African Affairs* 24.

Lynch M, 'Lives on Hold: The Human Cost of Statelessness' (Washington DC, Refugees International, 2005).

Lynch M and Southwick K, 'Ethiopia-Eritrea: Stalemate Takes Toll on Eritreans and Ethiopians of Eritrean Origin' (Washington DC, Refugees International, 2008).

Mabanga MM, 'Le Contentieux Constitutionnel Congolais' (Kinshasa, Editions universitaires africaines, 1999).

Mabeko-Tali J-M, '"Congolenses", "Congoleses", "Zairenses": L'immigration centrafricaine et la problématique identitaire angolaise' in Catherine Coquery-Vidrovitch and others (eds), *Etre étranger et migrant en Afrique au XXe siècle: enjeux identitaires et modes d'insertion*, vol 1 (Paris, L'Harmattan, 2003).

Mabogunje AL, 'Regional Mobility and Resource Development in West Africa' (Montreal, Centre for Developing-Area Studies, McGill University, 1972).

MacLean LM, *Informal Institutions and Citizenship in Rural Africa: Risk and Reciprocity in Ghana and Côte d'Ivoire* (Cambridge, Cambridge University Press, 2010).

Macmillan H, 'A Nation Divided? The Swazi in Swaziland and the Transvaal, 1865–1986' in Leroy Vail (ed), *The creation of tribalism in Southern Africa* (Oxford, James Currey, 1989).

Makoloo MO, 'Kenya: Minorities, Indigenous Peoples and Ethnic Diversity' (London and Nairobi, Minority Rights Group International and CEMIRIDE, 2005).

Makombo AN, 'Civil Conflict in the Great Lakes Region: The Issue of Nationality of the Banyarwanda in the Democratic Republic of the Congo' (1997) 5 *African Yearbook of International Law* 49.

Maksudyan N, 'The Fight over Nobody's Children: Religion, Nationality and Citizenship of Foundlings in the Late Ottoman Empire' (2009) 41 *New Perspectives on Turkey* 151.

Malkki LH, *Purity and Exile: Violence, Memory, and National Cosmology among Hutu Refugees in Tanzania* (Chicago, University of Chicago Press, 1995).

Mamdani M, 'The Ugandan Asian Expulsion: Twenty Years After' (1993) 6 *Journal of Refugee Studies* 265.

——, *Citizen and Subject: Contemporary Africa and the Legacy of Late Colonialism* (Princeton, Princeton University Press, 1996).

Mamdani M, 'Indirect Rule and the Struggle for Democracy: A Response to Bridget O'Laughlin' (2000) 99 *African Affairs* 43.

Mamdani M, 'Beyond Settler and Native as Political Identities: Overcoming the Political Legacy of Colonialism' (2001) 43 *Comparative Studies in Society and History* 651.

——, *When Victims Become Killers: Colonialism, Nativism, and the Genocide in Rwanda* (Princeton, Princeton University Press, 2002).

Manby B, 'Statelessness in Southern Africa' (Geneva, UNHCR, 2011).

——, 'Draft Zim Constitution Fails Citizenship Test': osisa.org, 11 October 2012.

——, 'Tanzanian Constitutional Review Proposes Radical Changes to Citizenship Law'; africanarguments.org, 15 April 2014.

——, 'Migration, Nationality and Statelessness in West Africa' (Geneva, UNHCR and IOM, 2015).

——, 'You Can't Lose What You Haven't Got: Citizenship Acquisition and Loss in Africa' in Audrey Macklin and Rainer Bauböck (eds), *The Return of Banishment: Do the New Denationalisation Policies Weaken Citizenship?* (Fiesole, Robert Schuman Centre for Advanced Studies, European University Institute, 2015).

——, *Citizenship Law in Africa: A Comparative Study* 3rd edn (New York, Open Society Foundations, 2016).

——, 'The Human Right to Citizenship: A Slippery Concept by Rhoda E. Howard-Hassmann and Margaret Walton-Roberts (Review)' (2016) 38 *Human Rights Quarterly* 526.

——, 'Legal Identity for All and Childhood Statelessness' in Laura van Waas and Amal de Chickera (eds), *The World's Stateless* (Tilburg, Institute on Statelessness and Inclusion, 2017).

——, 'Citizenship and Statelessness in the East African Community' (Geneva, UNHCR, 2018)

Manji AS, 'Imagining Women's "Legal World": Towards a Feminist Theory of Legal Pluralism in Africa' (1999) 8 *Social & Legal Studies* 435.

Manly M, 'UNHCR's Mandate and Activities to Address Statelessness' in Alice Edwards and Laura van Waas (eds), *Nationality and Statelessness under International Law* (Cambridge, Cambridge University Press, 2014).

Mann G, 'What Was the Indigénat? The "Empire of Law" in French West Africa' (2009) 50 *Journal of African History* 331.

Mann K and Roberts RL (eds), *Law in Colonial Africa* (Oxford, James Currey, 1991).

Mansfield ED and Snyder JL, *Electing to Fight: Why Emerging Democracies Go to War* (Cambridge MA, MIT Press, 2007).

Markakis J, 'Pastoralism on the Margin' (London, Minority Rights Group International, 2004).

Marshall TH, *Citizenship and Social Class and Other Essays* (Cambridge, Cambridge University Press, 1950).

Marshall-Fratani R, 'The War of "Who Is Who": Autochthony, Nationalism and Citizenship in the Ivorian Crisis' in Sara Dorman, Daniel Hammett and Paul Nugent (eds), *Making Nations, Creating Strangers: States and Citizenship in Africa* (Leiden, Brill, 2007).

Massey H, 'UNHCR and De Facto Statelessness' (Geneva, UNHCR, 2010).

Masunungure EV and Koga H, 'Zimbabweans' (Mostly) Tolerant Views on Citizenship' (Accra, Afrobarometer, 2013).

Mazrui A, 'Casualties of an Underdeveloped Class Structure: The Expulsion of Luo Workers and Asian Bourgeoisie from Uganda' in William A Shack and Elliott P Skinner (eds), *Strangers in African Societies* (Berkeley, University of California Press, 1979).
Mazrui A, 'Banditry and the Politics of Citizenship: The Case of the Galje'el of Tana River' (Mombasa, Muslims for Human Rights (MUHURI), 1999).
Mbao MLM, 'Human Rights and Discrimination: Zambia's Constitutional Amendment, 1996' (1998) 42 *Journal of African Law* 1.
M'Baye K, 'L'attribution de la nationalité sénégalaise "jure soli" et l'option de nationalité dans la loi sénégalaise de 7 mars 1961' (1961) 71 *Penant* 347.
Mbembe A, 'À propos des écritures africaines de soi' (2000) 77 *Politique africaine* 16.
McAuslan J, 'John Joseph Akar v. Attorney General' (1968) 12 *Journal of African Law* 89.
——, 'John Joseph Akar v. Attorney General' (1969) 13 *Journal of African Law* 103.
McCallin B and Montemurro M, 'Whose Land Is This? Land Disputes and Forced Displacement in the Western Forest Area of Côte d'Ivoire' (Oslo, Norwegian Refugee Council Internal Displacement Monitoring Centre, 2009).
McDougal MS, Lasswell HD and Chen L, 'Nationality and Human Rights: The Protection of the Individual in External Arenas' (1974) 83 *Yale Law Journal* 900.
McGovern M, *Making War in Côte d'Ivoire* (Chicago, University of Chicago Press, 2011).
——, *A Socialist Peace? Explaining the Absence of War in an African Country* (Chicago, University of Chicago Press, 2017).
McInerney C, 'Accessing Malagasy Citizenship: The Nationality Code and its Impact on the Karana' (2004) 19 *Tilburg Law Review* 182.
McNevin A, 'Undocumented Citizens? Shifting Grounds of Citizenship in Los Angeles' in Peter Nyers and Kim Rygiel (eds), *Citizenship, Migrant Activism and the Politics of Movement* (Abingdon, Routledge, 2012).
Melone S, 'La nationalité des personnes physiques', *Encyclopédie juridique de l'Afrique : Vol VI, Droits des personnes et de la famille* (Dakar, Nouvelles éditions africaines, 1982).
Mendy PK, 'Portugal's Civilizing Mission in Colonial Guinea-Bissau: Rhetoric and Reality' (2003) 36 *International Journal of African Historical Studies*, 35.
Merry SE, *Human Rights and Gender Violence: Translating International Law into Local Justice* (Chicago, University of Chicago Press, 2006).
Mhurchú AN, 'Citizenship beyond State and Sovereignty' in Engin F Isin and Peter Nyers (eds), *Routledge Handbook of Global Citizenship Studies* (Abingdon, Routledge, 2014).
Milano E, 'The Conferral of Citizenship En Masse by Kin-States: Creeping Annexation or Responsibility to Protect?' in Francesco Palermo and Natalie Sabanadze (eds), *National Minorities in Inter-State Relations* (Leiden, Martinus Nijhoff Publishers, 2011).
Miles WFS and Rochefort DA, 'Nationalism Versus Ethnic Identity in Sub-Saharan Africa.' (1991) 85 *American Political Science Review* 393.
Miller CL, 'Who Are the "Permanent Inhabitants" of the State? Citizenship Policies and Border Controls in Tanzania, 1920–1980' (PhD, University of Iowa, 2011).
Milner J, 'Can Global Refugee Policy Leverage Durable Solutions? Lessons from Tanzania's Naturalization of Burundian Refugees' (2014) 27 *Journal of Refugee Studies* 553.
Minnaar A de V, Hough M and de Kock CP, *Who Goes There? Perspectives on Clandestine Migration and Illegal Aliens in Southern Africa* (Pretoria, Human Sciences Research Council, 1996).
Misago J-P, Landau LB and Monson T, 'Towards Tolerance, Law, and Dignity: Addressing Violence against Foreign Nationals in South Africa' (Geneva, IOM, 2009).
Moyo S, Rutherford B and Amanor-Wilks D, 'Land Reform and Changing Social Relations for Farm Workers in Zimbabwe' (2000) 27 *Review of African Political Economy* 181.
Muller L, 'South African Courts Confirm the Right to Nationality of a Stateless Child – 20 Year Old Legal Principle Protecting Stateless Children Is Finally Implemented'; statelessness.eu, 13 September 2016.

Munaita W and Munala J, 'Identity and Articulations of Belonging: A Background Study on the Pemba of Coastal Kenya' (Geneva, UNHCR, 2016).

Murphy SD, Kidane W and Snider TR, *Litigating War: Arbitration of Civil Injury by the Eritrea-Ethiopia Claims Commission* (Oxford, Oxford University Press, 2013).

Murray CRG, 'In the Shadow of Lord Haw Haw: Guantánamo Bay, Diplomatic Protection and Allegiance' (2011) 1 *Public Law* 115.

Muzondidya J, 'Zimbabwe for Zimbabweans: Invisible Subject Minorities and the Quest for Justice and Reconciliation in Post-colonial Zimbabwe' in Brian Raftopoulos and Tyrone Savage (eds), *Zimbabwe: injustice and political reconciliation* (Cape Town and Harare, Institute for Justice and Reconciliation and Weaver Press, 2005).

Mvududu SC and McFadden P, *Reconceptualizing the Family in a Changing Southern African Environment* (Harare, Women and Law in Southern Africa Research Trust, 2001).

Nahum F, 'Ethiopian Nationality Law and Practice' (1972) 8 *Journal of Ethiopian Law* 168.

Namegabe Rugarabura P-R, 'Traditional Chieftaincy and Decentralisation in the Democratic Republic of Congo: Opportunities and Challenges' (PhD, Libera Università Internazionale degli Studi Sociali, 2008).

Nanz P, 'Mobility, Migrants and Solidarity: Towards an Emerging European Citizenship' in Seyla Benhabib and Judith Resnik (eds), *Migrations and Mobilities: Citizenship, Borders and Gender* (New York, NYU Press, 2009).

Ncube W, 'Defending and Protecting Gender Equality and the Family Under a Decidedly Undecided Constitution in Zimbabwe' in John Eekelaar and Ronald Thandabantu Nhlapo (eds), *The changing family: international perspectives on the family and family law* (Oxford, Hart Publishing, 1998).

Ndahinda FM, *Indigenousness in Africa: A Contested Legal Framework for Empowerment of 'marginalized' Communities* (The Hague, TMC Asser Press, 2011).

Ndakaripa M, 'The State and Contested Citizenship in Zimbabwe, 1980–2011' in Sabelo J Ndlovu-Gatsheni and Finex Ndhlovu (eds), *Nationalism and national projects in Southern Africa: new critical reflections* (Pretoria, Africa Institute of South Africa, 2013).

Ndaywel è Nziem I, 'La nationalité congolaise à l'épreuve du séisme des Grands Lacs' in Pamphile Mabiala Mantuba-Ngoma (ed), *La nouvelle histoire du Congo : Mélanges euroafricains offerts à Frans Bontinck*, vols 65-66–67 (Paris, L'Harmattan, 2004).

Ndegwa SN, 'Citizenship and Ethnicity: An Examination of Two Transition Moments in Kenyan Politics' (1997) 91 *American Political Science Review* 599.

Nellemann C, Redmond I and Refisch J (eds), *The Last Stand of the Gorilla: Environmental Crime and Conflict in the Congo Basin. A Rapid Response Assessment* (Nairobi and Oslo, UN Environment Programme & GRID-Arendal, 2010).

Neuberger B, 'The African Concept of Balkanisation' (1976) *14 Journal of Modern African Studies* (no. 3) 523–29.

Newitt M, *A History of Mozambique* (Hurst, 1995).

Ngai MM, *Impossible Subjects: Illegal Aliens and the Making of Modern America* (Princeton, Princeton University Press, 2014).

Ngang K, 'Understanding the Bakassi Conflict: A Showcase of Conflict Prevention in Practice' (Fiesole, European University Centre for Peace Studies, 2007).

Nguya-Ndila Malengana C, *Nationalité et citoyenneté au Congo-Kinshasa: le cas du Kivu* (Paris, L'Harmattan, 2001).

Nigeria National Conference 'Final Draft Conference Report' (Abuja, 2014).

Nigeria National Population Commission, 'Internal Migration Survey in Nigeria' (Abuja, 2010).

Nigeria Research Network, 'Indigeneity, Belonging, & Religious Freedom in Nigeria: Citizens' Views from the Street' (Oxford and Kano, University of Oxford and Development Research and Project Centre, 2014).

Nkiwane TC, 'Gender, Citizenship, and Constitutionalism in Zimbabwe: The Fight Against Amendment 14' (2000) 4 *Citizenship Studies* 325.

Noiriel G, 'Socio-histoire d'un concept: Les usages du mot "nationalité" au XIXe siècle' (1995) 20 *Genèses* 4.
Noor Mohammed NA, *The Legal System of the Somali Democratic Republic* (Charlottesvill VA, Michie, 1972).
Nugent P, *Africa since Independence* (Basingstoke, Palgrave Macmillan, 2004).
Nuytinck H, 'Les principes du nouveau droit de la famille au Burkina Faso' (1991) 806 *Penant* 258.
Nwachukwu I, 'The Challenge of Local Citizenship for Human Rights in Nigeria' (2005) 13 *African Journal of International and Comparative Law* 235.
Nwogugu EI, 'Recent Changes in Nigerian Nationality and Citizenship Law' (1976) 25 *International and Comparative Law Quarterly* 423.
Nyamnjoh FB, 'Local Attitudes towards Citizenship and Foreigners in Botswana: An Appraisal of Recent Press Stories' (2002) 28 *Journal of Southern African Studies* 755.
——, *Insiders and Outsiders: Citizenship and Xenophobia in Contemporary Southern Africa* (London, Zed Books, 2006).
——, 'From Bounded to Flexible Citizenship: Lessons from Africa' (2007) 11 *Citizenship Studies* 73.
Nyamu-Musembi C, 'Addressing Formal and Substantive Citizenship: Gender Justice in Sub-Saharan Africa' in Maitrayee Mukhopadhyay and Navsharan Singh (eds), *Gender Justice, Citizenship and Development* (Delhi and Ottawa, Zubaan and International Development Research Centre, 2007).
Nyers P and Rygiel K (eds), *Citizenship, Migrant Activism and the Politics of Movement* (Abingdon, Routledge, 2012).
Nylander AVJ, *The Nationality and Citizenship Laws of Nigeria* (Lagos, University of Lagos, 1973).
Nzongola-Ntalaja G, 'Citizenship, Political Violence, and Democratization in Africa' (2004). 10 *Global Governance: A Review of Multilateralism and International Organizations* 403.
Odinkalu CA, 'Natives, Subjects, and Wannabes: Internal Citizenship Problems in Post-Colonial Africa' in Rhoda E Howard-Hassmann and Margaret Walton-Roberts (eds), *The Human Right to Citizenship: A Slippery Concept* (Philadelphia, University of Pennsylvania Press, 2015).
Odoki Commission, 'Report of the Uganda Constitutional Commission' (Kampala, 1993).
OECD High Commissioner on National Minorities, 'The Bolzano/Bozen Recommendations on National Minorities in Inter-State Relations & Explanatory Note' (Vienna, Organisation for Security and Cooperation in Europe, 2008).
Okoli KC, 'Nigerian Citizenship Law: A Current Perspective' (1990) 34 *Journal of African Law* 27.
O'Laughlin B, 'Class and the Customary: The Ambiguous Legacy of the Indigenato in Mozambique' (2000) 99 *African Affairs* 5.
Olinga AD, *L'accord de Greentree du 12 juin 2006 relatif à la presqu'île de Bakassi* (Paris, L'Harmattan, 2009).
Oucho JO and Crush J, 'Contra Free Movement: South Africa and the SADC Migration Protocols' 48 *Africa Today* 139.
Pabanel J-P, 'La question de la nationalité au Kivu' (1991) 41 *Politique africaine* 32.
Pailey RN, 'Birthplace, Bloodline and beyond: How "Liberian Citizenship" Is Currently Constructed in Liberia and Abroad' (2016) 20 *Citizenship Studies* 811.
Parolin GP, *Citizenship in the Arab World: Kin, Religion and Nation-State* (Amsterdam University Press, 2009).
——, 'New Policy on Egyptian Citizenship for Children of Palestinian Fathers'; globalcit.eu.
Parry C, *Nationality and Citizenship Laws of The Commonwealth and of The Republic of Ireland* (London, Stevens & Sons, 1957).
Pedersen S, *The Guardians: The League of Nations and the Crisis of Empire* (Oxford, Oxford University Press, 2015).
Peil M, 'The Expulsion of West African Aliens' (1971) 9 *Journal of Modern African Studies* 205.
——, 'Ghana's Aliens' (1974) 8 *International Migration Review* 367.
——, 'Host Reactions: Aliens in Ghana' in William A Shack and Elliott P Skinner (eds), *Strangers in African Societies* (Berkeley, University of California Press, 1979).

Pelican M, 'Mbororo Claims to Regional Citizenship and Minority Status in North-West Cameroon' (2008) 78 *Africa* 540.
Pereira C, 'Understanding Women's Experiences of Citizenship in Nigeria: From Advocacy to Research', *Gender, Economies and Entitlements in Africa* (Dakar, CODESRIA, 2004).
Perrin D, 'Identité et transmission du lien national au Maghreb : Etude comparée des codes de la nationalité' (2007) 3 *L'Année du Maghreb* 479.
——, 'Beyond the Borders: Dual Nationality in Western Mediterranean Countries' in I Schäfer and JR Henry (eds), *Mediterranean Policies from Above and from Below* (Nomos, 2009).
——, 'Immigration and Citizenship Law in the Maghreb: Turning Aliens into Citizens' (Fiesole, Robert Schuman Centre For Advanced Studies, European University Institute, 2011).
——, 'Citizenship Struggles in the Maghreb' in Engin F Isin and Peter Nyers (eds), *Routledge Handbook of Global Citizenship Studies* (Abingdon, Routledge, 2014).
Pidatala K and others, 'Identification Systems Analysis Country Assessment: Zambia' (Washington DC, World Bank, Identification for Development Initiative, 2016).
Pierrot E-J, 'A Responsibility to Protect: UNHCR and Statelessness in Egypt' (Geneva, UNHCR, 2013).
Plender R, 'The Exodus of Asians from East and Central Africa Some Comparative and International Law Aspects' (1971) 19 *American Journal of Comparative Law* 287.
Polzer T, 'Local Government and Migration Management in Border Areas – Challenges and Opportunities for Public Service Provision' (Johannesburg, Forced Migration Studies Programme, University of the Witwatersrand, 2007).
——, 'Regularising Zimbabwean Migration to South Africa' (Johannesburg, Forced Migration Studies Program University of the Witwatersrand and Consortium for Refugees and Migrants in South Africa, 2009).
Queffélec A and Ould Zein B, 'La "Longue Marche" de l'arabisation en Mauritanie' (2001) 15 *Le français en Afrique*; http://www.unice.fr/.
Raftopoulos B, 'The State in Crisis: Authoritarian Nationalism, Selective Citizenship and Distortions of Democracy in Zimbabwe' in Amanda Hammar, Brian Raftopoulos and Stig Jensen (eds), *Zimbabwe's Unfinished Business: Rethinking Land, State and Nation in Zimbabwe in the Context of Crisis* (Harare, Weaver Press, 2003).
——, 'Nation, Race and History in Zimbabwe' in Sara Dorman, Daniel Hammett and Paul Nugent (eds), *Making Nations, Creating Strangers: States and Citizenship in Africa* (Leiden, Brill, 2007).
Ramos RMM, *Estudos de direito português da nacionalidade* (Lisbon, Coimbra Editora, 2013).
Ranger T, 'The Invention of Tradition in Colonial Africa' in EJ Hobsbawm and TO Ranger (eds), *The Invention of Tradition* (Cambridge, Cambridge University Press, 1983).
Read JS, 'Some Legal Aspects of the Expulsion' in Michael Twaddle (ed), *Expulsion of a Minority: Essays on Ugandan Asians* (London, Athlone Press, 1975).
Refugee Law Project, 'Critique of the Refugees Act 2006' (Kampala, 2006).
Renner-Thomas A, *Land Tenure in Sierra Leone: The Law, Dualism and the Making of a Land Policy* (Milton Keynes, AuthorHouse, 2010).
Robinson KE, 'The Public Law of Overseas France since the War' (1950) 32 *Journal of Comparative Legislation and International Law* 37.
Rothchild D, 'Kenya's Minorities and the African Crisis over Citizenship' (1968) 9 *Race & Class* 421.
Rutherford B, 'Shifting Grounds in Zimbabwe: Citizenship and Farm Workers in the New Politics of Land' in Sara Dorman, Daniel Hammett and Paul Nugent (eds), *Making Nations, Creating Strangers: States and Citizenship in Africa* (Leiden, Brill, 2007).
Rutinwa B, 'The Tanzanian Government's Response to the Rwandan Emergency' (1996) 9 *Journal of Refugee Studies* 291.
——, 'The End of Asylum? The Changing Nature of Refugee Policies in Africa' (2002) 21 *Refugee Survey Quarterly* 12.
Saada E, *Les enfants de la colonie: les métis de l'empire français entre sujétion et citoyenneté* (Paris, La Découverte, 2007).
Sadiq K, *Paper Citizens: How Illegal Immigrants Acquire Citizenship in Developing Countries* (Oxford, Oxford University Press, 2009).

San Martin P, 'Nationalism, Identity and Citizenship in the Western Sahara' (2005) 10 *Journal of North African Studies* 565.

Sanders ER, 'The Hamitic Hypothesis; Its Origin and Functions in Time Perspective' (1969) 10 *Journal of African History* 521.

Sanderson M, 'Key Threats of Statelessness in the Post-Secession Sudanese and South Sudanese Nationality Regimes' (2014) 19 *Tilburg Law Review* 236.

Santoir C, 'Le conflit mauritano-sénégalais : la genèse : le cas des Peul de la haute vallée du Sénégal' (1990) 26 *Cahiers des sciences humaines* 553.

Sawyer A, *The Emergence of Autocracy in Liberia: Tragedy and Challenge* (San Francisco CA, Institute for Contemporary Studies, 1992).

Schatz EJ, 'Reframing Vulnerability: Mozambican Refugees' Access to State-Funded Pensions in Rural South Africa' (2009) 24 *Journal of Cross-Cultural Gerontology* 241.

Schuck PH and Smith RM, *Citizenship Without Consent: Illegal Aliens in the American Policy* (New Haven CT, Yale University Press, 1985).

Scott JC, *The Art of Not Being Governed: An Anarchist History of Upland Southeast Asia* (New Haven CT, Yale University Press, 2009).

Scotton CMM, 'Some Swahili Political Words' (1965) 3 *Journal of Modern African Studies* 527.

Sedler RA, 'Nationality, Domicile and the Personal Law in Ethiopia' (1965) 2 *Journal of Ethiopian Law* 161.

Seely JC and others, 'Second-Class Citizens? Gender in African Citizenship Law' (2013) 17 *Citizenship Studies* 429.

Selby A, 'Commercial Farmers and the State: Interest Group Politics and Land Reform in Zimbabwe' (DPhil, Oxford University, 2006).

Shack WA and Skinner EP (eds), *Strangers in African Societies* (Berkeley, University of California Press, 1979).

Shafir G (ed), *The Citizenship Debates: A Reader* (Minneapolis, University of Minnesota Press, 1998).

Shah R, 'Britain and Kenya's Citizenship Law: A Conflict of Laws?' (1992) 6 *Tolley's Immigration & Nationality Law & Practice* 120.

——, 'Kenya's Citizenship Laws Revisited' (2012) 26 *Journal of Immigration Asylum and Nationality Law* 269.

Sharma VD and Wooldridge F, 'Some Legal Questions Arising from the Expulsion of the Ugandan Asians' (1974) 23 *International and Comparative Law Quarterly* 397.

Shepherd GM, 'The Comorians in Kenya: The Establishment and Loss of an Economic Niche' (PhD, London School of Economics, 1982).

Sierra Leone Truth and Reconcilation Commission, 'Report of the Sierra Leone Truth and Reconciliation Commission, Vol.2' (Freetown, 2004).

Sikainga AA, 'Citizenship and Identity in Post-Secession Northern Sudan' (2011) 86 *Bulletin of the Association of Concerned Africa Scholars* 11.

Sloane RD, 'Breaking the Genuine Link: The Contemporary International Legal Regulation of Nationality' (2009) 50 *Harvard International Law Journal* 1.

Sloth-Nielsen J and Ackermann D, 'Foreign Children in Care in the Western Cape Province' (Cape Town, Scalabrini Centre, 2015).

Smith AH, 'Prevention of Discrimination under Kenyan Law' (1971) 20 *International and Comparative Law Quarterly* 136.

Smith J and Charny JR, 'Sudan: Preventing Violence and Statelessness as the Referendum Approaches' (Washington DC, Refugees International, 2010).

Smith L, 'Voting for an Ethnic Identity: Procedural and Institutional Responses to Ethnic Conflict in Ethiopia' (2007) 45 *Journal of Modern African Studies* 565.

——, *Making Citizens in Africa: Ethnicity, Gender, and National Identity in Ethiopia* (Cambridge, Cambridge University Press, 2013).

Smith RM (ed), *Citizenship, Borders, and Human Needs* (Philadelphia, University of Pennsylvania Press, 2011).

Snyder JL, *From Voting to Violence: Democratization and Nationalist Conflict* (New York, Norton, 2000).

Somerville JJB, 'The Central African Federation' (1963) 39 *International Affairs* 386.

Southwick K, 'Ethiopia-Eritrea: Statelessness and State Succession' (2009) 32 *Forced Migration Review* 15.

Southwick K and Lynch M, 'Nationality Rights for All: Global Survey on Statelessness' (Washington DC, Refugees International, 2009).

Soysal YN, *Limits of Citizenship: Migrants and Postnational Membership in Europe* (Chicago, University of Chicago Press, 1994).

Spiro P, 'A New International Law of Citizenship' (2011) 105 *American Journal of International Law* 694.

Statistics South Africa, 'The Coverage and Quality of Birth Registration Data in South Africa: 1998–2005, Report No. 06-03-01' (Pretoria, 2007).

Stearns J, *From CNDP to M23: The Evolution of an Armed Movement in Eastern Congo* (Nairobi, Rift Valley Institute, 2012).

——, *North Kivu: The Background to Conflict in North Kivu Province of Eastern Congo* (Nairobi, Rift Valley Institute, 2012).

Stearns JK, *Dancing in the Glory of Monsters: The Collapse of the Congo and the Great War of Africa* (New York, PublicAffairs, 2011).

Steinberg J, 'South Africa's Xenophobic Eruption' (Pretoria, Institute of Security Studies, 2008).

Stone D, 'Enhancing Livelihood Security among Mauritanian Refugees in Northern Senegal: A Case Study' (Geneva, UNHCR, 2005).

Sumner B, 'Territorial Disputes at the International Court of Justice' (2004) 53 *Duke Law Journal* 1779.

Taiwo O, 'Of Citizens and Citizenship' in Okon Akiba (ed), *Constitutionalism and society in Africa* (Aldershot, Ashgate, 2004).

Tannenbaum J, 'Analysis of the Aliens and Nationality Law of the Republic of Liberia' (Washington DC, American Bar Association Rule of Law Initiative, 2009).

Tapinos GP, 'La population étrangère' in Georges Photios Tapinos, Philippe Hugon and Patrice Vimard (eds), *La Côte d'Ivoire à l'aube du XXIe siècle: Défis démographiques et développement durable* (Paris, Karthala, 2001).

Tari MS, 'Tuareg: The Tragedy of a Forgotten People'; amazighworld.org (n.d.).

Thomas L, 'Refugees and Asylum Seekers from Mixed Eritrean-Ethiopian Families in Cairo' (Cairo, Programme for Forced Migration and Refugee Studies, American University in Cairo, 2006).

Tirefort A, 'L'affaire « Daho-Togo »: Une fièvre de xenophobie en Côte d'Ivoire' in Catherine Coquery-Vidrovitch and others (eds), *Etre étranger et migrant en Afrique au XXe siècle*, vol 1 (Paris, L'Harmattan, 2003).

Tonah S, 'The Politics of Exclusion: The Expulsion of Fulbe Pastoralists from Ghana in 1999/2000' (Munich, Max Planck Institute, 2002).

Truth, Justice & Reconciliation Commission of Kenya, 'Final Report Vol. IIA' (Nairobi, 2013).

Tubiana J and Gramizzi C, 'Tubu Trouble: State and Statelessness in the Chad–Sudan–Libya Triangle' (Geneva, Small Arms Survey, 2017).

UN African Group, 'Draft Aide Memoire : African Group : United Nations Declaration on the Rights of Indigenous People' (Geneva, 2006).

UN Commission on Human Rights, 'Report on the Situation of Human Rights in Zaire by the Special Rapporteur, Mr. Robert Garretón, in Accordance with Commission Resolution 1996/77' UN Doc. E/CN.4/1997/6/Add.1 (Geneva, 1996).

——, 'Interim Report of the Special Rapporteur on the Situation of Human Rights in the Democratic Republic of the Congo' UN Doc. A/58/534 (Geneva, 2003).

UN Department of Economic and Social Affairs, 'Trends in International Migrant Stock: The 2013 Revision' (United Nations, 2013).

UN Economic Commission for Africa, 'Diversity Management in Africa: Findings from the African Peer Review Mechanism and a Framework for Analysis and Policy-Making' (Addis Ababa, 2011).

UN Human Rights Committee, 'General Comment No. 17: Rights of the Child (Art. 24)' (Geneva, 1989).

UN Office of the High Commissioner for Human Rights, 'Democratic Republic of the Congo, 1993–2003: Report of the Mapping Exercise Documenting the Most Serious Violations of Human Rights and International Humanitarian Law Committed within the Territory of the Democratic Republic of the Congo between March 1993 and June 2003' (Geneva, 2010).

UNHCR, 'Finding a Home on Ancestral Land: Somali Bantu Refugees Gaining Citizenship in Tanzania' (Geneva, 2010).

——, 'The Concept of Stateless Persons under International Law (The "Prato Conclusions")' (Geneva, 2010).

——, 'Statelessness Determination Procedures and the Status of Stateless Persons (The "Geneva Conclusions")' (Geneva, 2010).

——, 'Guidelines on Statelessness No. 4: Ensuring Every Child's Right to Acquire a Nationality through Articles 1–4 of the 1961 Convention on the Reduction of Statelessness' (Geneva, 2012).

——, 'Handbook on Protection of Stateless Persons under the 1954 Convention Relating to the Status of Stateless Persons' (Geneva, 2014).

UNICEF, 'Every Child's Birth Right: Inequities and Trends in Birth Registration' (Geneva, 2013).

van Acker F, 'La « Pembenisation » du Haut-Kivu : Opportunisme et droits fonciers revisités' (1999) *L'Afrique des Grands Lacs Annuaire 1998–1999* 201.

van der Beken C, 'Ethiopia: Constitutional Protection of Ethnic Minorities at the Regional Level' (2007) 20 *Afrika Focus* 105.

van der Laan HL, *The Lebanese Traders in Sierra Leone* (The Hague, Mouton, 1975).

van Pittius EFWG, *Nationality within the British Commonwealth of Nations* (London, PS King & Son, 1930).

van Waas L, 'The Stateless Tebu of Libya?' (Tilburg, Tilburg Law School, 2013).

——, 'The UN Statelessness Conventions' in Alice Edwards and Laura van Waas (eds), *Nationality and Statelessness under International Law* (Cambridge, Cambridge University Press, 2014).

Vandenabeele C and Lao CV, 'Legal Identity for Inclusive Development' (Manila, Asian Development Bank, 2007).

Vansina J, *Paths in the Rainforests: Toward a History of Political Tradition in Equatorial Africa* (Oxford, James Currey, 1990).

Vermeer-Kunzli A, 'Nationality and Diplomatic Protection' in Alessandra Annoni and Serena Forlati (eds), *The Changing Role of Nationality in International Law* (Abingdon, Routledge, 2013).

Verstraete M, *La nationalité congolaise* (Brussels, Académie Royale des Sciences d'Outre-Mer, 1959).

Verweijen J and Vlassenroot K, 'Armed Mobilisation and the Nexus of Territory, Identity, and Authority: The Contested Territorial Aspirations of the Banyamulenge in Eastern DR Congo' (2015) 33 *Journal of Contemporary African Studies* 191.

Verwilghen M, *Conflits de nationalités, plurinationalité et apatridie*, vol 277 (Hague Academy of International Law, 1999).

Vezzadini E, 'Genealogies of Racial Relations: The Independence of South Sudan, Citizenship and the Racial State in the Modern History of Sudan' (2011) 86 *Bulletin of the Association of Concerned Africa Scholars* 30.

Viljoen F and Louw L, 'State Compliance with the Recommendations of the African Commission on Human and Peoples' Rights, 1994–2004' (2007) 101 *American Journal of International Law* 1.

Vink M, de Groot R and Luk NC, 'MACIMIDE Global Expatriate Dual Citizenship Dataset' (Harvard Dataverse, 2015).

Vlassenroot K, 'Citizenship, Identity Formation & Conflict in South Kivu: The Case of the Banyamulenge' (2002) 29 *Review of African Political Economy* 499.

Vonk OW, *Nationality Law in the Western Hemisphere: A Study on Grounds for Acquisition and Loss of Citizenship in the Americas and the Caribbean* (Leiden, Brill, 2015).

wa Mutua M, 'Why Redraw the Map of Africa: A Moral and Legal Inquiry' (1995) 16 *Michigan Journal of International Law* 1113.

Waas L van, *Nationality Matters: Statelessness under International Law* (Antwerp, Intersentia, 2008).

Walker I, 'Comorians and Hadramis in the Western Indian Ocean: Diasporic Practices in a Comparative Context' (2012) 38 *Social Dynamics* 435.

——, 'Identity and Citizenship among the Comorians of Zanzibar, 1886–1963' in Abdul Sheriff and Enseng Ho (eds), *The Indian Ocean: Oceanic connections and the creation of new societies* (Hurst & Company, 2014).

Walker SG, 'From Refugee to Citizen? Obstacles to the Naturalisation of Refugees in Uganda' (Kampala, Refugee Law Project, 2011).

Walzer M, *Spheres of Justice: A Defense of Pluralism and Equality* (New York, Basic Books, 1983).

Weber E, *Peasants into Frenchmen: The Modernization of Rural France ; 1870–1914* (Stanford CA, Stanford University Press, 2007).

Weil P, 'Access to Citizenship: A Comparison of Twenty-Five Nationality Laws' in Thomas Alexander Aleinikoff and Douglas B Klusmeyer (eds), *Citizenship Today: Global Perspectives and Practices* (Washington DC, Carnegie Endowment for International Peace and Migration Policy Institute, 2001).

——, *Qu'est-ce qu'un Français? Histoire de la nationalité française de la Révolution à nos jours* (Paris, Grasset, 2002).

——, 'Le statut des musulmans en Algérie coloniale: Une nationalité française dénaturée' (Fiesole, European University Institute, 2003).

——, 'From Conditional to Secured and Sovereign: The New Strategic Link between the Citizen and the Nation-State in a Globalized World' (2011) 9 *International Journal of Constitutional Law* 615.

Weis P, *Nationality and Statelessness in International Law* 2nd edn (Leiden, Brill, 1979).

Weiss P, 'L'Opération Licorne en Côte d'Ivoire : Banc d'essai de la nouvelle politique française de sécurité en Afrique' (2004) V *Annuaire français de relations internationales* 313.

Weissbrodt D and Meili S, 'Human Rights and Protection of Non-Citizens: Whither Universality and Indivisibility of Rights?' (2009) 28 *Refugee Survey Quarterly* 34.

Whitaker BE, 'Citizens and Foreigners: Democratization and the Politics of Exclusion in Africa' (2005) 48 *African Studies Review* 109.

——, 'The Politics of Home: Dual Citizenship and the African Diaspora: Dual Citizenship and the African Diaspora' (2011) 45 *International Migration Review* 755.

Whitehouse B, *Migrants and Strangers in an African City: Exile, Dignity, Belonging* (Bloomington, Indiana University Press, 2012).

Wichmann N, 'Reforming the Swiss Citizenship Act: Mission Impossible' (Swiss Forum for Migration Studies, University of Neuchatel, 2013).

Widner JA, 'States and Statelessness in Late Twentieth-Century Africa' (1995) 124 *Daedalus* 129.

Willame J-C, *Banyarwanda et Banyamulenge: Violences ethniques et gestion de l'identitaire au Kivu* (Brussels and Paris, Institut africain-CEDAF and L'Harmattan, 1997).

——, 'Kivu : La Poudrière' in Colette Braeckman et al (eds), *Kabila prend le pouvoir* (Brussels, Groupe de recherche et d'information sur la paix et la sécurité (GRIP), 1998).

Willis J and Gona G, 'Pwani C Kenya? Memory, Documents and Secessionist Politics in Coastal Kenya' (2013) 112 *African Affairs* 48.

Wilson RR and Clute RE, 'Commonwealth Citizenship and Common Status' (1963) 57 *American Journal of International Law* 566.

World Bank, *World Development Report 2016: Digital Dividends* (Washington DC, 2016).

Wrubel TP, 'Liberia: The Dynamics of Continuity' (1971) 9 *Journal of Modern African Studies* 189.

Yéré H-M, '"Double Nationalité" and Its Discontents in Ivory Coast, 1963–66' in Emma Hunter (ed), *Citizenship, Belonging, and Political Community in Africa: Dialogues between Past and Present* (Athens OH, Ohio University Press, 2016).

Young C, 'Nation, Ethnicity, and Citizenship: Dilemmas of Democracy and Civil Order in Africa' in Sara Dorman, Daniel Hammett and Paul Nugent (eds), *Making Nations, Creating Strangers: States and Citizenship in Africa* (Leiden, Brill, 2007).

Zambakari C, 'Sudan and South Sudan: Identity, Citizenship, and Democracy in Plural Societies' (2015) 19 *Citizenship Studies* 69.

Zatzepine A, *Le droit de la nationalité des républiques francophones d'Afrique et de Madagascar* (Paris, Pichon et Durand-Auzias, 1963).

Zetterqvist J, 'Refugees in Botswana in the Light of International Law' (Uppsala, Scandinavian Institute of African Studies, 1990).

Zhou Y-Y, 'How Refugees Affect Conceptions of Citizenship in Africa' (Social Science Research Network, 2017).

Ziemele I, 'State Succession and Issues of Nationality and Statelessness' in Alice Edwards and Laura van Waas (eds), *Nationality and Statelessness under International Law* (Cambridge, Cambridge University Press, 2014).

Zimamoza Institute, 'Ethnic Cleansing In Zimbabwe: The Origins and Objectives of the Zimamoza Institute' (Harare, 2007).

Zoro-Bi E, *Juge en Côte d'Ivoire: désarmer la violence* (Paris, Karthala, 2004).

——, 'Je suis un Sidibé de Tiémélékro : L'acquisition de la nationalité ivoirienne à titre originaire : Critère juridique ou critère anthropologique?' in Jean-Bernard Ouédraogo and Ebrima Sall (eds), *Frontières de la citoyenneté et violence politique en Côte d'Ivoire* (Dakar, CODESRIA, 2008).

Zounmenou D and Kok N, 'Peace, Security and Cooperation Framework for the DRC: Hopes and Challenges'; issafrica.org, 8 March 2013.

LIST OF CITIZENSHIP LAWS

African nationality laws A list of current and former laws regulating nationality, as well as constitutions containing substantive provisions on acquisition and loss of nationality	
Algeria	Loi No.63-96 du 27 mars 1963 portant Code de la nationalité algérienne Ordonnance No.70-86 du 15 décembre 1970 portant Code de la nationalité algérienne Ordonnance No. 05-01 du 27 février 2005 modifiant et complétant Code de la nationalité algérienne
Angola	Lei da nacionalidade de 11 de novembro 1975 Lei No.2/84 da nacionalidade de 7 de fevereiro Lei No.13/91 da nacionalidade, de 11 de maio Lei No.1/05 da nacionalidade, de 1 de julho Constitution, 2010 Lei No.2/16 da nacionalidade da 31 de marzo
Benin	Loi No. 65-17 du 23/06/65 portant Code de la nationalité dahoméenne
Botswana	Constitution 1966 Citizenship of Botswana (Supplementary Provisions) Law No.39 of 1966 Citizenship of Botswana (Supplementary Provisions) (Amendment) Act No.56 of 1969 Citizenship Act No.25 of 1982 Constitution (Amendment) Act No.32 of 1982 Citizenship (Amendment) Act No.17 of 1984 Citizenship (Amendment) Act No.14 of 1995 Citizenship Act No.8 of 1998 Citizenship Amendment Act No.9 of 2002 Citizenship Amendment Act No.1 of 2004
Burkina Faso	Loi No.50-61-AN du 1 décembre 1961 portant adoption d'un Code de la nationalité voltaïque Zatu No. An VII 0013/FP/PRES du 16 novembre 1989, portant institution et application du Code des personnes et de la famille
Burundi	Décret-Loi No 1/93 du 10 août 1971 portant Code de la Nationalité Loi No. 1-013 du 18 juillet 2000 portant réforme du Code de la nationalité Constitution 2005

Cameroon	Ordonnance No.59-66 du 26 novembre 1959 portant Code de la nationalité camerounaise Loi No. 1968-LF-3 du 11 juin 1968 portant Code de la nationalité camerounaise
Cape Verde	Decreto-Lei No.71/76, de 24 de julho Decreto-Lei No.102/76, de 20 de novembro – Nacionalidade Originária Decreto-lei 31/87 de 28 de março Lei No.80/III/90 de 29 de junho de 1990 Decreto No.114/90, BO No.49, I Serie, de 08 de dezembro de 1990 Lei No.41/IV/92 de 06 de abril de 1992 Constitution 1992 (revised 1995, 1999 & 2010) Lei No.64/IV/92 de 30 de dezembro Decreto-Lei No 53/93 de 30 de Agosto de 1993 Decreto-Lei No.19/2000, 24 de Abril de 2000
CAR	Loi No. 61-212 du 27 mai 1961 portant Code de la nationalité centrafricaine Loi No.64-54 du 2 décembre 1964 Loi 63-406 fixant la nationalité des enfants nés de deux conjoints qui n'auraient pas contracté un mariage civil et dont la mère est centrafricaine Ordonnance No.1966-64 du 30 août 1966 modifiant la Loi 1961/212 du 20 avril 1961 portant Code de la nationalité Ordonnance No.84-022 du 12 avril 1984 abrogeant ordonnance no.66-64
Chad	Loi No.31-60 du 27 février 1961 portant Code de la nationalité tchadienne Décret No.16/PG du 28 septembre 1961 relatif au Code de la nationalité tchadienne Ordonnance No. 33/PG-INT du 14 août 1962 portant Code de la nationalité tchadienne Décret No. 211-PG.-INT. du 6 novembre 1963 portant application du Code de la nationalité
Comoros	Constitution, 2001, revised 2010 Loi No. 79-12 du 12 décembre 1979 portant Code de la nationalité comorienne Loi relative à la citoyenneté économique en Union des Comores, du 27 novembre 2008
Congo Republic	Loi No. 35-61 du 20 juin 1961 portant Code de la nationalité congolaise Décret No. 61-178 du 29 juillet 1961 fixant les modalités d'application du Code de la nationalité Loi No. 2-93 du 30 septembre 1993 modifiant l'article 30 de la loi No. 35-61 du 20 juin 1961 Loi No.32-2011 modifiant certaines dispositions de la Loi No.35-61 du 20 juin 1961 portant code de la nationalité congolaise

Côte d'Ivoire	Loi No.61-415 du 14 Décembre 1961 portant Code de la nationalité ivoirienne (telle que modifiée par la Loi No.64-381 du 7 octobre 1964, la Loi No.72-852 du 21 Décembre 1972, et la Loi No.2004-662 du 17 décembre 2004 et les décisions No.2005-03/pr du 15 juillet 2005 et No.2005-09/pr du 29 aout 2005) Constitution de la République de Côte d'Ivoire Loi No.2000-513 du 23 juillet 2000 Loi No. 2004-662 du 17 décembre 2004 modifiant et complétant la Loi 61-415 du 14 décembre 1961 portant Code de la nationalité Loi No.2004-663 du 17 décembre 2004 portant dispositions spéciales en matière de naturalisation Décision No. 2005-03/PR du 15 juillet 2005 relative au Code de la nationalité. Décision No. 2005-04/PR du 15 juillet 2005 portant dispositions spéciales en matière de naturalisation Décision No. 2005-09/PR du 29 août 2005 relative au Code de la nationalité Décision No. 2005-10/PR du 29 août 2005 relative aux dispositions spéciales en matière de naturalisation Loi No.2013-653 du 13 septembre 2013 portant dispositions particulières en matière d'acquisition de la nationalité par déclaration Loi No.2013-654 du 13 septembre 2013 portant modification des articles 12, 13, 14 et 16 de la Loi No.61-415 du 14 décembre 1961 portant Code de la nationalité
DR Congo	Constitution 1964 (« Luluabourg ») Décret-loi du 13 mars 1965 relatif à la déclaration acquisitive de la nationalité congolaise Décret-loi du 18 septembre 1965 portant loi organique relative à la nationalité congolaise Arrête du 30 novembre 1966 portant mesure d'exécution du décret-loi du 18 septembre 1965 portant loi organique relative à la nationalité congolaise Ordonnance-Loi No.71-020 du 26 mars 1971 relative à l'acquisition de la nationalité congolaise par les personnes originaires du Rwanda-Urundi établies au Congo 30 juin 1960 Loi No. 1972-002 du 5 janvier 1972 relative à la nationalité zaïroise Loi No. 1981-002 du 29 juin 1981 relative à la nationalité zaïroise DRC Décret-Loi No.197 du 29 janvier 1999 modifiant et complétant la Loi No.81-002 du 29 juin 1981 sur la Nationalité Congolaise Loi No. 04-024 du 12 novembre 2004 relative à la nationalité congolaise Constitution 2006
Djibouti	Loi No. 200/AN/81 portant Code de la nationalité djiboutienne. Loi No.79/AN/04/5eme L du 24 octobre 2004 portant Code de la nationalité djiboutienne

Egypt	Law No. 26 of 1975 concerning Egyptian nationality Law No. 154 of 14 July 2004 amending Law No. 26 of 1975 Decree No. 12025 of 26 July 2004 concerning certain provisions enforcing Law No. 154 Constitution 2014
Equatorial Guinea	Ley Fundamental 1982 Ley Fundamental 1991, amended 1995 Ley núm. 8/1990, de fecha 24 de Octubre, reguladora de la nacionalidad ecuato-guineana Ley Num.3/2011 de fecha 14 de Julio, reguladora de la Nacionalidad Ecuatoguineana Ley Fundamental 2012
Eritrea	Constitution 1997 Eritrean Nationality Proclamation No. 21/1992
Ethiopia	Constitution 1995 Nationality Law 1930 Proclamation No. 270/2002 concerning the rights of foreign nationals of Ethiopian origin Proclamation No. 378/2003 on Ethiopian Nationality
Gabon	Loi No.89/61 du 2 mars 1962 portant de la nationalité gabonaise Loi No. 37-1998 portant Code de la nationalité gabonaise
Gambia	Constitution 1965 Gambia Nationality and Citizenship Act No. 1 of 1965 Constitution 1970 Constitution 1997, amended 2001
Ghana	Ghana (Constitution) Order in Council 1957/277 Ghana Nationality and Citizenship Act 1 of 1957 Constitution (Consequential Provisions) Act (CA8) Ghana Nationality Act 62 of 1961 Ghana Nationality Decree, NLCD 191 of 1967 Ghana Nationality (Amendment) Decree NLCD 333 of 1969 Constitution of the Republic of Ghana 1969 Ghana Nationality Act 361 of 1971 Ghana Nationality (Amendment) Decree 1972 NRCD Constitution of the Republic of Ghana 1979 Constitution of the Republic of Ghana 1992 Constitution of the Republic of Ghana (Amendment) Act 527 of 1996 Citizenship Act 591 of 2000
Guinea	Ordonnance No.011 du 1 mars 1960 portant code de la nationalité guinéenne Loi 004/APN/83 du 16 février 1983, portant Code civil de Guinée

Guinea Bissau	Lei da nacionalidade No.1/76 de 4 de maio Lei da nacionalidade No.1/84 de 15 de fevereiro Constitution 1984 (modified 1991, 1993 and 1996) Lei da nacionalidade No.2/92 de 6 de abril Lei da nacionalidade No.6/2010 de 21 de junho
Kenya	Constitution 1963 Citizenship Act Cap170, 1963 Constitution 1969 Constitution of Kenya (Amendment) Act No.6 of 1985 Children's Act No.8 of 2001 Refugee Act 2006 Constitution 2010 Kenya Citizenship and Immigration Act No.12 of 2011 as amended by the Statute Law (Miscellaneous Amendments) Act No.12 of 2012 and the Security Laws (Amendment) Act No. 19 of 2014
Lesotho	Constitution 1966 Lesotho Citizenship Act 1967 Lesotho Citizenship Order No.16 of 1971 (amended 1993) Constitution 1993
Liberia	Constitution 1847 Aliens and Nationality Law, Title 3, Liberian Code of Laws 1956 Aliens and Nationality Law 1973 Constitution 1984
Libya	Law No.17 of 1954 on Nationality Law No.18 of 1980 pertaining to the resolutions of the Nationality Act Regulatory Code for Law No.18 of 1980 pertaining to the resolutions of the Nationality Act Law No.24 of 2010 on the Provisions of Libyan Nationality
Madagascar	Ordonnance No. 60-064 du 22 juillet 1960 portant Code de la nationalité malgache (modifiée par la Loi No. 1961-052; la Loi No.1962-005; l'ordonnance no.1973-049; et la Loi No.1995-021) Loi No. 1961-052 portant modification de l'article 93 du Code de la nationalité malgache, modifiant les articles 24, 58, 82 et 93 du Code de la nationalité
Malawi	Constitution 1964 Malawi Citizenship Act No.2 of 1964 Malawi Citizenship Act No.28 of 1966 Statute Law (Miscellaneous Amendments) Act No. 37 of 1967 Amendment Act No.5 of 1971 Amendment Act No.22 of 1992 Constitution 1994 (Act No.20 of 1994, as amended by Acts No.31 of 1994, 6 of 1995, 7 of 1995, 1 of 1997 and 38 of 1998)

Mali	Ordonnance No.55 du 24 novembre 1960 relative à l'attribution de la nationalité malienne à tous les ressortissants de la République du Mali Loi No. 62-18 AN-RM du 3 février 1962 portant Code de la nationalité malienne Loi No. 95-70 du 25 août 1995 portant modification du Code de la nationalité malienne Loi No.2011–087 du 30 décembre 2011 portant Code des personnes et de la famille
Mauritania	Loi No.61-112 du 12 juin 1961 portant Code de la nationalité mauritanienne tel que modifié par la Loi No.1962-157 et la Loi No.1976-207 Loi. No.2010-023 du 11 février 2010 abrogeant et remplaçant certaines dispositions de la loi 61-112 du 12 juin 1961 portant Code de la nationalité mauritanienne
Mauritius	Constitution 1968 Mauritius Citizenship Act 1968 Mauritius Constitution Amendment Act No.23 of 1995 Mauritius Citizenship Amendment Act No.24 of 1995
Morocco	Dahir No.1-58-250 du 6 septembre 1958 portant Code de la nationalité marocaine tel que modifié et complété par la Loi No. 62-06 promulguée par le dahir No. 1-07-80 du 23 mars 2007
Mozambique	Constitution 2004 Lei da Nacionalidade de 20 de Junho de 1975 alterada pela Lei No. 16/87 de 21 de Dezembro
Namibia	Constitution 1990 Namibian Citizenship Act No. 14 of 1990 Namibian Citizenship (Special Conferment) Act No.14 of 1991 Namibia Refugees (Recognition and Control) Act No. 2 of 1999 Namibian Constitution Second Amendment Act No. 7 of 2010
Niger	Loi No.61-26 du 12 juillet 1961 déterminant la nationalité nigérienne Ordonnance No.84-33 du 23 août 1984 portant Code de la nationalité nigérienne Ordonnance No.88-13 du 18 février 1988 Ordonnance No.99-17 du 4 juin 1999 portant modification de l'Ordonnance No.84-33 du 23 août 1984 portant Code de la nationalité nigérienne Constitution 1999 Loi No.2014-60 du 05 novembre 2014 portant modification de l'Ordonnance No.84-33 du 23 août 1984 portant Code de la nationalité nigérienne
Nigeria	Constitution 1960 Nigerian Citizenship Act 1960 Nigerian Citizenship Act 1961 Nigeria Constitution (Amendment) Decree No. 33 of 1974 Constitution 1979 Constitution 1999

Rwanda	Loi du 28 septembre 1963 portant Code de la nationalité rwandaise Constitution 2003, revised 2015 Loi organique No. 29/2004 du 03/12/2004 portant code de la nationalité rwandaise Loi organique No. 30/2008 du 25/07/2008 portant code de la nationalité rwandaise
SADR	No information
São Tomé and Príncipe	Lei no. 39/75 da nacionalidade de 15 de dezembro 1975 Lei no. 6/90 da nacionalidade de 13 de setembro de 1990 Constitution 2003
Senegal	Loi No. 61-70 du 7 mars 1961 déterminant la nationalité sénégalaise (modifiée par la Loi No.61-10 du 7 mars 1961, la Loi No.67-17 du 28 février 1967, la Loi No.70-27 du 27 juin 1970, la Loi No.70-31 du 13 octobre 1970, la Loi No.79-01 du 6 janvier 1979, la Loi No.84-10 du 4 janvier 1984, et la Loi No.89-42 du 26 décembre 1989) Loi No.2013-05 du 8 juillet 2013 portant modification de la Loi No 61-10 du 7 mars 1961 déterminant la nationalité sénégalaise
Seychelles	Constitution 1976 Citizenship Ordinance No. 9 of 1976 Constitution Decree 1979 Citizenship (Amendment) Regulations 1983 Constitution 1993 (as amended by Act 7 of 1994, Act 5 of 1995, Act 19 of 1995, Act 14 of 1996, SI 11 of 1998, Act 7 of 2000, SI 31 of 2000, SI 22 of 2001, SI 32 of 2002 and Act 7 of 2011) Citizenship Act No. 18 of 1994 (as amended by Act 11 of 2013)
Sierra Leone	Constitution 1961 Sierra Leone Constitution (Amendment) (No.2) Act 1962 Sierra Leone Citizenship Act, No. 4 of 1973, as amended by Act No.13 of 1976 Constitution 1991 Sierra Leone Citizenship Amendment Act No. 11 of 2006 Refugees Protection Act No. 6 of 2007 Child Rights Act No. 7 of 2007
Somalia	Law No.28 of 22 December 1962 on Somali Citizenship Somali Transitional Federal Charter 2004 Provisional Constitution 2012
South Africa	South African Citizenship Act No.44 of 1949 Constitution 1996 South African Citizenship Act No. 88 of 1995 South African Citizenship Amendment Act No.19 of 1997 South African Citizenship Amendment Act No.17 of 2004 South African Citizenship Amendment Act No.17 of 2010
South Sudan	Transitional Constitution of the Republic of South Sudan 2011 Nationality Act 2011

Sudan	Definition of Sudanese Ordinance 1948 Sudanese Nationality Act 1957 Sudan Nationality Decree No. 18 of 1993 Sudanese Nationality Act 1994 (amended by Act No.1 of 2006) Constitution 1998 Sudanese Nationality (Amendment) Act 2011
Swaziland	Constitution 1967 Constitution 1968 Swaziland Citizenship Act, No.17 of 1967 Swaziland Citizenships Order, No.22 of 1974 Swaziland Citizenship Act No.14 of 1992 Constitution 2005
Tanzania	Zanzibar Nationality and Naturalisation Decree 1911 Zanzibar Nationality Decree No.30 of 1952, amended by Act No.16 of 1958 Tanganyika Constitution 1961 Tanganyika Citizenship Ordinance 1961 Tanganyika Citizenship Ordinance (Amendment) Act, No.69 of 1962 Zanzibar Constitution 1963 Union of Tanganyika and Zanzibar Act 1964 Extension and Amendment of Laws Decree No.5 of 1964 Zanzibar Citizenship Decree No.5 of 1964 Zanzibari Act No.5 of 1985 Tanzania Citizenship Act No. 6 of 1995 Law of the Child Act No 21 of 2009
Togo	Loi No. 61-18 du 25 juillet 1961 relative à la nationalité togolaise Ordonnance 78-34 du 7 septembre 1978 portant Code de la nationalité togolaise Constitution 1992 Loi No.2007-017 du 6 juillet 2007 portant code de d'enfant
Tunisia	Décret No.34 du 26 janvier 1956 portant promulgation du Code de la nationalité tunisienne Décret-Loi No.63-6 du 28 février 1963 portant refonte du Code de la nationalité tunisienne. Loi No.63-7 du 22 avril 1963 ratifiant le décret-Loi No.63-6 du 28 février 1963 portant refonte du Code de la nationalité tunisienne, Loi No.71-12 du 9 mars 1971 modifiant les article 63 et 65 du Code de la nationalité tunisienne Loi No.85-791 du 14 novembre 1979 portant modification de l'article 30 du code de la nationalité Loi No.84-81 du 30 novembre 1984 modifiant l'article 32 du Code de la nationalité tunisienne Loi No.95-92 du 9 novembre 1995 relative à la publication du Code de la protection de l'enfant Loi No.2010-55 du 1er décembre 2010 modifiant certaines dispositions du Code de la nationalité tunisienne Constitution 2014

Uganda	Constitution 1962 Citizenship Act 1962 (Chapter 65) Constitution 1967 Constitution 1995 Uganda Citizenship and Immigration Control Act No.3 of 1999 (Chapter 66) Constitution (Amendment) Act 2005 Uganda Citizenship and Immigration Control (Amendment) Act 5 of 2009
Zambia	Constitution 1964 Citizenship of Zambia Ordinance No.61 of 1964 Constitution 1973 Citizenship of Zambia Act No.26 of 1975 (amended by Act No.17 of 1986 and Act No.13 of 1994) Constitution Act No.1 of 1991 as amended by Act No. 18 of 1996 and Act No. 20 of 2009 Constitution of Zambia (Amendment) Act No. 2 of 2016 Zambia Citizenship Act No.33 of 2016
Zimbabwe	Southern Rhodesian Citizenship and British Nationality Act No.13 of 1949 Citizenship of Rhodesia and Nyasaland and British Nationality Act No.12 of 1957 Citizenship of Southern Rhodesia and British Nationality Act No.63 of 1963 Citizenship of Rhodesia Act, 1965 Constitution of Zimbabwe, 1980 Constitution of Zimbabwe Amendment (No.3) Act No.1 of 1983. Citizenship of Zimbabwe Act No.23 of 1984 Constitution of Zimbabwe Amendment (No.11) Act No.30 of 1990 Constitution of Zimbabwe Amendment (No.14) Act No.14 of 1996 Citizenship of Zimbabwe Amendment Act No.12 of 2001 Citizenship of Zimbabwe Amendment Act No. 22 of 2001 Citizenship of Zimbabwe Amendment Act No. 23 of 2001 Citizenship of Zimbabwe Amendment Act No.1 of 2002 Citizenship of Zimbabwe Amendment Act, No 12 of 2003 Constitution of Zimbabwe Amendment (No.17) Act No.5 of 2005 Constitution of Zimbabwe Amendment (No.18) Act No.11 of 2007 Constitution of Zimbabwe Amendment (No.19) Act No 1 of 2009 Constitution of Zimbabwe Amendment Act No.20 of 2013

INDEX

In this book, and in the index, the terms 'citizenship' and 'nationality' have the same meaning. The term used in an international law context is most often 'nationality'; while in national contexts, the terminology follows that used in the country concerned (generally 'citizenship' in common law countries, and 'nationality' in civil law countries).

NB–page numbers given in **bold** refer to information in tables, and page numbers in *italics* refer to information in figures